ACCOUNTING:
A SURVEY

ACCOUNTING: A SURVEY

Henry E. Riggs

Professor of Industrial Engineering
and Engineering Management
Stanford University

McGraw-Hill Book Company

New York   St. Louis   San Francisco   Auckland   Bogotá   Hamburg
Johannesburg   London   Madrid   Mexico   Montreal   New Delhi
Panama   Paris   São Paulo   Singapore   Sydney   Tokyo   Toronto

Library of Congress Cataloging in Publication Data

Riggs, Henry E
   Accounting.

   Includes index.
   1. Accounting. I. Title.
HF5635.R56   657   80-19503
ISBN 0-07-052851-9

ACCOUNTING: A SURVEY

6789 HDHD 8987

This book was set in Bookman by Progressive Typographers.
The editors were Donald G. Mason and Edwin Hanson;
the designer was Jane Moorman;
the production supervisor was Phil Galea.
The drawings were done by J & R Services, Inc.
The cover was designed by Joseph Gillians.

About the Author

Henry Riggs' broad career background includes industry as well as academic positions. After receiving a B.S. in Industrial Engineering from Stanford University and an M.B.A. from Harvard Business School, Professor Riggs spent a number of years in industry both as a consultant and as a practicing manager. His experience includes such positions as consultant with Stanford Research Institute; Controller and later President of ICORE Industries, a manufacturing firm; and Vice-President for Finance of Measurex Corporation, a high-growth, high-technology producer of sophisticated control systems.

While employed in private industry Professor Riggs also taught part-time at the college level, until he joined the Stanford University faculty full-time in 1974. At Stanford he splits his teaching time between the Department of Industrial Engineering and Engineering Management and the Graduate School of Business. During his years as a teacher at Stanford, Professor Riggs has earned an excellent reputation as a teacher and developer of teaching materials and courses. In 1979 he was selected the Outstanding Teacher in the School of Engineering, and in 1980 he received the university's highest teaching award. Professor Riggs continues extensive contact with private industry through consulting and membership on several Boards of Directors. He currently chairs several corporate audit committees.

To the
memory of
G.W.R.
and
J.A.R.

Contents

List of Cases and Extended Exercises

Preface

This book is intended for use in a one-semester or one-quarter course for students seeking an understanding of the concepts of both financial accounting and cost/managerial accounting. In addition, the book is intended for those practicing managers who want to improve their understanding of the procedures for accounting and of the benefits and shortcomings of the accounting reports; the text is appropriate for management development programs in business and industry, for adult education courses, and for self-study.

The book grew out of a four-unit, one-quarter course in industrial accounting taught at Stanford University. Originally this course was designed for undergraduate engineering students. Increasingly, nonengineering majors and graduate engineering students have been attracted to the course, as they prepare themselves for decision-making within organizations of all kinds.

Such a course requires a concise, concept-oriented text that stresses the interpretation and use of financial, cost, and managerial accounting information. When no suitable text could be located, the author began to prepare and duplicate syllabus materials for the course. These materials, which have been thoroughly tested and improved as a result of students' comments and suggestions, have evolved into this book.

In summary, the text is designed more for the present and future user of accounting information than for the aspiring accountant. The text is not designed to be another introductory accounting text for use in the first of a comprehensive series of accounting courses offered in most undergraduate business departments. It covers in a single text both financial accounting and cost/managerial accounting; traditionally, these two areas of accounting are treated in separate courses using separate texts. This text asks the student to consider the purposes of financial information before studying a set of dogmatic rules for the development of that information, and it seeks to develop within the student a healthy skepticism regarding the usefulness of accounting data, as well as an appreciation for the benefits of that data.

For students who will proceed no further than this text in the study of accounting or financial control, this text provides both a satisfactory introduction and conclusion. They will have gained an understanding of the fundamental accounting concepts and of both the managerial uses and the limitations of accounting information. But the text also provides a sound foundation for other students who will proceed further in their study of management aspects of accounting.

The text does not purport to be comprehensive; a number of subjects that are of great interest to the professional accountant but of only marginal usefulness to the manager are intentionally omitted. For example, this book omits discussion of accounting for long-term equities, consolidated and consolidating statements, accounting for minority interests on an equity basis, statements of changes in financial position, transfer pricing, planning capital acquisitions, and automated data processing.

However, sophisticated topics relevant to management—topics such as valuation, price level adjustments, deferred income taxes, standard cost accounting, and overhead variances—are discussed concisely, with an emphasis on conceptual understanding rather than theory.

Accounting can be taught by the presentation in a relatively pedantic manner of a set of rules and procedures; the student is then asked to apply these rules to a set of simplified and generally unrealistic exercises. The rules and procedures are slow to "sink in," as the student has little appreciation of the dilemma which led to the establishment of the rule.

This text seeks to create a "need to know" by evolving the conceptual framework for accounting as the student considers the informational needs of the manager—first in the area of financial accounting and then, later in the book, in cost and managerial accounting. As the procedures and techniques of accounting are introduced and discussed, the role of compromises, estimates, assumptions, and omissions is stressed. The various cases and the presentation of alternative approaches to valuation are particularly helpful in conveying the message that accounting can only estimate the financial state of the enterprise and cannot be expected to reflect all that is important about the enterprise.

Chapters 1 and 2 of the book develop the reasons for keeping the financial score and the fundamental basis for scorekeeping: valuation of what the enterprise owns and what it owes. Chapters 3 through 8 (and several cases) develop a set of rules for financial accounting and then elaborate on certain of the key problems and sources of error in the financial statements. Chapter 9 and two accompanying cases are devoted to financial statement analysis. Chapters 10 through 12 develop a set of rules for cost accounting, after developing the "need to know," and the applications of cost accounting procedures are illustrated in several cases.

Finally, Chapters 13 and 14 emphasize the use of financial data in analysis of operations by and for management and in operational decision-making; again, several cases provide the student practice in utilizing managerial accounting techniques.

This book avoids much of the jargon of accounting while introducing and explaining the common terms that are the language of accounting. Key terms introduced in each chapter are listed and defined at the end of the chapter. Throughout, the book is addressed to the person who encounters in his or her daily work accounting data, reports, and information and who needs to interpret and use the products of the organization's accounting system. Illustrations in both the text and the problems are drawn from a wide variety of business and nonprofit organizations. The cases that are included at various points in the book add realism and stimulate the interest of present and future users of accounting information. Incidentally, any or all of the cases can be omitted without interrupting the flow of the book.

Problems at the end of each chapter are intended to provide both provocative questions for discussion and numerical exercises varying length and complexity.

Two comprehensive accounting exercises are included at the end of the book: the first, and longer, is devoted to financial accounting and the second to cost accounting. The problems and the extended exercises have proved invaluable in integrating the material and cementing the concepts in the students' minds. While the emphasis throughout the book is on concepts rather than mechanics, some pencil-pushing and number-crunching assure that students become participants in, and not simply observers of, accounting procedures. Moreover, the exercises build confidence in the student that accounting is not a mystery and that indeed the student is capable of operating a straightforward accounting system.

A comprehensive Instructor's Manual is available from the publisher for use by instructors who adopt the text.

As with all authors, I am indebted to my colleagues, my family, my student assistants through the years, the staff at McGraw-Hill, and the platoon of marvelous secretaries and typists who have helped me. I would also like to express my thanks for the many useful comments and suggestions provided by colleagues who reviewed this text during the course of its development, especially to Rosalind A. Cranor, Virginia Polytechnic Institute and State University; Thomas Boucher, Cornell University; Jack McPherson, Southern Technical Institute; Roger P. Murphy, Iowa State University; and Donna R. Rausch, University of Nebraska at Omaha. Finally, I am particularly grateful to the many students who signed up for my accounting course with reluctance (and often under some parental pressure); their subsequent enthusiasm for the material and their friendship toward me have been the real motivation behind this book.

Henry E. Riggs

ACCOUNTING: A SURVEY

1 Introduction: Why Keep Score?

Accounting. You probably already have a set of conceptions or prejudices about this subject. You may think it is the lifeblood of a modern industrial enterprise. Alternatively, you may view accounting information as mere history, with little relevance for forward-looking management. You may think that accounting data are very precise and represent the indisputable facts about an operation; or you may feel that, since accountants themselves often disagree, the results of their labors must represent little more than their individual opinions. You may equate accounting with your checkbook and monthly bank statement; or your savings account passbook; or your paycheck with its stub indicating various amounts withheld from pay; or the record of receipts and expenses for your club, charity, or association. You may be accustomed to reading published financial statements of corporations, perhaps in connection with common stock investments you have made or contemplate making. On the other hand, you may feel totally lost when confronted by these published financial statements, replete with large numbers and financial jargon that seems to speak only to the initiated.

Accountant. Again, the word may bring a variety of thoughts or images to your mind. Your mental image of the accountant may be based upon the Victorian clerk working for Ebenezer Scrooge, leaning over his desk while perched atop his tall stool. Alternatively, you may view the modern accountant as standing before a massive data-processing computer watching lights flash, tapes whirl, and printers spit forth financial facts at 1,000 lines per second.

Each of us is in contact with accounting data and information nearly every day of our lives. It is safe to say that these continual encounters— many of them baffling, and some of them simply unpleasant—have caused us to form opinions on what accounting is and is not, what it can and cannot do for us or to us, and what accountants must be like.

This book asks you to keep an open mind concerning both accounting and accountants. Those of you who are skeptics now may be persuaded by your study to conclude that accounting information, properly analyzed and interpreted, can be of substantial benefit to the users. Those of you who are now enthusiastic believers in the value of accounting may, after further study, want to temper your enthusiasm. You may conclude that account- ing information, like most other types of information, has its significant limi- tations.

Introduction to the Text

This book is intended for students seeking an understanding of the frame- work of accounting. It is designed more for the present and future user of accounting information than for the accountant. This user—you—may now be a business, engineering, or liberal arts major in college or graduate school; or a manager (or aspiring manager) in business, in industry, in gov- ernment, or in one of the many other types of organizations, both public and private, that dominate our society. For every professional accountant, there are a host of others who need to understand the basic concepts that the accountant uses in order to understand the accountant's messages. In- deed, most of us today have need both in our personal lives and in our jobs to interpret accounting reports and make use of financial data.

Some students will proceed no further than this text in the study of ac- counting or financial control; for them, this text provides both a satisfactory introduction and a conclusion. They will have gained an understanding of the fundamental concepts and the managerial uses of accounting informa- tion. Importantly, they will also have gained an appreciation of the inherent limitations of accounting techniques and therefore of the resulting informa- tion.

Other students will want to proceed further in their study; for them, this text provides a basic understanding upon which to build both greater tech- nical skills and greater sophistication in financial analysis. Of course, a few students will discover in the study of this material an interest in accounting as a career. This discovery may come as a surprise to them, for many people approach the study of accounting with great reluctance, thinking it a dry and lifeless subject with limited practicality.

This text is in a number of ways quite unlike traditional accounting texts. First, as already stated, it is designed with a view more to the needs of the nonaccountant than to the needs of the individual preparing for a professional accounting career. Second, it seeks to develop within the reader a healthy skepticism regarding the usefulness of accounting data, as well as an appreciation for the benefits of that data. Third, the text omits any serious discussion of a number of subjects that are of great interest to the professional accountant but of only marginal usefulness to the manager.

Fourth, and most importantly, it asks you to consider the need for and purposes of financial information before studying a set of dogmatic rules for the development of that information. Accounting can be taught, and often is, by the presentation in a relatively pedantic manner of a set of rules and procedures; the student is then asked to apply these rules to a set of simplified and generally unrealistic exercises. The rules and procedures are slow to sink in, for the student has little appreciation of the need for the rule or of the dilemma which led to the establishment of the rule. Moreover, not having wrestled with alternative rules and procedures, the student is likely to decide that the rules are unnecessarily arbitrary and that the data would be a good deal more useful if the rules were altered.

This text seeks to create a "need to know" by exploring financial data requirements first in the area of general, or financial, accounting and then later in the areas of cost and managerial accounting. This problem-first technique is analogous to providing food only after making the person hungry and is the opposite of the more common practice of introducing detailed technical material and then providing illustrations of and exercises on how it is used. The intention is to create an awareness on the reader's part that there is a need for data, that there is a body of knowledge that has developed for compiling these data, and that some rules and procedures must necessarily be laid down in order that the accountant and his or her "audience" can communicate.

So, the purpose of this text is not to convince you to become an accountant nor to teach you basic bookkeeping skills. The purpose is to make you a better user of accounting and financial information—gaining from it what is there to get, while being mindful of the information's shortcomings and limitations.

Scorekeeping

Accounting is analogous to scorekeeping. Managers of business enterprises are interested in the financial score; managers of athletic teams are interested in the game score. Nonmanagement members of the business enterprise, like their athletic counterparts, the players, are also interested in the score. Besides the active participants—both management and non-management—in business or in athletics, there are a host of other individuals who are also interested in the score—in athletics, the fans, the sportswriters, and the concessionaires selling beer and hot dogs; in business, the shareholders, the bankers, the customers, and the government.

We are interested in the score for a variety of reasons, but most importantly because we make decisions on the basis of the score. Managers—whether in business or athletics—will change strategies or tactics on the basis of the score. Customers, employees, and sports fans may renew their allegiances to a company or team or change allegiances on the basis of the score. Concessionaires at the playing field and suppliers to the business may change their own operating plans, basing their decisions on the record or score (e.g., rate of growth in sales, or won/lost record) of the business or team with which they are working.

Definition of Accounting

What are some elements of an appropriate definition of accounting, or financial scorekeeping? A useful definition needs to provide us with some guidelines as to what accounting both is and is not, what we can expect from our scorekeeping system, and what kinds of information or insights are simply beyond the reasonable scope of an accounting system.

Accounting is historical in perspective   The score of an athletic contest gives the results of what has happened in the game thus far, and not what may take place in the next period, inning, or minute; similarly, the accounting information shows only what has gone on in the business or other enterprise up to the date of the accounting reports. Thus, the accountant is really a historian.

Of course, history is relevant to the future. Plans for virtually all human endeavors—business, athletics, and international diplomacy are only examples—are better formulated after a careful review and analysis of history. It is important to recognize, however, that the accounting system cannot itself be expected to provide a crystal-ball view of the future. Sales forecasts, production plans, and expense budgets are all prospective; that is, they seek to describe what we expect, hope, or plan to occur in the future. These data are not in the accounting records. However, management's estimates of the future will utilize solid knowledge about the past as gained from analysis of the historical score.

Accounting deals in monetary measures, and accounting reports are expressed in monetary terms We will discover that much of importance about an enterprise cannot easily or usefully be expressed in **monetary terms.** This fact does not suggest that these events are less important than others which can be expressed monetarily, or that they are less relevant to the future planning for the enterprise. The hiring of a top scientist might be much more significant for an industrial enterprise than purchasing a new piece of laboratory equipment; however, we will have a good deal less trouble valuing in monetary terms the piece of laboratory equipment than we will valuing the newly hired scientist. Similarly, obtaining an appointment with the president of a company that is a major potential customer may be a much more significant event than shipping another in a long series of orders to one of our present customers, but clearly the first event is a good deal more difficult to value in monetary terms (we have only an appointment, not a sale) than is the second event (we can value both the goods shipped—the sale—and the resulting reduction in our inventory).

Accounting is performed for an entity The entity might be a business enterprise, an industrial concern, a church, a local governmental unit, the local fire department, the senior high school, the Parent-Teacher Association (PTA) of the senior high school, or your family. The entity must be precisely defined, and both the accountant and the user of the accounting information must take care not to confuse the entity of interest with other entities of close association or particular affinity.

Thus, if we are accounting for a partnership (for example, a law firm) we are accounting for the partnership's activities and not the personal activities of the partners. The partners may have other incomes and surely will have other expenses, but these are not incomes or expenses of the partnership. If the accounting entity is your family, the earnings and expenses of all the members of your family need to be included, and the resulting information will be different than if the accounting entity is you alone. If we are accounting for the PTA of the senior high school, we want to concern ourselves only with that organization—not the high school itself, not the citywide PTA organization, and not the national PTA. And we want to make sure that we include all activities that are a part of this PTA organization—the membership committee, the social committee, and so forth.

We also may, for accounting purposes, break up a large enterprise into elements, each of which will be treated as an accounting entity. For example, it would be normal procedure to define a single division of a large, multidivision industrial enterprise as an accounting entity. It will be useful for the division manager and his or her associates to keep the division's score separate from the score of the larger enterprise. Of course, the score must also be kept for the overall enterprise as well as for the divisional elements, but the accounting records and systems of the individual divisions can be readily combined to yield the financial score for the overall enterprise.

As another example, we might define as a separate entity the social committee of the PTA. Then we would isolate the financial transactions and events of this committee and design an accounting system that would produce quite different financial reports than those for the PTA as a whole —reports which, incidentally, may be more useful to the social committee chairman than to the PTA chairman.

Accounting requires certain actions   What are the actions the accountant undertakes? What verbs should we use to define accounting? The first verb that may come to your mind is *record*. We have spoken of accounting records, and therefore the accounting process must involve recording what goes on in the entity. But before the "goings on" of the enterprise can be recorded, they must be *observed;* that is, we must in fact ascertain what of monetary significance is happening. Once observed, the goings on must be translated into monetary terms such that they can be recorded; that is, they must be *measured,* and the measurement must be in terms of monetary units.

Once the goings on are recorded, however, the accountant's job is not completed. A sequential log of all that transpired in a business enterprise might satisfy certain legal requirements to keep records, but the log would not be very readable—it would be too long and would lack organization. Thus, the accountant *classifies* and then *summarizes* the data, so that data become information.

To recap, the action verbs that we need for our definition, listed in the order in which the actions are taken, are **observe, measure, record, classify,** and **summarize.**

We have been using the colloquial expression "goings on." What kinds of goings on of the business enterprise need to be observed, measured, recorded, classified, and summarized? Surely, transactions to which the entity is a party qualify: making a sale, paying a bill, receiving a check from a customer, lending or borrowing money, distributing the payroll, acquiring inventory, buying a machine tool, and so forth. Can we draw a box around our accounting entity and concentrate our attention solely on those activities that involve transactions with other entities? Not quite. While such transactions will indeed give rise to the great majority of accounting entries, we will need to take other accounting action to recognize changed conditions within the entity, changes which have not—at least not yet—involved transactions with outside persons or organizations. Several examples may help.

A piece of production equipment grows older and, as it does so, becomes of less benefit to the company.

Certain items in inventory fail to move for many months, and we recognize that their worth to the company has diminished or disappeared.

It may be appropriate to recognize our liability to pay salaries or payroll taxes before the date upon which they are actually due to be paid.

Stringing these elements together, then, we arrive at the following definition of accounting:

Accounting is the process of observing, measuring, recording, classifying, and summarizing the individual activities of an entity, expressed in monetary terms, and interpreting the resulting information.

The final clause of this definition, ("interpreting the resulting information,") is, of course, not solely the task of the accountant; the managers and all other persons interested in the financial score of the entity will be involved in interpreting the resulting information. Nevertheless, this final clause is added to the definition here to emphasize that part of the accountant's job is to extract meaning from the history that he or she is recording. Indeed, in this book we shall place major emphasis on this part of the accounting task.

Limitations of Accounting Information

Consider again the definition of accounting just presented. Does the definition suggest that the accounting or financial score tells the full story of the activities of the entity? Is there a suggestion that perhaps accountants themselves might disagree on the financial score? That is, are there limitations to both the completeness and the precision of the accounting information? Indeed there are.

Too frequently readers of accounting reports assume that the reports present the "truth" about the financial state of the organization. Even worse, they may believe that the reports present the "whole truth." Some accountants, possessing normal human motivations, may do little to disabuse the readers of these erroneous impressions.

First, we limit our observing and recording to those activities—transactions or changed conditions—that can be expressed in monetary terms. As suggested earlier, much goes on within any enterprise that cannot be expressed in monetary terms. Second, we limit our focus to the history of the particular entity; much that goes on outside the entity—for example, in the economy as a whole or within a competing organization—may have important future consequences for our entity.

Finally, we will soon discover that in the process of observing and measuring, the accountant will be required to make estimates, assumptions, compromises, and even intentional omissions. This situation is aggravated by the fact that the accountant is always working under time pressure: the usefulness of accounting information is a function in part of its timeliness. Thus, how precisely can the accountant value the obsolescing inventory mentioned earlier? Can the accountant be certain that some department manager has not entered into an agreement that obligates the company without informing the accounting department? Can the accountant be certain that all customers will pay their bills? Is it not possible that two reasonable people might disagree on the value to the company of a particular piece of machinery?

In fact, accounting can only estimate the financial state of the enterprise. It is unreasonable to expect the accounting documents to reflect all that is important about the history of the enterprise or to reflect that history in absolutely indisputable terms. Because accounting reports are often presented in very precise terms—down to the hundredth part of a dollar— we tend to associate with these reports a higher level of precision than they deserve. It is possible to be precisely wrong; it is also possible for vague accuracy to be highly useful!

Audiences for Accounting Information

Because a broad range of people and institutions are concerned about or interested in the financial score of an entity, the accountant serves many constituencies. Thus, accounting reports are addressed to multiple audiences. To illustrate, let's focus on an industrial corporation engaged in manufacturing. Who are the audiences for the financial reports of such a company, and for what kinds of questions do they seek input? That is, who cares, and what do they want to know?

Management Management has the most extensive demands for financial scorekeeping. Charged with the responsibility for day-to-day operations and long-range direction of the corporation, management must concern itself with an extensive set of issues and questions. Management is looking for rapid historical feedback to determine whether the company is operating according to plan. Are sales and expenses on target? If not, where are they out of line? Management is faced with a host of marketing decisions. Should it add a product? Delete another? Should it accept or decline a particular order? What price should it bid on job X? Should it adjust prices on product line Y? Should it increase or decrease promotional expenditures or other selling activities?

In addition to seeking information for operational decisions, management also requires data to monitor the current financial health of the company. How much cash does the corporation have? How much do customers owe it? Are they paying on time? How much does the company owe its suppliers? Is the company paying them on time? How much inventory does it hold? Does it have the ability to borrow additional money from the bank?

Furthermore, to the extent that any of the audiences discussed below —for example, investors, bankers, tax collectors—seek information on the company's financial score, management must necessarily be interested in the messages that the company's financial statements are conveying to these audiences. Thus, in preparing to deal with these outside audiences, management needs to take the viewpoint of each as it reviews the company's financial reports.

Investors The corporation's present shareholders are of course investors, but any persons or institutions who might buy shares of the company's stock are potential investors, and both groups seek certain fundamental financial information about the company. Is the company profitable? Is it sufficiently profitable so that the company can sustain or increase the dividend? What are the risks that the company will find it necessary to cut or eliminate the dividend, or, much worse, will become bankrupt? Alternatively, does the recent history of the company and its current financial condition point to strong increases in profits with perhaps attendant increases in the dividend and the market price of the stock?

Security analysts and brokers serve as advisers to present and potential investors and are therefore an important part of this audience. Indeed, strong evidence exists that the market price for a particular company's securities is determined by a relatively few professional investors and analysts who become thoroughly knowledgeable of the financial score of the company. This segment of the total audience for financial information, then, is both highly demanding and of critical importance to the company and its management.

Creditors We may think first of the bank as creditor to the company. In addition, trade suppliers—other companies selling "on credit" to the manufacturing enterprise—are also creditors. The position of the creditor is fundamentally different from the position of the investor. Creditors are interested in being repaid on time and, in the case of formal loans, with interest; but they do not share as investors (owners) do in the future growth and profits of the company.

The sooner the creditor expects to be repaid—that is, the shorter the maturity of the credit—the more the creditor will focus on the immediate financial position of the company (its liquidity) and the less concerned he or she will be with the longer-term prospects of the company. Conversely, if repayment is to occur some distance into the future—that is, if the loan has a long maturity—the lender needs to be concerned with both the short-term position and the long-term prospects for the company, since the long-term lender may not be repaid if the company incurs a string of loss years and fails as a viable business unit.

Tax collector   The various taxing authorities determine tax liability for the corporation as a function of sales, profits, property owned, payroll, and occasionally of other factors as well.   In the United States, taxes on profit, or income taxes, are exacted by the federal government, certain state governments, and some municipal governments.   Typically, property taxes are collected by the county or municipal government, while sales and payroll taxes may be imposed by one or more of the levels of government that characterize the political framework of the United States—federal, state, county, and municipal.

   The basis for calculating, and subsequently verifying, the tax liability of the corporation will be determined from the accounting records.   Thus, the preparer of the company's various tax returns is a user of accounting data; also, government tax auditors routinely demand access to the company's accounting records to verify the correctness of the company's tax payment.

   Two general comments should be made here with regard to taxes; each of these comments will be discussed more thoroughly as we proceed in our study.   First, management will, in virtually all cases, strive to minimize the company's current liability for taxes of all kinds.   This effort involves both postponing the payment of taxes as long as possible and taking advantage of various tax law provisions to reduce taxes.   Note that there is a world of difference between avoiding unnecessary taxes and evading required taxes!   However, because in a particular instance the applicability or effect of the tax law (particularly the income tax law) may be very unclear, the company's tax liability may not be determinable with certainty, and an inevitable adversary relationship grows up between company management and the tax collector.

   Second, tax laws must not be permitted to dictate accounting practice, particularly with respect to accounting for profits.   Income tax laws are enacted to raise revenue for a particular governmental unit and, in certain instances, to further national economic goals by providing incentives to business to take actions consistent with those goals.   Thus, the definition of profit in the income tax laws is typically at variance to some degree with the appropriate definition of profit for management and investors.   As a result, the company will normally be required to maintain in its accounting records certain information solely for the purpose of calculating its tax liability.

Others   Aside from these primary audiences, there exists a broad spectrum of other individuals and institutions interested in the financial score for the industrial manufacturing corporation. Customers will be interested in the general financial viability of the company, particularly if they are dependent upon the company for long-term source of supply. Employees will be similarly interested in the company's viability; a growing, profitable, and financially strong company represents an attractive employer. Labor unions, as representatives of the employees, will also have an avid interest in the financial results of the company, perhaps particularly just prior to contract negotiations, when the union is formulating its demands based at least in part on what it feels the company can afford. Managements of competing companies are also eager recipients of all indications of the financial score of the company, from mere rumors of sales, profits, or cash position to complete published financial statements.

Government regulatory bodies will also look to the company's accounting records for information. Companies are, of course, subject to varying amounts of regulation, depending primarily on their lines of business. Public utilities (electric, natural gas distribution, telephone, and so forth) are granted regional monopolies by the government and in return are subject to price and other regulation. This regulation is aimed at assuring service to users and an adequate return on investment to the utility's shareholders.

Transportation companies (airlines and railroads) and broadcasting companies (radio and TV) are regulated by both federal and state agencies. All companies whose securities are actively traded in organized markets are subject to various financial reporting requirements stipulated by the Securities and Exchange Commission, and both federal and state securities agencies will exercise some control on the sale of newly issued securities by all corporations. Antitrust legislation, while affecting primarily the large companies in the country, may also constrain the actions (particularly with regard to pricing) of even relatively small concerns. In its interactions with each of these regulatory bodies, management will be relying to a great extent on financial information obtained from the accounting records to advance the company's cause or to defend its position.

Finally, wage and price controls have been imposed in this and many other countries, and speculation abounds as to the nature and extent of such controls in the future. Wage and price controls can place a demanding requirement on the accounting system of all companies.

Conflicting Views of Various Audiences

Clearly, the various audiences are interested in quite different types of financial information. Moreover, because of the different viewpoints of the various audiences, a company may wish to convey quite different messages to different audiences.

For example, management of the company will typically be motivated to report to shareholders a strong profit picture. At the same time, management will seek to minimize taxes calculated as a percentage of profits. The desired message to the creditors may be that the company is in a strong financial position, perhaps entitled to more liberal credit terms; the desired message to the labor union may be that the company will be hard pressed to meet demands for substantial wage or fringe benefit increases.

We will see that, in fact, the accountant has certain latitude in reporting both profits and financial position. Using the example of the obsolescing inventory again, we will see that, if the accountant takes a relatively pessimistic view of the value of this inventory, both profits and financial position will be reported less glowingly to both shareholders and the income tax collector than if the accountant takes a relatively more optimistic view of the value of this same inventory. Of course, this and similar situations present opportunities for deception or, far worse, fraud. But no matter how honest and objective the accountant attempts to be in such situations, it is likely that his or her judgment will be colored by the conscious or unconscious consideration of the message that the resulting financial reports will convey to key audiences. After all, the accountant is subject to the same human frailties and is buffeted by the same human motivations that affect us all!

Accounting in a Business Environment

The accounting function in business is a service function, not an end in itself. The accounting department does not create sales, fabricate products, or engineer new products. It keeps score, and, as suggested earlier, its paramount task is to provide information and analyses to management that will assist management in the operation of the business enterprise.

Within the business environment, accounting is functional to the extent it assists management in managing toward the company's objectives. While an exhaustive discussion of business objectives would be out of place in this text, some consideration of typical business objectives will assist us in picturing accounting's role in the overall business organization.

Certainly an important (although not necessarily the prime) objective of business is to earn a profit. Actual behavior of business managements suggests that maximizing profits is not a widespread objective. Without arguing about whether business should or should not seek to maximize profits (or short-term versus long-term maximization of profits), managements seem to act as though they want their companies to be adequately (perhaps comfortably) profitable, but not necessarily maximally profitable. In any case, the accounting department should be able to assist managements in achieving profit targets; the accountant is *the* scorekeeper with respect to the objective of making profits.

In this connection, the accounting system needs to provide the base historical data for management to use in charting the future course of the company—setting targets—to the extent, at least, that the targets can be quantified in monetary terms. Presumably this course charting will involve the creation of financial plans and budgets. The accounting department must then be able to track actual performance of the enterprise against planned performance as expressed in budgets; moreover, it must provide this tracking with minimum delays (or in computer jargon, in as close to real time as possible) so that management can take corrective action when operations get off course.

The fundamental economic decisions that must be made by all business managements involve the most efficient allocation of the available resources, since resources are inevitably scarce. Incidentally, these decisions are faced by managements of all productive enterprises, whether within a "free" economy, a controlled economy, or a mixed economy. These scarce productive resources are money, existing productive capacity, and labor, including technical expertise, management expertise, and human muscle. Many analytical techniques, some quite sophisticated and requiring extensive computing power, are utilized to assist in making these resource allocation decisions. Much, though not all, of the data utilized in these mathematical models can and should be available within the accounting records. Indeed, the accounting system should be designed with a view to the various input data required by the company's present and future analytical tools, such as:

Discounted cash flow analyses of alternative investment opportunities

Simulation of a part of the company's operations

Economic order quantity analyses

Linear programming applied to a part of the company's production or distribution activities

All of these tools require extensive accounting data on costs and revenues for the company as a whole, for certain products, for certain departments, or for certain geographic regions.

Most businesses, of course, articulate other objectives to accompany the profit objective. At the risk of opening up arguments as to the appropriateness of various objectives, we can say that managements often do in fact pursue such other objectives as:

Maximizing sales or market share

Increasing economic power through sheer size

Creating or maintaining technical leadership or a unique scientific staff

Developing enhanced reputations or prestige for the company or its management

Perpetuating the enterprise for the benefit of employees, the community, the management, or the family

Assuring that present management members retain their jobs

Accounting may be of relatively little help in measuring the company's progress—keeping score—with respect to certain of these objectives. It is difficult to quantify in monetary terms economic power or reputation or prestige. Again, accounting reports tell only a part of the company's total story.

Accounting in Nonprofit or Governmental Environments

Our primary emphasis in this study of accounting will be on enterprises—manufacturers, service organizations, and sales organizations—that seek to make a profit. Of course, our economy and society are replete with organizations that are not profit-seeking—government units, educational institutions, charities, certain hospitals, churches and synagogues, clubs, foundations, fraternal and service organizations, political parties, and consumer or farmer cooperatives. While the accounting requirements, and therefore accounting systems, of these organizations are somewhat different from those of profit-seeking companies, they are not fundamentally different. Since the objectives of these nonprofit organizations are different, they may require different sorts of data and reports in order to assist their managements in tracking progress toward objectives. Yet all of these organizations take in revenue and incur expenses. The well-managed among them operate on a plan, and the plan involves a budget in monetary terms. The managements of these organizations have the same needs as their profit-seeking counterparts to monitor actual financial performance as compared to the budget. Nevertheless, some accounting conventions will be different for governmental, educational, or other types of nonprofit organizations. In general, a good deal more emphasis may be placed in these organizations on the flow of cash, where business will place more emphasis on the measurement of profit.

Useful Nonaccounting Information

Our definition of accounting suggests that we can look to the accounting records and reports only for those data and information that can be stated in monetary terms. Yet nonmonetary measures or records will be of vital assistance to managements of both for-profit and nonprofit organizations. Management should seek out the nonaccounting measures of performance or condition that can provide insights into the probable ability of the organization to meet its future objectives.

Returning to our analogy with athletic teams, we are concerned with other information about the team besides simply the score of the games played and the related statistics on individual team members. We are concerned about the age and health of the athletes. We are concerned about the depth of backup personnel for each of the critical positions. We are interested in which athletes perform best under varying climatic, competitive, or time conditions.

Similarly, business managements may be interested in such nonmonetary measures as the number of new customers, frequency of late deliveries, frequency of "stock outs," employee turnover, employee absenteeism, market share vis-à-vis competitors, educational background of technical and managerial personnel, number of sales calls per salesperson per day, percentage of contract proposals accepted, percentage of production capacity being utilized (by department), and reject rate or quality yield. Indeed, most businesses can define several nonmonetary key indicators of performance that management will want to monitor every bit as closely as data developed by accounting. The most significant of these key indicators are those that tend to serve as early warning signals, that is, those that foretell operating problems.

Importance of Personal Motivations

Management is defined by some as the process of planning, supervising, and controlling an organization in pursuit of its objectives. We have been discussing the role of accounting in providing data and analyses to assist management in its job, particularly in the areas of planning and controlling.

Yet, it is important to bear in mind that an organization is not an impersonal machine, but rather a collection of human beings. We have spoken of some of the objectives other than profit that might be accorded high priority by top management. Middle- and lower-level managers, salespersons, scientists and engineers, clerks, machine operators, and every other group in the overall organization will also have their collective and individual objectives.

Human behaviorists tell us that we are all motivated to satisfy our needs, whatever those needs may be. Information supplied by the accounting reports may help us to satisfy certain of our needs (e.g., I need to demonstrate that my department can operate on budget, and the accounting report verfies that it has) or it can threaten our need satisfaction (e.g., I need to maintain low overtime costs in my department because that is an objective to which I committed myself at the beginning of the year and the last accounting report shows no improvement in that expense category). An accounting report will create motivations within its readers; that motivation may be constructive to the overall goals and objectives of the organization (e.g., I'm going to take steps to increase sales of certain products because sales have been below target) or it may be destructive to the overall goals (e.g., I will subcontract certain production activities at a considerable sacrifice in total costs rather than incur additional overtime costs, since the high subcontract costs will not be charged to my department and management is "on my back" about overtime costs). The effectiveness of the accounting reports will be very much a function of the use to which management puts them. Reports can be used to threaten or coerce middle and lower levels of management, or they can be used to provide feedback to those levels of management to permit them to do a better job of managing.

Accountants are also motivated by the reactions of management to reports they generate. Too frequently, an adversary relationship builds up between accounting management and operating management: operating management disputes the veracity of the accounting numbers, and accounting management becomes defensive; operating management withholds information from the accounting department, and the accounting management delights in highlighting areas of poor operating performance. A healthy relationship exists when operating management looks to the accounting department for feedback and assistance, and the accounting department readily admits that the accounting process is not an exact science and that there may be many valid explanations as to why actual revenues and expenses deviated from the plan.

Summary

Accounting is the process of financial scorekeeping. More comprehensively, accounting is defined as the process of observing, measuring, recording, classifying, and summarizing the individual activities of an entity, expressed in monetary terms, and interpreting the resulting information.

This text is designed primarily for those seeking an understanding of the accounting framework in order to make productive use of accounting and financial information, rather than for those who seek to learn basic bookkeeping skills.

Accounting is not a complete story of the history of the enterprise, for, as the above definition suggests, it ignores those activities that cannot be measured and expressed in monetary terms. Furthermore, to a significant extent, it omits consideration of events or conditions outside of the entity, even though such events or conditions may impact significantly on the future of the enterprise. Nonmonetary, and therefore nonaccounting, measures of the company's activities and condition can also prove both revealing and useful.

While the accounting reports serve a myriad of audiences, the primary beneficiary of the information is the management of the enterprise. Secondary beneficiaries, but very key audiences, include investors (present and potential) in the company's securities, creditors to the company, and the various governmental taxing authorities. Other interested parties include customers, employees, trade unions, government regulatory bodies, and competitors. The informational requirements of these audiences vary widely.

The value of accounting reports to the primary audience, management, is as an aid in tracking the company's progress in pursuit of one or more of the corporate objectives. Furthermore, accounting data represent the key inputs for most analytical techniques employed by management to assist in making the fundamental economic decisions on the allocation of the enterprise's scarce productive resources.

Accounting techniques for government, education, charity, and other nonprofit organizations are not fundamentally different than those for profit-seeking enterprises. However, informational requirements and certain accounting conventions will vary, since the objectives of these nonprofit organizations are typically very different from the profit and related objectives of businesses within the private sector.

New Terms

Accounting The process of observing, measuring, recording, classifying, and summarizing the individual activities of an entity, expressed in monetary terms, and interpreting the resulting information.

Classify To categorize similar transactions, events, or conditions within the accounting system.

Entity The definition of the organization for which the accounting is being performed.

Measure To value the event, transaction, or condition that is to be acknowledged in the entity's accounting system.

Monetary terms The form to which the description of activities is limited in an accounting system; the measure used in valuing all that is to be included in the accounting records.

Observe To determine what transactions, events, or conditions need to be acknowledged in the entity's accounting system.

Record To evidence in the accounting system those events, transactions, and conditions that have been measured (valued).

Summarize   To combine and condense the data appearing in the accounting system in order to supply meaningful information to the various audiences.

Problems

1   As a manager, what questions do you face that accounting information may help you answer? Specifically, what information with respect to what questions can you expect to receive from your accounting system? What kinds of information or data that will be useful in answering these questions will probably *not* be supplied by your accounting system?

2   In what ways and for what purposes will the following individuals have contact with the accounting system of a manufacturing firm?
   a   The inventory (stores) clerk
   b   The project manager in design engineering
   c   The sheet-metal shop foreman
   d   The field sales engineer
   e   The secretary to the president
   f   The manager of the Cincinnati branch sales office
   g   The purchasing agent
   h   The product line manager in the marketing department
   i   The manager of warehouse and shipping

3   The illustrations in this text are based primarily on retailing and manufacturing enterprises. How might the relevant questions, and therefore the needs for accounting information, be different for:
   a   An individual managing his or her household finances
   b   A manager of a TV repair shop
   c   A university administrator
   d   A bank manager
   e   A manager of the city recreational department
   f   A doctor managing his or her own office
   g   A street vendor selling handmade jewelry

4   Assume that you are a security analyst for a major stock brokerage firm and have the responsibility for writing a report on the Baronet Company. You have just received Baronet's published financial statements. What specific questions do you think will be answered by a careful review of these financial statements? Now suppose that you have an opportunity to visit for one hour with the president of Baronet. What are some of the key questions that you would pose to the president? Can you characterize the differences between the questions that might be answered by the financial statements and the questions that you would pose to the president?

5   Assume that you are a shareholder in the Baronet Company and that you have the latest published financial statements for the company but no access to the management of the company or to security analysts' reports. Where might you seek additional information for use in making your decision to sell the shares you now own or buy more shares in the company?

6 Assume that you are an investigator for the antitrust division of the Justice Department of the federal government and are investigating a large manufacturer of glass containers. What information that would be useful to your investigation would you expect to obtain from published financial statements of that particular manufacturer and its competitors?

7 Assume that you are a sales tax auditor for the state government and are about to begin auditing the recent sales tax returns of a distributor of industrial supplies. The distributor is required to charge and collect sales tax on only certain types of sales transactions. What data and/or documents would you request of the distributor's accounting manager?

8 Do you think it would be relatively easy or difficult to measure in monetary terms each of the following transactions?

   a The purchase of a used truck

   b The exchange of a parcel of land owned by the company for many years for a 15-year lease on a newly constructed facility

   c The sale of newly issued common stock to an outside investor

   d The acceptance of an interest-bearing five-year note from a customer in settlement of his past-due account

   e The signing of a five-year employment contract with the company's chief scientist

   f The negotiation of a 10-year license on a product developed by the company to another company who agrees to pay 4% royalty on all sales of the product.

   g The acceptance of an order for 120 units of product **X** to be delivered at the rate of 10 units per month for the next year

   h The shipment of the first 10 units in connection with the order mentioned in (g)

   i The receipt of 400 pounds of raw material Z

   j The purchase of a one-year insurance policy providing comprehensive coverage on the company's facilities

   k The filing of a lawsuit seeking $20,000 damages from a supplier for breech of contract

9 Evaluate the following quotation: "Accountants are simply historians focusing on past events. Management is concerned with charting the future course of the business, not with worrying about past successes or failures. Therefore, the accountant's function is not vital to management, except to the extent that it causes the company to comply with various governmental regulations."

10 Assume that you have just received your monthly bill from the gasoline company whose credit card you carry. You recall signing each of the slips that are included with your bill. Consider the progress of these slips from the time you signed them in the gasoline station until they appear with your monthly bill. What transactions have occurred? What accounting action has been taken at the gasoline station? At the oil company? What transactions remain to be taken?

11 The text provides examples of several goings on within a company that do not involve transactions, but do give rise to the need for accounting action. Can you think of other examples of changed conditions, not involving transactions with outside entities, that might cause accountants to take action with respect to values in the accounting records?

12   The text suggests several types of nonaccounting, quantitative information that might prove useful to management.   In your personal life can you think of non-monetary, quantitative measures or information that might assist you in better managing your personal finances?

The Accounting Framework: The Concept of Value

W e have defined the accountant's task as observing, measuring in monetary terms, recording, classifying, and summarizing the individual activities of an entity. We have alluded to some of the problems of observing the goings on in a business enterprise, and we will return to this dilemma periodically. Similarly, we will have much to say about the accepted techniques of recording, classifying, and summarizing. This chapter focuses on the issue of measuring in monetary terms, or valuing. How does an accountant value what the enterprise owns, and how are its obligations valued? How is a monetary value assigned to all of the various transactions to which the enterprise is a party? Some of these valuations are straightforward and relatively indisputable. Others present very real dilemmas.

This chapter begins with a discussion of three valuation methods:

1 The *time-adjusted value* method, which views value as a function of the stream of future benefits and costs arising from the item owned or from the obligation.
2 The *market value* method, which equates value to the price at which the item owned could be bought or sold currently.
3 The *cost value* method, which equates value to the price paid for the item at the time it was originally acquired.

Application of the three alternative methods will not necessarily result in the same values. No single method is inherently more correct than the other two. However, the cost value method is the predominant method currently in use. In order to better understand the advantages and short-comings of this method, it is important to understand all three methods.

We shall begin with an explanation of the time-adjusted value method. This method is most easily visualized in terms of valuation of a promise to pay.

Valuing a Loan (or Note)

Consider the case of the valuation of a debt instrument from the point of view of the holder of the instrument, the lender or creditor.

How does the lender determine the value of the borrower's promise to pay interest on the outstanding debt and to repay the principal? These two sources of cash flow are fixed by agreement between lender and borrower both as to amount and timing, and thus the flows are very predictable, as-suming that the borrower represents a good credit risk. Because money has a time value (i.e., you would prefer to receive a dollar now rather than a year from now, since you can make use of that dollar in the intervening year), those flows of cash that the lender will receive at some distance in the future are of less value today than those flows that are due to be received relatively sooner. Interest tables are available that permit the lender to cal-culate the equivalent value today of flows occurring at various times in the future, at any interest rate that the lender selects as appropriate. Such values are referred to as *present values of future cash flows* or **time-ad-justed values;** this text will use the term *time-adjusted value* to refer to today's equivalent value, at a specified interest rate, of a flow of cash (inflow or outflow) that will occur in the future.

For example, assume that $1,000 has been lent in return for the bor-rower's promise to make interest payments of $50 at the end of each of the next three years and a return of the principal of $1,000 at the end of the third year. What is the value to the lender of this borrower's promise to pay? If the lender determines that 5% is the appropriate **equivalency rate** (that is, the rate to use in determining equivalencies, based upon a comparison of other opportunities available to the lender for deployment of its money), then the time-adjusted value of this series of flows is $1,000, since the lender will be receiving interest at the rate of 5% from now until the principal balance of the loan is repaid.[1] That is, the lender is indifferent

---

[1] In practice, the lender would set the interest rate on the loan (here, 5%) equal to its equiva-lency rate.

between having $1,000 now or the promise from a credit-worthy borrower to pay the following amounts:

$50 at the end of 12 months
$50 at the end of 24 months
and $1,050 at the end of 36 months.

If for any one of a number of reasons the lender decides that the rate to be used in calculating equivalencies has increased from 5% to, for example, 8%, then the time-adjusted value of that stream of promised payments will be less than $1,000. Standard interest rate tables (included and explained in the appendix to this chapter and widely used in the banking industry) reveal that at 8% the time-adjusted value of the payment stream is about $923. Conversely, if a lower rate is used, the time-adjusted value will be greater: at 3% it is about $1,057. In this case the lender is indifferent as to whether it has $1,057 now or the borrower's note, assuming it judges 3% to be the appropriate rate for calculating equivalency. This simple table may help explain this concept:

| Cash Flow | Timing | Equivalent Value Now of the Cash Flows at Alternate Equivalency Rates: | | |
		3%	5%	8%
$50	End of 12 months	48.54	47.62	46.30
$50	End of 24 months	47.13	45.35	42.87
$1,050	End of 36 months	960.90	907.03	833.52
		$1,056.57	$1,000.00	$922.69

Therefore, the lender will value this note differently, depending upon what it finds to be the equivalency interest rate applicable to the situation. If 8% is the appropriate rate, the lender would be willing to sell the borrower's promise to pay for any amount above $923 or, what amounts to the same thing, it would be willing to cancel the borrower's note if the borrower would agree to pay $923 or more now (that is, the lender would be willing to "discount" the note from its face value of $1,000 in order to get the early return of its money).[2]

The illustration above assumes a credit-worthy borrower. Now suppose that the lender realizes that in light of the borrower's financial position, employment prospects, and so forth, repayment on schedule is by no means assured. In this case the lender regards this loan as somewhat more risky than the average and feels that it must get a higher interest return in order to compensate for the higher risk. Therefore, the lender concludes that the interest rate for calculation of equivalency should be higher than 8%—say,

[2] For further discussion of these concepts, see the appendix to this chapter.

10%—to allow for this greater risk of repayment. Using a 10% equivalency rate, the lender values the note at about $876, and would be willing to discount the note all the way to $876 if by doing so it could secure immediate payment of that amount.

If the lender has a portfolio of notes, each having different risks and different schedules for the payment of interest and the repayment of principal, this technique of valuing the notes would be useful and meaningful to the lender. The resulting valuations would provide information to the lender that could assist it in negotiating with borrowers or in selling (discounting) the notes to other lenders.

Of course, borrowers can use the same technique to value their own promises to pay interest and principal to lenders. A borrower whose interest rate for equivalency is 8% would be willing to pay not more than $923 right now to be relieved of the obligation to make the scheduled payments of principal and interest. On the other hand, the borrower whose equivalency rate is 3% would be better off paying any amount up to $1,057 now (a premium of up to $57 over the face value of the note) since a 3% equivalency rate suggests that the borrower doesn't have other opportunities to invest cash at a return higher than 3%. Note that the repayment of a debt is essentially a risk-free "investment."

Valuing Common Stock Securities

Let's move now to the slightly more complex case of valuing another form of security, a share of common stock,[3] again from the point of view of the holder of the security, the shareholder or investor. What determines the value of a share of common stock? If the stock is publicly traded in organized markets (e.g., the New York Stock Exchange) the value is determined by the classic auction method: It is equal to what the buyer is willing to pay and the seller is willing to take for the share.

But this answer begs the question. How do the buyers and sellers judge what the value is to them, and thus whether they should buy or sell? Like the lender, the shareholder (or potential shareholder) will attempt to ascertain what flow of benefits will result from ownership of the share of stock. Presumably the benefits are dividends while the stock is owned and the market price (less selling commissions) at the time the owner elects to sell the stock (ignoring income taxes on dividends and capital gains or losses).[4] Thus, the value of the share of stock to the shareholder is the

---

[3] Evidence of partial ownership of a corporation.
[4] In a rational market, the price that future buyers will be willing to pay for the stock will also be a function of the expected cash returns. If all future buyers are treated as one, it can be seen that the future cash returns from ownership of the share of common stock are limited to divi-

time-adjusted value of the future cash flows, calculated at the interest rate that the shareholder thinks is appropriate for calculating equivalency. The selection of this interest rate will be influenced by the riskiness of the investment—that is, by the shareholder's assessment of the risk that the anticipated flow of dividend payments will not be realized—and by the returns available from competing investment opportunities.

As shareholders lower their interest rate equivalencies, they tend to bid up the price of shares. Moreover, those investors who are averse to taking high risks will be attracted to companies with relatively secure dividend payments and they will be willing to calculate the time-adjusted value of these dividends at relatively low equivalency rates, thus placing a high value on the security.

Valuing Personal and Company Assets

Consider the applicability of this method of valuation—that is, the time-adjusted value of future cash flows—to other **assets** owned by individuals, besides shares of common stock and debt instruments. Ownership by individuals is not fundamentally different from ownership by profit-seeking companies, and thus the time-adjusted value should be equally applicable to individuals and businesses.

The term *asset* appears for the first time in the paragraph above. We shall use the term to apply to all physical property, rights (e.g., patent and trademark rights), and any other resources that hold the promise of providing ongoing benefits to the owner in the future. Certainly shares of common stock and debt instruments represent assets to their respective owners. An automobile or household furniture or an account at the savings and loan association or even a pantry full of canned foods represents an asset to the person who owns it: each holds the promise of delivering benefits in the future. The car may become wrecked or the canned food in the pantry may spoil, but at the moment the owner has a reasonable expectation of future benefits flowing from the ownership of each of these items. Each of them, as an asset, has a value, and the accountant's task now is to consider methods for determining that value.

Can the time-adjusted value of an automobile be calculated? Yes; at least in concept the time-adjusted valuation method seems appropriate. The ownership of the automobile will give rise to certain future cash inflows

---

dends paid on the stock plus the liquidation payment to shareholders when the company is liquidated (an event that few managements or shareholders contemplate seriously). Thus, even for companies that are currently paying no dividends, the value of the common stock is a function of shareholders' expectations as to the amount and timing of such cash dividends in the future.

and outflows and will provide transportation benefits. These transportation benefits can be valued, perhaps by reference to the costs associated with transport by alternative methods such as taxicab, train, or bicycle. Other benefits, more difficult to value in monetary terms, might include convenience or status. If the time-adjusted method of valuation indicated that the value to the owner of the car was less than the amount it would be worth on the secondhand market, the owner might well be persuaded to sell the car; conversely, if the time-adjusted value turned out higher than its value to potential buyers, as reflected by its secondhand price, the owner would retain the car.

The example of the automobile illustrates the importance of the viewpoint of the evaluator. You might feel that the convenience associated with automobile ownership is very important to you, while your neighbor who seldom requires travel to out-of-the-way places or at odd hours places little value on the convenience aspect. As a result, you will tend to place a higher time-adjusted value on an automobile than will your neighbor.

You might be thinking that a far easier and more practical way of valuing your automobile would simply be to value it at its secondhand price; in this country, recent-vintage cars are valued in a pamphlet that is published monthly and subscribed to by virtually all auto dealers. Or, if your car is almost brand new and you are very proud of its up-to-date styling and accessories, you might argue that the value of the car is what you paid for it. Clearly, these are alternative methods of valuation, and we will consider them further in a moment; but these methods of valuation are not necessarily any more correct than the method based upon the time-adjusted value of the future flow of benefits.

Consider now the problems associated with valuing another asset that you own, your household furniture. Again, the time-adjusted value of the future flow of benefits to you of owning this furniture is one evidence of value, although it is not easily calculated. Used household furniture does not have the same ready secondhand market or readily ascertainable resale prices that used automobiles have; valuation by reference to resale market prices is a difficult technique to apply. As in the case of your automobile, the price you originally paid for the asset represents still another indication of value.

What of the pantry full of canned goods? You probably filled the pantry either because you were able to get a very attractive price on the food by buying in large quantities or by taking advantage of a particular sale, or because you sought the security of having a stock of food in the event of a tornado, hurricane, earthquake, enemy attack, food shortage, or rampant inflation. In any case, the benefits from owning this large stock of food will be stretched out into the future, and you have some idea of the timing and magnitude of the financial benefits to be derived from its ownership. Thus, calculating a time-adjusted value for this stock of food is feasible; indeed,

you probably went through such an exercise intuitively when you purchased the food, particularly if your motivation for buying the large stock of
food was to avail yourself of an attractive price opportunity. Of course, you
could value this hoard of food at the prices that you would have to pay
today to replace it or you could value it at the actual acquisition cost.
Again, as in the case of the automobile or of the household furniture, all
three methods of valuation are applicable.

We need now to look more closely at each of these valuation methods:
the *time-adjusted value* method, the **market value** method and the **cost
value** method.

TIME-ADJUSTED VALUE

Application of the time-adjusted method requires that the owner of the
asset (or the responsible accountant) forecast the future benefits that will be
derived from ownership of the asset. For certain assets, such as loans, investments in common stock, paid-up insurance policies, buildings or equipment leased to others, or customers' promises to pay, estimating future benefits is relatively easy. These benefits may be in the form of actual cash
flows or, as in the case of the paid-up insurance policy, the benefits may be
protection or the elimination of cash outflows that would be required in the
absence of the asset. Payment in advance of a year's rent on a building
creates an asset, the right to use the building for a year or, equivalently, the
elimination of the requirement to make monthly rental payments during the
year.

This method of valuation is particularly useful for assets that have a
substantially long life and a predictable benefit flow. A loan that requires
the borrower to make level payments, incorporating both principal and interest, at the rate of $1,000 per year for 10 years certainly does not have a
present-day value of $10,000 unless the lender assumes a zero interest rate
for equivalency (which implies that the lender has nothing else to do with the
money). Rather, the value of the loan depends upon the equivalency interest rate that the lender assigns to loans (investments) of this type:

Equivalency Interest Rate	Time-Adjusted Value
6%	$7,360
8%	6,710
10%	6,144
12%	5,650
15%	5,019

The higher the interest rate assumed, the lower the value of the loan.

Consider the applicability of this method of valuation to certain other
assets; for example, a machine tool owned by a manufacturing company

and a cellar of fine wines owned by an individual. In both cases the ownership of the asset promises a return of benefits stretched out into the future,
but measuring these benefits presents a real challenge.

The benefits to be derived from the ownership of the machine tool will
depend upon a host of factors, including:

1   The rate of obsolescence of the tool, which in turn will depend upon the
    rate of technological development by machine tool builders
2   The future demand for the product or products to be produced on the
    machine tool (this demand will in turn be dependent upon the rate of
    change in the company's product lines, changes in the competitive cli-
    mate, the strength of the economy, and changing consumer prefer-
    ences)

Similar problems are faced in the valuing of a cellar of fine wines. The
benefits to be derived from owning this asset are the personal pleasure of
consuming the wine and serving it to friends, but the value of these benefits
is somewhat less predictable, since it is dependent upon such factors as how
well the wine ages, the volume and quality of wines to be produced in upcoming years, and future supply-demand imbalances that may significantly
impact the cost of wines. Note that this method of valuation, while appealing in theory, may be much less useful in practice, at least for valuing such
assets as machine tools and wine cellars.

We have been focusing on the valuing of assets. Does the time-adjusted valuation method apply also to the valuation of obligations? Yes, as
we have already seen in a borrower's valuation of a promise to pay under a
loan agreement. The borrower's interest equivalency rate (determined by
reference both to uses for the borrowed money and also to alternative
sources of funds) is applied to the future cash flows to which the borrower is
obligated.

What other obligations might be similarly valued? Consider a company's obligation to perform warranty service on the products it sells. If the
company has been producing the warranted product for some time, a study
of the record of warranty service will provide a quite reliable basis for estimating the timing and magnitude of the warranty service that will have to
be performed. Of course, these estimates will need to be tempered by consideration of design or manufacturing changes which may increase or decrease the warranty risk to the manufacturer, but once the pattern of warranty expenditures—future cash flows—has been estimated, the
time-adjusted valuation method can be applied to arrive at a present-day
equivalent value.

Similarly, a company's obligation to make payments to employees who
have retired (i.e., pensions) or to others who are on vacation or sick leave

can be valued on a time-adjusted basis. Typically, the timing and amounts of these flows are predictable.

You may feel that these obligations, warranty and employee leave, need not be valued. Why not postpone any accounting for warranty or leave until the event occurs that requires the company to make an expenditure: when the product is returned for repair or when the employee commences the leave? While this is not an unreasonable point of view, there exists little doubt that the company will incur these expenditures, since inevitably a certain percentage of products will fail during the warranty period and employees do indeed take vacations or get sick or otherwise become entitled to paid leave. Moreover, it is today's shipments of products that give rise to the warranty service obligations and today's employment of personnel that requires the company to make certain payments at the time of promised leave. Thus, the fact that activities today are creating these future company obligations for warranty and leave payments and the fact that the timing and amount of these future expenditures are quite predictable suggest that the obligations should be valued and recorded.

Other types of obligations that are perhaps contingent or unpredictable might not be valued and recorded. Examples are the possibility of infringing another company's patent, the possibility that an income tax audit will result in the imposition of additional taxes, or the possibility that a current dispute with a supplier will result in additional payments to that supplier. Obviously, certain types of obligations will fall in a "gray area"—that is, two people might reasonably disagree as to whether or not the obligation should be recorded—and we shall need to come back to this issue in later chapters.

MARKET VALUE

Another method of valuing both assets and obligations involves the use of the market value, or price at which similar assets and obligations currently trade in the market place. That is, if we can determine the price at which the asset could be purchased or sold, that price could serve as the basis for valuation by the asset's present owner.

We have already considered the example of the used automobile for which there does exist a ready second market. Because very many used automobiles are traded in the secondhand market in this country every year, information is collected, compiled, and published as to typical, or market, prices for a variety of makes and models.

Of course, common stocks that are actively traded (referred to as being publicly held) have market prices. Loans are also bought and sold among financial institutions and individuals and thus have a market price. On the other hand, common shares in a company that is predominantly owned by a single family or loans of a specialized nature or loans between individuals are not necessarily actively traded in any organized market, and thus these types of securities do not have an easily determinable market price. However, even these securities do have some market price, that is, a price at which they could be bought or sold.

Thinking back over the other examples used in this chapter, we might agree that:

1   Household furniture surely has a market value. The classified advertisements in the daily newspaper indicate a relatively active, though largely unorganized, market for secondhand furniture. Persons knowledgeable about the used-furniture market could provide fairly reliable estimates of the market value.
2   The pantry full of canned foods easily can be valued at market prices by simple reference to today's price at the food market for the same items.
3   Secondhand machine tools of a standard configuration have a very ready market at predictable prices, much like used automobiles. However, market prices of machine tools tend to fluctuate quite widely, depending upon the state of the economy and the delivery schedules for equivalent new machine tools. This situation may be troublesome, since the use of this method of valuation would require that recorded accounting values fluctuate with these market prices. Also, specialized machine tools—perhaps tools that were custom-made for a particular user—may be of potential use only to the owner's competitors and so have a very limited market. Arriving at a reliable market price for such assets would be difficult.
4   The cellar of fine wines can be valued by reference to today's prices for a bottle of the same wine from the same vineyard in the same year. In fact, vintage fine wines are sold and traded quite regularly.

What about the problem of valuing the company's or an individual's obligations? We saw how the time-adjusted valuation method might be applied to warranty and employee leave obligations. Can the market value method also be applied to valuing these obligations?

A manufacturer of industrial or consumer devices which are subject to warranty could contract with another organization, perhaps one with an extensive network of service centers, to undertake the warranty work. Such a contract with an outside organization would fix a market price for this obligation: the price the manufacturer will pay to be relieved of the obligation to repair during the warranty period. In fact, contracts of this nature are entered into regularly in certain industries, such as the computer peripheral industry.

Contracting with outside firms, generally insurance companies, to fulfill pension obligations to employees is a more prevalent example of paying a market price in order to be relieved of a future obligation. Many organizations also contract with insurance companies for the payment of wages to employees in the event of extended sick leaves.

Therefore, we see that in many situations valuation by reference to the current market price for the asset or for relief from the obligation is feasible; undue effort or research is not required and the resulting values are quite defensible. This method has some strong appeal: it does not require predictions about the future, as the time-adjusted value method does, it is rooted in the reality of today's marketplace, and it is understandable, explainable, and not complex.

However, the method does have its shortcomings. The market for used tools such as the specialized machine tool mentioned above is very limited, and so the company may receive quite a low price for the asset in a sale. Does this imply that the specialized tool is of low value to the owning company, which, in fact, has no intention of selling it? In a more general sense, just how relevant are current market prices to the problem of valuing an asset, *if* the owner of the asset does not intend to sell it? The value of the specialized machine tool resides in its use, not in its resale. The fact that there may exist no other potential users of the specialized tool does not denigrate or destroy its usefulness to the company that now owns it.

At the other end of the scale, suppose that an asset owned by the company has a high resale, or market, value, but for any of a number of reasons the company cannot consider selling the asset. Again, it seems that the value in use is more relevant to the accountant's problem of asset valuation than is the higher market value that may exist, but not be realizable, for the asset.

Similarly, the household furniture and the pantry full of canned foods may have values to their particular owners that are higher than the market prices of strictly comparable items today. The furniture may have a sentimental value and the emergency supply of food may have a security value —important values to their owners perhaps, but not reflected in the market prices that others are willing to pay.

Thus, the market value method of valuation, while appealing, has limitations, as did the time-adjusted value method. We will consider now the cost value method, and then later return to a consideration of the advantages and disadvantages of each of the three methods.

COST VALUE

A more complete name for this method might be the *historical cost method*, since it calls for assets to be valued at the prices paid at the time they were acquired.

A decided advantage of the cost value method is that typically one can determine with both ease and accuracy what was actually paid for the asset. The acquisition prices of the securities, the automobile, the household furniture, the pantry full of canned goods, the machine tools (whether standard or custom), and the cellar of fine wines are known.

One quickly realizes that these historical cost values bear no necessary relationship to the values that would be assigned to assets by the time-adjusted value or market value methods. For example, if the automobile or household furniture was purchased long ago, its cost value may be considerably higher than current market value. On the other hand, if the automobile is now considered a classic or if the owner of the fine wine made a particularly astute purchase, current market prices may be considerably above the acquisition or historical cost value. Consider the problem of valuing a parcel of land, a building site. If the land was acquired some time ago, its original cost is probably very much below today's current market values, unless of course the pattern of development of the community or roadway system has left the parcel in less desirable surroundings, in which case the reverse may be true.

If the decline in the value of the asset results simply from the passage of time—for example wear, tear, and obsolescence on buildings or machine tools or vehicles—the accountant might simply value the asset at a declining percentage of its original cost, as the asset ages. This procedure is in fact widely followed by accountants through the process of recording in the accounting records each year an amount called *depreciation,* which serves to reduce the recorded value of the asset. This procedure is discussed in Chapter 7.

However, this systematic write-down in the value of an asset over its life takes care of only one set of causes of decline in asset value. In fact, a number of other factors create wide differences between market value and historical cost value. Probably the most important is inflation.[5] Inflation can cause an old asset recorded at historical cost to appear in accounting records to have substantially less value to the company than its cost of replacement. This condition frequently affects public utilities (electric, gas distribution, telephone) and producers of basic commodities such as steel and aluminum. The facilities built by these companies many years ago may continue to be productive, but the high rate of inflation in land and construction costs means that the cost value of newly constructed, equivalent facilities will be very much higher than the cost value assigned to the old facilities. This dilemma has been accorded increasing attention by the accounting profession in recent years, and some aspects of the professional deliberations on accounting for inflation are discussed in Chapter 8.

Can the cost method be used to value the company's or an individual's

---

[5] We might more generally speak of changes in purchasing power, thus including both inflation and deflation. However, the history of virtually all organized economies is one of persistent inflation at various rates, punctuated by relatively few periods of deflation.

obligations? By their nature obligations are settled in the future and have no historical cost, simply because history has not yet caught up with the obligations. A strict interpretation of the cost value method might then suggest the omission from the records of any such obligations that require the future expenditure of cash or the future performance of services. Such an interpretation is unsatisfactory, as obligations such as bank loans, promises to pay vendors, obligations under warranty provisions, and payment of wages to employees on vacation or sick leave would seem to be of major importance to the company. Moreover, it is not unduly difficult to measure the future cost of meeting these obligations.

Before we turn to consider the relative merits of the three valuation methods just discussed, we need to consider, at least preliminarily, the use to which these valuations of assets and obligations will be put. That is, what is the framework of our accounting system?

The Accounting Equation

We have been referring throughout this chapter to assets and obligations. Assets we have defined as physical property, rights, and financial resources that hold the promise of providing ongoing benefits in the future. We have considered a number of types of assets: securities, promises of customers to pay, production facilities such as machine tools and plant space, rights to the use of patents, protection for one year under an insurance policy. While we have not mentioned them before, it should be obvious that cash (whether in the drawer or in the bank) and inventory are critically important assets to all merchandising and manufacturing companies, and these assets should not be unduly difficult to value. Other important assets that the company might own are orders from customers and employment contracts with key personnel, although we will see that these assets are a good deal more difficult to value.

In any case, we know that our company owns a great number of physical "things" and intangible "rights" that we call *assets*. We also have suggested that the company has certain obligations—to its bank for money it has borrowed, to its vendors for inventory or services rendered, to its employees for wages and benefits earned but not yet paid, to customers in connection with product warranty provisions, and to others as well. These obligations to persons or organizations outside the entity for which we are accounting are referred to as **liabilities.**[6] The liabilities of a company are

---

[6] You may be inclined to argue that employees are part of, and not outside, the entity. While the employees are without doubt essential to the operation of the enterprise, they earn income and incur expenditures independent of the business entity for which we are accounting, and so are separate and distinct accounting entities.

typically discharged by the payment of cash, but they may also be discharged by the performance of a service, such as warranty repair. Liabilities comprise all that the accounting entity owes.

Thus, we define *assets* as that which the entity *owns,* and *liabilities* as that which the entity *owes.* We feel one way about assets—we are better off to own them—and quite the opposite way about liabilities—we would like to avoid them. Put another way, liabilities represent a call on the assets; if at any time we were to discharge the liabilities, we would do so by utilizing the assets then owned. A healthy company will own more than it owes—its value of assets will exceed the value of liabilities. Moreover, the difference between what it owns and what it owes, the net amount of assets that are not required to offset liabilities, is a measure of the *worth* of the company. This worth accrues to the benefit of the company's owners—in the case of a corporation, its shareholders. That is, the greater this difference between assets and liabilities, the better off are the shareholders collectively. We refer to this difference between assets and liabilities as **owners' equity,** and we can describe the fundamental **accounting equation** as follows:

Assets − liabilities = owners' equity

This statement must be true at all times. If assets of the company increase without any change in liabilities, owners' equity must increase, that is, the owners collectively must be in a better position than they were before the assets increased. If, on the other hand, the liabilities of the corporation increase without any corresponding change in assets, then the owners' equity must have declined.

Using simple algebra, we can rearrange the terms in the equation shown above, and arrive at the following restatement of the accounting equation:

Assets = liabilities + owners' equity

This form is, in fact, the more typical one. You may already be aware that most published financial statements in this country follow this format: assets listed first (or on the left), liabilities and owners' equity shown below (or on the right), with the totals being equal. This form of the equation suggests another way to describe the fundamental accounting equation: the assets represent the investments by the accounting entity in physical property, intangible rights, and financial resources; the liabilities and owners' equity represent the sources of funds that were used to make the investments. The left side of the equation shows what the company owns, and the right side shows how the ownership of the assets was financed.

More on Owners' Equity

But how, in fact, is owners' equity created? How can assets increase without an increase in liabilities, or how can liabilities decrease without a corresponding decrease in assets? (Both of these events will serve to increase owners' equity.) There are two ways that this increase in owners' equity can occur:

1 The owners can invest additional capital in the enterprise. If the enterprise is a sole proprietorship or partnership, the owners are the sole proprietor or the partners, and they simply agree to put more funds into the business. If the enterprise is formed as a corporation, additional shares of stock are created and sold to investors who may be attracted to buy into the corporation.
2 The enterprise can earn a profit. Take the simple example of a company buying merchandise for $1.00 and selling it for $2.00. If the company incurs no other expenses, it has made a profit of $1.00. If this $1.00 of profit is not removed by the owners, then it represents an addition to owners' equity.

These are the two important ways that owners' equity is increased. You will probably quickly see that there are also two primary ways in which owners' equity can be decreased:

1 The owners can withdraw funds from the business. The typical example is the payment of dividends to the owners of the capital stock of a corporation.
2 The company can incur a loss. If in the example above the merchandise that was purchased for $1.00 is sold for 75 cents (and the company incurs no other expenses), then the company has made a loss of 25 cents.

Therefore, owners' equity, in addition to being simply the difference between assets and liabilities of the enterprise, can also be defined as:

The sum of capital invested by the owners plus profits earned by the enterprise, less the sum of any losses incurred by the enterprise and any funds paid by the enterprise back to its owners.

Because much confusion arises as to the meaning of owners' equity, let's spend a minute emphasizing what owners' equity is *not*. First, owners' equity is *not* a pool of cash, not liquid funds that are available to be spent or repaid to shareholders. Remember that any financial resources owned by the company are considered to be assets. Thus, to determine whether in fact cash exists for spending or return to shareholders, we need to look at the assets of the company. If today the owners put additional capital into the company, the company's financial resources—assets in the form of cash—will increase by exactly the same amount as owners' equity will increase. If tomorrow the company uses this cash to purchase inventory, the company will be trading one asset for another, and owners' equity will remain unchanged; however, now the company will no longer have the liquid funds that it had before. This fact is revealed not by looking at the amount of owners' equity, but by considering the amount of cash and other liquid assets owned by the company.

Second, for reasons that will become clear, the valuation placed on owners' equity in the company's financial records may be substantially different from the value assigned to the ownership of the company by the financial markets. For a publicly traded corporation, the market value of the entire corporate entity is equal to the current trading price of a share of the corporation's stock times the number of total shares owned by investors. This *trading value* may well be considerably at odds with the value arrived at by substracting liabilities owned by the company from assets owned by the company. Recall that trading (market) prices for shares of common stock are a function of the investors' collective expectations about the future flow of benefits (primarily dividends) from ownership of the shares and the equivalency interest rate assigned by investors to this flow of benefits. (The equivalency rate will in turn be a function of investor psychology, conditions in the general economy, and conditions in the credit markets.) Moreover, the trading price of the common stock simply indicates the amount for which 100 or 200 shares of stock could be bought or sold. If you sought to purchase all the shares of a corporation, your demand would greatly exceed the available supply of shares and would cause the trading price to increase; conversely, if you sought to sell a very large number of shares, there might not exist in the market a sufficient number of buyers and the trading price would become depressed.

Thus, for reasons having to do with both the mechanics of establishing the trading price of the common shares and the difficulties associated with valuing the assets and liabilities of the corporation, it will be unreasonable to expect that the two valuations of owners' equity will agree—that is:

(Assets − liabilities) will not necessarily equal (trading price per share × number of common shares)

We shall reemphasize these points a number of times in this text.

Choosing among the Valuation Methods

Let's return now to consider the relative advantages and disadvantages of the three valuation methods presented earlier. Which one does the best job of valuing the assets and liabilities of the company? It is apparent from our discussion thus far that different valuation methods fit different situations. The time-adjusted value method seems well-suited to the valuation of common stocks, notes, and other investment securities. The market value method seems workable with respect to valuing automobiles, standard machine tools, a pantry full of canned goods, and perhaps even a cellar of fine wines. The cost value method seems workable with respect to most all assets and liabilities, but as the time period between acquisition date and evaluation date lengthens and the rate of inflation increases, we become less comfortable with the information provided by this method of valuation.

We need to choose some criteria to use in comparing these three valuation methods. While there is not agreement about the appropriate criteria, the following seven factors should serve as a sufficient basis for comparison.

CURRENTLY RELEVANT

The accounting information that will result from the valuation of assets and liabilities is used to make decisions, such as operating decisions by management, investment decisions by shareholders, and credit decisions by lenders. These decisions require currently relevant data, data that reflect today's situation and expectations. Almost by definition, the historical cost method suffers in fulfilling this criterion and the more ancient the history, the more it is likely to suffer.

FEASIBLE

It must be possible to develop the data required by the valuation method. If the future flow of benefits to be derived from an asset simply cannot be estimated, then the time-adjusted value method becomes unfeasible for that asset. An example is a patent on one feature of a potential new product. If the design of the remainder of the new product is never completed, or the resulting product proves to have no market or to be too expensive to produce, the patent in question may provide a very modest flow of future benefits. Alternatively, if the product gets designed, is producible, and meets a market need, the flow of benefits from the patent may be long and large. The accountant simply can't know now what the future holds for the patent.

The cost value method will typically prove to be highly feasible—data as to historical cost are readily available.

EFFECTIVE

While it may prove to be feasible to develop certain data required for time-adjusted valuation or market valuation, the expense incurred for the human power, computing power, or the service of outside experts such as appraisers may render one or more of the valuation methods cost-ineffective. For example, there is no question that data about the current market value of a chemical processing plant or of a trademark could be assembled; the asset could be advertised for sale, and offers solicited. But such a process would be costly, for a good deal of discussion and negotiation would have to transpire before a bona fide offer would be received. (Moreover, a bona fide offer might never be received, if it became known that the owner had no intention of selling the asset.)

Bear in mind with respect to all accounting information and reports that we cannot afford to spend more developing the information than the information is worth to us. This generalization certainly applies to the valuation of certain assets and liabilities that do not have a predictable flow of future benefits and do not have a readily available market price.

TIMELY

The usefulness of accounting information declines rapidly with time. Management needs information that will help it to make timely operating decisions, to correct problems, and to seize opportunities. Investors need information that will permit them to decide to buy, sell, or hold securities, and they want this information as soon as possible. An accounting report that tells the condition of the company six months ago is a lot less useful to its audience than one that tells the condition of the company two weeks ago. Accountants are willing, therefore, to sacrifice some accuracy in valuation in order to get rapid valuation.

FREE FROM BIAS

By now it must be clear that a good deal of latitude is available to the accountant in deciding what should be recorded and at what value. The ideal valuation method will be objective and sufficiently definitive so as to be little affected by an accountant's conscious or unconscious bias.

REPEATABLE

This criterion is closely related to the previous one. Again, if the valuation method is objective, it should be repeatable. If the valuation done today and the one performed next month or next year are consistent (but of course not necessarily identical), we will have more confidence in the resulting information.   If the valuation process repeated by another accountant leads to the same result, we will judge both the method and the information to be more reliable.

VERIFIABLE

As a matter of course, the financial records and statements of major enterprises are audited by independent, professional accountants.   In order that these auditors can fulfill their role of confirming that the financial reports fairly represent the company's position, the valuations of assets and liabilities by the company's own accountants must be verifiable by the outside accountants.   That is, tangible evidence that is subject to independent verification must be used in the valuation process.   Again, if the method used is objective, it will tend to satisfy the final three criteria—it will be free from bias, repeatable, and verifiable.

The Challenge of Alternative Valuation Methods

Clearly, none of the three valuation methods—time-adjusted value, market value, cost value—satisfies all of the seven criteria.   Thus, the choice among them is not clear-cut.   The first criterion, that data be currently relevant, seems best satisfied by the time-adjusted value and market value methods, and least satisfied by the cost value method.   However, the remaining criteria are probably best satisfied by the cost value method:

Uncovering historical cost data is clearly feasible.

Application of the method is cost-effective: once determined, the values don't change.

The data can be arrived at in a timely manner.

Historical costs are relatively free from bias; some arguments may arise as to what constitutes cost, but these arguments will typically be minor as compared with disagreements on the future flow of benefits.

Cost value determinations are repeatable, and since they don't change with time, they are consistent and reliable.

Cost data represent tangible evidence subject to independent verification.

Yet, the market value method also satisfies most, if not all, criteria with respect to the valuation of certain assets such as automobiles or standard machine tools. The market value of these assets is certainly currently relevant data; it is feasible and cost-effective to arrive at the data; the data are quickly available, objective, free from bias, repeatable, and verifiable. The time-adjusted value method also satisfies substantially all of the criteria in certain instances: few problems are encountered in applying this method to the valuation of a loan or of an employee pension, as the data required are available, objective, verifiable, and so forth.

On balance, we can conclude that the time-adjusted value method provides information that is most relevant to today's decision, but is extraordinarily difficult to apply to the valuation of very many assets and liabilities. The data required are not readily or inexpensively available, biases are inevitable, and as a result different individuals, each doing the most conscientious job possible, will arrive at different values. On the other hand, the cost value method appears to be the most reliable (we understand the source and can verify the accuracy of the data) although this method often compromises our first criterion, since historical cost simply may not be relevant to today's decision.

The challenge that faces the accountant is to develop accounting information and reports that combine the relevancy and usefulness that are inherent in the time-adjusted value method with the efficiency and reliability that are inherent in the cost value method. Thus, if the time-adjusted value method is to predominate in our accounting practice, we must find a way to make the time-adjusted valuations free from bias, objective, and verifiable, and to make the method efficient. If the cost value method is to predominate, then we must work on making the resulting information more useful to current decision making by the many audiences who depend on the accounting reports.

Dominance of the Cost Value Method

While we shall continue to explore the applicability of the three valuation methods, we need to recognize that current accounting practices and rules are built to a very large degree on the cost value method. In the vast majority of cases today, accountants are content to use historical cost data as the best evidence of what the company owns—the value of its assets—and what the company owes—the value of its liabilities. The method is expedient and pragmatic. At the same time, there exists wide agreement that the method is not wholly adequate. It is precise but, in the view of many, not sufficiently accurate.

There is ample evidence that accountants are embracing, to an increasing degree, the valuation procedures inherent in the other two methods. Market values, or replacement values of assets, are being accorded more attention as the business and financial communities wrestle with operating and investment decisions in times of rapid inflation. The future flow of benefits and costs is often now considered the most appropriate basis for valuation of certain liabilities. Thus, we have seen and will probably continue to see a movement away from strict adherence to historical cost valuations. The accountants' rule-making bodies, both public and private, have been conspicuously active in the last several years in promulgating new rules that attempt to overcome some of the deficiencies in the cost value methodology and to provide more objectivity to alternative methodologies. As we proceed in our discussion of accounting, we need to be ready to question the rules and conventions that dictate the techniques now in use. These rules and conventions are typically built on cost value methodology and are subject to change.

Summary

In this chapter we have focused on that part of the accounting task that involves valuing the various assets and obligations (liabilities) of the accounting entity, preparatory to recording in the accounting records the events and conditions of the enterprise. Three quite different methods might be used:

1   The time-adjusted value method, which seeks to determine the equivalent value today of the flow of benefits or costs that will arise in the future as a result of owning the asset or being subject to the liability.
2   The market value method, which looks to the price at which the asset or liability, in its present state, could be bought or sold in the market as the evidence of its value in today's accounting records.
3   The cost method, which relies on historical cost—that is, the cost of the asset or liability at the time it was originally acquired—to represent its value.

The resulting valuations are used to determine what the company owns (assets) and what it owes (liabilities); the difference between the two represents the worth attributable to the owners. Thus, the fundamental accounting equation can be written:

Assets − liabilities = owners' equity

There are two basic sources of financing for the assets owned by the enterprise: (1) the funds obtained from the company's creditors, as represented by the company's liabilities; and (2) funds obtained from the company's owners, either as cash invested over the years by the owners or profits earned on behalf of the owners but not paid out to them. Thus, the accounting equation can also be stated as:

Assets = liabilities + owners' equity

The simplest view of owners' equity is that it is just the difference between assets owned and liabilities owed. Owners' equity is also defined as capital invested in the business by its owners, plus the net of earnings made less losses incurred in operating the business, and less any amounts returned to the owners.

Seven criteria are suggested for judging the relative advantages and disadvantages of each of the three valuation methods to be used in valuing the company's assets, liabilities, and owner's equity. The ideal valuation method would provide information that is: (1) relevant to current decisions; (2) feasible in its derivation; (3) cost-effective (worth more than the cost to generate it); (4) timely; (5) free from bias; (6) repeatable; and (7) verifiable by independent persons. None of the three valuation methods is clearly preferable. The time-adjusted value method seems to provide the most currently useful data, but is often difficult to implement. The cost value method best satisfies those criteria dealing with objectivity and verifiability of the data, but frequently historical costs are not relevant to today's decisions.

In actual accounting practice, the cost value method is widely used. Currently accepted rules and techniques for valuation adhere closely to this methodology, but there is increasing pressure from both accountants and financial audiences for a correction of some of the shortcomings of the cost value method and for a movement in the direction of the time-adjusted value and market value methods.

Appendix: Calculating Time-Adjusted Values

Money is said to have a time value. One would rather receive a certain amount of money today than the same amount at a later date, say a year from today, since a return can be earned on the money during the intervening year. Similarly, one would prefer to delay the payment of a specified amount as long as possible so that a return can be earned on the money during the period of the delay.

If the rate of the available return is known, the advantage or disadvantage associated with accelerated or delayed receipts and payments can be calculated. That is, values of cash flows (receipts or payments) are a function of their timing and by appropriate adjustment the values can reflect differences in timing. The time-adjusted valuation method referred to in Chapter 2 requires that future cash flows that will arise because of assets owned or obligations undertaken be valued as of today, utilizing an appropriate equivalency (interest) rate.

Suppose, for example, that person X is the manager of a retail store. When the store has a small amount of excess cash, X invests it in a short-term deposit or security that earns interest at a specified rate, $r\%$ per year; when the store runs short of cash, X withdraws (disinvests) from this deposit or security the amount necessary to cover the cash deficiency. Now suppose that the owner of the building in which X's store is located offers to reduce (or discount) the store's rent if X will agree to pay the rent in advance. X wishes to determine the rent discount that would be attractive; that is, X wants to know the value today of this obligation due one year from now. This value will indicate to X how much to pay in rent today in lieu of a $2,000 rental payment otherwise due a year from today.

If X does not make the advance rental payment, the money will remain in the deposit or security that earns at the rate, r. X's equivalency rate is r. Therefore, the maximum amount, P, that X would be willing to pay today is that amount that would otherwise grow at the rate of r per year to $2,000 at the end of the year; to repeat, it is assumed that X will leave the amount P in the interest-bearing deposit or security if the advance rental payment is not made. Therefore, an equation for P is:

$$P(1 + r) = \$2,000$$

$$P = \frac{2,000}{(1 + r)}$$

If r is 8%,

$$P = \frac{2,000}{(1.08)} = \$1,852$$

We conclude that, if the building owner will accept less than $1,852 today in lieu of $2,000 a year from today, X will want to pay the rent in advance. P is referred to as the present worth or time-adjusted value of the future rental payment at rate r; that is, $2,000 a year from now has a time-adjusted value today of $1,852, assuming an interest rate of 8%.

Now suppose the building owner seeks payment in advance of rentals due at the end of each of the next three years. Certainly X will demand a a greater discount on the second year's rent than on the first, and a still greater discount on the rent that would otherwise not be due for three years. Therefore, X needs to know the time-adjusted value (or present value), P, of a stream of three payments, each of $2,000, occurring at one-year intervals, assuming an interest rate of r. P is the sum of the individual time-adjusted values for each of the three years:

$$P = \frac{2,000}{(1 + r)} + \frac{2,000}{(1 + r)^2} + \frac{2,000}{(1 + r)^3}$$

If r is once again 8%,

$$P = \frac{2,000}{(1.08)} + \frac{2,000}{(1.08)^2} + \frac{2,000}{(1.08)^3} = \frac{2,000}{(1.08)} + \frac{2,000}{(1.166)} + \frac{2,000}{(1.260)}$$

$$= 1,852 + 1,715 + 1,587 = \$5,154$$

If X's alternative use of the funds is the investment in the deposit or security earning 8%, X would be willing to pay an amount up to \$5,154 to be relieved of the obligation to make the three annual rental payments of \$2,000 each.

Assume now that the building owner is badly in need of cash, and, in the absence of the advance rental payment from X, would have to borrow money at very high interest rates. Under these conditions the owner might be willing to accept substantially less than \$5,154. That is, the time-adjusted value of these future receipts to the building owner is less than the value to X's company, if the owner assumes an interest rate, r, of greater than 8%. Indeed, the owner may have an equivalency rate well above 8%, if alternatively the owner would have to borrow at an interest rate of, say, 12%. Assuming an r of 12%, P for the building owner—the time-adjusted value of the next three annual rental payments—is:

$$P = \frac{2,000}{(1.12)} + \frac{2,000}{(1.12)^2} + \frac{2,000}{(1.12)^3}$$

$$= 1,786 + 1,594 + 1,424 = \$4,804$$

Note that the higher the interest, or equivalency, rate, r, used in the calculation, the lower the time-adjusted value of future payments.

Table 2A-1 contains factors for calculating the time-adjusted value of \$1 to be received or paid at various dates in the future and at various interest rates. Table 2A-2 contains factors for calculating the time-adjusted value of a *stream* of payments or receipts, each of \$1, occurring at annual intervals for the periods (n) indicated; these factors are also shown for various interest rates.

The use of these tables can be illustrated with the examples just discussed:

a   The time-adjusted value today of a cash flow of \$2,000 occurring a year from today can be calculated from Table 2A-1; the factor in the 8% col-

Table 2A-1
Time-Adjusted (Present) Value of One Dollar at the End of n Years

Year (n)	1%	2%	3%	4%	5%	6%	7%	8%	9%	10%	12%	14%	15%	Year (n)
1	0.990	0.980	0.970	0.962	0.952	0.943	0.935	0.926	0.917	0.909	0.893	0.877	0.870	1
2	0.980	0.961	0.943	0.925	0.907	0.890	0.873	0.857	0.842	0.826	0.797	0.769	0.756	2
3	0.971	0.942	0.915	0.889	0.864	0.840	0.816	0.794	0.772	0.751	0.712	0.675	0.658	3
4	0.961	0.924	0.888	0.855	0.823	0.792	0.763	0.735	0.708	0.683	0.636	0.592	0.572	4
5	0.951	0.906	0.863	0.822	0.784	0.747	0.713	0.681	0.650	0.621	0.567	0.519	0.497	5
6	0.942	0.888	0.837	0.790	0.746	0.705	0.666	0.630	0.596	0.564	0.507	0.456	0.432	6
7	0.933	0.871	0.813	0.760	0.711	0.665	0.623	0.583	0.547	0.513	0.452	0.400	0.376	7
8	0.923	0.853	0.789	0.731	0.677	0.627	0.582	0.540	0.502	0.467	0.404	0.351	0.327	8
9	0.914	0.837	0.766	0.703	0.645	0.592	0.544	0.500	0.460	0.424	0.361	0.308	0.284	9
10	0.905	0.820	0.744	0.676	0.614	0.558	0.508	0.463	0.422	0.386	0.322	0.270	0.247	10
11	0.896	0.804	0.722	0.650	0.585	0.527	0.475	0.429	0.388	0.350	0.287	0.237	0.215	11
12	0.887	0.788	0.701	0.625	0.557	0.497	0.444	0.397	0.356	0.319	0.257	0.208	0.187	12
13	0.879	0.773	0.681	0.601	0.530	0.469	0.415	0.368	0.326	0.290	0.229	0.182	0.163	13
14	0.870	0.758	0.661	0.577	0.505	0.442	0.388	0.340	0.299	0.263	0.205	0.160	0.141	14
15	0.861	0.743	0.642	0.555	0.481	0.417	0.362	0.315	0.275	0.239	0.183	0.140	0.123	15
16	0.853	0.728	0.623	0.534	0.458	0.394	0.339	0.299	0.252	0.218	0.163	0.123	0.107	16
17	0.844	0.714	0.605	0.513	0.436	0.371	0.317	0.270	0.231	0.198	0.146	0.108	0.093	17
18	0.836	0.700	0.587	0.494	0.416	0.350	0.296	0.250	0.212	0.180	0.130	0.095	0.081	18
19	0.828	0.686	0.570	0.475	0.396	0.331	0.277	0.232	0.194	0.164	0.116	0.083	0.070	19
20	0.820	0.673	0.554	0.456	0.377	0.312	0.258	0.215	0.178	0.149	0.104	0.073	0.061	20
21	0.811	0.660	0.538	0.439	0.359	0.294	0.242	0.199	0.164	0.135	0.093	0.064	0.053	21
22	0.803	0.647	0.522	0.422	0.342	0.278	0.226	0.184	0.150	0.123	0.083	0.056	0.046	22
23	0.795	0.634	0.507	0.406	0.326	0.262	0.211	0.170	0.138	0.112	0.074	0.049	0.040	23
24	0.788	0.622	0.492	0.390	0.310	0.247	0.197	0.158	0.126	0.102	0.066	0.043	0.035	24
25	0.780	0.610	0.478	0.375	0.295	0.233	0.184	0.146	0.116	0.092	0.059	0.038	0.030	25

Year (n)	16%	18%	20%	22%	24%	25%	26%	28%	30%	35%	40%	50%	Year (n)
1	0.862	0.847	0.833	0.820	0.806	0.800	0.794	0.781	0.769	0.741	0.714	0.667	1
2	0.743	0.718	0.694	0.672	0.650	0.640	0.630	0.610	0.592	0.549	0.510	0.444	2
3	0.641	0.609	0.579	0.551	0.524	0.512	0.500	0.477	0.455	0.406	0.364	0.296	3
4	0.552	0.516	0.482	0.451	0.423	0.410	0.397	0.373	0.350	0.301	0.260	0.198	4
5	0.476	0.437	0.402	0.370	0.341	0.328	0.315	0.291	0.269	0.223	0.186	0.132	5
6	0.410	0.370	0.333	0.303	0.275	0.262	0.250	0.227	0.207	0.165	0.133	0.088	6
7	0.354	0.314	0.279	0.249	0.222	0.210	0.198	0.178	0.159	0.122	0.095	0.059	7
8	0.305	0.266	0.233	0.204	0.179	0.168	0.157	0.139	0.123	0.091	0.068	0.039	8
9	0.263	0.225	0.194	0.167	0.144	0.134	0.125	0.108	0.094	0.067	0.048	0.026	9
10	0.227	0.191	0.162	0.137	0.116	0.107	0.099	0.085	0.073	0.050	0.035	0.017	10
11	0.195	0.162	0.135	0.112	0.094	0.086	0.079	0.066	0.056	0.037	0.025	0.012	11
12	0.168	0.137	0.112	0.092	0.076	0.069	0.062	0.052	0.043	0.027	0.018	0.008	12
13	0.145	0.116	0.093	0.075	0.061	0.055	0.050	0.040	0.033	0.020	0.013	0.005	13
14	0.125	0.099	0.078	0.062	0.049	0.044	0.039	0.032	0.025	0.015	0.009	0.003	14
15	0.108	0.084	0.065	0.051	0.040	0.035	0.031	0.025	0.020	0.011	0.006	0.002	15
16	0.093	0.071	0.054	0.042	0.032	0.028	0.025	0.019	0.015	0.008	0.005	0.002	16
17	0.080	0.060	0.045	0.034	0.026	0.023	0.020	0.015	0.012	0.006	0.003	0.001	17
18	0.069	0.051	0.038	0.028	0.021	0.018	0.016	0.012	0.009	0.005	0.002	0.001	18
19	0.060	0.043	0.031	0.023	0.017	0.014	0.012	0.009	0.007	0.003	0.002		19
20	0.051	0.037	0.026	0.019	0.014	0.012	0.010	0.007	0.005	0.002	0.001		20
21	0.044	0.031	0.022	0.015	0.011	0.009	0.008	0.006	0.004	0.002	0.001		21
22	0.038	0.026	0.018	0.013	0.009	0.007	0.006	0.004	0.003	0.001	0.001		22
23	0.033	0.022	0.015	0.010	0.007	0.006	0.005	0.003	0.002	0.001			23
24	0.028	0.019	0.013	0.008	0.006	0.005	0.004	0.003	0.002	0.001			24
25	0.024	0.016	0.010	0.007	0.005	0.004	0.003	0.002	0.001	0.001			25

Table 2A-2
Time-Adjusted (Present) Value of One Dollar per Year for n Years

Year (n)	1%	2%	3%	4%	5%	6%	7%	8%	9%	10%	12%	14%	15%	Year (n)
1	0.990	0.980	0.971	0.962	0.952	0.943	0.935	0.926	0.917	0.909	0.893	0.377	0.870	1
2	1.970	1.942	1.914	1.886	1.859	1.833	1.808	1.783	1.759	1.736	1.690	1.647	1.626	2
3	2.941	2.884	2.829	2.775	2.723	2.673	2.624	2.577	2.531	2.487	2.402	2.322	2.283	3
4	3.902	3.808	3.717	3.630	3.546	3.465	3.387	3.312	3.240	3.170	3.037	2.914	2.855	4
5	4.854	4.713	4.580	4.452	4.330	4.212	4.100	3.993	3.890	3.791	3.605	3.433	3.352	5
6	5.796	5.601	5.417	5.242	5.076	4.917	4.767	4.623	4.486	4.355	4.111	3.889	3.785	6
7	6.728	6.472	6.230	6.002	5.786	5.582	5.389	5.206	5.033	4.868	4.564	4.288	4.160	7
8	7.652	7.325	7.020	6.733	6.463	6.210	5.971	5.747	5.535	5.335	4.968	4.639	4.487	8
9	8.566	8.162	7.786	7.435	7.108	6.802	6.515	6.247	5.985	5.759	5.328	4.946	4.772	9
10	9.471	8.983	8.530	8.111	7.722	7.360	7.024	6.710	6.418	6.145	5.650	5.216	5.019	10
11	10.368	9.787	9.253	8.760	8.306	7.887	7.499	7.139	6.805	6.495	5.938	5.453	5.234	11
12	11.255	10.575	9.954	9.385	8.863	8.384	7.943	7.536	7.161	6.814	6.194	5.660	5.421	12
13	12.134	11.348	10.635	9.986	9.394	8.853	8.358	7.904	7.487	7.103	6.424	5.842	5.583	13
14	13.004	12.106	11.296	10.563	9.899	9.295	8.745	8.244	7.786	7.367	6.628	6.002	5.725	14
15	13.865	12.849	11.938	11.118	10.380	9.712	9.108	8.560	8.061	7.606	6.811	6.142	5.847	15
16	14.718	13.578	12.561	11.652	10.838	10.106	9.447	8.851	8.313	7.824	6.974	6.265	5.954	16
17	15.562	14.292	13.166	12.166	11.274	10.477	9.763	9.122	8.544	8.022	7.120	6.373	6.047	17
18	16.398	14.992	13.753	12.659	11.690	10.828	10.059	9.372	8.756	8.201	7.250	6.467	6.128	18
19	17.226	15.678	14.324	13.134	12.085	11.158	10.336	9.604	8.950	8.365	7.366	6.550	6.198	19
20	18.046	16.351	14.877	13.590	12.462	11.470	10.594	9.818	9.129	8.514	7.469	6.623	6.259	20
21	18.857	17.011	15.415	14.029	12.821	11.764	10.836	10.017	9.292	8.649	7.562	6.687	6.313	21
22	19.661	17.658	15.937	14.451	13.163	12.042	11.061	10.201	9.442	8.772	7.645	6.743	6.359	22
23	20.456	18.292	16.444	14.857	13.489	12.303	11.272	10.371	9.580	8.883	7.718	6.792	6.399	23
24	21.244	18.914	16.936	15.247	13.799	12.550	11.469	10.529	9.707	8.985	7.784	6.835	6.434	24
25	22.023	19.523	17.413	15.622	14.094	12.783	11.654	10.675	9.823	9.077	7.843	6.873	6.464	25

Year (n)	16%	18%	20%	22%	24%	25%	26%	28%	30%	35%	40%	50%	Year (n)
1	0.862	0.848	0.833	0.820	0.807	0.800	0.794	0.781	0.769	0.741	0.714	0.667	1
2	1.605	1.566	1.528	1.492	1.457	1.440	1.424	1.392	1.361	1.289	1.225	1.111	2
3	2.246	2.174	2.107	2.042	1.981	1.952	1.923	1.868	1.816	1.696	1.589	1.407	3
4	2.798	2.690	2.589	2.494	2.404	2.362	2.320	2.241	2.166	1.997	1.849	1.605	4
5	3.274	3.127	2.991	2.864	2.745	2.689	2.635	2.532	2.436	2.220	2.935	1.737	5
6	3.685	3.498	3.326	3.167	3.021	2.951	2.885	2.759	2.643	2.385	2.168	1.824	6
7	4.039	3.812	3.605	3.416	3.242	3.161	3.083	2.937	2.802	2.508	2.263	1.883	7
8	4.344	4.078	3.837	3.619	3.421	3.329	3.241	3.076	2.925	2.598	2.331	1.922	8
9	4.607	4.303	4.031	3.786	3.566	3.463	3.366	3.184	3.019	2.665	2.379	1.948	9
10	4.833	4.494	4.193	3.923	3.682	3.571	3.465	3.269	3.092	2.715	2.414	1.965	10
11	5.029	4.656	4.327	4.035	3.776	3.656	3.544	3.335	3.147	2.752	2.438	1.977	11
12	5.197	4.793	4.439	4.127	3.851	3.725	3.606	3.387	3.190	2.779	2.456	1.985	12
13	5.342	4.910	4.533	4.203	3.912	3.780	3.656	3.427	3.223	2.799	2.469	1.990	13
14	5.468	5.008	4.611	4.265	3.962	3.824	3.695	3.459	3.249	2.814	2.478	1.993	14
15	5.576	5.092	4.676	4.315	4.001	3.859	3.726	3.483	3.268	2.826	2.484	1.995	15
16	5.669	5.162	4.730	4.357	4.033	3.887	3.751	3.503	3.283	2.834	2.489	1.997	16
17	5.749	5.222	4.775	4.391	4.059	3.910	3.771	3.518	3.295	2.840	2.492	1.998	17
18	5.818	5.273	4.812	4.419	4.080	3.928	3.786	3.529	3.304	2.844	2.494	1.999	18
19	5.878	5.316	4.844	4.442	4.097	3.942	3.799	3.539	3.311	2.848	2.496	1.999	19
20	5.929	5.353	4.870	4.460	4.110	3.954	3.808	3.546	3.316	2.850	2.497	1.999	20
21	5.973	5.384	4.891	4.476	4.121	3.963	3.816	3.551	3.320	2.852	2.498	2.000	21
22	6.011	5.410	4.909	4.488	4.130	3.971	3.822	3.556	3.323	2.853	2.499	2.000	22
23	6.044	5.432	4.925	4.499	4.137	3.976	3.827	3.559	3.325	2.854	2.499	2.000	23
24	6.073	5.451	4.937	4.507	4.143	3.981	3.831	3.562	3.327	2.855	2.499	2.000	24
25	6.097	5.467	4.948	4.514	4.147	3.985	3.834	3.564	3.329	2.856	2.499	2.000	25

umn and the one-year row is 0.926. Therefore: $P = 2,000(0.926) = \$1,852$.

b The time-adjusted value today of a stream of three $2,000 cash flows occurring at the end of each of the next three years can be calculated from Table 2A-2; the factor in the 8% column and the three-year row is 2.577. Therefore: $P = 2,000(2.5770) = \$5,154$. For the building owner the factor is in the 12% column and the three-year row: 2.402. Therefore: $P = 2,000(2.402) = \$4,804$.

For purposes of accounting valuations, we are typically concerned with making time adjustments of future cash flows (inflows or outflows) to value them as of today. However, these same tables can be utilized to provide answers to the following types of questions:

1 If one places $100 today in an investment earning 10% per year, what will be the value of that investment in five years? Since the factors in Table 2A-1 indicate the value today of $100 to be received at some date in the future, the inverse of the factors indicates the value in the future of an amount placed at interest today. For example, the factor in the 10% column and five-year row is 0.621; the future value after five years of $100 placed at 10% interest today is:

$$100 \times \frac{1}{0.621} = \$161$$

2 If one borrows $10,000 today at an interest rate of 12%, how much will he or she be required to pay back (principal plus interest) at the end of each of the next eight years so as to just repay the loan in eight years, assuming that all eight payments are to be equal? Note that this is the typical form of a borrowing agreement in connection with a home purchase (the borrowing agreement is called a mortgage) or the purchase of an automobile or appliances (an installment purchase). Since the factors in Table 2A-2 indicate that value today of a stream of future payments or receipts, the inverses of the factors indicate the amounts to be paid or received in the future that are equivalent to a certain value today. In this example, the factor in the 12% column and eight-year row is 4.968; the stream of eight future annual payments required to discharge a $10,000 loan taken out today at 12% interest is:

$$10,000 \times \frac{1}{4.968} = \$2,013$$

3 If one places $10,000 today in an investment earning 12%, how much can he or she withdraw at the end of each of the next eight years and

have no amount left in the investment at the end of the eighth year? This is the same question as in 2 above, now phrased from the point of view of an investor rather than a borrower. The investor can remove $2,013 per year for each of the eight years.

4   If the seller of a residential building site agrees to accept either a lump-sum payment of $25,000 now or a payment schedule of $5,000 now and $3,300 per year at the end of each of the next 10 years, the seller is, in effect, offering to lend $20,000 (the difference between $25,000 and $5,000) to the buyer in return for the 10 annual payments of $3,300. What is the interest rate, r, inherent in this borrowing? Table 2A-2 provides factors to adjust to today's value the 10 annual payments. The factors in the 10-year row are:

   at 10%: 6.145
   at 12%: 5.650

Applying these factors to the stream of ten $3,300 annual payments, we get the following values for P:

   P (at 10%) = 6.145 × $3,300 = $20,279
   P (at 12%) = 5.650 × $3,300 = $18,645

Since the amount of the loan ($20,000) lies between these two values of P, the inherent interest rate on the loan must also lie between 10% and 12%. By interpolation we can estimate the rate at 10.3%. Thus, the tables can be used to estimate returns (interest rates) when both the time-adjusted (present) values and future values are known.

New Terms

Accounting equation   Assets = liabilities + owners' equity
Asset   The name given to all that is owned by the accounting entity.
Cost value   The value of an asset or liability arrived at by determining the price at which it was originally purchased (asset) or will be discharged (liability).
Equivalency rate   The interest rate used in time-adjusted valuations to adjust future benefits and costs to their value today (present value).
Liability   The name given to an obligation of (something that is owed by) the accounting entity.
Market value   The value of an asset or liability arrived at by determining the price at which it could be bought or sold today.
Owners' equity   The net value or worth of the owners' interest in the entity as expressed in the accounting records. Owners' equity is the sum of capital invested by the owners plus profits earned (or less losses incurred) less any funds

repaid by the entity to its owners. Owners' equity is also the difference between the total value of assets and total value of liabilities.

Time-adjusted value The value of an asset or liability arrived at by consideration of the future stream of benefits and costs associated with it, with appropriate adjustment for the timing of these future benefits and costs.

Problems

1 Which of the three valuation methods—time-adjusted, market, and cost—would you use to value:

a Your personal wardrobe

b Your half-ownership interest in a pleasure sailboat

c Your hi-fi system, assuming that you built it yourself

d Your three-year time-savings account that earns interest at 7% per year (an interest penalty will be charged against the account if you withdraw the funds before the end of three years)

e The installment loan on your car, which requires you to pay $83 per month for the next 15 months

f Your good health

2 Consider yourself as an accounting entity. Can you calculate your own owners' equity? If so, what assets and liabilities would you need to consider in arriving at your owners' equity?

3 The following "things" or "rights" are owned by a particular company. Do you think they should be valued in the company's accounting records, and, if so, what valuation method would you use?

a A trade name that is widely recognized and trusted by consumers

b A two-year employment contract with a well-known scientist employee

c A contract with a major supplier which requires that supplier to deliver 14,000 tons of material to the company at a fixed price over the next year; the fixed price is 20% below the price that the company would now have to pay to other suppliers for equivalent material

d A small parcel of land that is not large enough to serve as a building site

e Two hundred dozen pencils, representing about a 15-month supply, for use by office personnel

f A simple conveyor system that was built by the plant maintenance man during his spare time from scrap material that he found around the plant

g Obsolete material in inventory that was originally purchased for $300 and could now be sold to a salvage dealer for $40

h The five-year lease on the company's building, which has four and a half years remaining and calls for monthly rent of $2,000

i Electrical power distribution equipment that was installed at a cost of $5,000 in the company's leased building, but which could not be removed if the company vacates the building

4 The following liabilities or obligations are owed by a particular company. Do you think they should be valued in the company's accounting records, and, if so, what valuation method would you use?

a   The company's promise to deliver 10 units of product A by the fifteenth of next month

b   As in *a* above, and the company has agreed to a penalty of $100 per day for every day that it is late in delivery

c   A two-year employment contract with a well-known scientist (see question 3*b* above)

d   The expectation by the company's employees that they will receive a handsome end-of-year bonus

e   The $5,000 bill from the electrical contractor who installed power distribution facilities in the company's building (see question 3*i* above)

f   The five-year lease on the company's building, which has four and a half years remaining and calls for monthly rent of $2,000 (see question 3*h* above)

g   A contract with a major supplier which requires the company to accept delivery of and pay for 14,000 tons of material over the next year; the fixed price on this contract is 20% below the price the company would now have to pay to other suppliers for equivalent material (see question 3*c* above)

5   Is it possible for a company to have negative owners' equity? If so, how might this condition come about? What does this condition imply about the total value of assets owned and liabilities owed by the company?

6   Banks are business entities, just as are manufacturing and retailing companies. What are the principal assets owned by a bank? What are its principal liabilities? Who are the owners of the bank; that is, who benefits from the bank's owners' equity? If a bank's borrower fails to pay back the money borrowed, how would this situation affect the bank's assets, liabilities, and owners' equity?

7   What are the principal assets of a partnership engaged in legal practice? What are its principal liabilities? Who are the owners of the partnership?

8   Suppose you belong to a private social or tennis club. What are the principal assets owned by this club? What are its principal liabilities? Does the club have owners? If so, who are they? If not, is there no amount equivalent to owners' equity for your club?

9   You own a bond that pays you interest at the rate of 6% per year. Prevailing interest rates have increased since you purchased this bond to the level of about 8%. Would you now be inclined to value your bond at more or less than you paid for it? (You can verify your answer by noting the relationship between bond prices and interest rates quoted on the financial pages of a newspaper such as the Wall Street Journal.)

10   Are current market prices of assets generally equivalent to the cost to replace the assets? Why or why not?

11   Suppose that the market price method leads to a valuation of $400 for an asset that has an original cost of $500. If we use the cost value rather than the market value method of valuation, what effect will this decision have on the company's assets, liabilities, and owners' equity? Is this effect desirable or undesirable? To whom?

12   Since the time-adjusted value requires the accountant to forecast the future flows of benefits and costs, is this method of valuation inconsistent with the view that the accountant is a historian? Discuss your answer.

13 Suppose you are the independent auditor for a company, charged with the responsibility of verifying the valuations placed on the items below. For each of the three valuation methods, how would you go about the process of verification?

a The promise of a customer to pay $100 per month for the next 25 months to repay the $2,500 now owed by him to the company

b A five-year-old office building owned by the company and utilized by its sales office in Des Moines

c An inventory of merchandise that the company expects to sell to customers over the next three months and which will be replaced as it is sold by equivalent merchandise purchased from suppliers

14 Consider the asset described in 13a above. Which of the three valuation methods is likely to lead to the highest value for this promise to pay? Under what set of conditions would you expect the time-adjusted value to be lower than the market value?

15 Consider the asset described in 13b above. What factors might cause the building's time-adjusted value to its present occupants to be above its market value?

16 Consider the inventory described in 13c above. Under what conditions might the time-adjusted value of this merchandise to the company be less than the cost value? Would you expect the market value to exceed the cost value, to be less than the cost value, or typically to be the same as the cost value? Why?

17 Assume you are a banker considering making a five-year loan to a medium-sized manufacturing company. Would you prefer to have financial statements for the company prepared on the basis of time-adjusted values, market values, or cost values?

18 Assume that you are a banker considering lending $5,000 to a middle-income family. The money will be used to remodel the family's home. Would you prefer to have the family's financial statement prepared on the basis of time-adjusted values, market values, or cost values?

19 Identify each of the following as an asset, a liability, or owners' equity (from the viewpoint of the company):

a Income taxes for last year that have not yet been paid

b Vacation leave for employees, earned by them but not yet taken

c Amounts owed to the company by its suppliers for faulty merchandise that has been returned to the suppliers

d A license granted by a governmental regulatory agency that permits the company to engage in a certain business

e A loan by the bank to the company

f A loan by the company to one of its employees

g Common stock owned by this company in another, unrelated company

h Products which have been manufactured and are now in inventory awaiting sale

i Interest on a loan due to the corporation by an employee (see f above)

j Deposit paid to an equipment supplier for specialized equipment to be delivered next year

k Amounts owed to the company's outside lawyers

l Trucks used to provide delivery service to customers

m   Life insurance policy on the company president's life that will pay $100,-000 to the company in the event of the president's death

n   A house owned by the company and rented by the company to the sales manager's son

o   A loan from a shareholder to the corporation

p   An order from a customer for equipment to be manufactured and delivered next year and billed to the customer at that time

q   Earnings of the company during the first six months of this year when no dividends have been paid

20   The Ridlow Company is a small retailing firm. During one month the following events occurred. Analyze the effect of each event described on the assets, liabilities, and owners' equity of the Ridlow Company. For each, consider the appropriateness of the cost value as the measure of the value of the event.

> **Example:** Ridlow paid $1,100 to First National Bank: $1,000 as partial payment of the remaining principal balance of a loan, and $100 in interest for the month.
>
> > *Answer:* assets: decrease by $1,100
> >
> > liabilities: decrease by $1,000
> >
> > owners' equity: decreases by $100

a   A customer to whom goods had been sold in the previous month made a partial payment of $1,500 on her account.

b   Excess equipment carrying a value on the accounting records of $2,000 was sold for $2,000.

c   Sales of goods totaled $8,000, of which $3,000 was received in cash and $5,000 represented credit sales. The inventory sold in these transactions had been purchased by Ridlow for $5,500.

d   Wages earned by employees and paid during the month totaled $1,200. In addition, as required by law, Ridlow paid $150 in employment taxes.

e   Ridlow paid $1,000 to suppliers for goods received in previous months.

f   New inventory having an original cost of $6,000 was ordered and received. Of this amount, $2,500 was paid in cash and $3,500 remained owing to the suppliers. In addition, Ridlow placed orders during the month for inventory costing $4,000, but none of this merchandise had yet been received.

g   A supplier to whom Ridlow owed $5,000 agreed to defer payment for one year, provided Ridlow would agree to pay interest on the balance at the rate of 8% per year.

h   At the end of the month, 25 shares of common stock were sold to an employee for a cash payment of $5,000.

21   The Napa Corporation is a television repair firm located in a medium-sized town. During one month, the following events occurred. Analyze the effect of each described event on the assets, liabilities, and owners' equity of the corporation. For each, consider the appropriateness of the cost value as the measure of the value of the event. (See example at the beginning of problem 20.)

a   One repairman was paid a $50 bonus for making an evening visit to fix a customer's TV, which had not been properly repaired in the shop.

b   A shipment of invoice forms bearing the company's name and other specialized information was received. This supply of invoices cost $850 and should be sufficient to last for 18 months.

c A bill for $35 was received from Sherlock Trucking for delivery of the invoices mentioned in *b* above.

d The corporation paid dividends totalling $500 to its shareholders.

e The company invested $1,000 in excess cash in a short-term U.S. government note.

f The company purchased for cash materials used in the repair of TV sets. These materials cost $650.

g The company purchased for $5,000 in cash a new truck that had a list price of $5,600.

h The president of Napa purchased for $1,000 in cash 10 shares of common stock of Napa that were owned by the president's cousin.

i An employee to whom Napa had lent $200 disappeared and was rumored to have moved to a distant city.

j A young customer who owed $50 to Napa painted the woodwork on the exterior of the store in full "payment" of his account.

k The accountant for Napa estimated that the value of the repair equipment owned by the company had declined by $150 during the month.

22 A flower stand operated by an enterprising student at a shopping center near the college was in the following financial position at the end of March:

Assets: Cash	$ 250
Flower stand structure	1,250
Liabilities (amounts owed to flower suppliers)	300

During the month of April the following events occurred:

a Sales totaled $1,700. All sales were for cash.

b Flowers were purchased fresh each day, and the total of all flower purchases for the month was $900. Purchases were on credit.

c Rental of $100 was paid to the shopping center in cash.

d Wages paid in cash to the stand attendants totalled $600.

e Payments on account to the flower suppliers aggregated $850.

f The student estimated that the value of the flower stand structure had declined by $50 during the course of the month.

Trace through the effects on the assets, liabilities, and owners' equity of all of these events, and determine the financial position of the flower stand at the end of April. (See example at the beginning of problem 20.)

N EW CORP (A)

Consider how you would value the following transactions in connection with the start-up and initial functioning of New Corp. What effects would each have on the assets, liabilities, and owners' equity at New Corp?

You are the accountant for New Corp, and you have been

charged with the responsibility of developing financial information that will be useful to the internal management of this new manufacturing company, initially established on January 1, 19X5.

The president of the corporation, Mr. Armstrong, has written a note to describe each event or transaction that he thinks might be important to you. He is not an accountant and feels that in certain instances he may have supplied you too much or not enough information.

Mr. Armstrong has organized this business to manufacture and sell construction safety helmets. The helmets will be assembled from an injection-molded plastic shell, to be molded by New Corp, and certain cushioning and strapping components, purchased from outside suppliers. Mr. Armstrong has handed you the following notes:

JANUARY

1 Issued two stock certificates in exchange for cash, as follows:
   a 40 shares to my brother-in-law, Mr. Banta; received a check for $20,000.
   b 60 shares to me; company received my personal check for $20,000. (The price to me is lower than to my brother-in-law, as I am also making available to the corporation my helmet design and my full-time management services.)
   Both checks were deposited on January 2 in our account at First Bank.
2 Received from the state on January 2 a certificate of incorporation, permission to use the name New, and permission to sell 100 shares of stock. Also on January 2, issued to the state a check for $300 for filing fees. The legal work on this incorporation was done at no charge by a personal friend of mine.
3 On January 3, withdrew $20,000 from our bank account and purchased from the bank a certificate of deposit (a security used for short-term savings), maturing in 90 days and paying interest at maturity at the rate of 8% per year.
4 On January 5, entered into a lease with Sunshine Properties for office and manufacturing space totaling 5,000 square feet. The lease runs for two years at a monthly rental of $800 per month. Issued a check to Sunshine for $1,600 covering rental for the first month (January 19X5) and last month of the lease period.
5 On January 6, entered an order with Acme Tool for the purchase of an injection molding machine. The machine will be delivered in March and has a purchase value of $8,700, including sales tax.

6   On January 10, paid Stringer Electric $3,500 for the installation of lighting and electrical wiring in the rented space. This installation, which was performed on January 6 and 7, should serve our needs for as long as we occupy this space.

7   On January 13, hired Ted James as production foreman at a salary of $1,100 per month. Employment contract with Ted requires us to employ him for a minimum of one year and he is required to start work March 1. Ted will move his family to this locality in February and the company will pay the moving charges (estimated at $1,000) and will advance him $1,200 on his future salary to assist him in defraying other moving expenses. He will repay this salary advance, which I sent to him on January 15, at the rate of $100 per month beginning in March.

8   Purchased on credit and received from Silvia Office Supplies $650 worth of stationery, invoice forms, and incidental office supplies. These supplies should last us for about four months.

9   On January 18, entered an order with DuPont for plastic raw materials to take care of our first year's production. The aggregate purchase cost of the order is $18,000. Ten percent of the order will be delivered in February and the balance will be scheduled for delivery at our discretion over future months; also, we retain the option of canceling all or a portion of this balance without penalty.

10 On January 25, placed help-wanted advertisements in the local newspaper. These ads, costing a total of $320, will appear during the last two days of January and the first two days of February. We should receive the bill from the newspaper in about seven days.

11 On January 26, purchased a pickup truck for $2,500 cash.

12 On January 30, I signed an agreement with A. T. Taster for tooling and its associated patent for use on the molding machine. The tooling has been delivered and should be useful to us for an indefinite period. The agreement calls for us to pay Taster within 90 days $1,500 for the tooling (approximately his out-of-pocket cost) and 10 shares of stock of New Corp for the patent. (We must get permission from the state to issue these additional shares, but I anticipate no problem in obtaining this permission.)

13 On January 31, issued two checks to me: one for $350 as reimbursement for my out-of-pocket travel and entertainment expenses during January (the receipts are attached) and one for $1,000 (I plan to minimize the amount of cash I withdraw from the company, but I will need to take some each month to cover my living expenses.)

FEBRUARY

14 On February 2, received first shipment from DuPont against our order placed on January 18. The invoice, which actually arrived on February 7, shows an amount due of $1,890: $1,800 for the material and $90 for freight. (It is industry practice for the buyer to pay freight.) If we pay this invoice within 30 days, we can deduct 2% for prompt payment.

15 Confirmed with DuPont on February 4 a shipment date of March 10 for the next 10% of our January 18 order.

16 On February 5, we received permission from the state to issue 10 shares of stock of New Corp to A. T. Taster (see note 12) and the certificate was issued to him on that day.

17 On February 10, entered into a loan agreement with First Bank that will permit us to borrow up to $25,000 at 8% interest, provided we meet certain requirements spelled out in the loan agreement. Also on February 10, borrowed $9,000 under this agreement, with repayment due in one year.

18 On February 11, I arranged for a comprehensive insurance policy for the company with coverage to begin on March 1. Issued a check for $300 to cover the premium for the first six months.

19 Paid on February 12 the rent for February ($800) to Sunshine properties.

20 The lighting that was installed by Stringer (see note 6) has now been in for a month and is working fine. Also the truck (see note 11) is one month old. Do we need to take any accounting action?

21 On February 13, I hired Sally Simond as an office clerk at a salary of $600 per month, payable on the fifteenth of each month. She started work on February 15.

22 On February 15, purchased additional office supplies on credit from Silvia Co. These items, totaling $400, should also last for a number of months.

23 On February 25, Ted James's move was complete (see note 7) and I issued a $980 check to the moving company.

24 On February 25, issued a check to Silvia Office Supplies for $650 (see note 8).

25 Also on February 26, I purchased and took delivery of some strapping materials. I bought about a six-months' supply (perhaps more than I should have) from another helmet manufacturer who happened to have excess inventory. As a result, I had to pay only $4,000 (check issued on February 26) for materials that would have cost $4,500 if I had purchased them from our normal supplier.

26   On February 28, issued two checks to me: one for $225 for reimbursement for company expenses in February (receipts attached) and one for $300 (living expenses).   I have decided to set my salary at $1,200 per month beginning January 1, but I'll only take as much cash each month as I need to live on.   I'll pay the difference to myself after the business begins to show a profit.

3

The Products of the Accounting System

The previous chapter considered alternative methods of valuing the various events and conditions that we observe within the business entity. We turn now to a discussion of that portion of the accountant's task that involves recording, classifying, and summarizing. The values derived must be recorded in some systematic and organized manner if we are to gain real information from the accounting records, rather than just a jumble of financial data. The type of information we seek—the particular accounting reports—will dictate the system of classification of data. While there is an infinite variety of accounting reports that may prove useful to management, owners, creditors, and others, two key accounting reports are fundamental to virtually all systems. These two key reports are the **balance sheet** and the **income statement.**

Key Accounting Reports

The balance sheet details the financial position of the firm at a particular date. The form of the balance sheet is simply that of the accounting equation discussed earlier:

Assets = liabilities + owner's equity

A balance sheet tells how much the business owns and owes as of a particular date and therefore the balance of owners' equity. A comparison of the balance sheet at one date with the balance sheet of the same company at an earlier date reveals the change in financial position, including the change in total owners' equity. Recall that changes in owners' equity are typically occasioned by either (1) investment or withdrawal of funds by the owners or (2) the earning of a **profit** or **loss** by the company. Thus, if owners' equity has increased and the owners themselves have neither invested nor withdrawn from the business, then the company has been profitable during the period between the two balance sheet dates.

However, it is the other accounting report, the income statement, that provides us a more convenient and comprehensive source of information about the **earnings**[1] or losses of the business enterprise. Comparing balance sheets at two different dates reveals whether the company has been profitable between the two dates, but does not provide additional information as to why it was or was not profitable. The income statement is designed to provide that additional information so critical to the various audiences who read the statements. The income statement represents an elaboration of one section—the owners' equity section—of the balance sheet.

We will discuss in some detail in this chapter each of these two key accounting reports.

The Balance Sheet

The balance sheet might be, and sometimes is, more formally called a **statement of financial position.** It shows what the company owns and owes as of a single, particular date. All balance sheets are dated and the information contained therein is a "snapshot" of the financial condition of the company at that date. By the next day the stream of events and transactions within the company will have changed its financial position to some modest degree. Of course, most businesses don't find it necessary to draw up a balance sheet each day; monthly or even quarterly (three-month interval) balance sheets provide management, owners, and creditors with sufficiently timely information.

Each of the major sections of the balance sheet—assets, liabilities, and owners' equity—should provide as much or as little detail as is useful. Surely audiences want to know more than simply the aggregate value of all assets owned by the company; values by category of asset are useful. How

---

[1] The terms *earnings* and *profits* are used interchangeably.

much cash does the company hold?   How much **inventory?**   What is the total value of its productive plant and equipment?   Similarly, audiences want to know more about liabilities than their simple total.   How much is owed to trade creditors (vendors)?   To the bank?   To taxing authorities?   Finally, with respect to owners' equity a clear separation of the amount of owners' equity attributable to funds invested by the owners and the amount attributable to profits or losses from operating the business is useful.

But still more detail could be provided.   Perhaps management wants to keep separate track of various portions of the inventory; a manufacturing company might have separate categories for raw material, work in process, and finished goods inventory.   And perhaps the balance sheet should distinguish between cash in the bank and cash on hand in the cash registers, or between factory buildings and factory equipment, or between amounts due from customers in the short term and amounts that won't be received for some time.   The amount of detail in the accounting records needs to be balanced, of course, against the cost of operating a more elaborate and detailed accounting system; many companies err on the side of collecting and disseminating more detail than is truly useful.

Exhibit 3-1 provides a sample balance sheet of the Martin Company.   The nomenclature and format of this typical balance sheet require further discussion.

DEFINITION OF CURRENT AND NONCURRENT

Virtually all accounting systems, including the Martin Company's system, draw an important distinction between so-called current and noncurrent (or long-term) assets and liabilities.   **Current assets** are typically defined as those assets that will, in the normal course of business, be converted into cash or used up within the next 12 months.   Thus, amounts owed by customers that will be paid within the next year (typically labelled **accounts receivable**) are considered current.   If Martin has agreed that a customer's obligation to the company can be discharged by monthly payments over the next three years, only those payments that are to be received during the next year are considered current and the remainder are considered noncurrent or long-term.   Inventory will typically be sold within the next several months and thus inventory typically qualifies as a current asset.   The primary elements of current assets for both manufacturing and merchandising firms are cash, accounts receivable, and inventory.   Companies that sell only for cash (no credit sales) will have no accounts receivable; service companies may have little or no inventory.

The definition of **current liabilities** parallels that of current assets: those liabilities that must be discharged by the business within the next 12 months.   Amounts owed to vendors (typically labeled **accounts payable**) are current since they are usually due within 30 to 90 days.   If Martin has

Exhibit 3-1
THE MARTIN COMPANY, INC.
Balance Sheet
June 30, 19X1

ASSETS

Current assets		
Cash	$ 2,493	
Accounts receivable	18,610	
Inventory	9,308	
Prepaids	780	
Total Current Assets		$31,191
Investments		7,300
Property and equipment		22,730
Intangibles		2,670
Total Assets		$63,891

LIABILITIES AND OWNERS' EQUITY

Current liabilities		
Accounts payable	$ 5,350	
Salaries and employee benefits payable	2,480	
Taxes payable	1,855	
Notes payable within one year	5,000	
Total Current Liabilities		$14,685
Long-term debt		15,000
Owners' equity		
Invested capital	15,000	
Retained earnings	19,206	
Total Owners' Equity		34,206
Total Liabilities and Owners' Equity		$63,891

a loan with the bank that requires monthly repayments of principal over five years (generally referred to as a **term loan**), that portion of the principal that will be repaid within the next year is considered a current liability and the remainder is a long-term (noncurrent) liability.

What is the magic of the one-year time frame? None, particularly. This definition of current and noncurrent represents simply another convention of accounting that is widely accepted. Obviously, the job of reading and interpreting financial reports from a variety of companies is facilitated by the uniform adoption of conventions of this kind, and we will find that accounting in the United States is replete with such rules and conventions.

Does a company that has a predominance of current assets differ in any significant way from one that has a predominance of noncurrent assets? Or does one really care whether a company's liabilities are due within the next 12 months or thereafter? The distinction between current and noncurrent does not affect owners' equity—owners' equity is still the difference between total assets and liabilities; nevertheless, the distinction is most useful, particularly to creditors of the company. If a company has a high value of current assets and relatively few liabilities due within the next 12 months, the probability that this company will be able to meet its liabilities on schedule is a good deal higher than for another company that has high current liabilities and low current assets. The former company is said to be *liquid* and the second company *illiquid*. A liquid company minimizes the risk of running out of cash, and being unable to meet the string of obligations that are inherent in the operation of a business—meeting the payroll, acquiring supplies, paying on schedule for the utilities and telephone, and so forth.

Therefore, it is really the relationship between current assets and current liabilities that is more important than the absolute level of either. A measure of **liquidity** is the ratio of current assets to current liabilities, defined by financial analysts as the *current ratio,* and discussed further in Chapter 9. Accountants define the difference between current assets and current liabilities as **working capital.**

Generally, companies with low, or negative, working capital have difficulty meeting their day-to-day commitments and frequently they must scramble around to find the cash to pay their bills. Companies with a strong working capital position know that, even if a temporary slowdown in the pace of business occurs, or the collection of accounts receivable lags for a month or two, the company will probably not get in the embarrassing position of being unable to pay its bills. One needs to be a bit careful of this generalization; suppliers' bills and the payroll must be paid with cash and not with inventory! Thus, the composition of current assets—particularly the amounts of cash and of accounts receivable to be collected soon—in relationship to current liabilities is the more critical consideration.

Exhibit 3-1 indicates that the current assets owned by the Martin Company total $31,191 and the current liabilities total $14,685. Although the figure is not shown on the balance sheet, we can determine that the working capital is $16,506 at June 30, 19X1—the difference between current assets and current liabilities.

In summary, a careful review of current assets and liabilities will generally be revealing. Indeed, for an employee worrying about getting paid on time, or a banker considering making a short-term loan, or a supplier considering providing credit terms, this information on liquidity may be much more important than information about the profitability of the company or the present level of owners' equity. Note that a company may be profitable and growing, and yet be unable to meet its short-term liabilities because it simply has inadequate cash.

STATEMENT FORMAT

The typical format of balance sheets follows the accounting equation: assets are listed first, followed by liabilities and owners' equity. This is the convention that we will follow throughout this book. However, this convention represents simply a convenience and not a law of either nature or the government. Some companies choose to present their balance sheets in the format: assets − liabilities = owners' equity. Still others show working capital plus noncurrent assets equal to noncurrent liabilities plus owners' equity. Each of these formats is simply a variation on the equation: assets = liabilities + owners' equity. While there are good arguments in favor of each of these variations, we shall adhere to the more traditional format as shown in Exhibit 3-1.

The subcategories of assets and liabilities are listed on balance sheets in order of liquidity, with the most liquid assets and the most immediate liabilities listed first. Cash represents the ultimate in liquidity and is thus listed first among the Martin Company's assets. Accounts receivable are more liquid than inventory, which when sold creates an account receivable. **Prepaids** are typically not large in amount and represent payments made in advance for a service or right not yet received; for example, rent or insurance premiums paid in advance of the use of the rented facility or of the insurance protection are prepaid expenses. We will have more to say about prepaids later.

Long-term, or noncurrent, assets of manufacturing or merchandising companies consist largely of land and building facilities—offices, manufacturing plants, warehouses, and salesrooms—and of equipment—machine tools, display cases, automobiles and trucks, and office machines. Investments in other companies or in loans (for periods longer than one year) to employees, customers, or others also represent noncurrent assets. Finally, the company may own patents, trademarks, or other rights that have an ongoing life but are intangible in nature; for the Martin Company these have been lumped together as **intangibles.**

One might reasonably argue that certain of the noncurrent assets are in a sense more liquid than some of the current assets. For example, a used pickup truck (a noncurrent asset) may have a very ready secondhand market, with the result that the company could realize cash from its sale without delay. The reason that the truck is classified noncurrent is that, if the business continues to operate in the normal course, the truck will in fact *not* be sold. That is, the truck is owned because of its long-term usefulness in the company's operation, not with a view to its resale.

In contrast to the truck asset, portions of the current asset, inventory (particularly in-process inventory), are generally unsalable until turned into finished goods inventory. However, the in-process inventory is classified as current because the company expects to complete the manufacturing process and sell the inventory within the next 12 months.

Turning now to the liability side of the balance sheet, we see the separation of current and long-term liabilities at Martin Company. The labels used in the current liability section are, for the most part, self-explanatory. As mentioned above, *accounts payable* is the name given to amounts owing to suppliers as the result of purchasing supplies, inventory, and services for the day-to-day operations of the business. Within the owners' equity section of the balance sheet a distinction is made between (1) capital contributed to the company by its owners and (2) the earnings of the company.

ONCE AGAIN: WHAT IS OWNERS' EQUITY?

Exhibit 3-1 shows two items in the owners' equity section of Martin Company's balance sheet:

Invested Capital

Retained Earnings

For a corporation, **invested capital** is the sum of all monies received from shareholders in connection with the sale of new shares of common stock by the corporation.[2] In a partnership, invested capital is the sum of all investments by the partners. **Retained earnings** is the cumulative total of all earnings made and reinvested in the business (that is, not paid out to shareholders) since the formation of the corporation. Thus, retained earnings equals:

Cumulative profits earned by the company

less: any cumulative losses incurred by the company

less: cumulative dividends paid to the company's shareholders

Recall that owners' equity is also defined as simply the difference between total assets and total liabilities. Recall, too, that owners' equity does not represent a pool of cash available to management or the owners. Moreover, it is not necessarily equal to the market value of all of the shares of common stock of the corporation. If shareholder A decides, two years after purchasing new shares from the Martin Company, to sell the shares to investor B, the price per share will not be set by referring to the owners' equity section of the balance sheet. The market price per share may be higher or lower than the value suggested by the balance sheet, depending upon how eager A is to sell and B is to buy.

[2] Shares may have been sold at different prices per share over the years that the corporation has existed.

Note, too, that the transaction between shareholder A and investor B has no effect on Martin's owners' equity. A and B are different accounting entities than Martin, and Martin was not a party to the transaction between the two individuals. The sale from A to B may have been at either a higher or lower price than shareholder A paid for the shares originally, but this fact will not be recorded in Martin's accounting records. The capital invested in the Martin Company is whatever A paid in cash for the shares originally.

Incidentally, owners' equity is often referred to as **net worth,** or, for corporations, **shareholders' equity.** We will use these three terms interchangeably in this book.

Accounting Notation

After this brief introduction to the balance sheet and before turning to a discussion of the income statement, we need to introduce some additional accounting definitions, and the accounting conventions that have built up around these definitions.

DOUBLE ENTRY

You may have heard the phrase **double entry** bookkeeping. This phrase is used to describe the accepted method in the United States for recording accounting data. This process is not mysterious, and is derived directly from the accounting equation that we have been discussing.

Recall that if assets increase with no increase in liabilities, owners' equity must also increase—that is, the owners now own more without owing more, and are therefore better off. To record this event—an increase in an asset and an increase in owners' equity—requires two entries, hence the name *double entry*. It is also possible that an increase in an asset occasioned an increase in a liability: for example, the company borrowed money. In such an event, both an increase in the asset (cash) and an increase in the liability (loans payable) must be recorded. Notice that owners' equity is unaffected—the entity owns the amount of additional cash received but it owes the same amount to the lender, and therefore the entity is neither better nor worse off; no entry need be made to owners' equity, but only the double entry made to Cash and to Loans Payable. Another example may help explain this concept: Assume that a customer pays an amount owed to the company. In this instance, one asset has been swapped for another; cash increases and accounts receivable decreases. If the account receivable from this customer was valued at exactly the amount actually received in cash, then we have the following double entry:

Increase in Cash, by the amount received

Decrease in Accounts Receivable, by the amount received.

Here, neither the liabilities nor owners' equity section of the balance sheet is affected by the transaction, but nevertheless two entries are required to record completely the transaction.

How does double entry accounting differ from single entry accounting? A useful example of single entry accounting is the accounting that you probably do on your bank check stubs. On these stubs you record a deposit as a single entry and a withdrawal as a single entry. Your checkbook can still be balanced making only these single entries. Implicitly, however, when you make a deposit you are increasing your worth and when you make a withdrawal you are decreasing your worth. You are maintaining a very simple accounting system that involves a single asset, cash; when you increase cash you are increasing your worth or *equity* and when you decrease your cash, you are decreasing your worth. This single entry system is probably quite adequate for your purposes. In a more complex accounting system than your checkbook, however, a double entry system greatly simplifies the accounting task.

ACCOUNTS, LEDGERS, AND T ACCOUNTS

The accountant classifies the entries made in the accounting records by putting like entries in the same **account.** Thus, each subcategory of asset, liability, or owners' equity is represented by a separate account in the accounting records. Some typical account names are:

Cash on Hand

Cash on Deposit, First Bank

Cash on Deposit, Security Savings and Loan

Accounts Receivable — Trade

Accounts Receivable — Employees

Raw Material Inventory

Finished Goods Inventory

Supplies Inventory

Inventory on Consignment at Customer's

All of these accounts are current assets. For purposes of balance sheet presentation, the first three accounts listed above may be combined and shown simply as Cash; the next two may be combined as Accounts Receivable. Although these accounts are combined for the purposes of published financial statements, maintaining separation among them may be useful to the accountant and selected other audiences. For example, it is important to the treasurer of the company, who has the responsibility to manage the company's cash, to know how much cash is located where. Similarly, the manager of inventories needs detailed information on the value of inventory of various kinds. But for published financial statements, combining the last four accounts on the list above into a single account, Inventory, may be quite satisfactory.

A listing of all of the accounts used within a particular accounting system is referred to as the system's **chart of accounts.** The chart of accounts is a kind of road map of the accounting system; it lists all possible accounts available for use by the accountant and indicates the nature and extent of classification, or categorization, in the accounting records. Simple accounting systems may have only 20 or 30 accounts, but as the size of the organization and the complexity of the system increase it is not unusual to find that the chart of accounts has grown to hundreds of separate accounts.

The term **general ledger** refers to that set of accounting documents that details the increases, decreases, and current status of each of the accounts. Thus, all entries find their way to the general ledger. The accounting reports, including the balance sheet and the income statement, are made up from the balances that are shown in the general ledger. A subsequent chapter will discuss the detailed format of the general ledgers that are used in actual accounting systems. For now, though, it should be clear that the general ledger needs to show the amount and cause of the increases in each account, and the amount and cause of the decreases; this information will allow us to trace what is happening in the account and to calculate the balance in the account at any time.

Accountants have a shorthand format for general ledger accounts, known as the **T account.** These T accounts simply omit some of the detail that would appear in the accounts of an actual general ledger. Each account in the general ledger has its own T account. We shall use this format for illustrations in this book, and you are encouraged to use T accounts for the problems and exercises at the end of the chapters. The T account, true to its descriptive name, looks like a T:

Account Name

DEBITS AND CREDITS

The accounting equation suggests that assets be recorded "on the left" and liabilities "on the right":

Assets = liabilities + owners' equity

Following this suggestion, we will assume that asset accounts have balances on the left side of their T accounts, and liabilities and owners' equity accounts have balances on the right side of their respective T accounts. As a result, the sum of all of the left-hand balances will equal the sum of all the right-hand balances, and this equality will always be true because of the double-entry convention.

The terms *left-hand balance* and *right-hand balance* are neither convenient nor elegant, and thus accountants have given the names **debit** balance to left-hand balances and **credit** balance to right-hand balances. Asset accounts typically have debit balances, and liability and owners' equity accounts typically have credit balances; the sum of all debit balances will always equal the sum of all credit balances.

By using these names and placing debit balances on the left and credit balances on the right, we will be following accepted convention in the United States. All professions seem to promulgate their own particular conventions and definitions, and the accounting profession is no exception. You may ask, "Why can't I put assets on the right, and call the balances in asset accounts Charlie?" You can, so long as you remember what rules you have established for your accounting system and so long as no one else has to work with or seek information from it. However, as a practical matter, conventions of the type just described greatly facilitate communication; you are urged to accept these conventions and definitions and resist expressing your creativity in the design of the format of your accounting system!

In T account format, the current assets and current liabilities of the Martin Company at June 30, 19X1 would appear as in Exhibit 3-2.

Exhibit 3-2
Partial General Ledger of
THE MARTIN COMPANY, INC.
(In T-Account Format)

Cash	Accounts Receivable	Inventory	Prepaids
2,493	18,610	9,308	780

Accounts Payable	Wages and Employee Benefits Payable	Taxes Payable	Notes Payable within One Year
5,350	2,480	1,855	5,000

Note: The sum of these debit balances is not equal to the sum of the credit balances, because this is only a partial balance sheet.

How are transactions or events recorded in the T accounts? If a company borrows $2,000 on a short-term note, the transaction would be recorded in the company's T accounts as follows:

Cash		Notes Payable	
Balance[3]			Balance
2,000			2,000

Thus, an asset, cash, has been increased and a liability, notes payable, has been increased. An addition has been made to the debit balance of the asset and to the credit balance of the liability. A *debit entry* has been made in the asset account, Cash, and a *credit entry* in the liability account, Notes Payable. The double entry concept has been followed, as both a left-hand and a right-hand entry have been made, and thus the equality demanded by the accounting equation is maintained. It should be clear that the double entry concept demands that a complete recording in the general ledger involve equal debit and credit entries.[4]

Take another example: a customer pays $150 on her account. This transaction would be recorded by the company who receives the payment as follows:

Cash		Accounts Receivable	
Balance		Balance	150
150			

An increase in an asset, cash, has been matched by a decrease in another asset, accounts receivable. The increase in cash is a debit entry and the decrease in accounts receivable is a credit entry. A debit entry is matched by a credit entry; the accounting equality holds.

Still another example: The company pays $850 to a vendor, this amount currently being in the accounts payable balance. The company records this transaction:

Cash		Accounts Payable	
Balance	850	850	Balance

[3] The term *balance* is shown to indicate that the account had a debit (or credit) balance before the particular transaction was recorded.

[4] The transaction would be recorded by the bank making the loan in exactly the opposite way. The note is a receivable to the bank—an asset—and the company's cash deposit is a bank liability.

Both assets and liabilities have been decreased, and no change in owners' equity occurs. The decrease in the asset, cash, is a credit entry, and the decrease in the liability, accounts payable, is a debit entry. Again, the debit and credit entries are equal.

We can generalize that:

Asset accounts typically have debit balances.

Liability accounts and owners' equity accounts typically have credit balances.

An increase in an asset is created by a debit entry.

A decrease in an asset is created by a credit entry.

An increase in a liability or owners' equity account is created by a credit entry.

A decrease in a liability or owners' equity account is created by a debit entry.

Accordingly, we can define debit and credit entries as follows:

A debit entry will increase an asset account or decrease a liability or owners' equity account.

A credit entry will increase a liability or owners' equity account or decrease an asset account.

Notice that, again by convention, accountants do not use negative entries. That is, a decrease in assets is not represented by a negative debit entry, but rather by a credit entry. Of course, a credit entry is the opposite of a debit entry, just as a negative debit entry—if such were used—would be the opposite of a debit entry.

We have said that asset accounts typically have debit balances. Could they have credit balances, and, if so, what would a credit balance mean? Yes, certain asset accounts can temporarily have credit balances—that is, their typical debit balances can be forced by excessive credit entries to a negative position. A credit balance will occur in the account, Cash on Deposit, First Bank, when the bank account is overdrawn. Conceivably, an account receivable could incur a temporary credit balance, meaning that customers have overpaid their accounts, and the company owes them a refund. Similarly, liability accounts can have temporary debit balances. Finally, if a company has earned a cumulative loss or paid dividends in excess of cumulative profits, the retained earnings account in owners' equity will carry a debit balance.

You may be puzzled by the names that accountants have chosen for both balances and entries. Your past associations with the terms *debit* and *credit* may cause you to think of debits as "bad" and credits as "good": you have always been eager to earn "credits" and you may have experienced the bank "debiting" your checking account for service charges. Yet we have said that assets—which you probably think of as good—have debit balances and liabilities—which you probably think of as something to be avoided—have credit balances.

Can the popular and accounting definitions of these terms be reconciled? Think of the terms in the context of the owners' equity accounts. Owners' equity accounts typically carry credit balances; an increase in owners' equity (a good event) is recorded by a credit entry, and a decrease in owners' equity is recorded as a debit entry. If that orientation to the terms debit and credit doesn't help, perhaps you can try simply to block from your mind any emotional connotation of these two terms.

Incidentally, when the bank tells you that it is crediting (increasing) your bank account or debiting (decreasing) your bank account, its use of the terms is consistent from the *bank's* viewpoint with our definitions. Your account represents a liability of the bank (since it is obligated to give you your money on request); an increase in your bank account is an increase in the bank's liability, represented by a credit entry. Similarly, a decrease in your bank account, while represented by a credit entry to your asset account, Cash, is a debit entry (decrease) to the bank's liability account, Customer Deposits.

The Income Statement

The income statement is best visualized as an elaboration, or an expanded clarification, of the changes in the Retained Earnings account within the owners' equity section of the balance sheet. We have seen that certain events or transactions serve to increase owners' equity, while others decrease owners' equity. If, between one balance sheet date and the next, the cumulative monetary effect of the "increasing" transactions exceeded the cumulative monetary effect of the "decreasing" transactions, then the company earned a *profit* for the period. The balance sheet account entitled Retained Earnings will have increased by the amount of this profit, less any dividends paid to shareholders.

Then why is an income statement needed? Why doesn't the balance sheet alone give all necessary information? The balance sheet can show only the net effect on owners' equity of the very many types of transactions that serve to both increase and decrease owners' equity. Essentially nothing is learned about the magnitude and classification of either the increasing or decreasing transactions. Various audiences need the additional information that the income statement can provide.

The income statement is a statement of *performance,* whereas the balance sheet is a statement of *condition.* The income statement details how the company performed during the period covered by the statement. The balance sheet details the financial position of the company as of the date of the balance sheet.

Thus, while a balance sheet is a snapshot as of a particular date, the income statement is a "moving picture" of what happened during the period. Just as a balance sheet must carry a specific date to be meaningful, an income statement must clearly indicate the exact period for which it details the changes in owners' equity. Incidentally, the income statement is also commonly referred to as a **profit and loss statement** or **P&L;** or an **operating statement;** or an **earnings statement.** We shall use these terms interchangeably in this book, but with a preference for the term *income statement.*

DEFINITION OF REVENUE, SALES, AND EXPENSES

The term that accountants use for increases in owners' equity is **revenue;** the most important source of revenue for most firms is sales of goods or services to customers. Decreases in owners' equity are referred to as **expenses.** If revenues exceed expenses for a particular period, the company has earned a profit; conversely, if expenses exceed revenues, the company has incurred a loss for the period.

We have just said that sales transactions with customers are the key source of revenue for most companies. The company may also earn interest on its savings, or on its investments, or on its loans to employees or customers; interest thus earned is another source of revenue. The company may rent to others excess plant or office space, or may sell an old physical asset for more than the value at which the asset is carried in the company's general ledger; these events also create revenue.

Expenses are typically classified in a manner that will help management judge the performance of the various segments or departments of the business. A primary expense category is **cost of goods sold (COGS), or cost of sales (COS):** the expenses that can be traced directly to the goods or services provided to the customers. For a merchandising company using the cost value method, cost of goods sold equals the cost to the company of acquiring the particular items of inventory sold to the customer.

The determination of cost of goods sold for manufacturing or service companies is typically more difficult than for merchandising companies. Manufacturers or service firms need to include in cost of goods sold (or cost of services rendered) wages and related expenses of those personnel directly involved in creating the particular product or service being sold. Valuing services and manufactured products is a complex process, referred to as *cost accounting,* and subject to a rather separate though consistent set of rules and conventions. Illustrations at this stage in our study will be drawn primarily from merchandising companies in order to simplify our task.

Of course, both merchandising and manufacturing firms incur many other expenses that are not traceable directly to the product or service involved in the sales transactions. Typically these include selling expenses and administrative expenses. Depending upon how the business is financed, it may incur significant interest expenses. Tax obligations that are a function of profits earned by the company are still another form of expense. Note, however, that dividend payments to shareholders, although an appropriate and necessary form of return upon the capital invested by the shareholders, are traditionally not shown as an expense of the company. Although dividend payments do result in a decrease in the Retained Earnings account, they do not represent a diminution in the collective financial position of shareholders; cash formerly held by the corporation for the benefit of the shareholders is now paid to the shareholders in the form of dividends.

STATEMENT FORMAT

Exhibit 3-3 presents the income statement for the Martin Company in typical format. Note first that the net income, or net profit, of the firm was

Exhibit 3-3
THE MARTIN COMPANY, INC.
Income Statement
(First Half 19X1)
Period Jan. 1, 19X1 through June 30, 19X1

Sales, Gross	$116,410	
less: Returns and Allowances	3,075	
Net Sales		$113,335
Cost of Goods Sold		78,683
Gross Profit		34,652
Operating Expenses		
Selling and Promotion	18,005	
General and Administration	8,910	
Total Operating Expenses		26,915
Operating Profit		7,737
Other Income and Expense		
Interest and Dividend Income	363	
less: Interest Expense	917	
		554
Income before Taxes		7,183
Taxes on Income		3,060
Net Income		$ 4,123

$4,123 for the six-month period from January 1 through June 30, 19X1.   Exhibit 3-1 shows the retained earnings for Martin at June 30, 19X1 as $19,206.   Although we do not have the balance sheet for the Martin Company at December 31, 19X0,[5] we know that, if no dividends were paid by this company during the six-month period, the retained earnings at December 31, 19X0, must have been $15,083: $19,206 at June 30 less the $4,123 earned during these past six months.

The income statement tells much more, however, than simply the single profit figure.   The income statement begins with information on the sales transactions.   Since Martin is a merchandising company, it encounters sales returns and is required to make certain adjustments for quality, delivery problems, incorrect merchandise, and so forth.   Since the total of such returns and allowances is relatively significant for this company — about 2.6% of gross sales for the first half of 19X1 — the accountant for Martin has chosen to provide this information in the accounting records and on the income statement.   For other companies where returns are minimal, this additional refinement to the income statement may not be warranted.

Next, the income statement provides information on the cost of goods sold and **gross profit.**   Gross profit, sometimes referred to as **gross margin,** is simply the difference between sales revenue and the corresponding cost of goods sold.   It should be emphasized that the Cost of Goods Sold account carries the cost only of that merchandise sold during the period, and not the cost of merchandise acquired during the period.   That is, the Sales account matches the Cost of Goods Sold account.   Thus, the gross profit represents the cumulative total difference between purchase cost and sales price of all merchandise sold during the period.   Obviously, this information is useful to management.

Again, a great deal of additional detail could be provided in the revenue and expense sections of the accounting records, if management feels that the cost of generating this detail is warranted.   For example, information on sales by major product category, or by department, or by region, or even by individual salesperson, might be useful; indeed, an automatic data-processing system would permit multiple categorization of sales.   A parallel set of details could be developed for cost of goods sold, so that gross profit could be calculated by product line, by department, or by region.   This level of detail would be most helpful to management in making decisions about adding or deleting products, or allocating the promotional budget among the products or outlets, or determining whether salespersons should be dropped or added.

Before we move on, consider the entries required to record a sales transaction.   Again we must be true to our double entry convention and to

---

[5] The balance sheet at the close of business on December 31, 19X0 must be the same as the balance sheet at the start of business on January 1, 19X1.

the accounting equation. The sale for cash of merchandise having a sales price of $25 is recorded as follows:

Cash		Sales	
Balance			25
25			

The debit entry is to the asset account, Cash, and the credit entry is to the Sales account. This transaction represents the situation discussed earlier where the assets of the company have increased with no increase in liabilities, so that owners' equity has increased. If the sale had been on account or on credit—that is, if the customer did not pay cash, but promised to pay in the near future—the debit would have been to Accounts Receivable, but the credit would still have been to Sales.

The entries required to record cost of goods sold are not quite so obvious. Typically a company like Martin will sell merchandise from its inventory; if so, the sale creates a decrease in the asset account, Inventory. In order to properly match the sales revenue and the cost of merchandise sold, the following entries are made:

Inventory		Cost of Goods Sold	
Balance	15	15	

The debit entry is to the Cost of Goods Sold account, an expense account. The debit entry has served to decrease owners' equity and the credit entry has reduced the asset account, Inventory. The debit balance in the Inventory account was created when the merchandise was purchased from the company's suppliers.

Note that the sales price of the merchandise involved in this transaction exceeded its purchase cost—a desirable condition! That is, the credit to the Sales account was greater than the debit to the Cost of Goods Sold account. The owners of the business are better off to the extent of the difference, or the gross profit.

You might be thinking that we could take a shortcut through these entries: record simply a credit to a Gross Profit account for the difference between the sales value and the cost value of the merchandise. The accounting entries would then be as follows:

Cash		Inventory		Gross Profit	
Balance		Balance	15		10
25					

Note that here two credit entries balance a single debit entry. But, since the arithmetic sum of the two credit entries equals the single debit entry, the accounting equation is preserved: the net difference in assets (differences between accounts receivable increase and inventory decrease) is balanced by the increase in gross profit (equivalent to an increase in owners' equity). However, there is one undesirable feature of this last method of recording the transaction: some information has been lost. This last method would permit determination of neither total sales nor total cost of goods sold for the company. Exhibit 3-3 shows that total sales for the six months were $113,335 and the gross profit was $34,652, or 30.6% of sales. That information is both more complete and more useful than the information on gross profit alone.

To summarize, then, the $25 cash sale of merchandise that was valued in inventory at $15 is properly recorded as follows:

Cash		Inventory		Sales	Cost of Goods Sold	
Balance		Balance	15	25	15	
25						

Thus, two double entries are required: one to record the sale and one to record the matched cost of goods sold. Note that no account entitled Gross Profit is used here. The gross profit shown on the income statement (Exhibit 3-3) was calculated by the accountant when preparing the statement.

Refer again to Exhibit 3-3. Operating expenses for the Martin Company are shown here as Selling and Promotion expenses and General and Administrative expenses. Within each of these expense categories, the Martin Company undoubtedly has a number of individual expense accounts, each one appearing in Martin's chart of accounts. Within the Selling Expense section of the chart of accounts the following individual expense accounts might appear:

Salaries of Sales Personnel

Sales Bonuses and Commissions—Sales Personnel

Office Salaries

Rent Expense

Telephone and Telegraph Expense

Automotive Expense

Other Travel Expense

Entertainment Expense

Postage Expense

Supplies Expense

Advertising Expense

Brochure Expense

Miscellaneous Expense

Again, more or less detail can be included. For example, separate accounting of hotel expenses and air travel expenses, rather than combining them as Other Travel Expense, might be useful, or the accountant may decide to combine advertising and brochure expenses as a single account, Promotional Expenses.

The entries needed to record these expenses are straightforward. Assume the company pays in cash a $100 bonus to salesperson **X**. The recording for the company is:

Cash		Sales Bonuses and Commissions Expense	
Balance	100	100	

The decrease in the asset (credit entry) is balanced by a decrease in owners' equity (debit entry to an expense account). If the company purchases promotional brochures on "open account" for $175, the transaction is recorded thus:

Accounts Payable		Brochure Expense	
	Balance	175	
	175		

No change in assets has occurred, but the increase in liabilities (credit entry) is balanced by a decrease in owners' equity (debit entry to an expense account).

Exhibit 3-3 shows that the Martin Company earned an **operating profit** of $7,737 for the six months. Operating profit is calculated before considering other revenue and expenses that did not arise directly from the merchandising operations at Martin. Thus, the interest and dividend revenue from the investments that Martin holds (see the listing of assets on Exhibit 3-1) are not part of operating profit, since holding investments is not Martin's primary line of business. Similarly, the interest on the company's long-term and short-term debts (again, see Exhibit 3-1) are nonoperating expenses, although clearly very real expenses to the company. While these other incomes and expenses are not included in the calculation of operating profit, the tax laws require that they be included in determining taxable income. Thus, the next item on the income statement is Income (or Profit) before Taxes. Taxes on income are a function of the profit earned by the company and are the last expense item shown on the income statement. The net income—the bottom line on the income statement—represents the net improvement in the shareholders' position for the period, before any dividend return to those shareholders.

Good arguments can be and are made for presentation of the income statement in other formats. However, Exhibit 3-3 is currently the most typical and widely accepted format for merchandising companies. Income statements for manufacturing companies would look largely similar to the one for Martin. On the other hand, income statements for other types of businesses sometimes look quite different. For example, the primary sources of revenue and expenses for an insurance company or commercial bank are vastly different from those of a manufacturing or merchandising firm, and a bank's or insurance company's income statement would be designed to highlight information relevant to that particular business.

Reference has been made several times to the chart of accounts, and now all of the major categories of accounts that appear in the Martin Company's chart of accounts have been introduced: asset, liability, owners' equity, revenue (sales), and expense. Each of the revenue and expense accounts that the accountant decides to use in the accounting system will be included in Martin's chart of accounts, just as each of the asset and liability accounts that Martin uses appears in its chart of accounts. To repeat, the revenue and expense accounts are really subsets of the owners' equity category; the net difference between the two subsets becomes a part of retained earnings. Exhibit 3-4 presents a simplified chart of accounts for Martin. (The use of certain of these accounts, such as depreciation, will be taken up later.) Incidentally, if Martin's accounting system is automated, each of these accounts will be numbered and the numbers used to facilitate data processing.

It may now be more apparent to you why the chart of accounts for a company can involve hundreds of individual general ledger accounts: the company will probably want to include quite a lot of detail on revenues and expenses.

Finally, notice that the statements appearing in both Exhibits 3-1 and 3-3 show amounts only to the nearest whole dollar; that is, the cents have been omitted for presentation purposes. This practice is typical, although the accounting records themselves carry figures to the hundredth part of a dollar. Indeed, large companies may, for statement purposes, round off to the nearest thousand dollars, and very large companies in this country round off to the nearest million dollars in published financial reports.

THE ACCOUNTING PERIOD

Exhibit 3-3 is Martin's income statement for the six-month period from January 1, 19X1 to June 30, 19X1. That is, the **accounting period** to which

Exhibit 3-4
THE MARTIN COMPANY
Chart of Accounts

ASSETS

Cash on Hand
Cash on Deposit, First Bank
Accounts Receivable—Trade
Accounts Receivable—Other
Inventory—Department X
Inventory—Department Y
Prepaids
Land
Warehouse and Store Facilities
Depreciation—Warehouse and Store
  Facilities
Fixtures and Equipment
Depreciation—Fixtures and Equipment
Transportation Equipment
Depreciation—Transportation Equipment
Investments—Shares in Unrelated
  Companies
Investments—Municipal Bonds
Intangibles—Trademark

LIABILITIES

Accounts Payable—Trade
Accounts Payable—Other
Salaries Payable
Commissions and Bonuses Payable
Payroll Taxes Payable
Sales Taxes Payable
Property Taxes Payable
Income Taxes Payable
Short-term Notes Payable—Bank
Short-term Notes Payable—Other
Long-term Debt

OWNERS' EQUITY

Invested Capital
Retained Earnings

REVENUES

Sales—Department X
Sales Returns and Allowances—Department X
Sales—Department Y
Sales Returns and Allowances—Department Y
Interest Income
Dividend Income
Gain (Loss) on Sale of Physical Assets

EXPENSES

Cost of Goods Sold Expenses
  Cost of Goods Sold—Department
  X
  Cost of Goods Sold—Department
  Y
Selling Expenses
  Salaries of Sales Personnel
  Sales Bonuses and
    Commissions—Sales Personnel
  Office Salaries Expense
  Rent Expense
  Depreciation Expense
  Telephone and Telegraph
    Expense
  Automotive Expense
  Other Travel Expense
  Postage Expense
  Supplies Expense
  Promotional Expense
  Miscellaneous Expense
General and Administrative
  Expenses
  Salaries—Executive
  Salaries—Clerical
  Rent Expense
  Insurance Expense
  Depreciation Expense
  Telephone and Telegraph
    Expense
  Travel and Entertainment
    Expense
  Postage Expense
  Professional Fees Expense
  Miscellaneous Expenses
Other Expenses
  Interest Expense
  Other Nonoperating Expenses

this statement applies is six months long. An accounting period can be of any length and is the time period for which the company creates income statements. Probably the most typical accounting period is the calendar month. While most publicly owned companies publish financial statements for shareholders every three months (that is, each calendar quarter), for internal purposes the companies generally produce financial statements monthly. The Martin Company produces monthly statements; by simple combination it can then develop income statements encompassing longer periods, such as the six-month statement contained in Exhibit 3-3.

Most companies focus particular attention on their year-end balance sheet and annual income statement. Also, for reasons of convenience or because of seasonality in the business, many companies will define their financial, or fiscal, year differently than a calendar year. Retailers often end their years on January 31, while other companies may select September 30 as year-end. Later we will discuss the work of the independent auditor, whose primary work is in connection with the annual statements.

In recent years, accounting periods that are not tied to calendar months have come into fairly wide acceptance. The year may be divided into 13 four-week periods, with each four-week segment treated as an accounting period, or into four 13-week periods. With this definition of the accounting period, each period has the same number of business days, ignoring holidays, and thus operating results for the period are unaffected by the number of Saturdays and Sundays that happen to fall in the period. Periods defined in this way may be particularly useful for retailing firms and some service firms.

Income statements for accounting periods shorter than one year are generally referred to as **interim statements.**

One might argue for accounting periods longer than a year so as to encompass a full economic cycle. A one-year period permits the effect of seasonality to be included in each accounting year, but some years may be adversely affected by the economic cycles (recessions) while others are favorably affected (prosperity). Because economic cycles remain quite unpredictable in both frequency and duration, and because tax laws require companies to file returns annually, it is generally impractical to utilize 15-month, 18-month, or longer accounting periods.

One can make a more convincing argument for shorter accounting periods. Much can happen in a month, and management may be unwilling to wait a full month for feedback on operations. However, management must balance the cost of developing detailed financial reports more frequently than monthly with the benefits that these reports might have. Many managements conclude that partial financial statements on a more frequent basis—perhaps even daily—are necessary supplements to the more detailed monthly or four-week statements. These daily reports might pertain to cash position, sales, sales returns, and a host of nonaccounting data such as equipment downtime, number of overtime hours, rejection rates on production lines, and so forth.

When Is Income Earned?

Assume that the Martin Company, a merchandising operation, is a retailer. When customers come to one of Martin's stores, they select merchandise, purchase it for cash or on credit, and take the merchandise away with them. Martin does not typically receive orders from its customers in advance of delivery time, and direct selling activity is limited to the time when the individual customer is in the store. When should the Martin Company account for the gross profit on the merchandise sold (the difference between sales price and purchase cost)? Is it all earned at the moment that the customer buys and carries away the merchandise?

The cost valuation method does indeed require that the full amount of the gross profit should be recognized as earned when the sale to the customer is consummated—no part of the gross profit before, and none later. The managers at Martin's may have done an exceptionally clever job of selecting merchandise or negotiating price, and Martin Company may have spent thousands of dollars over the course of several weeks on newspaper and radio advertising to promote the merchandise. Nevertheless, 100% of the gross profit is assumed to be earned at the moment of the sale.

The time-adjusted value method would view the situation quite differently. Active promotion and advertising for a segment of merchandise inventory would probably increase the chance that the merchandise would be sold at attractive prices and decrease the risk that it would have to be disposed of at distress prices; as a result, the merchandise would increase in value even before the sale. Similarly, if the managers were able to obtain particularly attractive prices, perhaps by placing large orders or making early commitments, the time-adjusted value method might record a portion of the total gain to be realized long before the final sale. The market value method might also cause earlier recognition of a portion of the gain. In addition, both of these methods might reasonably cause Martin Company to record something less than the full gain as the customer left the store with the merchandise, since the company still faces the risk that the customer may return the merchandise or keep it but not pay for it.

In accounting for a manufacturer of large equipment, rather than a merchandising company, the differences between the time-adjusted value, the market value, and the cost value methods might be still more pronounced. The manufacturer of large equipment may receive orders from customers well in advance of delivery date, and the equipment ordered may be manufactured over a period of weeks or months. The cost value method insists that the critical moment in the entire transaction between buyer and seller is the moment of delivery. The time-adjusted and market value methods would recognize that the receipt of the order itself is a valuable event—the management and owners of the company undoubtedly think they are better off with the order than without it. Too, both methods would recognize that gross profit is earned progressively during those weeks or months that the large equipment is being manufactured.

One can argue that income is earned in a series of small steps, in the course of development, selling, manufacturing, order processing, shipping, and after-sale service. However, any two persons might have difficulty agreeing on just how much of the income has been earned at each step. The engineering design, embodied in drawings, has value, the inventory increases in value as manufacturing occurs, the selling process has much to do with adding value to the product, and after-sales service may be critical to keeping the product sold. But to measure objectively, without bias and in a manner that can be verified, each increment of value is exceedingly difficult. As a result, accountants find it necessary to return to the cost value method as being objective, verifiable, efficient, and timely.

In summary, the cost value method concentrates the recognition of earnings in any sales transaction at that moment when the goods are delivered or services provided in response to a firm order from the customer. Such a convention simplifies the accounting task, but it should be recognized that the convention is arbitrary.

Accrual Concept of Accounting

Consider again the simple method of accounting that you probably use to maintain your bank checking account. You tend to equate your worth with your cash balance. As your cash balance increases, you are better off. You earn wages as you work, but acknowledge those earnings only when you are paid, and your bank balance increases. Similarly, when you purchase $30 worth of food at the store, you consider that you have incurred an expense of $30, even though you will take home an inventory of food that will then be consumed over the coming days. You operate a simple **cash basis** accounting system.

Such a simple, cash-oriented system works quite adequately for certain professional services, such as doctors' offices, and for a few other types of businesses. All these businesses are characterized by having essentially no inventory or physical assets and one dominating expense category: salaries and wages.

The great bulk of business enterprises in this country must utilize a more complex accounting concept: the **accrual concept.** This concept requires that:

1 Revenue be recognized at the time that goods are delivered or services rendered, regardless of when the customer pays for the goods or services. The customer may pay in advance, simultaneously with delivery, or 30 or more days after being billed.
2 Expenses be recognized as soon as they are incurred, regardless of when the cash outflow occurs. An expense is incurred when the service is received. For example, rent expense associated with a company's rented facilities is incurred in the period the facilities are used, regardless of whether the rent was actually paid during the previous period or will be paid in a future period; similarly, management salaries expense is incurred when the work is performed by the managers, regardless of when the salaries are actually paid in cash.

Thus, in accrual accounting, in contrast to the accounting in your checkbook, the flow of revenues and expenses is not the same as the flow of cash into and out of the business. In order to properly determine the profit earned by an enterprise during an accounting period and to value assets and liabilities at the end of the period, revenues and expenses must be matched to the accounting period.

Therefore, revenue for the accounting period includes only those sales for which merchandise or services have been delivered during the period. Similarly, all expenses must be properly assigned to the period. Those expenses that were incurred in the previous period and paid for in this period are omitted and any expenses that should properly be assigned to a future period are omitted, even if the cash outflow occurred in this period.

EXAMPLES OF THE ACCRUAL CONCEPT

Some examples may help clarify the accrual concept. The simplest example is that of the credit sale. The critical transaction—delivery of merchandise—occurs during this period, although cash from the customer will be received in a subsequent period. As indicated earlier, the appropriate entries are:

> debit to Accounts Receivable
> credit to Sales

The matching of cost of goods sold to sales revenue also requires that the expense associated with giving up the merchandise to the customer be recorded in this period, even though the cash outflow to acquire the merchandise may have occurred in a previous period.   The entries to record the acquisition of inventory are:

> debit to Inventory
>
> credit to Accounts Payable (or Cash)

As another example, assume that the customer makes a $100 down payment against an order that will be delivered to the customer in the next accounting period.   The $100 receipt does not represent revenue to the company during this accounting period, because the critical sales transaction has not yet occurred (according to the assumptions of the cost value method).   Rather, the receipt of the $100 has created a liability for the company: the company must either make the delivery in the upcoming accounting period or return the customer's deposit.   The appropriate entries are:

> debit $100 to Cash
>
> credit $100 to Customer Advance (a liability account)

Note here that the increase in the asset is exactly matched by the increase in the liability, and owners' equity is unaffected.

Before leaving this example, consider the entries that will be required when the merchandise is finally delivered; i.e., when the sale is completed and the revenue appropriately recorded.   Assume that the total sale is $1,000 and the remaining $900 is paid in cash by the customer at the time of delivery.   The appropriate entries at that time will be (in T account format):

Cash		Customer Advances		Sales	
Balance 900		100	Balance		1,000

Here two debit entries balance the single credit entry to the Sales account.

Assume that today the company purchases and pays for a one-year comprehensive insurance policy that will provide coverage commencing with the next accounting period.   To record the payment in advance of the $120 annual premium, the appropriate entries are:

> debit $120 to Prepaid Expenses (an asset)
>
> credit $120 to Cash

One asset was swapped for another; no change occurs in either liabilities or owners' equity.   Some cash was given up in return for the right to future protection under the insurance policy.

Again, before leaving this example, consider the appropriate entry next month, when the benefit of one-twelfth of the insurance coverage will have expired. At that time the asset, Prepaid Expenses, will have declined in value to $110; an insurance expense of $10 will need to be included in next month's expenses, as follows:

Insurance Expenses		Prepaid Expenses (an asset)	
10		Balance	10

Obviously, at the end of 12 months, the prepaid expense account will have been written down to zero, and each of the months will have been charged with $10 worth of insurance expense.

As a final example, assume that, by agreement with the owner of the building, a company may delay monthly rental payments until 15 days following the end of the month. If the company uses a monthly accounting period, it will need to recognize the fact that it has received during this month the benefit of the use of the property, even though it does not have to pay rent until the next accounting period. Thus, the use of the facility this month has created a liability to the owner of the property. The appropriate accounting entries for this month are:

> debit the monthly rent to Rental Expense
>
> credit the monthly rent to Rent Payable (or Accounts Payable)

When next month the rental for this month is finally paid, the entries will be:

> debit to Rent Payable (or Accounts Payable)
>
> credit to Cash

Notice that these two entries next month—a decrease in an asset and a decrease in a liability—do not affect owners' equity. The effect on owners' equity—the expense—has been recorded this month.

Review again these four examples:

1 Recognition of sales, with the inflow of cash occurring in a subsequent period
2 Inflow of cash this period, with the corresponding sale to be recognized in a subsequent period
3 Cash outflow occurring prior to the accounting period when the expense will be recognized
4 Expense recognized this period, although cash outflow occurs in a subsequent period

Adherence to the accrual concept of accounting is essential for the accurate reporting of profit, and consequently the accurate valuation of assets and liabilities. However, it is this concept that gives rise to much disagreement among accountants and between accountants and their audiences, because it is often far from clear just when a sale was consummated or an expense was incurred. Some rules to assist in resolving these disagreements are discussed in the next chapter.

Example: Accounting for a Full Period

The relationship between the balance sheet and the income statement may be illuminated with a simple example of the accounting for a small business for a full accounting period, one month. The example, based upon the last problem in Chapter 2, also illustrates the use of T accounts (to represent general ledger accounts) and debit and credit entries.

Assume that you are accounting for the operations of a flower stand for the month of April. The flower stand sells all flowers for cash, and thus has no accounts receivable. It also buys new flowers each day, and thus carries no inventory over from one day to the next. The balance sheet for the flower stand at March 31 is:

Assets

Cash	$ 250
Stand (fixed asset)	1,250
Total assets	$1,500

Liabilities and Owners' Equity

Accounts payable	$ 300
Owners' equity	1,200
Total liabilities and owners' equity	$1,500

Exhibit 3-5 shows the T accounts for the flower stand. The balances at March 31 are shown in the four accounts listed on the balance sheet above. All other entries are described below, and each entry is labelled for easy reference with the appropriate letter.

a   Sales for cash totaled $1,700. (While the operator of the stand makes frequent bank deposits, the entry is shown as if only a single deposit were made at the end of the month.) The credit to Sales is balanced with the debit to Cash.

b   Flowers were purchased fresh each day, and the total of all purchases (on credit) for the month was $900. Since the stand had no beginning or

Exhibit 3-5
T-Accounts for Flower Stand

ASSETS

Cash		Stand (Fixed Asset)	
250	100 (c)	1,250	50 (f)
(a) 1,700	600 (d)		
	850 (e)		

LIABILITIES AND OWNERS' EQUITY

Accounts Payable		Owners' Equity	
(e) 850	300		1,200
	900 (b)		

REVENUE

Sales	
	1,700 (a)

EXPENSES

Cost of Goods Sold Expense		Rent Expense		Wages Expense	
(b) 900		(c) 100		(d) 600	

Decline in Value of Fixed Asset (expense)	
(f) 50	

ending inventory, these purchases represent cost of goods sold. The debit to Cost of Goods Sold (expense) is balanced with the credit to Accounts Payable.

c Rental of $100 was paid in cash to the shopping center. The debit to the expense account, Rent Expense, is balanced with a credit to Cash.

d Wages paid in cash to the stand's attendants totalled $600. The debit to the expense account, Wages Expense, is balanced with a credit to Cash.

e Payments of bills from the flower suppliers aggregated $850. Recall that flowers are purchased on credit; payments to suppliers during the month were less than credit purchases, and thus the Accounts Payable balance is higher at month-end. This transaction does not affect the income statement; the credit to Cash is balanced with a debit to Accounts Payable.

Exhibit 3-6
Financial Statements for Flower Stand

INCOME STATEMENT for April

Sales		$1,700
Cost of goods sold		900
Gross margin		800
Operating expenses		
Rent	100	
Wages	600	
Decline in value of fixed asset	50	750
Profit		$ 50

BALANCE SHEET at April 30

Assets

Cash		$ 400
Flower stand structure		1,200
Total Assets		$1,600

Liabilities and Owners' Equity

Accounts payable		$ 350
Owners' equity		
as of March 31	1,200	
Profit for April	50	
Total owners' equity (at April 30)		1,250
Total Liabilities and Owners' Equity		$1,600

f   The operator of the flower stand estimates that the value of the fixed asset (the physical stand) declined by $50 during the month. Note that no transaction is involved here; a review of the assets owned reveals that one of those assets should be valued lower at the end of the month than at the beginning. The credit entry to the fixed asset account is balanced with a debit to an expense account.

The accounting process has been completed for April and we can proceed to construct an income statement for the month and a balance sheet as of April 30, utilizing the balances that appear in the T accounts (general ledger accounts). These statements are shown in Exhibit 3-6.

Note that the flower stand made a $50 profit for the month of April. This amount does not appear in any T account but is derived on the income statement as the difference between sales and expenses. The amount also appears on the balance sheet in the owners' equity section as the balancing item.

Note also that total assets have increased during the month by $100.

This condition is neither good nor bad. This $100 increase in assets is balanced by a $50 increase in liabilities (accounts payable) and a $50 increase in owners' equity (profit for the month).

Summary

While a great assortment of accounting reports may be useful to various audiences, the two key accounting reports are the balance sheet and the income statement. The balance sheet is a statement of financial condition, providing a "snapshot" as of a particular date of the assets owned, liabilities owed, and balance of owners' equity. The comparison of two balance sheets, one at the beginning of an accounting period and the other at the end, reveals the total change in the company's retained earnings during the period. Adjusting this amount for any return that may have been paid to owners, one can determine the profit for the accounting period. However, this single profit figure tells little about the operations of the company. The income statement, on the other hand, is designed to do just that; it is a statement of performance for a particular accounting period.

Typical formats have developed for each of these statements, with some variation in format, of course, depending upon the company's particular business. The assets and liabilities of the company are listed on the balance sheet in order of decreasing liquidity, and a careful distinction is made between current and noncurrent assets and liabilities. The difference between these two amounts, the working capital of the company, indicates the company's overall liquidity, or ability to meet near-term obligations. On the income statement, the costs directly attributable to sales made during the period are matched against those sales to permit the calculation of gross profit. The operating expenses—e.g., selling and administrative—for the period are then subtracted from gross profit to derive operating profit. The bottom line of the income statement is net income after nonoperating income and expenses and after income tax expense—the final amount that serves to increase the Retained Earnings account of owners' equity.

We discussed earlier the reasons why the cost value method of valuation dominates actual accounting practice in this country, in preference to the time-adjusted value or market value methods. Other widely adopted accounting conventions are the accrual concept of accounting, and the double entry method. The double entry method follows directly from adherence to the fundamental accounting equation: a full accounting entry must involve equal debit and credit entries in order to preserve the equality. Typically, asset accounts carry debit balances, and both liabilities and owners' equity accounts carry credit balances. A debit entry (as distinct from debit balance) serves to increase an asset or decrease a liability or owners' equity account; a credit entry serves to increase a liability or owners' equity account or decrease an asset account.

The accrual concept of accounting requires that the revenues and expenses of a firm be matched to the accounting period when the revenues are earned and the expenses incurred, regardless of when cash is received or paid out. The cost value method assumes that income is earned only when a sale is realized, and a sale is realized at the single point in time when the goods or services are delivered to the customer. Thus, it is the transaction with an external party, the customer, that gives rise to revenue and earnings.

The categories of accounts into which entries are made are assets, liabilities, owners' equity, revenue, and expense. Each category will have from several to hundreds of individual accounts, depending upon the size and nature of the business and upon management's preferences. A full listing of all accounts utilized in the accounting system for a company is referred to as the chart of accounts and the set of records containing this account-by-account information is referred to as the general ledger.

New Terms

Account   The fundamental element of the accounting system that permits categorization and combination of like transactions and of like assets and liabilities. All accounts appear in the firm's general ledger.

Accounting period   The time period to which the income statement applies.

Accounts payable   The name given the liability account showing amounts due to the firm's suppliers (or vendors).

Accounts receivable   The name given the asset account showing the amounts due from customers.

Accrual concept (or basis)   The concept of accounting that, in contrast to the cash basis, requires that revenues and expenses be recognized in the accounting period when they are earned or incurred, regardless of whether the corresponding cash flow occurs within that accounting period.

Balance sheet   Statement of condition of an enterprise as of a particular date; expressed in the form of the accounting equation: assets = liabilities + owners' equity. An alternative name is *statement of financial position*.

Cash basis   A form of accounting that, in contrast to the accrual basis, requires that revenues and expenses be recognized in the accounting period when the corresponding cash flow occurs.

Chart of accounts   The listing of all accounts that are available in the general ledger.

Cost of goods sold (COGS)   The expense account containing the costs directly identifiable with the sales for the accounting period. An alternative name is *cost of sales*.

Cost of sales (COS)   An alternative name for *cost of goods sold*.

Credit (credit entry; credit balance)   Liability, owners' equity, and revenue (sales) accounts typically carry credit balances.   A credit entry increases a credit balance or decreases a debit balance.

Current assets   Those assets that will be converted to cash or used within the next twelve months.

Current liabilities   Those obligations of the enterprise that will be discharged within the next twelve months.

Debit (debit entry; debit balance)   Asset and expense accounts typically carry debit balances.   A debit entry increases a debit balance or decreases a credit balance.

Double entry   The type of accounting system that requires that each debit entry be balanced with a credit entry in order to preserve the accounting equation.

Earnings   Alternative name for *profit*.

Earnings statement   Alternative name for *income statement*.

Expense   A transaction that creates a decrease in owners' equity.

General ledger   The set of accounting records that details the current status of all of the accounts.

Gross margin   An alternative name for *gross profit*.   Gross margin may be expressed as a percentage: the percentage that gross profit is of net sales.

Gross profit   An amount equal to the difference between sales and cost of goods sold.

Income statement   Statement of performance of an enterprise for an accounting period; sales, cost of goods sold, and operating expenses are matched to the accounting period.   Alternative names are *operating statement, profit and loss (P&L) statement,* and *earnings statement*.

Intangibles   The name given to the asset accounts showing the values of certain rights or other intangible property such as patents, trademarks, and licenses.

Interim statements   Income statements for accounting periods shorter than one year and balance sheets at dates other than year-end.

Inventory   The name given the asset account for materials or merchandise owned by the enterprise and available for resale or use in manufacturing operations.

Invested capital   The name given to the owners' equity account showing the cumulative value of all investment in the enterprise by its owners.   In a partnership, this account might be called *partners' capital,* and in a corporation *common stock* or *capital stock*.

Liquidity   An enterprise's condition with respect to its ability to meet near-term obligations.   Liquid assets include cash, marketable securities, certain accounts receivable, and any other assets that will be or can be converted to cash in the near-term.

Loss   The amount by which entries that decrease owners' equity exceed those that increase owners' equity.   The opposite of a *profit*.

Net worth   An alternative name for *owners' equity*.

Operating profit   The amount of profit (or earnings) derived from normal operations of the enterprise, before the recognition of other (nonoperating) income and expense and before taxes on income.

Operating statement   Alternative name for the *income statement*.

Prepaids (or prepaid expenses)   Current asset accounts showing amounts paid in advance of the accounting period when the corresponding expenses will be recognized. (Examples: prepaid rent and prepaid insurance.)

Profit   The amount by which entries that increase owners' equity exceed those that decrease owners' equity. An alternative name is *earnings*.

Profit and loss (P&L) statement   Alternative name for the *income statement*.

Retained earnings   The name given to the owners' equity account showing cumulative earnings retained by the corporation. Net income increases retained earnings and dividends reduce retained earnings.

Revenue   A transaction, such as a sale, that creates an increase in owners' equity.

Shareholders' equity   An alternative name for *owners' equity* in the case of a corporation.

Statement of financial position   Alternative name for the *balance sheet*.

T account   A shorthand notation for a general ledger account.

Term loan   A loan (liability) having a maturity greater than one year.

Working capital   An amount equal to the difference between current assets and current liabilities. Working capital will be negative if current liabilities exceed current assets.

Problems

1   Classify the following assets and liabilities as either current or noncurrent (in certain instances, a portion may be current and the balance noncurrent), and explain your answer:

   a   Prepayment of $400 for a six-month insurance policy

   b   Loan payable to the bank, requiring equal monthly principal payments over two years

   c   An automobile owned by a manufacturing company and used by one of the salespersons

   d   An automobile owned by a used-auto dealer and available for resale

   e   Dividends declared by the company's board of directors and payable next month

   f   Investment in common stock of an unrelated corporation whose shares are widely traded on the New York Stock Exchange

   g   Investment in U.S. Treasury securities (federal government debt instruments) that trade actively in a public market and mature in 15 months

   h   Production equipment that has now been retired after many years of use and is available for resale

   i   A loan to the company from its president; the loan has a stated maturity of six months but both the president and others in the company feel that several years will pass before the company will be in a position to repay the loan

   j   A lease between the company and one of its customers, requiring the customer to pay $700 per month for 36 months

2   The key problem in determining profit for an accounting period is that of timing: deciding when revenues and expenses should be recognized. Insert, as appropriate, *increase* or *decrease* in the first blank of each of the following

statements, and *Asset, Liability, Revenue, Expense,* or *Owners' Equity* in the second blank of each statement.

a If an expenditure of cash occurs in the accounting period prior to the period when the corresponding expense is incurred, the expenditure serves to _____ a(an) _____ account and decrease the account Cash.

b If cash is received in the accounting period following the period when the corresponding revenue was recognized, the receipt of cash serves to _____ a(an) _____ account and increase the account Cash.

c If cash is received in the accounting period prior to the period when the corresponding revenue will be recognized, the receipt of cash serves to _____ a(an) _____ account and increase the account Cash.

d If an expenditure of cash occurs in the accounting period following the period when the corresponding expense was incurred, the expenditure serves to _____ a(an) _____ account and decrease the account Cash.

3 The following balances have been taken from the balance sheet of the Gothic Co. as of the end of its most recent fiscal year:

Current Assets	$450,000
Invested Capital	200,000
Long-term Liabilities	150,000
Other Noncurrent Assets	50,000
Property, Plant, and Equipment	325,000
Retained Earnings	275,000
Total Assets	825,000

Determine the amount of Gothic's current liabilities at year-end. What was the company's working capital at year-end?

4 The Frank Company, a manufacturing company, had total current assets of $250,000. Below are listed the balances in all accounts classified as either current assets or current liabilities, except for the Cash account. Determine the balance in the Cash account.

Accounts Payable	$ 35,000
Accounts Receivable	75,000
Inventories	100,000
Loans Payable	50,000
Prepaid Expenses	30,000
Salaries and Wages Payable	20,000

5 Prepare a balance sheet in conventional format for the Leopold Corp. as of August 31, 19X4 using the following data:

Accounts Payable	$ 40,000
Accounts Receivable	55,000
Accrued Vacation and Holiday Pay	8,000
Cash	10,000
Dividends Payable	5,000
Estimated Tax Liability	10,000

Interest Payable	3,000
Inventories	86,000
Invested Capital	100,000
Investment in Marketable Securities	5,000
Investment in Ramsey Co. (represents 20% ownership)	10,000
Land	12,000
Loan to Ramsey Company	5,000
Notes Payable	30,000
Patents and Trademarks	15,000
Plant and Equipment	36,000
Prepaid Insurance Premiums	2,000
Retained Earnings	40,000

6 Prepare a balance sheet in conventional format for the Flavell Company (a partnership providing data-processing services) as of March 31, 19X6, using the following data:

Accounts Payable	$ 2,000
Accounts Receivable	18,000
Accrued Insurance Premiums Payable	1,000
Cash	7,000
Computer Programs (developed by Flavell Company)	10,000
Data Processing Equipment (on lease)	30,000
Improvements in Rented Office Space	3,000
Investment by Partners	45,000
Lease Payable (data processing equipment)	28,000
License to Use Computer Programs (developed by others)	3,000
Office Furniture	5,000
Office Supplies Inventory	2,000
Prepaid Rent	1,000
Profit (before partner withdrawals): 1/1/19X6 through 3/31/19X6	5,000
Taxes (property) Payable	1,000
Withdrawals by Partners: 1/1/19X6 through 3/31/19X6	3,000

7 The founders of Leonard and Sons, Inc. invested a total of $50,000 upon formation of the company two years ago. No dividends have been paid. Now the company has total assets of $85,000, current assets of $35,000, current liabilities of $50,000, and long-term liabilities of $30,000. Would you say that the company has been successful during its first two years of operations? Explain.

8 The working capital of the Ramos Co. at May 31, 19X3 is $35,000. Current assets are $60,000, total assets are $125,000, and the company owes no long-term liabilities. What is the balance of owners' equity at May 31, 19X3?

9 The management of the Forest Corporation wishes to maintain a ratio of current assets to current liabilities equal to two, reducing its short-term borrowing so as to achieve this result. The corporation's cash balance is currently $30,000. Accounts payable are equal to $60,000 and the company is now borrowing $30,000 from the bank on a short-term loan. Inventory totals $100,000 and accounts receivable total $40,000. The only current asset accounts are Cash, Accounts Receivable, and Inventory; and the only current liability accounts are Accounts Payable and Short-term Bank Loan Payable. How much of its short-term bank loan should the company repay?

10 During 19X8 the total assets owned by the Leon Company declined from $135,000 to $125,000, while the total liabilities of the company increased from $55,000 to $65,000. Assuming that during the year no additional capital stock was sold by the Leon Company (that is, no new shareholder investment occurred) and the company paid dividends totaling $10,000, what can you say about the performance of the company during the year 19X8?

11 The Ralson Company expanded rapidly during 19X9 by investing in new plant and equipment and in manufacturing inventory. As a result, total assets increased from $400,000 at the beginning of the year to $700,000 at the end of the year. Total owners' equity at the beginning of the year was $200,000 and the company's net profit for the year was $50,000. Assuming the company paid no dividends during 19X9:

a What were the company's total liabilities at the end of the year, if no additional capital stock of the company was sold during the year?

b What were the company's total liabilities at the end of the year, if the company received $300,000 during the course of 19X9 from the sale of additional capital stock?

12 The Marshall Company earned a profit of $25,000 for the year 19X7, while the total assets of the company declined by $20,000 from the beginning to the end of the year. If the company sold no additional capital stock and paid no dividends during the year, by how much did the company's liabilities change? How is it possible that the company's assets could decline during the same year that a profit was earned?

13 The Bower Company's general ledger contained the following account balances (partial listing) at the end of June, 19X4. Construct an income statement in conventional format using the following data:

Administrative Expenses	$ 2,800
Cost of Goods Sold	16,500
Development Expenses	1,100
Interest Expense	500
Sales	25,000
Selling Expenses	3,300

What was Bower's gross margin for the period? Profit before tax?

14 The Reed Repair Company specialized in the repair of foreign-made automobiles. The company's general ledger at the end of 19X8 carried the following balances:

Accounts Payable	$ 4,800
Accounts Receivable	15,100
Cash	3,700
Decline in Value of Tools and Equipment, 19X8	200

Insurance Expense	200
Inventory of Parts	8,700
Owners' Equity (at January 1, 19X8)	19,500
Parts Expense	4,200
Prepaid Rent Expense	600
Property Tax Expense	300
Property Taxes Payable	1,500
Rent Expense	300
Repair Income	29,000
Telephone and Utility Expense	500
Tools and Equipment	3,300
Salaries Expense	4,000
Wages and Salaries Payable	3,100
Wages Expense	16,800

Construct in conventional format both an income statement for the year 19X8 and a balance sheet at year end, using the data above. What was Reed's profit for the year?

15 The Marks Consultants account for both revenues and expenses on the cash basis, rather than the accrual basis. Expenses consist solely of salaries and office rent; total cash paid out for these two expenses in 19X3 was $37,000. Total cash revenue from clients for the same year was $45,000. In addition, the company purchased $1,000 worth of new office equipment and determined that the value of existing office equipment had declined by $200 during the year. The balance sheet for the Marks Consultants at the beginning of the year 19X3 was as follows:

Cash	$5,000	Liabilities	0
Office Equipment	$4,000	Owners' Equity	$9,000
Total Assets	$9,000	Total Liabilities and	$9,000
		Owners' Equity	

Construct the company's balance sheet at year-end 19X3.

16 Record in T account format the following events or transactions, each of which is independent of all others. You should make only those entries required to record the particular event or transaction; do not include balances that may exist in the accounts as a result of earlier entries. Be certain that the sum of your debit entries is equal to the sum of your credit entries. Label each T account with the account name that you think is appropriate and indicate whether the account is an asset, liability, owners' equity, income, or expense account.

a The Bremer Co. sells for $5,500 merchandise that was valued in the company's inventory at $3,200.

b The Bremer Co. purchases inventory valued at $9,800, paying cash to the supplier.

c The Bremer Co. pays $800 rent on office space—$400 for this month and $400 for next month.

d The Bremer Co. pays wages and salaries totaling $2,700.

e The Bremer Co. pays the Bank of Centerville $5,200: $5,000 principal repayment on a loan and $200 interest for the current month.

f The Bremer Co. pays dividends to its shareholders totaling $1,100.

g The Bremer Co. purchases on open account inventory valued at $4,700.

h The Bremer Co. pays to its suppliers $3,000 for merchandise purchased on open account in previous months.

i The Bremer Co. receives $6,000 in cash from the sale of 100 shares of newly issued capital stock of the company.

j The Bremer Co. determines that the value of its equipment has declined by $450 during the month.

17 Following the instructions for question 16 above, record the following events or transactions.

a The Rector Co. receives a bill for $250 for janitorial service for the month.

b The Rector Co. pays $150 in payroll taxes for the previous month.

c The Rector Co. receives $700 from customer **X** in partial payment of that customer's account.

d The Rector Co. sells on open account merchandise having an aggregate sales price of $320.

e The Rector Co. borrows $2,000 from First Bank on a five-year term loan.

f The Rector Co. declares dividends totaling $1,500, with the intention of paying the dividend next month.

g The Rector Co. returns to its suppliers merchandise that is defective. Rector was originally billed $400 for this merchandise by the supplier, but the bill has not yet been paid.

h The Rector Company purchases an insurance policy for $1,500 in cash for one year of comprehensive protection, commencing next month.

i The Rector Co. receives supplies having a purchase cost of $600. These supplies were ordered last month, and the vendor's invoice is expected to arrive just after the end of this month.

j Rector Co. receives $100 as down payment from a customer who has requested delivery of certain merchandise next month.

18 Following the instructions for question 16 above, record the following events or transactions.

a The March Mercantile Co. accepts a used vehicle valued at $2,000 in full settlement of a customer's account receivable that has been valued at $2,500.

b The March Mercantile Co., after a careful review of all merchandise in inventory, determines that certain items that have been valued at $450 are now worthless.

c The March Mercantile Co. accepts from one of its customers the return of merchandise having an original sales value of $50. The customer had previously paid for the merchandise, but has agreed to accept a credit against future purchases rather than a cash refund.

d A one-year insurance policy purchased last month by March Mercantile for $2,400 in cash now has only 11 months of protection remaining.

e The March Mercantile Co. makes a $500 travel advance (loan) to one of its managers for a business trip that will be taken next month.

19 The following three events are somewhat unusual, and present problems both as to valuation and as to the particular accounts in the general ledger that will be affected.   Indicate which accounts you think will be affected, if any, and whether the entry will be a debit or credit.   Then describe how you would arrive at the value or values required for the entries.

a   The Brown Co. acquires from a local inventor a patent on a new device that Brown will produce in the coming years, in exchange for issuing to the inventor 500 shares of Brown Co. common stock.

b   The Redding Corporation leases a specialized machine tool from a lease financing company for five years, the estimated life of the machine tool. Redding estimates that the machine tool will have no value at the end of five years.   The lease requires 60 monthly payments of $275.

c   Mans Electronics, Inc. files a lawsuit against one of its suppliers for $50,000 for breach of contract.   The supplier has offered to settle for $10,000 but Mans has decided to take the matter to court.

20   In certain countries outside the United States, the typical balance sheet is presented in such a manner that the left-hand side of the accounting equation reads (instead of simply "assets"):

Working capital plus noncurrent assets

How would the right-hand side of such an accounting equation read?

N EW CORP (B)

Consider how you would value the following transactions in connection with the continued operation of New Corp. Prepare entries in T account format to record the transactions.

As Mr. Armstrong began in March 19X5 to produce and sell the safety helmets, he continued to record in note form all of the events or transactions that he thinks might be of use to you in your role as accountant. [See New Corp (A) for the first 26 notes.]

27   On March 1, our machine operators and assembly personnel—a total of six persons having an aggregate monthly salary of $5,100—started work. Our staff now consists of these six persons, Ted James (production foreman), Sally Simond (office clerk), and myself.

28   On March 1, commenced our first production run of 1,000 helments, due for completion on March 10.

29   On March 2, purchased and took delivery of miscellaneous office and plant equipment having a list price value of $4,550. The vendor agreed to accept $400 per month for 12 months, beginning April 1. Also on March 2, purchased on open account and took delivery of production supplies costing $1,700. These supplies are consumed in the course of production, generally in direct relationship to the number of labor hours.

30 On March 2, rented ancillary production equipment on a month-to-month basis at a monthly rental of $500. Paid March rent for this equipment.

31 On March 10, our first production run was completed, and I think our costs were in line. We used one-third of the DuPont material we received in early February (see note 14) and 5% of strapping materials (see note 25). Our six production workers (and James and I, as well!) were fully committed to this production run during these initial days. We have now commenced a second run of 2,500 due for completion on March 31. (Note: Consider how you would go about valuing this finished inventory; do not attempt T-account entries.)

32 On March 12, shipped 500 helmets to Lowe Industrial Supply (a distributor). Our price to Lowe is $5.00 per helmet, and that firm will resell to the ultimate industrial user at $7.50 per helmet. Our agreement with Lowe is that they may have 60 days to pay for this initial shipment, but our terms will be net 30 days on subsequent orders. Incidentally, we will have to pay Baxter (our independent sales representative) 5% commission on this order, but that payment can be delayed until we receive payment from Lowe. (Note: For purposes of this and the following note, assume that each helmet is valued in inventory at $3.00.)

33 On March 15, shipped 200 helmets (at a price of $4.50 per helmet) to Mammoth Supply Co. I lowered the price to Mammoth both because it is potentially a very large customer and because they agreed to pay in advance. Check received March 15.

34 On March 15, I drew the following checks:
a $800 rent to Sunshine Properties
b $600 salary to Sally Simond (see note 21)
c $1,890 to DuPont (see note 14)
d $8,900 (including $200 for installation) to Acme Tool for the injection molding machine ordered in January (see note 5) and received today.

35 Received the following additional orders during the month:
a March 18: 100 helmets at $5.00 per helmet from Glover. Shipment due April 15.
b March 23: 3,000 helmets at $4.50 per helmet from Ginger Co.; these helmets are scheduled for delivery at the rate of 500 per month beginning in May. In return for the price conces-

sion, they gave us a 20% down payment—check for $2,700 deposited on March 23.

36 On March 22, received another 10% of our order from DuPont and the associated invoice for $1,890 (including freight) and instructed DuPont to cut our April shipment to one-half the size received in February and March.

37 On March 31, I drew the following checks:
   a $800 to me as partial payment of March salary (see note 26)
   b Six checks totaling $5,100 for the six production workers (see note 27). (Note: Consider whether these wage payments are an expense of March. How might they be matched to revenues?)
   c $1,000 to Ted James: $1,100 salary less $100 repayment on the advance we made to him
   d $500 to A. T. Taster (partial payment for tooling: see note 12)
   e $400 to me for reimbursement of entertainment expense
   f $400 to Silvia Co. (see note 22)
   g $150 for utilities for the month of March
   h $1,700 for production supplies (see note 29)

38 Our equipment is now another month older. Also, we have only 5 months remaining on the insurance policy we bought and paid for last month (see note 18).

39 Remember that our certificate of deposit matures in early April (see note 3) and at that time we should receive about $400 interest on the deposit.

40 On March 31, borrowed $5,000 under our loan agreement with First Bank (see note 17). We will probably not be able to repay this loan for a number of months.

41 By March 31, we hadn't quite completed the second production run of 2,500 helmets. I am hopeful that these can be completed in early April. (Note: Consider how you would go about valuing this in-process inventory; do not attempt T-account entries.)

COMPUTER SERVICE ASSOCIATES

In January 1981 Earl McDonald and Gretchen Sasser began to discuss the possibility of joining together in a new business venture to provide computer programming and data-processing services to a limited group of customers in the Moline, Illinois area. At the time, both Earl and Gretchen were employed by the General Consolidated Manufacturing Company, producers of heavy farm equipment; while both worked in the data processing department of the company,

Earl's primary experience was in computer programming, and Gretchen's was in computer operations. Each had for years thought about starting a new computer service, but both now felt that a partnership arrangement could be more successful since their work experiences were complementary and between them they had a wide circle of acquaintances in the Moline area.

In February they gave notice to their employer and on March 1, 1981, they commenced their partnership operation, for which they coined the name Computer Service Associates, or CSA. They knew that the first few months of operations would be slow, but they focused their attention on attracting customers that could provide some immediate revenue to the partnership. They spent very little time worrying about the administrative records for their new company.

It is now August 31, 1981, six months after the CSA partnership was formed. Earl and Gretchen really have no idea whether their operation has been successful to date and they are beginning to be concerned about their ability to meet the various obligations that CSA continually incurs. CSA seems always to be short of cash, and Earl and Gretchen are uncertain whether the cash shortage is a danger signal. They have asked you, their friend , to help them analyze both their present financial position and also the progress that the company has made over the past six months. In conversations with Earl and Gretchen and by reviewing the meager records that exist around CSA's office, you develop the information contained in the balance of this case.

By August, CSA had developed two companies as quite steady customers and had done work for two other customers. One of these customers, Weintraub Construction Corporation, signed a contract with CSA in early June for the development over a six-month period of computer programs to improve the construction company's bidding procedure. The contract provides that CSA will deliver certain programs each month and Weintraub will pay CSA $1,000 per month for six months, with payments due on the last day of each month beginning in June. While the June and July payments have been received, the payment due on August 31 has not yet been received, although CSA has made the required delivery of programs. The other customers contract with CSA on a job-by-job basis. As the jobs are completed, Earl sends the customer an invoice. He retains a Xerox copy of this invoice in an Unpaid Invoices file until payment is received from the customer; when payment is received the invoice copy is marked ''paid'' and is moved to another file entitled Paid Invoices. At August 31 the Unpaid Invoices file contains the following invoices:

Date	Customer	Amount
August 23	Clyde Engineers	$1,450
August 15	Bruno Brothers	1,150
July 24	Clyde Engineers	800
June 30	Harris Corporation	1,660

You run an adding machine tape of the invoices in the Paid Invoices file and find that they total $4,850. You note that apparently Weintraub (the customer on a six-month contract) is not sent an invoice each month, as none appears in either file. In the course of conversation with Gretchen you learn that Micro Materials paid CSA $150 in April for services rendered that month, although no invoice exists for this amount.

Earl and Gretchen had been aware that a number of larger companies in the Moline area had considerable excess computing capacity and in June they were able to arrange to buy time on one of these computers at quite favorable terms. Thus, the partnership does not have, and does not anticipate acquiring, its own computer. The two partners worked out of their homes for the first month, but in April CSA rented a small office in a regional shopping center on the edge of Moline. By reading the rental agreement you learn that rental is $500 per month and CSA is required to rent the space for a minimum of two years, beginning April 1, 1981; apparently CSA deposited $500 with the owner of the building as security, this amount to be applied to the last month's rent (i.e., March 1983). Earl and Gretchen tell you that they contracted with a dealer in used office furniture and other office equipment for all the desks, chairs, typewriters, and other equipment in the office at a total purchase price of $4,000; the contract required CSA to pay half of this amount to the equipment dealer upon delivery and the balance in December 1981. The partners feel that the furniture and equipment will last for 4 years, after which it will be valueless, and therefore that the equipment should now be valued at only seven-eighths the amount paid for it.

CSA's check book stubs indicate that the current bank balance is $380[1] (CSA has no other cash). Certain check stubs have been improperly prepared and thus you are unable to develop complete information on cash payments made. Earl and Gretchen do recall the following:

1 Earl McDonald contributed $2,000 and Gretchen Sasser $4,000 to the partnership bank account on April 1.

---

[1] Note: Many cash transactions have occurred during the six months. Debits to cash were recorded when the partners' capital was invested and when customers paid for services. Credits were recorded as expenditures were made for assets, expenses, or the payment of liabilities. The resulting balance is $380.

2 In July, when the company's cash position got very tight, Gretchen Sasser loaned an additional $500 to the partnership. No formal loan agreement exists, no interest is being paid to Gretchen, and the partners haven't any idea when the $500 can be repaid to Gretchen.

3 Each of the two partners has been withdrawing $500 per month as salary ($1,000 per month in total). Five such monthly withdrawals have been made, but in view of the current cash balance, the August withdrawal has been postponed.

4 In April Earl McDonald received a check for $250 as a fee to him for assisting his close friend in the preparation of 1980 income tax returns for his friend's auto repair shop.

In looking through various files and on top of desks you discover the following:

1 Gretchen Sasser's personal savings account passbook. No withdrawals or deposits have been made in the last six months but on June 30 the savings bank credited the account with $30 for interest earned.

2 A letter agreement dated August 1 between CSA and Fred Sasser (Gretchen's husband). The agreement calls for Fred to rent space within CSA's office, beginning August 1, at the rental rate of $80 per month. Gretchen says that Fred has not yet paid either the August or September rent.

3 A file marked Unpaid Bills. Gretchen tells you that although she typically pays bills in this file on the 10th and 25th of each month, payments may be delayed depending upon the amount of cash available in CSA's bank account. The file contains the following:

Date	Vendor/Supplier	Amount	Explanation
August 30	Noonan Development	$500	September office rent
August 22	Illinois Bell Telephone	80	Telephone bill through August 20
August 20	Hofmann Manufacturing	600	Computer time for August 1—15

4 A stock of computer paper and specialized computer programming forms. Earl tells you that this stock is about one-half of the shipment received in mid-July. The company paid $840 for the full shipment.

5 Miscellaneous stationery, envelopes, and other office supplies. You decide to ignore these items of inventory since in total they probably have a value of less than $100.

The arrangement between CSA and Hofmann Manufacturing regarding CSA's purchase of time on Hofmann's computer provides, according to Earl, that CSA purchase a minimum of $1,000 of time per month for the months of August through December 1981. Hofmann bills CSA semimonthly (each 15 days) for the amount of time used, but not less than $500. The bill for the period August 15—31, 1981, has not yet been received, but Earl thinks it will total about $550. You cannot find the billings from Hofmann for months prior to August, but are assured by the partners that they have been paid.

ASSIGNMENT

1   Construct a balance sheet as of August 31, 1981 in as much detail as possible. (SUGGESTION: Do not attempt to reconstruct the T-account entries for the six months. Based upon the material in the case, identify and value all assets and liabilities as of August 31, 1981; you can then determine owners' equity by deduction.)

2   Construct as complete an income statement as you can for the six-month period. (Hint: You should be able to determine revenue for the six-month period and, from the balance sheet, the amount of the profit or loss for the period. In addition, you can isolate certain of the expenses and by deduction ascertain the aggregate total of all other expenses. You will not be able to separate cost of goods sold from operating expenses.)

3   What additional detailed information would you like to have that might be revealed by a more complete income statement? Construct the form of income statement that you would recommend for this company.

4   How has Computer Service Associates performed over the six-month period? Be specific. If you were Earl or Gretchen, would you be satisfied if performance during the next six months were the same as for the past six months?

5   Should Earl or Gretchen be concerned about the company's cash position? Explain.

6   Suppose that Gretchen Sasser (who has more invested in this business than her partner) is interested in buying out Earl McDonald and that McDonald has expressed a reluctant interest in selling. How much do you think that Gretchen should offer for Earl's share? Is this the same amount that you would recommend to Earl that he accept? How does this amount relate to the owners' equity at August 31 as stated on your balance sheet?

7   Now suppose that both Earl and Gretchen are offered very attractive positions and salaries if they will rejoin General Consolidated Manufacturing Company (their former employer); they decide to

accept the offers and therefore liquidate CSA. How much cash do you think will ultimately be returned to the two partners if they liquidate the business? How does this amount relate to the owners' equity at August 31 as stated on your balance sheet? How does it relate to the amount you recommended to Gretchen (see question 6) that she offer Earl for his share of the business?

Developing a Set of Rules for Financial Accounting

Up until this point in our study of accounting, we have emphasized that there may reasonably exist wide differences of opinion concerning the proper way to record a particular event or transaction in monetary terms. These differences may arise because different individuals observe and measure the same event in different ways. Also, the particular entries chosen to record an event or transaction may be affected by the use to which the resulting financial information will be put. For example, if the primary interest is in providing data to be used by the company's creditors, one might choose quite a different way to record a transaction than if the interest is in providing data that will be useful to management in making product pricing decisions.

This chapter recaps our discussion to date and develops certain basic concepts that are widely followed in accounting practice today. Finally, it mentions the various rule-making bodies in the United States that seek to interpret these concepts and promulgate more specific constraints and rules to guide professional accountants in their day-to-day practice.

Valuation Methods

Recall the format and derivation of the income statement (profit and loss statement); recall, too, that the valuation of assets and liabilities will determine the valuation of owners' equity, since owners' equity is simply the difference between assets and liabilities. As the income statement is nothing more than an amplification of the source and magnitude of the changes in the owner's equity account, the valuation of assets and liabilities must ultimately determine the magnitude and timing of the recognition of revenues and expenses on the income statement.

Thus, the two basic products of the accounting system—the balance sheet and the income statement—form one integral whole: the balance sheet providing a "snapshot" of the value of assets owned and liabilities owed as of a certain date, and the income statement providing details about the nature and extent of the changes in those assets and liabilities (and thus owners' equity) between two balance sheet dates.

We have investigated three logical bases for valuing assets and liabilities:

1 The time-adjusted value method requires that we determine the present value of the future stream of positive benefits (for assets) and negative benefits (for liabilities) by discounting these future benefits at an interest rate appropriate to the entity for which we are accounting.
2 The market value method requires that we determine the current market value of each asset and liability, a value which for assets will often approximate the replacement cost of the assets.
3 The cost value method accepts as the basis for valuation the original cost of the asset or liability. This method also recognizes that the original cost may need to be modified to record the decline in value of fixed assets over time, obsolescence of inventory, or other effects.

Most of us conclude that the time-adjusted value method provides the most intellectually satisfying basis for valuation. It seems to be the method that best recognizes the importance of the future in today's valuation. In this respect it is consistent with the realization that the major benefit of financial data and reports is to provide input for decision making regarding the future. Nevertheless, after struggling with the problems inherent in the process of determining the magnitude and timing of the future stream of positive and negative benefits, we are less confident of our ability to apply this method. We realize that the cost value method, in eliminating most of these problems of assessing the future, presents some very real advantages that greatly mitigate its disadvantages.

Professional accountants have struggled for years with these same dilemmas, and the struggle continues today. They have developed sets of both basic concepts and specific rules that provide a framework for resolving questions regarding individual accounting entries. This framework is based largely, but not entirely, on the cost value method. Moreover, the framework undergoes continuous evolution in a series of small steps as the accounting profession attempts to resolve for its members certain of the recurring dilemmas.

It is important to remember that these basic concepts and specific rules represent compromises between conflicting objectives that the accountant faces. An understanding of this framework and the reasons behind its various elements is essential if we are to interpret in an intelligent manner the financial data that we encounter as managers, stockholders, and members of the voting public. As we interpret financial information we must be cognizant of the limitations imposed by this framework of concepts and rules. We may not always agree with the rules as promulgated, but we must at least understand them.

Basic Concepts

Note in the discussion that follows that the basic concepts evolve directly from the definition of accounting that was presented in Chapter 1 and the distinction that was drawn in Chapter 3 between accrual and cash accounting systems.

Expression in monetary terms   Only those events and transactions that can be expressed in monetary terms can be recorded. The resulting accounting story about the business will necessarily be incomplete, since many of the most important business events cannot be reduced to monetary terms: the hiring and leaving of personnel, the discovery of a new process, product, or technique, the resolution of a key management disagreement. The future effects of the particular event may ultimately be expressable in monetary terms, generally in increased or decreased revenues or expenses, but the event itself may not be recordable in the accounting system.

Entity   The entity being accounted for, be it a business, a nonprofit organization, a person, a family, or a government unit, must be carefully defined, and only events affecting that specific entity should be measured and included in the accounting system. For a business, accounting is restricted to those events affecting that business; the effect that the same events might have on individuals and organizations outside of the business entity—including employees, stockholders, customers, labor unions, and suppliers—is ignored. For a governmental unit, accounting is confined to those events affecting that governmental unit, and ignores the effect that the same events might have on citizens served or individuals employed by the organization.

Going-Concern assumption   Unless an accountant knows for a fact to the contrary, accounting procedures are performed under the assumption that the entity will continue to operate for an indefinite period into the future, providing essentially the same services.   Because of this **going-concern assumption,** the accountant need not be concerned, for example, with the amount that would be received should the plants and equipment or other producing assets of the entity be sold, since the assumption is that the entity has no intention of selling those assets.   Instead, the accountant is concerned with valuing the assets in the context of the use to which they are now put.

Of course, should the decision be made to liquidate or sell the entity, the going-concern assumption is no longer valid, and the assets and liabilities must be reevaluated under this new assumption.   The values arrived at under this new assumption may be considerably different than under the going-concern assumption.   The assets may be valued substantially higher if they are currently very productive and are to be sold, or they may be valued substantially lower if they are generally unproductive and are to be abandoned or sold at a distress price.

Conservatism   When faced with reasonable doubt as to whether an asset or revenue should be stated at one value or another *lower* value, the accountant will exercise **conservatism** and choose the lower value; correspondingly, when faced with reasonable doubt as to whether a liability or expense should be stated at one value or another *higher* value, the accountant will choose the higher value.   That is, the accountant will opt for the choice which tends to result in lower owners' equity.   The key phrase in the first sentence of this paragraph is "reasonable doubt."

Note that this concept does not imply the accountant will purposely understate owners' equity, although some understatement may result from the application of this concept.   Rather, the accountant will take reasonable precautions to provide for probable losses and not to record revenues before they are earned.

The application of this concept leads to many arguments between accountants and business executives.   The business executive is typically optimistic, but this concept demands that the accountant lean in the direction of pessimism.   While the concept may be difficult to defend from the point of view of accounting theory or logic, it does provide a useful balance to the optimistic nature of most of us.   Moreover, to the extent surprises occur in business—unexpected or unanticipated events—these surprises most frequently, although by no means always, have the effect of reducing ownership equity, rather than increasing it. Thus, in practice it seems that the application of this concept of conservatism tends to result in greater realism in financial statements.

Accrual   As discussed in Chapter 3, it is possible to operate an accounting system using either the accrual concept or the cash concept. The cash concept requires that expenses be acknowledged and assets recorded only when the corresponding cash outflow occurs and that revenues be acknowledged only when the corresponding cash inflow occurs. By contrast, the accrual concept requires that expenses by acknowledged when, and as soon as, they are incurred, regardless of when the cash outflow occurs. Sometimes the expense and the cash outflow, or expenditure, occur simultaneously; in these cases, the cash concept and the accrual concept of accounting lead to the same result. At other times, the expense occurs before the expenditure is made—for example, when goods or services are purchased on credit and consumed prior to payment. Then the accrual concept will acknowledge the expense at the time of consumption, while the cash concept will recognize the expense at the time the vendor's invoice is ultimately paid. In other situations, the cash outflow occurs before the goods or services are consumed; for example, rental on a building may be prepaid or wages may have been paid to production workers who have produced goods which now are in finished-goods inventory and thus not yet shipped. Under these circumstances, the accrual concept will acknowledge the expense at the time the rented building is ultimately used or the finished goods inventory ultimately sold, while the cash concept will acknowledge the expense at the earlier date when the cash payments are made.

Similar distinctions can be drawn between the accrual and cash concepts with respect to revenue. The accrual concept will recognize revenue when the goods or services are provided to the customer, regardless of whether the customer has obtained the goods or services on credit, for cash at the time of delivery, or by advance payment. The cash concept will recognize revenue as the cash is actually received.

Note that the distinction between these two concepts is only a matter of timing, but timing is all-important. Most of the disagreements among accountants as to the appropriateness of accounting entries revolve around the question of timing. Even under the accrual concept, reasonable persons may disagree as to when consumption or delivery of goods or services actually occurred.

The accounting systems that we shall study all utilize the accrual concept. Nevertheless, there are many entities that do use the cash concept, and quite reasonably so. For example, as mentioned in Chapter 3, you probably run your personal "set of books," which may consist solely of your checkbook, on a cash basis. Certain professional and service companies maintain their records on a cash concept basis. Generally, for entities that have few or no fixed assets and little or no inventory and whose primary expenses are composed of wages and salaries that are paid frequently and on a regular basis, the cash concept is appropriate. In such cases, there exists a minimal difference in timing between incurring an expense and making the corresponding cash payment, and between delivering goods or services and receiving payment for them. Thus, the accrual concept and cash concept yield quite similar results.

Realization The **realization** concept dictates that revenue is all earned on the date when the particular goods or services are delivered or furnished.

In the absence of this concept, one might say that a portion of the revenue is earned when the order is received from the customer, additional portions are earned at each step in the manufacturing or servicing process, still more is earned when the product is shipped, and the final increment is earned when payment is received from the customer. The primary problem with such an alternative concept is the difficulty in determining the timing and amount of revenue to be recognized at each of the steps in the complete sales and collection cycle. There appears to be no objective way of making such determinations.

Intuitively we may feel that not all of the revenue, and thus not all of the profit, from a sales transaction is earned at one single moment in time. We instinctively know, and economists confirm, that each element or segment of the business has a hand in producing value. Nevertheless, by convention accountants make the simplifying assumption that all of the revenue is recognized at the date of exchange of the goods or services between seller and buyer

There are exceptions to this generalization. When the in-process time is very long and the value added at various stages in the process can be accurately and objectively measured, portions of the revenue may be recognized in advance of final delivery or exchange. Examples include large building or other construction projects or the fabrication of complex equipment such as space vehicles or nuclear generators. Also, if there is reasonable doubt that the supplier of the goods or services will ever receive cash in exchange—for example, because of financial failure of the customer or because the customer retains the right to return the goods following evaluation—the recognition of revenue may be delayed beyond the date of delivery or until the cash is finally received.

Matching Growing out of the concepts of accrual accounting and realization is the concept of **matching.** That is, when revenue is realized from a certain transaction, all related expenses must also be recognized; thus, the accountant matches revenues with the corresponding expenses. The expenses are recognized neither before nor after the date upon which the revenue generated by those expenses is realized. In practice, it is important only that the revenues and expenses be matched in the same accounting period. Again, reasonable persons may differ as to just which expenses are properly matched to what revenues, and thus practice will differ somewhat between different companies and different accountants.

Consistency Since the concepts or guidelines discussed above are not completely specific, the accountant is still left with a great deal of discretion with respect to recording particular transactions and events. Specific accounting rules only narrow, but do not eliminate, this discretionary area. The **consistency** concept requires that the accountant, once having decided upon a method of accounting for a particular transaction within a particular company, must continue consistently to employ that method for accounting for all similar transactions. The concept requires both consistency in handling the recording of similar transactions and consistency over time. The *consistency over time* concept facilitates the comparison of financial data from one accounting period to another. We will soon see that comparisons and trend analyses are two primary means of interpreting financial data. Were the concept of consistency to be relaxed, comparability would be lost and analysts would find themselves comparing the apples of one accounting period to the oranges of another.

Of course, conditions change over time, and to prohibit entirely any change in accounting policies and procedures would hinder accountants in their efforts to present more useful and meaningful data to the various audiences, including particularly management and the stockholders. The concept of consistency requires, instead, that upon determining that a change in accounting practice or procedure would enhance the usefulness of the financial data the accountant should thoroughly disclose the nature of the change and give the audiences an estimate of the effect of this change on the reported financial information.

Materiality The concept of **materiality** advises the accountant to focus time and attention on the material, or important, events in the business. The measuring, valuing, and recording of financial data cost money; if the benefit of the resulting data is less than the cost of collecting and processing it, then the accountant should cease the collection and processing. Rather than incurring the expenses inherent in detailed measurement, the accountant may simply decide to estimate the value of the event or transaction.

For example, it may be inefficient and uneconomic to track the use of low-value parts in an assembly process—parts such as nuts, bolts, and washers. Estimating the value of these parts withdrawn from inventory for a particular job may be completely satisfactory for management's purposes, because the value of the parts is immaterial in the context of the total enterprise.   Consequently, even a substantial error in the estimate will have an immaterial effect on the final financial statements.

Again, when an entity is billed monthly for certain services such as utilities and telephone, it may be unnecessary to determine how much of each billing falls in the current accounting period, the past accounting period, and the next accounting period.   If the amount of the bill is generally similar from month to month and the accountant makes certain that one bill is recorded each month (if the accounting period is a month), it will probably be unnecessary to allocate the bill between this month and last month or this month and next month.   Such an allocation will be expensive because the accounting system will have to collect additional information to serve as the basis for the allocation.   The effect of the allocation will probably be immaterial to the reported financial statements.

Specific Rules

In addition to these general concepts there are certain specific rules that have been promulgated by the accounting profession and agencies of the U.S. federal government in order to provide additional guidelines in particularly troublesome and controversial accounting areas.

The primary purpose of these rules is to promote consistency between companies in the way in which operating results and financial positions are reported to shareholders.   For internal management purposes, the company is free to develop data in any manner that it deems useful.   Public reporting of financial information, however, must follow these guidelines.

The **American Institute of Certified Public Accountants (AICPA),** an association whose membership is limited to professional, or certified, accountants, has been a strong force in this country in the formation of policies and procedures for accounting.   For many years, this association issued informal and nonbinding recommendations about policies and procedures.   In the late 1950s, as the need for unified adherence to more standardized procedures became more widely felt, the association organized the **Accounting Principles Board (APB).**   During the period from 1959 to 1973 this board issued 31 formal opinions that **certified public accountants (CPAs)** were required to follow.   Both the work of and the controversy surrounding the APB grew rather steadily during its 14-year existence, as the opinions issued dealt with very sensitive and difficult issues.

In the early 1970s the need for a more independent rule-setting body, one with industry and academic representation as well as CPA representation, was recognized.   On June 1, 1973, the **Financial Accounting Standards Board (FASB)** was established, consisting of seven full-time members that are appointed by a Board of Trustees. As with opinions of the APB, the pronouncements of the FASB must be followed by the professional accountants in this country. The FASB continues to tackle the very many thorny and unresolved accounting issues. The rules set forth thus far by the FASB have been met with a good deal of opposition, as well as support, and this situation will probably continue. Since different audiences for financial statements have different needs and objectives, it is unrealistic to hope that any rule that seeks to settle conclusively a highly controversial issue will be warmly embraced by all that the rule affects. There is widespread hope that the FASB will prove effective and efficient in order that the rule-setting function can remain in the private sector rather than be the subject of governmental laws and regulations. However, it is still too early to be certain that this hope will be realized.

Indeed, in recent years a governmental regulatory agency, the **Securities and Exchange Commission (SEC),** in its role as watchdog for the investing public, has become increasingly active in requiring certain standardized accounting procedures. These must be followed when companies issue financial statements to their public shareholders. While these procedures and guidelines need be followed by only those companies whose securities are traded in interstate commerce, virtually all major U.S. corporations fall into this category, and thus the requirements of the SEC become de facto guidelines for the entire accounting profession. The SEC has had significant impact on accounting practice over the years, and many feel that the SEC's role will become more dominant to the extent that the FASB proves ineffective or slow to resolve the many accounting dilemmas that remain.

Typically, the formal rules and procedures set forth by the APB, the FASB, or the SEC are of such a specialized nature that they need not be discussed in detail in this book. Among the areas now covered by these rules are the calculation of earnings per share, accounting for the value of fluctuating international currencies, accounting for research and development expenses, accounting for leases, and accounting for long-term receivables and payables under a variety of circumstances. The FASB, and possibly the SEC as well, will continue to promulgate rules in these and other areas in an attempt to reduce the diversity of accounting treatments and to improve the comparability of financial statements emanating from different businesses.

Before leaving the discussion of specific rules, we should note that other agencies of the U.S. federal government have insisted on certain standardized accounting procedures for those companies which they regulate or with which they contract. For example, companies engaged in defense and aerospace contracting with the federal government must submit to certain specified accounting procedures, as must the railroads that are regulated by the Interstate Commerce Commission.

The Role of the CPA Auditor

The independent and certified accountant plays a key role in ensuring that both the generalized concepts and the specific rules of accounting are followed by issuers of financial statements. All companies whose securities are widely traded—virtually all companies of significant size in this country—engage CPAs to audit their accounting records and systems and attest to their financial statements.

Certified public accountants are those accountants who have, through formal education, on-the-job experience, and rigorous testing, demonstrated competency in accounting to a level that warrants certification, or licensing, by the state. As members of a profession, CPAs are required to observe a code of professional ethics. Similar procedures are followed in other countries; chartered accountants in England or Canada are generally equivalent in background and function to CPAs in the United States.

The practice of public accounting is performed by those CPAs who offer their services for a fee and who remain independent from their clients. Although CPAs are hired and paid by their clients, their independent status requires that they not simply be advocates of the client, as might a lawyer or a physician. Rather, the CPA's code of ethics requires the CPA to discharge an obligation to the general public, while performing a service to the client. Thus, in certifying the correctness and fairness of publicly reported financial statements, the CPA is asserting that he or she has performed sufficient review of the accounting procedures and individual records so as to be satisfied that the financial statements fairly represent the position and condition of the firm. Should this assertion prove incorrect, and a member of the general public (typically an investor) thereby suffer financial loss by relying on the accountant's certification, the individual suffering the loss may bring legal action against the CPA for malpractice or incompetence. Therefore, the potential liability that the independent CPA assumes by virtue of this public responsibility is very large indeed.

The process of asserting the accuracy and fairness of financial statements is called **auditing,** and the audit function is the most important aspect of the independent CPA's public practice. This function does not require that the CPA prepare the financial statements for the company being audited (indeed, a CPA who prepared the statements would no longer be independent), but rather that the CPA review and test the accuracy of the statements prepared by the company's own management. Further, the audit function does not require that the CPA review each specific accounting entry, an effort which would clearly be very time consuming and expensive. Rather, CPAs employ well-developed and relatively standardized procedures that involve such activities as: (1) reviewing a random sample of routine transactions, (2) verifying by objective means a random sample of specific assets and liabilities (e.g., inventory, accounts receivable, and accounts payable), (3) reviewing the routine daily procedures of the accounting department, (4) checking out in detail any unusual transactions or accounting entries, and (5) making such other tests as may seem necessary or prudent given the nature of the particular company being audited. Further, to protect shareholders, creditors, and honest and competent members of management, the independent CPA utilizes procedures to test for fraud, as well as for simple error or slipshod accounting practice.

In the course of the auditing procedure, the independent CPA must be certain that the company is following the basic concepts outlined in this chapter—e.g., the company is properly and conservatively matching revenues and expenses—and that the company is following the specific rules of the APB, the FASB, and, if applicable, the SEC. Thus, the CPA is expected to guard against the intentional or unintentional over- or understatement of profit or misstatement of financial position. The independent CPA has a responsibility to the shareholder not to permit overstatement of profit, to the taxing authorities not to permit understatement of profit, and to the company's creditors not to permit an unrealistic presentation of the company's financial position. It should be clear, therefore, that many opportunities exist for disagreement to arise between the CPA performing the audit function and the company's managers who have prepared the financial statements being audited. The relationship between the independent CPA and the client is an unusual and often delicate one.

A CPA may practice professionally as an individual or as a member of a partnership. Partnerships vary in size from local two-person partnerships to very large, worldwide partnerships. The profession in this country is dominated by eight large firms that practice throughout this country and in many other countries of the world—the so-called "Big Eight"—but many strong regional and local firms also provide competent client service. In addition to performing the audit function, the larger accounting firms all provide consulting or advisory services, generally in the areas of tax return preparation, tax planning, management-information systems, data-processing systems, and routine or special accounting procedures.

Implications of These Concepts and Rules

Readers of financial statements have a strong tendency to accept formal statements as representing the "truth," with only a small margin of error. This tendency is even present among sophisticated and experienced financial analysts. Our discussion to this point has stressed that accountants must utilize estimates and approximations if they are to provide useful financial data in a timely manner. The concepts and rules discussed above help accountants exercise reasonable judgment, but surely they do not resolve all accounting dilemmas.

As the input data to the accounting system contain estimates and approximations, the output of the accounting system, the financial statements, are at best estimates—the balance sheet is an estimate of the value of assets and liabilities at a point in time, and the income statement is an estimate of the source and magnitude of the changes in owners' equity during the particular accounting period. To repeat, they are only estimates. To be *completely certain* of the level of profit and thus the value of owners' equity, the company would have to cease operations, liquidate the assets, and pay off all liabilities. Only then could one know for certain how much value remained for the owners of the company.

And yet, by following these rules and concepts, particularly the concept of consistency, accountants can provide extremely useful data to their audiences: to management, for making operating decisions; to stockholders, for making investment decisions; and to lenders, for making credit decisions.

Although the financial statements can provide much useful data for decisions, their readers should retain a healthy skepticism: in no sense do these statements convey absolute truth about the financial position or profitability of the business.

Summary

As accountants wrestle with the problem of valuing assets and liabilities, and thereby owners' equity (changes in which are described by revenues and expenses), certain generalized concepts and specific rules are followed.

Much attention was focused in earlier chapters on alternative valuation methods. In practice, the cost value method represents the most basic principal of accounting systems. The accounting concepts discussed in this chapter are therefore built on the cost value method. Nevertheless, accountants encounter situations where the time-adjusted value or market value methods are appropriate and sometimes these other methods are required by rules promulgated by professional authorities.

The key concepts that assist in resolving day-to-day accounting dilemmas are:

Expression in monetary terms

Entity

Going-concern assumption

Conservatism

Accrual

Realization

Matching

Consistency

Materiality

These key concepts will ensure comparability among financial statements emanating from *different* companies; the concepts will ensure even greater comparability among financial statements emanating over time from the *same* firm. Valuation procedures assume that a firm will continue in its present business. Several concepts require that accountants exercise care not to overstate either profit or the overall financial health of the firm. Finally, several of the concepts are aimed at the heart of the problem of determining when revenues and expenses—and therefore profits—should be recognized.

As further steps to meet these laudable objectives, the Financial Accounting Standards Board (and its predecessor, the Accounting Principles Board) was organized within the private (nongovernment) sector in the United States to establish specific rules to resolve (or help to resolve) crucial accounting dilemmas. The Securities and Exchange Commission, the federal agency that is the watchdog for the investing public, is also actively involved in formulating guidelines for the presentation of financial statements to shareholders and potential investors.

The independent certified public accountant (CPA) is employed by major companies in this country to audit the companies' accounting systems and attest that their financial statements can be relied upon by the public. In fulfilling their responsibilities to both client companies and the public, CPAs make certain that companies' accounting practices are in accord with both the general concepts discussed here and with the specific rules that are issued by both the professional and governmental regulatory authorities.

New Terms

AICPA (American Institute of Certified Public Accountants) An association of professional certified accountants in the United States.

APB (Accounting Principles Board) A body organized by the AICPA (American Institute of Certified Public Accountants) that was a predecessor organization to the FASB (Financial Accounting Standards Board).

Auditing The process carried out by certified public accountants of testing the accuracy of accounting records and systems and certifying the fairness of the resulting financial statements.

Certified public accountant (CPA) An accountant who has, through formal education, on-the-job experience, and rigorous testing, demonstrated competency in accounting and who has thereby been awarded certification by a state.

Conservatism   The accounting concept that requires the accountant to provide for probable losses, and not record revenues before they are earned, thus leaning in the direction of understating revenues and assets and overstating expenses and liabilities.

Consistency   The accounting concept that requires that all similar transactions and conditions be accounted for in the same manner over time.

FASB (Financial Accounting Standards Board)   An independent rule-setting body within the private (nongovernment) sector responsible for promulgating accounting regulations in the United States to which CPAs must adhere.

Going-concern assumption   The accounting concept that requires accountants to value assets and liabilities assuming the enterprise will continue its present set of activities, unless or until a decision to the contrary is made by the enterprise's management.

Matching   The accounting concept that requires the matching of revenue with all corresponding expenses.

Materiality   The accounting concept that advises the accountant to focus time and attention on valuing the material, or important, events or changes in condition which affect assets and liabilities. Materiality is judged in relationship to total values appearing on financial statements for the particular enterprise.

Realization   The accounting concept that requires revenue to be recognized as earned at the particular point in time when the goods or services are delivered or furnished.

SEC (Securities and Exchange Commission)   A U.S. government regulatory agency responsible for regulating securities markets and certain relationships between publicly owned companies and their shareholders.

Problems

1   Under what set of conditions might a cash basis accounting system be preferable to an accrual basis system?

2   Even when a company is following the cost value method, accepted accounting procedures require that the company value inventory (and selected other assets) at the lower of cost or market value. What is the justification for imposing this lower of cost or market rule?

3   Give three examples of expenditures which, at the time the expenditures are made, are not expenses for the business firm. Give three examples of expenses that, at the time the expenses are recognized, do not involve expenditures by the firm.

4   Assume that you must pay a 5% export duty on a certain export sale. When you record the export duty expense at the same time that you record the sale, what accounting concept are you following?

5   Assume that the decision has been made to liquidate a company (i.e., go out of business). What effect does this decision have on the accounting concepts fol-

lowed by the company? What effect do you think this decision would have on the valuation of the company's assets and liabilities, if any?

6 Some manufacturing companies treat property taxes as a part of the cost-of-goods-sold expense, while others treat them as operating expenses. Does this difference in practice violate the accounting concept of consistency? If so, under what conditions?

7 What accounting concept states that revenue is recognized not when a sales order is received, nor when a contract is signed, nor when the goods are manufactured, but only when the product is shipped or delivered to the customer?

8 *Multiple Choice.* Circle the letter which best answers the question. Circle only one letter for each question.

  A How do auditors verify the accuracy of a client company's accounts receivable?
    a By checking all credit invoices sent to customers
    b By checking all cash receipts from customers
    c By checking both invoices sent to and cash receipts from customers
    d By verifying balances directly with a random sample of customers
    e By verifying balances directly with all customers

  B The initials FASB stand for:
    a Financially Acceptable Social Behavior
    b Financial Accounting Standards Board
    c Federation of Auditing Systems Board
    d Financial Auditors and Suppliers Brotherhood
    e None of the above

  C The time-adjusted valuation method will yield a higher value for an asset than the market valuation method when the asset is owned by **X** and:
    a X's equivalency interest rate is lower than the rate for other typical owners
    b When the typical owner of such assets is willing to pay more for the asset than X is willing to pay
    c The economy is experiencing rapid inflation
    d When prevailing interest rates in the economy are low
    e None of the above

9 Explain the problems that you might encounter in applying the concepts of
  a Realization
  b Matching
to the following business:
    Your company produces and markets phonograph records and tapes of popular rock music groups. You contract with the music group, paying the group a fixed amount plus a percentage of the sales revenue. You sell to record and tape distributors who have the right to return any unsold records or tapes within the 12-month period following purchase.

10 Suppose you are the accounting manager for a magazine that offers three-year subscriptions for $15. Describe how you would account for the receipt of such a $15 payment. What are the key problems you foresee?

11 Using five different accounting concepts, indicate the accounting concept that requires the accountant to:

a Lean toward understating revenues and overstating expenses

b Use prepaid expense accounts

c Ignore historical cost when valuing an asset that will no longer be used by a manufacturing company because of a change in the company's business

d Refrain from changing accounting practice from period to period

e Record the expected telephone expense for this month, even though the corresponding telephone bill itself will not be received from the telephone company until next month

12 In certain instances, companies may treat research and development expenditures for new products as an asset (typically referred to as "capitalizing research and development") rather than as an expense. In terms of the accounting concepts discussed, what are the arguments in favor of such treatment?

13 How might an independent certified public accountant (CPA) go about obtaining verification of:

a Amounts owed to the company by its customers (accounts receivable)

b Value of inventory

c Amounts owed by the company to its suppliers (accounts payable)

d Value of cash

e Value of loans payable

14 The Bryant Sewing Machine Sales Company sells three basic models of a very popular sewing machine for home use. It also sells miscellaneous parts, supplies, and accessories for the sewing machines. Opening balances in the company's general ledger at May 1, 19X7, were as follows:

Account	Debit	Credit
Cash	$ 1,760	
Accounts Receivable	2,220	
Inventory—Model X (11 units)	3,300	
Inventory—Model Y (1 unit)	500	
Inventory—Model Z (7 units)	1,750	
Inventory—Miscellaneous	1,250	
Accounts Payable		$ 1,450
Invested Capital		6,000
Retained Earnings		3,330
Totals	$10,780	$10,780

The balances in Accounts Receivable and Accounts Payable were composed of the following:

Accounts Receivable:

S. Gamblin	$ 680
Y. Schmitz	400
P. Markus	200
L. Schick	300
A. McDonald	450
M. Cahill	190
	$2,220

Accounts Payable:
Apex Machine Co. $1,320
Daily Gazette   130
                     $1,450

Other accounts used by Bryant (that is, included in the company's chart of accounts) are as follows:

Advertising Expense

Cost of Goods Sold—Other

Cost of Goods Sold—Sewing Machines

Salaries Expense

Rent Expense

Sales—Other

Sales—Sewing Machines

Set up T accounts for the accounts listed above and enter the following May transactions directly in these accounts.
a   Enter the opening balances in their respective accounts
b   Paid rent for store and store equipment to T. Takata, $250
c   Received $300 from S. Gamblin, $300 from L. Schick, and $150 from A. McDonald, a total of $750
d   Sold four model X sewing machines, each at $450, for cash
e   Paid Apex Machine Co. $800 on account
f   Sold parts, supplies, and other miscellaneous inventory for a total sales value of $710, all received in cash
g   Sold one model Y sewing machine for $1,300 on credit to P. Markus. Sold one model Z sewing machine for $350 on credit to M. Cahill and one for $375 on credit to D. Mein, a new customer
h   Sold one model Z sewing machine to L. Schick for $350. L. Schick paid $150 cash and owes the balance
i   Purchased on credit from Apex Machine Co. the following:
Two model X at $300 each
Two model Z at $250 each
j   Placed advertising with Daily Gazette for the month at a total cost of $75. Payment for this advertising is due June 15
k   Sold one model X sewing machine for $450 cash
l   Paid salaries to employees for the month of May totaling $1,700 cash
m   Paid Daily Gazette $130 for advertising that appeared during April
n   Determined that miscellaneous inventory of parts, supplies, and accessories was $900 at the end of May, compared to $1,250 at the beginning of the month
Determine and record the balance in each T account. Prepare a balance sheet at May 31, 19X7 and an income statement for May.

15 The following transactions occurred during October, 19X4 at the Campbell Service Company. The balance sheet for the Campbell Service Company at September 30, 19X4 was as follows:

Assets		Liabilities and Owners' Equity	
Cash	$ 450	Accounts Payable	$ 1,600
Accounts Receivable	2,400	Notes Payable	3,000
Supplies on Hand	800	Wages and Salaries Payable	500
Equipment	5,100	Invested Capital	5,000
Truck	2,000	Retained Earnings	650
Total	$10,750	Total	$10,750

The general ledger at Campbell Service Company includes the following accounts besides those listed on the balance sheet above:

> Advertising Expense
> Bonus Expense
> Bonus Payable
> Decline in Value of Equipment (expense)
> Decline in Value of Truck (expense)
> Insurance Expense
> Interest Expense
> Prepaid Insurance
> Rent Expense
> Service Revenue
> Supplies Expense
> Utilities Expense
> Wages and Salaries Expense

Record the opening balances in the appropriate T accounts, and then make the entries required to record the following:

a Mr. Campbell invested an additional $2,000 in the business

b Rent in the amount of $700 was paid in cash for the month of October

c Supplies were purchased on credit at a cost of $300

d Credit customers were sent invoices totaling $2,300 for services rendered during the month

e Cash customers paid $1,000 for services rendered to them during October (Note: Total of credit and cash sales was $3,300.)

f Cash in the amount of $1,700 was received from customers for services rendered in previous months

g A six-month insurance policy, with coverage beginning on October 1, 19X4, was purchased for $300 in cash

h The invoice from the utility company in the amount of $380 was received and paid

i The accountant for Campbell estimated that the truck declined in value by $100 and the equipment declined in value by $250 during October

j   Additional equipment to be used in the service activity was purchased on credit at a price of $750

k   Wages and salaries earned by employees for the month totaled $1,300

l   Total cash payment of wages and salaries during the month was $1,200, including the $500 that was payable at the beginning of the month

m   Invoices from suppliers for supplies and equipment received in previous months were paid in the amount of $1,450

n   A count and valuation of supplies on hand at the end of the month revealed an end-of-month balance of $650

o   Campbell Service Company paid $550 to the bank from which the company was borrowing: $500 in principal repayment and $50 interest

p   Advertising for the month totalled $175, paid in cash

q   In return for extra services that he rendered to the company during October, Mr. Campbell agreed that the company would pay a bonus to the general manager equal to 10% of October's sales; this bonus is to be paid on November 10

Prepare an income statement for the month of October and a balance sheet as of October 31, 19X4.

Accounting Systems and Procedures

At this stage in the study of accounting, we turn to consider the elements of an operating accounting system and the common procedures used in assembling, organizing, and displaying financial data. That is, we shall consider some of the mechanics of bookkeeping and the procedures used to convert the vast stream of accounting data into useful financial information.

Bookkeeping techniques are a primary emphasis in many accounting textbooks, but here, where our focus is on the user of financial statements rather than on the practitioner of the accounting trade, only this chapter is devoted to the mechanics of accounting. Virtually everyone in an organization encounters and influences some part of the data flow that ends up in the accounting department. Purchase orders, labor time records, invoices sent to customers, bills received from vendors, checks received, and checks paid are all part of this data flow. Therefore, it is important that those who influence the flow of data have some sense for the way in which the documents containing the data are utilized by the accounting department. In other words, some understanding of the general functioning of an accounting system is important for the user of financial statements.

Recall the verbs used in our definition of accounting: *observe, measure, record, classify,* and *summarize.* Our discussion thus far has concentrated on the first two of those verbs: *observe* and *measure*. This chapter is concerned with the way in which as ets, liabilities, revenues, and expenses which have been measured and valued now become recorded in the accounting system, classified in some logical and useful manner, and summarized for the purposes of financial statements.

Chart of Accounts

Classification is key to the accounting process. Consider the very many transactions, and therefore the extensive volume of accounting data, that occur in any large organization. Hundreds or thousands of sales may be made each day. Hundreds or thousands of bills are received, checks paid out, and checks received. Many employees earn wages and salaries that are paid not daily but periodically. Many different types of fixed assets are owned. Money is borrowed and repaid and tax obligations are recorded and paid.

The accounting system must do more than simply collect and record the data. If the *data* are to be turned into *information,* they will need to be classified in ways that are useful to management, creditors, shareholders, tax collectors, and other readers of financial statements.

Chapter 3 introduced the idea of the chart of accounts, a kind of road map to the accounting system that indicates all of the accounts that are available to the accountant for the purpose of classifying the assets owned, liabilities owed, revenues earned, and expenses incurred. The chart of accounts defines both the nature and the extent of the classification that is built into the accounting records.

Establishing an accounting system generally begins with the drawing up of the chart of accounts. The particular set of ledger accounts (recall that the T accounts that we have been using to illustrate accounting entries are ledger accounts) will be a function of the type of business being conducted and the size and complexity of the organization. Some companies will want sales classified extensively so as to provide management with useful information for making product-line and sales-management decisions; other companies sell only a single product or service and need only one sales account in the chart of accounts. An organization that consists of many separate departments will typically want to categorize expenses not only by type of expense (for example, salary, telephone, travel, supplies, rent), but also by the department (machine shop, assembly shop, sales department, accounting department), since different managers are responsible for different segments of the enterprise.

Designers of accounting systems need to bear in mind that information costs money—not only to prepare but also to assimilate and interpret. An almost-inevitable tendency is to construct an elaborate chart of accounts in order to provide very complete classification of data. The computerization of an accounting system makes this urge still more irresistible, since the computer can classify and reclassify data with great speed. Too often, accounting reports prepared by computer are so voluminous as to be both intimidating and not terribly useful to the reader.

Recall that the reader wants the data summarized—*summarize* was the fifth and final verb used in our definition of accounting. The more detailed the classification, the less the data are summarized. The accountant designing the chart of accounts must make the cost versus benefit trade-offs between providing sufficient detail (classification) to be useful to the readers and summarizing the data to the point that financial reports can be prepared and interpreted efficiently. This is not an easy trade-off to make, and from time to time a company's chart of accounts needs to be revised to reflect changed conditions in the organization and changing informational needs.

The chart of accounts will typically be numerically coded to facilitate data processing. Each digit of the account code has meaning in indicating the account's classification. Exhibit 5-1 shows the general form of the chart of accounts for the Kidder Corporation, and Exhibit 5-2 shows detailed account names and numbers within certain account categories. Kidder is a small company and thus does not have an elaborate or extensive chart of accounts. Nonetheless, the company uses about 100 general ledger accounts. A larger company with many product lines, departments, and offices might have a chart of accounts of 1000 or more accounts. Such a company might, for example, want not a single set of accounts for general and

Exhibit 5-1
THE KIDDER CORPORATION
Chart of Accounts
Major Categories of Accounts

Account Number (Range)	Account Category
101–149	Current Assets
150–199	Noncurrent Assets
200–249	Current Liabilities
250–259	Long-term Liabilities
261–299	Ownership Equity
300–349	Revenue (Sales)
350–399	Cost of Goods Sold
400–699	Operating Expenses
400–499	Selling Expenses
500–599	Research and Development (R&D) Expenses
600–699	General and Administrative (G&A) Expenses
700–799	Other Income and Expense

Exhibit 5-2
THE KIDDER CORPORATION
Excerpts from Chart of Accounts

Account Number	Account Name
100–149	CURRENT ASSETS
101	Petty cash
105	Cash (Checking)—First Bank
107	Cash (Savings)—Provident Savings and Loan
111	Accounts Receivable—Trade
112	Allowance for Doubtful Accounts—Trade
113	Accounts Receivable—Other
115	Notes Receivable—Trade
117	Notes Receivable—Other
118	Travel Advances—Employees
121	Inventory—Raw Material
125	Inventory—In-process
131	Inventory—Finished Goods
141	Prepaid Expenses
145	Other Current Assets
147	Freight Clearing
300–349	REVENUE (SALES)
301	Sales—Product A
305	Sales—Product B
321	Sales—Special contracts
329	Other Sales
345	Sales Returns and Allowances
347	Sales Price Discounts
400–499	SELLING EXPENSES
401	Sales Commission Expense
411	Sales Salaries
413	Fringe Benefit Expenses—Sales
415	Travel and Entertainment Expenses
421	Advertising (Space) Expense
423	Promotional Literature Expense
425	Miscellaneous Supplies and Other Expenses
429	Miscellaneous Outside Services
431	Telephone and Telegraph Expenses
433	Occupancy Expense
435	Depreciation Expense

administrative (G&A) expenses, but expenses further classified to each of, say, seven departments comprising the general and administrative function.

Note in Exhibit 5-2 that the Kidder Corporation uses 15 current asset accounts, including three different inventory accounts, and a separation of receivables into a number of categories. The company has four classifications of sales: products A and B, special contracts, and the inevitable "other" category. The company's selling expenses are divided among 11 accounts. More extensive categorization here might have been useful. For example, field sales force salaries might have been separated from the salaries of the office support staff, and travel and entertainment expenses might have been further divided into air travel expenses, auto rental and taxi expenses, hotel expenses, meal expenses, and entertainment expenses. The sales manager might desire this additional detail, or tax reporting requirements might demand it (for example, a separation of entertainment expenses from other travel expenses). Once again, the chart of accounts must be developed with a view both to the needs of the users of financial statements and to the added costs associated with added detail.

The Elements of an Accounting System

Essentially all accounting systems are composed of three primary elements: **source documents, journals,** and **ledgers.** Moreover, the flow of data is the same in all accounting systems: from source document to journal to ledger. While the physical appearance of these elements may vary considerably depending upon the sophistication of the accounting system, the elements are present in a simple accounting system maintained by a single bookkeeper as well as in highly automated accounting systems that are maintained by computer.

SOURCE DOCUMENTS

As implied by the name, source documents represent the original evidence of a transaction to be recorded. What are the primary, recurring transactions in a merchandising or manufacturing company? There are essentially only four: (1) sales to customers, (2) cash received from customers (a transaction that occurs concurrently with the sale transaction in some instances), (3) incurrence of expense, and (4) cash disbursement, or the payment of cash (again, in some instances this transaction may be coincident with the incurrence of expense). Surely other transactions occur—money is borrowed and repaid, fixed assets are acquired and disposed of, and so forth—but the primary transactions that the accounting system should be designed to handle routinely are those which are listed above and will now be discussed further.

Sales   The primary evidence of a sale on credit is the **invoice** prepared for the customer.   Typically, this invoice is prepared on a multipart form and one or more copies of the invoice will be utilized as the source document for the sale.   Cash sales may be evidenced by a copy of a receipt given to a customer or by simply a cash register tape.

The invoice sent to the customer must contain all of the information required by the accounting system to classify the sale, as well as simply to record it.   For example, in addition to the customer's name, the date, and the amount of the sale, the invoice will need to show the type of product sold or service rendered, if the accounting system is to classify sales data by product type.   The invoice will also need to be coded by geographic region, or responsible salesperson, if the accounting system is to provide sales data classified by sales region or salesperson.   If the accounting system is computer-based, multiple classifications are easily accomplished.   Typically numerical codes will be assigned to the various products, customers, regions, and so forth in order to facilitate the data processing.

Other transactions may be triggered by the sales transaction and, if so, the invoice should contain the data required to record these associated transactions.   For example, if the customer is charged sales tax or is charged separately for freight, this information needs to appear on the invoice in order to facilitate the proper accounting entries.

Cash receipts   Most cash is received in the form of checks, rather than currency, and the check itself is a source document.   Most organizations, however, are anxious to deposit checks without delay, and thus a satisfactory source document is either a copy of the check or the voucher portion attached to most checks drawn by commercial or industrial organizations.

Just as the cash register tape or copy of the receipt given to a customer is evidence of a sales transaction, the same document is also evidence of cash received as a part of that transaction.

Incurrence of Expenses   An invoice (or bill) received from a vendor is evidence of an expense incurred, in the same way that an invoice sent to the customer is evidence of a sales transaction.   This expense needs to be recorded in a timely manner, frequently well in advance of the date when the bill is paid; thus, the vendor's invoice, and not the company's subsequent payment, must trigger the accounting entry to record the expense.

The vendor's invoice alone is not complete evidence as to the amount and validity of the expense.   It does not typically indicate whether the merchandise or services being billed were in fact ordered or authorized by the company. Furthermore, the vendor's invoice does not verify either that the merchandise has been received or that the prices charged are the agreed-upon prices. Therefore, the accounting department must often collect and match several documents to confirm that the vendor's invoice represents a bona fide expense of the company to be recorded in the accounting books. A copy of the company's **purchase order** sent to the vendor can confirm both the agreed-upon price and the fact that the products or services were indeed ordered. Thus, the organization's purchasing department needs to forward to the accounting department a copy of a purchase order sent to a vendor, and the vendor's invoice should appropriately reference the purchase order. Evidence is still required that the merchandise was in fact received. This verification document comes from the company's receiving department or stock room, and typically is based upon the **packing slip** (or packing list) that the vendor enclosed with the shipment, indicating quantities of each item shipped; the receiving clerk will note on the packing slip any discrepancies between the quantities shown and the quantities actually received. By matching data on the packing slip and the original purchase order to the vendor's invoice, the accounting clerk can verify that the expense is appropriate without having any further contact with either the purchasing department or the receiving department.

Extensive classification of expenses—by type of expense and responsible department—is typically useful. The data necessary to effect classification will appear on the purchase order or be noted by the accounting clerk on the vendor's invoice that is serving as the source document.

Wages and salaries represent important types of expenses that are evidenced by specialized source documents. The source document for an employee paid on an hourly basis (hourly or direct labor) is that employee's **time card,** showing not only the total hours worked, but, when appropriate, the particular activity on which he or she worked. Time cards are typically signed by the individual's supervisor to provide independent accuracy verification. The source document for salary expenses (for persons not paid on an hourly basis) will be some other document prepared by the individual or by the personnel department.

Cash disbursements As most cash payments are made by check rather than in currency, a copy of the firm's check is the logical source document for cash disbursements (payments).

Commercial and industrial organizations typically use a multipart form as a check, sending the original to the payee and retaining one or more (nonnegotiable) copies to serve as a source document. In a simple (for example, personal) accounting system, the check stub serves as the source document for the cash disbursement. Payments made in currency are infrequent and typically are made from a *petty cash fund*. Individual vouchers are prepared when cash is paid out from the petty cash fund and these vouchers serve as source documents in support of the checks drawn periodically to reimburse the petty cash fund.

JOURNALS

Journals are the accounting system's so-called *books of original entry.* That is, all transactions evidenced by source documents are recorded in one of the journals. (The term **register** is often used interchangeably with the term *journal.*)

An accounting system could be operated with a single journal, called a **general journal.** All transactions would then be listed in chronological order, referencing the appropriate source document. In an organization of any size or complexity, such a general journal would be voluminous and not very useful. A step toward classifying accounting data is accomplished within the journals through the use of specialized journals. While all accounting systems maintain a general journal for the recording of nonroutine transactions, most accounting systems use one or more specialized journals, often a specialized journal for each category of source document just discussed. That is, a company might use the following journals: **sales journal, cash receipts journal, expense journal** (or voucher register), **cash disbursements journal** (or **check register**), and general journal. Even more extensive classification of transactions may be appropriate. For example, many companies utilize an expense journal and a cash payments journal for nonsalary expenses and payments, but also a specialized **payroll journal** in which all payment of wages and salaries is recorded. This set of transactions is unlike other transactions, and is circumscribed by a large number of legal requirements; moreover, the wage and salary expenses are typically recognized at the same time payroll checks are drawn.

Exhibits 5-3 through 5-5 show examples of two specialized journals used by The Kidder Corporation, and of the general journal, and each is discussed briefly below.

The sales journal for the Kidder Corporation, shown in Exhibit 5-3, contains entries for the first several days of March. Note that the normal entry involves a debit entry to Accounts Receivable (account no. 111) and a credit entry to one of the sales accounts (account no. 301, 305, or 321). Essentially all debit entries to Accounts Receivable occur in this journal. Sales are being classified by type, and at the end of the month the summary totals at the foot of each of these three sales columns will indicate total sales for the month by product category.

This specialized journal also contains the record for certain nonsales transactions that are, by their nature, linked to the sales transactions. Kidder pays commissions to sales agents on certain types of sales. Proper matching of expenses and revenues demands that the commission expense be recognized in the same accounting period when the related sale is recog-

Exhibit 5-3

THE KIDDER CORPORATION

Sales Journal

| | DEBIT | | | | SALES | | CREDIT | OTHER | |
	#401 Commission Expense	#111 Acct. Rec'ble.	Date	Customer Name	#301 Product A	#305 Product B	#321 Special Contracts	#147 Freight Clearing	#225 Commissions Payable
		4,050	Mar. 1	Cox Supply Co.	4,000			50	
	150	3,200	Mar. 2	General Mammoth Corp.		3,200			150
		3,160	Mar. 4	Mansfield Distributors	2,480	650		30	
	100	3,900	Mar. 8	Foster Bros. Wholesalers	2,500	1,400			100
		2,600	Mar. 8	Williamette Supply Co.	2,600				

nized. The commission expense could be recorded in the expense journal, but a more convenient approach is to allow for the recording of commission expenses coincident with the recording of the related sales transactions. Such a procedure is permitted by the design of the specialized journal shown in Exhibit 5-3. Note that a column has been provided for account no. 401, Commission Expense, and for account no. 225, Commission Payable (a current liability). When the sales transaction on which an agent earns commission is recorded in the sales journal (for example, the sale on March 2 to General Mammoth), the appropriate debit to Commission Expense and credit to Commission Payable can be recorded simultaneously. The careful design of specialized journals can contribute to efficient processing within the accounting department.

Exhibit 5-4 illustrates a cash disbursements journal, often called a check register. The checks written by the Kidder Corporation are listed sequentially as a control procedure (or double check) that all of the company's prenumbered checks have been used properly and none has been used for the unauthorized withdrawal of funds. The most common debit will be to Accounts Payable and each transaction will necessitate a credit to Cash; thus, columns are dedicated to each of these two accounts. In certain instances, cash discounts for prompt payment may be earned (as discussed in the following chapter) and this information can also be recorded in this specialized journal by providing a separate Cash Discounts Earned column on the credit side (see checks no. 263 and 264). In situations where expenses were not previously recognized in other journals, the debit entries

Exhibit 5-4
THE KIDDER CORPORATION
Cash Disbursements Journal
(Check Register)

Date	Payee	Check No.	DEBIT Accounts Payable Amount	DEBIT Other Acct.	DEBIT Other Amount	CREDIT Cash	CREDIT Cash Discount Earned
Mar. 10	Overland Freight	259		147	100	100	
"	VOID	260					
"	Kennedy Trucking	261		147	50	50	
"	Dean and Bulheley	262		233	1,000	1,000	
"	Creative Publications	263	2,000			1,950	50
"	Ajax Webbing	264	2,500			2,450	50
"	Moore Supply	265		111	500	500	
Mar. 13	First Bank	266		251	600	950	
				721	350		

Exhibit 5-5
THE KIDDER CORPORATION
General Journal

Date		Description	Acct. No.	Debit	Credit
Mar.	3	Cash	105	10,000	
		Short-term Bank Borrowing	211		10,000
	8	Depreciation Expense	435	200	
		Accum. Deprec.—Office Equipment	167		200

will not be to Accounts Payable. Thus the specialized cash disbursements journal has been designed to permit debit entries to any account; the accountant need simply record the account number (as determined from the chart of accounts) and the amount of the debit. Check no. 265 records the refund of $500 to a customer and check no. 266 records the payment of principal and interest on a loan from First Bank.

Exhibit 5-5 illustrates a form of general journal, the journal used to record those transactions and adjustments (including corrections) that do not fit into one of the specialized journals. All accounting systems require a general journal, but the extent of its use will depend upon the number and design of the specialized journals employed by the system. Each entry in the general journal must show the account title and number and the amount of both the debit and the credit. Of course, no classification is being accomplished in this journal. The two entries shown in Exhibit 5-5 do not fit in any of the specialized journals: the first records the borrowing of $10,000 from the First Bank on a short-term basis and the second records the depreciation expense for the month on office equipment used by the sales department. Note that the second of these entries (to record depreciation) involved no transaction with an outside party. Kidder's accountant simply recognized that some of the original cost of the fixed asset should be recorded as an expense (that is, depreciation expense should be charged); all such recognitions, discussed at length in the following chapter, are typically recorded in the general journal.

GENERAL LEDGER

The third step in the process is to transfer the categorized data from the journals to the *general ledger*. The general ledger contains all of the accounts listed on the chart of accounts, as discussed in Chapter 3, and represents the fundamental "books" in the accounting system. All accounting data ultimately find their way to the general ledger, and financial statements are prepared from the summarized data contained therein.

At the end of the accounting period (for example, a month), the transfer from journal to ledger is accomplished in the following way:

1   First, the journals are totaled and double-checked to be certain that the sum of all debits equals the sum of all credits—that is, the journals are checked to be certain that they are in balance.
2   The totals of those columns in the specialized journals which have been devoted to a single account are transferred to the corresponding general ledger account. Note that the detailed individual entries are not transferred, only the totals; the specialized journals have permitted the accountant to group like transactions so that only the summarized totals need appear in the general ledger.
3   Other entries that appear in the specialized journals (see, for example, the Other Debits in Exhibit 5-4) and all entries in the general journal are transferred to the appropriate general ledger account.

At this point, the general ledger should be in balance (debits equal credits). All data from the source documents have flowed through one of the journals and now appear in classified and summarized fashion in the general ledger. The format of the general ledger is analogous to the T account that we have been using: debits on the left and credits on the right. General ledgers also provide space to record both the date of the entry and the journal (specialized or general) from which it came.

In properly summarizing and categorizing the data, the accountant also has left a "trail" from the general ledger back through the journals to the source documents, so that the detail behind each general ledger entry can be examined and the resulting balance can be verified. Such a trail is needed both by the accounting staff and by the company's independent auditors. Suppose the sales department manager or an auditor at Kidder wished to know exactly what caused the promotional literature expense to be so high during the month of March. This account, no. 423 in the general ledger, is shown in Exhibit 5-6. The balance in this account on February 28 (that is, after the first two months of the year) was $600. The entries for March net to a debit of $550, and thus indeed the March expense does seem high in relation to the expense for the previous two months. The entries in March are as follows:

1   On March 12 a $100 debit entry to this account was made on page 3 of the cash disbursements journal (CDJ 3).
2   Similarly, on March 21 a $150 entry was made on page 4 of that journal.
3   At the end of the month, the expense journal was summarized, and the column total ($400) related to this expense category was transferred to the general ledger (EJ).

Exhibit 5-6
THE KIDDER CORPORATION
General Ledger Accounts

Account No. 423
Promotional Literature Expense

Date	Explanation	Debit	Date	Explanation	Credit
Feb 28	Balance	600	March 31	GJ 2	100
March 12	CDJ 3	100			
March 21	CDJ 4	150			
March 31	EJ	400			

4   Also on March 31, a $100 credit entry was made, the detailed explana-
tion of which is contained on page 2 of the general journal (GJ 2); this
entry reduces the expense and is probably a correction.[1]

The accountant can now go back to these three journals—the expense,
cash disbursements, and general journals—and on the pages indicated determine each of the individual transactions that contributed to the total
$550 expense for the month.   The entries in the journals will in turn refer-
ence the particular source documents involved, and, if the auditor or sales
manager wants still more detail, these individual source documents can be
retrieved from the files.

SUBSIDIARY LEDGER

The general ledger balances, with respect to a company's various asset and
liability accounts, provide no detail on the composition of the amounts
owned and owed.   Thus, the Accounts Receivable balance in the general
ledger indicates the total amount owed to the company by all of its customers, but does not tell the accountant the amount owed by each customer.
The accountant must have this customer-by-customer information, since
late-paying customers must be pursued, and, if a customer is excessively
delinquent, the company will want to cease selling to that customer.
  Similarly, the company needs to know not only the total amount owing
to vendors (total Accounts Payable) but also the detailed amount owing to
each vendor.   Kidder may wish to know the amount of sales commission

---

[1] Entries are not erased from either journals or ledgers; rather, corrections are made by re-
versing the original (incorrect) entry and then proceeding with the correct entry.   A debit entry
is reversed by an equal credit entry to the same account, and a credit entry is reversed by a
debit entry to the same account.

owing to each agent, not simply the total amount of sales commissions payable as revealed in account no. 225 in the general ledger.

The detailed back-up data in support of a general ledger balance is maintained in a so-called **subsidiary ledger**—a ledger which elaborates on a particular general ledger account and reconciles in total with the balance contained in that account.   The most common subsidiary ledger is the Accounts Receivable subsidiary ledger.   It is organized by individual customer and records the detail of debits (arising from sales) and credits (arising from cash receipts) to each customer's account.   A simple type of subsidiary accounts receivable ledger can be maintained as follows: place a copy of each invoice sent to the customer in a file identified with the customer's name, and remove and destroy that copy as soon as payment of the invoice is received from the customer; the file should at all times contain all of that customer's unpaid invoices.   The total of the amounts on these invoices represents the balance due from that particular customer, and the total of all invoices remaining in all customer files equals the Accounts Receivable balance in the general ledger.

Any asset or liability account may be the subject of a subsidiary ledger.   While Accounts Receivable and Accounts Payable are the most common subsidiary ledgers, some accounting systems provide for subsidiary detail on inventory, fixed assets, and even cash (if the company maintains accounts in numerous banks).

Entries are made to these subsidiary ledgers at the time that the related journal entry is made, utilizing data contained on the source documents. When at the end of the accounting period the data are transferred from journals to ledgers, accountants *reconcile* the resulting general ledger balances with the detail already contained in the subsidiary ledgers.

The Accounting Cycle

At the end of an accounting period the accountant will need to construct financial statements for the period, but a good deal of extra work is required at period-end to get the accounting books in shape for this purpose.

Source documents have been arriving at the accounting department throughout the period, and data contained thereon have been processed through to the journals, both specialized and general, on a routine basis. Also, all subsidiary ledgers have been maintained on a current basis.   However, typically no entries have been made in the general ledger during the course of the accounting period.

At the end of the accounting period, information from the journals is transferred to the general ledger, as discussed earlier; in accounting parlance, data from the journals are *posted* to the general ledger.   The accountant can now construct a preliminary **trial balance,** a listing of all accounts in the general ledger and the debit or credit balance in each. This preliminary trial balance allows the accountant to be certain that the ledger is *in balance*—the debits equal the credits. The fact that the trial balance balances does not indicate that all entries have been made to the correct accounts, but simply that, in recording from source document to journal and in posting from journal to ledger, debit entries have been balanced with equal credit entries. Of course, if the trial balance fails to balance, the accountant knows that an error has occurred, and a hunt for the error or errors commences.

Also at this stage the accountant reconciles all subsidiary ledgers to their corresponding control accounts in the general ledger.

This first trial balance is referred to as "preliminary" because additional entries will have to be made before accounting for the period is complete and financial statements are constructed. These additional entries— referred to as *adjusting entries* or *end-of-period adjustments*—are discussed in some detail in the following chapter. Suffice to say here that these adjusting entries are not triggered by transactions with parties outside the organization and therefore are not the subject of typical source documents; rather, the entries are initiated by the accountant with the realization that certain events (including simply the passage of time) have occurred that necessitate adjustments in the values of assets or liabilities. Examples include the realization that a certain customer will be unable to pay, and thus Accounts Receivable needs to be adjusted, or that an interest obligation arises as a result of current borrowing, and thus Current Liabilities needs to be adjusted. These adjusting entries are recorded in the general journal and then posted to the general ledger. Now the accountant is able to construct a final trial balance (as still another check) and construct the financial statements for the accounting period in the manner discussed in earlier chapters.

Chapter 2 points out that the income statement is designed to amplify changes in owners' equity during an accounting period. Thus in a sense, income and expense accounts are a part of owners' equity. At the end of a fiscal year, all income and expenses are *closed* to the Retained Earnings account; that is, debit and credit entries are made in these accounts so as to drive their balances to zero, with the offsetting entries in Retained Earnings. These **closing entries** transfer net income for the year to retained earnings, and the income and expense accounts have a zero balance at the beginning of the new fiscal year.

Income and expense accounts can also be closed monthly, thus transferring each month's profit to retained earnings. This procedure is not typical, nor is it necessary in order to determine monthly profit. When these accounts are only closed annually, the profit for a particular month is determined by deduction. For example, the profit for the sixth month is derived by: (1) constructing a profit and loss statement from the income and expense account balances at the end of six months, (2) constructing a profit and loss statement from account balances at the end of five months, and (3) subtracting the five-month statement from the six-month statement.

Summary

While the emphasis in this book is on accounting concepts and interpretation of accounting data, some knowledge of the mechanics of bookkeeping is essential for all who must interact with and gain information from an accounting system.

The basic roadmap of the accounting system is contained in the chart of accounts that lists all available accounts; the extent and nature of the accounting classifications are codified in this account listing. The accountant needs to balance costs and benefits in deciding the amount of detail to be maintained in the accounting books.

The basic flow of accounting data is from source document to journal to general ledger. While there is a wide variety of source documents in use, each typically evidences one of the following four basic transactions: sale, incurrence of expense, receipt of cash, or payment of cash. Specialized journals may be constructed to facilitate the efficient processing of information, permitting similar transactions to be grouped. All accounting systems also utilize a general journal for recording those transactions that do not fit one of the specialized journals and for recording various adjusting (end-of-period) entries.

At the end of the accounting period, the data from the journals is posted to the general ledger and a preliminary trial balance is constructed. Certain end-of-period entries are typically then recorded in the general journal and posted to the general ledger before a final trial balance is constructed and the financial statements—income statement and balance sheet—are drawn up.

New Terms

Cash disbursements journal   A form of specialized journal in which the payments of cash are recorded. This journal is frequently referred to as a *check register,* as typically checks are recorded sequentially within the journal.

Cash receipts journal   A form of specialized journal in which the receipt of cash is recorded.

Check register   Another name for *cash disbursements journal.*

Closing entries   Those entries that serve to transfer net income for the period to retained earnings and cause all income and expense accounts to have zero balances at the commencement of the new accounting period.

Expense journal A form of specialized journal in which expenses are recorded.

General journal The journal in which are recorded all transactions and recognitions that do not fit into one of the specialized journals.

Invoice The document issued by the seller to the buyer specifying amounts owed by the buyer in connection with items provided or services rendered by the seller. Invoices are often referred to as *bills*.

Journals Books of original entry where data from source documents are recorded before being included in the general ledger. Accounting systems typically utilize both specialized journals and a general journal.

Ledger Refers to the *general ledger,* the fundamental "accounting books" of the organization. In an accounting system, data flow from source documents to journals to the general ledger.

Packing slip (or packing list) The document prepared by the seller and included with shipments to the buyer. The packing list details the quantity and description of all items included in the shipment.

Payroll journal A form of specialized journal in which wages and salaries expenses are recorded, together with the many transactions that are related to payroll.

Purchase order The document issued by the buyer to the seller specifying the particular item(s) or service(s) ordered, quantities, prices, terms of purchase, required delivery date, and so forth.

Register Another name for a specialized journal. For example, the cash disbursements journal may also be referred to as a check register.

Sales journal A form of specialized journal in which sales transactions are recorded.

Source documents The evidence of transactions with other entities. These documents (for example, invoices and checks) are used by accountants to obtain the data required to record the transactions.

Subsidiary ledger A set of records providing detail on the composition of a particular general ledger account. For example, an accounts receivable subsidiary ledger details by individual customer the amounts owed to the organization, and the sum of the balances in the subsidiary ledger agrees with the single balance in the Accounts Receivable account in the general ledger.

Time card The document maintained by individual workers detailing the hours worked and, in many instances, the job, task, or project worked on. Time cards are used by the payroll section of accounting as the source document for salaries and wages expenses.

Trial balance A listing of all accounts in the general ledger and their balances.

Problems

1 What is the role of journals in an accounting system? Why aren't data from source documents recorded directly in the general ledger?

2 Describe the data and information that you would expect to find in an Accounts Payable subsidiary ledger.

3 Specialized journals may be designed to facilitate recording similar transactions. For example, a company whose employees do a great deal of traveling might wish to design a specialized journal to record travel expenses. Design such a journal, indicating the information that you would expect to see in it.

4 Why are general ledger accounts typically assigned both a number and a name, rather than just a name?

5 Suppose that you just joined a company in its accounting department and wished to become familiar with its accounting system. What document or documents would you review first and why?

6 Describe and categorize the source document that would represent the original evidence of the following:

  a Wages expense for an inventory clerk

  b Sales revenue derived from merchandise shipped to a customer

  c Commission expense to be paid to one of the company's salespersons in connection with the sale described in *b*

  d Purchase of a fixed asset

  e Payment to a trade supplier for merchandise received in a previous accounting period

  f Payment received from a customer for merchandise shipped in a previous accounting period

  g Cash payment received from a retail customer for merchandise purchased in the store

  h Purchase of material for the company's inventory

7 The controller at a particular company wishes to establish a paperwork flow system that will permit the sales department to instruct the shipping department as to the exact items to be shipped to a customer and that will assure that the accounting department will accurately bill the customer for the merchandise shipped. Describe an appropriate paperwork system.

8 To assure accurate payment of vendors' invoices, the accounting department (typically, the accounts payable clerk) needs to obtain information from several different documents. What are those documents and what information is obtained from each?

9 At the end of an accounting period, what simple check should be performed on the accuracy of a set of subsidiary ledger accounts?

10 In what way or ways does the use of specialized journals increase the efficiency of the accounting function (that is, reduce the time required to complete the accounting cycle)?

11 Suppose that you were asked to set up an accounting system for a restaurant that serves both lunch and dinner and operates a bar. Prepare a simple chart of accounts for such an operation. What specialized journals, if any, would you recommend that the restaurant use?

12 Assume you owned a small apartment building consisting of twelve rental units. Prepare a simple chart of accounts for the business. Would you use any specialized journals? Any subsidiary ledgers?

13 The following questions relate to specialized journals:

  a In a check register, the credit entry is typically to what account?

b Describe the types of accounts to which debit entries are typically made in a check register.

c In a sales journal, what account is most frequently debited?

d In a sales journal, to what other accounts might debit entries be made? Describe the circumstances giving rise to these entries.

e How can a sales journal be used to classify and summarize accounting information in ways that might be useful to management?

f Why is a separate payroll journal frequently used, rather than including salary and wage expenses with other expenses in an expense journal?

g What debit and credit entries predominate in a cash receipts journal?

14 Describe a simple form of Accounts Payable subsidiary ledger that utilizes copies of the source documents.

15 If a departmental manager suspected that the repair expenses charged to her department in a particular month were incorrect, what procedure would the company's accountant have to follow to determine exactly what charges had been included in the Repairs Expense account?

16 This book has used (and will continue to use) T accounts to illustrate accounting entries. The set of T accounts is equivalent to what part of the accounting records in a formal accounting system?

17 The following are entries appearing in a general journal. Describe the event or condition that probably caused the accountant to make each entry. (Note: In journal entries, Dr = debit and Cr = credit.)

a	Dr	Bad Debt Expense	$150	
	Cr	Accounts Receivable		$150
b	Dr	Cash	$10,000	
	Cr	Invested Capital (owners' equity)		$10,000
c	Dr	Cash	$6,000	
	Cr	Marketable Securities		$6,000
d	Dr	Customer Down Payments	$2,000	
	Dr	Cash	$2,000	
	Dr	Accounts Receivable	$4,000	
	Cr	Sales		$8,000
e	Dr	Interest Expense	$50	
	Dr	Installment Contracts Payable	$400	
	Cr	Cash		$450
f	Dr	Accounts Payable	$250	
	Cr	Office Supplies Expense		$250
g	Dr	Retained Earnings	$1,000	
	Cr	Cash		$1,000
h	Dr	Purchases	$4,000	
	Cr	Accounts Payable		$3,600
	Cr	Cash		$400

6

Further Refinements to Financial Statements

In the last two chapters we developed a set of rules for financial accounting and discussed the systems that accountants use to "keep the books." This chapter introduces no new concepts; rather it presents some common refinements and adjustments to financial statements that are required by the rules discussed in Chapter 4.

The accounting concepts that give rise to these adjustments are primarily the concepts of accrual, matching, and conservatism. Accountants frequently need to transfer expenses and incomes from one accounting period to another in order to properly match the expenses and revenues of a period and to guard against the overstatement of earnings or assets. Thus, our key concern in this chapter will be timing: When shall revenues and expenses be realized?

The profitability of a firm on an interim basis (month, quarter, or year) can, of necessity, only be estimated. The total profitability of a firm can be determined with absolute certainty only after the affairs of the firm have been wound up, all assets converted to cash, and all liabilities paid. At that point, all cash remaining is the property of the shareholders and only then can the shareholders know the total return received from their investments. Of course, for most companies this day of reckoning—when the enterprise owns nothing but cash and has no obligations other than to stockholders—never arrives. Unless a company gets into financial difficulties and is liquidated in bankruptcy proceedings, the company continues to function—earning revenues, incurring expenses, owning assets, and owing liabilities. (The company may be sold as a going concern or merged, but these events do not cause the ultimate cash reckoning.)

Thus, in order to respond to the informational needs of shareholders, creditors, and (most importantly) management, accountants must estimate profitability on an interim basis. These audiences make important decisions on the basis of these monthly, quarterly, and annual financial statements. Accordingly, accountants put much effort into adjusting the general ledger at the end of each accounting period to accurately reflect the timing of revenues, expenses, and changes in the values of assets and liabilities.

This chapter focuses on the most common of these periodic adjustments, typically referred to as **end-of-period adjustments** or simply **adjusting entries.** Note that transactions themselves do not trigger these adjusting entries. Adjusting entries are initiated by the accountant, who recognizes the need to alter values in the general ledger in order to provide a more accurate picture (that is, a better estimate) of the performance of the enterprise and of its present financial position or condition. These adjusting entries are typically recorded in the general journal.

Prepaids and Accruals

The inflow and outflow of cash do not always follow the flow of revenues and expenses, respectively. As discussed earlier, when time passes between the flow of cash and the earning of revenue or incurrence of expense, an asset or a liability will result. These assets and liabilities will typically have to be adjusted in future periods to reflect changed conditions or simply the passage of time.

The names given to the balance sheet accounts affected by these timing differences are shown in Exhibit 6-1 and explained in the following sections.

LIABILITIES AND REVENUE

First, consider revenue. Most business in industrialized countries is conducted on a credit, rather than a cash, basis; the expectation is that the customer will pay for the goods or services sometime following their delivery. When a sale is made, an asset, accounts receivable, is increased (debited) to balance the increase in revenue (credit to sales). When the customer pays the invoice, the reduction in the asset account, Accounts Receivable, is

Exhibit 6-1
Balance Sheet Accounts Affected by Timing Differences

	Revenue	Expense
Cash flow occurs *before* revenue/expense is to be recognized	Unearned Revenue (liability)	Prepaid Asset (asset)
Cash flow occurs *after* revenue/expense is recognized	Accrued Receivable (or Accounts Receivable) (asset)	Accrued Liability (or Accounts Payable) (liability)

matched by the increase in another asset account, Cash. Two transactions (delivery of merchandise or services and receipt of cash) trigger two sets of entries. No adjustments are required.

Now suppose that the customer pays in advance of delivery for a portion or all of the goods or services. For example, a customer of the Tebbens Company is required to make a 20% down payment to Tebbens at the time of placing an order for specialized merchandise to be manufactured by the company. Here the flow of cash precedes the flow of revenue, rather than following it. When this payment, for example $200, is received by Tebbens, a debit entry to Cash is appropriate (increasing cash) but a credit entry to Sales is inappropriate, since the realization concept states that sales are recorded only when the goods or services are delivered. Tebbens is now obligated to the customer either to deliver the specialized merchandise or to return the $200. Thus, the appropriate credit entry is to a liability account that might be entitled **Unearned Revenue:** Customer Down Payments.[1] The entry at the time the cash is received (in T-account format) is:

Cash		Unearned Revenue: Customer Down Payments	
200			200

When the merchandise is subsequently delivered by Tebbens, this liability will be eliminated. Suppose that the full price of the merchandise is $1,000 and the balance will be paid by the customer on normal 30-day terms. Then, the entry at the time of delivery, again in T-account format, is:

Accounts Receivable		Unearned Revenue: Customer Down Payments		Sales	
800		200	Balance		1,000

[1] This account might also be called **Deferred Income.**

and the liability would thereby be eliminated. Once again, two transactions cause two sets of entries.

If Tebbens contracts with its customers to provide preventive and emergency service in return for an annual charge, the company needs to recognize the revenue from the service contract month by month throughout the contract period. Typically the annual service charge is paid in advance by the customer, thus giving rise to another unearned revenue (liability) in Tebbens' general ledger. Tebbens' accountant must be careful to make the adjusting entry each month that will recognize both the service revenue earned and the decline in the liability.

Other revenue may be earned as a function of time, with payment received periodically. For example, suppose Tebbens subleases part of its space for $400 per month, with the tenant to make quarterly payments in advance. Assume Tebbens receives a check for $1,200 (three months at $400 per month) on March 20, 19X4, as payment of rent for April through June. The debit entry is once again to Cash, but the Tebbens accountant would be incorrect to record $1,200 for rental income in March; the rental will actually be earned pro rata over the next three months. In the meantime, Tebbens has an obligation to the tenant to provide the space. Therefore, the appropriate entry at the time the cash is received is:

Cash	Unearned Revenue: Rental Income
1,200	1,200

Now step forward to the end of April, when the Tebbens accountant is considering end-of-period adjustments that may be necessary to correctly state the company's revenues and expenses for the month of April. In April Tebbens has earned $400 rental income from the sublease, even though no transaction occurred during the month. The accountant thus needs to make the following adjusting entry (shown in general journal format), both to recognize the revenue and to reflect the fact that Tebbens' obligation to the tenant has declined to $800 ($1,200 less $400 benefit already received by the tenant):

> Dr. Unearned Revenue: Rental Income $400
> Cr. Rental Income $400

ACCRUED ASSETS AND REVENUE

Alternatively, suppose that the terms of the sublease are that the tenant pays at the end of each quarter for the use of the space during that quarter. Once again the Tebbens accountant wants to recognize the fact that in April Tebbens earned $400 of rent, even though payment will not be received for two more months. The appropriate adjusting entry is:

Dr.   Accrued Rent Receivable $400
      Cr.   Rental Income $400

This entry recognizes that the tenant is obligated to Tebbens, and that Tebbens has an asset equal to the rent for the period of time that the tenant has already occupied the space. If similar adjustments are made at the end of May and June, the Accrued Rent Receivable account will grow to $1,200. When, at the end of June, the tenant pays $1,200 for the previous three months' rent, the Accrued Rent Receivable account will be credited and returned to a zero balance.

If a company such as Tebbens owns notes due from individuals or other firms, interest income from these notes will be accounted as illustrated above. When interest payments are received in advance, Tebbens recognizes a liability that is then reduced as the interest is earned with the passage of time. When interest is received in arrears (at the end of the period), Tebbens recognizes an asset (accrued interest receivable) that builds with the passage of time until discharged by the borrower's payment.

ACCRUED LIABILITIES AND EXPENSES

Thus far we have been concerned with the timing of revenues at Tebbens. Parallel problems exist in the timing of expenses. If Tebbens borrows from the bank under an agreement that provides for quarterly interest payments to be made at the end of the quarter, the accountant will need to make an adjusting entry during each month of the quarter so as to match the interest expense to the time period and to recognize the company's liability to pay this interest to the bank one or two months hence; that is, the accountant recognizes the **accrued liability.** Thus, if in October 19X5 Tebbens' total bank borrowing was $40,000 and the interest rate was 9% per annum (3/4 of 1% per month), interest expense of $300 should be accrued for October by the following end-of-period entry:

Dr.   Interest Expense $300
      Cr.   Accrued Interest Payable $300

PREPAID EXPENSE

If Tebbens pays in advance for goods and services to be delivered in subsequent accounting periods, a **Prepaid Expense** account[2] is created. This asset is then adjusted as the expense is matched to the appropriate accounting period. For example, Tebbens purchases a one-year property insurance policy, providing comprehensive coverage from July 1, 19X5

---

[2] Prepaid expenses are also referred to as **deferred expenses.**

through June 30, 19X6. If payment of $1,800 is made in advance during June 19X5, the reduction in cash must be accounted for, although no expense is then incurred. Thus, the asset, cash, is exchanged for another asset, a prepaid. The entry is:

Cash		Prepaid Insurance Premiums	
Balance	1,800	1,800	

Beginning in July 19X5, Tebbens' accountant will recognize a pro rata portion of the cost of the insurance policy as an expense of each month by making the following adjusting entry:

Dr.	Insurance Expense	$150	
	Cr.	Prepaid Insurance Premiums	$150

With the final adjusting entry in June 19X6, the prepaid asset created by the June 19X5 payment will be reduced to zero.

REMINDER: CONCEPT OF MATERIALITY

Throughout our discussion of adjusting entries, bear in mind the concept of materiality. If the adjustment would not make a material difference to expenses (or revenues) or to assets (or liabilities), then the adjustment can be ignored. Examples abound of situations in which an adjusting entry is theoretically appropriate but practically unnecessary, based upon considerations of materiality. If Tebbens pays $72 for an advertisement that will appear in the telephone directory classified section (the "Yellow Pages") for the following year, it is theoretically correct to prorate this expenditure through the year, showing $6 per month for advertising expense. But such adjustments are so immaterial for most companies as to be unwarranted; the $72 payment can simply be reflected as an expense in the particular accounting period when it is made.

Monthly billings for utility, telephone, and similar services represent another example. The utility company's billing cycle may not coincide with a calendar month (for example, the cycle may be from the 14th day of one month through the 13th day of the following month), and so theoretically the bill should be split between the two months to which it applies. However, if Tebbens' utility bill does not vary greatly from month to month this refinement is probably unnecessary. So long as one utility bill is included in each month, the accountant has done a satisfactory job of matching utility expenses to the accounting period.

Salaries are very often the largest single expense item for a company. Salaries are typically paid weekly, biweekly or semimonthly. Some adjusting entries may be required at month-end to reflect earned but unpaid salaries: a debit to the Salary Expense account, offset by a credit to Salaries Payable. These adjustments are frequently quite material.

Adjusting Asset Values

As conditions change and time passes, accountants find it necessary to revise asset valuations. Most commonly these adjustments are made at the end of the accounting period. The most important of these adjustments is the depreciation of fixed assets. Because of the complexity of this topic and the extensive interaction between the income tax laws and depreciation accounting procedures, a thorough discussion of the accounting for fixed assets is postponed to the next chapter, Chapter 7.

Consider other assets. We have just considered the need to create a prepaid asset account when the flow of cash precedes the accounting period in which the corresponding expense should be recognized. This prepaid asset account, as discussed, needs to be adjusted for the expense recognition of subsequent accounting periods.

A company may own other assets, aside from fixed assets, whose value will diminish over time. For example, suppose Tebbens purchases a patent from an inventor for $9,000. Since a patent by law in the United States has a life of 17 years from issuance date, the new owner, Tebbens, will want to recognize a decline in the value of this patent as the years go by. In fact, Tebbens may decide that the useful life of the patent is substantially shorter than its legal life, since the useful life will be a function of the rate of technological change within the particular industry. Assume that Tebbens determines the patent's useful life to be five years, or 60 months. The accountant would then reduce—or **amortize**—the value of this patent on a month-by-month basis, and the month-end adjusting entry to recognize patent amortization will be:

> Dr.   Amortization Expense, Patents $150
> Cr.   Patent (asset) $150

CONTRA ACCOUNTS

The accountant may wish to preserve information about the original cost of the patent in the general ledger. If so, the credit side of the patent amortization entry would not be made directly to the Patent account, but rather to a **contra account,** Allowance for Amortization. Contra accounts are designed to adjust the value of assets (or liabilities), and appear in the general ledger just after the associated account being adjusted. The balance sheet statement itself may contain both amounts or simply the net of the two accounts. Note that although the contra account, Allowance for Amortization, will appear in the asset section of the general ledger, it will typically carry a credit balance. After one year of amortization, the balances in Tebbens' general ledger will be:

	Balance
Patent	$9,000 Dr
Allowance for Amortization	1,800 Cr

and the balance sheet may indicate the value of the patent either as:

Patent, net	$7,200

or:

Patent	$9,000	
less: Allowance for Amortization	$1,800	$7,200

The use of the contra account provides additional information to the reader of the financial statement; the reader learns both what the company paid for the patent ($9,000) and the extent to which its value has been amortized (one-fifth).

ALLOWANCE FOR DOUBTFUL ACCOUNTS

A prevalent end-of-period entry for companies whose sales are predominantly for credit (rather than for cash) adjusts the value of the firm's accounts receivable to allow for probable uncollectible accounts, or bad debts. Extending credit to customers almost inevitably exposes a company to bad-debt losses. The extent of those losses will depend upon the nature of the customer group, as well as the care with which the company screens the credit-worthiness of its customers before agreeing to extend credit.

The concept of matching suggests that the expense (or loss) associated with accounts that prove ultimately to be uncollectible should be matched to the period when the sale was originally made. Of course, if the seller knew at the time of the sale that a customer would not pay, the seller would not extend credit; the buyer would be required to pay cash or would simply be turned away. Thus, it is impossible to identify in advance exactly which accounts will prove uncollectible, and yet the accountant knows that, on a probabilistic basis, some portion of the accounts receivable will never be collected. With this knowledge, the accountant needs to undertake an adjustment to the Accounts Receivable balance. Failure to make this adjustment will result in an overstatement of an asset, thus violating the concept of conservatism, as well as inadequately matching expenses to revenues.

The accountant will need to exercise judgment in developing some rule for decisions regarding this end-of-period adjustment. The company's history of bad-debt losses will provide a useful guide, but this historical pattern needs to be tempered with such considerations as the state of the economy, changes in credit-granting policies of the firm, and changes in the mix of customers. For example, the accountant at Tebbens may determine that a conservative estimate of bad-debt losses is $\frac{1}{2}$ of 1% of credit sales for the period. Thus, if credit sales for February 19X8 are $460,000, the estimate of the value of those receivables which will ultimately prove uncollectible is: (.005 × 460,000) = $2,300, and the end-of-period adjusting entry is:

Dr.	Bad Debt Expense	$2,300	
	Cr. Allowance for Doubtful Accounts		$2,300

Note that once again a contra account is used in order to preserve in the accounting records the gross value of all accounts receivable. After this adjustment, the subsidiary ledger for Accounts Receivable will continue to reconcile with the general ledger account, since the Allowance for Doubtful Accounts is a pooled, or overall, adjustment, not an adjustment of amounts owed by particular customers. Note, too, that the effect of this adjustment is to include as an expense of February 19X8 a provision for bad debts that is a function of the month's credit sales, even though the firm will not know which of the credit sales proved uncollectible until several months later.

If the accountant is conservatively high in estimating bad-debt losses, the credit balance in the contra account, Allowance for Doubtful Accounts, could grow to unreasonable proportions. Therefore, the decision rule regarding bad-debt adjustments typically contains a second provision that the total balance in the Allowance account will not exceed a certain percentage of the Accounts Receivable balance. Thus, the complete decision rule might read as follows:

> The Allowance for Doubtful Accounts shall be increased each month by one-half of one percent of the credit sales for the month, provided, however, that the increase in the Allowance account shall not result in the total Allowance exceeding five percent of outstanding accounts receivable.

The use of the contra account, Allowance for Doubtful Accounts, eliminates any profit-and-loss effect in the particular month in which an account is finally determined to be uncollectible. Assume that in February 19X8 the Tebbens Company learns that a customer who had purchased $1,700 of merchandise in late 19X7 (that is, several months previously) has encountered financial difficulties and probably will never pay the $1,700 account currently outstanding. The customer's promise to pay is therefore valueless, and the accountant should eliminate this asset from the general ledger. The entry to recognize this write-off of a receivable is:

Dr.	Allowance for Doubtful Accounts	$1,700	
	Cr.	Accounts Receivable	$1,700

Two facts should be noted about this entry: (1) the *net* value of the Accounts Receivable (the gross amount less the Allowance for Doubtful Accounts) is unaffected; and (2) no expense account is debited in this entry, since both the debit and credit are to asset accounts. Thus, the profit in February 19X8 is not impacted by the discovery that a particular receivable created in an earlier period is a bad debt.[3]

INVENTORY CONTRA ACCOUNTS

Just as accounts receivable values are adjusted to allow for probable noncollection in the future, so inventory values may be adjusted for spoilage, shrinkage, obsolescence, and similar phenomena that affect the worth of inventories. A cost of carrying inventory is the risk of obsolescence. The proper matching of expenses to accounting periods suggests that when the risk of obsolescence is high, some inventory obsolescence expense should be acknowledged in each accounting period, even though management will not be able to determine exactly which items become obsolete until some time in the future. As in the case of Allowance for Doubtful Accounts, a contra account, perhaps entitled Allowance for Obsolete Inventory, can be created. A balance in this account can be built up by the application of a decision rule that relates this period's obsolete inventory expense to the level of purchases and to inventory balances. (This decision rule may need to be altered to provide for larger increases in the Allowance when the firm decides to replace one product line with another or when some other event is anticipated that will increase the risk of obsolescence.) When in a future accounting period particular items in inventory are determined to be obsolete, both the Inventory account and the contra account, Allowance for Obsolete Inventory, will be adjusted, with no impact on the firm's profitability during that period.

Liabilities Created by Today's Operations

Accountants need to be alert to obligations that the firm may be undertaking because of operations today, even though performance under these ob-

---

[3] Suppose that the customer owing $1,700 does, in fact, finally make a partial payment of $500, but only after Tebbens has written off the customer's account. Obviously, Tebbens will accept the payment. Typically, a debit entry will be made to the Cash account, and a credit entry to the Allowance account.

ligations may be postponed for months or years. Primary examples are employee pensions and product warranties. In both of these cases, the firm undertakes only a contingent obligation to perform: expenditures for warranty repair will be required only if the product proves defective, and pension payments will be required only when the set of conditions specified in the pension agreement have been met.

One might be inclined to ignore these contingent future liabilities, since companies, after all, obligate themselves in a myriad of ways every day. The issuance of purchase orders implies a promise to pay; the hiring of a scientist or manager under an employment agreement obligates the company to pay future salaries. These obligations are not reflected in the accounting records, however, until, in the first case, the products or services have been received and, in the second case, the scientist or manager has actually performed services and thereby earned a salary.

The cases of pensions and warranties are fundamentally different. Expenditures for warranty repair arise only because of the past delivery to customers of products or equipment. Thus, a part of the total cost of the products or equipment delivered is the cost associated with performing on the warranty provided to the customer. This warranty cost, then, should be matched to the period when the sale was made and not to the period when the defect is brought to light by the customer.

The exact amount of the warranty obligation, of course, is not known in advance. Typically, companies will encounter warranty repair on only a small percentage of their products. Accountants must exercise judgment to determine, in a probabilistic sense, the future warranty obligation that will arise from today's shipments. If, for example, warranty expenditures have historically amounted to about 1% of sales, then in a month when sales total $850,000 the appropriate end-of-period adjusting entry will be:

Dr.	Warranty Expense	$8,500	
	Cr.	Allowance for Warranty	
		(or Warranty Reserve)	$8,500

When the warranty work is performed sometime in the future, the costs associated with that work will be debited to the Allowance (or Reserve) account (a liability account), and not to an expense account; thus, the profit in that future period will be unaffected by the necessity to repair products that were shipped in earlier periods.

Note that the Allowance (or Reserve) account is not a contra account. No asset values are being adjusted. Rather, the accountant is recognizing as a liability an obligation to perfom in the future as a result of today's operations.

The accounting for pension obligations is similar. The exact dollar amount of the obligation to provide pensions in the future to present employees, however, may be even more difficult to predict than warranty obligations. Pension payments will typically be made years, rather than months, in the future, and the payments may be a function of the length of service of the employee, the age at time of retirement or death, and the final salary rate of the employee at retirement or death. Nevertheless, if by working today an employee earns the right to a future pension, then the employer needs to recognize as an expense of today the obligation to pay that future pension.[4]

Other employee benefits require similar recognition of liabilities for future payments. For example, most companies have carefully defined vacation and sick-leave policies. A company that provides its employees with two weeks of paid vacation leave per year may provide that an employee accrues ten-twelfths of a day of vacation for each month of work. The wages or salary paid to a vacationing employee in August is not an expense of August, but rather an expense of the months during which the vacation leave was accrued. Proper matching suggests that the company's obligation to pay wages and salaries during vacations should be recognized month by month by debiting Vacation Expense and crediting Vacation Wages and Salaries Payable. Then when an employee whose salary is $200 per week takes a two-week vacation, the payment to the employee will be accounted for as follows:

Cash		Vacation Wages and Salaries Payable	
Balance	400	400	Balance

Accounting for one other employee benefit illustrates the difficulty accountants face in proper matching and the extent to which they must exercise judgment in assigning expenses and revenues to particular accounting periods. Many companies make bonus or profit-sharing payments to key employees at year-end. Are these payments appropriately recognized as expenses of the final month of the year, or should they be recognized pro rata throughout the year? On the one hand, if the company is relatively certain that bonuses will be paid at year-end, failure to spread the impact of these bonuses throughout the year will result in an overstatement of profit in each of the first 11 months of the year, offset by a drastic understatement of profit in the twelfth month. On the other hand, early in the year the company may not have a clear view of the total of bonuses to be paid at year-end, since bonuses are a function of the company's profits. The accoun-

---

[4] Many employers will pay insurance companies to provide their employees with pensions. In such cases, the employer is paying today to relieve itself of these future obligations, by shifting the obligation to the insurance company. In the absence of such arrangements, employers may create their own pension funds. Typically, these funds are managed by a trustee (for example, a bank) and the pension trust is treated as a separate accounting entity.

tant is faced with a difficult dilemma, the resolution of which will almost surely not satisfy all of the audiences of the financial statements. Typically, if the profit-sharing payments or bonuses are highly predictable because of the company's size and stability, such year-end payments will be accrued throughout the year; by year-end the general ledger will contain an amount in the Bonuses Payable liability account approximating the amount of the payments. In other situations the accountant may have no practical alternative but to wait until year-end to recognize the bonus expense.

Deriving Cost of Goods Sold by End-of-Period Adjustment

A particularly common end-of-period adjustment is one that derives cost of goods sold expense in situations where detailed inventory values are not maintained day-to-day in the accounting records.

Chapter 3 discussed in some detail the concept of accounting for cost of goods sold, particularly the importance of matching Cost of Goods Sold to Sales so that the gross margin (or gross profit) provides a true indication of the margin earned on the revenue of the period. That discussion indicated that a $4,000 credit sale of equipment having a value in finished goods inventory of $2,500 is accounted for as follows:

Dr.	Accounts Receivable	$4,000	
Dr.	Cost of Goods Sold	2,500	
	Cr. Sales		$4,000
	Cr. Finished Goods Inventory		2,500

Note that this method of determining Cost of Goods Sold, referred to as the **perpetual inventory method,** requires that the accountant be able to identify the cost associated with each sale. This requirement presents no problem in the illustration above: the equipment is of large dollar value and relatively few sales are made. Consider, alternatively, a variety store or supermarket grocery store that sells thousands (or tens of thousands) of items each day. Tracking the costs associated with each of these items would be an onerous chore. Moreover, the cost of such tracking would probably be out of proportion to the value of the information derived.[5]

An alternative method of determining cost of goods sold exists. A firm

---

[5] The advent of low-cost computers and mass memories, and of universal product codes and laser-based devices to read the codes, may make feasible the maintenance of perpetual inventory values in accounting records, but to date most such systems have been used for control of physical inventory and not for maintenance of accounting records.

can reasonably assume that the cost of items sold in a particular accounting period is equal to the amount purchased into inventory, less any increase in inventory or plus any decrease in inventory. Stated another way, the total amount of merchandise available for sale in the period equals the amount in inventory at the beginning of the period plus the amount purchased during the period; this total is either sold or remains in inventory at period end. Or, equivalently, cost of goods sold equals:

Beginning inventory

plus: net purchases

less: ending inventory

In fact, the accountant cannot be certain that items not remaining in inventory at period end were sold; they might have been lost, stolen, misplaced, or discarded for some reason. Such inventory "shrinkages" are typically small compared to the amount actually sold, but this method of determining cost of goods sold will not permit isolation of the amount of such shrinkages.

The advantage of this method of determining cost of goods sold is that it requires less accounting; cost of goods sold is determined only once each accounting period, rather than at the time of each sale. The disadvantages are three. First, we lose the ability to determine the margin on individual sales, and can determine only the overall margin for all sales during the period. Second, the accounting records provide no evidence of the amount of inventory shrinkages. Finally, the method requires that inventory be physically counted and valued at the end of each accounting period, a tedious and often time-consuming job.[6] Note that the ending inventory for one accounting period becomes the beginning inventory for the following accounting period.

This method of determining cost of goods sold as performed for the Roberts Company is illustrated in Exhibit 6-2. Throughout the month of October 19X3 the Roberts Company has recorded no entries in the Cost of Goods Sold account and has debited to the Purchases account (rather than the Inventory account) all merchandise acquired. The Purchases account is a type of temporary expense account—temporary in the sense that, after the end-of-period adjustment described presently, it will have a zero balance. Note, too, that during the month Roberts returned to its suppliers items valued at $1,500; this amount is shown in the Purchase Returns ac-

---

[6] If the perpetual inventory method is used, physical inventories must also be taken from time to time in order to determine the amount of inventory shrinkage due to breakage, pilferage, and similar causes. However, items may be counted on a rotating basis (referred to as cycle counting), and they need not all be counted at the end of each accounting period. Estimates of inventory shrinkage will typically be adequate for interim financial statements.

Exhibit 6-2
ROBERTS COMPANY

Trial Balance at October 31, 19X3

	Dr.	Cr.
Cash	$ 5,000	
Accounts receivable	15,000	
Inventory	9,800	
All other assets	16,700	
All liabilities		$25,000
Total owners' equity		20,000
Sales		43,000
Cost of goods sold	—	
Purchases	29,000	
Purchase returns		1,500
All other expenses	14,000	
	$89,500	$89,500

Value of Inventory at October 31, 19X3:	$10,500
(This amount was determined by	
physically counting and valuing all	
items in inventory at October 31.)	

Cost of Goods Sold, October 19X3:

Beginning inventory	$ 9,800	(see trial balance above)
plus: Purchases	29,000	(see trial balance above)
less: Purchase returns	(1,500)	(see trial balance above)
Ending inventory	(10,500)	(see note above)
Cost of goods sold	$26,800	

End-of-Period Adjusting Entry:

	Dr.	Cr.
Dr. Inventory	$10,500	
Dr. Purchase Returns	1,500	
Dr. Cost of Goods Sold	26,800	
Cr. Inventory		$ 9,800
Cr. Purchases		29,000
	$38,800	$38,800

count, rather than as a reduction in Inventory. Net purchases for the month, therefore, were $27,500.

No entries were made during the month in the Inventory account, since merchandise acquired was debited to the Purchases account and no accounting has yet been made for merchandise sold. Thus, the amount shown in the Inventory account on the trial balance is the value of the inventory at the end of the last accounting period—that is, the value of inventory at the close of business on September 30, 19X3, which is also the value of inventory at the commencement of business on October 1.

The accounting records do not reveal the value of inventory owned by Roberts at October 31. Rather, the personnel at Roberts must now count and value the physical items in inventory at that date. Assume this value is $10,500; then the value of merchandise sold must have been: $9,800 + $29,000 − 1,500 − $10,500 = $26,800.

The derivation of the cost of goods sold is shown in Exhibit 6-2, together with the end-of-period adjusting entry required to record cost of goods sold. Note that this end-of-period adjustment reduces to zero both the Purchases and Purchase Returns accounts (described above as temporary expense accounts) and revalues the Inventory account to the appropriate balance at October 31.

Had the accountant at Roberts not made the end-of-period entry but rather simply treated net purchases as equal to Cost of Goods Sold, the inventory values on Roberts' October 31 balance sheet would have been understated, with a corresponding understatement in the profit.

Exhibit 6-3 illustrates in T-account format the effect of the adjusting entry on the preliminary trial balance, and Exhibit 6-4 shows the resulting financial statements.

Exhibit 6-3
ROBERTS COMPANY
General Ledger with Adjusting Entry Recorded

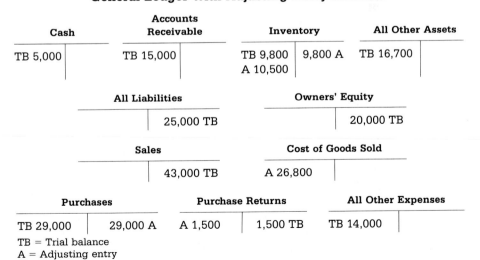

Cash	Accounts Receivable	Inventory	All Other Assets
TB 5,000	TB 15,000	TB 9,800 | 9,800 A A 10,500	TB 16,700

	All Liabilities	Owners' Equity
	25,000 TB	20,000 TB

	Sales	Cost of Goods Sold
	43,000 TB	A 26,800 |

Purchases	Purchase Returns	All Other Expenses
TB 29,000 | 29,000 A	A 1,500 | 1,500 TB	TB 14,000 |

TB = Trial balance
A = Adjusting entry

Exhibit 6-4
ROBERTS COMPANY
Financial Statements

Balance Sheet at October 31, 19X3

ASSETS		LIABILITIES AND OWNERS' EQUITY	
Cash	$ 5,000	All liabilities	$25,000
Accounts Receivable	15,000	Owners' Equity (at	20,000
Inventory	10,500	September 30, 19X3)	
All other assets	16,700	Net income, October 19X3	2,200
	$47,200		$47,200

Income Statement
Month ended October 31, 19X3

Sales	$43,000
Cost of Goods Sold	26,800
All other expenses	14,000
Net income	$ 2,200

Discounts for Prompt Payment

Another refinement that does not involve end-of-period adjustments but does affect the timing of the recognition of revenues and expenses is the handling of discounts allowed or earned because of prompt payment. Standard terms of sale or purchase frequently provide that the buyer may deduct a small percentage of the invoice amount if the invoice is paid within a specified number of days; the discount is a reward for paying quickly. Typical **cash discount** terms are "2%, 10 days/net, 30 days," meaning that the invoice may be discounted by 2% if payment is made within 10 days of the invoice date and, alternatively, the full (net) amount of the invoice is due in 30 days.

The accounting issue here is again one of timing. When shall the discount be reflected: at the time of purchase/sale or when payment is finally made or received? The concept of matching once again provides the guide.

If the Tebbens Company offers its customers a 3% discount for paying within 10 days of invoice date, and most customers avail themselves of this attractive discount,[7] Tebbens is in essence discounting its sales; it is reason-

---

[7] When a buyer fails to take a discount for prompt payment, the buyer is in essence borrowing from the supplier for a period of days in return for giving up the discount. Thus, a buyer who does not pay promptly an invoice subject to "3%, 10 days/net, 30 days" terms is "paying" 3% for the privilege of borrowing from the supplier the face amount of the invoice for an additional

able to assume that in normal circumstances Tebbens will receive only 97% of the invoice amount. If so, Tebbens should use the so-called **net method** of accounting for discounts allowed—that is, the sale itself should be recorded net of the discount, as illustrated in Exhibit 6-5, part A. If, on the other hand, the discount terms offered to customers are 1/2%, 10 days/net, 30 days—relatively unattractive terms.[8]—and customers only infrequently pay within 10 days and take the 1/2% discount, then the **gross method** of accounting for sales should be utilized: any discounts taken by the customers should be recorded only when the customer's payment is in fact received. The gross method of accounting for cash discount terms is illustrated in Exhibit 6-5, part B.

Note in Exhibit 6-5, Part B that the gross method presumes that cash discounts will typically not be taken; discounts that are taken by the customer are treated as expenses of the period when the cash is received or are debited to a contra account to Sales. The net method, on the other hand, never records as a sale that portion of the invoice that will typically be discounted (in this illustration, $30); thus, the net method is conservative in the recognition of revenue. If, finally, the customer does not take advantage of the discount, then in that future period when the payment is received the $30 of income not recorded at the time of the sale is finally recognized.

The situation with respect to cash discounts for prompt payment for *purchases* of goods or services is exactly parallel. If the cash discount available is so attractive that the company will in all normal circumstances pay in time to earn the discount, then the company will want to use the net method of recording these purchases or expenses. Otherwise, the gross method is more appropriate. Note that, while the *net* method of recording *sales* is more conservative, the *gross* method of recording *expenses* is more conservative—the benefit of the discount is deferred until the accounting period in which the payment is finally made.[9]

The cash discount dilemma is another illustration of the timing problem continually encountered by accountants. Interim financial results can be substantially affected by the judgment exercised by accountants in resolving these dilemmas. However, the requirement that accountants be consistent significantly reduces the problem. For example, the profit earned

---

20 days—from the 10th to the 30th day following invoice date. Paying 3% for 20 days of borrowing is equivalent to paying about 54% annual interest rate (there are about eighteen 20-day periods in a year and $18 \times 3\%$ equals 54%). Thus, passing up discounts of this magnitude is a very costly financial policy; the buyer would do well to raise additional debt or equity capital so as to have sufficient funds available to take advantage of attractive cash discount terms.

[8] Not all cash discount terms are attractive. Here the buyer is giving up 1/2% for the use of the supplier's money for an additional 20 days. These terms equate to about a 9% annual interest rate, a rate that the buyer is likely to find quite acceptable.

[9] Note that the net method of accounting for discounts on purchases highlights discounts *lost,* while the gross method highlights discounts *taken.* Information on discounts lost (opportunities not taken) may be particularly useful to management.

Exhibit 6-5
Accounting for Cash Discounts

Part A: Net Method

Sale: $1,000   Terms: 3%, 10 days/net, 30 days

Recording the sale

A/R		Sales	
970			970

Recording the receipt of cash, discount taken

A/R		Cash	
	970	970	

Recording the receipt of cash, discount *not* taken

A/R		Cash		Other Income	
	970	1,000			30

Part B: Gross Method

Sale: $1,000   Terms: ½%, 10 days/net, 30 days

Recording the sale

A/R		Sales	
1,000			1,000

Recording the receipt of cash, discount taken

A/R		Cash		Discounts Allowed[1]	
	1,000	995		5	

Recording the receipt of cash, discount *not* taken

A/R		Cash	
	1,000	1,000	

[1] An expense account or a contra account to sales.

during a particular month will be virtually identical regardless of whether the gross or net method of accounting for cash discounts is used, so long as no *change* in method is undertaken during the period. If the net method is used, the amount recorded as expenses or purchases will be less than under the gross method but will approximate the difference between (1) the expenses and purchases that would have been recorded using the gross method, and (2) the discounts that would have been earned (an Other Income account) using that method.

Exceptions to the Accrual and Realization Concepts

Chapters 3 and 4 discuss briefly the cash basis accounting method. This method recognizes sales or revenue only when cash is received, regardless of when merchandise was delivered or service rendered, and expenses only when cash is paid out. While generally accepted accounting principles require accrual accounting rather than cash basis accounting, many businesses, particularly small businesses and professional service firms, do utilize the cash basis method. These firms typically do not have public shareholders to whom they must report in accordance with generally accepted accounting principles. Moreover, under certain circumstances the cash basis method is permissible for income tax reporting. This method is typically conservative in the recognition of profit and it is simple. While our emphasis throughout this book is on the accrual concept, it is important to remember that the cash basis method is appropriately used in certain types of enterprises.

Still other types of businesses also find the realization concept not totally applicable to their circumstances. Recall that the realization concept requires that revenue be recognized on the date when the particular goods or services are delivered or furnished. Some businesses, such as heavy construction, encounter very long in-process time. For example, a large concrete dam is only "delivered" once, when complete; the construction project may proceed over several years. The primary contractor on such a job will typically employ a **percentage-of-completion method** of accounting. Rather than recognizing revenue only at the end of the project —and then recognizing an enormous amount of revenue—the contractor will recognize a portion of the revenue in each of the accounting periods throughout the project. Great care must be taken to match the expenses to each accounting period as revenue is being recognized.

Some businesses operate under **cost-plus contracts;** that is, the amount charged to the customer is a function of the costs incurred, typically cost plus a fixed fee or cost plus a percentage of cost. Consulting firms, auditing firms, research centers, and some contractors frequently have cost-plus contracts with their customers. In these circumstances, revenue for interim accounting periods while the contract is in process is relatively easy to determine. The recognition of revenue, therefore, will typically not be delayed until the end of the contract, but will be recognized period by period as the costs are incurred.

Summary

This chapter introduced no new accounting concepts, but rather discussed the application of certain accounting concepts to particularly troublesome areas of accounting. The recurring problem that must be addressed is the proper timing of revenues and expenses—that is, the concepts of accrual and matching. Accounting conventions that have evolved to handle these prevalent timing problems recognize the accountant's need to be conservative, to anticipate expenses but not to accelerate revenues.

The discussion in this chapter highlights the difficulty of attaining the goal of precise matching of revenues and expenses. The exercise of judgment is necessary. However, two other concepts discussed in Chapter 4 mitigate the effects of differences in judgment. First, the concept of materiality eliminates the need for absolute and complete matching; the accountant need be concerned only with timing adjustments that will have a material effect on the statement of profit or on the balance sheet. Second, the concept of consistency dictates that once a particular recurring timing problem has been resolved the resolution remain consistent from period to period.

The accountant's task is not limited solely to recording transactions between the accounting entity and other individuals or businesses. In order to satisfactorily state revenues, expenses, assets, and liabilities, the accountant must in addition undertake certain adjustments to the general ledger to reflect changed conditions or simply the passage of time. These end-of-period adjustments have been categorized in this chapter as:

1 Adjustments to unearned revenue (liability) accounts and prepaid asset accounts
2 Adjusting asset values. Examples:
   a Fixed assets (discussed in the following chapter)
   b Other assets: amortization
   c Accounts receivable: allowance for doubtful accounts
   d Inventory: obsolescence and other adjustments
3 Recognition of liabilities created by today's operations. Examples: allowances for warranty expenses and pensions and other employee benefits

Where perpetual inventory records are not maintained within the accounting system, cost of goods sold may be determined by deduction and recorded as an end-of-period entry. Cash discounts for prompt payment with respect to both purchases and sales can be accounted for by either the gross or net method; the choice is made by determining which method will result in the more realistic timing of revenues and expenses. Finally, cash basis accounting and revenue recognition on a percentage-of-completion or cost-plus basis represent exceptions to the accrual concept and the concept of realization.

New Terms

Accrued liability   An obligation that arises when an expense is recognized in one period although the cash outflow will occur in a subsequent period. Examples are accrued tax, interest, and rental liabilities.

Adjusting entries   An alternate name for *end-of-period adjustments*.

Allowance for Doubtful Accounts   A contra account used to adjust the value of the asset account, Accounts Receivable, for amounts that will prove to be uncollectible.

Amortize (amortization)   To prorate the value of an asset over a succession of accounting periods. For example, a patent will be amortized from its original cost to a zero value over the useful life of the patent. A prepaid expense associated with an insurance policy will be amortized (reduced in value systematically) over the term of the policy.

Cash discounts (or discounts for prompt payment)   Small discounts (typically 2% or less) allowed by certain suppliers to customers who pay invoices within a prescribed number of days.

Contra account   An account used to adjust the value of another account while preserving the original balance in that account. Allowance for Doubtful Accounts is a contra account to Accounts Receivable and carries a credit balance, even though it appears among the asset accounts.

Cost-plus contract   A contract providing that the price charged is a function of the cost of performing the contract—cost plus a fixed fee or cost plus a percentage of cost. Costs and related revenues are typically recognized as the costs are incurred and not solely at the completion of the contract.

Deferred expense   An alternate name for *prepaid expense*.

Deferred income (or deferred revenue)   A liability that arises when cash is received in an accounting period prior to the period when the corresponding income (revenue) is to be recognized.

End-of-period adjustments   Entries occurring at the end of the accounting period and initiated by the accountant (rather than being triggered by transactions); these entries are necessary to adjust values of assets and liabilities and to match revenues and expenses.

Gross method (of accounting for cash discounts)   The method that recognizes sales or purchases at their face (or full) value, with any cash discounts allowed or earned accounted for in the period when cash is finally received or paid out (see *net method*).

Net method (of accounting for cash discounts)   The method that recognizes sales or purchases at a value net of the available cash discount, with any discounts not taken by customers and discounts lost on purchases accounted for in the period when cash is finally received or paid out (see *gross method*).

Percentage-of-completion method   A method of recognizing sales (or revenue) on an extended contract (e.g., research or construction) in proportion to the percentage of the contract completed, rather than recognizing the entire sale (all revenue) only at the completion of the contract.

Perpetual inventory method   A method of accounting for each inventory increase or decrease as it occurs.   Alternatively, inventory values may be adjusted only at period-end in connection with the determination of cost of goods sold for the period.

Prepaid expense   An asset that arises when cash outflow occurs in an accounting period prior to the period when the corresponding expense is to be recognized.

Unearned revenue (or income)   An alternative name for *deferred income* (or *deferred revenue*).

Warranty reserve   A liability account that arises when warranty expenses are matched to revenue at the time of shipment, although performance of warranty repair will occur in future periods.   Expenditures for warranty reduce this liability and do not appear as expenses of the future periods.

Problems

1   Determine cost of goods sold for April by the end-of-period adjustment method, using the following information.   Record in T-account format; if you place existing balances in your T accounts, be certain to circle them so that they will not be confused with entries required for this recognition.

Opening inventory balance, at April 1	$7,300
Purchases, during April	5,500
Purchase returns, during April	200
Closing inventory, at April 30	7,700

2   Determine and record in T-account format the appropriate entries to recognize cost of goods sold for January, using the end-of-period adjustment method. The general ledger at January 31 reveals the following balances:

Accounts Payable	$18,000 Cr
Accounts Receivable	31,000 Dr
Cash Discounts Allowed	100 Dr
Cost of Goods Sold	0
Inventory	29,600 Dr
Purchases	22,000 Dr
Purchase Returns	500 Cr
Sales	21,000 Cr
Sales Returns	1,000 Dr

Note: This is *not* a complete trial balance.
Inventory increased during the month by $6,500.

3   Cline Corporation rented a portion of its building to the Walker Company, the rental period to begin at the first of this month. The rental rate is $200 per month, and Cline just received a check from Walker for $1,200 covering the first six months' rent. As the accountant for Cline, what accounting entries would you make when you receive the $1,200 check?

4 The Morris Motor Company has just received notice that Mr. Combs has declared personal bankruptcy and therefore will undoubtedly not pay his $450 account balance. As the accountant for Morris, what entry, if any, would you make when you received this news

   a Assuming that Morris utilizes an Allowance for Doubtful Accounts account

   b Assuming that Morris does *not* utilize such an Allowance for Doubtful Accounts account

5 Refer to question 1 above. Assume that you have already made the entries required by that question. Assume that you *now* discover inventory valued at $500 that you failed to include in your ending inventory valuation. Make an appropriate correcting entry.

6 The Zorn Group wishes to maintain an allowance for doubtful accounts in its accounting records. The company estimates that 2% of its credit sales will prove uncollectible; it further feels that the Allowance account should not be permitted to accumulate to more than 6% of the company's Accounts Receivable balance. What entries, if any, would you make for the month of December, given the following information:

Accounts receivable balance at December 1	$85,000
Allowance for Doubtful Accounts balance at Dec. 1	4,800
Bad debts written off during December	500
Credit sales, December	75,000
Cash collected in December on accounts receivable	60,000

7 The Myers Marine Works was pleasantly surprised to receive $200 from Charlie Cook in partial payment of a $600 balance that Cook owed to Myers. Myers had previously written off this account as uncollectible. What entries would you make as the accountant for Myers when you received the $200 check, assuming you expected to receive no more?

8 A customer slipped on the sidewalk in front of Zukin's Hardware Store and broke his arm. He has sued Zukin for negligence, asking $20,000 in damages. Zukin's lawyer, who originally stated that Zukin would undoubtedly win the suit, now feels that Zukin can probably settle out of court for about $1,000, but that this settlement will not be reached for several months. As the accountant for Zukin, would you make any accounting entries at this time? Why or why not?

9 The Nelson Corporation purchased a one-year insurance policy for $4,800 in cash on January 1, 19X6. If coverage under the policy is for calendar year 19X6 and Nelson treats each month as an accounting period, what accounting entries should be made in August 19X6 regarding this insurance policy?

10 The Darrell Company follows a policy of accruing for year-end bonuses during each month of the year. Year-end bonuses have become a tradition at Darrell and typically amount to 6% of annual salary for all employees when the company experiences a profitable year. The winter months, including February, are generally unprofitable for Darrell, while the balance of the year is highly profitable. February of this year is also expected to be unprofitable. Total salary payments for the month are $16,000. Assume that you are the accountant for Darrell and are working on adjusting entries for the month of February. Would you make an adjusting entry in February regarding year-end bonuses? If so, what would it be? If not, why not?

11 The Darrell Company is required by agreement to pay group health insurance for its employees in the amount of $20 per month per employee. Payment is required on the fifteenth of the following month for all employees who worked more than 120 hours during the previous month. Assuming that 15 employees worked more than 120 hours in February, indicate what adjusting entries should be made at the end of February with respect to group health insurance.

12 The Palmer Partners' preliminary trial balance (balance in each general ledger account before adjusting entries) at the end of March 19X5 is shown below. The accountant for Palmer, a retailer of fresh vegetables, has gathered the following information as she considers possible month-end adjusting entries.

PALMER CORPORATION
Preliminary Trial Balance
(Before Adjustments)
March 31, 19X5

Account	Dr.	Cr.
Cash	$ 5,000	
Merchandise Inventory, March 1	5,500	
Prepaid Insurance Expense	500	
Prepaid Rent Expense	0	
Supplies Inventory	600	
Store Fixtures	9,000	
Accounts Payable		$ 3,870
Bank Loan Payable		1,800
Wages Payable		0
Payroll Taxes Payable		0
Partnership Capital		11,500
Sales		76,000
Cost of Goods Sold	0	
Purchases	60,000	
Purchase Returns		1,200
Wages Expense	12,100	
Rent Expense	750	
Insurance Expense	0	
Interest Expense	0	
Supplies Expense	0	
Depreciation Expense	0	
Payroll Tax Expense	0	
Miscellaneous Expense	920	
Total	$94,370	$94,370

a A count and valuation of inventory of vegetables at March 31 revealed a total on hand of $5,300.

b Supplies inventory (bags, ties, and so forth) was $450 at March 31.

c Wages earned but unpaid at March 31 totaled $1,300.

d Payroll taxes due on the tenth of April will be 5% of all wages earned during March.

e Rental for the cash register is $50 per month, but is paid only every three months. The last payment was on January 31 for the three months prior thereto, and the next payment will be due April 30.

f The bank loan payable at February 28 was $2,000, and the payment to the bank in March of $200 had been debited to the Bank Loan Payable account. In fact, the $200 payment was composed of $20 of interest and $180 of principal repayment.

g Depreciation on the store's fixtures for the month of March was $200.

h Palmer paid rent to the landlord during March of $750. Although this payment covered rent for both March and April, the full $750 was charged as an expense in March.

i On January 1, Palmer purchased for $600 an insurance policy providing coverage for the entire year.

Make adjusting entries, as you deem appropriate, and construct an income statement and balance sheet in conventional format. *Note:* Palmer closes its books monthly; thus, the balances in the income and expense accounts on the trial balance are applicable to the month of March only.

13 Shown below is the trial balance for the Parola Corporation at July 31, 19X2, after some, *but not all,* end-of-period entries have been made for the month. Parola closes its profit and loss accounts monthly.

a What was Parola's profit for the month, before giving effect to any of the adjustments described below?

b What was Parola's working capital at July 31, 19X2, before giving effect to the adjustments described below?

c If inventory at July 31, 19X2 was $15,500, what was cost of goods sold for the month?

d A $500 account owed to Parola by Nelson Co. is deemed to be uncollectible. What effect will this determination have on the company's total assets?

e Note the balance in the Dividends Payable account. (1) To what account was the debit entry made when this liability was established? (2) To what account will the credit entry be made next month when this liability is discharged?

f Parola uses the gross method of recording cash discounts with respect to both sales and purchases. If the company had always used the *net* method of accounting for cash discounts on sales (but the gross method for purchases), what accounts on the trial balance *besides* Discounts Allowed would be affected by this change, and in which direction?

g Assuming that all sales made are on credit, rather than for cash, about how many days (rough estimate) do you think it takes customers, on the average, to pay their bills to Parola? (*Hint:* Consider the balances in the Sales and Accounts Receivable accounts.)

Trial Balance

	Dr.	Cr.
Cash	$ 12,000	
Accounts Receivable	60,000	
Allowance for Doubtful Accounts		$ 2,100
Inventory	14,500	
Prepaid Expenses	2,300	
Fixed Assets	47,800	
Allowance for Depreciation		12,800
Accounts Payable		7,400
Dividends Payable		4,000
Taxes Payable		3,000
Miscellaneous Accruals		8,800
Capitalized Value of Lease Obligations		17,000
Capital Stock		20,000
Retained Earnings		58,100
Sales		49,000
Purchases	11,800	
Purchase Returns		1,200
Salary Expense	31,400	
Depreciation Expense	1,200	
Occupancy Expense	800	
Utilities Expense	1,600	
Interest Expense	100	
Discounts Allowed	500	
Discounts Earned		100
Gain/Loss on Sale of Fixed Assets		500
Total	$184,000	$184,000

h What two accounts on the trial balance are most likely to be the subject of subsidiary ledgers?

i Prepaid and accrual accounts typically arise because of timing differences between the flow of cash and the flow of expenses. What accounting concept requires recognition of these timing differences?

14 *Multiple Choice.* Select those debit and credit entries (shown in general journal format) that you think best record the end-of-period entry described. (*Hint:* Develop your answer in T-account format and then select the journal entries that correspond.)

a Marcus Mercantile determines cost of goods sold by the end-of-period adjustment method at the end of each month. During the month just ended, Purchases totaled $18,000, Purchase Returns totaled $1,000, and Inventory declined by $3,000. Sales totaled $27,000, Sales Returns totaled $2,000. The entries required to record cost of goods sold are:

  1   Dr: Purchases $18,000
  2   Dr: Purchase Returns $1,000
  3   Dr: Sales $27,000

4	Dr:	Sales Returns $2,000
5	Dr:	Inventory $3,000
6	Dr:	Cost of Goods Sold $17,000
7	Dr:	Cost of Goods Sold $8,000
8	Dr:	Cost of Goods Sold $20,000
9		Cr:	Purchases $18,000
10		Cr:	Purchase Returns $1,000
11		Cr:	Sales $27,000
12		Cr:	Sales Returns $2,000
13		Cr:	Inventory $3,000
14		Cr:	Loss/Gain Account $5,000
15		Cr:	Loss/Gain Account $8,000
16		Cr:	Loss/Gain Account $10,000

b The Chatfield Company this month paid $4,000 in connection with a trade show that will occur early next year, charging the $4,000 to Promotion Expense. The accountant has decided that this amount is properly an expense of next year, not this month. To make this change (correction), the entries are:

1	Dr:	Promotion Expense $4,000
2	Dr:	Prepaid Promotion Expense $4,000
3	Dr:	Accounts Payable $4,000
4	Dr:	Loss/Gain Account $4,000
5		Cr:	Promotion Expense $4,000
6		Cr:	Prepaid Promotion Expense $4,000
7		Cr:	Accrued Promotion Expense Payable $4,000
8		Cr:	Loss/Gain Account $4,000
9	No entry required at this time.

15 *Multiple Choice.* (See instructions in problem 14.) The transactions described must be accounted for in light of adjusting entries made at the end of earlier accounting periods.

a The Walters Computer Co. sells and services small business computers, providing its customers a one-year warranty against defects. At the time of sale of a computer, an addition is made to the Allowance for Warranty Expense account to provide for future warranty expenditures. Walters has just provided replacement parts valued at $5,000 to one of its customers. One-half of these parts represented warranty replacements and the other half are billed to the customer at $4,000.

1	Dr:	Warranty Expense $2,500
2	Dr:	Allowance for Warranty Expense $2,500
3	Dr:	Cost of Parts Sold $5,000
4	Dr:	Cost of Parts Sold $2,500
5	Dr:	Accounts Receivable $4,000
6	Dr:	Accounts Receivable $2,500
7	Dr:	Loss/Gain Account $1,000
8	Dr:	Inventory $5,000
9		Cr:	Inventory $5,000
10		Cr:	Sales $5,000
11		Cr:	Sales $4,000

12	Cr:	Allowance for Warranty Expense $2,500
13	Cr:	Warranty Expense $2,500
14	Cr:	Loss/Gain Account $1,500
15	Cr:	Loss/Gain Account $4,000

b On September 5, the Miller Mining Company pays wages that had been accrued as of August 31. Total wages accrued equals $7,100; net cash payments to the miners is $5,800, the difference being $1,000 income tax withheld and $300 trade union dues withheld. The withheld amounts will be paid later in September.

1	Dr:	Accrued Wages Payable $7,100
2	Dr:	Prepaid Wages $7,100
3	Dr:	Wages Expense $7,100
4	Dr:	Wages Expense $6,100
5	Dr:	Cash $5,800
6		Cr:	Cash $6,100
7		Cr:	Cash $5,800
8		Cr:	Income Tax Payable $1,000
9		Cr:	Trade Union Dues Payable $300
10		Cr:	Trade Union Dues Expense $300

c The Schwartz Bros. accounts for sales net of the cash discount offered to customers: 5% if paid within 10 days. Schwartz receives $100 in cash from a customer who did not take the discount.

1	Dr:	Cash $100
2	Dr:	Cash $95
3	Dr:	Discounts Allowed $5
4		Cr:	Other Income $5
5		Cr:	Sales $95
6		Cr:	Sales $100
7		Cr:	Accounts Receivable $100
8		Cr:	Accounts Receivable $95

d The Board of Directors of Rummel Corporation declared a dividend last month, to be paid this month. Rummel closes its books monthly. Rummel now pays this dividend in the amount of $10,000.

1	Dr:	Dividend Expense $10,000
2	Dr:	Dividends Payable $10,000
3	Dr:	Retained Earnings $10,000
4	Dr:	Prepaid Expense $10,000
5		Cr:	Prepaid Expense $10,000
6		Cr:	Owners' Equity $10,000
7		Cr:	Cash $10,000
8	No entry required at this time.

16 Selected financial data for the accounting years 19X5 and 19X6 for a commercial janitorial service are:

	19X5	19X6
For the year:		
Total Revenue	$150,000	$200,000
Gross Margin	75,000	100,000
Profit	9,000	12,000

On December 31:

Cash	10,000	10,000
Accounts Receivable	15,000	20,000
Total Assets	75,000	80,000
Accounts Payable	5,000	5,000

These financial results were determined using accrual accounting. If the janitorial service had used cash rather than accrual accounting, do you think its profits in 19X6 would have been $12,000, more than $12,000, or less than $12,000? Why?

17 Record in T-account format the transactions or recognitions described. Label each account as follows: A = asset; L = liability; I = income; E = expense; OE = other owners' equity. Do *not* place in the T accounts any amounts that are not a direct result of this transaction or recognition (i.e., omit balances that exist prior to this entry).

a Koze Construction returned supplies to the Fishman Company requesting credit against future purchases. The original purchase, earlier this month, had been for $7,000; the bill was paid within 10 days of receipt and thus Koze took a 2% cash discount and paid only $6,860 to Fishman. Koze determines cost of supplies used by the end-of-period adjustment method and uses the gross method of accounting for discounts. Make entries for Koze to record the return.

b The Macmillan Merchandisers sold on credit to Second Street Store merchandise having a sales value of $200. Macmillan granted customers terms of 7%, 10 days/net 30. Because customers almost always took advantage of the discount, Macmillan recorded sales net of cash discounts. Macmillan determined cost of goods sold by an end-of-period adjustment. Make entries for Macmillan to record this sale.

c Following the conservative rule that inventory should be valued at the lower of cost or market, Macmillan Merchandisers determined that the valuation of 100 units of item M in its inventory should be adjusted. Some facts regarding item M's value are:

Original purchase cost:	$3.00 per unit
Current cost (if replaced):	$2.50 per unit
Current price quoted by Macmillan to its customers:	$2.75 per unit

Make the adjusting entry for Macmillan Merchandisers.

18 Shown on the following two pages is the trial balance for the Kalison Floor Covering Company at June 30, 19X8. Kalison retails carpets in a medium-sized city. It occupies rented facilities and offers credit to some of its customers.

a Describe in *journal entry* format the adjusting entries (if any) required by each of the following statements.

1 Upon careful review of the accounts receivable subsidiary ledger at month-end, the accountant for Kalison Floor Covering Company decided that $150 of receivables would probably prove uncollectible and should be written off. He also discovered a $50 credit balance in the account of V. Brazda; the account had been written off in March as un-

KALISON FLOOR COVERING COMPANY

	PRELIMINARY TRIAL BALANCE		ADJUSTMENTS		ADJUSTED TRIAL BALANCE	
	Dr.	Cr.	Dr.	Cr.	Dr.	Cr.
Accounts Payable		$16,100				
Accounts Receivable	$14,800					
Accrued Salaries Payable						
Advertising Expense	1,650					
Allowance for Depreciation—Leasehold Improvements		1,600				
Allowance for Depreciation—Truck						
Allowance for Doubtful Accounts		250				
Bad-Debt Expense	170					
Cash	500					
Cost of Goods Sold						
Deferred Revenue		980				
Depreciation Expense	120					
Fixed Assets—Leasehold Improvements	5,280					
Fixed Assets—Truck	4,000					
Interest Expense	30					

Interest Payable		40					
Inventory	21,500						
Invested Capital		10,000					
Notes Payable—Bank		5,000					
Notes Payable—Finance Company		2,000					
Prepaid Expenses	800						
Purchases	13,700						
Purchase Returns		300					
Retained Earnings		7,520					
Salaries Expense	3,200						
Sales		24,500					
Sales Returns	1,400						
Utilities and Telephone Expense	390						
Rent Expense	750						
Totals	$68,290	$68,290					

collectible, but Brazda did, in fact, make the $50 payment in June.

2   Kalison determined cost of goods sold by the end-of-period adjustment method. A physical inventory was taken at June 30, 19X8 and valued at $17,800.

3   At June 30, 19X8, Kalison held a total of $980 of down payments by customers on special orders of carpets. In reviewing these balances at month-end, the accountant discovered that an advance payment of $150 by D. Auker had not been recorded on the $650 invoice submitted to D. Auker in June when the carpet was delivered. Thus, the company could anticipate a payment from D. Auker of only $500, not the $650 that was billed.

4   Interest of $30 was paid to the finance company on June 30. Also, interest on the bank note (at the rate of 12% per year) is due quarterly (i.e., at the end of every three months); the next payment is due on July 31, 19X8.

5   At the end of June, salaries earned but not yet paid to Kalison employees total $280. These salaries will be paid in July.

b   Make the adjustments to the trial balance and construct an income statement and a balance sheet, both in conventional format.

19   A trial balance for Mingo Corporation at June 30, 19X7, was:

a   The company's accountant has not yet determined cost of goods sold for the period. The physical inventory valuation at June 30 is $3,500. Record the necessary adjusting entry at June 30 in *journal entry* format.

b   After making the adjustment required in *a* above, construct for Mingo Corporation a balance sheet at June 30, 19X7, and a six-month income statement (January through June 19X7) in conventional format.

c   Assume now that after constructing the financial statements Mingo's accountant discovered the following errors. *If* these errors were *corrected*, would Mingo's profit be increased or decreased?

	Dr.	Cr.
Accounts Payable		$ 4,000
Accounts Receivable	$ 6,000	
Accumulated Depreciation		1,500
Accrued Liabilities		1,000
Capital Investment		8,500
Cash	1,000	
Cost of Goods Sold	0	
Expenses (Operating)[1]	2,500	
Fixed Assets	7,000	
Inventory	3,000	
Purchases[1]	4,000	
Retained Earnings		1,500
Sales[1]		7,000
Total	$23,500	$23,500

[1] For the Period January 1 through June 30, 19X7.

1   $200 of inventory was overlooked when the June 30 physical inventory valuation was taken
2   No depreciation has yet been accumulated for a fixed asset purchased in May
3   A deferred income (liability) account was not reduced by 25% as it should have been

Fixed-Asset Accounting

Assets that are used by their owners in the process of manufacturing products or performing services and that have a useful life longer than one year are considered *fixed assets*. Fixed assets are fundamentally different from current assets. Unlike accounts receivable, fixed assets are not turned directly into cash; unlike inventory, fixed assets are not acquired to be resold. A company's purpose in owning fixed assets is to use them for a number of years and not to earn a profit in their purchase and resale.

The accrual concept of accounting requires that fixed assets be **capitalized** when acquired—that is, the expenditure must be treated as an asset and not an expense. The valuation of a fixed asset at the time of its acquisition is relatively straightforward; however, the initial valuation cannot remain unchanged over time. The value of a typical fixed asset declines over the time that the firm owns it. To avoid distorting reported income at either the acquisition date of the asset or at the date when the asset is finally disposed of (probably for a fraction of its original cost), the value of the fixed asset must somehow be reduced periodically and in steps throughout its life.

A retail store can purchase inventory and maintain the value of that inventory at its acquisition cost throughout the time it is owned, since the normal expectation is that the store will sell the inventory at a price higher than its cost. The same store, however, cannot purchase a delivery truck, use it for several years, and expect to sell the truck for more than a fraction of its original cost. Thus, while the retail store need not record a decline in the value of its inventory over time, the store does need to account systematically for the decline in the value of the delivery truck.

Fixed-asset accounting is tremendously important for firms that are fixed-asset-intensive. For example, electric power utilities invest very much more in property, plant, and equipment (fixed assets) than they do in current assets (such as accounts receivable and inventory). The way in which they allocate as expenses portions of the value of those fixed assets over the years they are owned will have a major impact on the utilities' year-to-year reported profits. On the other hand, in a professional service firm—a labor-intensive enterprise—fixed-asset accounting will be relatively unimportant, since the firm owns few fixed assets and the primary expenses are personnel salaries and related expenses.

Alternative Valuation Methods

Let's return to the three valuation methods discussed in Chapter 2: the time-adjusted value method, the market value method, and the cost value method.

The first two of these methods will automatically recognize a decline in the value of fixed assets throughout their years of use. A firm utilizing the time-adjusted value method recomputes at the end of each accounting period the remaining stream of benefits to be derived from owning the asset. As the asset grows older, the remaining period over which benefits will be realized shortens, and thus the time-adjusted value of the remaining benefits decreases. A firm utilizing the market value method similarly redetermines at the end of each accounting period the then-current market value of the fixed asset. As the asset grows older or begins to wear, its market value will typically decline and this fact will be acknowledged in the firm's accounting records. Under either of these two methods, the decline in the value of the fixed asset during each accounting period will be recorded as an expense of that period.

Appealing as these two methods of valuation may be in concept, they are extremely difficult to implement, as discussed in Chapter 2. Moreover, the cost valuation method is currently the only method that is acceptable for financial statement purposes in the United States.[1]

---

[1] Chapter 8, "Accounting for Price-level Changes," discusses the reporting of replacement values of fixed assets, still another valuation method, which is being advocated by certain authorities in the United States. Chapter 8 points out that high inflation rates in recent years have caused some accountants and economists to argue that fixed-asset valuations reported under the historical cost method are unrealistic and therefore depreciation expenses are understated.

Turning, then, to the use of historical costs in the valuation of fixed assets, we realize that some procedure must be devised to cause a *write-down* in the capitalized value of the asset during its years of use. That is, accountants must allocate over the years that the fixed asset is owned, the difference between its original cost and the amount that the accountant anticipates will be realized when the asset is sold or scrapped at the end of its use. This procedure is referred to as **depreciation accounting.**

Depreciation accounting can be defined as the rational, equitable, and systematic allocation over the years that the owner expects to use the asset of the difference between the asset's acquisition cost and its estimated salvage value. The American Institute of Certified Public Accountants (AICPA) refers to depreciation as a "process of allocation, not valuation."[2] By this the AICPA means that the value of the fixed asset appearing on the firm's balance sheet (assuming depreciation has been properly recorded) will bear no necessary relationship to the asset's market value. The presumption is that the firm does not expect to sell the asset until the end of its years of use, and thus interim market values are irrelevant. The asset's estimated market value at the time that the asset will be disposed of is relevant to depreciation accounting; that value is equal to the salvage value used in the depreciation calculation.

Impact of Accounting Rules and Concepts

As a prelude to a discussion of the specific steps required in accounting for depreciation, consider the impact on fixed asset accounting of the various accounting rules and concepts discussed in Chapter 4. If these rules are indeed useful in resolving accounting dilemmas, they should provide guidance in understanding some of the accepted procedures for fixed asset accounting.

ACCRUAL AND MATCHING

We have already recognized that it is the accrual concept, coupled with the requirement to utilize historical cost, that gives rise to the need for depreciation accounting. The expense associated with the ownership of a fixed asset must be matched to the benefit derived from the asset's use.

Typically, depreciation expense, that is, the allocation of a portion of the value of the fixed asset, is matched to the accounting period. Depreciation is thus calculated as a function of time, since the period of use of the asset is defined in terms of time—for example, eight years or fifteen years.

The usefulness of certain assets, however, might better be defined in

[2] AICPA, *Accounting Research Study*, No. 7, 1965.

terms of units of work rather than time.   For example, an injection molding tool might be capable of producing 10,000 parts, after which it will be so corroded or worn that it must be replaced; the time period over which these 10,000 parts will be manufactured is a function of market demand.   In this situation, the difference between the acquisition cost of this tool and its scrap value after producing 10,000 parts might be matched against parts production, rather than time; if so, 1/10,000 of this difference would be charged as an expense for each part manufactured.

CONSISTENCY

The definition of depreciation accounting speaks of the use of a rational, equitable, and systematic procedure.   A procedure meeting these require-ments must be consistent from accounting period to accounting period. However, methods of calculating depreciation may vary for different classes of assets: buildings may be depreciated using a different procedure from tools and fixtures, and transportation equipment may utilize a still dif-ferent procedure.

CONSERVATISM

The requirement that managements lean in the direction of understating both profit and the value of assets suggests that, in formulating deprecia-tion-accounting policies, managements should bear in mind that higher de-preciation expenses will result in more conservative financial statements. Higher depreciation expenses result from (a) assuming fewer years of use, (b) estimating lower disposition (salvage or scrap) values, and (c) recognizing more depreciation expense in the earlier years of ownership and less in the later years.

MATERIALITY

Inexpensive assets as well as high-priced assets may provide benefits to their owners for more than a single accounting period.   Hand tools, desk-top staplers, and simple hand-held calculators have extended lives, just as do buildings, trucks, computers, and machine tools.   Not all long-lived assets, however, need be treated as fixed assets—that is, not all need to be capitalized and then depreciated.   Typically, those assets with an acquisi-tion cost below some threshold level (for example, $100 or $1,000) will be treated as expenses—in the jargon of accounting, they will be *expensed*. This treatment substantially reduces accounting costs, and no material dis-tortion of reported profits or fixed asset valuations will result.   Thus, the expensive procedure of capitalizing and depreciating is reserved for those assets that have a material acquisition cost and useful life.

GOING-CONCERN ASSUMPTION

As stated earlier, depreciation accounting procedures pay no heed to interim market valuations of fixed assets, since the assumption is made that the firm will continue to be a going concern and will continue to use the asset in its intended manner.   If either of these assumptions should cease to be valid, the accountant must reassess the value of the asset, acknowledging the new set of circumstances.

Suppose an asset being depreciated over five years is rendered obsolete after two years by a technological advance.   If the asset is of no further use to its owner and cannot be sold to another user or sold for scrap, the asset has zero value to its present owner and the owner's accounting records should reflect this fact.   The accountant must record as an expense of the period when the asset's obsolescence is recognized any remaining undepreciated value of the asset.   If the present owner of the asset decides to make a premature disposition of the asset (that is, before the end of the number of years of use originally estimated), the accountant should reflect this decision to offer the asset for sale rather than continue to use it.   The decision may necessitate a substantial write-down in the value of the asset, and a corresponding expense, in the accounting period in which the decision is made.

Calculating Depreciation Expense

The definition of depreciation accounting given earlier requires the determination of four factors: (1) the acquisition cost of the asset—its **initial cost,** (2) the estimated years of use of the asset—its **useful life,** (3) the estimated value of the asset at the end of its estimated useful life—its **salvage value,** and (4) the rational, equitable, and systematic method of allocating this difference between acquisition cost and salvage value—its depreciation method.   While the fourth factor, the depreciation method, requires the most discussion, the first three factors also present some difficulties that need to be explored.

INITIAL COST

The initial cost may need to include more than simply the cash purchase price of the fixed asset.   Initial cost must also include any other outlays required to get the asset into a position and condition where it is productive. Thus, freight charges and installation costs are normally included in the initial cost of the asset, so that these expenditures are depreciated over the life of the asset rather than being reflected as an expense of the accounting period when the asset was acquired.

Major overhauls or rebuilding of existing fixed assets should be treated as fixed asset expenditures, if the result of the refurbishing is to increase substantially the useful life of the asset. Thus, a major overhaul of a machine tool or the replacement of the roof of a factory should typically be capitalized and depreciated.

USEFUL LIFE

The accountant next needs to determine the period over which the asset will be depreciated, that is, its life. The concern here is with the useful life of the asset, the period of time that it will be productive to its present owner. This useful life may be a good deal shorter than the asset's total life—that is, less than the total time from the asset's initial creation until its final owner discards or demolishes it. A truck may have several owners during its total life, but the depreciable life for each of those owners is equal to the time that each owner uses the truck.

The life of an asset is typically dictated by either wear or obsolescence. A truck may truly wear out. The motor, transmission, and other mechanical parts may deteriorate to the point that the truck is not reliable or is not worth repairing; if so, the owner will cease using it and its useful life to the present owner will terminate. A second owner—one more tolerant of breakdowns or willing to effect repairs—may now purchase the truck, thus commencing another useful life of the truck for this second owner.

Unlike a truck, a computer will probably not wear out, but it is likely to obsolesce. The computer may be capable of operating for 20 or 30 years, but its useful life to an owner may be only five years, at the end of which time technological improvements in computers will give the owner strong motivation for replacing the old computer with a new one.

The life of a specialized production tool may be determined by neither wear nor technological change, but by changes in demand for the product or service produced by the tool. For example, the fixtures and tooling required to make a child's toy that is heavily promoted by television advertising during one Christmas season may have a relatively short useful life simply because the demand for the toy is expected to evaporate when the promotional program is terminated. The fixtures are neither worn nor technologically obsolete, but they are no longer useful.

We will discuss shortly the relationship between depreciation accounting and the income-tax laws, but it should be pointed out here that income-tax regulations in the United States provide certain guidelines as to appropriate depreciable lives for various classes of assets. Many accountants accept these guideline lives for lack of other specific evidence as to useful lives; however, in many situations, shorter or longer lives may be more appropriate for the equitable distribution of the difference between original cost and salvage value. The income tax laws should not determine accounting policy. Depreciable lives longer than the guideline lives will not be challenged by the taxing authorities; shorter lives may well be challenged for use in calculating taxable income, but they will be allowed if the taxpayer can demonstrate that the shorter life is appropriate in the particular circumstances.

SALVAGE VALUE

If the determination of useful life is difficult, the estimation of the probable market value of the asset at the end of that useful life will be that much more difficult. Fortunately, for many (but certainly not all) assets, the estimated salvage value is a relatively small percentage of the initial cost (for example, 10%); thus, an error in its estimation will not have a material impact on depreciation expense and asset valuation.

Salvage values are determined by many factors that are difficult to predict. A commercial building may have an estimated useful life of 40 years. Its market value at the end of that period will very much depend not only on the condition of the building itself but the condition of the neighborhood in which the building is located. If the building happens to be located in a part of the city that has developed into a high-rent, retail-commercial area, the building may have a market value well in excess of its initial cost.[3] On the other hand, the owner may now find that the building's location is undesirable and prospective buyers cannot be found. It is unlikely that the owner can accurately forecast these conditions 40 years in advance.

The salvage value of standard machine tools will be determined by the condition of the used-machine-tool market at the end of their useful lives. Prices of used machine tools vary widely, generally in response to basic economic cycles in the country. In recession periods, prices will be low; during times when the demand for machine tools to expand productive capacity exceeds the ability of the machine tool manufacturers to supply new tools, the prices of used machine tools may approach or exceed the cost of new tools.

Of course, rates of inflation (or deflation) will have a major impact on salvage values. In the next chapter we will discuss the effect of price level changes on fixed-asset accounting.

In many situations it is appropriate to assume zero salvage value. A specialized asset, useful to its present owner but unlikely to be useful to others, should carry a zero salvage value. **Leasehold improvements**— that is, lighting, electrical equipment, and other improvements installed in rented facilities—should normally be depreciated over the term of the lease to a zero salvage value, as the lessee will derive no continuing benefit from the improvements after moving out of the facility.

---

[3] The cost value method would not permit acknowledgment of an estimated salvage value greater than the asset's initial cost.

DEPRECIATION METHOD

The depreciation method selected by the firm will determine how the total depreciation expense is spread among the accounting periods throughout the asset's useful life.   The three fundamental methods that we need to consider are: **straight-line, accelerated,** and **units-of-production.**

The straight-line method is explained by its name: the value of the asset is reduced from initial cost to salvage value in a straight-line manner over the asset's useful life.   If the asset has a 10-year life, one-tenth of the depreciable value will be assigned as depreciation expense during each year of life (or 1/120th of depreciable value during each month of life).

The accelerated method assigns greater depreciation expense during the early years of the asset's life, and lower depreciation expense during the asset's later years.   The arguments for the use of accelerated depreciation and the common conventions for applying this method will be discussed presently.

The unit-of-production method assigns depreciation expense in proportion to the amount that the asset is used.   This method requires that the life of the asset be defined in terms of volume of usage during the period of ownership—for example, hours of operation of the machine, units produced by the equipment, or miles traveled by the vehicle.   The amount of depreciation expense to be recognized during any accounting period will be a function of the amount of usage during that period.   For example, if a particular tool's life is defined as the production of 450,000 units, depreciation expense on this asset during a year when 75,000 units are produced will be 16.7% (75,000 ÷ 450,000 = 16.7%) of the difference between initial cost and salvage value of the asset.   The unit-of-production method of depreciation is not in common usage today.

Arguments for accelerated depreciation   Straight-line depreciation is both simple and apparently equitable.   What are the arguments in favor of using accelerated depreciation?   Recall that the objective in depreciation accounting is simply to allocate in a rational and systematic manner the difference between initial cost and salvage value over the life of the asset.   It is *not* an objective to reflect in the accounting records an approximation of the asset's declining market value.   Although accelerated depreciation may come closer than straight-line depreciation to approximating market values, this circumstance should not serve as an argument for the accelerated depreciation method.   It is illogical to argue that the accelerated method better approximates market values when that is not the objective.

There are, however, two rational arguments for the use of accelerated depreciation.   First, the asset may well have more usefulness to its owner during the early years of its life, before the effects of wear and technological obsolescence have had much chance to take their toll.   Toward the end of its life, the asset may be assigned to a stand-by role, with the primary pro-

ductive load being assumed by newer, and perhaps technologically superior, assets.   A second argument is that maintenance expenses are likely to
increase over the life of the asset.   If the total cost of owning and operating
an asset (including both depreciation and maintenance) is to be spread eq-
uitably over the life of the asset, more depreciation might be recognized
early in the asset's life in order that depreciation expense will be lessened
as maintenance expenditures increase later in the asset's life.

Moreover, accelerated depreciation is consistent with the key accounting concept of conservatism.   Accelerating depreciation expenses will typically have the effect of reducing reported profits.   If the company is growing and thus continually adding to its stock of fixed assets, accelerated
depreciation will lead to conservatively stated profits throughout the growth
phase of the company.

Accelerated depreciation is widely used, and the two most common
conventions employed are **sum-of-the-years'-digits** depreciation and **declining balance** depreciation.

Sum-of-the-years'-digits (SOYD)   This clever (and perhaps somewhat
contrived) convention determines the depreciation expense each year as a
decreasing fraction of the difference between initial cost and salvage value.
The fraction is defined as follows: the numerator is the remaining years of
life of the asset (including the current year) and the denominator is the sum
of all the digits in the life of the asset.[4]   For example, an asset with a seven-
year life will be assigned depreciation during its first two years using the
following fractions:

$$\text{Year 1:} \quad \frac{7}{7 + 6 + 5 + 4 + 3 + 2 + 1} = \frac{7}{28}$$

$$\text{Year 2:} \quad \frac{6}{28}$$

Declining-balance   While the sum-of-the-years'-digits convention reduces the fraction each year, the declining-balance convention holds the
fraction constant but reduces the base to which the fraction is applied.   The
base each year is the initial cost less depreciation accumulated to date —
that is, the remaining book value of the asset.   The fraction is set by reference to the straight-line method.   The most common rate of declining-balance depreciation is the so-called double-declining balance, meaning that
the fraction is twice (double) the straight-line rate.

Thus, an asset with a 10-year life incurs depreciation at the rate of one-
tenth per year under the straight-line method and two-tenths or one-fifth

---

[4] The formula for the sum of the digits is: $\dfrac{n(n + 1)}{2}$, where n = life in years.

under the double-declining-balance convention. However, the amount of the depreciation expense declines year by year because the one-fifth fraction is applied each year to the current book value, a declining amount. For example, an asset with an initial cost of $8,000 and a useful life of 10 years would incur the following depreciation expenses for each of the first three years of its life, assuming double-declining-balance depreciation:

Year 1: $\frac{1}{5}$($8,000) = $1,600
Year 2: $\frac{1}{5}$($8,000 − $1,600) = $\frac{1}{5}$($6,400) = $1,280
Year 3: $\frac{1}{5}$($8,000 − $1,600 − $1,280) = $\frac{1}{5}$($5,120) = $1,024

Two additional refinements to this convention should be noted. The first is designed to cope with the fact that the unswerving application of the declining-balance convention would never permit an asset to be depreciated to zero. In the example above, depreciation in each of the remaining seven years of the asset's life would be:

Year 4: $\frac{1}{5}$($4096) = $819
Year 5: $\frac{1}{5}$($3277) = $655
Year 6: $\frac{1}{5}$($2622) = $524
Year 7: $\frac{1}{5}$($2098) = $420
Year 8: $\frac{1}{5}$($1678) = $336
Year 9: $\frac{1}{5}$($1342) = $268
Year 10: $\frac{1}{5}$($1074) = $215

and the remaining undepreciated balance at the end of 10 years (the end of the useful life of the asset) would be $859. This result is not satisfactory if the anticipated salvage value of the asset is zero. To correct this situation, accountants typically switch from the declining-balance convention to the straight-line method during that year when the straight-line method would result in greater depreciation expense. In the example above, note that after the fifth year of the asset's life its undepreciated balance (book value) is $2,622. If at this point the switch is made to the straight-line method and zero salvage value is assumed, this balance will be depreciated over the remaining five years of life, one-fifth each year. During the sixth year of the life of the asset, depreciation calculated under the straight-line method is exactly the same as under the double-declining-balance convention, $524. However, if the switch is made, depreciation expense will stay at the $524 level for the remainder of the asset's life rather than following the declining pattern shown above; the asset will then have no depreciable value remaining (zero book value) at the end of its life.

A second refinement is that under this declining-balance convention salvage values are ignored when determining depreciation expense. When the switch is made to the straight-line method, however, the asset is then

Exhibit 7-1
Illustration of Alternative Depreciation Methods

Initial Cost of Asset: $26,000 (includes freight and installation)
Useful Life: 10 years
Estimated Salvage Value: $2,000

	Year	Depreciation Calculation	Annual Depreciation Expense	End-of-Year Book Value
STRAIGHT-LINE	1	$\frac{1}{10}(26,000 - 2,000)$	$ 2,400	$23,600
DEPRECIATION	2	$\frac{1}{10}(26,000 - 2,000)$	$ 2,400	21,200
	3	$\frac{1}{10}(26,000 - 2,000)$	$ 2,400	18,800
	4	$\frac{1}{10}(26,000 - 2,000)$	$ 2,400	16,400
	5	$\frac{1}{10}(26,000 - 2,000)$	$ 2,400	14,000
	6	$\frac{1}{10}(26,000 - 2,000)$	$ 2,400	11,600
	7	$\frac{1}{10}(26,000 - 2,000)$	$ 2,400	9,200
	8	$\frac{1}{10}(26,000 - 2,000)$	$ 2,400	6,800
	9	$\frac{1}{10}(26,000 - 2,000)$	$ 2,400	4,400
	10	$\frac{1}{10}(26,000 - 2,000)$	$ 2,400	2,000
		Total	$24,000	
SUM-OF-YEARS'-DIGITS	1	$\frac{10}{55}(26,000 - 2,000)$	$ 4,364	$21,636
	2	$\frac{9}{55}(26,000 - 2,000)$	3,927	17,709
	3	$\frac{8}{55}(26,000 - 2,000)$	3,491	14,218
	4	$\frac{7}{55}(26,000 - 2,000)$	3,054	11,163
	5	$\frac{6}{55}(26,000 - 2,000)$	2,618	8,545
	6	$\frac{5}{55}(26,000 - 2,000)$	2,182	6,363
	7	$\frac{4}{55}(26,000 - 2,000)$	1,745	4,618
	8	$\frac{3}{55}(26,000 - 2,000)$	1,309	3,308
	9	$\frac{2}{55}(26,000 - 2,000)$	873	2,435
	10	$\frac{1}{55}(26,000 - 2,000)$	435	2,000
		Total	$24,000	
DOUBLE-DECLINING-	1	$\frac{2}{10}(26,000)$	$5,200	$20,800
BALANCE	2	$\frac{2}{10}(20,800)$	4,160	16,640
	3	$\frac{2}{10}(16,640)$	3,328	13,312
	4	$\frac{2}{10}(13,312)$	2,662	10,650
	5	$\frac{2}{10}(10,650)$	2,130	8,520
	6	$\frac{2}{10}(8,520)$	1,704	6,816
	7	$\frac{2}{10}(6,816)$	1,363	5,452
	8[1]	$\frac{1}{3}(5,452 - 2,000)$	1,151	4,301
	9	$\frac{1}{3}(5,452 - 2,000)$	1,151	3,150
	10	$\frac{1}{3}(5,452 - 2,000)$	1,150	2,000
		Total	$24,000	

[1] Change to straight-line method and depreciate to estimated salvage value over remaining life.

depreciated to its anticipated salvage value. This situation is illustrated in Exhibit 7-1, which compares straight-line and accelerated depreciation.

The double-declining-balance convention results in slightly more depreciation during the early years than the SOYD convention, but the extent of the difference depends upon the life of the asset and its salvage value, and (as indicated in Exhibit 7-1) the SOYD method may lead to higher depreciation after the first several years.

Example Exhibit 7-1 illustrates the straight-line depreciation method and the two common accelerated depreciation conventions for an asset having an initial cost of $26,000, a 10-year useful life, and an estimated salvage value at the end of its useful life of $2,000. Total depreciation over the life of the asset is, of course, the same under all three methods — $24,000, the difference between initial cost and estimated salvage value. Thus, once again the difference among the alternative accounting methods is in the *timing* of the recognition of expenses.

Note that midway through the life of the asset, its book value (initial cost less depreciation accumulated to date) under the straight-line method is $14,000, but under the accelerated methods its book value is only about 60% of that amount.

Allowance for Depreciation

Thus far we have focused on determining the amount of depreciation expense to be recognized each year throughout the life of an asset. We now need to consider the accounting entries to record the expense and the corresponding decline in the book value of the asset.

Depreciation is accumulated in a contra account (see Chapter 6 for a discussion of contra accounts) in order to preserve within the general ledger the information as to the initial cost of the asset. Thus, using the example illustrated in Exhibit 7-1, the accounting entry (in journal entry format) to record depreciation expense under the SOYD convention during the third year of the life of the asset is:

Dr.	Depreciation Expense	$3,491	
	Cr. Allowance for Depreciation		$3,491

After this entry is made, the general ledger balances with respect to this asset (in T-account format) are:

Fixed Asset		**Allowance for Depreciation**	
26,000			11,782

The balance in the Allowance account is equal to the sum of the depreciation expense in each of the first three years, and the difference between these account balances, $14,218, is the book value of the asset, as shown in Exhibit 7-1.

The contra account is typically labeled **Allowance for Depreciation.** It is sometimes incorrectly referred to as **Reserve for Depreciation.** It should be clear that the balance in this contra account is not a reserve in the sense of being a pool of cash available for the purchase of a replacement asset. The purpose of the contra account is simply to adjust (or offset) the corresponding asset valuation.

Note that the entry to record the depreciation expense and the corresponding increase in the allowance (contra) account is not triggered by a transaction. Rather, this entry is one of the series of adjusting or end-of-period entries that accountants must initiate (as discussed in the preceding chapter) in order to properly state profit for the accounting period and asset values at the end of the period.

Many accountants and business persons refer to depreciation expense as a source of cash. It is not. Cash is paid out when the asset is originally acquired. Depreciation is an expense but one which does not *consume* cash, a so-called **noncash charge** or expense. Profit earned by a company is a source of cash; that is, to the extent sales exceed expenses, cash is generated by the business, ignoring for the moment changes in the balances of accounts receivable, accounts payable, and other elements of working capital. However, cash generated by business operations is typically more than the operating profit. The cash flow from operations exceeds reported profit by the amount of noncash expenses. Total cash flow from operations, then, may be viewed as operating profit *plus* noncash expenses. In this sense only can depreciation be considered a source of cash.

Accounting for the Disposition of Fixed Assets

Our discussion thus far has assumed that the asset will be owned until the end of its estimated useful life, at which time it will be sold (or scrapped) for its estimated salvage value. It is, in fact, unlikely that the actual ownership of an asset will conform exactly to the estimates made of life and salvage value. We need, therefore, to consider the accounting entries to be made when the original life and salvage value assumptions do not work out precisely.

Sometimes an asset is owned for a period longer than its estimated life. When the asset has been fully depreciated—that is, when the allowance for depreciation is built up to the point that the asset's book value equals its estimated salvage value (or, if zero salvage value is assumed, until the allowance equals the initial cost)—no additional depreciation expense is recognized. The balances in both the asset account and the contra account simply remain unaltered so long as the company uses the asset.

Refer again to the example in Exhibit 7-1. If after 12 years the asset is finally retired at a salvage value of $2,000, the accounting entry at the time of retirement will be:

Dr.	Cash	$2,000	
Dr.	Allowance for Depreciation	24,000	
	Cr. Fixed Asset		$26,000

These entries in the fixed asset and contra accounts will exactly offset the initial cost and accumulated depreciation balances that were contained therein.

Frequently an asset is sold prior to the end of its estimated useful life. This sale may be occasioned by a change in the company's business that eliminates the need for the asset or by technological changes that cause the company to reequip with a more up-to-date asset. Assume, for example, that a cattle rancher owns a piece of ranching equipment with useful life and initial and salvage values conforming to the assumptions in Exhibit 7-1. Now, suppose that the rancher sells this equipment after six years. Sales of productive assets are fundamentally different from sales of the ranch's products. The cattle rancher is in the business of selling cattle, not in the business of buying and selling the trucks and other ranching equipment owned by the ranch. Thus, when the ranching equipment is sold by the rancher, the sale is viewed as an occasional sale, not in the normal course of business, and is not recorded in the same manner as a sale of cattle. Almost inevitably, the sale will occur at a price above or below the book value of the asset at the time of the sale; thus, typically the owner will recognize some gain (profit) or loss upon disposing of the asset.

GAIN (LOSS) ON DISPOSITION OF FIXED ASSETS

Assume that the equipment referred to in Exhibit 7-1 is sold after six years at a price of $8,000. Exhibit 7-1 indicates that the owner will record a loss on this sale, if the owner has been depreciating on a straight-line basis, but a gain if either of the accelerated depreciation conventions was used. The book values after six years are:

If depreciated straight-line	$11,600
If depreciated SOYD	6,363
If depreciated double-declining-balance	6,816

Any gain or loss on this sale is recorded in an account entitled Gain (or Loss) on Disposition of Fixed Assets. Assuming the straight-line depreciation method was used, the appropriate entries at the time of the sale, in journal entry format, are:

Dr.	Cash	$ 8,000	
Dr.	Allowance for Depreciation	14,400	
Dr.	Loss on Disposition of Fixed Asset	3,600	
	Cr. Fixed Asset		$26,000
	Total	$26,000	$26,000

If the double-declining-balance depreciation convention had been used, the entry at the time of the sale would have been:

Dr.	Cash	$ 8,000	
Dr.	Allowance for Depreciation	19,184	
	Cr. Gain on Disposition of Fixed Asset		$1,184
	Cr. Fixed Asset		26,000
	Total	$27,184	$27,184

Note that no entry was made in either the Sales or the Cost of Goods Sold accounts. Gain (or loss) on disposition of fixed assets is considered a nonoperating revenue or expense, and accordingly is typically shown below the operating profit line on the company's income statement.

TRADE-IN

The accounting entries to reflect the sale of an asset for cash are relatively straightforward. Complications arise when the disposition is part of a barter transaction, since evidence about true value may be difficult to obtain. This dilemma occurs frequently when one asset is traded in on another— that is, when part of the payment for the new asset is the transfer of ownership of the old asset to the seller of the new asset.

Suppose that a restaurant trades in a piece of equipment having an initial cost of $13,000 and a current book value of $5,000 on a new piece of restaurant equipment having a list price of $21,000. After much negotiation, the equipment dealer agrees to accept the restaurant's old equipment plus $14,000 in cash for the new piece of equipment. Apparently the equipment dealer is ascribing a value of $7,000 to this trade-in, the difference between the list price of the new equipment and the cash balance to be paid by the restaurant. If so, the restaurant has realized a $2,000 gain on the disposition of the old asset, as the book value of this asset is only $5,000. The restaurant's accounting entries to record this entire transaction would then be:

Dr.	Fixed Asset (new equipment)	$21,000	
Dr.	Allowance for Depreciation		
	(old equipment)	8,000	
Cr.	Fixed Asset (old equipment)		$13,000
Cr.	Gain on Disposition of Fixed Assets		2,000
Cr.	Cash		14,000
	Total	$29,000	$29,000

Now assume further that in the absence of an old piece of equipment to trade in, the restaurant could have negotiated with the dealer for a discount off the $21,000 list price. If so, there is some question whether the equipment dealer really was ascribing a value of $7,000 to the trade-in or whether the $7,000 difference between the list price and cash to be paid was the sum of a price discount and the value of the trade-in. The accountant for the restaurant may have a difficult time making the separation, but some estimate will be necessary to properly record this transaction. Assume, finally, that the restaurant believes that the dealer would have accepted $19,500 in cash and no trade-in. We now have evidence that the dealer actually valued the trade-in at only $5,500, and the restaurant realized a correspondingly smaller gain on the trade-in of the old equipment. All of these assumptions lead to the following entries:

Dr.	Fixed Asset (new equipment)	$19,500	
Dr.	Allowance for Depreciation		
	(old equipment)	8,000	
Cr.	Fixed Asset (old equipment)		$13,000
Cr.	Gain on Disposition of Fixed Assets		500
Cr.	Cash		14,000
	Total	$27,500	$27,500

Note that the new equipment is recorded at its equivalent cash purchase price, which is somewhat less than its list price. The gain on disposition is now substantially lower. Recall the admonition of accountants to be conservative—that is, to choose among possible accounting entries so as to state conservatively the value of assets and of profits. Conservatism is better served by the second set of entries than the first. Here again the accountant is called upon to exercise judgment in assigning values to assets.

TIMING IN THE RECOGNITION OF A LOSS

When an asset is no longer useful to its owner, the value of the asset on the owner's books should be adjusted accordingly. Suppose, for example, that in 19X4 the Camus Company purchased computer card punch equipment at an initial cost of $85,000, and that it has been depreciating this equipment over a 10-year estimated useful life. If, five years later, in 19X9, Camus replaces its computer system so that card input is no longer used, the card punch equipment is no longer useful to Camus. Camus' management, after determining that only a very nominal amount could be obtained by the sale of this now-obsolete equipment, may decide to retain the equipment in storage. Without debating the wisdom of this decision, we need to consider what accounting entry, if any, should now be made. It is not appropriate to continue to depreciate this equipment in the normal fashion, as the card punch equipment is no longer productive. With respect to these particular assets, the going-concern assumption no longer applies. If the accountant ascertains that the equipment has no market value (or scrap value), the remaining book value of this equipment should be written off— that is, expensed. This expense should be recognized at the time the computer system is revamped, for it was that event that rendered the punch card equipment valueless to Camus.

Income Tax Considerations

Tax laws in the United States contain many provisions having to do with fixed assets. Thus, tax considerations are important to management in the decisions regarding the acquisition, depreciation, and disposition of fixed assets. In fact, certain tax laws are designed to spur investment in fixed assets by providing tax incentives. While it is important to understand these considerations, it is also important to recognize that the tax laws should not be permitted to establish accounting policy for a company.

Tax laws are enacted for the purpose of generating tax revenue in a manner consistent with government economic policy. They are not meant to dictate to companies how they should account for fixed assets, and certain provisions of the tax laws may be inconsistent with sound accounting practice.

As a result, the way in which we account for fixed assets for the purposes of reporting company performance to shareholders and creditors (financial accounting) may be quite different from that which is reflected in the company's income tax returns (tax accounting). Most companies end up maintaining two sets of books—appropriately, legally, and openly. The reconciliation of these two sets of books is discussed in Appendix A of this chapter.

Recall the objective of depreciation accounting: to allocate in a rational, systematic, and equitable manner the difference between initial cost and estimated salvage value over the life of the asset. The company's objective when determining the depreciation expense deduction on its income tax returns is quite different: it is to minimize taxes and postpone the payment of taxes as long as possible. Every taxpayer is expected to make use of the opportunities presented by the tax laws to minimize income tax payments. The same can be said for every corporation. To do otherwise is both foolish and inconsistent with management's obligations to corporate shareholders. Further, because money has a time value (as discussed at length in Chapter 2), taxpayers seek to postpone the payment of taxes as long as possible in order that they can have the use of the money during the period of postponement.

Therefore, when determining its taxable income, a company will typically seek to accelerate depreciation to the extent possible, thereby decreasing its taxable income (by increasing expenses) and decreasing its tax liability. Remember that depreciation expense is a noncash expense; therefore, an increase in depreciation expense has no cash cost and in fact produces a cash savings by reducing income taxes. Thus, accountants speak of depreciation offering a **tax shield**—higher depreciation expenses shield more of the corporation's earnings from taxation. Furthermore, a company will have an incentive to minimize gains (which are taxable) on the disposition of fixed assets and maximize losses (which are tax deductible) on disposition.

Understandably, therefore, the income-tax laws and regulations in this country are filled with provisions that determine both the extent to which depreciation can be used as a tax shield and how fixed assets are to be accounted for at acquisition and at disposition.

INCOME-TAX LAWS

The tax laws as they relate to fixed-asset accounting are much too complex to discuss in detail. Our purpose here is simply to indicate the general types of provisions that one can expect to encounter.

First, the law requires that assets which meet certain tests be capitalized and not expensed—that is, treated as fixed assets. The law requires that freight, installation, and similar expenditures also be capitalized. Inevitably, gray areas exist where taxing authorities may argue for capitalization while management will argue that the expenditure should be deductible immediately as an expense of the current period.

Second, the law establishes certain guidelines as to the useful lives over which various classes of assets should be depreciated. While management has an incentive to use as short a depreciable life as possible in order to maximize the depreciation tax shield in the early years of the asset's life, the tax authorities will expect a careful justification of the use of a life shorter than that established in the guidelines contained in the tax regulations.

The United States tax laws spell out in detail the maximum rate at which assets can be depreciated. Sum-of-the-years'-digits and declining-balance (at twice the straight-line rate) conventions are specifically permitted for most new assets, except real estate. Any depreciation method that results in a slower rate of depreciation than these two conventions yield will not be challenged by the tax authorities; conventions that result in more rapid depreciation probably will be challenged.

In certain situations a gain recognized on the sale of a fixed asset will be treated as ordinary income and taxed accordingly. In other situations the gain will be treated as a so-called **capital gain.** Capital gains are also taxed, but at a lower rate. Losses on disposition may also be treated differently under varying circumstances.

The specific provisions regarding these matters as they apply to a broad range of new and used assets in various industries and under alternative circumstances fill many volumes. It is critical that management obtain sound tax advice regarding these issues.

INVESTMENT TAX CREDIT

One set of provisions of the U.S. income-tax laws that has been prominent in recent years relates to what is referred to as the **investment tax credit** on fixed assets. These provisions permit the firm that acquires certain productive fixed assets to deduct from its tax liability a percentage of the initial cost. For example, an industrial firm acquiring a new machine tool at an initial cost of $15,000 and entitled under the particular circumstances to a 10% investment tax credit can reduce its income tax liability by $1,500 (10% of $15,000) in the year in which the asset is acquired. Note that the $1,500 does not simply reduce taxable income as $1,500 of depreciation expense would; rather, it is a direct reduction of taxes and is therefore much more valuable to the firm.

Investment tax credits do not affect future depreciation expenses for the asset. In the example above, the industrial firm will be able to depreciate over the life of the asset the full difference between the $15,000 acquisition cost and the estimated salvage value of the machine tool, in addition to availing itself of the one-time investment credit at the time of acquisition.

Investment tax credits have been enacted by the Congress to provide an incentive to invest in productive assets. Presumably, legislators feel that a higher level of expenditure on productive assets is in the national interest to stimulate the U.S. economy and to make U.S. industry more competitive in world markets.

LIMITATIONS ON DEDUCTIONS AND TAX CREDITS

Tax laws and regulations are replete with provisions that limit the total amount of deductible expenses and tax credits available to a taxpayer, whether the taxpayer is an individual, a partnership, or a corporation.

Certain alternate taxes may be imposed upon a taxpayer that will mitigate the apparent benefits to be derived from investment tax credits, rapid depreciation, capital gains upon disposition, and so forth. Careful tax planning is required to be certain that anticipated tax savings are in fact realized.

One further limitation should be kept in mind. Tax shields and tax credits are of no value to a taxpayer who, in the absence of shields or credits, would not be required to pay tax. Thus, accelerated depreciation may be of no benefit to an unprofitable corporation. If the company has no taxable income, accounting procedures that serve to increase the company's loss will provide no cash benefit to the corporation.[5] The point is that a tax deduction or tax credit is only of value to the taxpayer if and when the deduction or credit can serve to reduce actual cash tax payments.

Summary

While the time-adjusted and market value methods of asset valuation account routinely for the decline in value of a fixed asset over the life of that asset, the historical cost method of valuation requires that the accountant utilize some arbitrary but systematic procedure to allocate over the asset's life the difference between the initial cost of the asset and its estimated salvage value. Depreciation accounting does not attempt to reflect in the accounting records the market values of assets, but seeks simply to make rational, systematic, and equitable allocations of the costs of owning the fixed assets.

Depreciation accounting requires the determination of (1) initial cost, (2) estimated useful life, (3) estimated salvage value at the end of the useful life, and (4) the depreciation (or allocation) method. Difficulties are encountered in each of these determinations. Three alternative methods of depreciation are straight-line, accelerated, and units-of-production. The most common conventions for accelerating depreciation expenses are sum-of-the-years'-digits and declining-balance. Depreciation is accumulated in a contra account so as to preserve in the accounting records information on the initial cost of the asset.

At the time of disposition of an asset, any difference between the amount realized in the sale or scrapping of the asset and the asset's book value (initial cost less accumulated depreciation) is recorded as other income

---

[5] The U.S. tax law does permit most taxpayers to "carry back" and "carry forward" any taxable losses. For example, if a company incurred a $1 million pretax loss in 19X7 after several years of large pretax profits, the company could carry back the $1 million current loss and apply for a refund of some income taxes paid previously. If pretax profits over the past several years had not totaled $1 million, the company could then carry forward the loss and apply it against future years' profits in order to reduce income tax payments in those future years. The law limits the number of years of carry-back and carry-forward available to the taxpayer.

and expense typically in an account entitled Gain (or Loss) on Disposition of Fixed Assets.

Because depreciation expense is a noncash expense but a deductible expense for income tax purposes (that is, a tax shield), a taxpayer will seek to maximize depreciation for tax purposes while the taxing authorities will seek to limit the use of this tax shield. As a result, tax laws in the United States are replete with provisions regarding the capitalization, depreciation, and disposition of fixed assets.

Appendix A: Deferred Income Taxes

Chapter 7 discusses the likelihood that many corporations will use one depreciation method in financial accounting and another in tax accounting. These different methods result in timing differences in the recognition of expenses. These timing differences give rise to so-called **deferred income taxes,** as described below and illustrated in Exhibits 7A-1 and 7A-2.

Suppose that the Markel Company starts operations on January 1, 19X3, purchasing fixed assets on that date in the amount of $100,000. Assume further that these assets have a five-year life and zero salvage value. Markel elects to use straight-line depreciation for financial accounting purposes, and sum-of-the-years'-digits depreciation for purposes of determining taxable income. Finally, assume that Markel records $700,000 of revenue for the year 19X3, earns $90,000 in profit before depreciation and before income taxes, and will be subjected to a 40% income tax rate.

Exhibit 7A-1 indicates that pretax profit will be $70,000 when straight-line depreciation is used (financial accounting) and $56,667 if SOYD depre-

Exhibit 7A-1
Effect of Depreciation Method on Pretax Profit
MARKEL COMPANY

	Financial Accounting (Straight-line Depreciation)	Tax Accounting (SOYD Depreciation)
Revenue	$700,000	$700,000
Operating Profit before depreciation and income taxes	90,000	90,000
less: depreciation expense[1]	20,000	33,333[2]
Taxable Income	$ 70,000	$ 56,667

[1] Assumes $100,000 of fixed assets, acquired on January 1, 19X3, with an estimated useful life of five years and zero salvage value.

[2] $\frac{5}{15}$($100,000) = $33,333.

ciation is used (tax accounting). Now the accountant is faced with a dilemma: What is the appropriate income tax expense to record for financial accounting? Markel's actual cash tax payment with respect to 19X3 operations will be $22,667 (40% of $56,667). Yet the accountant knows that, to the extent higher depreciation is recorded early in the life of the assets, lower depreciation will be recorded later in the assets' lives; accordingly, to the extent Markel's tax liability is less in 19X3 when the assets are new, it will be more later (assuming no additional assets are acquired). Over the life of the assets, $100,000 in depreciation expenses will be recorded; the difference between the two depreciation methods is simply timing—timing in reference to expenses and timing in reference to cash tax payments.

If the $22,667 tax expense is used for financial accounting, after-tax net income will be recorded at $47,333 ($70,000 less $22,667). The *apparent* tax rate on the $70,000 of pretax income is about 35% ($22,667 ÷ $70,000) rather than the 40% provided by law. Late in the life of the asset, actual cash tax payments will be higher, and the apparent tax rate will exceed the 40% provided by law.

There is no doubt that Markel is well-advised to use accelerated depreciation for tax purposes. If it does, it will pay only $22,667 in taxes in 19X3, rather than the $28,000 (40% of $70,000) that it would have to pay if it used straight-line depreciation for tax purposes. It is to Markel's advantage to pay the lower taxes now, even though it will have to pay correspondingly higher taxes in the future (i.e., late in the life of the assets).

Thus, the question is not whether Markel should use SOYD depreciation in figuring its tax liability; the question is how income taxes should be handled for financial accounting purposes. The proper (and conservative) method is to record a tax liability of greater than $22,667 for the current year, 19X3; however, that portion of the tax liability in excess of $22,667 is recorded as a liability that is not currently payable. Applying the legal tax rate, 40%, to the pretax profit calculated assuming straight-line depreciation results in a tax expense provision of $28,000; of that amount $22,667 should be shown as a current liability of Markel, and the balance, $5,333, should be shown as a deferred income tax payable. Exhibit 7A-2 shows the effect of this accounting treatment on Markel's balance sheet at December 31, 19X3.

If Markel grows and periodically adds to its stock of fixed assets, it can be shown that the amount of deferred income taxes will continue to grow. Thus, many growing companies view deferred income taxes as permanently deferred. On the other hand, if we make the somewhat unreasonable assumption that Markel buys no new fixed assets in the years 19X4 through 19X7 and that its revenues and expenses remain at their 19X3 level, Markel's cash tax liability for 19X6 and 19X7 will be greater than the tax expense shown on the company's financial statements (statements that utilize straight-line depreciation). Thus, the Deferred Income Tax account

Exhibit 7A-2
Illustration of Differences between Tax and Financial Accounting
MARKEL COMPANY

	Tax Accounting, 19X3
Taxable Income	$56,667
Tax Expense	22,667

		Financial Accounting, 19X3
Taxable Income		$70,000
Income Taxes		
Currently Payable	$22,667	
Deferred	5,333	28,000
Net Income		$42,000

Balance Sheet at December 31, 19X3

Current Assets	XXXX	Current Liabilities	
Noncurrent Assets	XXXX	Income Tax Payable	$22,667
Total Assets	XXXX	All other current liabilities	XXXX
		Total Current Liabilities	XXXX
		Deferred Income Taxes	5,333
		Owners' Equity	XXXX
		Total Liabilities and Owners' Equity	XXXX

Exhibit 7A-3
Changes in Deferred Income Tax Account
MARKEL COMPANY

	19X3	19X4	19X5	19X6	19X7
Tax Accounting					
Profit before depreciation and income taxes	$90,000	$90,000	$90,000	$90,000	$90,000
less: depreciation expense (SOYD)	33,333	26,667	20,000	13,333	6,667
Taxable income	56,667	63,333	70,000	76,667	83,333
Tax expense (40% rate)	$22,667	$25,333	$28,000	$30,667	$33,333
Financial Accounting					
Profit before depreciation and income taxes	$90,000	$90,000	$90,000	$90,000	$90,000
less: depreciation expense (straight-line)	20,000	20,000	20,000	20,000	20,000
Profit before income taxes	70,000	70,000	70,000	70,000	70,000
Income taxes—current	22,667	25,333	28,000	30,667	33,333
—deferred	5,333	2,667	0	(2,667)	(5,333)
Net income	$42,000	$42,000	$42,000	$42,000	$42,000
Year-end balance of deferred income taxes	$ 5,333	$ 8,000	$ 8,000	$ 5,333	0

will build during the early years and decline late in the life of the assets, as shown in Exhibit 7A-3.

In some circumstances, the opposite effect to the one illustrated in this appendix occurs: expenses recognized for financial accounting in one period cannot be deducted for income tax purposes until a subsequent period. This situation is handled by the use of a Prepaid Income Tax account (an asset) rather than a Deferred Income Tax account (a liability). As an example, warranty expenses are typically not allowable deductions for income tax purposes until the warranty repairs are actually performed. If a company accrues an Allowance for Warranty, as described in Chapter 6, a timing difference will occur between warranty expenses for financial accounting and warranty expenses for tax accounting.

In summary, when different accounting policies are employed for financial accounting and for tax accounting, timing differences in income tax expenses will typically result. These timing differences are recognized by increases and decreases in the Deferred or Prepaid Income Tax accounts.

New Terms

Accelerated depreciation   Methods of depreciation that result in greater depreciation expenses in the early years of the asset's useful life and lower depreciation expenses in later years. The two common methods of accelerated depreciation are *declining-balance* and *sum-of-the-years'-digits*.

Allowance for depreciation   The contra account to fixed assets, which reflects the cumulative depreciation of the assets during their lives.

Capital gain   The difference between the cost of an asset (or, in certain circumstances, its book value) and the appreciated value received for the asset at the time of its sale. Capital gains are subject to different taxation than ordinary, or earned, income.

Capitalization (capitalize)   The accounting process by which an expenditure is recorded as an asset (to be subsequently depreciated or amortized) rather than as an expense.

Declining-balance   A method of accelerated depreciation that results in a depreciation expense equal to a specified fraction of the book value (initial cost less accumulated depreciation to date) of the asset, an amount which declines each year.

Deferred income taxes   An income tax liability that is not currently payable and typically results from differences in accounting procedures for determining income for financial accounting and for tax accounting.

Depreciation accounting   The rational, equitable, and systematic allocation over the years an asset is owned of the difference between the asset's cost of acquisition and its estimated salvage value.

Initial cost   An amount that includes the purchase price of the asset and all ancillary costs required to get the asset into a position and condition where it is productive.

Investment tax credit   A provision of the U.S. tax law that permits the acquirer of certain fixed assets to reduce its income-tax expense by a specified percentage of the initial cost of the assets.

Leasehold improvements   Those fixed assets that arise when a lessee invests in lighting, partitions, or other building improvements within a facility (typically a building) that is leased and not owned.   These improvements are owned by the lessee and not the lessor.

Noncash charge (or noncash expense)   An expense, such as depreciation or amortization, that is not accompanied by an expenditure of cash.

Reserve for depreciation   An alternative, but somewhat inappropriate, name for *Allowance for Depreciation,* a contra account to fixed assets.

Salvage value   The value of an asset at the end of its useful life, which is determined by the amount received by the present owner from the sale of the asset to a subsequent owner or from scrapping the asset.

Straight-line depreciation   A method of depreciation that results in equal depreciation expense in each accounting period of the asset's useful life.

Sum-of-the-years'-digits (SOYD)   A method of accelerated depreciation that results in depreciation expense equal to a fraction of the difference between initial cost and estimated salvage value, where the numerator of the fraction is the remaining life of the asset and the denominator is the sum of all of the digits representing the years of useful life of the asset.

Tax shield   A noncash expense (or charge) that is deductible for income-tax purposes.   Such an expense does not consume cash but rather, because it is deductible, reduces cash outlays for income taxes.

Units-of-production depreciation   Methods of depreciation that result in depreciation expense being a function of usage of the asset during the particular accounting period.

Useful life   The period of time during which an asset is useful to and used by its present owner; useful life is often only a portion of the total life of the asset.

Problems

1   Discuss the following statement: "The purpose of charging depreciation on a fixed asset each year is to reflect in the accounting records the approximate decline in the market value of the asset as it grows older."

2   What effect does the choice of depreciation method have on the income tax liability of the company?

3   In order to calculate the depreciation expense for a certain period on a particular asset, what factors must be determined or estimated, in addition to the depreciation method?

4   Discuss the difference between the total life of an asset and its useful life. Which life is longer?

5   Which method(s) of depreciation do you feel is (are) most consistent with the accounting concept that demands conservatism?

6   Record in T-account format for Tamm Corporation the following transaction: The Tamm Corporation sold a piece of production equipment that it has used for three years to the Merrill Company. Merrill has agreed to pay Tamm $800 next month and $800 at the end of six months. Tamm will incur a $150 expenditure in removing the equipment from its plant. The original price of the equipment was $5,000 and it has been depreciated on the sum-of-the-years'-digits method, assuming a five-year useful life and $500 salvage value.

7 If, in the second year of the life of an asset, the depreciation charge on the asset is $800, what method of depreciation is being used, assuming the asset had an original cost of $4,000, an estimated life of five years, and an estimated salvage value of $1,000?

8 Calculate the depreciation during the second year on a computer that was purchased for $10,000 and is being depreciated by the double-declining-balance method over a life of five years, assuming that the owner anticipates that he will be able to sell the computer at the end of five years for $2,000.

9 A certain machine acquired on January 1, 19X8 by Castle Construction Company has a first cost of $150,000, an estimated life of 15 years, and an estimated salvage value of $30,000. Compute the depreciation charges for each of the first two years of life by:

  a The sum-of-the-years'-digits method
  b The double-declining-balance method
  c The straight-line method
  d The units-of-production method, assuming the machine has a life equivalent to 20,000 hours of use and the machine was used for 2500 hours during 19X8 and 2200 hours during 19X9

10 Record in T-account format the following transaction: the Mitchell Company purchased a large punch press for $4,500, payable in 30 days. The company paid $400 in cash to the trucking company for delivery of the press and $600 in cash to riggers and electricians for installation of the equipment.

11 The following transactions and events occurred at the Walden Foundry Corporation in July 19X8. During this month Walden moved from its old facility to a new plant that was constructed to the company's specifications on a site owned by the company. The move also signaled a substantial increase in capacity for Walden. Prepare T-account entries to record the events and transactions.

  a The old facility was sold for $98,000. The land on which the old facility was located had been purchased many years before at a cost of $10,000. The building had an original cost of $40,000, and depreciation in the amount of $23,000 had been accumulated against the building. The purchaser of the old facility gave Walden $78,000 in cash and a second mortgage note on the facility in the amount of $20,000.

  b Certain equipment used in the old facility but not appropriate for the new facility was sold for $18,000 in cash. This equipment appeared on the company's records at an original cost of $35,000 less accumulated depreciation of $16,000.

  c A new furnace was purchased for the newly constructed plant at a cost of $45,000. Walden paid freight expense of $3,000 and installation expense of $8,000. All payments were in cash.

  d A forklift truck that had been owned by the company for three years was sent out for a major overhaul. The forklift had an original cost of $4,000; it had been depreciated on a straight-line basis for three years, assuming a four-year life and a 20% salvage value. The overhaul, which cost $1,500 (paid in cash), was expected to extend the life of the forklift for an additional two years.

e Because the configuration of the new plant was different from that of the old facility, the company's material-handling equipment had to be modified and portions had to be replaced. Certain conveying equipment that originally had been purchased for $2,500 and had accumulated depreciation of $1,200 had been traded in on other new conveying equipment. The vendor of the conveying equipment allowed Walden a trade-in value on the old equipment of $1,500 against the $8,500 purchase price of the new equipment. Walden's plant engineer estimated that the old equipment could have been sold to a secondhand dealer or another industrial concern for about $1,000. Record both the purchase of the new equipment (payment due in 30 days) and disposition of the old equipment.

f The installation of the conveying equipment was accomplished by Walden's own work force. A total of 100 hours was accumulated by the work force against this task. These workers earned an hourly wage of $5.50; normal fringe benefits, including payroll taxes and group insurance, totaled another $1.50 per hour. Typically the time of these same workers was charged to customers at the rate of $11.00 per hour.

g The landscape contractor with whom Walden contracted for landscaping the new facility at a fixed price of $5,000 offered to accept only $4,500 for the work if Walden agreed to pay at the completion of the work rather than 60 days following completion, as had been specified in the contract. Walden accepted this offer and made the $4,500 cash payments.

h A large grinder installed at the old facility could not be used in the new plant, and Walden sold the grinder for $2,500 in cash, under the condition that Walden deliver the grinder to the purchaser. The grinder, which the company had purchased many years ago for $3,000, was fully depreciated with no allowance for salvage value. Walden paid $200 in cash for removal of the grinder from the old plant and $300 for transport to the purchaser's plant.

i Costs of the new facility were the following: land, $34,000; improvements to the land, including drainage and sewers, as required by the city ordinances, $7,000; building, $158,000; building improvements, including air conditioning, some movable partitions, and electrical bus ducts, $23,000. The entire project (cost totaled $222,000) was financed with a $175,000 first mortgage, and the balance of $47,000 was paid in cash by Walden.

12 Refer to question 11*d* above. Calculate the depreciation for the fourth year of the life of the forklift, assuming that its estimated salvage value at the end of its extended life will be $500.

13 Refer again to Walden's move as discussed in question 11 above. The actual move from the old to the new facility took four working days and required the effort of Walden's work force as well as the services of a rigging company hired by Walden. Walden paid the rigging company a total of $8,000; the work force spent a total of 300 hours on the move. Hourly rates applicable to this work force are detailed in question 11*f* above. How would you account for this move? What alternative do you see to accounting for the move as simply an expense?

14 Refer to question 11*i* above. Calculate the depreciation expense for the first two years on Walden's new building facility assuming that the building itself will have a 40-year life with 20% salvage value and the building improvements will have a 15-year life with no salvage value. Make your calculations for both straight-line depreciation and double-declining-balance depreciation. Which of these depreciation methods would you recommend to Walden? What factors would you suggest Walden consider in choosing a depreciation method?

PROBLEMS FOR APPENDIX A

15 Assume that in 19X5 the Wagner Corporation had gross revenues of $50 million, all in cash, and that cash outlays for operating expenses (excluding income taxes) totaled $32 million. (The foregoing cash outlays do not include depreciation, a noncash expense.) Depreciation would be $8 million calculated by the sum-of-the-years'-digits method and $5 million calculated by the straight-line method. A 50% income tax rate applies to all taxable income. Compute the 19X5 profit and cash flow after income taxes under each of the following assumptions:

a Straight-line method of depreciation used for both financial and tax accounting

b Sum-of-the-years'-digits method of depreciation used for both financial and tax accounting

c Straight-line method of depreciation used for financial accounting purposes and sum-of-the-years'-digits method for tax accounting, with an allowance in the accounting records for deferred taxes

16 The Prestige Corporation uses straight-line depreciation for financial accounting and sum-of-the-years'-digits depreciation for tax accounting. If the corporation acquires machinery having an original cost of $40,000, an eight-year life, and a 10% salvage value, what will be the balance in the deferred income tax account attributable to this asset after two years? Assume Prestige's incremental tax rate is 35%.

17 A company determines that its income tax expense for financial accounting is $115,000, but its immediate tax liability as revealed on its tax return is $105,000. Record in general journal format the adjusting entry that should be made at year-end to record income taxes.

18 Refer to question 8 above. If the company used straight-line depreciation for financial accounting and double-declining-balance depreciation for tax accounting, how much would its reported earnings be increased, assuming the company's incremental tax rate is 40%?

P| ATTON CORPORATION

Louise Kaplan reviewed the trial balance at March 31, 19X3, and was encouraged with what she saw. Earlier in the week she had expressed to Ed Marchik, the firm's accountant, her eagerness to "get a handle" on the company's first-quarter profitability just as soon as she could. Louise and her father, Morris Kaplan, had purchased the Patton Corporation late in 19X1 from the Patton family. The two owners were generally pleased with, but also apprehensive about, their progress in improving the firm's profitability.

COMPANY BACKGROUND

The Patton Corporation had been founded in the late 1940s by Julius Patton and operated by him until his death in early 19X1. The company had always been in the soils engineering business, although its mix of customers had evolved significantly over the years. At the time that the Kaplans bought the company its business was concentrated in soils-engineering work in connection with commercial and industrial construction projects in the three-county area around Harrisburg. Clients included present owners of real estate, prospective developers of commercial and industrial property, architectural and engineering firms, and construction companies. Timely response to client requests for soil studies was important in the business, as of course were the accuracy and dependability of Patton's studies. Patton's business had deteriorated in the last several years of Mr. Patton's life. Nevertheless, at the time the Kaplans purchased the business its reputation was still quite strong. Indeed, one of the major assets that the Kaplans purchased was Mr. Patton's customer list indicating the nature and extent of work done for each, the key contact person in each client organization, and background information on each client.

The Kaplans purchased the company for $50,000 and took control on January 1, 19X2. The purchase price was paid to Patton's estate: $20,000 in cash (from the Kaplans's savings) and a $30,000 note payable from the company to the estate. The $30,000 note was due in six equal annual installments beginning in 19X4; interest at the rate of 10% per year on the outstanding balance was due at the end of each year. During the early months of 19X2 the company had to borrow $20,000 on a short-term note from the Harrisburg National Bank; this loan had since grown to $23,000.

The Kaplans were putting great emphasis on improving the firm's reputation for high quality and rapid service. The company's profitability in 19X2 had been satisfactory but not up to the owners' original expectations. Louise had budgeted for a substantial increase in profitability in 19X3.

FIRST-QUARTER OPERATIONS

Louise and her father paid particular attention to quarterly financial results. While certain data regarding revenues and selected expense categories were developed and reviewed carefully each month, Ed Marchik had been instructed to place primary emphasis on an accurate determination of profit for each calendar quarter. In early April 19X3, Ed worked long hours to complete the recording of all transactions for the preceding month and to transfer data from the journals to the general ledger. He had just completed the preliminary trial balance shown on the attached worksheet when Louise entered his office. Seeing the worksheet on his desk, Louise said, "Great, Ed, I see you've finished the accounting for our first quarter. How did we do?"

Ed replied that it was too early to tell. "Until I've had a chance to develop and record the quarter-end adjusting entries, we won't really know."

Looking over Ed's shoulder, Louise reviewed the trial balance and commented, "But revenues and the major expenses are shown right there. Revenues were over $175,000—a heck of an improvement over last year. And total project labor was less than $60,000. If we just add up all the expenses on what you call your preliminary trial balance, we ought to be able to determine our profit. It looks good to me."

"Now don't jump to conclusions, Louise," said Ed. "Some of those expenses are understated — for example you can see that we haven't recorded any depreciation expense yet — and some other expenses may be overstated. Give me a little more time and I'll develop a reliable income statement for the first quarter and a balance sheet at March 31 for you."

"What do you have left to do?" asked Louise. "We need to know."

Ed was beginning to get impatient with Louise, just as Louise was impatient at the delay in receiving the financial statements. He explained that at the end of each accounting period — in Patton's case, at the end of each quarter — an accountant developed and recorded certain standard journal entries relating to recurring adjustments of prepaids and accruals. The accountant also carefully reviewed each of the general ledger accounts to see if perhaps other nonrecurring adjustments needed to be made in order to portray accurately the financial performance for the period (the income statement) and the financial position at the end of the period (the balance sheet).

Louise thought to herself that perhaps Ed was being unduly cautious and conservative in making these adjusting entries. While she was anxious that the financial statements be correct, she was also anxious to prove to herself, the rest of the family, and the loan officer at the Harrisburg National Bank that the company was making progress in improving profitability. She said, "Would you mind ex-

PATTON CORPORATION
Trial Balance Worksheet
March 31, 19X3

Account	Account Name	Preliminary Trial Balance		Adjustments		Adjusted Trial Balance	
		Dr.	Cr.	Dr.	Cr.	Dr.	Cr.
1010	Cash	$ 10,600					
1020	Accounts Receivable	81,500					
1021	Allowance for Doubtful Accounts		$ 1,600				
1025	Travel Advances—Employees	2,200					
1030	Supplies Inventory	7,700					
1040	Prepaid Expenses	2,000					
1051	Equipment—Office	13,500					
1052	Equipment—Field	28,100					
1059	Accumulated Depreciation—All Equipment		8,300				
1061	Intangible Assets	3,600					
1062	Accumulated Amortization—Intangibles		1,200				
1501	Accounts Payable—Trade		10,200				
1511	Bank Loans—Short-Term		23,000				
1521	Interest Payable		500				
1523	Accrued Wages and Salaries Payable		15,800				
1525	Accrued Bonuses Payable		—				
1531	Customer Advance Payments		3,000				
1533	Deferred Income		2,000				
1541	Miscellaneous Accrual		8,300				
1561	Dividends Payable		—				
1571	Notes Payable—Long-Term		30,000				
1591	Capital Stock		20,000				
1595	Retained Earnings		4,700				

Account	Description	Debit/Amount	Credit/Amount
2010	Revenue—Engineering Projects		175,200
2020	Other Revenue		—
2101	Project Labor—Professional	41,700	
2111	Project Labor—Staff	15,900	
2120	Supplies—Project	6,100	
2130	Subcontract Expense—Project	12,300	
2201	Professional Salaries—Nonproject	32,000	
2211	Other Salaries and Wages—Nonproject	16,700	
2221	Office Supplies Expense	2,000	
2231	Depreciation Expense—Office Equipment	—	
2232	Depreciation Expense—Field Equipment	—	
2241	Advertising and Promotion Expense	8,900	
2242	Dues and Subscriptions Expense	1,400	
2244	Rent Expense	3,900	
2245	Occupancy Expense (utilities, insurance, etc.)	2,800	
2246	Staff Training Expense	3,500	
2247	Vehicle Operating Expense	2,000	
2248	Telephone Expense	1,600	
2249	Travel Expenses	3,700	
2250	Bonus Expenses	—	
2251	Miscellaneous Income		700
2253	Interest Expense	800	
2255	Bad-Debt Expense	—	
2257	Amortization Expense	—	
	Totals	$304,500	$304,500

plaining these adjustments to me, Ed?   I really need a better understanding of our financial statements in order to be able to answer the
bank's questions."

Ed replied that not only would he be pleased to explain his reasoning behind the various adjusting entries, but in addition he could
benefit from a dialogue with Louise.   "When I develop these adjusting entries, I really need to know the firm's plans, problems, and commitments as seen by top management," said Ed.   "While financial
statements are historical documents, the values we assign to certain
assets and liabilities are going to be substantially influenced by the
company's future plans."

RECURRING ADJUSTMENTS

"Let's begin with that list of adjusting entries that we make every
quarter," said Ed.   "The format of the first several adjusting journal
entries each quarter is exactly the same.   This procedure assures us
that we won't overlook any of these important adjustments."

Ed explained to Louise each of the following seven recurring (or
routine) adjusting entries:

1   A portion of the acquisition cost of the firm's long-term assets
    (principally equipment and vehicles) was assigned to each ac-
    counting period.   This allocation of original cost was referred to
    as *depreciation* and was accumulated in a contra account enti-
    tled Accumulated Depreciation.   Depreciation of the office
    equipment for the first quarter of 19X3 was $600 and deprecia-
    tion of the field equipment (including vehicles) was $1,800.
2   The firm maintained an Allowance for Doubtful Accounts.   Ed
    explained that this account ought to be equal to about 2.5% of
    Accounts Receivable, as he felt that about one out of 40 cus-
    tomer accounts would prove to be uncollectible.   He therefore
    proposed to increase this Allowance (contra) account by about
    $400.   Louise asked if they shouldn't review outstanding cus-
    tomer balances to see exactly which accounts might prove un-
    collectible.   Ed responded that he would do that later as he re-
    viewed each general ledger account; the write-off of specific
    customer accounts was not a recurring, predictable entry.
3   Included among the prepaid expenses was the $1,200 remaining
    balance of the $3,600 annual premium on a general insurance
    policy.   The cost of this insurance policy was amortized (allo-
    cated) across its 12-month term at $300 per month.
4   Interest on the note due to the former owners (see above for
    terms of the note) was accrued for the quarter.

5 As office supplies were purchased, their cost was expensed to account no. 2221. At the end of each quarter, Ed made a rough count of the office supplies inventory and made any necessary adjustment to increase or decrease the Supplies Expense account and the Supplies Inventory account (account no. 1030). He determined that currently the inventory of office supplies was about $300 less than at the end of December 19X2.

6 The value assigned to the customer list of the former owners, an intangible asset, was being amortized over a three-year period at the rate of $300 per quarter.

7 The company's Board of Directors, consisting of Louise, her father, her brother, who was not active in the business, and an old family friend, typically met late each quarter and frequently declared a dividend. Louise confirmed that the Board did meet late in March and declared cash dividends on the company's common stock totaling $1,000. The dividend was to be paid in late April.

NONRECURRING ADJUSTMENTS

These were the only recurring journal entries that Ed made routinely each quarter. He then began to consider what other adjustments to asset or liability accounts might be appropriate.

8 Ed asked Louise about the status of negotiations with Stanley Mueller. Mr. Mueller, a commercial building developer, had expressed dissatisfaction with a job performed by Patton in mid-19X2. Louise's father had agreed with the customer that if Patton's work proved upon further investigation to have been faulty, Patton would refund $2,000 to Mr. Mueller. At the time of that agreement, Ed had reduced contract revenues by this $2,000 amount and established a corresponding Deferred Income account. Louise confirmed that Mr. Mueller was now satisfied with Patton's work and that the company no longer faced the possibility of returning $2,000 to Mueller.

9 Patton's management had for some time been discussing the need to redecorate a portion of the company's offices, replacing the carpet and certain furniture. The estimated cost of this redecorating was $4,500. Ed wondered whether it might not be desirable to begin to accrue — at the rate, say, of $500 per month — for this anticipated expenditure. Louise, with her concern for near-term reported profits, argued that no entry should be made — and certainly no expense recorded — until the redecorating project was actually accomplished.

10   Ed, always on the lookout for future expenditures that should be recognized as an expense of the current period, asked Louise what management's plans were for paying a year-end bonus. Louise responded that, if the company generated substantially greater profits in 19X3 than in 19X2, as she felt quite certain it would, management was likely to authorize year-end bonuses totaling about $6,000. Ed argued that a pro rata portion of this year-end bonus should be recognized as an expense during each accounting period throughout the year. Louise felt that bonuses were properly reflected as an expense in that accounting period when they were declared; thus, she felt that only when and if bonuses were in fact paid in the fourth quarter of the year should they be recognized as an expense.

11   Louise wondered if there weren't expenses charged to the current quarter that properly belonged in future accounting periods. She mentioned that Patton had contracted and paid for exhibit space at a midsummer convention. She asked Ed how the $300 cost of this exhibit space had been accounted for. Ed reviewed the company's Check Register and found that the cost had been charged to account no. 2241, Advertising and Promotion Expense. Louise argued that this amount should be shown as a prepaid expense, not as an expense of the current quarter. Ed said, "That seems like a small amount to worry about. We can't be 100% exact in our allocation of expenses. You've made the commitment for the exhibit space and can't get a refund even if you cancel. Anyway, showing this $300 as an expense of the first quarter is conservative."

12   Louise was concerned that Ed was being just too conservative, recognizing expenses before they should be recognized. She asked Ed how he had accounted for the $1,500 tuition paid for a continuing education course that Louise would be attending in late summer. Again, after reviewing the Check Register, Ed confirmed that this amount had been expensed to account no. 2246, Staff Training Expense.

13   Ed asked Louise about some subcontracting work that had been done by the Camus Company on a project recently completed and billed by Patton. Ed recalled that Patton had not yet received Camus's invoice. Louise confirmed that the work had been done and that the amount to be charged by Camus would be about $1,600. Louise wondered if any accounting action needed to be taken prior to the receipt of Camus's invoice, but Ed assured her that the concept of matching of expenses and revenues demanded that this amount be recognized as an expense of the current period.

14 Ed mentioned to Louise that payment from the Wallace Construction Company was now almost 150 days past due. Louise recalled that at a Chamber of Commerce luncheon the previous week she had heard that Wallace had filed for bankruptcy. Reluctantly, Louise agreed with Ed that this receivable in the amount of $500 should be written off as uncollectible.

After some additional review of the preliminary trial balance, Louise and Ed could find no other adjustments that needed to be made — or even potential adjustments that they could argue about! Ed said, "Give me a couple of hours to finish this trial balance worksheet and construct financial statements. I should have the final results for you by the end of the day."

ASSIGNMENT

a Prepare in general journal format the adjusting entries that you think should be made as of March 31, 19X3.
b Record these entries in the adjustment columns on the attached trial balance worksheet. Complete the worksheet.
c Prepare financial statements from the adjusted trial balance.
d A final journal entry to record income-tax expense is typically made at this stage, after the firm's pretax profits have been determined. Record in general journal format the appropriate adjusting entry, assuming Patton's income tax rate is 40%. (Do not bother to reflect this final entry on either the worksheet or in your financial statements.)
e If Patton had failed to make these end-of-period adjusting entries, would its first-quarter profits have been overstated or understated, and by how much?
f Review your financial statements. If you were Louise or her father, would you be pleased with the results of the first quarter of 19X3? Do you have any particular concerns about the company's current financial position?
g Two accounts to which no adjustments were made are the Travel Advances (1025) and Customer Advance Payments (1531) accounts. Illustrate in general journal format how these accounts might be used if the following occurred:
    1 An employee turns in an expense report showing total travel expenses of $700; this employee had been provided with a $500 travel advance.
    2 A customer who in a previous accounting period made a $1,000 down payment to Patton with respect to a job to be per-

formed during this accounting period, is now billed $4,000 for the completed project.

h Suppose that Patton maintained its accounting records on a cash rather than an accrual basis. Do you think Patton's revenues for the quarter would be higher or lower on a cash basis? Why? Would the company's profits for the quarter be higher or lower? Why?

8

Accounting for Price Level Changes

Inflation and *deflation* are the terms used to describe increases and decreases in general price levels in an economy. In periods when *general* price levels are changing, the price of *specific* assets or liabilities also will typically increase or decrease, although not necessarily in proportion to the change in general price levels. The historical cost method of valuation takes no account of these general or specific price changes. When the rate of inflation or deflation in an economy is low —say, 1 or 2% per year—valuation distortion because of price level changes will be minor. Such was the situation in the United States for many years; during those years accounting for price level changes was given little attention by either accountants or managers. In recent years, however, the rate of inflation has accelerated markedly in the United States and in many other developed countries around the world. The inflation problem that was thought to be unique to less-developed and somewhat unstable economies has become a problem for most countries. As a result, the inadequacies of historical cost valuations have become more apparent and accountants have devoted considerable attention to methods for accounting for inflation.

Inflation's Effects on Historical-Cost Financial Statements

The problem of price-level changes is, of course, most significant with respect to those assets and liabilities that are held for a considerable time — fixed assets, long-term liabilities, and, to a lesser extent, inventory. The distortion occurs not only in the balance sheet but also in the income statement. For example:

1   If inventory was purchased some months ago and the inflation rate has been high in the meantime, the amount recorded on the company's balance sheet for the asset (inventory) will now be low in relation to current purchase prices. When the item is sold, its price to the customer will reflect the intervening inflation. Thus, as the accountant matches sales and costs of goods sold in the income statement, today's sales price will be matched against the historical purchase cost. The company's gross margin will appear high in comparison with the gross margin that would result from matching today's sale price with the *replacement* cost of the inventory. The information relevant to management is the relationship between today's sales price and today's replacement cost of the item, information which is not revealed in an accounting system based upon historical cost valuations. The use of historical costs, then, will tend to understate the amount of inventory and overstate profits during periods of rapid inflation.

2   A similar situation pertains with respect to fixed assets. Historical costs will tend to understate the amount of the asset on the balance sheet and depreciation based upon these historical costs will be less than depreciation based upon replacement costs. Many persons believe that in periods of inflation accounting based upon historical costs understates the depreciation expense on the income statement, thus resulting in an overstatement of profits.

3   Long-term liabilities are affected in the opposite manner. The repayment terms of most long-term liabilities require the borrower to repay a fixed amount on a set schedule: for example, $10,000 per year for 10 years. In periods of rapid inflation, the amount to be repaid annually, $10,000, remains unchanged, but the purchasing power of that $10,000 declines each year. In effect, the obligation to pay $10,000 per year becomes progressively less painful as inflation occurs. Note that in the case of liabilities, the lender is being harmed by the effects of inflation, but the borrower is in essence benefited. However, to the extent that inflation is anticipated, the lender will attempt to mitigate this effect by charging higher interest rates.

Recall that two of the important accounting concepts discussed in Chapter 4 were *matching* and *consistency*. It is these two concepts that suggest the need to adjust for price-level changes. In the inventory example just mentioned, the current sales price is matched against the historical cost value; in effect, the sale is valued on the basis of today's dollar and cost of goods sold is valued on the basis of the less-inflated dollar of some time ago. The readers of financial statements might be better served through improved matching, with both the sale and the costs of goods sold valued in monetary units of equivalent purchasing power—for example, today's dollar value.

The accountant is also concerned about consistency between accounting periods. In the third example above, the long-term liability each year is valued at the then-current value of the dollar. If inflation is eroding the value of the dollar, only balance sheets prepared on the basis of equivalent purchasing power—that is, using a consistent monetary measure—would reflect the fact that the liability is becoming progressively less of an obligation to the company, as it is being repaid with progressively cheaper dollars.

The aggregate effect on reported profits of U.S. companies of the high rate of inflation that prevailed in the United States in the late 1970s was reported by *Business Week* magazine in a special report dated March 19, 1979 and entitled "The Profit Illusion":

> On paper, U.S. business earned a record . . . $118 billion after [taxes in 1978] . . . 16 percent more than it earned in 1975. . . . If the tax collector, shareholders and makers of new capital goods could be paid with paper, then corporations would be sitting pretty today. . . .

> Unfortunately, taxes, dividends, and the cost of new growth have to be paid for with hard cash, and that is where cold reality intrudes, because only on paper did last year produce a boom in corporate profits. Fully one-third of the earnings that companies reported for 1978 were an illusion—gains created by inflation and out-of-date accounting methods. More than $42 billion of last year's after-tax earnings simply vanish after phantom inventory gains are extracted and depreciation expense is raised to reflect more accurately the true cost of replacing aging assets at a time when inflation is raging unchecked.[1]

Accounting for price-level changes is a very complex subject that might be thought to be beyond the scope of this book. The pervasiveness of high inflation rates in recent years, however, demands some general discussion of the common approaches to price-level accounting.

Over the past decade, much debate has occurred concerning the most effective method of allowing for inflation in accounting valuations. As yet, no consensus has emerged. The accounting profession (and in the United

---

[1] *Business Week,* March 19, 1979, p. 108.

States, the Securities and Exchange Commission) has moved toward providing inflation-adjusted accounting reports as supplementary information
to readers; the primary financial reports continue to be those prepared on
the basis of historical costs. It seems unlikely that in the near future the
cost method will be abandoned as the primary basis for day-to-day accounting. Changing price levels will be accounted for by adjustments to historical cost data, not by abandoning the cost method of accounting.

Alternative Approaches to Inflation Accounting

A great variety of proposals has been put forth by accountants, government
regulators, and managers to deal with valuations in an inflationary environment. Although, as just mentioned, opinion is divided as to the preferred
method, the various proposals are based largely on one or a combination of
two basic approaches: (1) making **specific-price adjustments**—that is,
attempting to adjust for specific price changes of inventory and fixed assets;
and (2) making **general-price-level adjustments** that attempt to reflect in
the financial statements the effects of inflation in terms of equivalent purchasing power, without concern for changes in prices of individual assets
and liabilities. While a comprehensive discussion of each of these approaches is indeed beyond the scope of this book, the reader should have
some familiarity with the objectives and nature of each.

SPECIFIC-PRICE ADJUSTMENTS (SPA)

This approach requires that specific nonmonetary assets be revalued.
Cash and accounts receivable—both monetary assets—are unaffected,
and adjustments are typically limited to inventory and fixed assets (property, plant, and equipment). Making specific-price adjustments for inventory and fixed assets owned by an enterprise appears easier than it is in
practice.

The time-adjusted value method discussed in Chapter 2 provides just
such a specific adjustment. If the stream of net benefits associated with
ownership of particular items in inventory or particular fixed assets were expressed in terms of today's value of the dollar and the benefit stream were
adjusted for time, the resulting value would be inflation-adjusted. Unfortunately, as we have seen, this valuation method is unreliable and subject to
bias in many situations because the expected future net benefits to be
derived from ownership are difficult to estimate.

Several other methods of making specific-price adjustments are possible, but unfortunately they do not necessarily all result in equivalent adjust-

ments. For some assets, a current price may be obtainable. For example, an item in inventory that cost $1.00 but whose replacement would now cost $1.25 could be adjusted to its current price, $1.25. For certain other assets, particularly certain fixed assets, price indices may be available that will allow historical costs to be inflated to a reliable current value; this approach to specific-price adjustment is appropriate for certain industrial plant assets.

On the other hand, many other assets, particularly aging equipment, would not typically be replaced in kind; that is, if technological improvements have occurred since the original acquisition, the owner of the asset would take advantage of the improvements at the time of replacement. Thus, the appropriate specific-price adjustment should be based upon the current cost of building or acquiring equivalent productive capacity, and not the cost of duplicating the exact physical asset now owned. Determining equivalent productive capacity may be difficult, time-consuming, unreliable, and subject to bias.

Assuming that satisfactory specific-price adjustments can be arrived at for inventory and fixed assets, the accountant can reflect these adjustments in the balance sheet valuations. Then, however, the accountant must determine how these revaluations—gains or losses that result from holding or owning the inventory and fixed assets—should be reflected in the income statement. If the application of specific-price adjustment (SPA) accounting results in higher valuations for inventory and fixed assets, as it normally will in periods of inflation, owners' equity must also increase; the accounting equation, "assets = liabilities + owners' equity," must be satisfied, and the increased value of these two classes of assets does not trigger a decline in value of other assets nor an increase in liabilities.

Is this increase in owners' equity a profit? Yes, but a profit that arises from inflation and not from the company's operation. Proponents of SPA accounting feel that a clear separation of these two elements of profit— operating profit and inflationary gains arising from holding assets—is of significant benefit to management, shareholders, prospective investors, and other readers of financial statements. The earlier quotation from the *Business Week* article captures the concern that financial analysts have regarding the overstatement of profits, based on historical costs, in times of rapid inflation.

Exhibit 8-1 illustrates in a highly simplified case the comparison of financial statements prepared on the basis of historical costs with those prepared using SPA accounting. Assume that the Allport Corporation merchandises only one type of product and makes only two purchases and two sales during the year 19X6, a year when the purchase cost of the product being sold escalates from $1.00 at the beginning of the year to $1.60 at the end of the year. The current or replacement value of the company's fixed assets has also inflated substantially during the year.

Exhibit 8-1
Comparison of Historical Cost and
Specific Price Adjustment Accounting
ALLPORT CORPORATION

Transactions during 19X6

Purchases:	March 19X6	1500 units at $1.20
	September 19X6	2000 units at $1.40
Sales:	March 19X6	2000 units at $2.00
	September 19X6	1000 units at $2.30

Inventory Position

January 1, 19X6:   1000 units (at $1.00 per unit)
December 31, 19X6:   1500 units

	Historical Cost Accounting	SPA Accounting
Balance Sheet (at December 31, 19X6)		
Cash and accounts receivable	$3,000	$ 3,000
Inventory	2,100[1]	2,400[2]
Fixed assets	4,000	6,000
	$9,100	$11,400
Liabilities	$4,000	$ 4,000
Owners' Equity		
As of January 1, 19X6	4,200	4,200
Profit, 19X6	900	400
Inflationary Gains, 19X6	0	2,800
	$9,100	$11,400
Income Statement (year ended December 31, 19X6)		
Sales	$6,300	$ 6,300
Cost of goods sold	3,500[3]	3,800[4]
Operating expenses	1,500	1,500
Depreciation	400	600
Profit	$ 900	$ 400
Inflationary Gains—Inventory		$ 600[5]
Fixed Assets		2,200
Total Inflationary Gains		$ 2,800

[1] 1,500 units at $1.40
[2] 1,500 units at December replacement cost of $1.60
[3] 1,000 units at $1.00; 1,500 units at $1.20; and 500 units at $1.40
[4] 2,000 units sold in March when current value was $1.20 plus 1,000 units sold in September when replacement cost was $1.40.
[5] 1,000 units gained $.20 between January 1 and sale in March; 500 units gained $.20 between purchase on March and sale in September; and 1,500 units gained $.20 between purchase in September and December 31.

Note that the profit from operations under SPA accounting is only $400, as compared with the $900 profit based upon historical costs. This difference in profit is attributable to (1) the fact that cost of goods sold is calculated using the replacement cost of the product that prevailed at the time of the sale (in this example the sales and purchases occur conveniently in the same month, and thus the purchase price indicates the adjusted value for purposes of valuing cost of goods sold); and (2) higher depreciation expense, based upon the replacement cost of the fixed assets rather than their historical original cost. SPA accounting does, however, lead to substantial inflationary gains. The value of all inventory increased by $600 during the months that it was owned. Note that half of this gain has not yet been realized—the company continues to hold 1,500 units of inventory that were purchased for $1.40 and are now valued on the balance sheet at $1.60 per unit—while the other half has been realized on inventory that grew in value between the date it was acquired and the date it was sold. The separation of realized and unrealized inflationary gains, which is not shown on Exhibit 8-1, may also be appropriate.

In this example, income taxes have been ignored. The income-tax laws and regulations in the United States are based upon historical costs, and thus all $900 of Allport's profit would be taxed. That is, the $300 realized gain on the inventory is taxable, and the additional $200 of depreciation expense shown on the SPA income statement is not an allowable deduction. In certain other countries, inflation adjustments to income may be permitted when calculating taxable income—for example, an escalation, or indexing, of depreciation expense.

In practice, the application of SPA accounting for companies that have large investments in fixed assets or inventory can have substantial financial impact. For example, in 1976 International Telephone and Telegraph (ITT) indicated that the replacement cost of its year-end inventory was $74 million higher than its historical cost of $2,370 million, a 3% difference. More importantly, "depreciation expense computed on average replacement costs would be $463 million for the year 1976 compared with $293 million on an historic cost basis."[2] This $170 million difference is equivalent to almost 21% of ITT's pre-tax profit for that year.

Specific-price adjustment accounting has not met with much enthusiasm from managements who find the task of compiling the data onerous and expensive. Moreover, managers tend to question both the validity of the data, particularly in light of the assumptions that lie behind the estimates, and the usefulness of the data to shareholders, security analysts, and other readers of financial statements. The following view expressed in ITT's 1976 Annual Report is apparently quite widely held:

> In the Corporation's view, the replacement cost [specific price adjustment] data . . . has been estimated in a reasonable manner; however, it is also management's opinion that these estimates are of limited value because of the subjectivity involved in their development under the present guidelines.[3]

---

[2] Annual Report, International Telephone and Telegraph Corporation, 1976, p. 38.
[3] Ibid.

If the problems associated with making the specific price adjustments required in this approach to inflation accounting can be overcome, the approach has the advantage of providing useful data to management in the form of improved matching of revenues and expenses. Because of the problems encountered in effecting SPA accounting, however, auditors have difficulty verifying the resulting values and thus tend to favor approaches that are more objective and free from potential bias. The general price-level adjustment approach is therefore typically preferred by auditors.

GENERAL-PRICE-LEVEL ADJUSTMENTS (GPLA)

A prime objective of financial accounting is to provide comparable data for successive accounting periods in order that financial trends can be observed and comparisons can be struck. This objective requires that accounting practices be consistent from period to period. In times of rapid price changes, however, the basic monetary unit in which assets and liabilities are measured does not remain consistent. In periods of inflation the purchasing power of the dollar declines with time. An asset purchased for $1,000 five years ago is not comparable to an asset purchased for $1,000 today, as more purchasing power was spent to acquire the five-year-old asset than to acquire the new asset. Or, viewed in another way, if the five-year-old asset were to be replaced today at the same cost in purchasing power, its cost would be substantially more than $1,000.

Some accountants argue that financial statements ought to be expressed in terms of equivalent purchasing power in order to facilitate comparisons over time. Such statements are relevant to shareholders, since they have particular interest in the company's ability to provide purchasing power in the form of dividends. A $1.00 dividend today is of less value to the shareholder than a $1.00 dividend last year, not only because of the time value of money but also because inflation has caused today's $1.00 dividend to have less purchasing power than last year's dividend.

The general-price-level adjustment (GPLA) approach to the problem of accounting for changing prices is to recompute financial statements in equivalent monetary units (in the United States, in constant dollars). Adjustments are not restricted solely to inventory and fixed assets, but are made to all assets and liabilities and to revenues and expenses. The adjustments can take the form of restating prior years' financial statements in terms of today's dollar value, or restating the current financial statements in terms of the value of the dollar in some base year.

The index used to make the price adjustments is a general one, such as the Gross National Product price deflator or the Consumer Price Index, rather than an index relevant to the specific asset or liability being adjusted. The purpose of the adjustment is not to reflect changes in cost, market, or replacement values of individual assets and liabilities. Historical costs continue to be the basis for the valuation; the historical costs are simply adjusted to reflect changed purchasing power of the monetary unit (dollars, yen, marks, francs, etc.). **General price indices** are readily available and reliable. Their application to the revaluation of an asset or liability is straightforward, objective, verifiable, and essentially free from bias. As a result, auditors tend to be more comfortable with this approach to accounting for inflation and deflation than with the various specific price adjustment methods.

Exhibit 8-2 indicates how a plant site (nondepreciable asset) might be valued in terms of constant purchasing power. Assume the site was acquired in 19X2 for $2 million. The firm's financial statements would continue to carry this asset at its original, historical cost. If annual inflation rates were as shown on the second line of Exhibit 8-2, a general price level index for the economy would be approximately as shown in the following line, increasing from a base of 100 in 19X2 to 145 in 19X6. The plant site can be revalued either in terms of 19X6 purchasing power or in terms of 19X2 purchasing power, as shown in the exhibit. Note that the trend information is the same whether valuation is in 19X6 dollars or 19X2 dollars. Remember too that the market value or resale value of this plant site is not reflected in these adjustments; the adjustment has been applied to the historical cost without reference to current values. The market value of the plant site might be affected by a host of factors other than simply inflation — principally the pattern of industrial and land development in the surrounding area.

General Motors in its 1978 Annual Report provided supplementary information to illustrate the effect of price-level changes (that is, declining purchasing power of the dollar) on the company's sales and profits over a six-year period. Exhibit 8-3 shows both reported sales and profits (in accordance with generally accepted accounting principles, based upon historical costs) and GPLA figures, where revenues and costs have been adjusted to 1973 as a base year, using the Consumer Price Index (CPI).

Note that sales, as reported, grew from almost $36 billion in 1973 to

Exhibit 8-2
Illustration of Revaluation of an Asset
in Constant Purchasing Power

	19X6	19X5	19X4	19X3	19X2
Plant site valued at historical cost ($000)	$2,000	$2,000	$2,000	$2,000	$2,000
Approximate annual rate of inflation	9%	10%	12%	8%	—
General price index	145	133	121	108	100
Revalued plant site in constant purchasing power					
in 19X6 dollars	$2,000	$1,834	$1,669	$1,490	$1,379
in 19X2 dollars	$2,900	$2,660	$2,420	$2,160	$2,000

Exhibit 8-3
Impact of GPLA Accounting on the Income Statement
of General Motors Corporation
($ in billions)

	1978	1977	1976	1975	1974	Base Year 1973
Sales, as reported	$63.2	$55.0	$47.2	$35.7	$31.5	$35.8
Sales, in constant dollars[1]	43.1	40.3	36.8	29.5	28.4	35.8
Net Income, as reported	$ 3.5	$ 3.3	$ 2.9	$ 1.3	$ 1.0	$ 2.4
Net Income, in constant dollars	2.4	2.4	2.3	1.0	0.9	2.4

[1] Adjusted by applying the Consumer Price Index.
Source: Annual Report, General Motors Corporation, 1978, p. 18

over $63 billion in 1978, an apparent average annual growth rate of 12%. In terms of equivalent purchasing power, however, sales grew from $36 billion to $43 billion over the six-year period, a "real" (inflation-adjusted) growth rate of only 3.8% per year. The impact of GPLA accounting on profits is even more dramatic. In terms of equivalent purchasing power, 1978 profits were essentially identical to 1973 profits, although the as-reported profits grew from almost $2.4 billion to about $3.5 billion, an apparent annual growth rate of 7.9% over the period.

General Motors' management provides in the Annual Report the following interpretation of the data shown in Exhibit 8-3:

> Financial reporting is, of necessity, stated in dollars. It is generally recognized that the purchasing power of a dollar has deteriorated in recent years and, accordingly, the costs of raw materials and other items as well as wage rates have increased and can be expected to increase further in the future to compensate for the decline. It is not as generally recognized, however, that profit dollars also are subject to the same degree of reduction in purchasing power. Far too much attention is given to the absolute levels of profits rather than the relation of profits to other factors in the business and to the general price level. . . . Constant dollar profits have not increased in recent years in line with the changes in sales volume. . . . The result has been a further erosion of GM's profit margin from 6.7% in 1973 to 5.5% in 1978.[4]

Requirement for Price-Level Accounting in the United States

From 1976 to 1979 the Securities and Exchange Commission required larger companies in the United States to take a step in the direction of SPA

[4] Annual Report, General Motors Corporation, 1978, pp. 18–19.

accounting by providing supplementary financial information based upon replacement costs. While these companies were not required to prepare full income and balance sheet statements using replacement costs, they were required to indicate the impact on cost of goods sold of using replacement inventory values rather than historical costs, and the impact on depreciation expense of using replacement values for fixed assets.

The SEC removed this requirement in 1979 in response to the adoption by the Financial Accounting Standards Board (FASB) of a broader requirement entitled "Financial Reporting and Changing Prices" and referred to as *Financial Accounting Standard (FAS) No. 33*. This standard, once again applicable only to larger companies, requires that both SPA and GPLA information be reported on a supplemental basis. The standard is lengthy and detailed regarding the procedures to be followed in arriving at the specific prices required for SPA accounting and in applying the Consumer Price Index in GPLA accounting.

Interestingly, neither the FASB nor the SEC requires that this supplemental information be audited. As mentioned earlier, auditors are reluctant to verify price-adjusted statements, particularly those based upon SPA accounting, because of the number and subjectivity of the estimates required.

The FASB acknowledges that this supplementary information is not easily interpreted by readers. Thus, *FAS No. 33* requires that management provide an explanation and analysis of the information's significance within the particular company.

Finally, *FAS No. 33* stresses the experimental nature of the required information and the need to educate both preparers of financial statements and their audiences. This statement will undoubtedly be subjected to further change and interpretation, as accountants and managers wrestle with the problem of adequately reflecting in financial statements the effects of changing price levels.

Inventory Accounting Conventions

We turn now to consider a specific set of conventions that is widely followed in the valuation of inventory. These conventions involve no price adjustment, either SPA or GPLA, but do compensate in part for the effects of price-level changes. The conventions involve alternative assumptions as to the flow of historical costs through the accounting system.

The **first-in, first-out (or FIFO)** convention assumes that those historical costs first arriving in inventory (that is, the oldest historical costs) are the first to flow to cost of goods sold; the corollary assumption is that the last prices (the most recent prices) remain in inventory. **The last-in, first-out**

(or LIFO) convention assumes just the opposite: the most recent (last-in) prices are assumed to appear first in cost of goods sold, and the oldest (first-in) prices remain in inventory.

In inflationary periods, as prices rise the higher prices will be reflected sooner in cost of goods sold if the LIFO convention is used. Thus, the matching of sales and cost of goods sold is enhanced by the LIFO convention, since the prices reflected in cost of goods sold more closely approximate the replacement, or current, cost of the inventory being sold. This improved matching will generally be advantageous to management in making various production, investment, and marketing decisions—particularly pricing, as well as product-selection decisions. Profits, too, are more conservatively stated in times of inflation using the LIFO convention than using the FIFO convention.

During the recent years of high inflation rates the LIFO convention has come into widespread use for the two reasons just suggested. First, LIFO values cost of goods sold more currently, while FIFO values inventory more currently; typically management relies more on profit-and-loss-data than balance-sheet data in making operating decisions. Second, LIFO will lead to lower profits and therefore lower income tax expense in periods of inflation. Bear in mind that the conventions will have the opposite effects on profits and taxes in periods of deflation (declining prices).

Note that these conventions do not abandon the use of historical costs: under both FIFO and LIFO only historical costs are used in the valuation of both inventory and cost of goods sold. The difference between FIFO and LIFO is simply the assumption made about the flow of these costs. Note too that the convention refers only to the flow of dollars, and not to the flow of the physical items in inventory. Good inventory management practice typically requires that the older inventory be used up before the newer inventory; thus, when retail store shelves are stocked, the older merchandise is moved to the front and the newer merchandise is placed at the back of the shelf. The physical flow of inventory, then, is generally first-in, first-out, but the accountant still has the choice of using either FIFO or LIFO to account for the monetary flows.[5]

Chapter 6 discusses the two basic methods of accounting for cost of goods sold and inventory: (1) determining cost of goods sold and inventory values by end-of-period adjustment, and (2) maintaining perpetual inventory records, reducing inventory, and charging cost of goods sold as each sale is made. FIFO and LIFO conventions can be used with both methods,

---

[5] A valuation between FIFO and LIFO can be accomplished by use of *average costs*. Each time inventory is acquired, a new average cost is computed—an average of the value of the quantity of the item now on hand and the value of the new purchase. This weighted-average cost is then used to value cost of goods sold until the next purchase is made, at which time another average is calculated. While the method requires a good deal of computation, if inventory records are maintained on a computer, the method can be implemented quite easily.

Exhibit 8-4
FIFO and LIFO Conventions: Cost of Goods Sold Determined
by End-of-Period Adjustment
(July 19X4)

	PURCHASES			SALES	
Date	Quantity (Units)	Price/Unit	Purchase Value	Date	Units
7/2	200	$1.00	$ 200	7/3	80
				7/5	120
7/14	300	1.05	315	7/9	160
				7/13	100
7/21	200	1.10	220	7/17	100
				7/18	80
				7/22	100
7/27	250	1.12	280	7/26	80
	950		$1,015	7/29	100
					920

Opening Inventory = 300 units at $.95/unit or $285
Ending Inventory = 300 units + 950 units purchases − 920 units sold = 330 units

1 Valuation of Ending Inventory

	FIFO			LIFO	
Units	Price/Unit	Value	Units	Price/Unit	Value
250	$1.12	$280	300	$0.95	$285
80	1.10	88	30	1.00	30
330		$368	330		$315

2 Valuation of Cost of Goods Sold

	FIFO	LIFO
Opening inventory	$ 285	$ 285
plus: Purchases	1,015	1,015
less: Ending inventory	368	315
Cost of goods sold	$ 932	$ 985

as illustrated in Exhibits 8-4 and 8-5. These exhibits relate to the valuation of a single inventory item that is experiencing very rapid inflation—its price increases from $1.00 to $1.12 per unit during the course of a single month.

Note in Exhibit 8-4 that ending inventory is valued at the most recent prices under FIFO, since the assumption is made that the older prices have flowed to cost of goods sold. The opposite assumption is made in valuing ending inventory under LIFO: the oldest prices (including the full value of opening inventory) are used to value inventory, with the assumption that the most recent prices have flowed to cost of goods sold. The cost of goods

Exhibit 8-5
FIFO and LIFO Conventions:
Cost of Goods Sold by Perpetual Inventory
(July 19X4)

Opening Inventory: 300 units at .95/unit of $285
Purchases: as listed in Exhibit 8-4

SALES / COST OF GOODS SOLD

		FIFO			LIFO		
Date	Units	Source of Price	Price/Unit	COGS Value	Source of Price	Price/Unit	COGS Value
7/3	80	Opening inventory	$0.95	$ 76	Purchase on 7/2	$1.00	$ 80
7/5	120	Opening inventory	0.95	114	Purchase on 7/2	1.00	120
7/9	160	(100) Opening inventory	0.95	95	Opening inventory	0.95	152
		(60) Purchase on 7/2	1.00	60			
7/13	100	Purchase on 7/2	1.00	100	Opening inventory	0.95	95
7/17	100	(40) Purchase on 7/2	1.00	40	Purchase on 7/14	1.05	105
		(60) Purchase on 7/14	1.05	63			
7/18	80	Purchase on 7/14	1.05	84	Purchase on 7/14	1.05	84
7/22	100	Purchase on 7/14	1.05	105	Purchase on 7/21	1.10	110
7/26	80	(60) Purchase on 7/14	1.05	63	Purchase on 7/21	1.10	88
		(20) Purchase on 7/21	1.10	22			
7/29	100	Purchase on 7/21	1.10	110	Purchase on 7/27	1.12	112
				$932			$946

Ending Inventory

		FIFO			LIFO		
	330	(80) Purchase on 7/21	$1.10	$ 88	(40) Opening inventory	$0.95	$ 38
					(120) Purchase on 7/14	1.05	126
		(250) Purchase on 7/27	1.12	280	(20) Purchase on 7/21	1.10	22
					(150) Purchase on 7/27	1.12	168
		(330)		$368	(330)		$354

sold under LIFO is indeed higher by $53 ($985 versus $932). The difference in valuation of ending inventory must be exactly the same $53, since opening inventory values were the same. Note that the two conventions utilize the same set of historical costs, simply making different assumptions as to the timing of the cost-of-goods-sold expense.

Exhibit 8-5 applies the FIFO and LIFO conventions to a perpetual-inventory situation. Each sale must be matched with its cost of goods sold determined from the most recent purchase price of the item. Once again, the LIFO convention results in higher cost of goods sold—higher by $14; and, once again, $14 is the amount of the difference in ending inventory valuation under the two methods. Note that under the LIFO convention a lower price was used on July 9 and 13 because the most recent purchases had been used up in the valuation of cost of goods sold on July 3 and 5.

Both FIFO and LIFO conventions are acceptable methods of accounting for inventory under the accounting profession's generally accepted accounting principles. Footnotes to the financial statements should specify the particular company's method of inventory valuation and the reader should be aware of the convention when interpreting financial results, particularly during periods of rapidly changing prices.

The LIFO convention, as mentioned above, leads to a higher cost of goods sold and therefore lower profits than the FIFO convention during inflationary periods. Lower profits in turn result in lower income-tax expense. Both FIFO and LIFO conventions are permitted under the current income tax laws in the United States. Two restrictions apply, however. First, a company is constrained by tax regulations from switching freely between the two conventions in an attempt to take advantage of periods of increasing and periods of decreasing prices. Second, the law requires that, if a company uses the LIFO convention in reporting for income-tax purposes, it must also use the LIFO convention for reporting profits to shareholders. This requirement that tax and financial accounting be the same is unusual. In virtually all other instances, accountants are free to select accounting methods for tax reporting purposes that will minimize tax obligations consistent with the tax laws and to select alternative accounting methods for public reporting purposes. Certain managements have been willing to forego the tax savings (in actuality, a postponement of taxes, rather than an outright savings) associated with the LIFO convention because they have been unwilling to accept the lower reported profits that result from its application in inflationary times.

Summary

As the world has experienced higher inflation rates in recent years, the need to account for these price-level changes has grown. The problem arises from accountants' concern with both the matching concept and the need for consistency. Matching of revenues and expenses is difficult when inventory and fixed assets are purchased in one period and used in a later period in the production of revenue. Comparability between financial statements prepared in different years is weakened when the monetary unit used in their preparation is unadjusted for changing price levels (purchasing power).

While consensus has not been reached on the optimum method of adjusting for price-level changes, the two primary methods being advocated are: (1) specific-price adjustments and (2) general-price-level adjustments. The first method attempts to reflect the specific price changes in such balance sheet items as inventory and fixed assets and to account separately for profits arising from operations and for gains that result from holding these assets during inflationary periods. The second method makes no reference to the changes of prices of individual assets, but seeks to reflect in the financial statements the changing purchasing power of the monetary unit by adjusting historical cost financial statements through the use of broad indices such as the Consumer Price Index. At this time, accountants, managers, and government regulators appear to favor the reporting of inflation-adjusted (and deflation-adjusted) financial data as only supplementary data. A company's accounting and primary reporting continue to be based upon historical costs.

Accounting for inventory and cost of goods sold in periods of changing prices is a widespread problem. Two conventions—FIFO and LIFO—make opposite assumptions regarding the flow of costs from inventory to cost of goods sold. FIFO leads to higher reported profits in inflationary periods than does LIFO, and to higher valuations of inventory. LIFO tends to provide financial data more useful to management in making operating decisions while minimizing income tax expenses; for both of these reasons, LIFO has come into wider usage in recent years.

Appendix A: Accounting for Currency Fluctuations

Another problem related to, and in effect arising from, price-level changes is that of accounting for currency exchange-rate fluctuations. The rate of exchange between two currencies is likely to change when the rate of inflation in the two countries is different. If country A is experiencing 5% inflation while inflation in country B is running 10% per year, the currency of country B is likely to lose value—become devalued—in terms of the currency of country A.

All multinational firms, and even many smaller companies, will have operations—or at least own assets and liabilities—in countries other than their home country. Yet these companies maintain their consolidated financial records in terms of the currency of the home country. Thus, all assets, liabilities, incomes, and expenses (and therefore owners' equity) that are denominated in another currency must be translated into the home-country currency for financial statement purposes. If a multinational company operates a foreign subsidiary, the subsidiary's financial statements must be maintained in terms of the foreign currency, but they also must be translated into the company's home currency for purposes of consolidated financial reporting of the worldwide operations.

Over the last 10 years, international currencies have fluctuated widely. Companies based in countries with strong currencies, such as Switzerland, have seen their foreign assets (denominated in the foreign currency) lose substantial value in terms of the Swiss franc, even while the assets have maintained their value in terms of the local currency.

Suppose a company located in a strong currency country (SCC) sells machinery to a customer in a weak currency country (WCC), with the understanding that the customer has one year to pay. At the time of the sale the exchange rate between SCC and WCC is 1:3—that is, one unit of SCC currency will purchase three units of WCC currency. The receivable from the customer is denominated as 30,000 units of WCC currency, but the selling company values the sale at 10,000 units of SCC currency. Stepping forward a year to the time when the customer pays, suppose that the prevailing exchange rate is then 1:4—that is, the currency of WCC has devalued vis-à-vis that of SCC, and one unit of SCC currency will now purchase four units of WCC currency. The customer pays the outstanding receivable: 30,000 units of WCC currency. When the machinery manufacturer converts this payment into SCC currency, it will receive only (30,000 ÷ 4) = 7,500 units of SCC currency. Thus, during the course of the year, this account receivable has declined in value from 10,000 to 7,500 in terms of SCC currency, although to the customer the account payable continued to be 30,000 units of WCC currency.

Alternatively, suppose the machinery manufacturer located in SCC had borrowed 150,000 units of WCC currency (when the exchange rate was 1:3), promising to repay at the end of one year. The borrower converts into local SCC currency immediately (50,000 units) and uses the funds productively. A year later, when the borrower must repay and the exchange rate is 1:4, the borrower will need to convert only 37,500 units of SCC currency into WCC currency in order to repay the loan: 37,500 units × 4 = 150,000 units of WCC currency. The machinery manufacturer has fared very well on this transaction, while losing on the receivable arising from the sale described in the previous paragraph.

These two brief examples illustrate one way that a firm can "hedge" its position—that is, minimize the financial impact of currency fluctuations: it can owe as much in the foreign currency as it owns. This hedging strategy is followed by many companies. Highly organized foreign exchange futures markets permit other approaches to hedging. Nevertheless, very many companies experience gains and losses as a result of currency fluctuations, and they must account for these gains and losses.

Accounting for currency devaluations and upward revaluations continues to be a somewhat controversial area. Exactly what exchange rates should be used in translating particular assets and liabilities? And when should the gains or losses arising from these fluctuations be recognized in the income statement? In the illustrations above, the loss on the receivable and the gain on the borrowing transaction must be completely accounted for by the end of the year. Should a portion of the gain or loss be accounted for during the year as the exchange rate was moving from $1:3$ to $1:4$—that is, before the gain or loss is finally realized through the receipt or payment of cash? Or should the recognition of gain or loss be postponed until the entire transaction is closed out? When nonmonetary assets and liabilities, such as fixed assets, that are owned in a foreign country are translated into the home currency for the purposes of consolidated financial reporting, should they be translated at the exchange rate prevailing at the time of their purchase or at the exchange rate today? These issues continue to be debated.

In summary, varying rates of price-level changes among countries lead to changes in currency exchange rates. These changing rates present problems in valuing assets and liabilities that are denominated in currencies other than a company's home-country currency. Controversy persists as to the method and timing of recognizing gains and losses from these currency fluctuations as a company translates the financial statements of foreign operations into units of home-country currency for the purposes of worldwide financial reporting.

New Terms

First-in, first-out A convention utilized to value inventory and cost of goods sold that assumes that the oldest prices in inventory are the first prices reflected in cost of goods sold.

General price indices Indices such as the Consumer Price Index or the Gross National Product price deflator that are designed to reflect the impact of inflation and deflation on price levels in general; these indices are used in *general-price-level adjustments (GPLA)* accounting.

General-price-level adjustments (GPLA) A method of accounting for price-level changes (inflation or deflation) by reflecting changed purchasing power of the monetary unit in the valuation of assets and liabilities.

Last-in, first-out A convention utilized to value inventory and cost of goods sold that assumes that the most recent prices in inventory are the first prices reflected in cost of goods sold.

Specific-price adjustments (SPA) A method of accounting for price level changes (inflation or deflation) by reflecting the changed prices of individual assets.

Problems

1 From the viewpoint of financial accounting, would you say that the FIFO method of inventory valuation should be regarded as more accurate than either the LIFO or average cost method? Discuss your answer.

2 What are the primary benefits and drawbacks of using the LIFO method of inventory valuation during periods of inflation?

3 If the LIFO method of inventory valuation leads to lower income tax expense in periods of increasing inflation (by comparison with the FIFO method), why are some managements reluctant to adopt LIFO?

4 If a company is considering the choice between FIFO and LIFO inventory valuation-methods in a period of continuing inflation, which method will:

   a Minimize income tax expense

   b Provide more useful information to management for pricing decisions

   c Provide more useful information regarding valuation of inventories

5 Describe how in 19X7 you would develop SPA data for the following assets owned by an automotive manufacturing company. Indicate what difficulties you might encounter.

   a Sheet aluminum used for certain parts of the automobile and purchased three months ago

   b A fuel pump manufactured in 19X4 and maintained in inventory to fill spare parts orders, although the pump is no longer used on current models

   c The final 2000 automobiles of the 19X6 model year that should be sold over the next two months

   d A word processing typewriter system purchased in 19X2 for the sales department; substantial improvements in speed and capacity have been incorporated in similar devices available in 19X7

   e A building in Princeville built 35 years ago and now housing one of the company's foundries

   f A forklift truck purchased in 19X5

   g An automatic warehouse system custom-built and installed for the company in 19X4

   h The land in midtown New York City purchased 25 years ago and now the site of the corporate headquarters building

6 Discuss the advantages and disadvantages of the two methods of adjusting for price changes (SPA and GPLA) at a major retailing company, from the point of view of:

a The company's banker, lending on a short-term basis with inventory as collateral for the loan

b A shareholder to whom dividends on the company's common stock represent 25% of his total income

c The merchandising vice president who has primary responsibility for pricing policies at the company

d An economist concerned with evaluating the effects of inflation on the profitability of the retailing industry

7 Is SPA accounting likely to have major or limited impact on the financial statements of the following firms? Explain.

a A large legal partnership founded 75 years ago

b An electric public utility, whose generating capacity was constructed 20 years or more ago

c An electric public utility in a rapidly growing geographic area whose generating capacity has been constructed within the past 10 years

d A retailing firm whose store facilities are all rented

e A retailing firm whose store facilities are all owned

f A motor manufacturer whose plant facilities are all rented (compare to *d* above)

g A machine tool manufacturer whose plant facilities are all owned (compare to *e* and *f* above)

8 Refer to Exhibit 8-1. Assume that all facts remain as described in this exhibit, except that the September purchases and sales were as follows:

> Purchases: 2000 units at $1.50
> Sales: 1000 units at $2.50

and the replacement cost of the product in December is $1.75. Determine the effect of these changes on the December 31 balance sheet and the income statement for 19X6.

9 Refer to Exhibit 8-2. If the annual rate of inflation had been as follows:

19X3	8%
19X4	12%
19X5	12%
19X6	15%

what would be the value in 19X6 of the plant site in constant purchasing power

a In 19X6 dollars?

b In 19X2 dollars?

10 The Moody Company operated in March 19X9 in a country experiencing very rapid inflation. Shown at the top of page 235 are the inventory transactions for one particular item the company carries. Calculate cost of goods sold for this item for March and the value of ending inventory under each of the following conditions:

a perpetual inventory, FIFO valuation

b perpetual inventory, LIFO valuation

| Date | PURCHASES | | SALES |
	Quantity (Units)	Cost	Quantity (Units)
March 1	100	$ 500	
10	200	1,020	
15			200
25	150	780	
30			200
Totals	450	$2,300	400

11 The Chu Corporation wholesales a standard industrial commodity that is subject to rather sharp price fluctuations as local demand and supply conditions change. At the beginning of February 19X4 the company had in inventory 7,000 pounds of this commodity, valued in the accounting records at $14,000. During February the following inventory transactions occurred:

| Date | PURCHASES | | SALES |
	Quantity (Lbs.)	Cost	Quantity (Lbs.)
Feb. 2			1,500
4	1,000	$ 2,100	
10	500	950	
11			2,000
16			1,000
17	1,000	2,000	
18			1,500
22	2,000	3,800	
25	1,000	2,100	
28			500
Totals	5,500	$10,950	6,500

Calculate cost of goods sold for the month and ending inventory under each of the following conditions:

a Perpetual inventory, FIFO valuation

b Perpetual inventory, LIFO valuation

c Cost of goods sold determined by end-of-period adjustment, FIFO valuation

d Cost of goods sold determined by end-of-period adjustment, LIFO valuation.

12 The Universal Utility Corporation owns one electric generating plant that was built 20 years ago. The original cost of the plant was $30 million, and accumulated depreciation to date is $12 million (annual depreciation expense is $600,000).

a Assume that the replacement cost of this generating plant is now $50 million and that the estimated life of such a plant would not be materially different from the 50-year life estimated for the original plant. If the Universal Utility Corp. wishes to utilize SPA accounting by reflecting replacement costs, rather than original costs, in its accounting records, what accounting entries would you recommend to reflect this change? What would be Universal's depreciation charge on this plant next year, assuming such a change were made?

b   Assume that in the 20 years since the generating plant was built a widely used index of purchasing power has increased from 100 to 200. If Universal Utility wishes to utilize GPLA accounting to reflect purchasing power erosion in its accounting records, what accounting entries would you recommend? What would the current year's depreciation expense be for this generating plant, assuming this purchasing power adjustment is made?

PROBLEMS FOR APPENDIX A

13   The Cooper Company maintains its books in U.S. dollars but has an account receivable expressed in hycas (a hypothetical foreign currency). The value of the receivable is 1000 hycas, and the sale occurred when the exchange rate was 4 hycas per dollar.

a   Record in T-account format the sale and the account receivable in dollars

b   Assume that in a subsequent period the receivable is still outstanding but the exchange rate has now changed to 5 hycas per dollar. What entry, if any, should be made in Cooper's general ledger at this time?

14   If the exchange rate between currency A and currency B changes from 2 units of A = 1 unit of B to 2.5 units of A = 1 unit of B:

a   Will a borrower located in country A and borrowing currency B be helped or hurt by this change?

b   Will a company located in country A and owning a deposit in a bank in country B and denominated in currency B be helped or hurt by this change?

c   How can a company located in country B protect (hedge) the value of its accounts receivable denominated in currency A?

Financial Statement Analysis

The first eight chapters of this book have discussed the guidelines for, and some problems surrounding, the preparation of financial statements. These statements—the balance sheet and the income statement—are constructed to provide useful information to the firm's various audiences, particularly management, shareholders, and creditors. This chapter discusses the various common techniques used to extract meaningful observations and conclusions about an enterprise's financial health and operating results.

The audiences for financial statements are concerned primarily with measuring how well the company is progressing in satisfying the dual objectives of (1) earning profits and (2) maintaining a sound financial position. These two objectives may not be given equal weight. One company might put more emphasis on profitability at some sacrifice in financial position, while another might put greater emphasis on financial stability and security at some sacrifice in current profitability. But all audiences must be interested in both corporate objectives. If financial soundness is ignored, the company's risk of failure will escalate; if the firm's profitability is ignored, its financial soundness will eventually become impaired.

We learn about a company by comparing financial data. It is the relationship among amounts on the income statement and balance sheet that conveys information—much more so than individual totals plucked from either statement. If we are told that a particular company has $1 million of assets, we know that the sum of its liabilities and owners' equity is also $1 million, but we learn virtually nothing about either its financial condition or its profitability. If we are also told that this company's owners' equity (or net worth) totals $500,000, we can deduce the relationship among equity, liabilities, and assets; we see that one-half of the company's assets have been financed by borrowing, and thus we have learned something about the company's financial position. If we are also told that the company earned $75,000 in profit in the fiscal year just ended, we now know something about the rate of profitability, or the return on the $1 million investment in assets.

Suppose we are told that another company has $800,000 of accounts receivable. We do not know if that amount is high or low. If we are now told that sales in the most recent fiscal year were $10 million, we know that accounts receivable are about 8% of annual sales, and we can hypothesize about the average length of time the company's customers take to pay their bills. Again, it is the comparison and not the absolute number that is useful in the analysis process.

Ratio Analysis

The fundamental method of analyzing financial statements is by the calculation of ratios. This chapter discusses in detail some of the most common ratios used and categorizes them by the type of information that they reveal.

Actually, ratio analysis is not an entirely new subject in this book. In the discussion of the products of the accounting system (the income statement and the balance sheet) in Chapter 3 we defined *current assets* and *current liabilities* in a parallel manner. This parallelism was purposeful, since the resulting ratio of current assets to current liabilities is meaningful. In the same chapter we defined *gross margin;* the ratio between gross margin and sales—the gross margin percentage—is another relevant ratio. In Chapter 6 we discussed the importance of consistent valuation between inventory and cost of goods sold; the ratio between these two values provides some indication of the rate at which a company is using, or "turning over," its inventory.

Analysts of financial statements learn rather quickly to think in terms of ratios. Current assets are instinctively compared to current liabilities. Cost of goods sold is automatically compared to total sales as a measure of gross profitability, and to total inventory as an indication of the rate of inventory usage.

The ratios themselves are calculated in a straightforward manner. The interpretation of the ratios, however, requires the exercise of judgment, and one's judgment is sharpened by experience. An analyst who has studied a variety of financial statements—statements of companies in different industries and in both prosperous and recession periods—will be able to glean more reliable judgments from a particular set of statements than will an inexperienced analyst. This chapter, including the exercises at the end, can provide you with a first step in gaining financial analysis experience.

Categorization of Ratios

There are about as many financial ratios as there are analysts calculating them. We shall discuss and categorize here only the most commonly employed ratios. The four primary categories in terms of the information that they are designed to provide are:

1 Liquidity: How able is the company to meet its near-term obligations?
2 Working capital utilization: How efficiently is the company using the various components of its current assets and current liabilities?
3 Capital structure: What are the company's sources of capital?
4 Profitability: How profitable is the company in light of both its sales and its invested capital?

To illustrate the calculation and meaning of the various ratios, we will analyze the financial statements of the Hewlett-Packard Company (HP) for the fiscal years ending October 31, 1978 and 1979. The income statements (statement of earnings) and balance sheets for the company for these two years are shown in Exhibits 9-1 and 9-2, but the financial notes accompanying these statements have been omitted.

Hewlett-Packard is a large and rapidly growing company which describes itself in the company's 1979 Annual Report as "a major designer and manufacturer of precision electronic equipment for measurement, analysis and computation . . . [whose] 4,000 products . . . are sold worldwide and have broad application in the fields of science, engineering, business, industry, medicine and education."[1] Founded in the late 1930s, HP has been one of the brightest success stories among high-technology companies, having grown so rapidly that by 1978 it was ranked by *Fortune* magazine as the 184th largest industrial company in the United States. In recent years

---

[1] 1979 Hewlett-Packard Company Annual Report, inside cover.

Exhibit 9-1

HEWLETT-PACKARD CO.

CONSOLIDATED STATEMENT OF EARNINGS

For the years ended October 31, 1979 and 1978
(Millions except per share amounts)

	1979	1978
Net sales	$2,361	$1,737
Costs and expenses:		
Cost of goods sold	1,106	808
Research and development	204	154
Marketing	362	264
Administrative and general	291	215
	1,963	1,441
Earnings before taxes on income	398	296
Taxes on income	195	143
Net earnings	$ 203	$ 153
Net earnings per share	$ 3.43	$ 2.63*

*Restated to give retroactive effect to the 2 for 1 stock split in June, 1979.

Exhibit 9-2
HEWLETT-PACKARD CO.
CONSOLIDATED BALANCE SHEET
October 31, 1979 and 1978
(Millions)

ASSETS

	1979	1978
Current assets:		
Cash	$ 30	$ 9
Temporary cash investments, at cost which approximates market	218	180
Notes and accounts receivable	491	371
Inventories:		
Finished goods	120	99
Purchased parts and fabricated assemblies	358	257
Other current assets	52	36
Total current assets	1,269	952
Property, plant and equipment, at cost:		
Land	53	44
Buildings and improvements	412	338
Machinery and equipment	257	201
Leaseholds and leasehold improvements	102	80
Construction in progress	68	58
	892	721
Accumulated depreciation and amortization	301	245
	591	476
Other assets	40	34
	$1,900	$1,462

LIABILITIES AND SHAREHOLDERS' EQUITY

	1979	1978
Current liabilities:		
Notes payable and commercial paper	$ 147	$ 85
Accounts payable	109	71
Employee compensation, benefits and other accrued liabilities	237	171
Accrued taxes on income	106	88
Total current liabilities	599	415
Long-term debt, less current portion included in notes payable (1979—$9; 1978—$7)	15	10
Deferred taxes on income	51	35
Commitments and contingencies		
Shareholders' equity:		
Common stock, par value $1 a share, 80 million shares authorized	59	29
Capital in excess of par value	267	247
Retained earnings	909	726
Total shareholders' equity	1,235	1,002
	$1,900	$1,462

the company has compiled a highly enviable financial record: strong growth rate, excellent profitability, and sound financial position.

The ratios discussed below are particularly applicable to manufacturing enterprises. Companies engaged in different industries will find some of these ratios irrelevant; other ratios, not discussed here, may be highly relevant. For example, a commercial bank must concern itself with the ratio between loans outstanding and customer deposits—the loan-to-deposit ratio—since customer deposits provide the funds that the bank lends to its borrowers.

LIQUIDITY

A company unable to meet its obligations as they come due runs the risk of becoming bankrupt. Trade suppliers and employees must be paid on time; interest and principal payments on borrowed money must be made when due. A company that has substantial liquid assets in relationship to its near-term obligations is said to have strong **liquidity,** or to be very liquid. Note that a company might be very illiquid, and thus be exposed to a high risk of failure, even while making substantial profits. Liquidity is a measure of financial position or condition, while profitability is a measure of return.

Current ratio   Probably the most widely quoted of all financial ratios is the **current ratio:**

Current ratio = current assets ÷ current liabilities

Recall that current assets are those assets that are either presently the equivalent of cash or within the next 12 months will be used up or turned into cash. Cash, accounts receivable, and inventory are the primary current assets, listed in order of decreasing liquidity. Current liabilities are those obligations which must be met within the following 12 months, including primarily accounts payable, wages and salaries payable, short-term bank borrowing, current portion of long-term debt, and miscellaneous accruals. The higher the current ratio the greater the margin of safety—that is, the more likely the company is to have sufficient liquid assets to meet its obligations as they come due.

Note that current assets do not include all the cash that the company will receive during the next 12 months, nor do the current liabilities include all obligations that must be met over the next 12 months. Sales occurring tomorrow, next week, and next month will result in cash receipts long before the end of 12 months, and over the coming weeks and months employees and vendors will have to be paid amounts not now included in current liabilities. Thus, the current ratio does not define comprehensively the ability of the company to meet all near-term obligations; it is only an indicator, albeit perhaps the most important such indicator.

Hewlett-Packard's current ratio at the end of its 1979 fiscal year was:

Current ratio = 1269 ÷ 599 = 2.1

Acid-test (or quick) ratio Another measure of liquidity is the **quick ratio,** often referred to also as the **acid-test ratio:**

Quick ratio = (cash + marketable securities + accounts receivable)
÷ current liabilities

Note that the denominator of this ratio is the same as for the current ratio: current liabilities. The numerator, however, includes only the most liquid of the company's current assets. No asset can be more liquid than cash! In addition, many companies also own assets that might be referred to as **cash equivalents:** short-term investments of temporary or permanent cash reserves in excess of immediate needs. These investments in U.S. Treasury Bills or other interest-bearing securities are highly marketable and can be converted into cash on virtually a moment's notice. Thus, **marketable securities** are considered part of the company's quick assets.[2] Accounts receivable are also arbitrarily considered as quick assets, since they will normally be collected (converted to cash) soon, typically within 90 days.

Note that the primary difference between the numerators of the current and quick ratios is the exclusion of inventories from the quick ratio. A service company that owns little or no inventory might therefore have a quick ratio that is approximately the same as its current ratio. Note also that a company that makes most of its sales for cash (for example, certain retail stores) may have few or no accounts receivable in comparison to another company whose customers buy on credit. Typically, the sale-for-cash company will have a lower quick ratio than the other, but this fact does not necessarily mean that the former company is illiquid. We shall reemphasize frequently in this chapter that financial ratios must be interpreted in light of the company's particular business and circumstances.

The quick (or acid-test) ratio at HP at October 31, 1979 was:

Quick ratio = (30 + 218 + 491) ÷ 599 = 1.2

HP's "temporary cash investments . . . ," valued at $218 million, are assumed to be equivalent to cash.

---

[2] The company may own other marketable securities that are not cash equivalent. For example, when company A purchases on the open market shares of common stock of company B, company A is presumably making a long-term investment in company B; thus, this asset would not be included in company A's current assets.

WORKING CAPITAL UTILIZATION

Current assets, particularly accounts receivable and inventory, represent major investments for many companies. At HP, current assets at October 31, 1979 represented 67% of total assets. The more efficiently the company uses its current assets—that is, the faster it collects from its customers and the less inventory it requires to accomplish its sales—the less capital the company will require.

For many companies, borrowing from trade creditors (that is, accounts payable) represents a major source of capital. While there are practical limits to this source of capital, the more the company utilizes this typically non-interest-bearing source of capital, the less it will have to obtain from sources to whom it must pay a return.

The difference between current assets and current liabilities is defined as *working capital,* and the ratios discussed below consider the efficiency with which the primary elements of working capital are utilized.

Accounts receivable collection period Most manufacturing companies offer credit to their customers. The longer the customers take to pay their bills the more the manufacturer has invested in accounts receivable. A comparison of sales volume with outstanding accounts receivable indicates how promptly customers are paying.

The **accounts receivable collection period** ratio is calculated as follows:

$$\text{Collection period (in days)} = \frac{\text{accounts receivable}}{\text{average sales per day}}$$

where

Average sales per day = annual sales ÷ 365

The collection period indicates the number of days of sales remaining uncollected (and therefore in accounts receivable) at the end of the accounting period. Stated another way, the ratio indicates the average number of days between the time that a customer is invoiced and the time that payment is received. Actual periods between invoice date and collection date will vary widely, with some customers paying very promptly and others taking a distressingly long time to pay. The mean of a frequency distribution of customer payments (number of days from invoice date to payment date) approximates the collection period expressed in number of days.

Several cautions are in order regarding the interpretation of the accounts receivable collection period. First, the annual sales should include only sales made on credit; if the company has substantial cash sales, an appropriate adjustment of the sales data must be made. Second, note that the formula above utilizes annual sales. Sales for shorter periods than a year (for example, fiscal quarters) can be used with only minor and obvious adjustments to the formula; however, if a business is seasonal, substantial distortion of the collection period ratio may occur at certain times of the year. For example, suppose that the ratio is calculated just after the conclusion of the company's busiest season. Average sales per day have been higher during this busy season than for the year as a whole; moreover, the high rate of sales in the most recent weeks has contributed to a high accounts receivable balance at the end of the period. Thus, the collection period can be greatly distorted by seasonality effects, as illustrated in Exhibit 9-3. Note that the collection period calculated at the end of each quarter, and based upon the sales for just that quarter, is consistent at 45.6 days. However, the year-end accounts receivable balance is inflated as a result of high sales in the final quarter; when this balance is compared to the average sales per day for the year (5.48), the resulting collection period is quite misleading.

A similar distortion can result when a company is growing rapidly. The accounts receivable collection period is the first ratio that we have encountered which draws data from both the income statement and the balance sheet. Recall that the income statement is a record of performance *for a period,* while the balance sheet is a statement of condition at the *end of a period.* The balance sheet therefore will be a function of the activity level at the *end* of an accounting period while the income statement records performance *throughout* the period. Consider the hypothetical company illustrated in Exhibit 9-4. This company grew in sales volume by $3,000 per month—from $100,000 in December of last year to $136,000 in December of this year. Note that the accounts receivable balance at each month end was just equal to sales in the most recent month; by inspection we see that the average collection period was in fact one month, or about 30 days. However, a comparison of average sales per day for the entire year with the accounts receivable balance at year-end results in a collection

Exhibit 9-3
Effect of Seasonality on Accounts Receivable Collection Period

Fiscal Period	Sales	Average Sale per Day	Accounts Receivable at End of Period	Collection Period[1]
Quarter 1	$ 400	4.38	$200	45.6 days
Quarter 2	400	4.38	200	45.6 days
Quarter 3	400	4.38	200	45.6 days
Quarter 4	800	8.77	400	45.6 days
Full Year	$2,000	5.48	400	73.0 days

[1] Accounts Receivable ÷ Average Sales per day

Exhibit 9-4
Effect of Growth on Accounts Receivable Collection Period

Month	Sales ($000)
Dec. (19X1)	$ 100
Jan. (19X2)	$ 103
Feb.	106
Mar.	109
Apr.	112
May	115
June	118
July	121
Aug.	124
Sept.	127
Oct.	130
Nov.	133
Dec.	136
Total, 19X2	$1,434

Accounts receivable balances

Dec. 31, 19X1	$100
Dec. 31, 19X2	136

$$\text{Collection period, based upon year-end A/R} = \frac{136}{1434 \div 365} = 34.6 \text{ days}$$

$$\text{Collection period, based upon average A/R} = \frac{(100 + 136) \div 2}{1434 \div 365} = 30.0 \text{ days}$$

period that overstates the true situation: the collection period appears to be 34.6 days instead of 30 days. The analyst can make an adjustment that typically will compensate adequately for the effect of steady growth, by using an average accounts receivable balance, instead of the year-end balance. If the analyst has available the balance sheet for the previous year-end as well as the current balance sheet, as we do in the case of HP, an average can be struck between these two numbers.[3] Thus, the better formulation of the accounts receivable collection period ratio is:

$$\text{Collection period} = \frac{(\text{opening A/R} + \text{ending A/R}) \div 2}{\text{annual sales} \div 365}$$

The efficiency of investment in accounts receivable at HP can be evaluated by the following:

---

[3] An even more accurate average would be obtained by averaging the 13 month-end accounts receivable balances from December 19X1 through December 19X2, but these data are unlikely to be available to the analyst.

RATIO BASED ON YEAR-END A/R

$$\text{A/R collection period} = \frac{\text{accounts receivable}}{\text{annual sales} \div 365}$$

$$= \frac{491}{2361 \div 365} = \frac{491}{6.47} = 76 \text{ days}$$

RATIO BASED ON AVERAGE A/R

$$\text{A/R collection period} = \frac{(\text{opening A/R} + \text{ending A/R}) \div 2}{\text{annual sales} \div 365}$$

$$= \frac{(491 + 371) \div 2}{2361 \div 365} = \frac{431}{6.47} = 67 \text{ days}$$

Inventory turnover   Most manufacturing and merchandising companies invest substantial amounts in inventory in order to serve customers and assure uninterrupted flow of manufacturing processes. Significant costs are associated with carrying inventory: cost associated with storage, insurance, risk of obsolescence, and the capital tied up. Thus, in deciding just how large a stock of merchandise and parts to carry, a company makes a trade-off (whether explicitly or implicitly) between the costs and benefits of carrying inventory.

When inventory is sold to customers, inventory values are reduced and a charge is made to Cost of Goods Sold. A comparison of inventory and cost of goods sold, then, can provide an indication of the rate at which inventory is being utilized—that is, the speed with which inventory is moving from receipt to final sale.

This **inventory turnover** ratio is quite parallel to the accounts receivable collection period. The collection period ratio compares sales and accounts receivable balances, with both amounts valued at sales prices; the inventory turnover ratio compares cost of goods sold and inventory balances, with both amounts valued at cost prices.

The inventory turnover ratio is typically expressed in "times-per-year," but an alternate form of the ratio is the **inventory flow period** ratio, expressed in "number of days." The ratio in times-per-year is:

$$\text{Inventory turnover} = \frac{\text{cost of goods sold}}{\text{inventory}}$$

and in number of days, the ratio is:[4]

---

[4] This ratio can also be calculated as: $\dfrac{365}{\text{inventory turnover (in times-per-year)}}$.

$$\text{Inventory flow period} = \frac{\text{inventory}}{\text{cost of goods sold} \div 365}$$

The inventory turnover ratio is subject to the same types of distortions arising from seasonality and growth as the accounts receivable collection period. A retail store enjoying substantial December holiday trade will build inventories in the fall with the anticipation of high sales in November and December. Its apparent rate of inventory usage at the end of October will be very different from an inventory turnover calculated on the basis of the depleted inventory balances of January 31. Growth in sales typically necessitates an increasing investment in inventory; to compensate, inventory turnovers should be calculated on the basis of average inventory balances, rather than year-end balances.

Hewlett-Packard grew substantially in 1979. Its inventory utilization ratios, based upon average inventory, are:

$$\text{Inventory turnover} = \frac{\text{cost of goods sold}}{(\text{opening inventory} + \text{ending inventory}) \div 2}$$

$$= \frac{1106}{(120 + 358 + 99 + 257) \div 2} = \frac{1106}{417} = 2.65 \text{ times per year}$$

$$\text{Inventory flow period} = \frac{(\text{opening inventory} + \text{ending inventory}) \div 2}{\text{cost of goods sold} \div 365}$$

$$= \frac{(120 + 358 + 99 + 257) \div 2}{1106 \div 365} = \frac{417}{3.03} = 138 \text{ days}$$

Assessing the adequacy of a company's inventory turnover is difficult because the nature of the particular business affects so greatly the rate of flow of inventory. At one extreme, a dairy had better have a very rapid turnover of inventory if its milk, butter, and cheese are to remain fresh until purchased by the consumer. At the other extreme, a shipbuilding firm requiring a year or two to complete the fabrication and assembly of a large ship will necessarily have very large inventories in relationship to its annual volume of activity.

Some published financial statements do not provide a separation of product and period costs. If an analyst does not have available cost-of-goods-sold data, the inventory turnover ratio can be calculated using sales, rather than cost of goods sold, in the numerator. The numerator and denominator are now not expressed in comparable terms: the numerator is valued at sales prices, including the company's gross margin, but the denominator (the inventory) is valued at cost prices. While the resulting ratio does not, in fact, indicate the number of times per year that the company's inventory turns over, a comparison of this ratio over a number of years may prove useful in assessing changes in the rate of inventory flow over time. (Bear in mind that changes in gross profit margins will also affect the ratio.)

Accounts payable payment period   A major determinant of a company's working capital position is the amount of trade, or vendor, credit utilized. Just as a comparison of sales and accounts receivable reveals the average collection period, a comparison of credit purchases and accounts payable reveals the average **accounts payable payment period**—the time that a company takes to pay its suppliers. This payment period can be compared to the normal terms of purchase to assess how well the company is meeting its obligations to its suppliers.

Unfortunately, total credit purchases are typically not revealed in published financial statements and may not even be readily available within the company. However, a *proxy* for credit purchases may be used—that is, another value, more readily available, that tends to increase or decrease coincident with credit purchases. Cost of goods sold represents a reasonable proxy, if the large majority of credit purchases is goods and merchandise for resale.

We do not have data on HP's credit purchases for 1978 and 1979, and we know that cost of goods sold includes major amounts of production labor and overhead in addition to materials purchased on credit. Thus, cost of goods sold is a quite imperfect proxy for credit purchases. Nevertheless, based upon year-end Accounts Payable totals, we can calculate the payment period as follows:

$$\text{A/P payment period} = \frac{\text{accounts payable}}{\text{cost of goods sold} \div 365}$$

$$\text{A/P payment period (1979)} = \frac{109}{1106 \div 365} = 36 \text{ days}$$

$$\text{A/P payment period (1978)} = \frac{71}{808 \div 365} = 32 \text{ days}$$

Based upon these data alone, it would appear that HP paid its vendors somewhat more slowly in 1979 than in 1978. However, many factors may account for this change, including a surge of purchases at year-end 1979, more rapid growth in 1979 than 1978, or a change in the mix of materials included in cost of goods sold.

Working capital turnover   The **working capital turnover** ratio provides the financial analyst with a summary view of the efficiency with which the company is using its net investment in current assets less current liabilities.

$$\text{Working capital turnover} = \frac{\text{sales}}{\text{average working capital}}$$

If this ratio, expressed in times-per-year, decreases, the company is investing more in working capital per dollar of sales; if the ratio increases, the company is making more efficient use of its working capital. Again, this ratio is subject to the same types of distortion from seasonality and growth that plagued the ratios just discussed.

In 1979 Hewlett-Packard's working capital turnover was:

Working capital turnover

$$= \frac{\text{sales}}{(\text{opening working capital} + \text{ending working capital}) \div 2}$$

$$= \frac{2361}{[(1269 - 599) + (952 - 415)] \div 2} = \frac{2361}{603.5} = 3.9 \text{ times per year}$$

Other asset turnover measures Still other asset turnover measures may prove useful to the financial analyst. A comparison of sales and net investment in fixed assets provides an indication of the number of dollars of annual sales realized from the company's investment in productive assets. The higher the **fixed asset turnover** ratio, the more effectively the company is utilizing its fixed assets. Finally, a global measure of the utilization of assets can be derived from a **total asset turnover** ratio—the relationship between sales and total assets. These two ratios, although they do not measure working capital utilization, are mentioned here because we will refer to them at the end of this chapter when we discuss the linkage among ratios.

For Hewlett-Packard in 1979 these ratios were:

$$\text{Fixed asset turnover} = \frac{\text{sales}}{\text{average net fixed assets}}$$

$$= \frac{2361}{(591 + 476) \div 2} = \frac{2361}{533.5} = 4.4 \text{ times per year}$$

$$\text{Total asset turnover} = \frac{\text{sales}}{\text{average total assets}}$$

$$= \frac{2361}{(1900 + 1462) \div 2} = \frac{2361}{1681} = 1.40 \text{ times per year}$$

The total asset turnover ratio at HP has remained quite constant in recent years at about 1.3 to 1.4, suggesting that, as this company grows, its investment in assets grow apace. If the ratio continues to hold in future years, HP can expect to have to invest 71 cents $(\frac{1}{1.40})$ in assets for every $1.00 increase in annual sales.

CAPITAL STRUCTURE RATIOS

Capital structure ratios help the analyst evaluate the "liabilities + owners' equity" side of the balance sheet—that is, how the company is being financed. These ratios help assess the financial riskiness of the business as well as the potential for improved returns through the judicious use of debt.

When a company borrows money, it undertakes a firm, iron-clad obligation to pay interest on the borrowed funds and to make principal repayments on schedule. Failure to make these various payments when due (that is, default on the provisions of the loan agreement) subjects the company to the risk of bankruptcy. By contrast, when a corporation obtains additional funds by the sale of new capital stock, it undertakes no such firm obligation to its new shareholders; these shareholders will receive dividends only if and when declared by the corporation's board of directors. Failure to pay dividends does not constitute default and does not subject the company to the risk of failure. Thus, from the point of view of the corporation, financing through the issuance of common stock is much less risky than financing through borrowing.

However, the judicious use of borrowing can benefit shareholders. If a company can borrow funds at an interest rate equal to $x\%$ and invest those funds to earn at a rate greater than $x\%$, then this incremental return will result in a higher return on shareholders' invested capital. This phenomenon, known as debt leverage, is explained and illustrated more fully in Appendix A to this chapter.

The point to bear in mind is that the use of borrowed funds is inherently neither good nor bad. The greater the use of borrowed funds—that is, the greater the use of **debt leverage**—the greater the financial risk to which the company is exposed, but also the greater the potential return to shareholders. Decisions on the amount of debt to be utilized by a corporation—that is, capital structure decisions—are a matter of judgment, judgment that must be exercised by the corporation's board of directors and management.

Total debt to owners' equity ratio The debt of most corporations is composed of both current liabilities and long-term debt; owners' equity consists of both capital invested by the owners and earnings retained in the business. The ratio between the two sums indicates the relative contribution of creditors and owners to the financing of the company. For

Hewlett-Packard, the **total debt to owners' equity** ratio in 1979 and 1978 was:

$$\text{Total debt to owners' equity} = \frac{\text{current liabilities} + \text{long-term debt}}{\text{total shareholders' equity}}$$

$$(1979) = \frac{599 + 15}{1235} = 50\%$$

$$(1978) = \frac{415 + 10}{1002} = 42\%$$

Total debt to total assets ratio A closely related ratio compares total debt to the total value of all assets owned by the company, thus indicating the percentage of total assets represented by liabilities. Since assets = liabilities + owners' equity, the **total debt to total assets** ratio provides no new information that was not inherent in the total debt to owners' equity ratio. For HP, this ratio in 1979 and 1978 was:

$$\text{Total debt to total assets} = \frac{\text{current liabilities} + \text{long-term debt}}{\text{total assets}}$$

$$(1979) = \frac{599 + 15}{1900} = 32\%$$

$$(1978) = \frac{415 + 10}{1462} = 29\%$$

The remainder of HP's assets (68% in 1979) were financed by owners' equity.

Long-term debt to total capitalization ratio This ratio requires the careful definition of both the numerator and denominator. Long-term debt is that portion of total borrowings having a maturity longer than one year (and therefore not included in current liabilities). **Total capitalization** is defined as the total of permanent sources of capital within the business. Current liabilities are not considered a permanent source of capital, since they arise spontaneously from the operations of the enterprise—amounts owing to trade creditors and employees and miscellaneous accruals would not be present if the company were not actively engaged in trade. Total capitalization, then, is defined as long-term debt plus owners' equity.[5] This

[5] The definition is actually somewhat more complex. Certain corporations have outstanding both preferred and common shares; while a discussion of the differences and relative advantages of each form of security is beyond the scope of this book, preferred stock is typically included as a part of owners' equity for the purpose of calculating capital structure ratios. Deferred taxes (see Appendix to Chapter 7) typically appear on the balance sheet between long-term debt and owners' equity. Some analysts will include deferred taxes as part of total capitalization and others will omit them entirely. Since by the nature of these deferred taxes most companies will not be required to make these payments in the foreseeable future, deferred taxes have been omitted here.

ratio indicates the percentage that *permanent,* or long-term, borrowed funds are of total permanently invested capital. For Hewlett-Packard in 1979 and 1978, this ratio was:

$$\text{Long-term debt to total capitalization} = \frac{\text{long-term debt}}{\text{long-term debt} + \text{owners' equity}}$$

$$(1979) = \frac{15}{15 + 1235} = 1\%$$

$$(1978) = \frac{10}{10 + 1002} = 1\%$$

HP obtains virtually all of its permanent financing from owners' equity, having made a policy decision to minimize the use of long-term debt.

Times interest earned   An indication of the ability of a corporate borrower to service its debt — that is, to pay interest when due — is obtained by comparing the company's annual interest expense with the company's earnings before the payment of interest or income taxes. The ratio assumes that **earnings before interest and taxes**[6] (often abbreviated EBIT) approximate the company's cash flow that will be available for debt service (an assumption which for any of a number of reasons may not be accurate). The higher this ratio, the greater is the safety margin, and the lower the risk that the company will be unable to service its debt. As this ratio declines, the greater is the risk that some untoward event such as an economic recession will cause the company to be unable to meet its interest payment obligations. Hewlett-Packard utilizes very little borrowed funds and thus its **times interest earned** ratio is very, very high. Public utilities such as telephone or gas and electric companies by their nature rely heavily on borrowed capital, and this ratio is very relevant in judging the financial risk inherent in the company's capital structure. For example, in 1978 the Southern Company, an electric power utility, had EBIT of $473 million and net interest payments of $310 million, and thus its times interest earned ratio was:

$$\text{Times interest earned} = \frac{\text{earnings before interest and taxes}}{\text{annual interest expense}} = \frac{473}{310} = 1.53$$

PROFITABILITY

The ratios dealing with liquidity, working capital utilization, and capital structure focus primarily on an assessment of the company's financial position. By contrast, the profitability ratios seek to measure the company's performance, or the rate at which it is earning financial returns.

[6] Pretax operating profit is used since current U.S. tax law permits interest to be deducted in computing taxable income.

Two types of profitability ratios are useful. The first measures profit in relation to sales levels and is obtained by comparing data solely within the income statement; the second measures profit in relation to investment and involves comparisons of income statement and balance sheet data.

Percentage relationships on income statement   The ratio of net income to total sales is a useful indicator of the company's rate of profitability. In addition, the percentage that each of the line items on the income statement bears to total revenue, or sales, also provides useful insights. For example, the gross margin percentage indicates the relationship between sales revenue and product cost. Sales expense as a percentage of sales revenue reveals what percent of the sales dollar the company spends on selling and marketing activities.

Exhibit 9-5 provides a percentage analysis of Hewlett-Packard's income statements for the years 1979 and 1978. Note the consistency between the two years, in spite of substantial growth. The company's gross margin—the difference between sales and costs of goods sold—was 53% (100% less 47%) in the most recent year, a healthy gross margin. The company spends quite heavily both on research and development and on marketing—9% and 15%, respectively—because of the nature of its very technical products. Net earnings at 9% of sales ranks Hewlett-Packard among the higher-earning manufacturing companies.

These percentages are greatly dependent upon the nature of the particular business. Consider the probable percentages for a large food retailer: cost of goods sold will be a very high percentage of sales, research and development expenses will be essentially nonexistent, and net earnings as a percentage of sales will be very small, typically 1–2%. Thus, as we

Exhibit 9-5
Percentage Analysis of Income Statement
HEWLETT-PACKARD CO., 1979 AND 1978

	1979	1978
Net sales	100%	100%
Cost and expenses		
Cost of goods sold	47	45
Research and development	9	9
Marketing	15	15
Administrative & general	12	14
Interest	—	—
	83	83
Earnings before taxes on income	17	17
Taxes on income	8	8
Net earnings	9%	9%

shall discuss shortly, comparisons between companies engaged in dissimilar businesses can be very misleading.

Return on sales   Note particularly the last of these percentage relationships, net income to total sales, or **return on sales (ROS).**   We shall refer to this ratio later in this chapter when we consider the linkage among ratios.

Return on equity   Turning now to consider profitability as related to investment, we find the most fundamental ratio is that of net income to total owners' equity, the so-called **return on equity (ROE).**   In order to compensate for growth, the ratio compares earnings for the year to average equity, or

$$\text{Return on equity} = \frac{\text{net income}}{(\text{opening equity} + \text{ending equity}) \div 2}$$

Hewlett Packard's return on equity in 1979 was:

$$\text{Return on equity} = \frac{203}{(1002 + 1235) \div 2} = \frac{203}{1118.5} = 18.1\%$$

The ROE ratio compares net income, after payment of all expenses including interest and taxes, with the total book value of the shareholders' investment, including both invested capital and earnings retained by the business.   Since presumably all shareholders invest for a return, even companies within different industries can be compared on the basis of ROE.

Return on equity does not, however, indicate the degree of risk inherent in the return.   A shareholder might be quite willing to accept a lower ROE in exchange for a lower risk.   Appendix A to this chapter describes how the use of greater debt leverage leads both to higher risk and potentially to higher ROE.

Note also that this ratio compares net income to *book* shareholders' equity.   An investor might have to pay more or less than equivalent book value for a share of stock, as market values of securities bear no necessary relationship to book values.   Thus, the ROE may not indicate for a particular investor the rate of return on an actual investment in the securities of the firm.

Return on assets   The return on equity for a company will be influenced by its capital structure.   As explained in Appendix A, a company employing high debt leverage is typically subject to wider swings in ROE than another company obtaining its permanent capital primarily through shareholders' equity.   An analyst may wish to factor out the influence of capital structure when appraising the company's ability to generate earnings on investment. If so, total assets may be used as the measure of investment—the total amount owned by the company, whether financed through debt or owners' equity.

The **return on assets (ROA)** ratio compares earnings to total assets. However, net income cannot be used as the numerator in this ratio, since net income is profit *after* payment of interest and the amount of interest paid is a function of the capital structure of the company. Thus, the analyst should again use earnings before interest and taxes (EBIT). Return on assets is defined as:

$$\text{Return on assets} = \frac{\text{earnings before interest and taxes}}{(\text{opening assets} + \text{ending assets}) \div 2}$$

At Hewlett-Packard in 1979, return on assets was

$$\text{Return on assets} = \frac{398^7}{(1462 + 1900) \div 2} = \frac{398}{1681} = 24\%$$

Bear in mind that the return on assets percentage and the return on equity percentage are not comparable, since ROA is a before-tax percentage and ROE is an after-tax percentage.

Interpreting Ratios

Experienced financial statement analysts instinctively observe ratios as they review financial statements; that is, they learn to think in terms of ratios as they scan financial statements, searching for strengths and weaknesses in the company's financial condition and operating performance. Not every ratio will provide useful information. For example, the observation that a particular company's current ratio conforms to typical industry averages may simply lead to the conclusion that liquidity is neither a particular problem nor a strength of the company. Further analysis may reveal a relatively long collection period—suggesting that the company is encountering problems in obtaining prompt payment from customers—and a relatively low total debt to owners' equity ratio, suggesting that the company has low financial risk and low debt leverage. These observations are useful and may suggest to the analyst areas for further inquiry: Why are customers paying slowly? Could the company benefit from further debt leverage? And so forth.

[7] Earnings before taxes on income is used here. HP's Statement of Earnings does not reveal interest expense.

Ratios need to be calculated accurately, but not with undue precision. A collection period calculated to the nearest whole day, rather than to the second decimal point, is quite adequate to suggest the general rate of customer collections. Values on the income statement and balance sheet are significantly affected by a host of variables such as seasonality (as previously discussed), price-level changes, and random events occurring just prior to the balance sheet date. Minor changes in most ratios are not significant.

NO ABSOLUTE STANDARDS

We have not yet addressed a question which undoubtedly has by now occurred to you: What *should* be the value of these various ratios? What represents an appropriate current ratio, or total debt to total assets ratio, or collection period, or return on equity?

Unfortunately, these questions cannot be answered. The adequate level of liquidity or appropriate amount of debt leverage is a function of the nature of the business, stage of development of the company, philosophy of the management and owners, and many other factors. While some "conventional wisdoms" do exist—such as that a manufacturing company should have a current ratio of 2.0 and a quick ratio of 1.0—these "wisdoms" are dangerous. Some companies achieve very adequate liquidity at a current ratio much less than 2.0—for example, service companies with very low inventories or companies that sell for cash and thus have no accounts receivable. Other companies need to have a current ratio well in excess of 2.0 in order to assure adequate liquidity—for example, companies whose manufacturing processes require large inventories.

Not only are we frustrated in seeking absolute standards for the various ratios, but in addition we typically cannot conclude for most ratios that "the higher the better" or "the lower the better." One might be inclined to think that the higher the current ratio, the more sound is the company's financial condition. Certainly a high current ratio indicates strong liquidity, but an excessively high current ratio suggests inefficient use of the current assets. Or, one may be inclined to conclude that the shorter the collection period, the better. However, if the company is achieving this rapid collection from customers by refusing to sell to any but the most credit-worthy of customers and then by harassing customers to pay quickly, the company may be suffering loss of sales volume as a result of its collection policies. Or, one may be inclined to conclude that the lower the total debt to total assets ratio, the healthier the business. Low debt leverage does indicate low financial risk, but many companies can and should avail themselves of the benefits of debt leverage; for them very low debt ratios may reveal that financial policies are unnecessarily timid.

Thus, judging the appropriateness of a particular ratio is not an easy matter. An analyst's judgment is aided by two techniques, however: reviewing trends over time, and comparing the ratios of one company to those of similar companies in the same industry.

TRENDS

Suppose that both company A and company B now have a current ratio of 2.0. The two companies apparently have equivalent liquidity. Now suppose that the current ratios for these two companies over the past three years have been:

	Two years ago	One year ago	This year
Company A	1.4	1.8	2.0
Company B	2.6	2.2	2.0

Interpreting the present current ratio in light of the trend in that ratio may lead to a different conclusion. Now company A's liquidity seems somewhat more comfortable, since it has been strengthened over recent years, while company B's liquidity has been deteriorating.

Exhibit 9-6 shows the trend in selected ratios for Hewlett-Packard over the past five years. These ratios have been quite stable over this period, but some trends are discernible. Liquidity has declined somewhat from 1975 levels, but both accounts receivable collection and inventory turnover have improved steadily during the five years. Total debt to total assets has increased somewhat, but the company continues to have low debt leverage. HP's profitability suffered somewhat as a result of the recession of the mid-1970s, but improved again in recent years.

Analyses of other companies might reveal more dramatic trends.

Exhibit 9-6
Trends in Financial Ratios
HEWLETT-PACKARD CO., 1975–1979

	1975	1976	1977	1978	1979
Liquidity					
Current Ratio	2.8	2.6	2.6	2.3	2.1
Working Capital Utilization					
A/R Collection Period (days)	74	71	67	68	67
Inventory Turnover (X per year)	2.3	2.4	2.4	2.5	2.7
Capital Structure					
Total Debt to Total Assets	24%	25%	26%	29%	32%
Profitability					
Return on Sales	8.5%	8.1%	8.8%	8.8%	8.6%
Return on Equity	16.4%	14.7%	16.2%	16.8%	18.1%

Exhibit 9-7
Trend in Capital Structure Ratio:
1974–1978
LOCKHEED AIRCRAFT COMPANY

Year	Ratio of Long-Term Debt to Total Capitalization
1974	97%
1975	92%
1976	80%
1977	72%
1978	59%

Exhibit 9-7 shows the trend in the long-term debt to total capitalization ratio for Lockheed Aircraft Corporation, a company that encountered such severe financial problems in the early 1970s that a governmental guarantee of the company's debt was required to reduce the risk of financial failure. Note the sharp reduction in debt leverage over the five-year period, from a disastrously high level to a moderately high level.

COMPARISON WITH SIMILAR COMPANIES

A company's ratios must be interpreted in light of the particular industry in which the company is engaged. It would be irrelevant to compare Hewlett-Packard to an electric power utility. Utilities typically have large amounts of fixed assets and relatively little working capital; their fixed asset and total asset turnovers are generally low, but they avail themselves of substantial debt leverage and thereby earn competitive returns on equity. Light manufacturing companies, such as HP, have substantially greater investment in current assets than in fixed assets and HP has chosen to emphasize equity rather than debt financing.

On the other hand, it might be revealing to compare HP's ratios to other companies of comparable size whose business is closely related to "precision electronic equipment for measurement, analysis and computation." That is, it can be useful to compare companies in similar businesses and of similar size—for example, direct competitors. Many trade or industry associations obtain from their membership, typically on a confidential basis, detailed information regarding financial ratios, and compile, categorize, and publish these data in summary form for the benefit of their members. Certain agencies of the government and some banks provide similar industry financial ratio data. Such data can prove invaluable to the analyst in providing a benchmark for comparison.

The American Electronics Association periodically surveys its members for financial ratio information and publishes the results of the

Exhibit 9-8
Industry Comparative Ratios
1978–1979

	HP	Industry[1]
Current ratio	2.1	2.6
A/R collection period (days)	67	63
Inventory turnover (times per year)	2.7	3.2
Total asset turnover (times per year)	1.4	0.9
Gross margin	53%	38.9%
Profit before tax ÷ total sales	17%	11.3%
Return on assets	24%	17.8%

[1] Includes data from 132 companies, each with sales in excess of $20 million per year; these companies are involved in many different types of electronic manufacturing. Data shown are medians. Source: 1978—1979 Operating Ratios Survey, prepared by the American Electronics Association.

survey to participating members. The 1978–1979 survey provides some useful comparative data for HP, as shown in Exhibit 9-8. While HP's total asset turnover is substantially above industry average, its inventory turnover is well below average and its collection period is slightly below average. On the other hand, HP is substantially more profitable than the industry average according to the three ratios shown in Exhibit 9-8.

Linkage Among Financial Ratios

It may by now have occurred to you that there must be linkages among the ratios that we have been discussing. For example, if a company can achieve a higher total asset turnover ratio, it will be able to reduce its total investment in assets, thus requiring less capital; if this condition can be reflected in lower total owners' equity, then return on equity will be enhanced. A capital structure employing more debt (that is, higher debt leverage) can result in higher return on equity. Also, if a company can improve its return on sales without changing its total asset turnover or capital structure, this condition may be reflected in higher return on equity.

These interrelationships or linkages can be expressed in a simple algebraic expression:

$$\text{Return on equity} = \frac{\text{net income}}{\text{total sales}} \times \frac{\text{total sales}}{\text{total assets}} \times \frac{\text{total assets}}{\text{total equity}}$$

The first of these three ratios is the return on sales (ROS) ratio discussed earlier; the second is the total asset turnover ratio; and the third is an indication of debt leverage.[8] Note that this entire expression must be true, since by the rules of algebra total sales and total assets cancel out of the equation and the ratio of net income to total equity—the definition of return on equity (ROE)—remains.

The reasons to focus on this expression are two: (1) return on equity is the fundamental measure of how well the company is doing in earning returns on the shareholders' funds entrusted to management, and (2) the three individual ratios, or fractions, suggest some alternative approaches for management to improve return on equity. This second point deserves further elaboration.

The first fraction indicates that ROE will be improved if ROS is improved, that is, if the company earns more profit per dollar of sales. The second fraction focuses on asset management: if the company can achieve the same sales with lower investment in assets, the right-hand side of the balance sheet can be reduced (i.e., less debt and equity capital will be required); this phenomenon will also improve ROE. Finally, if the company utilizes relatively more debt and less equity in its capital structure—that is, if it undertakes greater debt leverage—ROE will be increased. Remember, however, that this action will also increase the company's risk of failure.

We have already calculated Hewlett-Packard's ROE for 1979 at 18.1%. This value can also be derived using the three fractions described above:

$$\text{ROE} = \frac{203}{2361} \times \frac{2361}{1681} \times \frac{1681}{1119}$$

$$= 8.6\% \times 1.4 \times 1.5$$

$$= 18.1\%$$

Suppose HP could improve its net profitability in relationship to sales to 9.5%; this change would improve the company's ROE from 18.1% to 20.0%. Or, suppose the company could, by careful control of assets, improve its asset turnover from 1.4 to 1.5; if this reduction in asset investment were reflected by proportionate decreases in both debt and equity so that the company's debt leverage remained unchanged, ROE would be improved from 18.1% to 19.4%. Finally, if management had elected to assume greater financing risk by increasing debt leverage so that the ratio of assets to equity was 2.0 instead of 1.5, ROE would be increased to 24.1%. And, if all of these changes were undertaken, ROE would grow to 28.5%. For a variety of reasons these changes may be impractical or undesirable, but the linkage equation is useful in focusing attention on the importance of:

---

[8] Since the difference between the numerator and denominator of this fraction equals total liabilities, the higher this ratio, the greater is the company's level of debt, and therefore the higher is the company's debt leverage.

Return on sales

Asset utilization

Debt leverage

in the determination of the company's fundamental measure of profitability, return on equity.

Investment Ratios

Our discussion has thus far been limited solely to ratios utilizing data from the company's financial statements. Investors, and therefore management as well, are also interested in the relationship between the company's financial results and the market price for its common stock.

Common stock market prices are determined by the interactions of buyers and sellers. The shares of larger companies are traded on organized exchanges that are auction markets, such as the New York Stock Exchange or the London Stock Exchange, while the shares of smaller companies trade in other formal and informal manners. In all cases, market prices are a function of the prices that potential investors are willing to pay and the prices that present stockholders are willing to accept for shares of stock. The market price bears no necessary relationship to the data that appear in the company's accounting records.

Market prices for common stocks are quoted in per-share amounts. To make comparisons between accounting data and market prices, the analyst needs to translate certain accounting data to a per-share basis.

EARNINGS PER SHARE

Published financial statements provide data on **earnings per share (EPS)**—that is, net income attributable to each share of common stock.

$$\text{Earnings per share} = \frac{\text{net income}}{\text{number of shares of common stock}}$$

If the number of shares outstanding increased or decreased during the year, an average number of shares should be used in the denominator.

In 1979 Hewlett-Packard earned net income of $203 million and at year-end had outstanding 59,148,000 shares.

$$\text{Earnings per share} = \frac{\$203,000,000}{59,148,000} = \$3.43$$

This figure appears at the bottom of the income statement in Exhibit 9-1.

This EPS calculation is somewhat more complex for companies having contracts that may require them to issue additional common shares. This situation may occur because a company has granted rights to certain investors or members of management to purchase shares of common stock at set prices. These rights are typically embodied in stock options, warrants, and convertible securities; a more complete description of these instruments is beyond the scope of this book. If the company has prospered since the time these rights were granted, the set prices may now be significantly below current market prices. As these investors or managers exercise their rights, the to-be-issued shares will participate in the future earnings and dividends of the company. Accountants have devised a rather complex method for calculating EPS, giving effect to these additional shares that will eventually be issued, and refer to the resulting value as **earnings per common and common equivalent share.** Although Hewlett-Packard has some stock options and similar instruments outstanding, the company's earnings per share and earnings per common and common equivalent share are not materially different.

BOOK VALUE PER SHARE

A company's **book value per share** is simply shareholders' equity divided by the number of shares outstanding. For Hewlett-Packard at the end of 1979, the book value was:

$$\text{Book value per share} = \frac{\text{total shareholders' equity}}{\text{number of shares outstanding}}$$

$$= \frac{1,235,000,000}{59,148,000}$$

$$= \$20.88$$

A share's market price may be quite different from its book value per share, either above or below. A comparison between market price and book value may be revealing to the investor.

DIVIDENDS PER SHARE

Dividends are declared by a company's board of directors if, as, and when the board feels that such a payment is in the best interests of the company and its shareholders. Dividends are declared in per-share amounts and thus no conversion is required. In 1979 Hewlett-Packard paid total dividends of 35 cents per share.

PAYOUT RATIO

A company's **payout ratio** is the ratio of dividends per share to earnings per share, and indicates the percentage of the firm's earnings that are being paid out to shareholders as dividends. That portion not paid as dividends is, of course, retained and reinvested in the business. A company's **earnings retention ratio** is simply (100% − payout ratio). HP's payout ratio in 1979 was:

$$\text{Payout ratio} = \frac{\text{dividends per share}}{\text{earnings per share}}$$

$$= \frac{\$.35}{\$3.43} = 10.2\%$$

HP's payout ratio is low; the company is retaining most of its earnings (89.8%) to finance its high rate of growth.

PRICE/EARNINGS RATIO

The **price/earnings (P/E) ratio,** or **earnings multiple** as it is sometimes called, is the ratio of market price per share and earnings per share. Hewlett-Packard's stock is traded on the New York and Pacific Coast Stock Exchanges and the average of the highest and lowest trading prices throughout the 1979 fiscal year was $49\frac{1}{4}$. Using this value for average market price, the company's price/earnings ratio was:

$$\text{Price/earnings ratio} = \frac{\text{market price}}{\text{earnings per share}}$$

$$= \frac{49.25}{3.43}$$

$$= 14.4$$

A stock's market price is not a valid indicator of whether the stock is expensive or inexpensive relative to other stocks because the number of shares of stock outstanding is a function of (1) the prices at which the company sold shares in earlier years and (2) additional shares that may have been granted to shareholders (typically in the form of stock splits or stock dividends). Suppose companies A and B are identical in all respects except that A has twice as many shares outstanding as B. We would expect the market price of A to be one-half the market price of B. Since the earnings-per-share of A would also be one-half that of B, the price/earnings ratios of the two companies would be identical. Thus, stocks can be compared on the basis of price/earnings ratios, while they cannot be compared on the basis of absolute market prices.

If a stock has a high P/E ratio, this fact is evidence that investors are willing to pay a high multiple of current earnings to participate as shareholders in the future of the company. Hewlett-Packard's P/E ratio of 14.4 was above the average ratio in 1979 for all common stocks traded on the New York Stock Exchange. Apparently investors were willing to bid up the price of the HP shares because they felt that the company's prospects for growth in sales, earnings, and dividends were above average.

YIELD

A common stock's **yield** is the ratio of dividends per share and market price. HP's yield in 1979 was:

$$\text{Yield} = \frac{\text{dividends per share}}{\text{market price per share}}$$

$$= \frac{\$.35}{49.25} = 0.7\%$$

HP's yield is very low—less than 1%. Apparently individuals are investing in the stock not with a view to current cash return but with a view to future growth in the company, which growth may be reflected in higher market prices in the future. Note that part of the reason that HP's yield is low is that its market price is high.

Interpreting Investment Ratios

Price/earnings ratios and yields do not determine market prices of common stocks; rather, they are determined *by* and calculated *from* the market prices. Therefore an investor cannot decide to buy or sell particular securities solely on the basis of these ratios. Investment decisions—purchases and sales—are based upon investors' expectations about the future. The auction markets conducted by the world's stock exchanges are amazingly efficient in quickly reflecting in market prices of securities any changes in the collective expectations of investors.

Financial statements are historical documents and thus all ratios discussed here are historical. Ratios can assist investors in assessing the future and formulating their expectations but, because they may not reliably predict the future, they cannot be used mechanistically to make investment decisions.

A stock with a high P/E and a low yield may prove to be a good invest-ment if the company grows and prospers and its share price appreciates. On the other hand, it may prove to be a poor investment if investor expecta-tions of growth and profits are not realized and its share price declines (or appreciates only modestly); in the latter case the P/E ratio will probably de-cline over time.

Conversely, a stock with a low P/E may prove to be a good investment if the company's future performance exceeds the modest investor expecta-tions reflected in today's low P/E. Or, an investor attracted by a current high yield will be disappointed if the company's future operations do not permit the present dividend to be maintained; if the dividend is reduced, the stock's yield may remain unchanged but only because the share price has fallen—an unfavorable outcome for the investor.

Summary

The fundamental tool of financial statement analysis is the calculation of ratios. It is the comparison between amounts appearing on the financial statements, rather than their absolute level, that is meaningful to the ana-lyst in gaining insight into the two key questions: How sound is the com-pany's financial position, and how well is the company performing in earning returns on the capital employed?

Very many different ratios are in active use. Ratios that are highly rel-evant to certain industries or companies may be of marginal or no interest in other circumstances. The most common ratios, grouped into the four cate-gories discussed in this chapter, are:

Liquidity
 Current ratio
 Acid-test ratio (or Quick ratio)

Working capital utilization
 Accounts receivable collection period
 Inventory turnover
 Accounts payable payment period
 Working capital turnover

Capital structure
 Total debt to owners' equity
 Total debt to total assets
 Long-term debt to total capitalization
 Times interest earned

Profitability
   Percentage relationships on income statement
   Return on sales (ROS)
   Return on equity (ROE)
   Return on assets (ROA)

A number of caveats apply to the interpretation of ratios. Ratios that compare data from the income statement with data from the balance sheet (for example, the working-capital-utilization ratios) can be significantly distorted by seasonability and by high growth rates. No absolute standards exist for ratios; indeed, with respect to most ratios one cannot even conclude that the higher the better, or the lower the better. Judgment is required to know when a particular ratio is providing a danger signal or revealing a particular strength about a company.

Trends in ratios will typically reveal additional information about a company, particularly trends in the liquidity and capital structure ratios. Comparisons between similar companies in like industries can also be helpful. However, the analyst needs to bear in mind that the optimum level of a ratio will depend very much on the nature of the particular business in which the company is engaged, as well as on the company's future plans, management policies, and so forth.

Certain of the ratios discussed in this chapter are interrelated, or linked. Return on equity can be viewed as the product of (1) return on sales, (2) total asset turnover, and (3) leverage.

A company's financial performance also needs to be related to the investors' perception of the company as revealed in the market price established by the actions of potential buyers and sellers of the company's shares. Two important ratios from an investment viewpoint are price/earnings (P/E) ratio and yield.

Appendix A: Financial or Debt Leverage

This appendix provides a brief explanation and illustration of the risks and benefits of the use of borrowed funds—that is, the leverage associated with the use of debt.

The greater the use of debt within the company's capital structure, the more leveraged is the company. This **debt leverage** may in certain circumstances benefit the shareholders and in other circumstances lead to financial failure. If on a consistent basis the company is able to earn a return on its investments in excess of the interest rate that it must pay on borrowed funds, this incremental return over the cost of the borrowed funds

benefits the company's shareholders. Leverage has worked positively for
the shareholders.

On the other hand, the higher the company's debt, the greater its fixed
obligations to pay interest and principal. If the company's operating performance is erratic or encounters difficulties, the company may not be able
to comply with the terms of its borrowing agreements; if the company de-
faults on its loan agreements and its lenders demand adherence to the
terms of the borrowing contracts, the company may suffer financial ruin.

Exhibit 9A-1 details the capital structure of two hypothetical companies
that are identical in all respects except that company R has chosen to minimize debt leverage by borrowing no long-term funds and company S has
chosen to borrow one-half of its permanent capital. Company S is said to
be more highly leveraged than company R.

Exhibits 9A-2 and 9A-3 show the effects of leverage in periods of strong
operating performance (periods of prosperity) and in periods of weak performance (periods of recession). In the prosperous times illustrated in
Exhibit 9A-2, return on assets is 20% for both companies, well in excess of
the interest rate paid by company S on borrowed funds. As a result, company S, the more leveraged company, produces for its shareholders higher
returns on investment (ROE of 21% versus 12.5%), even though its total
profit in dollars is lower than that of Company R. Thus, debt leverage has
worked to the benefit of company S's shareholders in prosperous times.

In the recessionary times illustrated at the top of Exhibit 9A-3, both
companies earn a return on assets (5%) below the cost of (interest rate on)
borrowed funds, and thus company S's return on equity suffers by compari-

Exhibit 9A-1
Alternative Capital Structures, Companies R and S

Assets	Company R	Company S
Current assets	$ 5,000,000	$ 5,000,000
All other assets	5,000,000	5,000,000
Total assets	$10,000,000	$10,000,000
Liabilities and Owners' Equity		
Current liabilities	$ 2,000,000	$ 2,000,000
Long-term debt[1]	0	4,000,000
Owners' equity	8,000,000	4,000,000
Total liabilities + owners' equity	$10,000,000	$10,000,000
Ratios		
Current ratio	2.5	2.5
Total debt to owners' equity	25%	150%
Total debt to total assets	20%	60%
Long-term debt to total capitalization	0	50%

[1] Interest rate = 8%

Exhibit 9A-2
Effects of Debt Leverage in Period of Prosperity

	Company R	Company S
Sales	$22,000,000	$22,000,000
Total operating expenses	20,000,000	20,000,000
Operating profit	2,000,000	2,000,000
Interest expense	0	320,000
Profit before taxes	2,000,000	1,680,000
Income taxes (50% tax rate)	1,000,000	840,000
Net income	$ 1,000,000	$ 840,000

Ratios

	Company R	Company S
Return on assets	$\dfrac{2,000,000}{10,000,000}$	$\dfrac{2,000,000}{10,000,000}$
	$=20\%$	$=20\%$
Return on equity	$\dfrac{1,000,000}{8,000,000}$	$\dfrac{840,000}{4,000,000}$
	$=12.5\%$	$=21.0\%$

Exhibit 9A-3
Effects of Debt Leverage in Periods of Recession

MILD RECESSION	Company R	Company S
Sales	$16,000,000	$16,000,000
Total operating expenses	15,500,000	15,500,000
Operating profit	500,000	500,000
Interest expense	0	320,000
Profit before taxes	500,000	180,000
Income taxes (50% tax rate)	250,000	90,000
Net income	$ 250,000	$ 90,000

Ratios

	Company R	Company S
Return on assets	$\dfrac{500,000}{10,000,000}$	$\dfrac{500,000}{10,000,000}$
	$=5\%$	$=5\%$
Return on equity	$\dfrac{250,000}{8,000,000}$	$\dfrac{90,000}{4,000,000}$
	$=3.13\%$	$=2.25\%$

SEVERE RECESSION	Company R	Company S
Sales	$13,000,000	$13,000,000
Total operating expenses	13,500,000	13,500,000
Operating profit (loss)	(500,000)	(500,000)
Interest expense	0	320,000
Profit (loss) before taxes	(500,000)	(820,000)

son with company R (2.25% versus 3.13%). Debt leverage has in this case worked to the detriment of company S's shareholders.

If both companies follow the policy of paying 50% of net incc ̂ as cash dividends on common stock, company S's dividend payments will be "levered" favorably when conditions described in Exhibit 9A-2 prevail and unfavorably under conditions described in Exhibit 9A-3.

If the mild recession illustrated at the top of Exhibit 9A-3 turns into a deep recession or depression, as illustrated in the lower part of Exhibit 9A-3, both companies might incur operating losses. This eventuality would be a good bit more serious for company S than for company R. Company S must make substantial interest payments on its borrowed funds each year; these obligations are absolute. Failure to make these payments may result in company S's being declared bankrupt. Company R, facing no requirements for the payment of interest, is exposed to less risk of financial failure.

New Terms

Accounts payable payment period The average time period from receipt of merchandise or service to cash payment of the associated invoice. It is calculated as follows:

$$\frac{\text{Average accounts payable}}{\text{Average credit purchases per day}}$$

Accounts receivable collection period The average time period from invoice date to cash collection date. It is calculated as follows:

$$\frac{\text{Average accounts receivable}}{\text{Average sales per day}}$$

Acid-test ratio The ratio of the sum of cash, cash equivalents (including marketable securities), and accounts receivable to current liabilities. An alternative name for this ratio is *quick ratio*. The ratio measures a company's liquidity.

Book value per share The amount of shareholders' equity attributable to each share of common stock. It is calculated as follows:

$$\frac{\text{Total shareholders' equity}}{\text{Number of shares of common stock outstanding}}$$

Capital structure The composition of the capital employed in the business.

Cash equivalents Short-term investments that are highly marketable and can quickly be converted to cash.

Current ratio The ratio of current assets to current liabilities. It is a measure of the company's liquidity.

Debt leverage The extent to which the company relies upon borrowed funds (debt) for financing. Companies with high debt leverage are exposed to greater financial risk but also enjoy the potential of greater returns to shareholders.

Earnings before interest and taxes (EBIT) A company's earnings before the payment of (1) interest on borrowed funds and (2) income taxes. This quantity is used in calculating the times interest earned ratio and the return on assets ratio.

Earnings multiple Another name for *price/earnings ratio*.

Earnings per common and common equivalent share A form of earnings-per-share (EPS) calculation that gives effect to the company's contractual obligations to issue additional shares of common stock to certain investors or members of management.

Earnings per share (EPS) The net income attributable to each share of common stock. It is calculated as follows:

$$\frac{\text{Net income}}{\text{Average number of shares of common stock outstanding}}$$

Earnings retention ratio The percentage of the company's earnings reinvested in the business and not paid out as dividends. It is calculated as follows:

$$\frac{(\text{Earnings per share}) - (\text{dividends per share})}{\text{Earnings per share}}$$

or

$$100\% - \text{payout ratio}$$

Fixed-asset turnover A measure of the efficiency with which the company is using its net investment in fixed assets. It is calculated (in times per year) as follows:

$$\frac{\text{Sales}}{\text{Average net fixed assets}}$$

Inventory flow period The average time period from receipt of inventory to its shipment. The ratio is calculated as follows:

$$\frac{\text{Average inventory}}{\text{Average cost of goods sold per day}}$$

Inventory turnover The number of times per year that the firm's inventory turns over. It is calculated as follows:

$$\frac{\text{Cost of goods sold}}{\text{Average inventory}}$$

Liquidity The extent to which a company has funds available to meet its obligations as they come due. The most popular measures of liquidity are the current and quick (acid-test) ratios; the higher these ratios, the more liquid is the company.

Long-term debt to total capitalization   A financial ratio that measures debt leverage. It is calculated as follows:

$$\frac{\text{Long-term debt}}{\text{Total capitalization}}$$

Marketable securities   Those investment securities for which a ready market exists. United States Treasury securities and certain other interest-bearing short-term investments are marketable securities that are considered cash equivalents.

Payout ratio   The ratio of dividends per share to earnings per share. This ratio indicates the percentage of the company's earnings paid out in dividends.

Price/Earnings (P/E) ratio   The ratio of market price per share to earnings per share. This ratio is also referred to as the *earnings multiple* that investors are willing to pay for the company's common shares.

Quick ratio   An alternative name for the *acid-test ratio.*

Return on assets (ROA)   A measure of the company's return on investment that is independent of the company's capital structure. It is calculated as follows:

$$\frac{\text{Earnings before interest and taxes}}{\text{Average total assets}}$$

Return on equity (ROE)   A measure of the company's return on investment. It is calculated as follows:

$$\frac{\text{Net income}}{\text{Average shareholders' equity}}$$

Return on sales (ROS)   A measure of the company's rate of profitability on sales. It is calculated as follows:

$$\frac{\text{Net income}}{\text{Total sales}}$$

Times interest earned   A financial ratio that measures a company's ability to meet its interest payment obligations. It is calculated as follows:

$$\frac{\text{Earnings before interest and taxes}}{\text{Annual interest expense}}$$

Total-asset turnover   An assessment of the efficiency with which the company is using its total investment in assets. It is calculated (in times per year) as follows:

$$\frac{\text{Sales}}{\text{Average total assets}}$$

Total capitalization The total of permanent sources of capital within the business; it is nominally equal to long-term debt plus total shareholders' equity.

Total debt to owners' equity A financial ratio that measures debt leverage. It is calculated as follows:

$$\frac{\text{Current liabilities} + \text{long-term debt}}{\text{Total shareholders' equity}}$$

Total debt to total assets A financial ratio that measures debt leverage. It is calculated as follows:

$$\frac{\text{Total debt}}{\text{Total assets}}$$

Working capital turnover A measure of the efficiency with which the company is using its net investment in current assets less current liabilities. It is calculated (in times per year) as follows:

$$\frac{\text{Sales}}{\text{Average working capital}}$$

Yield The ratio of dividends-per-share to market price per share.

Problems

1 Indicate whether each of the following statements is True or False.

   a If a company uses $50,000 of its cash balance to reduce its accounts payable, its working capital will thus be increased.

   b If a company could get its customers to make large down payments (advance payments) with their orders, the company would probably improve its current ratio.

   c The current ratio and the acid-test ratio of a company will be approximately the same if the company maintains no inventory.

   d The book value of a share of common stock is equal to the total assets of the company divided by the number of shares of common stock outstanding.

   e The times interest earned ratio relates sales revenue to interest expense.

   f Price/earnings (P/E) ratios are a better measure of the relative value of common stock securities than are the absolute prices of the securities.

   g The current ratio is a better measure of liquidity than is the total debt to owners' equity ratio.

   h Working capital is the difference between assets and liabilities.

   i The action of declaring and paying cash dividends on common stock has the combined effect of reducing the current ratio and increasing the total debt to owners' equity ratio.

   j A company whose sales are steadily declining will have an accounts receivable collection period based upon period-end accounts receivable that is shorter than the same ratio based upon average accounts receivable.

2 If the ratio of net income to total assets of a company is approximately the same as its return on equity, what can you tell about the composition of the company's balance sheet?

3 Assuming a company needs to raise a certain amount of capital for its operations, what factors would you, as a member of management of the firm, consider in deciding how much of that capital should be obtained through increased borrowing and how much should be obtained through the sale of additional shares of common stock?

4 Several years ago the Financial Accounting Standards Board (FASB) began to require companies to capitalize most leases of fixed assets—that is, companies were required to include the time-adjusted value of the future lease payments as a liability and to depreciate the value of the fixed asset over its useful life. Prior to that time, such leases were generally not accounted for on the balance sheet; the monthly rental under the lease was simply shown as an expense when paid. Indicate what effect this new requirement has had on the following ratios for a company that leases many assets. Would the ratio be higher than before, lower than before, or unaffected?
  a Accounts receivable collection period
  b Total debt to total assets ratio
  c Current ratio
  d Total-asset turnover ratio

5 If the P/E ratio of a company's stock is 8 and its dividend-payout ratio is 60%, what is the stock's yield?

6 If the Wong Corporation's Board of Directors votes a 2 for 1 stock split, each shareholder will be sent one additional share of stock for each share then owned.
  a What effect would you expect this action to have on the market price of the company's common stock?
  b What accounting entries would be necessitated by this action?
  c What effect would you expect this action to have on the P/E ratio of the company's common stock?

7 Company M has the following ratios as of the end of fiscal year 19X8:
Return on equity = 20%
Return on assets = 8%
What observations can you make about the capital structure of company M?

8 If company Q has a current ratio of 2.2 and an acid-test ratio of 1.9, what observation(s) can you make about the composition of that company's current assets and current liabilities?

9 Suppose that company Y with current ratio of 1.5, acid-test of 0.8, and total current liabilities of $2,000,000 decides that its cash balance of $20,000 is inadequate. To improve its cash position, the company considers borrowing $200,000 on a short-term loan and adding this amount to its cash account. What would be the effect of this transaction on company Y's current ratio and acid-test ratio?

10 A financial analyst for the Brace Company has available the following information for a recent fiscal year:

Return (before tax) on assets: 10%
Total debt (current and long-term) to total assets: 60%
Accounts receivable collection period: 73 days
Return (before tax) on sales: 12%
Total assets: $1,200,000
Working capital: $200,000

Determine:
a Accounts receivable balance (in $)
b Return (*before tax*) on shareholders' equity
c Current ratio, if current assets are 50% of total assets
d Long-term debt (in $)

11 The following data are provided to you, a financial analyst, with respect to the Seiler Corporation for 19X5.

Current assets $500,000   Current liabilities $300,000
Total assets $1,000,000   Total liabilities and owners' equity $1,000,000

Ratios	
Acid-test	1.0
Return on equity	10%
Long-term debt to owners' equity	1.0
Total asset turnover	2.0
Income taxes as percent of before-tax income	50%
Interest rate on long-term debt	10%
Gross margin as percent of sales	50%

Calculate:
a The value of inventory (assume that the company has no prepaid expenses)
b Net income for 19X5
c Total debt to total assets ratio
d Accounts receivable collection period in days (Assume for this calculation only that the company has zero cash and marketable securities; use year-end rather than average accounts receivable.)
e Operating profit (assume that none of the current liabilities is interest bearing)
f Inventory turnover in times per year (Use year-end inventory, as calculated in a above, rather than average inventory.)

12 Given the following information for company R, prepare an income statement for the year in as much detail as possible:

Times interest earned	8 times
Return on equity	10%
Inventory turnover	4 times
Accounts receivable collection period	60 days
Total accounts receivable (avg.)	$300,000
Total inventory (avg.)	$300,000

Total debt (interest rate: 6%) (avg.)	$300,000
Total equity (avg.)	$750,000

13 You are given the following information about a company as of the end of its fiscal year:

Sales in most recent year	$1,000,000 (all were credit sales)
Accounts receivable collection period	45 days, based upon end-of-year receivables
Cash	$25,000
Current ratio	2.5
Gross margin	30%
Current assets (consisting of cash, accounts receivable, and inventory only)	$500,000
Noncurrent assets	$300,000
Noncurrent liabilities	$100,000

Calculate:

a The acid-test (quick) ratio

b Inventory turnover based upon end-of-year inventory

c The ratio of total debt to shareholders' equity

14 Construct a balance sheet for the Forrester Company as of December 31, 19X3 in as much detail as possible, utilizing the following information (make estimates where necessary; state any assumptions you make).

Ratios

Current ratio	2.3
Acid-test ratio	1.5
Accounts receivable turnover (based upon year-end accounts receivable)	8 times per year
Return on equity	16%
Yield on common stock	3%
Total debt ÷ total equity	1.0
Net profit ÷ total assets	8%
Net profit ÷ net sales	10%
Sales for year ended 12/31/X3	$8,000,000
Working capital at 12/31/X3	$1,300,000
Cash plus marketable securities at 12/31/X3	$500,000

15 The following ratios and selected account balances are provided for the Kennedy Company:

Accounts receivable collection period	50 days
Inventory turnover	6 times
Return on equity	8%
Return on total assets (before tax)	7%
Total debt ÷ owners' equity	1.0

Accounts receivable (avg.)	$820,000
Inventory (avg.)	$610,000
Shareholders' equity (avg.)	$1,000,000

Construct an approximate operating (profit-and-loss) statement in as much detail as possible.

16 The following data were taken from the financial statements of the Jose Company for the calendar year 19X5. Data were also collected on average values of certain financial ratios for companies operating in Jose's industry. Calculate the corresponding ratios for Jose and in a brief paragraph evaluate the management of Jose on the basis of ratio comparisons.

Balance Sheet, December 31, 19X5

Cash	$ 90,000
Accounts receivable	160,000
Inventory	350,000
Other current assets	20,000
Total current assets	620,000
Net fixed assets	310,000
Total assets	$930,000
Accounts payable	$100,000
Notes payable (interest at 7%)	90,000
Other current liabilities	60,000
Total current liabilities	250,000
Long-term debt (interest at 9%)	110,000
Capital stock	200,000
Retained earnings	370,000
Total liabilities and owners' equity	$930,000

Income Statement, Year Ended December 31, 19X5

Sales	$1,400,000
Cost of goods sold	1,050,000
Gross margin	350,000
Selling expenses	130,000
General and administrative expenses	110,000
Operating profit	110,000
less: Interest expense	15,000
Profit before taxes	95,000
less: Income taxes	45,000
Net income	$50,000

Ratio	Industry Average
Current ratio	2.5
Total debt ÷ total assets	60%
Times interest earned	7 times

Collection period	50 days
Inventory turnover	4 times
Total asset turnover	1.2 times
Net Income ÷ total sales	3.4%
Earnings before interest and taxes ÷ total assets	10.2%
Return on equity	9.8%

17   Refer to the following financial statements in answering the questions below.

ATKINSON COMPANY
($000)

	Years Ended Dec. 31	
INCOME STATEMENTS	**19X2**	**19X3**
Sales	$2,610	$2,450
Cost of goods sold	1,640	1,560
Gross margin	970	890
Operating expenses	815	780
Operating profit	155	110
Other income and expense	20	20
Profit before taxes	135	90
Taxes on income	60	35
Net income	$ 75	$ 55

	As of December 31	
BALANCE SHEETS	**19X2**	**19X3**
Assets		
Current Assets		
Cash	$ 15	$ 15
Accounts receivable	265	275
Inventory	380	350
Total current assets	660	640
Property, plant, and equipment, net	240	240
Total assets	$ 900	$ 880
Liabilities & Owners' Equity		
Current liabilities	$ 400	$ 360
Long-term liabilities	200	200
Owners' equity	300	320
Total liabilities and owners' equity	$ 900	$ 880

a   Assume Atkinson's only interest-bearing debt is the long-term liability with a 10% interest rate. What was the company's times interest earned ratio in 19X3?

b   Assuming Atkinson neither purchased nor sold capital stock during 19X3, how much did the company pay out in dividends to its shareholders?

c If Atkinson had 100,000 shares of common stock outstanding at December 31, 19X3 and the price/earnings ratio of the stock on that date was 12, what was the common stock's apparent yield?

d Indicate whether you think Atkinson's operations *improved* or *deteriorated* in 19X3 in comparison with 19X2 with respect to:

	Improved	Deteriorated	No Change
1 Liquidity	_____	_____	_____
2 Debt leverage	_____	_____	_____
3 Profitability on sales	_____	_____	_____
4 Collection period	_____	_____	_____

18 Shown below are the financial statements for Gamble Paper Company for the years 19X5 and 19X6.

	Year Ended December 31	
INCOME STATEMENT	**19X5**	**19X6**
Sales	$4,850,000	$5,120,000
Cost of goods sold	3,010,000	3,120,000
Gross profit	1,840,000	2,000,000
Selling, general, and administrative expenses	1,210,000	1,230,000
Operating profit	630,000	770,000
Other income and expense	(20,000)	(25,000)
Profit before taxes	610,000	745,000
Taxes on income	280,000	350,000
Net profit	$ 330,000	$ 395,000

	As of December 31	
BALANCE SHEET	**19X5**	**19X6**
Assets		
Current assets		
Cash	$ 200,000	$ 220,000
Marketable securities	50,000	50,000
Accounts receivable	690,000	740,000
Inventory	750,000	800,000
Prepaid expenses	20,000	25,000
Total current assets	$1,710,000	$1,835,000
Property, plant, and equipment	4,350,000	5,200,000
less: Accumulated depreciation	1,760,000	2,180,000
	2,590,000	3,020,000
Other assets	100,000	110,000
Total assets	$4,400,000	$4,965,000

Liabilities and Owners' Equity		
Current liabilities		
Accounts payable	$320,000	$340,000
Taxes payable	80,000	85,000

Bank loan payable	0	300,000
Other payables	280,000	330,000
Total current liabilities	680,000	1,055,000
Mortgage payable (interest at 9%)	1,320,000	1,200,000
Deferred income taxes	160,000	180,000
Capital stock plus paid-in capital (140,000 shares outstanding)	1,400,000	1,400,000
Retained earnings	840,000	1,130,000
Total liabilities and owners' equity	$4,400,000	$4,965,000

a Name *and* calculate (for 19X6) the *single* ratio that you think best indicates:
   (1) Gamble's liquidity
   (2) Gamble's efficiency of inventory utilization
   (3) The extent of Gamble's debt leverage
   (4) The "margin" that Gamble achieves on what it sells
   (5) Efficiency of Treasurer in collecting amounts due from Gamble's customers
   (6) Return on investment for Gamble's shareholders
   (7) Whether Gamble pays its trade creditors in a timely manner
b Did the Gamble Company pay a dividend in 19X6? If so, how much?
c What is the book value at December 31, 19X6 of Gamble's
   (1) Fixed assets
   (2) Common stock (per share)
d What were Gamble's earnings per share in 19X6?
e State one plausible reason why Gamble has substantial deferred income taxes.
f Assume that Gamble switched from the cost value to the market value method of valuing its fixed assets. As a result, at the end of year 19X6 fixed assets were increased by $1,000,000 and accumulated depreciation by $400,000.
   (1) What is the effect of this switch on Gamble's working capital at December 31, 19X6?
   (2) What is the effect of this switch on the ratio of total debt to shareholders' equity at December 31, 19X6?
   (3) What is likely to be the effect of this switch on Gamble's earnings per share in 19X7? Explain briefly.
g You are considering investing in the common stock of Gamble. What is the most important piece of *additional* information you need (i.e., information that you do not now have)?
h Suppose that at the beginning of 19X6, the Gamble Company provided to the bank that holds the mortgage on the company's plant (see the balance sheet) 20,000 shares of common stock of Gamble Company in exchange for cancellation of $500,000 of the mortgage payable. (This transaction would cause the December 31, 19X6 balance sheet to be different from that shown.) Discuss *briefly* how Gamble's 19X6 profitability would have been different from that shown, as a result of this transaction.
19 The balance sheets for Jennifer Janitorial Service Co., Inc. at December 31, 19X2 and June 30, 19X3 are shown below, together with the corresponding *six-month* income statement.

JENNIFER JANITORIAL SERVICE CO., INC.

BALANCE SHEET ($000) Assets	Dec. 31 19X2	June 30 19X3
Cash	$ 20	$ 25
Accounts receivable	630	780
Inventory	150	160
Prepaid expenses	30	40
Total current assets	830	1,005
Property, plant and equipment, net	275	280
Total assets	$1,105	$1,285

Liabilities and owners' equity		
Current liabilities	$ 490	$ 470
Long-term liabilities	100	200
Deferred income taxes	10	15
Owners' equity		
Invested capital (50,000 shares)	200	200
Retained earnings	305	400
Total liabilities and owners' equity	$1,105	$1,285

INCOME STATEMENT ($000)	Six Months Ended June 30, 19X3
Sales	$3,220
Cost of goods sold	2,302
Gross margin	918
Operating expenses	
Selling	380
Administrative	340
	720
Operating profit	198
Other income and expenses	10
Profit before tax	188
Income tax expense	63
Net income	$125
Earnings per share	$2.50

a Assume Jennifer borrowed the additional $100,000 of long-term debt on
January 1, 19X3, at an interest rate of 12% per annum. If on January 1,
19X3, Jennifer had instead sold 2,500 shares of common stock at $40 per
share and thus avoided the additional long-term borrowing,

   (1)   What would Jennifer's earnings per share have been for the six months
        ended June 30, 19X3

   (2)   What would Jennifer's total capitalization be at June 30, 19X3

Long-term liabilities	_____
Invested capital	_____
Retained earnings	_____
Total	_____

b Is the company's debt leverage higher at December 31, 19X2, or at June 30, 19X3? Illustrate your answer.

c Estimate the payout ratio during the first half of 19X3.

d If on June 30, 19X3, Jennifer's price/earnings ratio is 10, what is the ratio of book value to market value of Jennifer's common stock? (For the purpose of calculating market value, assume annual earnings at twice the six-months' earnings shown.)

e Calculate the following financial ratios on an annualized basis. (*Remember* that the income statement is for a six-month period.)

(1) Return on assets

(2) Return on equity

(3) Quick (acid-test) ratio at June 30, 19X3

(4) Average collection period (in days)

COMPARING AND CONTRASTING FINANCIAL STATEMENTS

I. Condensed financial statements for the following five companies appear on the next two pages:

    1. Safeway Stores, Inc., a major food retailer (supermarket chain)

    2. The Southern Company, a large electric-power public utility operating in the southeastern U.S.

    3. Richardson-Merrell Inc., a diversified pharmaceutical manufacturing company

    4. Inland Steel Company, an integrated producer of basic steel products

    5. Morrison-Knudsen Co., Inc., a major contracting firm concentrating on large-scale construction projects

A. What are your observations for each set of financial statements with respect to:

    1. Liquidity

    2. Use of working capital

    3. Financial leverage (capital structure)

    4. Profitability with respect to sales

    5. Profitability with respect to investment

B. Determine which of the attached financial statements (A through E) is applicable to each of the companies. What ratios or other evidence lead you to your conclusion?

C. The closing market price (on the New York Stock Exchange 45 days following year end) and annualized dividend for each of the companies was:

	Market Price per Share	Annualized Dividend per Share
Safeway Stores	$49	$2.20
Southern Company	$16¼	$1.46
Richardson-Merrell	$24¼	$ .90
Inland Steel	$46¼	$2.60
Morrison-Knudsen	$25	$1.10

    1. Calculate for each company:
      a. The price-earnings ratio
      b. The yield
      c. The payout ratio
      d. The book value per share
    2. Consider the difference among these ratios. What do they tell you about the companies or about investors' judgments regarding the companies?

D. What else would you like to know about each company to assist in your appraisal? What factual information might be available in the library, from a book, or directly from the company? If you could interview the president of each of these companies for ten minutes, what would be the key questions that you would ask?

II. Related questions

A. A footnote to the balance sheet of Safeway Stores (company B on Exhibits) indicates that the annual rent on the company's leased stores is about $121 million. Assuming that the company is obligated for 13.5 more years on these leases and that the appropriate equivalency rate for Safeway Stores is 8%, one can calculate the time-adjusted value of the leasehold (asset) and corresponding lease obligation (liability) to be $977 million.

    1. If these leases were capitalized, that is, shown on the balance sheet, what would be the effect on Safeway's debt-equity ratio (total debt ÷ total shareholders' equity)?
    2. If these leases are capitalized, should operating profit be adjusted for the purposes of the return on assets calculation? How and why? What would be the return on assets?
    3. Would the capitalization of the leases have any effect on the current ratio of the company? How and why?

B. If Inland Steel (company A on the Exhibits) had been concerned about its debt leverage in late 1976, it might have sold an issue of common stock and used the proceeds to repay some long-term

CONSOLIDATED BALANCE SHEETS

(Dollar amounts in millions)

	A	B	C	D	E
Current assets					
Cash and cash equivalents	$ 72	$ 82	$ 19	$121	$ 199
Accounts receivable	219	40	177	112	226
Inventory	317	756	—	136	276
Other current assets	19	80	13	13	3
Total current assets	627	958	209	382	704
Property, plant, and equipment	1,285	733	96	173	7,320
Other assets	157	18	42	112	48
Total assets	$2,069	$1,709	$347	$667	$8,072
Current liabilities	$ 323	$ 696	$161	$149	$ 701
Long-term debt	480	103	64	79	3,744
Deferred taxes and other deferrals	160	61	7	21	792
Preferred stock	2	—	—	—	768
Common stock equity	1,104	849	115	418	2,067
Total liabilities and owners' equity	$2,069	$1,709	$347	$667	$8,072
As of	Dec. 31, 1976	Jan. 1, 1977	Dec. 31, 1976	June 30, 1977	Dec. 31, 1976

284

STATEMENTS OF INCOME

(All dollar amounts in millions except earnings per share)

	A	B	C	D	E
Sales	$2,388	$10,442	$975	$836	$2,206
Cost of goods sold	2,071	8,375	915	331	1,480 ⎫
Gross margin	317	2,067	60	505	⎬
Selling, general, and administrative expenses	136	1,870	26	377	
Operating profit	181	197	34	128	726
Other income and expense (including interest)	30	6	10	19	361
Income before taxes	151	191	24	109	365
Taxes	47	85	11	52	167
Net income	$ 104	$ 106	$ 13	$ 57	$ 198
Number of shares (thousands)	20,553	26,044	2,697	23,554	120,000
Earnings per common share	$5.06	$4.07	$4.82	$2.42	$1.65
For the year ended	Dec. 31, 1976	Jan 1, 1977	Dec. 31, 1976	June 30, 1977	Dec. 31, 1976

borrowing. If the company had sold 5,000,000 shares of common stock at $33 per share in December 1976 and then used the proceeds to reduce its long-term borrowing, how would these transactions have changed the following ratios for Inland Steel at December 31, 1976?

1. Long-term debt to total capitalization
2. Return on year-end shareholders' equity

C. Suppose now that Inland Steel's (company A) accounts receivable collection period was reduced from about 33 days to 25 days and the resulting cash inflow was used to reduce outstanding accounts payable. Calculate for Inland Steel before and after this transaction:

1. Current ratio
2. Acid-test ratio
3. Working capital

What is the effect on the company's liquidity?

D. Assume that both Richardson-Merrell (company D) and Inland Steel (company A) switch from the cost basis of accounting for assets and liabilities to the market value (or replacement value) basis during the late 1970s when inflation continues at a high rate. Which of the two companies will experience the greatest financial statement impact from this change? Why?

III. Attached are the financial statements for 1978 and 1979 for Crocker National Corporation, the corporate name for Crocker National Bank, a major west coast bank. Conventional ratios are not all applicable to the analysis of banks. Define some ratios that you think would be appropriate. Consider the nature of the banking business. What would be logical measures of the bank's earnings? Its financial risk (or leverage)? It liquidity? Its return to shareholders? Which of the conventional ratios are applicable to banks?

emotech, Inc.

Hemotech produces a limited line of medical laboratory instruments. In founding the company, Paul Barnett, the president, sought to develop a line of automated products that would perform those key laboratory tests most frequently required in clinic and hospital labs. He felt that there was a large market for instruments that could quickly and accurately perform these repetitive tests.

At present, the company's only product is Hemostat, a multitask blood analyzer which performs blood-sugar, pH, and several other blood-chemistry tests. Hemostat can complete these tests in one-third the time required by a lab technician and achieves the same level of accuracy. (In practice accuracy is higher with Hemostat, since testing becomes so monotonous that technicians often make mistakes.) Hemotech also supplies the chemical reagents necessary to run the Hemostat units.

Barnett, who earned a B.S. in chemical engineering and a Master's degree in biomedical engineering, had worked for some time as a researcher with a large pharmaceutical and medical supply firm before founding Hemotech. In early 19W9 during the course of discussion with a practicing pathologist who ran his own lab, Barnett learned about new products on the market which were designed to remove some of the burden of repetitive blood testing. Although many medical journals were running reports and advertisements on these new devices, the pathologist, Dr. David Sawyer, expressed apprehension about their speed and accuracy.

Barnett was intrigued by Sawyer's comments and the possible approaches toward improving the existing technology in this area. He began spending increasing portions of his free time "tinkering" on paper with plans of his own. Finally, in January of 19X0, Barnett sent copies of these plans to Sawyer, along with an estimate of operating times, costs, and expected accuracy. Barnett was so encouraged by Sawyer's response that he decided to undertake the task of building a prototype. Within several months, with the help of Steve Davis, a friend who was a machinist and owned some equipment, Barnett produced a working model of his analyzer. Dr. Sawyer was even more impressed with the working device. Barnett's machine was capable of performing more tests than most of the analyzers on the market, yet required only one-half the time and delivered greater accuracy.

Late in 19X0, the three decided to incorporate as Hemotech. Barnett invested $25,000 of his savings in addition to his design and prototype in exchange for 70% of the stock. Davis invested his equipment plus a building in a nearby industrial area, which he had used in a previous business venture. These assets were valued at $65,000 and he received 15% of the stock. Dr. Sawyer invested $65,000 in cash for a 15% share of stock. Barnett became president and general manager, Davis, vice-president and production manager, and Dr. Sawyer agreed to serve as a consultant to the company.

After production was begun, the first months of business were slow and difficult. Sales were low, as could be expected for a new firm entering a technical field. Barnett concentrated on sales and felt that building a reputation for excellence based on a superior product would be the surest route to long-term success. Barnett kept the sales price of the Hemostat low in order to encourage sales.

Sales began to pick up at a very strong rate. As sales grew, so

CROCKER NATIONAL CORPORATION
(AND SUBSIDIARIES)

Consolidated Balance Sheets

(In thousands)	December 31, 1978	December 31, 1979
Assets		
Cash and due from banks	$ 1,637,469	$ 2,129,664
Time deposits with other banks	515,604	544,169
Investment securities (approximate market value of $1,044,507 and $1,054,476 at December 31, 1978 and 1979, respectively) (Note 1):		
United States treasury securities	425,760	381,702
Securities of U.S. government agencies and corporations	41,795	62,612
Obligations of states and political subdivisions	613,279	661,275
Other	34,777	37,817
Total investment securities	1,115,611	1,143,406
Trading account securities (Note 1)	22,414	24,829
Loans:		
Commercial loans	3,723,689	4,061,990
Real estate construction loans	450,676	634,915
Real estate mortgage loans	1,760,128	2,321,175
Consumer instalment loans	1,818,066	2,301,610
Foreign loans (Note 13)	1,412,624	1,457,917
Total loans	9,165,183	10,777,607
Less: Unearned discount	262,219	238,722
Reserve for possible loan losses (Note 2)	88,911	105,396
Net loans	8,814,053	10,433,489
Funds sold	348,215	143,406
Factored accounts receivable (Note 2)	413,566	393,667
Equipment lease financing (Note 2)	201,313	250,154
Premises and equipment (Note 3)	180,658	193,439
Customers' acceptance liability	379,407	496,400
Other real estate owned	8,919	6,319
Accrued interest receivable and other assets	287,933	379,708
Total	$13,925,162	$16,138,650

The accompanying summary of significant accounting policies
and notes are an integral part of these Statements.

CROCKER NATIONAL CORPORATION
(AND SUBSIDIARIES)

	December 31, 1978	December 31, 1979
Liabilities and Shareholders' Equity		
Deposits:		
Demand deposits	$ 3,507,062	$ 3,920,421
Savings deposits	2,414,065	2,264,960
Time certificates of deposit of $100,000 or more	2,674,940	2,292,899
Other time deposits	1,199,689	1,496,280
Foreign office deposits (Note 13)	1,416,598	2,542,260
Total deposits	11,212,354	12,516,820
Funds purchased (Note 4)	501,473	965,567
Other borrowed funds (Note 4)	505,648	608,960
Liability to factored clients	250,431	228,813
Bank's acceptance liability	379,407	496,400
Accrued expenses and other liabilities (Notes 6 and 11)	267,301	427,110
Long-term debt (Note 5)	239,939	234,982
	13,356,553	15,478,652
Commitments and contingent liabilities (Note 14)		
Preferred stock subject to mandatory redemption:		
$3 cumulative convertible preferred stock, 1,200,000 shares authorized, 908,864 and 319,962 shares outstanding at December 31, 1978 and 1979, respectively (Note 7)	45,443	15,998
Preferred stock not subject to mandatory redemption:		
$2.1875 cumulative convertible preferred stock, 2,000,000 shares authorized, 2,000,000 and 1,999,700 shares outstanding at December 31, 1978 and 1979, respectively (Note 7)	50,000	49,993
Common stock, $10 par value (Notes 7 and 8)	120,258	130,846

	Number of Shares			
	December 31, 1978	December 31, 1979		
Authorized	20,000,000	20,000,000		
Issued	12,025,828	13,084,648		
In treasury	(214,894)	(182,698)		
Outstanding	11,810,934	12,901,950		

	December 31, 1978	December 31, 1979
Paid in surplus	116,768	140,668
Retained earnings (Note 9)	241,650	327,177
	528,676	648,684
Less treasury stock, at cost	5,510	4,684
Preferred stock not subject to mandatory redemption, common stock and other shareholders' equity	523,166	644,000
Total	$13,925,162	$16,138,650

The accompanying summary of significant accounting policies
and notes are an integral part of these Statements.

CROCKER NATIONAL CORPORATION
(AND SUBSIDIARIES)

Consolidated Statements of Income

(Amounts, except per share, in thousands)	1978	1979 (Note)
Interest Income		
Interest and fees on loans	$ 880,597	$1,199,304
Interest on time deposits with other banks	38,495	62,153
Interest on investment securities:		
United States treasury securities	30,771	34,464
Securities of U.S. government agencies and corporations	2,556	4,280
Obligations of states and political subdivisions*	28,166	31,315
Other	2,383	2,544
Interest on trading account securities	4,936	5,184
Interest on funds sold	18,902	36,515
Income on factoring operations	43,026	47,069
Equipment lease financing income	21,256	19,592
Total interest income	1,071,088	1,442,420
Interest Expense		
Interest on deposits:		
Savings deposits	119,967	121,669
Time certificates of deposit of $100,000 or more	184,634	266,254
Other time deposits	71,863	101,132
Foreign office deposits	88,441	207,304
Interest on funds purchased (Note 4)	51,520	88,366
Interest on other borrowed funds (Note 4)	17,984	46,880
Interest on long-term debt	18,596	18,301
Total interest expense	553,005	849,906
Net interest income	518,083	592,514
Provision for possible loan losses (Note 2)	45,420	54,425
Net interest income after provision for possible loan losses	472,663	538,089
Other Operating Income		
Trading account profits (losses) and commission income	(906)	1,775
Service charges on deposit accounts	32,103	39,619
Trust and investment division income	19,033	22,710
Gain on sale of Los Angeles headquarters building (Note 10)	—	40,114
Other income	27,740	31,262
Total other operating income	77,970	135,480
Operating Expense		
Salaries	191,746	232,874
Employee benefits (Notes 8 and 11)	41,565	50,833
Occupancy expense (Note 3)	36,126	42,709
Equipment expense (Note 3)	32,786	34,083
Other operating expense	118,810	136,325
Total operating expense	421,033	496,824
Income before income taxes and securities transactions	129,600	176,745
Provision for income taxes (Note 6)	54,358	59,718
Income before securities transactions	75,242	117,027
Securities transactions net of income tax benefit of $4,344 and $140, respectively (Note 6)	(3,411)	(129)
Net income	$ 71,831	$ 116,898
Net income applicable to common stock (Note 12)	$ 66,639	$ 110,745
Average common shares outstanding	11,778	12,381
Earnings per common share (Note 12)		
Primary:		
Income before securities transactions	$5.95	$8.95
Net income	5.66	8.94
Fully diluted:		
Income before securities transactions	5.31	7.86
Net income	5.08	7.85
Cash dividends declared per share		
Common	$1.80	$2.00
$3 Preferred	3.00	3.00
$2.1875 Preferred	1.50	2.19

*Interest exempt from federal income taxes.
Note: The after-tax gain on the sale of the Los Angeles headquarters building was $27.7 million, equal to $2.26 primary and $1.85 fully diluted earnings per common share.

The accompanying summary of significant accounting policies and notes are an integral part of these Statements.

too did the need for more working capital and funds for plant expansion. Hemotech established an early and close relationship with Central Valley Bank (CVB). The bank showed confidence in Hemotech's future growth and in 19X2 made an initial loan to the company.

The loan, only the first of several which Hemotech would need to keep pace with accelerating sales, enabled the company to set up new production and packaging equipment for its Hemostat reagent business. Barnett felt that the reagents would represent an increasing share of total sales. Demand would be steady and predictable, since it depended on the number of units already sold.

Through 19X2 sales continued to expand at a high rate. Production was nearing plant capacity. Barnett knew that if he did not expand capacity, production costs, mostly in the form of overtime payments, would increase dramatically. When Barnett approached CVB for an additional loan in order to expand capacity, CVB granted the company only a modest increase in short-term credit. Barnett turned to other sources.

Barnett had already invested all his savings in the firm. However, Davis was able to raise $100,000 ($50,000 by mortgaging his home and an additional $50,000 from a friend, Mike Jones) and lend this amount to the company. Dr. Sawyer also invested an additional $50,000 in common stock. With this increased financing Hemotech was able to continue its vigorous expansion program through 19X3 and into 19X4.

By early 19X4 Barnett began to explore the possibility of expanding sales to the West Coast and possibly even abroad. After months of discussions and negotiations, Hemotech entered into a marketing agreement with a large international medical-supply conglomerate— Hospital Supply International (HSI). Hospital Supply International agreed to buy Hemostat units at wholesale prices and distribute them through its West Coast outlets and a limited number of overseas outlets. Though the profit contribution of these units would be lower than if Hemotech sold them direct, related selling and administrative expenses would also be lower.

In early 19X4, CVB, responding to Hemotech's performance in 19X3 and their new marketing agreement with HSI, approved a five-year term loan to finance plant expansion. This brought the total outstanding loan to $300,000.

Like many other firms, Hemotech was hit by the double problem of recession and high inflation in 19X4. Sales growth slowed and production costs increased. Hemotech showed a modest loss for the year. In 19X5, as the economy began to strengthen, Hemotech's sales rose substantially and the company returned to profitable operations.

In 19X6, by agreement among all the shareholders, the loans out-

HEMOTECH INC.
Balance Sheet ($000)
December 31,

	19X1	19X2	19X3	19X4	19X5	19X6	19X7
CURRENT ASSETS							
Cash	$ 1.3	$ 3.6	$ 7.2	$ 8.6	$ 10.5	$ 12.3	$ 14.0
Accounts receivable	18.4	47.2	96.7	106.1	157.0	181.0	245.3
Inventory	25.3	55.1	70.8	71.5	143.6	185.7	278.3
Total current assets	45.0	105.9	174.7	186.2	311.1	379.0	537.6
FIXED ASSETS							
Plant and equipment	123.6	185.3	327.7	514.6	597.1	746.3	930.5
Less: depreciation	(13.7)	(21.2)	(37.1)	(59.2)	(108.4)	(142.6)	(188.1)
Total	109.9	164.1	290.6	455.4	488.7	603.7	742.4
Total assets	$154.9	$270.0	$465.3	$641.6	$799.8	$982.7	$1280.0
CURRENT LIABILITIES							
Accounts payable	$ 13.9	$ 21.0	$ 44.3	$ 43.6	$ 74.8	$115.7	$ 185.0
Notes payable	—	40.0	50.0	50.0	100.0	100.0	213.0
Total current liabilities	13.9	61.0	94.3	93.6	174.8	215.7	398.0
LONG-TERM LIABILITIES AND OWNERS' EQUITY							
Long-term debt (bank)	0.0	70.0	70.0	250.0	300.0	400.0	450.0
Other long-term debt (due to shareholders)	0.0	0.0	100.0	100.0	100.0	0.0	0.0
Owners' equity							
Capital stock	150.0	150.0	200.0	200.0	200.0	300.0	300.0
Retained earnings	(9.0)	(11.0)	1.0	(2.0)	25.0	67.0	132.0
	141.0	139.0	201.0	198.0	225.0	367.0	432.0
Total liabilities and owners' equity	$154.9	$270.0	$465.3	$641.6	$799.8	$982.7	$1280.0

HEMOTECH INC.
Income Statement ($000)
Years Ending December 31,

	19X1		19X2		19X3		19X4		19X5		19X6		19X7	
Sales	$107	100%	$323	100%	$576	100%	$635	100%	$978	100%	$1189	100%	$1567	100%
Cost of goods sold	56	52	184	57	338	59	382	60	580	59	662	56	878	56
Gross margin	51	48	139	43	238	41	253	40	398	41	527	44	689	44
Selling, G&A expenses	39	36	91	28	155	27	162	26	248	25	315	26	394	25
Development expenses	21	20	32	10	51	9	56	9	65	7	95	8	130	8
Other expenses	0	0	18	6	19	3	38	6	48	5	58	5	57	4
Profit before taxes	(9)	(8)	(2)	(1)	13	2	(3)	(.5)	37	4	59	5	108	7
Income taxes	0	0	0	0	1	—	0	0	10	1	17	1	43	3
Profit after taxes	$(9)	(8%)	$(2)	(1%)	$12	2%	$(3)	(.5%)	$27	3%	$42	4%	$65	4%

$$\text{asset turnover} = \frac{\text{sales}}{\text{assets}} = \frac{1567}{1280} = 1.22 \Rightarrow .81 \text{ in capital}$$
to increase
sales $1.00

$$\frac{1567}{1131} = 1.39 \Rightarrow .71 \leftarrow \text{using} \frac{\text{last yr + this yr}}{2}$$

293

standing from Davis and Jones were converted into capital stock. The distribution of ownership was then as follows: Barnett 54%, Davis 19%, Sawyer 19%, and Jones 8%. With the increase in shareholders' equity and decrease in debt, Hemotech negotiated with CVB for additional short-term and longer-term borrowing in 19X6 and again in 19X7.

Now, in late January of 19X8, Paul Barnett is concerned about the rapid growth that Hemotech has experienced over the past seven years and the level to which the bank loans have grown. In preparation for a meeting next week with the loan officer at Central Valley Bank, Barnett has committed himself to a thorough review of the company's financial position. He knows that the bank loan officer will press him for specific operating and financing plans for 19X8.

10

Introduction to Cost Accounting

The first nine chapters of this book have focused on what is popularly called *financial accounting:* developing financial statements for use by management, present and potential investors, and present and potential creditors. We turn now to the subject that is popularly called **cost accounting.**

Cost accounting is concerned with developing detailed information on the cost of producing a product or service. Traditionally, cost accounting is treated as a subject quite apart from financial accounting; however, cost accounting is, in fact, just a subset of financial accounting. Just as a subsidiary ledger is part of the general ledger, so are the cost accounting data a part of the total set of financial or accounting data. Just as the income statement provides further amplification and clarification of the changes in owners' equity between one date and another, so do the cost accounting reports provide further amplification and clarification on the valuation of cost of goods sold and inventory.

In our discussion of financial accounting, we saw that a particular transaction might be recorded in a number of different ways—for example, LIFO inventory accounting might be used instead of FIFO accounting, or accelerated depreciation instead of straight-line depreciation. The resulting financial statements—both the balance sheet and the income statement—are affected by these choices. Similarly, in cost accounting we face choices. We may arrive at quite different answers to the question "What does the product cost?" depending upon our choice among alternative costing procedures.

The Critical Factor: Conversion

Up to this point in our study of accounting, we have succeeded in developing financial statements for a variety of companies without referring to cost accounting. Why do we now need to consider a new set of accounting techniques? Why and where are these techniques to be used?

The companies that have been used as examples thus far have, in the main, been merchandising or service companies, not manufacturing companies. That is, they have been involved in buying and reselling (i.e., merchandising) products or in providing a service such as appliance repair, janitorial service, or legal counsel. Merchandising companies purchase products in a finished state and resell them in the same finished state; an inventory item is not processed and thereby converted into a different product. Service companies typically carry little or no inventory and they, too, are not involved in transforming inventory from one condition to another.

In contrast, a manufacturing company is involved in inventory **conversion.** It buys raw materials or semifinished goods from its suppliers and, as a key part of its operations, transforms these raw materials or semifinished goods to a higher stage of completeness prior to sale to its customers. In effecting this conversion, the manufacturing company fabricates, processes, assembles, or otherwise transforms the materials—at each step adding value. Thus, at the end of the manufacturing process, the transformed or converted inventory—now called finished goods inventory—should properly be ascribed a greater value than the value of the unconverted, or raw, materials. Note that in a manufacturing company, the accountant must therefore be concerned with the cost of goods that the firm *produces* as well as with the cost of goods *sold.*

A manufacturing company will typically own inventory at various stages of completion. For example, a manufacturer of safety helmets carries raw-material inventory (plastic resins and strapping material), in-process—or partially completed—inventory (for example, helmet shells that have been formed but not finished or assembled), and finished goods inventory (helmets awaiting shipment to customers).[1]

To value properly the assets of a manufacturing company, the increas-

---

[1] Material which is considered "raw" to this manufacturer—for example, the plastic resin—would be considered finished materials to the company's supplier, the resin producer. It is essential to bear in mind the entity for which the accounting is being done.

ing value of the inventory as it moves from its raw state to more finished states must be accounted for. Each of the valuation models we have studied—the time-adjusted value model, the market value model, and the cost model—recognizes that the conversion process increases the value of the inventory.

The term *cost accounting* implies the use of the cost model, the basis of cost accounting procedures in general use today. Thus, the profit earned by a manufacturing company from the purchase of the raw materials, their conversion to finished goods, and the sale of those finished goods to customers is recognized only when the critical transaction occurs, the ultimate sale to the customer. In the conversion process materials move from the raw state to progressively more complete states; the cost model requires that the costs incurred in effecting this conversion be reflected in increased value of inventory.

But what are the costs incurred? Surely they include the cost of all the materials that end up in or on the finished product. But how about incidental supplies consumed in the manufacturing process? Surely they include the wages paid to machine operators and assemblers who work directly on the product. But how about the wages of others who are employed in and around the manufacturing operations? And how about rent on the manufacturing building, depreciation on the equipment, and heat, light, and power in the factory? Should these be considered part of the costs to be added to inventory? These questions will be considered later in this chapter and in the subsequent chapters on cost accounting. Bear in mind that the final answer to the question "How much does the product cost?" will depend on how these questions are answered.

What Questions?   Why?   For Whom?

Early in our discussion of financial accounting we asked: What decisions are going to be made on the basis of the financial information supplied? Why does the financial information influence these decisions? Who is going to make these decisions? To whom are these data supplied?

Consider these same questions with respect to cost accounting information. It is easy to answer the question, "For whom?". Unlike the multiple audiences for financial accounting, there really is one key audience for cost accounting information: internal management—that is, operating management within the manufacturing company.

Financial accounting requires cost data for the valuation of inventory and cost of goods sold, but these data could be supplied by the simplest of cost accounting systems. More elaborate cost accounting systems are justified only if they supply information useful to management in a multitude of

ways. The cost accountant and the cost accounting department exist primarily to serve operating management, providing data and analyses that
are useful to those managers who are responsible for making the day-to-day
operating decisions.   There are typically no outside authorities—stockholders, banks, security analysts, or governmental regulators—requiring
that these data be assembled.

Two of the relevant questions to be answered by cost accounting data
are "What is the value of inventory?" and "What are the manufacturing
costs that should be matched against sales revenues?" (i.e., "What was the
cost of goods sold for the period?").   But there are many other operating
questions for which the cost accounting information can be useful.

The marketing department is faced with a number of key decisions.
What shall it charge for the product or service?   Which products should it
promote?   Should it drop a certain product from the line?   How much extra
should it charge to supply a modified version of a standard product?   While
the cost of the product is by no means the sole criterion for detemining selling price or the composition of the product line, it is an important consideration.   The marketing manager will be inclined to promote those products in
the line which offer the greatest margin between selling price and manufacturing cost.   The manager will consider dropping a product from the line
when that margin gets very small or turns negative.   And if conditions in
the marketplace suggest a price below manufacturing cost, the marketing
department may have to rethink its plans!

Certain companies sell their products or services at *cost plus*—that is,
at a price equal to the cost of producing the product or providing the service, plus a fixed amount of profit, or plus profit calculated as a percentage
of the cost.   Many defense contractors and certain construction companies
price on this basis.   If so, both supplier and customer must agree on the
definition of the "cost" of the product or service.

Manufacturing managers are faced with quite different decisions than
are marketing managers.   Shall the company perform a certain part of the
manufacturing process itself, or shall it subcontract to an outside firm?
(This decision is typically referred to as a *make-or-buy* decision.)   Should
the company invest in new equipment?   Should it upgrade existing production equipment?   Should it produce one long production run of 100 pieces
or two shorter production runs of 50 pieces each?   To answer these questions, the decision maker is concerned with the current level of production
costs and with how costs will be affected by each of the alternatives being
considered.   Incidentally, the cost data relevant to these manufacturing decisions may be somewhat different from the cost data relevant to the marketing decisions outlined above.

Other questions that haunt manufacturing managers are: Is the company operating efficiently?   Are operations more efficient this year than

last? This month than last month? In plant A than in plant B? On product X than on product Y? Are operations generally proceeding in accordance with plan? The cost accountant can help answer these questions. For example, cost accounting can alert operating management to deviations from plan on an "exception" basis so that the operating manager can concentrate attention on these exceptions, evaluating reasons why a certain department or product or project is operating substantially better or worse than the plan.

Moreover, cost accounting can supply the manufacturing department with detailed data on the number of labor hours and number of machine hours spent in producing various products. These data on times are needed by the production-control group to schedule both the facilities and the work force.

The cost accounting department can also assist the design engineers. A review of the costs of existing products provides a basis for evaluating the probable cost of a new or redesigned product. Working together, the cost accountant and the industrial engineer (or value engineer) may be able to spot opportunities for significant cost reductions through redesign of the product, changes in the method of manufacture, or substitution of materials. A comprehensive base of cost accounting data can be invaluable to engineering departments interested in contributing to increased profits.

In providing this cost information, cost accountants are not constrained by rules imposed by outside authorities. External audiences—stockholders, creditors, and government regulators—are in general unconcerned with the specific cost accounting procedures employed by a company. As a result, a body of generally accepted accounting principles does not exist with respect to cost accounting. The cost accountant is free to arrange and rearrange the cost data in ways that the "customer" (the line manager) finds useful. Detailed cost information is generally considered confidential by the manufacturing company (with some notable exceptions) and cost information from others in the industry is generally not publicly available. Therefore, there is little concern for comparability in cost information from company to company. It is important, however, that the accounting methods within a single manufacturing company be consistent in order that the data on different products, from different departments, and from different accounting periods be comparable.

At the same time the cost accountant must be careful in answering the question "What does product X cost?" The accountant must understand the use to which the cost information will be put, and must also be certain that the person asking the question understands what is included and excluded from the cost of product X. We turn now to focus on this last issue: Which of all the expenses of a firm are properly considered as costs of manufacturing the firm's products?

Product versus Period Costs

The cost model requires that inventories be valued at the cost of acquiring those inventories. For raw inventories, the purchase price plus the cost of transporting the materials to the plant generally represent the acquisition cost. The situation is more complex with respect to partially completed (so-called *in-process*) inventories and finished goods inventories. Here the costs of conversion to their present state are properly included in the cost of acquiring those inventories.

These costs of conversion are defined as **product costs** and are utilized in valuing inventories and cost of goods sold. As a manufacturing company increases its in-process and finished goods inventory, it reflects certain of its expenditures—expenditures associated with the production or conversion process—as an increase in an asset (inventory) rather than as an expense (a reduction in owners' equity). When a unit is removed from finished goods inventory and sold, the proper matching of revenues and expenses requires that cost of goods sold reflect the product cost of the unit (with a corresponding credit entry to the inventory account), even if the unit was manufactured in a previous period. Thus, certain of the expenses (cost of goods sold) of the current period may represent expenditures of a previous period when the goods were manufactured.

Most expenditures by the firm that are not product costs are considered **period costs.** Production, or the conversion process itself, is only one of the activities that go on in typical manufacturing companies. In addition, the company may be engaged in the design of new products, in selling the products being produced, in warehousing and shipping the product to the customer, in after-sale service, and in general administration of the affairs of the company. These period costs are expenses of the particular accounting period in which they are incurred, subject, of course, to the rules of accrual accounting and matching that were discussed in earlier chapters.

Elements of Product Cost

Certain expenditures are clearly includable as product costs: those expenditures that can be traced directly to the product. The cost of all materials that end up on, in, or part of the final product—defined as **direct materials**—are surely product costs. The cost of all metal, plastic, fabric, rubber, and other parts that comprise an automobile represent product costs. But what about lubricants or coolants used on machine tools, or a catalyst used in a chemical reaction, or solder flux and welding rods, or the chemicals used in a plating operation? In a number of these cases, it is difficult or impossible to trace these materials to the final product. Even though solder flux, welding rod, and plating chemicals (or a portion of each of them) end up in the final product, measuring how much went to each unit produced is difficult and expensive. It is more efficient simply to define these materials as indirect, rather than direct, materials. As discussed below, **indirect materials** are no less a part of product costs than direct materials.

By similar reasoning, labor can be separated into direct and indirect components. **Direct labor** includes time spent on those actvities that can be traced directly to the product: for example, direct-labor wages are paid to operators of machine tools used to produce the product, assemblers who physically put together the finished product, or operators of a refiner, paper machine, rolling mill, chemical plant, or other continuous process unit. But what about wages paid to the tool-room attendant, the stock clerk in the storeroom, the production supervisor, or the production scheduler? Typically, it is difficult or impossible (or at least expensive) to trace the activities of these individuals to each unit of production, determining how much time each spent on each unit. It is frequently more efficient simply to define these categories as **indirect labor,** rather than direct labor.

Thus far we have defined direct materials and direct labor as elements of product cost. We have, in addition, suggested that there is another element, indirect costs, and that included in these indirect costs are indirect materials (material that cannot be traced directly to the product) and indirect labor. There are still other production expenditures that cannot be traced directly to the product but need to be included in product costs: for example, heat, light, and power within the factory, rental on the factory, insurance on the equipment, repair and maintenance expenditures, and expenditures incurred in operating the factory first-aid station. These expenditures are necessitated by the existence of the conversion, or production, activities. These expenditures, together with the indirect material and indirect labor discussed earlier, are the third element of product costs, **indirect production costs (IPC).**

This third element, indirect production costs, is called variously factory **overhead,** production overhead, factory **burden,** indirect manufacturing expenses, and similar names. In practice, these labels are used interchangeably. The terms *overhead* and *burden* seem to connote undesirable or even unnecessary costs, and thus are avoided here. Indirect production costs are no more desirable or undesirable than direct material and direct labor costs, nor are they typically any less necessary. As manufacturing operations become more highly automated, IPC comprises an increasing proportion of total product costs, sometimes exceeding the sum of the direct material and direct labor elements.

Just as a gray area exists between direct production costs (labor and material) and IPC, a gray area also exists between IPC and other indirect expenses that are not production-related. Remember that product costs include only those expenditures incurred in connection with the manufacture of the product, and exclude expenditures that are related to nonmanufacturing activities—activities such as designing the product, selling it, and servicing it. These other expenditures are treated as period costs; they are not included in cost of goods sold, even though the activities giving rise to these expenditures are unquestionably essential to the process of earning a profit from the sale of the product.

Timing of Expenses

It should be reemphasized that the timing of the recognition of product costs is fundamentally different from the timing of the recognition of period costs. Product costs become expenses during the accounting period in which the physical unit (that is, the product) is sold, not when it is manufactured. Period costs are expenses of the accounting period when they are incurred; this treatment is the same for manufacturing companies as for merchandising and service companies.

Note that in a period when inventory is growing—that is, the number of units manufactured exceeds the number sold—certain manufacturing expenditures will be reflected in the Inventory account (an asset); cost of goods sold will be less than the total of manufacturing expenditures. Similarly, when inventory declines, more goods are sold than produced; cost of goods sold will include some manufacturing expenditures of previous periods, and costs of goods sold for the period will be greater than manufacturing expenditures during the period.

We have seen that there is a gray area between product and period costs. Fortunately, it is not terribly important how these gray area costs are classified; it is more important that their classification be consistent from accounting period to accounting period, from product to product, and from department to department, in order that comparability be maintained. It is important to recognize however, that the classification does affect the timing of expenses and therefore of profit. To the extent more expenditures are categorized as product costs, fewer will be categorized as period costs and thus:

in periods when inventory grows, more expenditures will be reflected in the Inventory account (an asset), and fewer will be expenses of the period—therefore, profit will be greater; and

in periods when inventory levels decline, both the reduction in inventory and the value of cost of goods sold will be higher—therefore, profit will be lower.

Variability of Cost with Volume

Within the elements of product cost, a useful distinction is drawn between those costs that are variable with volume and those that are fixed regardless of volume. That is, as volume of production (total output) is increased within relatively narrow limits, some costs will necessarily increase, while other costs will generally not increase (i.e., they will remain fixed at least over the short run, measured typically in months, not years). The classic example of a **variable cost** is direct material: the amount of material required is a direct function of the volume of units manufactured. The classic example of a **fixed cost** is rent or depreciation on the factory: the rent expenditure is independent of the volume of units manufactured. Even if one wanted, one could not quickly expand the size of the factory to accommodate a modest increase in the rate of production.

Bear in mind that the terms *variable* and *fixed* as used in this context refer only to the behavior of costs with changes in *volume*. Costs may vary for many other reasons, such as the passage of time, the rate of inflation or deflation, the number of persons employed, or the size of the production facility. However, as the terms are used in cost accounting, the variability referred to is solely with respect to volume of activity.

This distinction between fixed and variable costs is important because sometimes it is appropriate to omit the fixed elements of product cost when answering the question "What does the product cost?" For example, if a factory is operating at well below capacity, the company may be wise to accept a contract even if the price is below total—the sum of fixed and variable—product costs, so long as the price is above variable costs. Also, analyses of capital investment proposals require information on differences in costs and revenues among the alternatives being studied, and frequently fixed product costs are irrelevant to the decision. Chapter 14 discusses these and other operating decisions requiring information with respect to variable product costs.

How variable are each of the elements of product cost? Direct material typically, but not always, is wholly a variable cost. That is, the amount of material utilized in or on the product is variable on a one-for-one basis with the volume of production. Direct labor, too, is generally assumed to vary directly with volume of production. However, this assumption implies that the production organization will add or remove persons from the direct labor force in direct proportion to volume, or that the production workers will be paid on a "piece-rate" basis (a certain amount per unit produced). Many production operations fit these assumptions.[2] But

[2] Even when *sales* volume fluctuates frequently and widely, it is often possible to minimize variations in the rate of *production* by building inventory when sales are low and drawing down inventory when sales are high.

in other cases skilled members of the direct labor force are considered indispensable; volume would have to decline dramatically before they would be laid off. In such cases, a large portion of direct labor costs may in fact be fixed.

Indirect production costs are in most instances composed of both variable and fixed elements. We have already mentioned that rent or depreciation on the factory space is typically a fixed cost. So too is the production superintendent's salary, and depreciation on the production equipment, and perhaps expenses of the production control department. At the other end of the spectrum, production supplies such as lubricants, coolants, shop rags, and so forth are generally variable with the volume of production—the greater the output, the more supplies will be consumed. Often power consumption, equipment maintenance, and costs of operating the stockroom are also directly variable with the volume of production.

But many elements of IPC are really semivariable with volume—they are neither entirely fixed nor do they vary in direct proportion to volume. Some may change in a "step" function. For example, the stockroom force may be able to handle a modest increase in volume, but when the increase exceeds this modest amount, another person must be hired. In the case of equipment maintenance, a certain amount must be performed simply to take care of the ravages of time, but as volume increases, so too typically does the need for maintenance on the production equipment.

In general, fixed IPC tends to be related to capital equipment (e.g., depreciation on fixed assets), while variable IPC tends to be related to labor (e.g., factory supervision and supplies consumed by the labor force). Thus, fixed IPC will represent a high proportion of total IPC in such fixed-asset-intensive operations as highly automated factories, and the reverse will be true in very labor-intensive situations such as assembly operations. We will find it useful to force a categorization of all elements of IPC, even the semivariable elements, into fixed and variable components. This categorization permits the development of an algebraic expression with a fixed-cost term and a variable-cost term, as follows:

$$\text{IPC} = F + vX$$

where F is the fixed costs, X is the rate of production (measured in physical units, dollars, hours, gallons, pounds, or other suitable units) and v is rate of change in IPC with changes in production volume.[3] Such an equation simplifies both the job of forecasting total IPC at various production volumes and the analysis of actual production costs as compared to the operating plan.

---

[3] Far more elaborate mathematical expressions could be developed to describe the relationship between IPC and production volume, but only in rare cases is such additional sophistication warranted.

For example, if the Procter Company determines that the fixed elements of IPC (including the fixed component of semivariable elements) total $25,000 per month and that IPC varies at the rate of $3.50 per unit produced, then IPC for the month should be:

$$IPC = 25,000 + 3.50 \text{ (units produced)}$$

In a month when 12,000 units are produced, total IPC expenditures should be:

$$IPC = 25,000 + 3.50 \text{ (12,000)} = \$67,000$$

The Flow of Costs

Our focus is on the costs incurred in converting materials from one state to another. This conversion typically does not take place instantaneously. Rather, production stretches over a time period that may be as short as minutes or hours or as long as months or, under unusual circumstances, years. During this period in-process inventory is increasing in value—additional direct material, direct labor, and IPC are being added to the in-process inventory as it moves toward its finished state.

Direct material, then, flows from raw-material inventory into in-process inventory and finally into finished goods inventory. When the material is in-process its value is being increased, and this fact is recognized by the addition of direct labor and IPC to the in-process inventory asset account.

Figure 10-1 shows a highly simplified flow chart. Take time to understand the flows depicted on the chart. Note particularly the three categories of inventory—raw, in-process, and finished goods—and the fact that all three represent assets on the balance sheet.[4] Product costs only become expenses when the final product is sold. By contrast, the period costs —expenditures incurred by the selling, engineering, and administrative departments—never end up as part of the value of inventories and are expenses of the period regardless of how much product is manufactured or sold.

The flow chart shows an opening balance in each of the inventory accounts and debit and credit entries to each of these accounts during the period. The closing balances in the inventory accounts may be greater or less than the opening balances; that is, more raw material may have been purchased than used (A more than B), or the reverse may be true. Again,

---

[4] Sometimes purchased material is used directly upon receipt, and thus raw-material inventory is at or near zero; similarly, the finished product may be shipped directly from the factory floor to the customer, and thus finished goods inventory may be at or near zero.

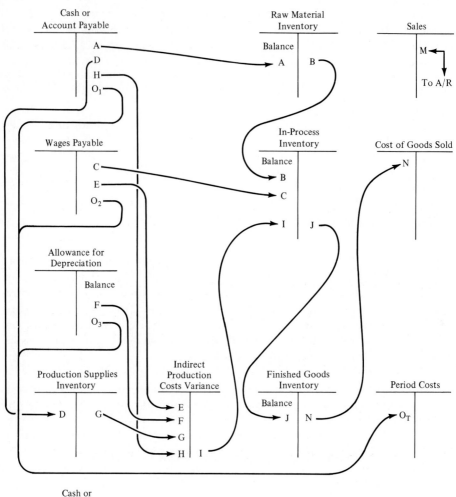

Figure 10-1 Cost Accounting Flow Chart

Note: Profit for period equals M less N less O_T.

LEGEND

A. Purchase of raw material
B. Commitment of certain raw material to production (direct material)
C. Direct labor wages
D. Purchase of production supplies
E. Indirect labor wages
F. Depreciation of production equipment and factory space

G. Production supplies actually consumed
H. Other indirect production costs
I. Indirect production costs (IPC) allocated (or absorbed) into in-process inventory
J. Value of finished goods completed during the period

M. Sale of finished products .
N. Cost of finished goods inventory sold
O. Period costs, including miscellaneous expenses (O_1), nonproduction labor (O_2), and depreciation on nonproduction assets (O_3)

more production may have been completed during the period than started, with the result that in-process inventory declined during the period.

Finally, if the amount of physical product sold exceeded the amount produced, N must be greater than J, and finished goods inventory declined. This fact means that included in cost of goods sold for this period are some of the production expenditures incurred in previous accounting periods. Or, stated another way, the total of production expenditures incurred during this period was less than the amount shown in cost of goods sold, and the corresponding offset is the decline in the value of the asset, inventory. Similarly, if production exceeded sales, then J must be greater than N, and finished-goods inventory increased. If so, a portion of the production expenditures incurred in this accounting period is being put into inventory (an asset of the firm). Or, stated another way, of the total production expenditures incurred during this period, a portion remains in inventory to be recognized as an expense (cost of goods sold) in future periods when the goods are sold to customers.

In this latter case—where production exceeds sales—one may be inclined to feel that expenses are understated and profit overstated, since a portion of production expenditures is recorded as an asset. But the assets of the firm have indeed increased and no misstatement of profit occurs unless the items now in finished goods inventory prove ultimately to be unsalable.

Allocation of Indirect Production Costs

One account on the flow chart shown in Figure 10-1 deserves special attention: the account entitled **Indirect Production Costs (IPC) Variance.** The handling of indirect costs, or overhead, presents particular problems in most cost accounting systems.

By the very nature of their being indirect, rather than direct, costs, the indirect production costs are difficult to assign to production output. It is relatively easy to determine the values of direct material and direct labor to be assigned to a particular unit of output, since the material contained therein can be measured and the direct labor hours can be counted. It is not so easy to determine how much of the factory rent or of the shop superintendent's salary should be assigned to a unit of output.

Consequently, cost accountants must select some rational method of allocating IPC among all that is produced. The allocation method should be consistent and fair. Bear in mind that the resulting IPC portion of the product cost is, however, an allocation, and that the amount allocated is necessarily rather arbitrary—a different method of allocation would result in a different product cost.

Typically, cost accountants find it useful (and even necessary) to make the IPC allocation *before* they know exactly how much was spent on IPC or how much was produced. They want to be able to determine how much things cost as the "things" are being produced throughout the accounting period, rather than waiting until the end of the accounting period. To do so requires that IPC be allocated to the various portions of production *during* the accounting period and not simply at the end of the accounting period. That is, to provide timely data on the flow of costs and on final cost of items or services produced, IPC must be allocated throughout the accounting period—before actual IPC expenditures are known. This requirement is particularly apparent for a company that performs custom manufacturing or service and prices its output as a function of cost; such a company does not want to wait until the end of the accounting period to total up and allocate actual IPC before rendering invoices to its customers.

Therefore, accountants typically predetermine the basis for allocating IPC and then use this basis throughout the accounting period to assign IPC to in-process inventory (see again the flow chart in Figure 10-1). Of course, the amount assigned to in-process inventory (or, in more typical accounting parlance, the amount of IPC absorbed into in-process inventory) is likely to be slightly different from the actual sum of expenditures on IPC cost elements. If so, a small debit or credit balance will remain in the IPC Variance account. The procedures for allocating IPC and the meaning of the IPC Variance account will now be discussed in more detail.

IPC VEHICLE

The first step in the allocation process is the determination of the **IPC vehicle**—the means of assigning IPC from the general pool to the particular segments of production. The most common vehicles are direct-labor hours, direct-labor dollars, machine hours, and units of production. The vehicle chosen must be directly identifiable with segments of production, and must be common to all items produced or services delivered; it should represent a fair or equitable basis for the allocation, or **absorption,** of IPC. In a shop where direct-labor hours is the IPC vehicle, if item A requires twice as many hours of direct labor as item B, item A will be assumed also to cost twice as much in terms of IPC—or, again in typical accounting parlance, item A will absorb twice as much IPC as item B.

Although direct-labor hours or dollars are the most common IPC vehicles, particularly in labor intensive manufacturing or servicing environments, other vehicles may also be appropriate. For example, in a custom printing plant, printing press machine hours may be most appropriate; much of the overhead will be connected with the presses themselves, and the amount of IPC that a particular printing job should absorb is assumed to be a function of the number of hours of press time that the job requires.

A producer of safety helmets might use units of production as the appropriate IPC vehicle; each helmet would then be assigned the same amount of IPC.

IPC RATE

Next, the **IPC rate** must be predetermined; that is, the cost accountant must determine before the outset of the accounting period the amount of IPC that each unit of the IPC vehicle will carry. This calculation requires that total production for the accounting period be estimated, based upon the company's overall manufacturing plan. This planned activity level is then used to determine both (a) the expected, or budgeted, level of IPC expenditures to accomplish the planned output, and (b) the quantity of the IPC vehicle—for example, the number of direct-labor hours or machine hours—that will be utilized during the accounting period. The IPC rate, then, is simply (a) divided by (b)—the budgeted IPC expenditures divided by the budgeted volume of the IPC vehicle.

For example, assume that a particular manufacturing operation expects to require 1,500 hours of direct labor per month to accomplish its planned production. To support this level of activity, the managers of the operation expect to spend $18,000 per month on indirect production costs. The resulting IPC rate for this operation, assuming that direct-labor hours is the IPC vehicle, will be $12 per direct-labor hour ($18,000 ÷ 1,500 hours). When "costing" a particular item produced in this manufacturing operation, $12 of IPC is allocated to an item for each direct-labor hour that is required to produce it.

Extending the example, an item that contains $58 of direct material and requires 4.5 direct-labor hours to produce (wage rate of $7.00 per hour) will have the following cost:

Direct material	$58.00
Direct labor (4.5 × 7)	31.50
IPC (4.5 × $12)	54.00
Total product cost	$143.50

Note that this IPC rate will be used throughout the accounting period. In some particular month the number of direct-labor hours may differ somewhat from the 1,500-hour estimate, and the amount actually spent on IPC cost elements may not total exactly $18,000. Differences between actual operations and planned operations (both in terms of the rate of activity as measured by direct-labor hours and the amount spent on IPC) are reflected in the IPC Variance account. Typically IPC is *not* reallocated at the end of the month to eliminate this variance.

IPC VARIANCE

Since actual operations almost always differ somewhat from plan, some debit or credit balance in the IPC Variance account is to be expected. Consider the sources of the debit and credit entries in the IPC Variance account shown in Figure 10-1. As the superintendent's salary is earned, the rent is paid, and depreciation on production equipment is recognized, the IPC Variance account is debited. (The corresponding credits are to Wages Payable, Cash, and Allowance for Depreciation.) As hours of direct labor are expended in completing in-process inventory, IPC is allocated to (absorbed by) the in-process inventory: $12 of IPC for each hour of direct labor. Throughout the period, a series of credit entries is made to the IPC Variance account as the IPC is absorbed into in-process inventory (the corresponding debits being made to the in-process inventory account). At the end of the accounting period, the credit amount in the IPC Variance account represents the total amount of IPC absorbed by production during the period.

Suppose that in a particular month, the total amount spent on IPC cost elements was $18,800 and the amount of IPC absorbed was $19,200. The IPC Variance account would then show the following balances at month-end:

IPC Variance	
18,800	19,200

The IPC Variance account has a net $400 credit balance.[5] Production during the period absorbed more IPC than was actually spent. Note that there are two possible explanations of this situation:

1   More was produced than originally anticipated, and thus more direct-labor hours were used, each of which absorbed $12 of IPC. In fact, this must have been the case. The total IPC absorbed was $19,200; at an absorption rate of $12 per direct-labor hour, the work force must have spent 1,600 direct-labor hours, 100 more hours than originally planned.

2   Less was spent on IPC than originally planned. At first glance, it might appear that the opposite is true: $18,800 was spent and the company planned to spend only $18,000. However, since certain elements of IPC are variable with volume of activity and total production activity was above the planned level, expenditures in excess of $18,000 should be expected.

---

[5] This credit balance in the variance account is frequently referred to as a *favorable variance* in the sense that it represents a negative expense. A debit balance would be referred to as *unfavorable*.

Appendix B of Chapter 12 discusses the method for isolating these two effects, the first being a *volume* effect and the second a *spending* effect. For our purposes now we simply need to recognize that IPC has been **over absorbed** for the month—more IPC was absorbed than spent—with the result that the IPC Variance account has a small credit balance. We cannot yet make any judgments regarding management's efficiency in controlling IPC.

The IPC variance is typically charged to Cost of Goods Sold for the period. (In this case, the credit balance represents a negative expense and serves to reduce cost of goods sold.)

It is worth repeating that IPC is not redistributed at the end of the accounting period to eliminate any IPC variance. In the example above, in order for the IPC variance to be zero, the IPC rate would have had to have been a bit less than the $12 rate used: $18,800 actually spent divided by 1,600 hours of actual direct labor equals $11.75. This 2% difference (or error) in the assignment of IPC is simply not significant; remember IPC accounting is, in any event, only an allocation process. The use of a predetermined IPC rate assures timely cost-accounting data; that advantage is well worth the disadvantage of generating small balances in the IPC Variance account.

Cost Accounting in Other Functions and in Other Industries

The techniques of cost accounting that are used to determine the cost of manufacturing a product also apply to certain nonmanufacturing activities. Analogous cost accounting techniques are widely used in the construction industry. Direct material, direct labor, and indirect construction costs are incurred in excavating, carpentry, concrete work, and landscaping. Some combination of these activities is involved in the construction of a building, a road, or a dam. The contractor may be building one instead of multiple units of a product, and the inventory (the construction project) doesn't physically move as it nears its finished goods state, but in other respects the situations in construction and manufacturing are very similar.

Service industries are interested in determining the cost of providing the service. A plumber expends direct materials, direct labor, and indirect costs in completing a certain repair job, and needs to account for these expenditures as a basis for billing the customer. A lawyer incurs direct labor (the lawyer's time and perhaps that of associates, aides, and stenographers) as well as indirect costs (rent, telephones, and insurance, for example) in completing an assignment for a client; again cost accounting data are needed for billing purposes.

Within the manufacturing company, cost accounting techniques are useful to "cost" other activities outside the factory. For example, how much does it cost to develop a new product? How much does it cost to make a sale? Just as manufacturing managers are interested in knowing production costs, so sales managers and engineering managers have need for data on the costs of developing products or effecting sales. However, it is more difficult to cost these tasks because, unlike most production tasks, they are quite unprogrammed. The materials and labor hours needed to complete a production task can be estimated with some accuracy; the same is not true of selling or of creative engineering. How difficult is the technical problem; how many different approaches will be tried before a solution is found; how creative is the engineer who is assigned to the task? How enthusiastic are customers about the product; how much do they know about the company and about its competitors; how large is the order; how capable is the salesperson?

Nevertheless, even for these unprogrammed engineering and selling functions it is useful to collect historical-cost information. Knowledge of the amount of labor, material, and indirect expenses utilized on an engineering-design project helps the company keep track of how it is employing its technical resources and provides input for forecasting and budgeting in the future. Cost accounting is unable to determine the cost of producing a sale, since there is no sure way to predict whether a sales call will lead to a sale. However, "making a sales call" is a definable task for which cost data can be collected, and these data are helpful in planning future selling activity.

Applicability of Financial-Accounting Guidelines

As mentioned earlier, there are no professionally sanctioned rules applicable to cost accounting similar to the generally accepted accounting principles applicable to financial accounting. The audience for cost accounting reports is internal management, and the cost information can be compiled and presented in whatever ways are useful to management's decision-making processes.

Nevertheless, the nine basic concepts of financial accounting presented in Chapter 4 do apply to the area of cost accounting.

Expression in monetary terms Cost accounting tells only that portion of the manufacturing story of the firm that can be expressed in monetary terms. Much is relevant to production activity that cannot be expressed in monetary terms—for example, the condition of the equipment, the skill level of the personnel, and the layout of the facility.

Entity Cost accounting is concerned with only a portion of the entity—the production activity. The limits of that activity must be defined carefully, as discussed in the next chapter.

Going-concern assumption This assumption is particularly important to the valuation of in-process inventories and finished goods inventories, as their valuation would generally be decidedly lower if the "going concern" assumption were removed. A partially completed unit typically has little value unless one assumes that it will ultimately be completed and sold.

Conservatism When in doubt as to the proper cost-accounting treatment, choose that alternative that will minimize or postpone the recognition of profit.

Accrual All cost accounting techniques rest on the accrual, rather than cash, basis of accounting.

Realization Only costs of conversion, not profit, are included in the valuation of in-process and finished goods inventory. All revenue and profit is earned on the particular date when the goods or services are delivered or furnished.

Matching The purpose of cost accounting as it relates to the valuation of inventories and cost of goods sold is to better match the cost of producing goods and services to the realization of revenue from their sale.

Consistency The cost accountant is not bound by rigid rules, but rather is free to assemble cost data in ways that seem most useful. But if the user of the cost information is to be able to make comparisons and observe trends of costs to assist in decision making, the data must be presented in a consistent manner.

Materiality The cost accountant, perhaps more than the financial accountant, has a tendency to violate this concept. There is almost no limit to the detail and apparent precision that can be included in cost accounting reports. It is imperative to strike a balance at the point of diminishing returns from increased detail, bearing in mind that:

a Information costs money. Operating personnel must keep detailed records; these records must be processed. Final reports must be prepared and reproduced. Reports must be digested by the audience (user). The more detailed the output, the more detailed must be the input and the more time must be spent in record keeping, processing, and analysis.

b   Masses of data tend more to confuse than to illuminate. Too often, the intended user of the data throws up his or her hands when presented with massive cost-accounting reports, either because they are difficult to understand or because time pressures inhibit thorough analysis.

c   Apparent precision is often spurious precision. It should be clear by now that in all areas of accounting assumptions must be made and the accountant must be content with less-than-complete information. For example, assumptions are made as to the variability with volume of certain indirect production costs, and labor-time reporting from the factory personnel will inevitably contain inaccuracies. The more these data are manipulated, allocated, and processed, the more the final cost accounting reports take on an aura of precision. In fact, of course, imprecise input data cannot be turned into precise output information.

Summary

Cost accounting is not an end in itself. While financial accounting reports —particularly the balance sheet and income statement—do represent a kind of end product, cost accounting seeks to provide information to operating managers to assist them in decision making. Different cost information may be appropriate for different decisions. The uses to which the cost accounting information may be put are quite varied: from valuing inventories to determining pricing to judging production efficiencies to making product design and product line decisions.

The focus of cost accounting is on the conversion, or production, process. The product costs—composed of direct material, direct labor, and indirect production costs (IPC)—are the costs incurred in that conversion process. We can think of these product costs as flowing through the production process, from raw-material inventory, to in-process inventory, to finished goods inventory, and finally, when the product is sold, to cost of goods sold.

Analysis of cost accounting information requires knowledge of those product costs that vary as a function of production volume (variable costs) as distinct from those that do not (fixed costs). Separation of IPC into variable and fixed components is particularly troublesome.

IPC costs are allocated to production output by means of a predetermined IPC rate, utilizing an IPC vehicle such as hours or dollars of direct labor, machine hours, or units of production. An IPC Variance account will typically result from this allocation process, as the amount of IPC absorbed by (allocated to) production will generally not equal exactly the actual IPC expenditures for the accounting period.

Cost accounting techniques are applicable to a broad range of activities outside manufacturing, and are fully consistent with the basic financial accounting concepts.

New Terms

Absorption (of IPC) The allocation of IPC to individual jobs or processes by means of an IPC rate. The job (or process) is said to have "absorbed IPC."

Burden An alternative name for *indirect production costs (IPC)*.

Conversion Transformation of raw material to in-process and finished goods inventory. This transformation adds value to the inventory in the form of labor and indirect production costs (IPC).

Cost accounting The set of accounting techniques concerned with developing detailed information about the cost of a product or service.

Direct labor Wages paid for time spent on production activities that can be identified directly with products manufactured or services performed. Direct labor is a product cost, generally assumed to be variable.

Direct materials The portion of product costs represented by the cost of materials that end up on, in, or part of the final product. Direct materials are a variable product cost.

Fixed costs Those costs that remain unchanged with modest changes in volume of productive activity.

Indirect labor Wages paid for time spent that is not identifiable directly with products manufactured or services performed. Indirect labor is an IPC element.

Indirect materials Materials consumed in the course of manufacturing or servicing which are not identifiable with individual units produced or services performed. Indirect materials is an IPC element.

Indirect production costs (IPC) That portion of product costs that cannot be identified directly with products manufactured or services performed. IPC is allocated to products and services by means of a predetermined IPC rate.

IPC rate The amount of IPC to be allocated to each unit of the IPC vehicle. IPC rates are generally predetermined as follows:

$$\text{IPC rate} = \frac{\text{Estimated IPC expenditures at planned volume}}{\text{Estimated quantity of IPC vehicle at planned volume}}$$

IPC variance The difference between actual IPC expenditures and IPC absorbed during the period. When actual IPC exceeds absorbed IPC, the variance has a debit balance and IPC is said to have been underabsorbed.

IPC vehicle The basis upon which IPC is allocated to production jobs and processes. Common IPC vehicles include direct labor hours, direct labor wages, machine hours, and units of production.

Overabsorption (underabsorption) of IPC A condition evidenced by credit (debit) balances in the IPC variance account: IPC absorbed has exceeded (fallen short of) total IPC expenditures for the period.

Overhead (production overhead, factory overhead) An alternative name for *indirect production costs (IPC)*.

Period costs Expenditures of a firm that are not considered product costs. Period costs are matched to the accounting period, while product costs are matched to sales.

Product costs The costs of manufacturing a product or performing a service. Product costs are used to value inventories and costs of goods sold.

Variable costs Those costs that vary directly and proportionately with modest changes in volume of productive activity.

Problems

1 How might cost accounting information assist a marketing manager in arriving at answers to the following questions:
   a What price to charge for a new product soon to be introduced (The new product will be similar in function to an existing product, but will be technically superior and more expensive to manufacture than the existing product)
   b The minimum price to quote on a large special order from a potential customer with whom the company does not now do business
   c Whether to promote product M in preference to product N

2 Assume that you are an engineer at a high-technology company. How might cost accounting information assist you in arriving at answers to the following questions:
   a Whether to recommend to management that a particular part be manufactured by the company or subcontracted to an outside supplier
   b What will be the return on investment from a new machine being considered by the manufacturing department
   c What will be the return on investment from a new product that the development and marketing staffs are considering
   d Whether a particular work group is operating efficiently or inefficiently

3 Cost accounting techniques are highly useful in tracking costs and efficiencies in manufacturing, as materials are converted from one stage of completeness to another. How might cost accounting techniques be useful in the following types of operations:
   a A building construction company
   b A TV repair shop
   c The audit department of a major independent accounting firm
   d A university
   e A commerical airline
   f A winery
   g A motion-picture production studio

4 The Fulton Fabrication Company manufactures steel weldments used in the construction of commercial and industrial buildings. The company's work is "custom"—that is, a weldment is produced only upon firm order from the customer, using the customer's design. Sales are to large general contractors. For each of the following cost elements, indicate whether you think the cost

should be classified as a *product cost* or a *period cost*. If the cost element should be classified as a product cost, should it be considered direct labor, direct material, or indirect production cost? If the cost element should be considered an indirect production cost (IPC), would you consider it to be a variable cost, a semivariable cost, or a fixed cost? State any assumption that you make.

a Depreciation on the fabrication plant

b Depreciation on the delivery trucks

c Welding supplies used in the fabrication process

d Steel withdrawn from the company's inventory for a specific job

e The wages paid to welders working on a specific job

f The wages paid to inspectors (there is one inspector for every 20 welders)

g The wages paid to the stockroom supervisor

h The wages paid to the stockroom clerks; the time required of stockroom clerks varies with the amount of activity in the company's shops

i The wages paid to the delivery truck drivers

j The salary paid to the manufacturing vice-president

k The salaries paid to the production shop foremen

l The cost to refill gas cylinders; the gas is used in the welding process

m The salaries paid to the cost accounting department

n The salaries paid to the production scheduling department

o The utilities for the plant

p Rental paid on the office facility; the facility is jointly occupied by the administrative personnel, the sales department, the manufacturing vice-president and his or her staff, and the production scheduling department

q Wages paid to the plant clean-up crew

r The cost of group health insurance for all employees (part of the company's fringe benefits)

s Fees paid to a computer-service bureau for processing inventory records; the monthly fee is a function of the number of inventory transactions for the month

t Interest expense associated with the installment purchase of two forklift trucks used in the plant

u Monthly lease of a small crane used in the plant

5 In a public statement justifying a price increase on a particular model of automobile, an officer of the automobile manufacturing company said, "Our costs have risen significantly in the past year, largely due to inflation but partly due to the redesign of the car required by federal regulation. Our costs are now $6,500 on this car that we are pricing at $7,000." What costs do you suppose this speaker is including when he speaks of "our total costs"? Is he including period costs? If so, how can the company determine "period costs per automobile"? Would it be possible to design a cost accounting system that treated all costs as product costs?

6 Two companies are identical in size and in products manufactured. They differ only in the design of their cost accounting systems, with company R defining more cost elements as product costs, and company S defining more cost elements as period costs. For the year 19X7, the companies have prepared the following estimates.

	Company R	Company S
Estimated sales (units)	50,000	50,000
Estimated production (units)	55,000	55,000
Inventory at beginning of 19X7 (units)	10,000	10,000
Estimated product cost	$250,000	$170,000
Estimated period costs	$130,000	$210,000

If these estimates are realized in the coming year by both companies:

a Which company will report higher profits?

b Which company will have higher inventory values at the end of 19X7?

c Which company will report higher gross margins?

7 Assume a company anticipates sales of $6 million and operating profits of $50,000 in year 19X1. It considers $50,000 to be an inadequate profit, but is reluctant to reduce its plant capacity and indirect-labor force (i.e., cut manufacturing overhead) because it anticipates substantially increased demand for its products in year 19X2. Is it possible that the company could increase its reported profits in 19X1 by increasing its inventory, even though sales remained at $6 million? Explain your answer.

8 Indicate whether each of the following costs is fixed or variable (as those terms are used in cost accounting):

a Materials used in the products manufactured; prices of these materials are expected to inflate at the rate of 5% per year

b Rental on manufacturing space; the rental is escalated each year as a function of the Consumer Price Index

c Depreciation on machine tool W; the capacity of this machine tool (as measured in units produced) is continually expanding as the company improves its manufacturing techniques and product design

d Wages paid to product-assembly personnel; in accordance with the union contract, the wage rate will not change for three years

e Wages paid to a group of particularly skilled production personnel; in accordance with the union contract, these workers are guaranteed 40 hours of work per week for 50 weeks of the year

f Sales commissions, at 5% of sales revenue, paid to independent sales agents

g Piece-work wages that are paid to production workers; these workers are paid a certain amount per unit of production, rather than an hourly wage

9 The Krupp Corporation's cost accounting system uses machine hours as the IPC vehicle. The corporation's manufacturing plan for 19X1 calls for the machines to be used an aggregate of 72,000 hours; planned expenditures for IPC are $705,600 for the year.

a What should Krupp's IPC rate be for 19X1?

b Suppose the corporation had chosen direct-labor wages as the IPC vehicle and expected total direct-labor wages in 19X1 to be $510,000. What would Krupp's IPC rate be for 19X1?

c How would you decide between machine hours and direct-labor wages as the IPC vehicle?

10 After a careful study of the variability of its IPC cost elements the McKee Company determined that expected IPC for a particular month could be described by the following formula:

$$IPC = \$51,500 + 2.4 \text{ (direct-labor hours)}$$

where direct-labor hours is the IPC vehicle and a measure of the company's total output for the month.

a What would McKee's IPC rate be for January when 27,000 direct-labor hours were expected?

b If in a subsequent month, March, the plant's activity (as measured in direct-labor hours) was expected to decline by 10% from January's level, what would the IPC rate be for March? Does the IPC rate increase by 10%? Why or why not?

11 One of the factories belonging to the Magasi Corporation experienced an IPC variance of $5,160 (debit) in September 19X7. The total IPC absorbed during the month was $268,925.

a What were actual IPC expenditures at this factory in September?

b If the IPC vehicle is direct-labor wages and the IPC rate is $1.55 per direct-labor wage dollar, what were total direct-labor wages for the month?

c If the IPC rate was established (predetermined) on the basis of a planned activity level of $175,000 in direct-labor wages, was activity in September above or below the planned level? What was the planned level of IPC expenditures upon which the IPC rate was based? Were actual IPC expenditures in September above or below this planned level?

N EW CORP (C)

In early April 19X5, as Mr. Armstrong was about to commence the third production run of safety helmets [see New Corp (B)], he became concerned with the need to determine with some accuracy the cost of producing safety helmets. He has expressed to you, his accountant, his need for more detailed cost data to assist him in making certain operating decisions: pricing of the standard safety helmet and of special orders for helmets; whether to produce certain elements of the helmet at New Corp or continue to subcontract; when to hire additional production personnel; the advisability of redesigning the helmet to reduce its cost.

You have assured Mr. Armstrong that you can design a cost accounting system that will be appropriate to the needs of the company and that you will implement this system for the month of April.

The notes below refer to observations that you have made on the manufacturing process at New Corp. Shown below are those notes from the month of April that may affect your accounting. [See New Corp (A) and (B) for the first 41 notes.]

42 In reviewing the first production run [see note 31 of New Corp (B)], you observe that:

  a DuPont material costing $630 was apparently sufficient for the production of 1,000 helmets

  b Strapping material costing $200 was apparently sufficient for the production of 1,000 helmets

  c Ted James, the production foreman, indicates that he assigned production personnel as follows:

  (1) One operator (hourly wage: $7.50) and one helper (hourly wage: $4.50) to operate the injection-molding machine.

  (2) Two persons to assemble helmets. Hourly wage for each assembler: $4.75.

  (3) One person to perform the various material functions of receiving, storing, packing, and shipping. The amount of work to be done by this person is highly dependent upon the rate of production. New Corp will have to hire part-time personnel to assist this person as the rate of production increases. Hourly wage: $4.75.

  (4) One person to perform miscellaneous tasks in the production department, including maintenance, repair, material movement. Hourly wage: $4.20. The amount of work to be performed by this person is relatively independent of the level of production of helmets.

Ted James assumes 173 working hours (four and a third weeks) in a typical month.

43 To get some idea of the level of IPC (production overhead), you note that:

  a It costs New Corp approximately $1,100 per month to operate the plant and office:

Rent	$800
Depreciation of leasehold improvements	$ 60
Utilities	$150
Property taxes and insurance	$ 90

The production operations occupy about 80% of the available space (the balance being office space) and consume about 80% of the utilities.

  b Ted James spends most of his time (approximately 80%) working on production, with the balance spent on general administration. Of course, one could say that Mr. Armstrong, Ms. Simond (office clerk), and you (the accountant) are also involved in production.

  c The following equipment is utilized in production:

    (1) Injection molding machine; monthly depreciation: $195

    (2) Miscellaneous machinery; monthly rent: $500

    (3) Truck and tooling; monthly depreciation: $150

  d Miscellaneous production supplies are required in each of the operations. At present employment levels, the cost of these supplies runs about $600 per month, or about 90 cents per hour spent by the molding machine operator, the helper, and the two assembly personnel.

  e During early March, production was at the rate of about 3,000 helmets per month. As the production staff gains experience, typical output for the present equipment and level of employment should be about 4,000 helmets per month. If the injection molding machine is run on overtime and additional assembly personnel are hired, output could probably be pushed to a maximum of 6,000 helmets per month.

44 Utilizing the data outlined above, you should be able to provide Mr. Armstrong with an appropriate IPC rate. (As a first step, select an IPC vehicle.)

45 The second production run of 2,500 helmets was completed in early April, and a third run of 2,000 units was commenced immediately. In about mid-April, when this third production run was just completed, Mr. Armstrong asked you to determine unit costs on this run, as he felt that labor efficiency had improved significantly. A review of time cards reveals the following labor time expenditures on this production run:

Machine operator and helper:	78 hours each
Two (2) assemblers:	80 hours each

Mr. Armstrong suggests that you assume direct-material costs per unit have remained unchanged (see 42a and 42b).

46 Mr. Armstrong informs you that he has had an offer from an import/export firm to purchase 2,000 safety helmets at $2.50 per helmet. The firm will accept delivery any time during the next six months; the firm will export the helmets to the Far East, a market that New Corp has no other way to serve. You have promised to advise Mr. Armstrong whether to accept this offer.

47 Later in the month Mr. Armstrong discussed with you his idea for a redesign of the helmet to reduce costs. This redesign would reduce the use of strapping materials by 25% and cut the time for assembly by about 25%. Mr. Armstrong indicated that the cost of the redesign project (including sophisticated new tooling) would be about $10,000, and you promised to do an analysis to help Armstrong to decide whether to proceed with the project.

11 Alternative Structures of Cost Systems

A cost accounting system that is appropriate for one manufacturing enterprise may be distinctly inappropriate, or even unworkable, in other manufacturing environments. In this chapter we will consider alternative ways in which cost accounting systems can be structured to fit the particular characteristics of various manufacturing and service enterprises and the needs of their managements.

Examples of Manufacturing Companies

Picture the production activity in each of the following companies and the diversity of tasks among them.

A manufacturer of a standard line of men's dress shirts Shirts of different sizes, colors, and styles are produced. The raw inventory (cloth, accessories, packing material) proceeds through the various steps in the process (cutting, sewing, packing) and emerges as finished shirts. Cutting and sewing equipment, together with assembly fixtures, constitute the production fixed assets.

A manufacturer of specialized machinery, such as large printing presses A number of different types of presses are manufactured, some standard models and others specially configured for a particular customer. Giant and small machine tools are required, painting and plating facilities, large assembly floors, and extensive material handling capacity, including cranes and a fleet of forklift trucks. Raw material inventory consists of purchased metal plate and rod, castings, hardware, and major purchased components such as motors, gears, and rollers. In-process inventory consists of machined parts and finished subassemblies in the storeroom, as well as partially assembled presses on the assembly floor. The larger presses may be in process for a number of months. Presses are shipped to the customers upon completion, and thus no finished-goods inventory of presses is maintained. However, since the company sells a large volume of spare parts to users of the presses, a finished-parts inventory is maintained.

An oil refinery producing standard products Unlike manufacturing (discussed in the last two examples), which occurs in a series of discrete steps, refining is a continuous process. The raw material is crude oil, together with various catalysts, chemical agents, and additives. In-process time is relatively short by comparison with the earlier examples, and the direct labor force is smaller for the equivalent value of product produced. Only a few operators are required to monitor the process, though a staff of technicians and repair personnel are available in case of trouble. The process runs around-the-clock, seven days per week.

A specialty chemical firm, producing custom pharmaceuticals for sale by others This company has chemical formulation facilities and several packaging lines, producing a limited number of products under contract to large pharmaceutical houses, which in turn market the products under their own trade names. The raw-material inventory consists largely of chemicals and packaging materials. The in-process time is brief, and the finished goods are shipped directly from the packaging line to the customer. The chemical formulation requires a relatively few skilled operators, while the packaging lines require a large number of semiskilled personnel. Volume of activity fluctuates widely as the company responds quickly in filling customers' orders.

Assembler of electronic instruments This company manufactures no metal parts or electronic components, all of which are purchased from its suppliers; these parts and components constitute the company's raw materials. The company's labor force consists of a large number of skilled and semiskilled assemblers, electronic technicians, and support personnel in the stockroom, scheduling department, and maintenance department. The manufacturing equipment consists of assembly fixtures, soldering equipment, simple hand tools, and electronic test equipment.

Need for Alternative Structures

Meeting the information needs of the managements of a heterogeneous group of manufacturers requires that the cost accounting systems be structured to accommodate the peculiarities of each company. An amazing variety of cost accounting systems is in use today, some highly sophisticated and some very simple, some very useful and some a waste of effort. The usefulness of the information system is not a function of its complexity; some simple systems are highly effective and have the added virtues of being inexpensive to operate and easy to understand.

Given this great variety among cost systems, we need to develop some categorization scheme to understand them. Three fundamental parameters of cost systems can be isolated. These parameters are best stated in terms of the following questions:

1 What is the definition of the task for which cost data are to be collected? The answer will indicate whether to use **job order costing** or **process costing.**
2 What expenditures shall be defined as part of indirect production costs (IPC) and what shall be excluded (i.e., treated as period costs)? The answer here will determine the choice among **full absorption, variable,** and **prime costing** systems.
3 For the purposes of valuing cost of goods sold and inventory, should product costs be defined as the actual costs incurred or as some predetermined or budgeted cost? That is, shall inventory and cost of goods sold be valued at what it actually costs to make the product, or at what it should cost? Here the choice is between **actual costs** and **standard costs.** (While it may seem intuitively obvious to you that actual costs should be used, please withhold judgment, for a number of benefits derive from the use of standard costs.)

The balance of this chapter is devoted to exploring these three questions and each of the alternative costing methods just mentioned. By answering these questions in light of the needs and peculiarities of the company, the cost accountant defines the major structural elements of the cost accounting system. As a building architect must answer certain fundamental structural questions in the early stages of designing a house—shall it be

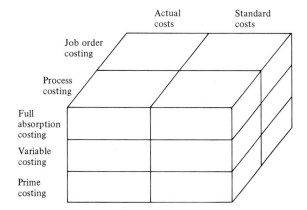

Figure 11-1 Alternative Cost Accounting Structures

brick or wood? Shall it be one or two stories? Shall it face east or north?—so the cost accountant needs to answer these three fundamental structural questions early in the program of designing a cost accounting system.

Note that all three of the questions must be answered in order for the structure of the cost accounting system to be completely defined. Figure 11-1 presents a three-dimensional matrix to assist in categorizing cost accounting systems. Each cell represents an acceptable alternative structure.

Definition of Task

When a task can be described as producing a given number of units—that is, described in terms of the output—the *job order costing system* is appropriate. When a cabinetmaker receives an order to fabricate a special kitchen cabinet for a home, that order is defined as a job in the cost accounting system and all costs incurred on that job are collected—direct labor, direct material, and indirect production costs (IPC). In a machine shop, a *job order* might be defined in terms of a subtask: perform the required drilling operations on a lot of 100 parts. This lot of parts may have already been milled—another job order would have collected the costs of the milling operations—and may subsequently be further processed on other job orders. Thus a job may encompass a single activity (drill one hole in a lot of parts) or multiple activities (fabricate, assemble, and finish a kitchen cabinet) and may involve a single unit (kitchen cabinet) or many units (100 machined parts). In all cases, the job is defined in terms of output of a unit or units in a specified stage of completeness.

When the task is defined as operating a manufacturing process for a specified time period but without reference to the quantity of output, the *process costing system* is appropriate. A coal-burning electricity-generating plant produces kilowatts of power and typically runs continuously. The plant's task is not defined in quantity of power output (kilowatthours) but rather in terms of the length of time "on line." Costs of operating the plant for a segment of time can be collected. As another example, consider the oil refinery mentioned at the outset of this chapter. This process is also typically continuous and the refining task is not defined as producing so many gallons of gasoline plus so many gallons of kerosene, plus so many gallons of fuel oil, and so forth; rather, the task is defined as operating the refinery for a certain period of time. Since the process is continuous, it is impractical to collect costs for a set number of gallons of output. In the case of the producer of custom pharmaceuticals, the task is defined as operating the chemical formulation facility for a certain period, rather than as producing so many grams, pounds, or gallons of a chemical compound. In process costing, the costs of operating the process are collected for a specified period of time rather than for a specified amount of output.

To recap, a job order costing system fits a manufacturing operation where the task can be defined as completing one or more discrete steps in the manufacture of a certain number of units. By contrast, a process costing system fits a continuous production process, where the task is defined as operating the process for a certain period of time or until a certain amount of raw material is consumed.

The cost per unit of production is determined differently under the two systems:

In job order costing, the cost per finished unit of output is determined by dividing the total costs incurred on the job by the number of units produced on that job. The job's costs are collected for as long as that job is unfinished (or open)—as short as hours or as long as months. Thus, the cost of drilling one metal part is determined by dividing the cost of drilling the whole lot of parts by the number of parts produced (100 in the earlier example).

In process costing, the cost per finished unit of output (often defined in bulk-measurement terms such as a gallon, a kilogram, or a square yard) is determined by dividing the costs incurred in operating the process for the prescribed period by the output derived from the process during that period. The process's costs are collected without reference to how much or how little output was actually produced. Thus, the cost of a pound of the chemical compound produced by the pharmaceutical company is determined by dividing the total cost of operating the formulation facility for a period (for example, one day) by the number of pounds of the compound produced during that day.

COST FLOWS: JOB ORDER COSTING

Figure 11-2 presents a typical flow chart for a job order cost system, for instance for the shirt manufacturer mentioned earlier. The three departments might be cutting, sewing, and packing. The overall task of making so many shirts of a certain model and color might be segmented into jobs (or subtasks) defined as performing a certain function (e.g., sewing) on the prescribed number of shirts of the given model and color. The total cost of a single shirt is determined by combining the costs collected on several jobs (cutting, sewing, and packing) and dividing the total by the number of shirts produced; this total cost per shirt can also be arrived at by summing the cost per unit on each of the three jobs. Jobs can be defined to include greater or less scope; the overall task might be segmented into larger jobs (e.g., making so many shirts of one color and so many shirts of another color) or smaller jobs (sewing only the side seams on the body of the shirt).

As indicated in Figure 11-2, the shirts move from department to department, increasing in value as they proceed. The department T accounts are

Figure 11-2   Flow Chart: Job Order Cost System

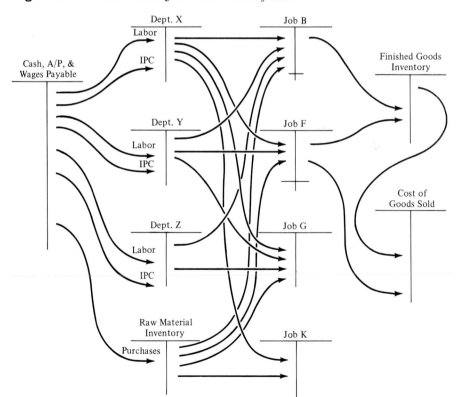

simply temporary accounts, collecting labor and indirect production costs prior to their assignment to individual jobs.[1] The amounts shown in all of the job accounts at any point in time represent the value of in-process inventory. At the end of the accounting periods, jobs G and K are still "open." Some or all of the work to be done on job G by departments X, Y, and Z has been completed, but no work has yet been done by departments Y and Z on job K. When complete, the jobs are "closed," and the balance in the account is moved to finished-goods inventory (e.g., job B) or to cost of goods sold (as in the case of those shirts produced on job F that were shipped directly to customers).

COST FLOWS: PROCESS COSTING

Figure 11-3 presents a typical flow chart for a process cost system. The company may consist of a single process (e.g., the oil refinery) or a number of processes. If there are a number of distinct processes, as illustrated in Figure 11-3, each process typically constitutes a separate department. Collecting costs for a process simply involves collecting all the costs for the corresponding department for the prescribed time period. Generally, a complement of workers is assigned to a process department; virtually all of these workers are considered direct labor, since their activities are directly involved in the process. Incidentally, labor time reporting and the determination of indirect production costs are generally easier and less expensive in a process costing system than in a job order costing system.

The flows in Figure 11-3 indicate that material is processed through process A, as a first step, and then transferred to process B for further processing; between processes it may be stored in a semifinished state as in-process inventory. The output of process B is split between finished-goods inventory and process C; that is, the output of process B is a finished product, but a portion of this finished product is further processed and then shipped directly to the customer.

Valuing in-process inventory is more difficult in process costing than in job order costing. In process costing, the cost accountant may be in doubt at the end of the accounting period as to how much of the department's material, labor, and IPC for the period should be assigned to work still contained within the process; this determination is critical, since the balance of the costs represents the cost of the output for the period. A simplifying assumption is often made: No change in in-process inventory has occurred (that is, the same amount of work in the same state of completion remains in process at the end of the period as at the beginning).

---

[1] If a predetermined IPC rate is used, as described in Chapter 10, an IPC variance balance (debit or credit) is likely to remain in each department.

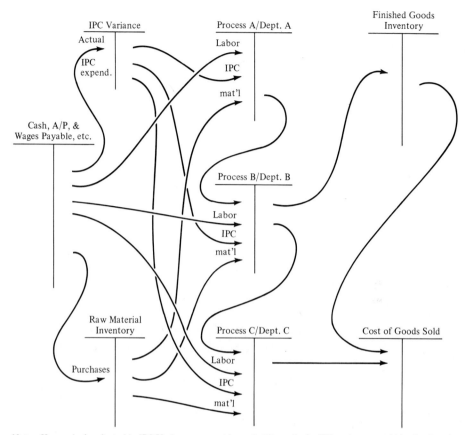

Note: Here a single, plantwide IPC Variance account is used. Alternatively, IPC variances could be developed for each process (department), as was the case in Figure 11-2.

Figure 11-3   Flow Chart: Process Cost System

It is quite possible for job order costing to be used in one area of a manufacturing operation and process costing to be used in another area of the same operation.   In the example of the specialty chemical firm that produces custom pharmaceuticals for sale by others, the chemical processing may be best accounted for by the process costing method, while the contract packaging may be best accounted for by the job order costing method.   The nature of the manufacturing activity generally signals quite clearly which of the two methods is appropriate.   However, either method may prove satisfactory in some instances, for example, for plastic extrusion operations, manufacturers of certain electronic components, or processors of certain agricultural products.

Inclusion of Indirect Production Costs

Chapter 10 discussed the extent to which product costs vary with changes in volume of production. We noted that indirect production costs (IPC) are composed of both fixed and variable elements. (For our purposes, semi-variable costs can be factored into their fixed and variable components.) Variable IPC are assumed to increase and decrease directly with increases and decreases in volume, and fixed IPC are assumed to remain unchanged as moderate changes in volume occur.[2]

As mentioned in the previous chapter, the separation of variable and fixed elements of product costs is significant because certain types of analyses focus solely on variable product costs. One increasingly popular cost accounting structure simply omits entirely the fixed component of IPC from the definition of product costs. This method, which we will call *variable costing,* defines product costs to include direct material, direct labor, and variable IPC. The fixed IPC is treated as an additional period cost. Thus all product costs as defined under the variable costing structure are variable with volume, and all fixed costs are excluded from the definition of product costs.[3]

The contrast here is between the variable costing structure and the *full absorption costing* structure. The phrase *full absorption* signifies that all of the production costs—material, labor, and all IPC, whether fixed or variable—are defined as product costs and are "absorbed into" the cost of the product.[4]

The structure referred to here as *variable costing* is frequently referred to in accounting literature as the **direct costing** method. This term, *direct costing,* is avoided here because in fact this method does not include solely direct costs in the definition of product cost; indirect production costs are included to the extent that they are variable with production volume.

Variable costing is not now sanctioned by the accounting profession as a generally accepted accounting principle for the valuation of inventory and cost of goods sold. This fact does not preclude the use of variable costing for internal management reporting; but it does require that during the preparation of financial statements for external audiences certain adjustments be made to the values for inventory and cost of goods sold in order to state

---

[2] These assumptions become less and less acceptable the wider the swings in production volume from a normal, or average, level.

[3] Assuming direct material and direct labor are truly variable with production volume, as is the typical, though not universal, situation.

[4] Remember that even full absorption costing omits from product costs all expenditures not production-related. The question "What does product X cost?" is presumed to seek only the cost of manufacturing the product, not the cost of designing it, selling it, or servicing it (though knowledge of the cost of performing these other functions might also be useful to management).

them at their equivalent full absorption costs. Fortunately, these adjustments are not difficult to make, and, in spite of this inconvenience, variable costing is gaining wider acceptance in industry.

ADVANTAGES OF VARIABLE COSTING

Why this increasing enthusiasm for variable costing? First, the clear and consistent separation of variable and fixed manufacturing costs means that data are readily at hand for those many analyses that require a focus on incremental or variable costs: make-or-buy decisions, capital-investment decisions, and certain marketing decisions. These decisions are discussed at greater length in Chapter 14.

Second, consider the effect of changes in production volume on full absorption cost, as illustrated in Exhibit 11-1. As production volume decreases, the fixed production costs are spread over fewer units of output, with the result that each unit bears a larger share, and therefore costs more. As volume increases, the same fixed production costs are now spread over more units of output, with the result that each unit bears a smaller share, and therefore costs less. This change in product cost with changes in volume is generally not useful and may lead to unfortunate decisions. For example, if costs are used as a basis for pricing, a company utilizing full absorption costing may be inclined to increase prices when production volume declines (with the result that orders may decline further) and decrease prices when production volume increases. Under variable costing, all fixed production costs are treated as period costs, and the unit cost will be largely unaffected by changes in the volume of production.

On the one hand, the fact that certain production costs are fixed makes them no less real. There is no question that the variable costing method (or structure) states product costs as lower than does the full absorption

Exhibit 11-1
Product Cost at Alternative Volumes:
Full Absorption and Variable Costing

	Typical Volume: 2000 Units per Month	"Slow" Period: 1500 Units per Month	"High Demand" Period: 2500 Units per Month
Direct material ($2.00 per unit)	$ 4,000	$ 3,000	$ 5,000
Direct labor ($1.00 per unit)	2,000	1,500	2,500
Variable IPC ($1.50 per unit)	3,000	2,250	3,750
Fixed IPC	4,000	4,000	4,000
	$13,000	$10,750	$15,250
Product cost per unit:			
Full absorption cost	$6.50	$7.17	$6.10
Variable cost	4.50	4.50	4.50

method.   Variable costing simply omits from product costs certain of the costs incurred in manufacturing.

On the other hand, if the level of fixed costs cannot be changed in the short run—that is, if in fact they are fixed regardless of production output —it may make more sense to treat them as period costs, in the same way that selling expenses and administrative expenses are treated.

DANGERS OF VARIABLE COSTING

While valid arguments exist for the use of variable costing, there are also dangers.   First, since product costs are lower under variable costing than under full absorption costing, cost of goods sold will be stated lower and total period costs higher.   Thus, margins (sales less product costs) will appear more favorable under variable costing than under full absorption costing, but period expenses will be correspondingly higher.   If, in the example illustrated in Exhibit 11-1, the selling price is $10.00 per unit, the margin at typical volume will be 35% if full absorption costing is used and 55% if variable costing is used.   Therefore, pricing decision rules need to be altered when a company changes to variable costing; if a company has been satisfied with a 40% margin calculated on the basis of full absorption costs, it may need a 50 or 60% margin calculated on the basis of variable costs.

In situations where fixed IPC costs represent a very major portion of total product costs—e.g., in a highly automated, capital-intensive plant utilizing low-cost material and very little direct labor—the difference between full absorption cost and variable cost will be extreme.   Variable costs alone may not be very useful.

Finally, variable costing and full absorption costing will result in different operating profits if in-process or finished-goods inventories increase or decrease during the period.   When finished-goods inventory increases during a month, full absorption costing will include in the valuation of that inventory a portion of the month's fixed production costs; variable costing will treat all fixed production costs as period expenses of the month.   Thus, in times of expanding inventories, profit will be higher if calculated under full absorption costing; the reverse is true when inventories decline.

Exhibit 11-2 illustrates the effect on operating profit of the use of the two methods.   Part A of the exhibit assumes that production exceeds sales, that is, finished-goods inventory increases.   Part B makes the opposite assumption.   In the case where production exceeds sales, profits are $400 higher under full absorption costing than under variable costing.   The corresponding offset is to the value of finished-goods inventory.   The 200 units added to finished-goods inventory are valued at $11.00 each under full absorption costing and $9.00 each under variable costing; this difference of $2.00 per unit, times the 200 units added to inventory, yields a $400 higher inventory valuation under full absorption costing.

Exhibit 11-2
The Effect on Profit of Changes in Inventory:
Full Absorption and Variable Costing

	Full Absorption Costing	Variable Costing
ASSUMPTIONS		
Product cost/unit		
Direct labor	$ 4	$ 4
Direct material	3	3
Variable IPC	2	2
Fixed IPC	2	0
Total	$ 11	$ 9
Fixed IPC (period cost)	—	$ 2,000
Selling price/unit	$ 20	$ 20
Other period costs	$ 6,000	$ 6,000
Opening inventory (1000 units)	11,000	9,000

A. Inventory increases as production (1000 units) is greater than sales (800 units)

Sales	$16,000	$16,000
Product costs	8,800	7,200
Margin	7,200	8,800
Period costs	6,000	8,000
Operating profit	$ 1,200	$ 800

B. Inventory decreases as production (1000 units) is less than sales (1100 units)

Sales	$22,000	$22,000
Product costs	12,100	9,900
Margin	9,900	12,100
Period costs	6,000	8,000
Operating profit	$ 3,900	$ 4,100

PRIME COSTING

The definition of product costs can be narrowed one step further: omit all indirect production costs—fixed and variable—from product costs. Thus, a third alternative structure treats *all* IPC as period rather than product costs. This structure is called *prime costing* and is not widely used. However, the term *prime cost* is frequently employed to refer to the sum of direct materials and direct labor.

To summarize this discussion, Exhibit 11-3 shows the elements of product cost that are included in each of the three altenative structures: prime costing, variable costing, and full absorption costing.

Exhibit 11-3
Alternative Definitions of Product Costs

	Costing Method		
COST ELEMENT	Prime	Variable	Full Absorption
Direct material	X	X	X
Direct labor	X	X	X
Variable IPC		X	X
Fixed IPC			X

Actual versus Standard Costs

Having made the choice between job order costing and process costing and between full absorption costing and variable costing, the cost accountant now faces one more decision about the cost accounting structure: Shall actual production costs or standard production costs be used? That is, in valuing inventory and cost of goods sold, should the product costs be those actually incurred to produce the product, or should inventory and cost of goods sold be valued using standards representing what it should have cost to produce the product?

Remember that this decision is independent of the choice between job order costing and process costing and between full absorption costing and variable costing. As illustrated in Figure 11-1, one could structure a job order, full absorption costing system using either actual or standard costs; a job order, variable costing system using either actual or standard costs; a process, full absorption costing system using either actual or standard costs; and so forth.

Thus far we have been tracking actual material costs as materials flow from raw inventory, to in-process inventory, to finished-goods inventory. As actual direct labor hours are spent, each is valued at the actual direct labor rate paid, and this direct labor cost is reflected in increased value of the in-process inventory. The predetermined IPC rate is applied to the actual quantity of the IPC vehicle incurred by the production process or the production job, and this IPC actually absorbed is also reflected in increased value of the in-process inventory.

Alternatively, we could track standard costs of material, labor and IPC as they flow through in-process inventory to finished goods inventory. To employ such a standard cost system requires that:

1   Standards be set: that is, the cost accountant or an industrial engineer must determine in advance (prior to actual production)

a   The number of direct labor hours required per unit of output and the wage rate per hour
b   The number of pounds, kilos, meters, feet, or pieces of direct material required per unit of output and the price per pound, kilo, meter, foot, or piece
c   The appropriate amount of IPC to be assigned to each unit of output
2   The differences between actual costs and standard costs be accounted for in some appropriate, and hopefully useful, manner

We shall consider these requirements in the course of discussing the pros and cons of standard and actual cost systems in this chapter and again in the following chapter as we discuss cost variances.

ADVANTAGES AND DISADVANTAGES OF STANDARD COST SYSTEMS

The primary disadvantage of standard cost systems is the necessity to set standards: predetermining the standard costs for all the various products manufactured by the company. If inventories and cost of goods sold are to be valued at what they *should* cost to produce, rather than what they actually *did* cost, then someone must determine what they *should* cost. Depending on the variety of the products produced, and the complexity of the manufacturing processes, this setting of standards—predetermining what the product should cost before it is produced—may be quite complex and costly. However, mitigating this disadvantage is the fact that the cost standards themselves are useful data that are readily available to assist management in making a host of everyday operating decisions such as:

1   Pricing both standard products and products that are to be customized for a particular customer
2   Make-or-buy decisions (i.e., whether or not to subcontract certain manufacturing or servicing activities)
3   Product redesign to reduce cost or to enhance performance
4   Production scheduling, for which the standard labor times and standard machine hours are necessary data inputs

The advantages of standard cost systems are numerous. Most importantly, standard cost systems provide information to line operating management on the differences between incurred (actual) costs of production and budgeted (standard) costs of production. This information can be extremely useful. If standard direct labor costs are an accurate measure of how much labor *should* be expended to produce a unit (or group of units), the difference between actual direct labor cost and standard direct labor cost for a certain manufacturing step is relevant to members of manage-

ment responsible for efficiency and cost control. Analysis of this difference, or variance, on each particular job will help management pinpoint
troublesome production jobs; analysis of the sum of the variances on all
jobs within a particular department will help management evaluate departmental efficiency. A similiar analysis of variances can be performed with
respect also to direct material and IPC.

In addition, two primary shortcomings of actual cost systems are overcome by the use of standard costs. First, under an actual cost structure,
physically identical units in finished-goods inventory may have different
values if they were produced on different job orders (job order cost structure) or during different periods (process cost structure). This difference is
more confusing than useful. The cost model requires that a unit in inventory be valued at its *historical cost*—the cost of direct labor, direct material,
and IPC incurred in making the unit. A standard cost system simply defines historical cost as equal to what it *should* cost to produce the unit: the
unit's predetermined or standard cost. Recall the discussion in Chapter 8
of the problem of valuing merchandise purchased at different prices and
the techniques devised to accommodate this problem—the first-in, first-out
(FIFO) and last-in, first-out (LIFO) methods. The same problem arises in
valuing manufactured products: units produced at different times are likely
to have different actual costs. The use of standard costs, however, essentially eliminates the problem by valuing identical units at identical costs.

A second shortcoming of actual cost systems is that record keeping is
extensive, cumbersome, and costly. Standard cost systems are typically
easier and less expensive to operate. As we shall see in the next chapter,
differences between actual and standard costs are drawn off, or isolated, at
each step of the manufacturing process. Once this difference, or variance
as it is called, is removed, no longer is there a need to keep track of the actual costs of each processing step as manufacturing proceeds step by step
from raw material to finished-goods inventory.

We shall delay the illustration of cost flows in a standard cost accounting system until Chapter 12, which considers in some detail the development and interpretation of cost variances. Cost flows for a standard cost
system are illustrated in Appendix A of Chapter 12.

In summary, standard cost systems are gaining in popularity over actual cost systems for three primary reasons:

1   The variance information (to be discussed in detail in Chapter 12) is use-
    ful to management in pointing up "exception areas"—products or de-
    partments where costs are not in line with the plan.
2   Standard cost systems are typically less expensive to operate because of
    the ease of accounting for cost flows and because like items are valued
    identically (at standard) in inventory and cost of goods sold, although

they may have been manufactured at different times and therefore at different actual costs.

3   The standard costs represent handy reference data for managers in many different functional areas—for marketing management in making pricing and product-line decisions, for purchasing agents in making purchase decisions, for production schedulers in "loading" the shop, and for top management in making investment decisions.

Illustrations of Alternative Structures: New Corp

New Corp is a young, small manufacturer of safety helmets (often referred to as "hard hats") for the construction industry. New Corp molds the shell for the helmet from a plastic resin that it purchases from a major chemical company. It also buys strapping materials for the head-support device which the company's assemblers fabricate and assemble into the plastic shell to complete a helmet.

The production activity at New Corp is better defined in terms of a series of jobs—injection mold so many helmet shells, assemble so many safety helmets, and so forth—than as a process. Either variable costing or full absorption costing could be used. New Corp has been operating an actual cost system, as no cost standards have been established. However, a standard cost system could be implemented at New Corp and might be appropriate.

Exhibit 11-4 illustrates a simple job order, full absorption, actual cost system in operation at New Corp during March 19X5, soon after the company was formed. The exhibit begins with data on production and sales for the month: (a) no jobs were in-process at the beginning of the month, (b) job M, calling for 1,000 helmets, was started, completed, and sold during the month, (c) job N, calling for 1,200 helmets, was started but not completed during March, and thus remains in-process at month-end. The exhibit then describes and illustrates in T-account format the accounting transactions (both financial and cost) for the month. Note particularly the entries in the two job accounts (classified as in-process inventory) and in the IPC variance account. Exhibit 11-4 concludes with New Corp's income statement for March and the balance sheet at March 31, 19X5.

Take time to review Exhibit 11-4 in detail before proceeding to the more complex Exhibits 11-5 through 11-7. These later exhibits are designed to assist you in further understanding the mechanics of job order cost accounting and also the differences between variable and full absorption costing structures. They assume a somewhat more elaborate cost ac-

Exhibit 11-4
NEW CORP
Cost Accounting: March 19X5

DATA ON PRODUCTION AND SALES

Sales   1,000 helmets at $5.00 each = $5,000
Production   Job M: injection mold and assemble 1,000 helmets;
                      all are sold.
                      Job N: injection mold and assemble 1,200 helmets;
                      job remains in process at month-end.
IPC rate: $1.50 per direct labor dollar

Product costs:	Job M	Job N
Direct labor	$1,100	$ 480
Direct material	850	500
IPC	1,650	720
	$3,600	$1,700

DESCRIPTION OF ACCOUNTING TRANSACTIONS
(Recorded in T accounts below)

1 Direct labor wages of $1,580 were paid in cash; job M charged with $1,100 and job N with $480.
2 Raw materials totaling $1,500 were purchased on credit.
3 Raw materials totaling $1,350 were issued to in-process inventory; job M charged with $850 and Job N with $500.
4 Accounts receivable of $6,000 were collected.
5 Accounts payable of $1,800 were paid.
6. Indirect production expenditures were $2,400 for the month: $2,000 in cash and $400 on credit. (Note debit entry in IPC variance account, not the job accounts.)
7 IPC was absorbed into jobs at IPC rate of $1.50 per direct labor dollar. (Note credit entry in IPC variance account.)
8. Sales totaled 1,000 units at $5.00 per unit, or a total of $5,000, all on credit.
9 The units sold comprised all of the production on job M; therefore, job M is closed and cost of goods sold is recognized.
10 Nonmanufacturing period expenses of $750 were paid in cash.

GENERAL LEDGER (T-ACCOUNT FORMAT)[1]
Assets

Cash		Accounts Receivable		Raw-Material Inventory	
(Bal) 2,000	1,580 (1)	(Bal) 7,000	6,000 (4)	(Bal) 3,000	1,350 (3)
(4) 6,000	1,800 (5)	(8) 5,000		(2) 1,500	
	2,000 (6)				
	750 (10)				

In-Process Inventory		Fixed Assets	

Job M		Job N	
(1) 1,100		(1) 480	
(3) 850		(3) 500	
(7) 1,650		(7) 720	
	3,600 (9)		

(Bal) 5,000

Liabilities and Owners' Equity

Accounts Payable		Owners' Equity	
(5) 1,800	2,000 (Bal)		17,000 (Bal)
	1,500 (2)		
	400 (6)		

Sales and Expenses

Sales		Cost of Goods Sold		Period Expenses	
	5,000 (8)	(9) 3,600		(10) 750	

IPC Variance	
(6) 2,400	1,650 (7)
	720 (7)

FINANCIAL STATEMENTS

Income Statement: March 19X5

Sales		$5,000
Cost of goods sold	3,600	
IPC variance[2]	30	3,630
Gross margin		1,370
Period expenses		750
Operating profit		$ 620

Balance Sheet at March 31, 19X5

Assets		Liabilities and Owners' Equity	
Cash	$ 1,870	Accounts payable	$ 2,100
Accounts receivable	8,000	Owners' equity at Feb. 28	17,000
Inventory		Profit, March	620
Raw material	3,150		$19,720
In-process (job N)	1,700		
Fixed assets	5,000		
	$19,720		

[1] (Bal) represents opening balance in accounts at March 1. Numbers appearing in parentheses beside each T-account entry refer to description above. Closing entries have been omitted.

[2] The difference between $2,400 actual IPC incurred and $2,370 IPC absorbed by jobs M and N.

Exhibit 11-5
NEW CORP (MAY 19X5)
Data on Production and Sales

Sales

1,200 helmets at $5.00 each =	$ 6,000
500 helmets at $4.75 each =	2,375
700 helmets at $5.10 each =	3,570
2,400	$11,945

Production

Job A—Injection mold 1,000 helmets
Job B —Injection mold 1,500 helmets
Job C—Assemble 1,000 helmets
Job D—Injection mold 1,200 helmets
Job E —Assemble 1,500 helmets

Note: Job D remained in-process at month end. The 1,000 helmets produced on jobs A and C were all sold. Of the 1,500 helmets produced on jobs B and E, 1,400 were sold. (Thus, 100 remained in finished-goods inventory at May 31.)

Inventory, Beginning

Raw material
   Plastic resin $1,500 (240 lb @ $6.25/lb)
   Strapping material $735 (3,500 sets @ 21¢/set)
In-process inventory: None
Finished-goods inventory: None

Purchases of raw material

Plastic resin: 500 lb at $6.35/lb
Strapping material: 2,000 sets at 19¢/set

Direct wages paid

	Hours Worked	Per Hour	Total
Molding machine operator	172	$7.53	$1,295
Molding machine helper	172	4.50	774
Assembler #1	125	4.80	600
Assembler #2	125	4.76	595
			$3,264

Total selling, development, and administrative expenses $2,131

Material and labor committed to jobs

	A	B	C	D	E	Total
			Job			
Direct labor						
Molding machine operator	50 hr	73 hr	—	49 hr	—	172 hr
Molding machine helper	50 hr	73 hr	—	49 hr	—	172 hr
Assembler #1	—	—	51 hr	—	74 hr	125 hr
Assembler #2	—	—	51 hr	—	74 hr	125 hr
Direct material						
Plastic resin	102 lb	150 lb	—	110 lb	—	362 lb
Strapping material	—	—	1,010 sets	—	1,500 sets	2,510 sets

IPC rate

Estimated IPC for normal month: Variable $1,350

Fixed   3,400

$4,750

Estimated direct labor wages, normal month $3,300

IPC rate, variable costing $= \dfrac{1,350}{3,300} = 0.409$ per direct labor $

IPC rate, full absorption costing $= \dfrac{4,750}{3,300} = \$1.439$ per direct labor $

Actual indirect production costs (IPC) for May:

Variable:

Supplies	$600	
Stores labor	817	
		$1,417

Fixed

Miscellaneous labor	$722	
Plant rent, utilities	880	
Plant superintendent	880	
Equipment rental	845	
Depreciation	150	
		$3,477
Total		$4,894

counting environment at New Corp. More jobs are involved; the complete manufacture of a lot of helmets now requires two jobs—one comprising the injection-molding task and the other the assembly task. The components of direct labor, direct material, and IPC are shown in detail, and the IPC rate is derived and then applied.

Exhibit 11-5 presents information on operations and actual costs for the month of May 19X5. Exhibit 11-6 assumes the use of a job order, actual, variable costing systems. Exhibit 11-7 continues with a job order, actual

Exhibit 11-6
NEW CORP (MAY 19X5)
Cost Accounting Structure: Job Order, Variable, Actual Costs

	Job					
JOB COST REPORT	A	B	C	D	E	Total
Direct labor						
Operator @ $7.53/h	$ 376	$ 550	—	$ 369	—	$1,295
Helper @ $4.50/h	225	329	—	220	—	774
Assembler 1 @ $4.80/h	—	—	$245	—	$355	600
Assembler 2 @ $4.76/h	—	—	243	—	352	595
Subtotal	601	879	488	589	707	3,264
Direct material[1]						
Plastic resin	637	939	—	699	—	2,275
Strapping material	—	—	212	—	315	527
Variable IPC[2]	246	360	200	241	289	1,336
Total	$1,484	$2,178	$900	$1,529	$1,311	$7,402
No. units produced	1,000	1,500	1,000	in-process	1,500	
Cost/unit	$1.484	$1.452	$0.900	—	$0.874	

OPERATING STATEMENT	$	%
Sales (2,400 units)	$11,945	100
Cost of goods sold		
Product costs (variable costing)		
1,000 units @ (1.484 + 0.900)[3] = 2,384		
1,400 units @ (1.452 + 0.874)[4] = 3,256	5,640	47
IPC variance[5]	81	1
Fixed IPC	3,477	29
Total cost of goods sold	9,198	77
Gross margin	2,747	23
Selling, development, and administrative expenses	2,131	18
Operating profit	$616	5

[1] Assuming FIFO; for the plastic resin, 240 lb at $6.25 used before the new purchase at $6.35/lb.
[2] IPC Rate = $0.409 per direct labor dollar (see Exhibit 11-5).
[3] Sum of unit cost of jobs A and C.
[4] Sum of unit cost of jobs B and E.
[5] IPC variance: IPC absorbed (see above) $1,336
           Actual IPC (see Exhibit 11-5).   1,417
                               $ 81 Dr

system, but now full absorption rather than variable costs are used. The illustration of a standard cost system is delayed until Chapter 12.

Notice in Exhibit 11-5 that in-process and finished-goods inventories have increased during the month: 2,500 units were completed, while only 2,400 were sold, and the value of in-process inventory goes from zero to a positive value. This inventory change will cause full absorption costing to state profits higher for the month than does variable costing. Note also that

Exhibit 11-7
NEW CORP (MAY 19X5)
Cost Accounting Structure: Job Order,
Full Absorption, Actual Costs

JOB COST REPORT

			Job			
	A	**B**	**C**	**D**	**E**	**Total**
Direct labor[1]	$ 601	$ 879	$ 488	$ 589	$ 707	$ 3,264
Direct material[1]	637	939	212	699	315	2,802
Total IPC[2]	865	1,265	702	848	1,017	4,697
Total	$2,103	$3,083	$1,402	$2,136	$2,039	$10,763
No. units produced	1,000	1,500	1,000	in-process	1,500	
Cost/unit	$2.103	$2.055	$1.402	—	$1.359	

OPERATING STATEMENT	$	%
Sales (2,400 units)	$11,945	100
Cost of goods sold		
Product costs (full absorption)		
1,000 units @ (2.103 + 1.402)[3] = 3,505		
1,400 units @ (2.055 + 1.359)[4] = 4,780	8,285	69
IPC variance[5]	197	2
Total cost of goods sold	8,482	71
Gross Margin	3,463	29
Selling, development, and administrative expenses	2,131	18
Operating profit	$1,332	11

[1] Same as under variable costing (see Exhibit 11-6).
[2] IPC Rate = $1.439 per direct labor $ (see Exhibit 11-5).
[3] Sum of unit cost of jobs A and C.
[4] Sum of unit cost of jobs B and E.
[5] IPC variance: IPC absorbed (see above) $4,697
                    Actual IPC (see Exhibit 11-5).   4,894
                                                   $ 197 Dr

the IPC rate has been predetermined, based upon estimated IPC expenditures and activity levels. The fact that actual IPC expenditures were higher than estimated and the quantity of the IPC vehicle (direct labor wages) was below the estimate caused the debit IPC variances that appear on Exhibits 11-6 and 11-7.

Exhibit 11-6 utilizes variable costing. On the job cost report, the actual costs of labor and material committed to each job are charged to that job. IPC is absorbed by each job through the application of the IPC rate (developed in Exhibit 11-5) to the job's direct labor wages. The cost per unit is derived by dividing total job costs by the number of units produced on the job. Note that the completion of a helmet requires two jobs: one for injection molding and one for assembly. For example, a lot of 1,000 helmets was injection-molded on job A and assembled on job C; the total cost of a helmet produced in this lot is obtained by adding the cost per unit on these two jobs. The cost-of-goods-sold section of the operating statement contains three elements: the variable product costs of the 2,400 units sold (*not* of the 2,500 units completed), the IPC variance (IPC was underabsorbed), and the actual fixed IPC cost, treated as a period cost.

Exhibit 11-7 utilizes full absorption costing. Labor and material costs are the same as under variable costing, but the IPC rate is now based upon the sum of variable and fixed IPC elements. The cost-of-goods-sold section of the operating statement contains only the full absorption product costs of the 2,400 units sold and the IPC variance; fixed IPC has been absorbed by the jobs and therefore does not appear as a separate line on the operating statement.

Now compare Exhibits 11-6 and 11-7. Note that product costs are much lower under variable costing (47% of sales) than under full absorption costing (69% of sales). Nevertheless, both the gross margin and operating profit are higher under full absorption costing. This difference is caused by the fact that a portion of the fixed IPC that is treated as a period expense under variable costing has been included in the valuation of in-process and finished-goods inventory at month-end under full absorption costing. The $716 difference in profit ($1,332 less $616) is equal to the difference in these inventory values:

	Valuation of Inventory		
	Variable Costing	Full Absorption Costing	Difference
In-process inventory (job D)	$1,529	$2,136	$607
Finished-goods inventory (100 units)	232	341	109
			$716

Incidentally, in a month when in-process and finished-goods inventories decline, full absorption costing will state profits lower than will variable costing.

Costing Joint Products and By-Products

Before concluding the discussion of structures of cost accounting systems, we need to explore briefly a particular problem that arises when two or more different end products emerge from a single process or single job order. These different end products are referred to as **joint products.** Some examples of joint products are the various distillates that are derived from a catalytic cracking tower processing oil; the end products made from a steer, including the various cuts of meat and the hide; and the various grades of agricultural products that are realized from a sorting or classifying operation. When one of the end products realized is not specifically sought by management and is of substantially less value than the primary product or products, it is referred to as a **by-product,** a special kind of joint product. Joint products typically emerge from a continuous process, where the process costing structure is used, but joint products may also be realized from a single job order.

The dilemma faced in costing joint products is to decide what portion of the total labor, material, and IPC incurred is properly assignable to each of the joint products, or to the by-product. Some logical method of allocation is normally used, sometimes based upon the relative sales values of the joint products, or their relative weights, or some other criterion. By-products may be allocated zero cost, or the amounts realized from the sale of the by-product may be offset against the costs of operating the process.

There is no precisely correct or accurate method of assigning costs to joint products. The allocation method is inevitably arbitrary. As a result, joint product costs are not very useful for making management decisions.

Summary

Cost accounting systems are fashioned to provide that information most useful to the company's operating management, given the company's situation in the marketplace and the nature of its production activities. As a result, a very wide diversity of cost accounting systems is employed across the broad spectrum of industry, from large companies to small companies, and from heavy-equipment manufacturers to producers of consumer products, to petrochemical processors. This chapter identifies three key parameters of the structure of cost accounting systems. Decisions with respect to the following three parameters define the structure of the system:

1 What are the limits of the task for which data are collected? Is this task defined in terms of a job order — produce so many parts or units, without fixing the elapsed time required — or as a process — operate the process for a specified period of time, without fixing the amount of output to be obtained?

2 With respect to indirect production costs, which indirect expenditures should be included and which should be excluded? If all indirect manufacturing expenditures are excluded, the resulting system is referred to as a *prime costing system;* such systems are not in common use. If only variable IPC is included in product costs (and fixed IPC is treated as a

period cost), the resulting system is referred to as a *variable costing system*. If both fixed and variable components of IPC are included in product costs, the resulting system is referred to as a *full absorption costing system*.

3   Shall inventory and cost of goods sold be valued at actual costs or standard costs? That is, shall variances between actual costs and standard costs be developed at each step of the manufacturing process so that standard costs rather than actual costs flow through to finished-goods inventory and to cost of goods sold? The use of standard costs facilitates the comparison of actual and planned production results, and helps pinpoint the causes of deviation from plan.

At the outset of this chapter, examples of five quite different production activities were described. Reread those first few pages containing the examples. What structure is appropriate for the cost accounting system for each of these companies?

1   A manufacturer of a standard line of men's shirts. The job order cost system seems to fit. The differences between variable and full absorption costing are probably not great in such a labor intensive (as opposed to capital equipment intensive) operation. It would seem that standard costing would be of substantial benefit to management in monitoring material usage and labor efficiency. Product cost standards should be relatively easy to set, as even new shirt models would not involve radically different production techniques.

2   A manufacturer of large printing presses. Job order costing is required. Either variable or full absorption costing would be appropriate. Here both custom and standardized products are manufactured, although even the custom presses contain standard components. In this situation a combination of standard and actual costing systems might be employed: standard costs to value the standard presses and the standard components of the custom presses, and actual costs to value the customizing activity (since it probably would not pay to set standards for each custom assignment). A custom press, when shipped to the customer, would then be valued (for cost of goods sold) at the standard cost of the standard components and the actual cost of special components and of assembly labor.

3   An oil refinery producing standard products. This continuous process requires process costing. Full absorption costing is probably preferable to variable costing, as most of the fixed costs are associated with the refinery capital equipment and can be allocated to production in terms of number of processing hours. Either standard or actual costing fits the situation. Joint products or by-products probably emanate from this process and, if so, some method must be devised to allocate the total process costs to the various joint products.

4   A chemical specialty firm, producing custom pharmaceuticals for sale by others.   Without knowing more about the particular processes, we cannot determine whether the tasks are better defined as discrete jobs or as continuous processes.   It is possible that either job order or process costing would be appropriate, or process costing might best fit the chemical processing lines while job order costing might best fit the packaging lines.   Since volume of activity varies widely, variable costing might be more appropriate than full absorption costing in order that product costs not be unduly influenced by volume of production.   If the products processed by the firm are continuously changing, actual costing may be preferable to standard costing.

5   Assembler of electronic instruments.   Here a job order, variable, standard costing system appears appropriate.   Since this operation is again labor intensive, rather than capital intensive, there will be relatively little difference between variable costs and full absorption costs; management decisions might be facilitated, however, by the use of variable costing.   If the company produces a standard line of instruments, the company can benefit from the use of standard costing.

Clearly, a wide variety of structures is possible.   Indeed, even within a single company it may be appropriate to use different structures for different segments of the business.   In designing the cost accounting system the information needs of the users, line operating management, should be emphasized.   These information needs are in turn dictated by the nature of the manufacturing process or of the service and by the degree to which the company's management relies on cost accounting reports.   Furthermore, in such industries as public utility, defense contracting, and transportation, the cost accounting system will also be influenced by the demands of external audiences, particularly government regulatory and contracting agencies.

New Terms

Actual costs   Product costs composed of actual direct material costs and actual direct labor wages plus an allocation of IPC based upon actual quantity of the IPC vehicle.   Actual costing (a cost accounting structure) contrasts with *standard costing*.

By-products   A category of *joint products* consisting of products of substantially less value than the other joint products emanating from a process or job order.

Direct costing   An alternative name for *variable costing*.

Full absorption costing   A cost accounting structure that defines product costs to include all IPC costs, both variable and fixed.   Full absorption costing contrasts with *variable costing*.

Job order   The definition of a task that specifies both the work to be performed and the number of units to be worked on. In *job order costing*, all costs associated with performing the defined task are collected. Job order costing contrasts with *process costing*.

Joint products Two or more different end products emanating from a single process or single job order. The cost of each of the joint products is derived by allocation.

Prime cost The sum of direct material and direct labor costs. All IPC is excluded from prime costs.

Process costing A cost accounting structure that collects all costs associated with the process for a period of time; the quantity to be produced during this time is not fixed. Process costing contrasts with *job order costing*.

Standard costs Predetermined product costs representing what it should cost (sum of direct material, direct labor, and IPC), rather than what it actually does cost to produce a product or perform a service. Standard costing (a cost accounting structure) contrasts with *actual costing*.

Variable costing A cost accounting structure that defines product costs to exclude fixed IPC costs. Fixed IPC is treated as a period cost. Variable costing contrasts with *full absorption costing*.

Problems

1 Indicate whether each of the following statements is True or False:
   a Prime costs include, in addition to the costs of manufacturing, a fair allocation of selling and administrative costs per unit.
   b Valuation of in-process inventory at the end of the accounting period is simpler in job order costing than in process costing.
   c If inventory is growing and variable costing is used, reported profits will be lower than if full absorption costing is used.
   d Process costing collects all costs of manufacturing for a particular time period, without reference to the amount or number of products produced, while job order costing collects all costs of manufacturing a predetermined amount or number of products without reference to the time period.
   e A standard cost accounting system is typically more expensive to operate than an actual cost accounting system.
2 Do you feel that variable costing provides better information for sales policy decisions (e.g., pricing and promotion) than full absorption costing? Explain.
3 What are the advantages of using a standard costing system rather than an actual costing system? What are the disadvantages?
4 Described below are some manufacturing or service operations. What cost accounting structure would you recommend for each, and why?
   a An architectural design office consisting of four architects, two draftspersons, and one secretary
   b A large aluminum smelting operation
   c A construction company specializing in building roads
   d A manufacturer of a line of private aircraft

e A manufacturing plant devoted solely to 17-inch television sets
f An auto shop specializing in engine rebuilding
g A sewage-treatment plant

5 Assume that the Mathews Company experiences wide seasonal fluctuations in sales. As a result, during the peak season monthly sales will run at twice the rate of monthly sales during the slow season. However, the company's monthly production rate remains relatively constant throughout the year. The company is debating between the use of variable costing and full absorption costing. Will the company's fluctuations in monthly profit be less under one of these methods of costing? If so, which one? Why?

6 If, in a particular country, both variable costing and full absorption costing are acceptable methods of accounting for tax purposes and you seek to minimize your tax payments, which method of costing would you select, and why?

7 In both actual and standard cost accounting systems, we use a predetermined IPC rate to include indirect manufacturing costs (or factory burden) in product costs. Why do we use a predetermined rate rather than allocating the actual costs to the products produced?

8 The Fry Freezer Company produces two models of freezer and operates a job order costing system. In preparing for its new fiscal year, 19X6, the company has developed the following estimates:

	Freezer Model	
	A	**B**
Estimated sales (units)	10,500	7,000
Estimated production (units)	11,500	8,500
Material cost per unit	$110	$130
Labor hours, category M (per unit)	4 h	4 h
Wage rate per hour, category M	$6	$6
Labor hours, category N (per unit)	4 h	7 h
Wage rate per hour, category N	$9	$9

INDIRECT PRODUCTION COSTS (ESTIMATE FOR THE YEAR)

Fixed

Salaries	$ 75,000
Rent	30,000
Depreciation	15,000
Other	8,000
Subtotal	128,000

Variable

Miscellaneous indirect labor	18,000
Supplies	32,000
Other	10,000
Subtotal	60,000
Total	$188,000

Determine the IPC rate and the standard costs of model A and model B under each of the following assumptions:

a Full absorption costing system, where the IPC vehicle is units of production (assume that, for this purpose, a unit of model A is equivalent to a unit of model B)

b Full absorption costing system, where the IPC vehicle is material cost in dollars

c Full absorption costing system, where the IPC vehicle is labor hours (assume that, for this purpose, an hour of category M labor is equivalent to an hour of category N labor)

d Full absorption costing system, where the IPC vehicle is labor cost in dollars

e Variable costing system, where the IPC vehicle is units of production (see assumption in **a** above)

f Variable costing system, where the IPC vehicle is labor cost in dollars

9 Refer to problem 8.

a If selling prices are established by applying a certain pecentage markup to standard unit costs, which of the IPC vehicles outlined in **8a** through **8d** above will result in the greatest difference between the prices of model A and model B? Explain.

b Assume that the IPC vehicle selected is labor cost (in dollars) and that the estimates of sales and production volume (in units) are realized. Will the operating profit of Fry in 19X6 be higher or lower if variable costing is used instead of full absorption costing? If the estimated indirect production costs are realized, how much will be the difference in operating profit in 19X6?

10 The Agrigrow Chemical Company operates an actual, process, full absorption cost accounting system. The company produces a single product, a fertilizer for agricultural use. Record in T-account format the opening balances and all transactions and recognitions for May 19X2. Construct an income statement for the month and a balance sheet at May 31, 19X2.

a Opening balances in the general ledger at April 30, 19X2:

Cash and other assets		$ 10,000
Accounts receivable		20,000
Inventories		
Raw	10,000	
In-process	5,000	
Finished	15,000	30,000
Fixed assets		
At cost	75,000	
Accumulated depreciation	(12,000)	63,000
Total assets		$123,000
All liabilities		$ 42,000
Owners' equity		81,000
		$123,000

b The IPC rate at Agrigrow is $1.50 per direct labor dollar.

c Transactions and recognitions for the month:

(1) Raw materials were purchased for $8,000, on credit.

(2) Raw materials valued at $7,000 were issued into production.

(3) Direct labor wages of $4,000 were paid in cash.
(4) Indirect production costs were:
    a Supplies (purchased on credit) $1,000
    b Indirect labor (wages paid in cash) $2,000
    c Depreciation expense $2,000
    d Other indirect costs (all paid in cash) $1,500
(5) In-process inventory was the same at the end of the month as at the beginning ($5,000).
(6) Sales (all on credit) were $18,000. Cost of goods sold, determined by the perpetual inventory method, was $13,300.
(7) Selling, general, and other operating expenses for the month totaled $4,000, all paid in cash.
(8) Collections on accounts receivable totaled $19,000 and payments of liabilities totaled $8,000.

11 Refer to problem 10. What would Agrigrow's profit have been in May if it had used a variable costing, rather than a full absorption costing system? Assume that:

a Variable IPC elements are supplies and indirect labor, and that the IPC rate was 70 cents per direct labor dollar

b The opening balances in the general ledger were the same as shown in problem 10 except:

In-process inventory	4,000 Dr.
Finished-goods inventory	12,000 Dr.
Owners' equity	77,000 Cr.

c Cost of goods sold (variable costing basis) for the month was $10,500

12 The Vesper Electrical Co. is an electrical subcontractor for major commercial buildings. During September 19X4 the company worked on three jobs, no. 124, no. 126, and no. 129. Job 129 was started during the month and not completed by the end of the month. The other two jobs were in process at the beginning of the month and completed during the month. The company operates a job order, variable, actual cost accounting system. The company's final trial balance at August 31, 19X4 was as follows:

	Dr.	Cr.
Cash and other assets	$ 17,000	
Accounts receivable	46,000	
Jobs in process (inventory)		
Job 124	31,000	
Job 126	16,500	
Fixed assets	83,700	
Accumulated depreciation		$ 38,100
Current liabilities		39,900
Long-term liabilities		47,000
Invested capital		20,000
Retained earnings		49,200
	$194,200	$194,200

The company maintained no raw-material inventory, as all material was purchased for specific jobs. The company's IPC rate was $6.00 per direct labor hour. Transactions for the month were:

a Materials purchased on credit for the jobs were:

Job 124	$ 6,000
Job 126	14,100
Job 129	10,600
	$30,700

b Direct labor hours and dollars (paid in cash) charged to the jobs were:

	Hours	$
Job 124	2,100	18,900
Job 126	1,200	10,700
Job 129	800	7,100
	4,100	$36,700

c Jobs 124 and 126 were completed, turned over to the prime contractor and billed for:

Job 124	$89,000
Job 126	60,000

d Expenditures on variable IPC totaled $23,300 ($11,000 paid in cash and $12,300 purchased on credit).

e Fixed IPC for the month was:

Depreciation	$ 2,000
Rental of equipment	16,000 (paid in cash)
Other	4,500 (paid in cash)
	$22,500

f Collections on accounts receivable totaled $30,000. Payment of current liabilities totaled $29,800. Payment of long-term liabilities totaled $1,500.

g Administrative and other operating expenses totaled $6,000, all paid in cash. Interest payments were $1,000.

h At midmonth the company borrowed an additional $70,000 on a short-term note. This note was still outstanding at month-end. The company experienced wide swings in accounts receivable, short-term bank loans, and amounts due to vendors because of the irregular pattern of its business.

Record the above in T-account format and construct an income statement for September 19X4 and a balance sheet as of September 30, 19X4.

13 Refer to problem 12. If Vesper had used a full absorption costing system, its trial balance would have been as shown above except for the following three accounts:

Job 124	34,000 Dr.
Job 126	18,000 Dr.
Retained earnings	53,700 Cr.

The company's IPC rate (including both fixed and variable elements of IPC) would have been $12 per direct labor hour. Perform the accounting, in T-account format, for Vesper for September, assuming full absorption costing. Construct an income statement for September and a balance sheet as of September 30, 19X4.

14 A summary of transactions for January 19X7 for the Larson Company is shown below. The company operates a job order, actual, full absorption costing system, and determines cost of goods sold by the end-of-period adjustment method. The individual job accounts appear in a subsidiary ledger; you should record all entries affecting jobs in the master account, Work-in-Process Inventory. (All dollar figures are in thousands of dollars.)

a Opening balances in the general ledger at January 1, 19X7, were:

Accounts receivable	$36,000 Dr.
Inventories	
Raw material	10,000 Dr.
In-process	10,000 Dr.
Finished-goods	5,000 Dr.
Fixed assets, at cost	14,000 Dr.
Accumulated depreciation	5,000 Cr.
All other assets (including cash)	15,000 Dr.
Accounts payable	13,000 Cr.
All other liabilities	14,000 Cr.
Owners' equity	58,000 Cr.

b Raw materials purchased on account:$17,000

c Paid in cash the following (all relate to January's activity):

Machine repairs	$ 1,000
Direct labor	7,600
Indirect labor	1,500
Administrative costs	2,500
Salespersons' salaries	1,500
Miscellaneous indirect production costs	500
Total	$14,600

d Paid accounts payable: $18,000 (in cash)

e Depreciation charged on machinery: $1,000

f Received $32,000 from customers on account; sales on account for the month were $24,000. (The company had no cash sales.)

g Raw material withdrawn from warehouse and put into production jobs: $15,000

h IPC rate: 60% of direct labor cost.

i Aggregate cost of units produced (i.e., completed) during month and transferred to finished-goods inventory (Note: this is *not* cost of goods sold.): $31,000

j Any overabsorbed or unabsorbed overhead (IPC variance) is charged to cost of goods sold for the month.

k Ending inventories:

Raw material inventory, ending	$12,000
In-process inventory, ending	?
Finished-goods inventory, ending	17,000

Assignment

1 Record opening balances and the transactions and other necessary entries in T-account format.

2 Prepare an income statement for January and a month-end balance sheet.

3 Determine the value of ending in-process inventory.

12 Developing and Analyzing Cost Variances

The previous chapter discussed the shaping of a cost accounting system to fit a company's particular informational needs. In this chapter we will discuss the development and analysis of data that can assist managers in monitoring the performance of their organizations.

The cost accounting system fulfills two important and related functions:

1 Providing the product cost data required for the accurate valuation of inventory and cost of goods sold. In this context, the cost accounting system supports in a major way the financial accounting of the enterprise.
2 Providing information to management regarding current operations. When properly developed and presented, this information assists management in determining when and to what extent operating plans need to be altered.

Our focus in this chapter is on the second of these two cost accounting functions.

Variances and Management by Exception

A basic tenet of management practice suggests that managers focus attention not on those areas that seem to be operating in accordance with the company's plans, but rather on those areas that seem to be operating at odds with plans. Referred to as **management by exception,** this technique requires that the company's accounting system be able to differentiate between those segments of the business that are "on-plan" and those that are not. Moreover, the cost accounting system should be able to highlight the magnitude and probable cause or causes of deviations from plan.

Any formal comparison of actual and planned results can be referred to as a **variance.** Our concern in this chapter is with techniques for analyzing variances to obtain information useful to management.

Standard cost systems, introduced in Chapter 11, are particularly useful to the management-by-exception concept. Properly designed, a standard cost accounting system can develop a series of variances—general ledger accounts that compare actual performance (that is, actual costs) with planned performance (that is, the expected level of costs, or standard costs) for particular segments of the operation. Recall that these systems require the formal development of standards and these standards become an integral part of the accounting system. Variances can be developed, for example, for individual departments in a manufacturing or servicing company. Then, within the individual department, variances can be developed with respect to specific products, specific functions, and individual cost elements (for example, labor or material) that are of critical concern to management. These variance data permit managers at all levels in the organization—department managers, division managers, general managers—to focus on exception areas. Variances at or near zero signal on-target performance. Large variances demand management attention to determine the causes of the deviation from plan and the possible need for corrective action.

Variance analysis techniques apply to period costs as well as to product costs. Budgeting the selling, administrative, and other operating expenses of an enterprise involves, in effect, setting standards for these period costs. Techniques of budgeting (setting budget levels) are discussed in the next chapter, but the techniques discussed here for analyzing variances are as applicable to period costs as to product costs.

We should recognize that even in companies that do not use standard costing and do not develop explicit budgets, management typically is operating on some type of implicit plan. This implicit plan may often be simply to repeat last year's actual results. The managers of a mature company operating in a stable market environment may view last year's actual results as the best guide to this year's operations. If so, last year's actual results represent a reasonable yardstick for judging this year's perform-ance, even though management may seek to improve cost performance in some areas during the current year. In this situation the cost accountant may find it useful to develop variance reports that highlight differences be-tween this year and last year. Management can then focus attention only on those segments of the business where significant variations between the two years are occurring.

Thus, variances may highlight differences between actual and stan-dard, or budgeted, costs, or when appropriate, they may highlight differ-ences between current actual costs and actual costs during a previous ac-counting period (typically the corresponding period of the previous year).

Interpreting Variance Balances

Exhibit 12-1 shows a variance report for the month of July 19X2 for one de-partment, department M, within the Andover Manufacturing Company. Andover uses an actual, rather than a standard, cost accounting system. The company does not use a formal budgeting procedure, but finds it useful to compare each month's results with results for the corresponding month of the previous year.[1] To simplify our discussion, assume that department M produces only one product, Malex, and that Malex is produced entirely within this department.

On Exhibit 12-1 and throughout our discussion of variances we will fol-low the normal convention of enclosing variance amounts in parentheses when the variance reduces the profit of the company. Thus, in the case of expense variances, when current actual expenditures are in excess of plan (or, in the case of our Andover example, in excess of last year's expendi-tures), the amount of the excess is enclosed in parentheses. When later in our discussion we deal with sales or revenue variances, the parentheses will indicate revenue below the budget or plan.

We see immediately from Exhibit 12-1 that department M's total ex-penses in 19X2 exceeded by a fair margin the 19X1 level. We may be in-clined to jump to the conclusion that the department performed poorly dur-ing July 19X2, since expenditures exceeded the previous year's level by $2,080. However, additional analysis is appropriate before reaching con-clusions regarding the department's performance. The causes of variation in expenditures between the two years need to be isolated in order to pin-point the particular corrective action that should be taken, if indeed any action is warranted.

---

[1] Andover Manufacturing Company might also find it useful to compare July 19X2 to June 19X2 (i.e., to the previous month). However, if monthly operating results are influenced by seasonality or by the varying number of working days in a month, the more useful comparison may be with the corresponding month of the previous year.

Exhibit 12-1
ANDOVER MANUFACTURING COMPANY VARIANCE REPORT
July 19X2
Manufacturing Department M

	Actual July 19X1	Actual July 19X2	Variance[1]
Direct labor wages	$ 9,000	$ 9,600	($ 600)
Direct materials used	13,500	14,800	(1,300)
Indirect production costs			
Supervisory labor	1,100	1,100	—
Fringe employment costs	2,020	2,220	(200)
Supplies	600	700	(100)
Maintenance expenses	2,000	1,800	200
Heat, light, and power	850	950	(100)
Rent and other occupancy costs	3,050	3,030	20
	$32,120	$34,200	($2,080)
Units of Malex produced	4,000	4,320	320 units

[1] Indicates effect on earnings. Amounts in parentheses reduce earnings.

Note an item of nonfinancial information appearing at the bottom of Exhibit 12-1: the number of units of Malex produced in each of the two months. The department produced 320 more units (8% more) in July of 19X2 as compared to the previous July. Thus, management should expect some expenditures to be higher in July 19X2. One major cause of expense variation is variations in volume of activity—in this case, variations in the number of units of Malex produced. This change in volume of output may alone explain certain of the variances; direct labor wages and direct materials used should be directly proportional to the volume of output. This volume variation may also influence some of the IPC elements, such as supplies expense, heat, light, and power, and fringe employment costs. On the other hand, it seems unlikely that volume of production would affect rent and other occupancy costs, assuming the department's physical facilities are the same in both years.

In addition to volume of productive activity, another cause of variation between *actual* and *plan* (or in the case of Andover, between one year's actual and the previous year's actual expenditures) might be changes in price. Andover may be paying its direct labor force higher wage rates in 19X2, or perhaps changes in the work force have caused the average wage rate in the department to be more or less than the previous year. A third cause might be changes in efficiency. Therefore, in addition to the effect of the variation in volume, two other factors influence direct labor wages: the efficiency of the labor force and the wage rates paid to the employees. Obviously, the same types of effects may influence direct materials used: Andover may be more efficient or inefficient in the use of materials, and in addition Andover may be paying more or less for the materials used in Malex than was paid in 19X1. Methods of isolating the effects of volume of production or activity, price or wage rate, and efficiency or usage will be discussed presently.

Before leaving Exhibit 12-1, however, we need to focus again on the meaning of variance balances. Variance balances enclosed in parentheses are popularly referred to as **negative** (or *unfavorable* **variances**—negative in the sense that they reduce the profit of the enterprise. Similarly, variances that add to profit are popularly referred to as **positive** (or *favorable*) **variances.** This nomenclature is both understandable and unfortunate. So-called negative and positive variances, or unfavorable and favorable variances, simply indicate that actual expenditures were at variance from the plan. They do not necessarily indicate either good or poor performance. For example, in Exhibit 12-1 note that volume of production increased by 8%, while total direct labor wages increased by only 6.7%; thus, while the total variance is negative when July 19X2 is compared to July 19X1, labor efficiency must have improved and/or the labor wage rates paid must have been lower than during July 19X1.

Consider also the variance in maintenance expenses. Andover spent $200 less on maintenance during July 19X2 than during July 19X1. Reduced maintenance expenditures are not necessarily favorable to the long-term health of the company's plant and equipment. If reduced expenditures on maintenance were achieved by improved efficiency in performing maintenance or because extra care in the use of equipment resulted in less demand for maintenance, then indeed the variance shown on Exhibit 12-1 is favorable. On the other hand, if the lower expenditures were achieved by simply deferring needed maintenance or cutting preventive maintenance, this variance from planned expenditure levels may be unfavorable, even though the financial result was an increase in profit in July 19X2.

Finally, the magnitude of the variance must be considered. It is likely that virtually all variance accounts will carry some balance at the end of an accounting period. If the magnitude of the variance is small, as compared with the total level of expenses, little significance should be ascribed to the variance. The concept of materiality certainly applies to variance analysis. For example, in Exhibit 12-1 the $20 favorable variance in rent and other occupancy costs is hardly material in relationship to the $3,030 total in the account or the total departmental expenditures of $34,200; with respect to this cost element, department M was about on-plan for the month of July 19X2.

Separating Price and Usage Variances

As mentioned above, even when the level of production activity is exactly in line with plan, actual expenditures may deviate from plan for one or a combination of the following reasons:

1 Rate of usage deviated from plan. Reasons for the deviation might include wastage or scrappage, resulting in greater usage of direct materials; improved labor efficiency, resulting in less direct labor; efficient use of equipment, resulting in fewer kilowatthours of power consumed; carelessness or inefficiency, resulting in the consumption of more production supplies.
2 The price paid per unit of input deviated from plan. For example, quantity discount terms resulted in lower prices for a certain material component; a recent labor union agreement caused wage rates to be higher than planned; a power company rate increase resulted in higher charges per kilowatthour.

If standards or budgets are established with respect both to usage and to price, then separate variances can be generated. While such refinement is not warranted for all variances, it is frequently appropriate for direct labor and direct materials. These two cost elements typically represent the major expenditures in manufacturing companies; moreover, the necessary data are generally at hand. In arriving at product cost standards, the cost engineer must determine the number of hours of direct labor required, as well as the labor wage rate, and an estimate of the quantity of materials (measured in terms of number of items, weight, length, or area), as well as of the price of the materials per unit of measure.

With respect to direct labor, separate **wage rate variances** and **labor efficiency** (or *usage*) **variances** are obtainable; with respect to direct material, **purchase price variances** can be isolated from **material usage variances.** Theoretically, price and usage variances could be calculated for all of the other expenses shown in Exhibit 12-1 for department M (expenses that comprise the indirect production costs for the department). However, establishing separate usage and price standards for the IPC elements would be difficult and the resulting information would be of marginal usefulness to operating management.

Exhibit 12-2 illustrates the separation of usage and price variances in department M of the Andover Manufacturing Company in July 19X2. Standard prime costs for one unit of Malex are shown in part A of Exhibit 12-2. Note that separate standards have been established for the quantities and the prices of the inputs (material and direct labor). Further detail on the actual results for the month of July are shown in part B of the exhibit. These data are sufficient for detailed analysis of labor and material variances for department M.

Part C of Exhibit 12-2 derives a single variance for each of direct material and direct labor. These variances show the combined effect of variations in price (wage rate) and usage (efficiency). The actual material cost of $14,800 for the month compares with the standard cost of $15,034 (4,320 units produced[2] times standard material cost per unit of $3.48) resulting in a credit, or favorable, balance of $234. This single variance doesn't indicate whether the favorable balance resulted from lower material prices or reduced usage of material, or some combination of the two, or possibly, from some inefficiency in the use of material that was more than offset by actual prices being well below standard. Similarly, the total labor variance for the month is a debit of $139, but the effects that wage rate variations and labor efficiency or inefficiency had on this combined variance are not revealed.

Part D of Exhibit 12-2 illustrates the separation of price and usage variances. The price (wage rate variance) compares actual and standard prices (wage rates) for the actual volume of material (labor) used. The credit entry in the purchase price (wage rate) variance is offset by the debit entry to the usage variance. The usage variance compares actual and standard usage, both valued at standard prices (wage rates).

[2] Note that the standard cost has been adjusted for actual volume produced—4,320 units of Malex.

Exhibit 12-2
ANDOVER MANUFACTURING COMPANY
July 19X2

A   Standard Prime Costs (Per Unit of Malex)

Material	Standard Quantity	×	Standard Price	=	Standard Material Cost
Item A	24 grams		$0.10/gram		$2.40
Item B	2 units		$0.54 each		1.08
Subtotal, material					$3.48

Labor	Standard Hours	×	Standard Wage Rate	=	Standard Labor Cost
Skill P	0.21 hours		$7.00		$1.47
Skill Q	0.12 hours		6.00		0.72
Subtotal, labor					$2.19
Total standard prime cost					$5.67

B   Actual Results, July 19X2

Quantity produced (from Exhibit 12-1)	4,320 units
Direct material used	
Item A	103,000 grams
Item B	8,700 units
Total material cost (from Exhibit 12-1)	$ 14,800
Direct labor hours used	
Skill P	895 hours
Skill Q	510 hours
Total labor cost (from Exhibit 12-1)	$ 9,600

C   Combined Variances for Material and Labor

Material Variance		Labor Variance	
Actual total material cost $14,800	Standard material cost of output 4,320 units × $3.48 = $15,034	Actual total labor cost $9,600	Standard labor cost of output 4,320 units × $2.19 = $9,461
	Balance = $234 Credit	Balance = $139 Debit	

D   Separate Price and Usage Variances

Material Purchase Price Variance		Material Usage Variance[2]	
Actual total material cost[1] $14,800	Actual material quantity used × standard prices A: 103,000 grams × $0.10 = $10,300 B: 8,700 units × $0.54 = $4,698 Total A + B = $14,998	Actual material quantity used × standard prices $14,998	Standard material cost of output[3] 4,320 units × $3.48 = $15,033.60
	Balance: $198 Credit		Balance: $35.60 Credit

Labor Wage Rate Variance		Labor Usage (Efficiency) Variance[5]	
Actual total labor cost[4] $9,600	Actual hours worked × standard wage rate P: 895 hours × $7.00 = $6,265 Q: 510 hours × $6.00 = $3,060 Total P & Q = $9,325	Actual hours worked × standard wage rate $9,325	Standard labor cost of output[6] 4,320 units × $2.19 = $9,460.80
Balance: $275 Debit			Balance: $135.80 Credit

See next page for footnotes.

Footnotes to Exhibit 12-2:

[1] Actual material quantity used times actual prices
[2] This variance can be verified as follows:

Material	Standard Quantity	Actual Quantity	Physical Quantity Variance	Standard Price	Variance (in $)
A	4,320 units × 24 grams/ Malex = 103,680	103,000	680 grams	$0.10/gram	$68.00
B	4,320 units × 2 units/ Malex = 8,640	8,700	(60) units	$0.54/unit	(32.40)
					$35.60

[3] Standard quantity (for output achieved) times standard material prices
[4] Actual hours worked times actual wage rates
[5] This variance can be verified as follows:

Skill	Standard Hours	Actual Hours	Variance in Hours	Standard Wage Rate	Variance (in $)
P	4,320 units × 0.21 hours/ Malex = 907.20	895	12.20	7.00	$ 85.40
Q	4,320 units × 0.12 hours/ Malex = 518.40	510	8.40	6.00	50.40
					$135.80

[6] Standard hours (for output achieved) times standard wage rate

Note that the credit in the total material variance is the result both of actual prices below standard ($198 credit) and of efficient usage of material ($36 credit). On the other hand, the efficient use of labor ($136 credit) was more than offset by the unfavorable wage rate variance ($275 debit) that resulted from actual wage rates higher than standard rates.

Note also that the arithmetic sum of these separate price and usage variances shown in part D is equal to the corresponding total variance derived in part C:

Material purchase price variance	$198 credit
Material usage variance	36 credit
Total material variance	$234 credit
Labor wage rate variance	($275) debit
Labor usage (efficiency) variance	136 credit
Total labor variance	($139) debit

Thus, the single variance has been decomposed into its two component parts.

Still more detailed analysis is possible. Price and usage variances for each of material items A and B and for each of labor skills P and Q could be developed if actual expenditures for the month were available at this level of detail. (Certain of this detail is shown in the footnotes for Exhibit 12-2.) For example, assume that of the $9,600 spent on labor during July, $6,310 represented wages paid to the employees representing skill P, while $3,290 was paid to those representing skill Q. The total labor variance for the month ($139 debit) consists of a $40.40 favorable balance with respect to skill P and $179.60 unfavorable with respect to skill Q. A more detailed analysis of the labor variances shows:

Wage rate variance, skill P	($ 45.00)
Wage rate variance, skill Q	(230.00)
Total wage rate variance	($ 275.00)
Efficiency variance, skill P	$ 85.40
Efficiency variance, skill Q	50.40
Total labor efficiency variance	$135.80

This additional detail can be incorporated into the cost accounting system, at some additional cost, if management decides the benefits outweigh the costs. If management feels that the total labor wage rate variance is sufficient, the cost accounting system and the resulting management reports should not be burdened with the additional detail concerning individual skills.

Indeed, management may in certain instances find even the amount of detail contained in part D of Exhibit 12-2 to be excessive. For example, if wage rates are dictated by a long-term labor union agreement, management may be confident that department M's wage rate variance from month to month will be at or close to zero. When a new labor union agreement is negotiated, standard wage rates will be revised accordingly and once again wage rate variances will be nil. In this case, the cost accounting system might be designed to yield only a single labor variance, as indicated in part C of Exhibit 12-2. When interpreting this single labor variance, management will be aware that any debit or credit balance is attributable solely to efficiency (usage) variation.

A strong argument in favor of separating price and usage variances is that the two effects—price and efficiency—are the responsibility of different managers within the organization. Material prices are negotiated by the purchasing department; the efficiency with which materials are used— that is, the extent of spoilage, wastage, or rework—depends upon the care and competence of the direct labor force. If corrective action is indicated by the variances, action will be taken in the purchasing department if the problem relates to price and by the supervisor of department M if the problem relates to usage. Another argument in favor of separation is that a favorable price variance might lead to an unfavorable usage variance if, for example, the company purchased lower-cost but inferior materials, resulting in high wastage or spoilage. On the other hand, the reverse might be true.

In summary, any expense variance, including variances with respect to IPC cost elements, can be broken down into its price and usage components if (a) separate quantity and price standards can be established and (b) the benefit to management of this additional detail outweighs the cost of generating it.

Isolating Volume Effects

As discussed earlier, cost variances are frequently created simply by the fact that actual volume of activity differed from the planned volume. If a particular cost is variable—that is, if it varies in direct proportion to the level of production activity—adjustments for changes in volume are necessary to develop a meaningful cost variance. Other cost elements are fixed —that is, the amount to be spent is independent of the volume of activity— and volume effects need not be isolated for these cost elements.

Cost accountants encounter relatively little difficulty in dealing with those costs that are wholly variable with volume and those that are wholly fixed. To repeat, the adjustment for volume fluctuations is straightforward for variable costs and no adjustments are required for fixed costs. The situation is somewhat more complex when dealing with the many cost elements that are semivariable—that is, the cost elements that vary with volume but not in direct proportion to volume. As an example, consider an expense outside of manufacturing: salespersons' compensation. Assume that the sales force is paid a certain base salary plus a 1% commission on sales—a common method of compensating salespersons. The base salary is a fixed cost and the commission is a variable cost; total compensation is semivariable. If sales volume increases 10% during a particular period, salespersons' compensation will increase, but by less than 10%, since only the commission portion of the compensation is influenced by volume.

Exhibit 12-3 contains a variance report for July 19X2 for one sales group, group T, at the Andover Manufacturing Company. Once again, Andover wishes to compare the current level of expenditures with the previous year's levels, developing variances between the two accounting periods. At first glance, it would appear that group T controlled expenses rather poorly in the month of July 19X2: expenses were $630 above expenses in July 19X1, or about 7% higher. However, sales in July 19X2 were considerably ahead of the previous year: $34,000, or about 26%.

If all of the cost elements were fixed—that is, independent of volume— the $630 variance would suggest relatively poor expense control. Conversely, if all of the cost elements varied in direct proportion to sales vol-

Exhibit 12-3
ANDOVER MANUFACTURING COMPANY
Sales Group T
Variance Report, July 19X2

	Actual July 19X1	Actual July 19X2	Variance
Salespersons' compensation	$ 5,300	$ 5,900	$ (600)
Freight expense	800	980	(180)
Travel and telephone expense	1,100	1,200	(100)
Training expense	700	420	280
Rent and other occupancy costs	650	680	(30)
Total	$ 8,550	$ 9,180	$ (630)
Sales volume	$130,000	$164,000	$34,000

ume, group T did an excellent job of expense control in July 19X2: sales increased by about 26% while expenses increased by only 7.4%. Neither conclusion is warranted. In fact, several of the cost elements are semivariable and further analysis is required.

What is the extent of variability of each of the expenses? Salespersons' compensation is semivariable. Freight expense is probably directly and proportionally variable: the more Andover ships to its customers, the higher its freight charges. The variability of travel and telephone expense is difficult to assess: travel costs and telephone tolls are primarily a function of the number of salespersons employed, but the volume of sales may also be a factor.[3] Rent and other occupancy costs are probably fixed, wholly independent of the volume of sales realized. Training expense is also independent of sales volume; training expense will vary from period to period, but as a function of turnover of sales personnel or of management's decision to invest more or less in training, not as a function of sales volume.

Exhibit 12-4 expands the variance report shown in Exhibit 12-3 to isolate the volume effects from the expense control effects. This analysis suggests that $549 of the total $630 variance was accounted for by the sales volume increase.

Note that the volume effect with respect to salespersons' compensation must have been 1% of the change in sales volume, since the sales force is paid commissions at the rate of 1% of sales. The remainder of the variance, $260, must represent a change in the base compensation of the sales force, perhaps as a result of inflation.

---

[3] One may be inclined to argue that the number of salespersons on the staff necessarily varies with sales volume. More typically, however, the size of the sales force is determined by management judgment, and adding or eliminating a sales position is not *caused* by changes in sales volume. Thus, changes in the size of the field sales force may *result* in, but not be *caused* by, variations in sales volume.

Exhibit 12-4
ANDOVER MANUFACTURING COMPANY
Sales Group T
Volume-Adjusted Variance Report, July 19X2

	Actual 19X1	Actual 19X2	Total Variance	Volume Effect	Expense Control Effect
Salespersons' compensation	$5,300	$5,900	($600)	($340)	($260)
Freight expense	800	980	(180)	(209)	29
Travel and telephone expense	1,100	1,200	(100)	—	(100)
Training expense	700	420	280	—	280
Rent and other occupancy costs	650	680	(30)	—	(30)
Total	$8,550	$9,180	($630)	($549)	($81)
Sales volume	$130,000	$164,000	$34,000	$34,000	—

Freight expense in July 19X1 was $800, or just over 0.6% of sales. Since this cost element is fully variable with sales, this same percentage should apply to the July 19X2 period. Thus, the sales increase should cause freight expense in July 19X2 to be $1,009, or $209 higher than the July 19X1 level. In fact, freight expense was less than this volume-adjusted level by $29. Group T performed well during the month in controlling freight expense.

Exhibit 12-4 assumes that the remainder of the cost elements are fixed —that is, independent of sales volume—and thus volume effects need not be isolated. Travel and telephone expenses were $100 above the previous year's level. Valid reasons may exist for this higher level of expenditures (inflation, more sales calls completed, or high telephone expense because of a great deal of contact with a distant customer), or the higher expenses may have resulted simply from lax expense control.

Analysis of the training expense variance is more difficult. Recall the discussion of maintenance expenses in the earlier example involving manufacturing department M. The fact that group T spent less on training in July 19X2 than during the corresponding month of the previous year may indicate that less training was needed (because of less turnover among salespersons); if so, the variance represents good performance. On the other hand, all salespersons and supervisors may have been too busy or preoccupied with other matters to get around to the training that was needed; if so, the variance does not necessarily represent good performance.

The $30 (5%) variance in rent and other occupancy costs is minor. If the weather in July 19X2 was a great deal warmer than in July 19X1, the power to operate the air-conditioning system in the offices might account for the variance, or the power company or the landlord may have increased prices.

Other Variances

Any comparison between actual results and budgeted or expected results can be termed a variance. Our discussion here has not been exhaustive in touching on all the possible types of variances that are used in practice.

Management may find it useful, for example, to develop variances with respect to revenues or sales, as well as with respect to costs and expenses. A deviation from expected or planned total sales revenue can result from a variation in the number of units sold (volume effect) or from a variation in the sales price realized (sales price effect), or from some combination of the two. Using procedures that parallel our earlier discussion, these two effects can be isolated and reported to management.

Another example involves so-called *mix* variances. If several different materials are combined in a process to create a final product, one could predetermine a standard mix of these materials. A debit material variance might be caused by greater use of a higher-priced material in substitution for a lower-priced material, even though the total pounds of raw material used were in accordance with the standard quantity. Thus, in addition to volume, purchase price, and usage variances, a material mix variance could be calculated. Mix variances can also be calculated with respect to labor, when a variety of skill levels are called for in staffing a certain process or job, and for sales revenue, when a company markets several different product lines.

Some Final Caveats

As we conclude this discussion of variance analysis, several caveats with regard to the development and interpretation of variances need to be reemphasized.

First, remember that it costs money to develop, compile, and analyze accounting detail. These costs must be balanced against the benefits received from having the additional information. Striking the balance between too little and too much detail is a challenge for the cost accountant and for operating management.

Second, the business jargon that refers to debit variances as unfavorable or negative and credit variances as favorable or positive can be misleading. Any deviation from standard—favorable or unfavorable—is worth investigating; the standard represents the plan and operating management should understand the reasons for deviations from that plan, whether the deviations add to or reduce profits.

Third, before variances are hastily judged to be favorable or unfavorable, the accuracy of the standards must be considered. Variances can arise strictly from poorly set standards. Standards and budgets may be little better than off-the-head guesses at companies operating with understaffed accounting departments or in volatile industries with rapidly changing product lines. In other companies with a history of cost information and a staff of industrial engineers assisting in the establishment of standards, the cost standards may be very accurate indeed.[4]

Regardless of how the standards or budgets are set, they should be reviewed periodically for reasonableness. This review will take into account changes in the products, manufacturing methods, and staffing. Generally, standard product costs are reviewed when a major error is suspected and otherwise not more frequently than once per quarter nor less frequently than once per year.

Finally, bear in mind that employees are motivated both positively and negatively by standard costs and by budgets. Some managements argue that standards and budgets should be set low (tight) to spur employees to be more efficient; they feel that high (loose) standards and budgets promote, or at least condone, a lax or sloppy attitude toward cost control. Other managements argue that tight standards and budgets are likely to be ignored by employees as being unreasonable and therefore irrelevant. A more complete discussion of the interrelationship between cost accounting and employee motivation will be taken up in the next chapter.

Summary

Management's task of determining when and to what extent corrective action needs to be taken can be greatly facilitated by the development of relevant cost and revenue variances. A variance provides a systematic comparison of actual results—costs or revenues—and planned, or budgeted, results. While standard cost accounting systems are particularly useful in highlighting variances, variance analysis techniques are applicable in a wide variety of circumstances. Even when management does not develop an explicit budget or plan, comparisons of one year's results with the previous year's results may yield useful variance data.

---

[4] The accuracy required will depend upon the use to which the standards are put. In some companies, standard labor times represent the basis for compensating employees—either as piecework (so much per unit produced) or as a group bonus; if used in this manner, the standards must be set with great precision, probably using detailed time studies or other sophisticated engineering techniques.

The primary causes of variances are:

1 *Volume.* Costs that are variable with volume of productive activity will deviate from original plan when volume deviates from plan. With an understanding of the expected behavior of costs with changes in volume, these volume effects can be separated from the spending effects. The resulting comparison of actual expenditures to a volume-adjusted standard is particularly useful to management.
2 *Price.* The price paid per unit of input (for example, per kilogram of material or per hour of labor) may be at variance with the plan.
3 *Rate of usage.* More or less of the input factor (for example, material or labor) may have been used to achieve the planned production level.

The separation of price and usage variances is particularly useful with respect to direct labor and direct material. Since both cost elements are typically assumed to vary directly with volume of production, standard cost accounting systems automatically adjust for volume by the way in which these variances are generated.

In a standard cost accounting system, improving labor efficiency will generally result in favorable labor efficiency (usage) variances, while increasing labor wage rates will result in unfavorable wage rate variances. Similarly, reduced wastage or scrappage will result in favorable direct material usage variances, while increasing purchase prices for material will result in unfavorable purchase price variances.

For IPC and various operating expenses a separation of price and usage variances is theoretically possible, although not typically useful. Rather these two variances are combined in a single spending variance. Since IPC in a full absorption cost system consists of both fixed and variable cost elements, isolation of the volume effect is somewhat more complex. Procedures for separating the volume and spending effects for IPC (or overhead), utilizing the predetermined IPC budget equation, are discussed in Appendix B to this chapter.

Although revenue (or sales) variances have not been discussed in detail in this chapter, it should be obvious that volume and price (selling price) effects can be separated.

The construction of a cost accounting and management reporting system should focus on those variances that are particularly useful, given the circumstances of the company. In analyzing variances, management should bear in mind the probable accuracy of the standards or budgets. Further, management should focus attention on all significant variance balances, since any substantial deviation from plan—whether the variance adds to or reduces profit—deserves investigation. Favorable or positive variances are not necessarily desirable or indicative of good performance, while unfavorable or negative variances may be justified or inevitable and do not necessarily indicate poor management performance.

Appendix A: Cost Flows through Standard Cost Variances

Chapter 11 illustrated cost flows for various alternative cost accounting structures. However, since cost flows in standard cost accounting systems are so influenced by the construction of the variance accounts, illustration of the standard cost accounting flows was postponed until now.

FLOWS WITHOUT SEPARATION OF PRICE AND USAGE VARIANCES

Figure 12A-1 illustrates cost flows for a standard cost system. The example shown assumes process costing (in contrast to job order costing) and as-

Figure 12A-1   Cost Flows: Standard Cost System—Without Separation of Price and Usage Variances (Assumes Process, Variable Costing System)

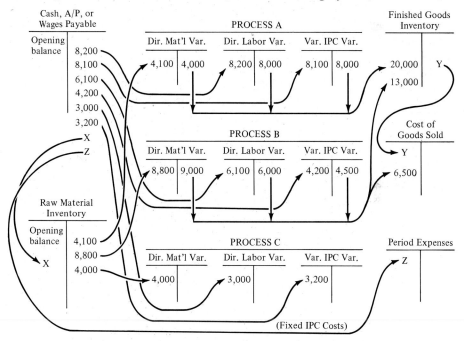

Table of Standard Costs (per lb. produced)					
Process	Dir. mat'l	Dir. labor	Var. IPC	Total	Lbs. produced this period
A	$2	$4	$4	$10	2,000
B	6	4	3	13	1,500
C	4	2	3	9	Still in process

sumes variable costing (in contrast to full absorption costing).   A comparison of this exhibit to Figure 11-3 of Chapter 11 (page 329), which shows a flow chart for a process cost system using actual costs, will help highlight the differences between a standard and an actual cost accounting system.

Several simplifying assumptions are made in presenting the flows on Figure 12A-1.

1   Beginning in-process inventory is zero for all processes and ending in-process inventory is zero for processes A and B.   Output from process C has been zero during this period, and thus for process C all costs incurred during the period remain in process at the end of the period. (This set of assumptions is convenient, although not realistic.)
2   Each of processes A, B, and C produces a finished product.   The output from each process flows to finished goods inventory or cost of goods sold, rather than to another process.

Take time to study the flows on this chart and note particularly the following:

1   Standards are set for each of the product cost elements for each of the processes—see table of standard costs.
2   As a result, variances for each of the cost elements can be determined for each of the processes, but note that in this exhibit price and usage (efficiency) variances have not been separated.
3   Because this is a variable costing system, fixed IPC is charged as a period expense and not included in the product costs.
4   Within process A, actual direct material expenditures were $100 over standard, direct labor was $200 over standard, and variable IPC was $100 over standard.   Debit variances thus totaled $400 on 2,000 pounds, or 2% of the standard cost value of the output from the process.   One or a combination of factors may explain these variations from standard.   Spoilage or general inefficiency are two obvious possibilities.
5   Within process B, actual direct material expenditures were $200 lower than standard, and variable IPC was $300 lower than standard, but direct labor was $100 over standard.   Again, a number of factors may explain these variances.
6   Within process C, variances cannot yet be determined since processing is not complete and the amount of output to be realized is not yet known.
7   Of the output from process B, 1,000 pounds valued at the standard cost of $13 per pound was sent to finished goods inventory and 500 pounds was shipped directly to the customer.
8   The value of finished goods inventory shipped during the period ($Y) is equal to the number of pounds of finished products actually shipped

times the standard cost per pound ($10 for product A, $13 for product B, and $9 for product C).

The balance in each variance account at the end of the period is typically closed into period expenses. That is, the difference between actual and standard is treated as a period cost, even though some of the units produced may be sold in a subsequent period. Alternatively, the balances may be carried as assets (debit balances) or liabilities (credit balances) if it is assumed that variances generated in subsequent interim accounting periods will tend to offset these balances; this assumption might be particularly appropriate for a seasonal business.

Some reasons for the variances shown on Figure 12A-1 were suggested above. Bear in mind also that the cause of a variance may simply be a poor standard. Setting standards is a difficult task, subject to much human error. The standard costs can be tested for reasonableness as they are used repeatedly over a number of periods.

COST FLOWS THROUGH PRICE AND USAGE VARIANCES

Figure 12A-2 presents the cost flows for the same example illustrated in Figure 12A-1; in this figure, however, the material and labor variances are separated into their price (wage rate) and efficiency (usage) components.

In reviewing these flows, note particularly:

1 A companywide purchase price variance and a companywide wage rate variance are shown. Since the prices of raw material and the wage rates paid to direct labor are generally outside the control of the process supervisor, it may be useful to collect all of the price (wage rate) variations in plantwide variance accounts. This plantwide information about materials will be of interest to the purchasing department, while information about wages will be of interest to the industrial relations department. Alternatively, these variances could be developed for each process.

2 The raw-material inventory is valued at standard costs, and thus the purchase price variance is calculated at the time the material is received as raw material, not at the time it is moved from raw-material inventory to in-process inventory. Since the valuation of inventories is facilitated by the use of standard costs,[5] it is generally more convenient and less expensive to value raw material inventories at standard rather than actual cost. Moreover, it is useful to management to know the purchase

---

[5] The problems associated with valuing inventories as price levels fluctuate (see Chapter 8) are eliminated.

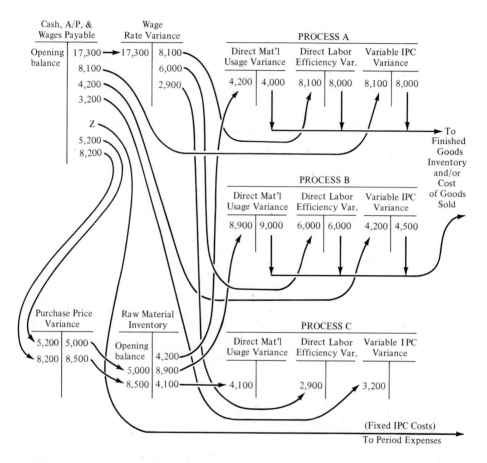

Figure 12A-2 Cost Flows: Standard Cost Systems—With Separation of Price (Wage Rate) and Usage (Efficiency) Variances (Assumes Process, Variable Costing System)

price variance as soon as possible—that is, when the material is first received. Alternatively, raw materials could be valued at actual cost and the purchase price variance isolated at the time the materials are started into production. Note that the wage rate variance is calculated as the direct labor is entered into production, since direct labor cannot be inventoried in a "raw" state. Thus, the method and timing of calculating the price variance for direct material typically does not parallel the method and timing of calculating the labor wage rate variance.

3   The credit entries to the wage rate variance account and the debit entries to direct labor efficiency variances are equal to the actual direct labor hours spent in each process times the standard wage rate. Similarly, the credit to the purchase price variance and the debit to raw material inventory are equal to the actual physical volume of materials pur-

chased times their standard prices; the credit to raw-material inventory and debit to direct material usage variances are also actual physical volumes (issued to the processes) times their standard prices. (In this illustration, these values are all assumed.)

4 Figure 12A-2 shows a $200 debit balance in direct material usage variance for process A. Total direct material variance shown in Figure 12A-1 was only $100 debit, and thus the unfavorable usage variance was partially offset by a favorable purchase price variance. For process B, on the other hand, the favorable material usage variance of $100 (see Figure 12A-2) was supplemented by a favorable purchase price variance to yield the total $200 favorable material variance shown in Figure 12A-1.

5 A similar analysis of wage rate and labor efficiency variances in the three processes reveals:

	Wage Rate Variance[1]	Labor Efficiency Variance[2]	Total Labor Variance[3]
Process A	100 debit	100 debit	200 debit
Process B	100 debit	0	100 debit
Process C	100 debit	—	—
	300 debit		

[1] Derived by deduction. Note that the total agrees with the wage rate variance shown in Figure 12A-2.
[2] See Figure 12A-2
[3] See Figure 12A-1

6 Note that the credit to each of the usage (efficiency) and IPC variances in Figure 12A-2 is equal to the credit in the corresponding total variances in Figure 12A-1. These credits are the standard costs (as shown in the Table of Standard Costs) of the three products produced times the number of pounds produced, and are offset by the sum of debits to finished-goods inventory and to cost of goods sold.

7 The IPC variances are the same in the two figures, as no attempt has been made to separate price and usage variances for IPC.

8 Process C has produced no finished product for the period, and thus material usage and labor efficiency variances for that process cannot yet be determined, since it is not now known how much more cost will be added to the process or how much final product will be realized. While the efficiency (usage) variances cannot be determined, the price (wage rate) variances have been isolated; the material and labor hours remaining in process C are valued at standard price and wage rates.

THE EFFECTS OF TIGHT AND LOOSE STANDARDS

The magnitude of variances will be greatly influenced by the philosophy inherent in standard setting. If standards are set tight (low, that is, difficult to achieve) negative (debit) variances will typically occur. Managements who believe in tight standards anticipate substantial debit variances and plan accordingly.

Tight standards lead to low product costs—therefore low values for inventory and cost of goods sold—but offsetting debit variances. Profits of the company will be unaffected by the tightness or looseness of standards *only* if production volume equals sales volume and thus inventories neither grow nor decline during the period. However, if inventories grow and standards are set tight, the value added to inventory will be low (by comparison with the value under looser standards) and the debit variances generated in the production of these inventoried products will be treated as a period expense, reducing profit.

To illustrate these effects, assume that a company incurred actual production costs for a particular month of $47,000; it sold 90% of its output and placed the other 10% in inventory. The income statement and balance sheet implications of tight and loose standards are as follows:

	Tight Standards	Loose Standards
Standard costs (assumed)	$45,000	$48,000
Variances	(2,000)	1,000
Income Statement Effect		
Cost of goods sold[6]	40,500	43,200
Variances	(2,000)	1,000
Total	42,500	42,200
Balance Sheet Effect		
Increase in inventory[7]	4,500	4,800

The $300 lower profit with tight standards is matched by the $300 lower value of inventory. Opposite effects result from reductions in inventory.

Appendix B: The Particular Problems of IPC: Volume and Spending Variances

The analysis of cost variances that relate to indirect production costs (IPC) is often particularly confusing, and thus deserves special attention in this appendix.

Complexity is introduced because, as discussed in Chapter 10, IPC consists of both fixed and variable cost elements. To develop meaningful data for control of overhead, or IPC, the cost accounting system must be able to isolate the effect on IPC of variations in volume of activity. Note

---

[6] 90% of production, valued at standard costs.
[7] 10% of production, valued at standard costs.

that this complexity relates only to full absorption cost systems and not to variable cost systems; by definition, IPC in variable cost systems consists solely of variable indirect manufacturing expenditures. The balance of this appendix, then, assumes a full absorption cost system.

Analysis of IPC variances is further complicated by the fact that IPC rates are predetermined; that is, the IPC rate utilized in the valuation of inventory and cost of goods sold is determined before the actual volume of activity for the period is known. Since the IPC rate is predetermined, it cannot be adjusted for actual volume.

Recall again why IPC rates are predetermined, that is, determined in advance of the start of the accounting period. In order to provide timely data on production costs and on final product costs of items or services produced, indirect production costs must be allocated to the various manufacturing jobs or processes throughout the accounting period. Note that while a standard cost accounting system requires that *all* product cost elements be predetermined—direct material, direct labor, and IPC—an IPC rate is predetermined *even* in an actual cost accounting system.

Recall how an IPC rate is established. First, the level of production activity for the period is determined, based upon the company's overall manufacturing plan. This planned level of activity is then used to estimate (a) the quantity of the IPC vehicle (e.g., direct labor hours, or machine hours, or direct material cost) that will be utilized during the period, and (b) the expected, or budgeted, level of IPC to accomplish the production plan. The budgeted IPC divided by the budgeted volume of the IPC vehicle yields the predetermined IPC rate. For example,[8] assume department L at Andover Manufacturing expects to require 1,500 hours of direct labor time per month to accomplish its 19X3 production plan. To support this level of activity, the department estimates that total IPC expenditures will be $18,000 per month (including variable, semivariable and fixed IPC cost elements). The resulting IPC rate for department L in 19X3 is $12 per direct labor hour ($18,000 ÷ 1,500 hours).

This $12 rate is then used throughout the accounting period. Since the IPC vehicle is direct labor hours, if a particular job (for example, job 246) in department L consumes four hours of direct labor, job 246 is charged with IPC in the amount of four times the IPC rate, or $48; to use the common jargon of cost accounting, job 246 absorbs $48 of IPC. In general journal format, the accounting entry is:

Dr	Job 246	$48
Cr	IPC variance	$48

Throughout the accounting period, a whole series of such entries is made,

---

[8] This example was also used in Chapter 10, where IPC rates and the IPC variance account were first discussed.

as direct labor is expended on the various jobs worked on in the department. At the end of the period, the credit balance in the IPC variance account represents the total amount of IPC absorbed by all jobs.

The debit balance in the IPC variance account is the total amount actually expended during the same period on IPC. Assume that for department L in October 19X3 the final IPC variance account balances are:

IPC Variance

18,800	19,200

At first glance, one might conclude that the department L supervisor did a good job of controlling IPC expenses: the amount actually expended, $18,800, was less than the amount absorbed into production jobs, $19,200. However, under Andover's full absorption cost system the IPC costs include both variable and fixed cost elements, and thus imbedded in this single cost variance are at least three effects:

1 *Volume.* If department L was more active this month than planned— that is, utilized more direct labor hours, the IPC vehicle—more IPC was absorbed than planned.
2 *Price.* For example, prices per kilowatthour for power, or wage rates for indirect labor, may have been more or less than the prices and wage rates that were utilized in making the original estimates of IPC.
3 *Usage or efficiency.* Andover may have used more or less power, more or fewer hours of indirect labor, or more or less supplies per unit of productive activity than estimated when the IPC rate was established.

To separate the second and third effects—price and usage—would require establishing standard prices (wage rates) and standard usage quantities (kilowatts, indirect labor hours, volume of supplies) for *each* item included in indirect production costs. This degree of sophistication in standard costing is most frequently not warranted. The price and usage effects are combined in a single variance and separated from the volume effect. For convenience, the combined price-and-usage variance will be referred to here as the **IPC spending variance.** Bear in mind that this separation of spending and volume effects applies both to actual and standard costing systems.

The task, then, is to separate the single IPC variance shown previously into the two components just described: IPC spending variance and **IPC volume variance.** That is, the overabsorption/underabsorption effect (volume effect) must be isolated from the spending effect. The $400 credit balance shown in the IPC variance account for department L is accounted for by some combination of:

1 Production activity being above or below expected levels for the month
2 Total spending on IPC (including both prices paid and amounts used) being more or less than planned

Note that the really useful information for management is a comparison of actual IPC spending with a *revised* estimate of appropriate IPC expenditures, revised to account for the actual volume of activity. An isolation of the volume effect will highlight the spending effect.

IPC BUDGET EQUATION (LINE)

To accomplish this objective requires an ability to rebudget or reestimate IPC expenditures on the basis of the actual level of activity in department L in October 19X3.[9] The data utilized in establishing the IPC rate at the beginning of 19X3 should indicate the degree of variation in total IPC expenditures with changes in volume; that information should, in turn, facilitate the rebudgeting of IPC. Figure 12B-1 illustrates these estimates graphically.

At the beginning of 19X3, the cost analyst at Andover Manufacturing estimated total IPC expenditures at several levels of production activity; these data were needed for the companywide budgeting process that led finally to the plan calling for production activity at the level of 1,500 direct labor hours per month. The analyst estimated that total IPC expenditures at this planned production level would be $18,000. He further estimated that at 1,300 direct labor hours, total IPC expenditures would be $17,200, or $800 less, and at 1,700 hours, total IPC expenditures would be $18,800, or $800 more. These points are all shown on Figure 12B-1 and are labeled A, B, and C, respectively. By fitting a line to these three points, the analyst can develop an algebraic expression for the **IPC budget line.** The intersection with the y-axis (at $12,000) determines the fixed cost portion of IPC. The slope of the line, equivalent to $4.00 per direct labor hour, represents the variable cost portion of IPC.[10]

The form of this IPC budget line was discussed in Chapter 10:

$$IPC = F + vX$$

In this example, the equation becomes:

$$IPC = \$12,000 + \$4.00 \times (\text{direct labor hours})$$

[9] The relevant comparison is not with the original estimate of $18,000 of IPC per month, since activity levels turned out to be above the original estimate.
[10] Note that $4.00 would be the IPC rate in a variable cost system, since all fixed IPC costs would be charged as period expenses.

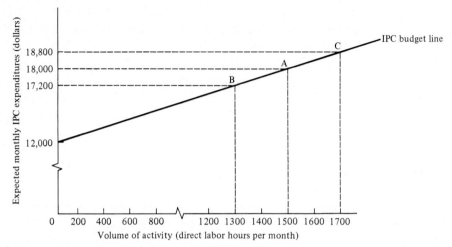

IPC budget equation: Total monthly IPC expenditures = $12,000 + $4 (direct labor hours)

Figure 12B-1 Andover Manufacturing Company, IPC Budget Estimates: Department L (19X3)

The slope and shape of this budget line will be valid for only modest variations in production activity (for example, 20% above or below the planned level). If actual production exceeds or falls short of the planned level by a wide margin (for example, 50%), the straight-line relationship between IPC and volume probably will not continue. Nevertheless, the straight-line approximation shown in Figure 12B-1 is adequate for most purposes[11] and allows total expected IPC expenditures to be recalculated at various levels of production activity.

Andover Manufacturing now has the information needed to separate the single IPC variance into its spending and volume variances: a basis for recalculating or rebudgeting the IPC based upon the actual volume of production within department L in October 19X3. A comparison of this rebudgeted IPC (or volume-adjusted IPC budget) to actual IPC expenditures will indicate how well department L controlled its spending on IPC.

Assume that during October 19X3 department L utilized 1,600 direct labor hours. Indeed, the sum of the credit entries in the IPC variance account indicates that direct labor hours must have numbered 1,600: each direct labor hour absorbed $12 of IPC and total IPC absorbed during the month was $19,200, or 1,600 hours times $12 per hour. Activity at the rate of 1,600 direct labor hours is somewhat above the original plan of 1,500.

Accordingly, total IPC expenditures for October should logically be

[11] With more data points a more complex curve (and resulting budget equation) could be developed to describe the variation in IPC with variations in volume. Typically, such added sophistication and complexity is not warranted.

above the original plan or $18,000 per month, since certain of the IPC cost elements are variable with volume. However, total IPC expenditures should not be as high as the amount of IPC absorbed (i.e., 1,600 hours times $12 per hour) since certain other IPC cost elements are fixed and should remain unaffected by this increased production activity.

According to the IPC budget line (and equation), what should have been spent on IPC in October, given that the volume of activity was equivalent to 1,600 direct labor hours instead of 1,500 hours? Substituting 1,600 hours in the equation yields a volume-adjusted IPC budget of $18,400:

Rebudgeted IPC = $12,000 + $4(1,600) = $18,400

IPC SPENDING AND IPC VOLUME VARIANCES

The single IPC variance shown earlier can now be separated as follows:

IPC Spending Variance		IPC Volume Variance	
Actual IPC expenditures	Volume-adjusted IPC budget	Volume-adjusted IPC budget	Absorbed IPC (IPC rate × quantity of IPC vehicle)
18,800	18,400	18,400	19,200

Note several things about these two variances:

1 The accounting system continues to be in balance (i.e., debits = credits), since the credit in the IPC spending variance is equal to the debit in the IPC volume variance.

2 The algebraic sum of the two separate variances is equal to the total IPC variance:

$$\begin{aligned}
\text{IPC spending variance} &= (\$400) \text{ debit} \\
\text{IPC volume variance} &= \underline{800} \text{ credit} \\
\text{Total IPC variance} &= \$400 \text{ credit}
\end{aligned}$$

3 IPC volume variance is always favorable when actual production activity exceeds plan and always unfavorable when production falls short of plan. Here the IPC volume variance gives only one message to management: volume of activity was above plan. This message is probably not news to management and is itself not worth the analysis. However, only by isolating the IPC volume variance can the IPC spending variance be highlighted. The $800 volume variance is equal to the 100 hours of direct labor by which actual production activity exceeded plan, times the $8.00 of fixed IPC absorbed per direct labor hour; the $8.00 figure is

derived from the production plan: $12,000 of fixed IPC and 1,500 hours of direct labor, or (12,000 ÷ 1,500) = $8.00 of fixed IPC per direct labor hour.

4   The IPC spending variance is indeed useful to management. Management now knows that IPC expenditures during October 19X3 were $400 more than the adjusted spending plan—that is, adjusted to reflect actual volume of activity.

This more detailed variance analysis is depicted graphically in Figure 12B-2. This graph is similar to the IPC budget graph in Figure 12B-1 but contains a line not shown on the earlier graph: the **IPC absorption line.** This line begins at the origin and passes through point A—the same point A shown on the graph in Figure 12B-1 (1,500 hours and $18,000 of IPC); its slope is the IPC rate, $12 per hour.

In Figure 12B-2, point P is the level of actual IPC expenditures for October, assumed earlier at $18,800. Point Q represents the rebudgeted IPC for October, based upon 1,600 direct labor hours. Point R represents the amount of IPC absorbed into department L jobs during October; note that the $12 IPC rate was used even though this rate was, in effect, too high since it resulted in an overabsorption of IPC. Exhibit 12B-1 describes the IPC variance analysis in algebraic terms.

Figure 12B-2   Andover Manufacturing Company, Department L, October 19X3, Graphical Depiction of IPC, Variance Analysis

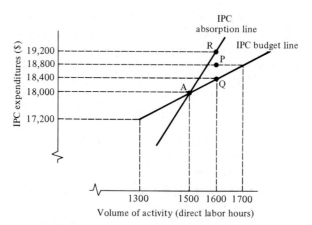

EXPLANATION

Point P = Level of actual IPC expenditures, October 19X3 = $18,800
Point Q = Volume-adjusted IPC budget = $18,400
Point R = Absorbed IPC (1,600 Hours X $12 per hour) = $19,200
IPC spending variance = point Q − point P = $400 unfavorable
IPC volume variance = point R − point Q = $800 favorable
Total IPC variance = point R − point P = $400 favorable

Exhibit 12B-1
ANDOVER MANUFACTURING COMPANY
Department L, October 19X3
Algebraic Analysis of IPC Variances

Let X_E = estimated volume of production, measured in terms of the IPC vehicle
  F = estimated fixed cost (in dollars)
  v = estimated rate of variation of IPC with changes in volume (equivalent to the slope of the IPC budget line in Figure 12B-2)

Then:

$$\text{IPC Rate} = \frac{F + vX_E}{X_E} = \frac{12,000 + 4.0\,(1,500)}{1,500} = 12.00$$

If X_A = actual volume, measured in terms of the IPC vehicle
and P = actual expenditures on IPC elements
Then:

IPC Spending Variance		IPC Volume Variance	
P	$F + vX_A$	$F + vX_A$	$\dfrac{F + vX_E}{X_E} X_A$
= 18,800	= 12,000	= 12,000	$= \dfrac{12,000 + 4.0\,(1,500)}{1,500} 1,600$
	+ 4.0 (1,600)	= 4.0 (1,600)	= (12.00) 1,600
	= 18,400		= 19,200

We have spent a good deal of time on this complex and detailed topic of IPC variance analysis. Why? Because the technique of separating spending and volume variances is relevant to many businesses and other organizations, including manufacturing, consulting, auto repair shops and many other service firms. The management of each of these operations faces the task at the end of each accounting period of evaluating cost performance. Unless management clearly understands the meaning of *overabsorbed* and *underabsorbed* overhead—and is prepared to isolate volume effects from spending effects—management is likely to be led to some erroneous conclusions.

EXAMPLE: VARIANCE ANALYSIS IN AN AUTO REPAIR SHOP

Exhibit 12B-2 presents a cost analysis report for the Harris Auto Repair Shop for the months of March and April 19X6. Business was slow for Harris Auto in March, but picked up briskly in April. Gross margin was below plan in March and well above plan in April, as might be expected with the swing in volume of activity. The issue facing management is the

Exhibit 12B-2

HARRIS AUTO REPAIR

Mechanics' wage rate = $10 per hour
Overhead rate[1] = 80% of wage rate or $8 per mechanic hour
Customer billing rate = 125% of cost (labor and overhead)
= $22.50 per mechanic hour

| | March 19X6 | | April 19X6 | |
	Budget	Actual	Budget	Actual
Sales	$90,000	$78,750	$90,000	$101,250
Labor expense	40,000	35,000	40,000	45,000
Overhead absorbed	32,000	28,000	32,000	36,000
Overhead variance	—	(2,000)UNF	—	1,500F
Gross margin	$18,000	$13,750	$18,000	$21,750
Mechanic hours	4,000	3,500	4,000	4,500

OVERHEAD VARIANCES

March 19X6   **April 19X6**

Overhead Variance	
30,000	28,000
Balance:	
2,000 Dr.	

Overhead Variance	
34,500	36,000
	Balance:
	1,500 Cr.

Overhead Spending Variance		Overhead Volume Variance	
30,000	30,250[2]	30,250	28,000
	Balance:	Balance:	
	250 Cr.	2,250 Dr.	

Overhead Spending Variance		Overhead Volume Variance	
34,500	33,750[3]	33,750	36,000
Balance:			Balance:
750 Dr.			2,250 Cr.

[1] Overhead rate determined as follows:
Expected overhead expenditures when wages paid to all mechanics total $40,000/mo.
  Variable cost elements = $14,000
  Fixed cost elements = 18,000
    Total = $32,000

Therefore, overhead budget equation = $18,000 + \frac{14,000}{40,000}$ (mechanic wages); overhead

rate = $\frac{18,000 + (14,000/40,000)\,(40,000)}{40,000}$ = $0.80 per dollar of mechanic wages.

[2] Volume-adjusted overhead budget = $18,000 + \frac{14,000}{40,000}$ (35,000) = $30,250

[3] Volume-adjusted overhead budget = $18,000 + \frac{14,000}{40,000}$ (45,000) = $33,750

interpretation of the overhead variance accounts[12] for the two months. Overhead variance was unfavorable in March by $2,000 and favorable by $1,500 in April. Volume alone may have accounted for these variances: volume was low in March, thus leading to an underabsorption of overhead costs, while April's high volume created an overabsorption condition. On the other hand, good or poor expense control at the auto repair shop might have been the cause. The volume effects need to be isolated so that management can judge performance in the control of overhead expenses.

Exhibit 12B-2 shows the derivation of the overhead budget equation, as well as the use of the equation in determining the revised budget, or volume-adjusted budget, for overhead for each month.

The overhead variance analysis shows that in spite of the overall negative, or unfavorable, overhead variance in March, Harris Auto actually spent $250 less than plan—the overhead spending variance was $250 credit. Furthermore, although April's sales level and gross margin were very favorable compared to budget, control of spending on overhead was unfavorable—the overhead spending variance is $750 unfavorable. Had overhead spending in April been on plan, gross margin for the month would have been $22,500, or $750 more than actually earned.

New Terms

Direct labor variance   The variance that compares actual expenditures on direct labor to standard direct labor costs. This variance can be separated into its wage rate and efficiency components.

Favorable (unfavorable) variances   Credit (debit) balances in variance accounts. The value judgments implied by these terms can be misleading.

IPC absorption line   Describes the rate at which IPC is absorbed by production activity. The slope of the line is the IPC rate.

IPC budget equation (line)   Describes algebraically (graphically) the variation of planned IPC expenditures with changes in production volume. The equation is used both to predetermine the IPC rate and to rebudget IPC for purposes of IPC variance analysis.

IPC spending variance   A comparison of actual IPC expenditures to volume-adjusted (rebudgeted) IPC expenditures.

IPC volume variance   A comparison of volume-adjusted (rebudgeted) IPC expenditures to IPC absorbed by production during the period.

Labor efficiency variance   A comparison of actual and standard direct labor hours, both valued at standard wage rates.

Management by exception   A practice of focusing management attention primarily on those segments of an operation that are not operating in accordance with plan.

---

[12] The popular term *overhead* is used in place of IPC in this example.

Material usage variance A comparison of actual and standard material quantities used, both valued at standard prices.

Material variance The variance that compares actual expenditures on direct materials to standard direct material costs. This variance can be separated into its price and usage components.

Negative (positive) variances Alternative names for *unfavorable* or *debit* (*favorable* or *credit*) *balances* in variance accounts. The value judgments implied by these terms can be misleading.

Purchase price variance A comparison of actual and standard prices for the actual quantity of material acquired.

Variance An account wherein actual results (expenses or revenues) are compared to planned results.

Wage rate variance A comparison of actual and standard wage rates for the actual number of hours of labor utilized.

Problems

1 Assume that you are designing a process, variable, standard cost accounting system. Why might you decide to use a single material variance account rather than separate material price and material usage variances?

2 If a company that charges its variances to cost of goods sold at the end of each accounting period increases its finished goods inventories during a period of rapid inflation, will the company's profits tend to be stated higher by the use of standard costing or actual costing? Why?

3 The Lamont Company produces a single product, M, and utilizes a job order, standard, full absorption cost accounting system. The following data apply to the month of July 19X9.

Variances:	Purchase price	$ 600 credit
	Material usage	1,100 debit
	Direct labor	200 debit
	IPC	1,100 credit
	Sales price[1]	3,100 credit

IPC rate: $2.50 per unit of M (rate used throughout 19X9)
Sales in July: 22,000 units
Volume of production in July: 21,000 units

[1] Sales price variance is the variance between the expected price to be realized from the sale of M to customers and the actual price realized.

a What reason might the company have for using only a single labor variance?

b What conclusions (stated briefly) do you draw from each of the following variances?

Purchase price
Material usage
Direct labor
IPC

    c What were the total IPC expenditures for the month?

    d If actual direct material usage was $43,100 in July and actual direct labor cost for the month was $31,700 (and assuming zero in-process inventories at the beginning and end of the month), construct the standard cost for one unit of **M** (full absorption costing).

    e Consider the sales price variance:

        1 Is this variance favorable or unfavorable (as we have been using these terms)?

        2 If the standard selling price for a unit of **M** is $9.00, by what percent did the actual sales price exceed or fall short of the standard during the month of July?

4 The following T accounts appeared in the general ledger of the Mason Corporation at June 30, 19X7.

Purchase Price Variance		Material Usage Variance		Labor Variance		Material Mix Variance	
44,000	42,500	42,000	43,000	10,000	8,000	43,000	44,000

IPC Variance		Finished Goods Inventory		Sales Price Variance		Cost of Goods Sold	
30,000	34,000	83,000 86,000	81,000	162,000	160,000	81,000	

Jobs-in-Process	
37,000	

    a Describe the cost accounting system used at Mason Corporation.

    b Do you think raw-material inventory increased or decreased during the period? Why?

    c How efficient was the company in utilizing its labor force? Discuss.

    d What was the total amount charged to the company by its suppliers for material purchases in June?

    e What is the IPC rate, assuming that standard labor dollars is the IPC vehicle?

    f Discuss (briefly) the significance of the sales price variance account.

    g Discuss (briefly) the significance of the material mix variance.

5 The Jennifer Janitorial Company uses a single labor variance. The balances in this account for an accounting period are:

Labor Variance	
1,497,000	1,485,000

If actual hours worked were 241,200 and the standard hourly labor wage rate was $6.25:

    a What was the labor efficiency variance for the period? (indicate debit or credit)

    b What was the wage rate variance for the period? (indicate debit or credit)

6 The Dunhill Company pays its sales force a 5% commission on sales in addition to modest base salaries. The company budgeted total selling expenses of $97,000 in March 19X0 when sales were expected to total $1,100,000. Actual results in March 19X0 are sales of $1,250,000 and selling expenses of $103,600. If all selling expenses other than commissions are fixed, how well did Dunhill control its selling expenses in March 19X0? Explain.

7 The Livingston County Hospital Board of Trustees reviewed the following data for the hospital's commissary (food preparation and serving) for November 19X4:

	Budget	Actual
Number of meals served	9,200	8,800
Total expenses	$28,450	$27,790

a The hospital's controller reminded the board that certain commissary expenses are fixed and therefore total expenses were only 2.3% below budget, while the number of meals served was 4.3% below budget. What would fixed commissary expenses have to be in order for actual expenses in November 19X4 to represent on-budget performance?

b If in a subsequent month the number of meals served exceeds the November budget by 5%, how much should the trustees expect total commissary expenses to be for that month?

8 To develop a sales price variance, the Brandt Co. accounted for each sale as follows:

Dr Sales price variance: Units sold times standard price
    Cr Sales: Units sold times standard price

Dr Accounts receivable: Actual value of sale
    Cr Sales price variance: Actual value of sale

a Explain the meaning of a debit balance in the sales price variance account at the end of an accounting period.

b In a particular accounting period, what was the average discount from list price provided to customers if actual sales were $116,300 and the sales price variance account balance was $4,850 debit?

c Indicate in T-account format the debit and credit entries that would have to be made to determine both a sales price variance and a sales volume variance for an accounting period.

9 The Fast-Fill Gasoline Co. set monthly sales volume and price standards for each of its retail gas stations. Prices were actually changed frequently during the month in response to competitive conditions but the standard prices were set for each grade for the month. Standards for August, 19X3 for station J were:

Grade	Volume (gal)	Price/gal	Revenue
A	21,500 (15.4%)	$1.35	$ 29,025
B	73,000 (52.3%)	1.30	94,900
C	45,000 (32.3%)	1.27	57,150
	139,500 (100.0%)		$181,075

Actual results for August, 19X3 were:

Grade	Volume (gal)	Revenue
A	20,100 (14.7%)	$ 27,035
B	71,500 (52.3%)	93,665
C	45,200 (33.0%)	57,420
	136,800 (100.0%)	$178,120

Calculate (a) the total sales price variance for the month, (b) a sales mix variance, and (c) a volume variance for the month. (Suggestion: Calculate the variances in the order indicated; the three variances should add to the total difference of $2,955 between budget revenue and actual revenue.)

10 The Brightmor Paint Company's most popular paint is manufactured from three primary ingredients. The standard cost of a liter of paint is:

Ingredient	Amount Used (Liters)	Standard Cost
B	0.4	$0.30
M	0.3	0.65
S	0.3	0.15
Total	1.0	$1.10

On a particular job to produce 2,000 liters of this paint, the following quantities of material were used:

Ingredient	Amount (Liters)
B	822
M	573
S	605
Total	2,000

Calculate a material mix variance for this job.

11 The Douglas Company operates a process, standard, variable costing system. Process A (also referred to as department A) produces product X using raw materials P and R. The following data apply to the month of July 19X5.

Beginning and ending in-process inventory		0
Material purchases		
Material P:	Quantity	450 pints
	Dollars	$1,100
Material R:	Quantity	100 pounds
	Dollars	$520
Material usage:	Material P	460 pints
	Material R	89 pounds
Labor usage:	Hours	860
	Dollars	$4,450
Variable IPC expenditures		$3,650

Standard prime cost per pound of product X output:
Direct labor $10.00 (at $5.00 standard wage rate per hour)

Direct material: Material P $2.50 (at standard price of $2.50 per pint)
                  Material R $1.00 (at standard price of $5.00 per pound)
IPC vehicle: pound of product X produced
Variable IPC rate: $8.00 per pound of product X
Amount of product X produced in July: 450 pounds

Assignment: Calculate all relevant variances.

12 The Standard Company manufactures a single product which it processes in a single department. The standard cost of the product has been computed as follows:

Raw materials:	5 pounds @ $1.00 per pound	$ 5.00
Direct labor:	3 hours @ $6.00 per hour	18.00
Indirect costs:	$12.00 per direct labor hour	36.00
Total standard cost per unit		$59.00

All inventories of this company are recorded at standard costs; the inventories at October 1, 19X9 are:

Raw materials:	5,000 pounds @ $ 1.00		$ 5,000
Work in process:			
Raw materials:	100 units @ $ 5.00	$ 500	
Direct labor:	100 units @ $ 9.00	900	
Indirect costs:	100 units @ $18.00	1,800	3,200
Finished goods:	200 units @ $59.00		11,800

The following are transactions for the month of October, 19X9.
a Purchased 50,000 pounds of raw materials at a price of $1.01 per pound
b Started 10,000 units into process; however, because of spoilage it was necessary to issue 51,000 pounds of raw material
c As of October 1, 19X9, the work force was granted a wage increase of 30 cents per hour. This increase had not been anticipated when the standard cost of $6.00 per hour had been set up. Furthermore, only 29,500 hours were utilized by the work force.
d During the month 9,900 units were completed and transferred to finished goods. (Assume the 100 additional units in in-process inventory are half-completed.)
e The predetermined IPC rate was $12 per direct labor hour.
f Actual indirect costs for the month were:

Indirect labor	$145,000
Depreciation	140,000
Heat, light, and power	37,000
Other	24,000
	$346,000

g In October, 9,700 units were sold for $90 per unit.

Assignment: Calculate cost of goods sold for the month. Include all the relevant variances, as the company follows the practice of charging all variances to cost of goods sold each month.

13 The Seiler Company operates a manufacturing operation consisting of a single department producing products A and B. Its cost accounting system is an actual, full absorption, job order system. For a recent period, the Seiler Company reported the following results:

Sales	$10,000
Cost of goods sold	7,375
Variances	75[1]
Gross margin	2,550
Selling expenses, variable	300
Selling expenses, fixed	700
Other period expenses	1,200
Profit before taxes	$ 350

[1] IPC variance

Production for the period consisted of:

Job 8: 100 units of product A

Job 9: 50 units of product B

Job 10: 130 units of product A

The cost accounting system revealed the following information with respect to actual costs on these three jobs:

	Job 8	Job 9	Job 10
Direct labor	$1,060	$ 280	$1,300
Direct material	1,580	740	2,150
Variable IPC[1]	530	140	650
Fixed IPC[1]	530	140	650
Total	$3,700	$1,300	$4,750

[1] IPC rate = 100% of direct labor (half variable and half fixed).

The company sold all of the output from jobs 8 and 9 and one-half of job 10. The company had no beginning finished goods inventory, but one-half of job 10 was in inventory at the end of the period. There was no in-process inventory at either the beginning or the end of the period.

Assume that the standard cost per unit for products A and B was as follows:

	A	B
Direct labor	$10	$ 6
Direct material	16	15
Variable IPC	5	3
Fixed IPC	5	3
Total	$36	$27

Reconstruct the income statement based upon a *full-absorption, standard, job order* cost system.

14   The following information pertains to the manufacturing and selling activity of the Burdick Company for a single month. Burdick produces product P from raw materials A and B in a continuous process.

> Actual direct labor for the month: 1700 hours; $5,285
> Actual material purchases:
>   Raw material A   4,500 lb; $ 4,725
>   Raw material B   7,000 lb; $13,300
> Actual IPC expenditures: $17,900
> IPC rate: $2.00 per unit of P produced
> Price of product P: $6.50 per unit
> Sales of product P for the month: 8,000 units
> Inventory of raw material and finished product:

	Beginning	Ending
A	0	200 lb
B	0	1,500 lb
P	0	1,000 units

In-process inventory is zero at both the beginning and end of the period.   The total of other (nonmanufacturing) expenses for the period: $12,500.

a   Assuming inventories are determined on a FIFO basis by end-of-period adjustment, determine the ending inventory valuation for materials A and B and product P and the income statement amounts (in format indicated) *assuming* an actual, full absorption process cost accounting system:

> Inventory values: A $_____
>   B $_____
>   P $_____
> Income statements:
>   Sales $_____
>   Cost of goods sold $_____
>   IPC variance $_____
>   Gross margin $_____
>   Period costs $_____
>   Profit before tax $_____

b   Assume that inventories are maintained at standard costs, and the standard cost of product P is as follows:

> Direct labor (0.2 hours) $ .60
> Direct material: A (0.5 lb)   .50
>   B (0.6 lb)   1.20
> IPC   2.00
>   _____
> $4.30

Determine the ending inventory valuation for materials A and B and product P, and construct an income statement (list names of variance accounts and amounts for each) *assuming* a standard, full absorption process costing system.

c Assume the variable IPC rate is $.80 per unit and that actual variable IPC costs for the period were $7,000. Determine the ending inventory valuation for materials A and B and product P, and construct an income statement (list names of variance accounts and amounts for each) *assuming* a standard, variable process costing system.

15 The Gamble Company operated a standard, process cost system, utilizing full absorption costs. Variance accounts were closed to Cost of Goods Sold each month. Two products, A and B, were manufactured, having standard costs as follows:

	A	B
Direct material	$10	$16
Direct labor	40	24
IPC	20	40
Total	$70	$80

A single raw material, having a standard purchase price of $1.00 per pound, was used in the manufacture of both products. All inventory values were carried at standard. The standard direct labor wage rate at Gamble was $8.00 per hour.

The following are statements related to the month of April 19X4:

a On April 1, balances in the company's general ledger were as follows:

	Dr	Cr
Raw materials inventory	$ 25,000	
Goods-in-process inventory	70,000	
Finished goods inventory	86,000	
Other assets	400,000	
Accounts payable		$ 40,000
Wages payable		16,000
Other liabilities		200,000
Shareholders' equity		325,000
	$581,000	$581,000

b The inventory changed during April as follows (in number of units):

	Product A	Product B
Units started	800	1,200
Units completed	1,100	1,000
Units sold	1,000	1,200

Therefore:

Goods in process	300 decr.	200 incr.
Finished goods	100 incr.	200 decr.

c During April, the company bought and received 40,000 pounds of material, paying $12,000 cash of the total bill of $41,500, leaving $29,500 still payable as of April 30.

d The materials warehouse issued 30,000 pounds of material to the production department during the month.

e Direct labor incurred during April totaled 7,400 hours, and direct labor expense was $60,000. Indirect labor expense was $20,000. Wages paid were $76,000.

f Indirect production costs for April, other than indirect labor, were $50,000. Of this amount $38,000 was credited to Other Assets and $12,000 to Accounts Payable.

g As indicated in *b* above, production schedules for April called for 800 units of A and 1,200 units of B to be started through production during the month, and the 30,000 pounds of material was all used for this purpose. (Assume all required raw material is withdrawn from raw-material inventory at the beginning of the production job.)

h Administrative and selling expenses were $40,000. The offsetting entry was to Accounts Payable.

i Standard cost sheets showed that standard costs representing work done on products during the month were charged to those products as follows: labor, $70,000; IPC, $64,000.

j Receivables in the amount of $200,000 were collected in April (both debit and credit entry to Other Assets). Accounts Payable in the amount of $38,000 were paid during April.

k April sales were 1,000 units of A for $106,000 and 1,200 units of B for $130,000. The offsetting entries were to Other Assets.

Assignment

1 Set up T accounts and record the opening balances and the above transactions. Calculate and prepare a schedule of all variance accounts.

2 Prepare an income statement for April.

3 Prepare a balance sheet as of April 30.

Problems for Appendix A

16 Assume that in a rapidly growing company, a standard cost accounting system is used, with all variances charged to profit and loss each accounting period. A debate has arisen among management as to whether standards for direct labor should be set tight (i.e., such that the work force will only rarely be able to perform tasks within the standard number of hours) or should be set loose. If the standards are set tight, under what conditions will the reported profit for the period:

  a Be more than reported profit if standards are set loose

  b Be less than reported profit if standards are set loose

  c Be the same as reported profit if standards are set loose

17 Refer to the situation described in problem 16. What other factors would you consider in deciding whether to set standards tight or loose?

Problems for Appendix B

18 The higher the fixed element of IPC as a percentage of total IPC, the greater the potential for significant overabsorption or underabsorption of IPC (assuming a full absorption accounting system). Explain.

19 To establish the IPC rate and the IPC budget for a certain department, the Bark Manufacturing Company developed the following estimates by an analysis of the behavior of the various IPC elements in relation to direct labor cost:

Estimated annual IPC = \$432,000
Estimated annual direct labor cost = \$240,000

$$\text{Monthly IPC budget} = \frac{432,000}{12} + (0.8)\left(\text{Actual direct labor cost} - \frac{240,000}{12}\right)$$

In a subsequent month, the actual IPC spent was \$34,000 and the actual direct labor cost was \$16,000. Compute the total IPC variance, the IPC spending variance, and the IPC volume variance.

20 The IPC variances for Marion Corp. in January 19X7 are:

IPC Spending Variance	\$ 0
IPC Volume Variance	3,000 Credit

  a Was production in January higher or lower than normal?

  b How did actual IPC expenditures in January compare with the amount that would be budgeted for IPC at normal volume?

    _____ higher _____ lower _____ the same _____

    can't determine from data provided.

21 The Total IPC Variance account for the Congleton Company in a particular month was as follows:

Total IPC Variance

25,300	26,000

The company's IPC rate had been established using the following estimates for a normal month:

Expected fixed IPC = $15,000
Expected variable IPC = 10,000
IPC vehicle = Direct labor hours
Expected direct labor hours = 5,000

Separate the total IPC Variance into its spending and volume components.

22 Refer to question 21 above, and assume the company used a variable rather than a full absorption cost accounting system.

a What would be the company's IPC rate?

b What additional information would you need to calculate the IPC variance under variable costing?

23 The Porter Electric Corporation has a total IPC variance in July 19X8 of $700 Credit. The IPC vehicle is units of production; production in July was 105% of the normal number of units. The IPC rate is $7.00 per unit and the company's IPC budget equation is: 30,000 + 2.00 (units).

a What was the "normal" (expected) monthly volume of production?

b What was the IPC Volume variance in July 19X8?

c What was the IPC Spending variance in July 19X8?

24 Refer to problem 8 in Chapter 11. Assume that in 19X6 Fry operated a full absorption costing system where the IPC vehicle was units of production. Actual results for the year were as follows:

Production of model A	12,000 units
Production of model B	8,700 units
Actual fixed IPC costs	$127,000
Actual variable IPC costs	$ 61,000

Calculate:

a Total IPC variance

b IPC Spending variance and IPC Volume variance, if the IPC budget is described as:

$128,000 + (3) (units of production)

25 Refer to problem 24 above. If Fry had in 19X6 operated a variable costing system, where the IPC vehicle was units of production, and actual results for the year 19X6 were as detailed above, what would Fry's IPC variance have been for the year?

26 A company that has an IPC rate (full absorption) of $2.50 per unit produced, used the following estimates to derive this rate:

Expected volume = 20,000 units per month

Expected fixed IPC = $30,000 per month

a Derive an IPC budget equation for the company.

b What would the company's IPC rate be for a variable costing system?

PTIMUM INDUSTRIES

Arthur VanWest, a young consultant with the accounting firm of Ernst and Waterhouse, was involved in the early stages of a study of the cost accounting system at Optimum Industries. Ernst and Waterhouse had been performing the annual audit for Optimum Industries (OI) for a number of years. When the president of OI indicated to the audit partner at Ernst and Waterhouse that perhaps the cost accounting system at OI should be updated to reflect changes in the nature of the company's operations, the partner suggested that the consulting arm of the Ernst and Waterhouse firm might be helpful to OI. After some further discussion, a consulting arrangement was agreed upon and VanWest was assigned to perform the initial study.

From a review of the Ernst and Waterhouse audit papers and a short discussion with the president of OI, VanWest learned something about the background and current operations at Optimum Industries. The company's fundamental business was the manufacture and sale of electrical wire and cable. Optimum drew its own wire from copper bar stock, applied plastic jacketing to the wire, and performed the several steps required to manufacture multiconductor cables.

BACKGROUND

In the early years of the company, its operations were much less integrated; that is, the company simply fabricated and sold wire, purchasing predrawn wire from others and selling jacketed wire to other cable fabricators. Over the years, however, the company had developed a wire drawing capability in order to supply its own needs and then began to sell drawn but unjacketed wire to other manufacturers for a variety of uses. In 19X2, when cable was in short supply in the economy, OI developed a cable fabrication capability to accommodate certain of its better customers; this activity had flourished in subsequent years to the point that cable now represented a sizeable percentage of OI's sales.

The manufacturing activity at OI was divided into four departments: wire drawing, wire jacketing, cable fabrication, and packaging and shipping. Both the wire drawing and the wire jacketing departments supplied other departments at OI—drawn wire was transferred to the jacketing department and jacketed wire was transferred to the cable fabrication department. These two departments also supplied customers outside the company.

PRESENT COST ACCOUNTING SYSTEM

VanWest quickly realized that Optimum Industries operated a job order cost accounting system in all departments. No standard costs were available for any of the operations, although VanWest felt that, given the nature of the manufacturing processes, standards could be set with relative ease. The actual costs collected for each job were on a full absorption basis, with a single plantwide overhead (or indirect production costs) rate used in all four departments.

FINANCIAL RESULTS

The company's income statement for May 19X7 is shown in Exhibit 1. OI's net income for the month was almost 6% of sales. The month of May, however, was traditionally a strong month at OI; sales and profits tended to be seasonal, with the busy season from about February through July, just in advance of the busy construction season. Exhibit 2 shows abbreviated balance sheets for the company for both April 30 and May 31, 19X7.

Exhibit 1
OPTIMUM INDUSTRIES
May 19X7
Income Statement

Sales	$247,000
Cost of goods sold	158,700
Overabsorbed IPC[1]	1,200
	157,500
Gross margin	89,500
Operating expenses:	
Selling[2]	27,400
Administration	18,900
Development	14,800
	61,100
Operating profit	28,400
Interest expense	5,700
Other income and expenses	(1,100)
	4,600
Profit before income taxes	23,800
Taxes on income	9,100
Net income	$ 14,700
Earnings per share	23¢

[1] Credit balance in IPC Variance account: IPC charged to production exceeded actual IPC expenditures.
[2] Includes sales commissions at the rate of 5% on all sales.

Exhibit 2
OPTIMUM INDUSTRIES
Balance Sheets (Abbreviated)

ASSETS	April 30, 19X7	May 31, 19X7
Current assets		
Inventories		
Raw and in-process	$ 285,400	$ 288,000
Finished-goods	106,900	101,700
All other current assets	587,000	598,300
Total current assets	979,300	988,000
Fixed assets		
At cost	710,000	715,000
less: accumulated depreciation	(214,000)	(222,500)
	496,000	492,500
All other assets	116,500	117,500
Total assets	$1,591,800	$1,598,000
LIABILITIES AND SHAREHOLDERS' EQUITY		
Current liabilities	$ 559,600	$ 566,100
Long-term liabilities	570,000	555,000
Owners' equity	462,200	476,900
Total	$1,591,800	$1,598,000

The company had been growing quite rapidly in recent years and OI had undertaken substantial long-term borrowing to finance this growth. The management at OI was generally satisfied with the company's earnings level, as management believed that OI's return on assets and return on equity were in line with, or better than, OI's competitors. Nevertheless, OI's management anticipated increasing competition in the market and was anxious to improve its manufacturing efficiency. It was this concern that caused the management to initiate a thorough review of the cost accounting procedures at OI.

PRODUCTION AT OPTIMUM INDUSTRIES

VanWest felt that he needed to obtain additional background information on each of the production departments, and on recent activity within the plant. Knowing that OI used a single plantwide overhead (IPC) rate, VanWest decided he had better get an understanding of the composition of that rate; in answer to his questions he was provided a copy of the plant's Indirect Production Cost Report for the month of May (Exhibit 3). He was encouraged to see that the company apparently appreciated that certain overhead cost elements varied with volume of production activity, while others were essen-

Exhibit 3
OPTIMUM INDUSTRIES
Indirect Production Cost (IPC) Report (Plantwide)—May 19X7

IPC COST ELEMENTS

Variable

Indirect labor	$8,300
Supplies	1,300
Power	1,900
Miscellaneous	700
	$12,200

Fixed

Factory management	$ 7,200
Rent	7,800
Other occupancy	5,700
	$20,700
Total IPC Expenditures	$32,900
IPC absorbed (at $9.85	
per direct labor hour)	$34,100
Overabsorbed IPC	$ 1,200

tially fixed and therefore independent of the amount of production activity. He noted that OI had overabsorbed IPC during the month of May, a normal situation during peak production months.

Wire drawing Many of OI's competitors did not draw their own wire, but instead bought predrawn wire from other suppliers, including OI. OI's management believed that the company's wire drawing capability represented a significant competitive advantage. The key to efficient operations in the wire drawing department was continuous, uninterrupted operation.

Copper bar stock was purchased from large copper companies and was drawn down in a series of steps to progressively smaller diameters. The department manager sought to run the first several drawdown stages on a continuous basis, typically 24 hours per day, five days per week; the operation might be operated seven days per week during peak periods and reduced to four days per week during the slow season. Later stages in the drawdown process, in which smaller and smaller wire diameters were achieved, were operated on a somewhat more intermittent basis, depending upon demand from customers.

Production control issued jobs for each stage of the drawdown process. For the early stages of drawdown, however, a new job was started immediately following the completion of the previous job with no interruption in actual production. VanWest noted that each of these jobs seemed to call for the same quantity of wire and the departmental manager was unable to describe to VanWest the basis for establishing quantities on these job orders. When VanWest inquired of the production control department, he was told that quantities for each job in these early drawdown stages were not influenced by customer demand, but were arbitrarily established at the equivalent of about three days of production. Thus, typically the department ran these drawdown processes continuously and completed about ten jobs, each for the same quantity, in the course of a month. VanWest made a note to himself to investigate the possible use of process costing in this department, in place of the present job order costing system.

Wire jacketing The wire jacketing department obtained drawn wire from the wire drawing department and jacketed the wire with a variety of plastic jackets. Optimum purchased plastic resins to be extruded over the wire from a number of different suppliers. Different jacketing materials were used, depending upon whether the particular application required heat resistance, abrasion resistance, resistance to ultraviolet light degradation, or some combination of these and other characteristics.

Optimum maintained a substantial inventory of finished wire in order to provide rapid delivery to customers. About 100 different wire types were inventoried; these wires were described in OI's catalog and customers ordered by reference to OI's catalog number. As a matter of policy, OI avoided custom wire jacketing jobs for customers, believing that its competitive advantage lay in efficient manufacture of its standard product line.

Production was scheduled and individual job orders were issued by production control in response to two sources of demand: (1) inventory restocking requirements, as determined by the inventory control department, and (2) requirements of the cable fabrication department for jacketed wire to be included in cables. All jacketing was performed to OI's own specifications, described by OI's catalog number. Typical job quantities were in the range from 5,000 to 50,000 meters and seldom did jobs remain in process for more than two weeks.

Exhibit 4 is the operating report for the wire jacketing department for May 19X7. The report shows total charges to the department for the month—$115,000 of direct labor, direct material, and indirect production costs. Work in process in the department increased by $1,200 during the month and at the end of the month

Exhibit 4
OPTIMUM INDUSTRIES
Wire Jacketing Department Operating Report—May 19X7

CHARGES TO DEPARTMENT

Direct material	$ 75,800
Direct labor	16,100 (2,345 hours)
Indirect production costs	23,100
	$115,000

WORK-IN-PROCESS	Material	Labor	IPC	Total
April 30, 19X7	$14,600	$5,080	$7,420	$27,100
May 31, 19X7	15,200	5,325	7,775	28,300
Increase	600	245[1]	355	1,200

WORK COMPLETED

Job Number	Product	Quantity[2]	Total Job Cost
783	A46	400	$ 26,400
784	M103	250	23,300
785	A58	50	6,800
788	A46	400	25,700
789	A33	150	13,100
791	M101	200	18,500
			$113,800

[1] 36 hours of direct labor
[2] In hundreds of meters

charges to jobs that remained in-process (i.e., work that had been started but not yet completed) totaled $28,300. Six jobs were completed during the month, as indicated on the report.

Cable fabrication Optimum produced a limited line of standard cables, manufactured to its own specifications and described in its catalog. The company also fabricated custom cables in accordance with customer specifications.

Cables varied in complexity from simple cables containing only a few conductors sheathed in a relatively inexpensive plastic jacket to cables containing a large number of specialized wires sheathed in a jacket capable of withstanding very difficult environmental conditions. For use in assembling the cables, the department obtained drawn but unjacketed wire from the wire drawing department and jacketed wire from the wire jacketing department. It also obtained special wire from other suppliers and occasionally a customer would supply part of the wire to be incorporated in a custom cable. Plastic resin for the cable sheathing was once again obtained from outside suppliers.

Production control issued job orders to the cable fabrication department in response to two sources of demand: (1) inventory restocking requirements for catalogued cables as determined by the inventory control department, and (2) purchase orders from customers for custom cables. Typical job quantities were substantially smaller than in the wire jacketing department, but in-process times were often longer because of delays in obtaining all of the materials for inclusion in the cables.

STANDARD COSTS

Soon after he started his study at OI, VanWest realized that the wire jacketing department represented a good environment for standard costing. Knowing that he would need to be able to demonstrate to the client the practical use of a standard cost accounting system if his recommendations were to be accepted, VanWest decided that he would need to develop, or to have developed, a set of standard costs for the wires produced in the wire jacketing department. He enlisted the help of the industrial engineering department manager in developing some of the data about labor times and material costs required to produce these standard wires. With these data VanWest was able rather quickly to develop the standard product costs by catalog product as shown in Exhibit 5.

Exhibit 5
OPTIMUM INDUSTRIES
Estimated Standard Costs: Wire Jacketing Department
(In Dollars per Hundred Meters)

		Labor			
Catalog Product	Material[1]	Hours[2]	$	IPC[3]	Total
A33	$58.20	1.62	$10.94	$15.96	$ 85.10
A46	42.31	1.24	8.37	12.21	62.89
A58	98.90	2.05	13.84	20.19	132.93
A81	57.38	1.62	10.94	15.96	84.28
M101	64.60	1.70	11.48	16.75	92.83
M103	66.40	1.48	9.99	14.58	90.97
M106	52.90	1.87	12.62	18.42	83.94

[1] Material cost in wire jacketing department includes the standard cost of all drawn wire obtained from the wire drawing department and the standard purchase price of materials obtained from outside suppliers.
[2] Standard wage rate, wire fabrication, is $6.75 per hour.
[3] At $9.85 per direct labor hour.

FURTHER STUDY

With his present understanding of the operations at OI and with the accounting data he had gathered for the most recent month, May 19X7, VanWest formulated the following questions that he felt he needed to consider as the next steps in his consulting assignment.

1   In the wire drawing department, should job order costing continue to be used or should OI switch to process costing? Is there a way in which both methods might be used within the department?

2   Should the company continue to use actual costing, or should OI switch to standard costing? In what areas does standard costing fit particularly well? In what areas does the present actual costing system provide advantages? Could a combination of standard and actual costing be used in the cable fabrication department?

3   What variance information could be developed for the month of May in the wire jacketing department utilizing the standard costs shown in Exhibit 5? (Estimate the variances for the month.) Would these variance data be useful to management? How expensive would it be to operate a standard cost accounting system in this department?

4   Would reported financial results have been different for the month of May 19X7 if standard costs (as shown in Exhibit 5) had been used in the wire jacketing department? Can the effect on profits for the month be quantified? If not, what additional information needs to be gathered to make this determination? What effect would this change have on the May 31 balance sheet?

5   Shown below are the inventory records for May for three of the company's most popular wire catalog items. The dollar values are determined on a FIFO basis, using actual costs.

   a   If inventory valuations were kept on a LIFO basis, using actual costs, what effect would this change have (with these three

Catalog Product	April 30, 19X7 Quantity[1]	Balance ($)	Additions to Inventory Job No.[2]	Additions to Inventory Quantity[1]	Sales from Inventory Quantity[1]	Sales from Inventory $	May 31, 19X7 Balance Quantity[1]	May 31, 19X7 Balance $
A33	110	9,600	789	150	125	10,910	135	11,789
A81	300	25,500	—	—	90	7,650	210	17,850
M101	0	0	791	200	70	6,475	130	12,025

[1] Hundreds of meters
[2] See Exhibit 4

products only) on profits and ending inventory valuations?

    b If standard costing had been in use for some time at OI (see standard costs in Exhibit 5), how would profits and ending inventory valuations be affected with respect to these three products only? Should the LIFO or FIFO basis of valuation be used with standard costs, or does it matter?

6 Exhibit 1 is the operating statement for May on a full absorption basis. If the company had been using variable (direct) costing, what line items on the financial statements would be affected and would they be increased or decreased?

7 If October represents the seasonal trough for OI (that is, the month of lowest production volume), are profits likely to be different under full absorption costing than under variable costing? Which is likely to result in higher reported profits in October? Under what conditions?

8 How is the use of variable costing going to affect OI's pricing decisions? By way of example, assume that the cable fabrication department is offered a custom job for the month of October (slow production period) at a price of $89.50 per hundred meters; the estimated cost of this custom job is $95.10 per hundred meters on a full absorption cost basis and $79.80 per hundred meters on a variable cost basis.

9 Might the use of variable costing change certain production decisions? Would such changes be appropriate? By way of example, assume that in October (slow production period) OI's controller argues that the company should be producing well in excess of its sales volume in order to build inventory and improve the company's reported profits. Does producing for inventory increase the company's profits in October under variable costing? Under full absorption costing? What are the advantages and disadvantages of producing for inventory during seasonal slow periods?

T HE KILLIAN COMPANY

Early in May 19X7, the president of the Killian Company welcomed the controller into his office to discuss the company's operating statement for April. The president knew that April sales had been about 5% above forecast, and thus he anticipated that April's operating profit would be well above the planned level of $57,000. Upon reviewing the April operating statement, however, the president was dismayed to see that the profit was, in fact, below plan. The president questioned the accuracy of the statement, and suggested that perhaps some double-counting of expenses had occurred.

The controller assured the president that the figures had been carefully checked and that he was confident of the statement's accuracy. He went on to say, "Remember, Sam, that material shortages last month caused us to have to shut down two of the production lines for more than a week. So, although sales were above our targeted level, production was well below normal. As a result, our charge for unabsorbed overhead[1] sharply reduced our profits. This problem is inevitable when our factory operations are out of phase with our sales. The opposite effect—overabsorbed burden—occurs when we have a good production month, that is, when production volume exceeds normal."

The president was obviously not satisfied with the controller's explanation. "These statements just won't make sense to the managers around here," he said. "When we have a good sales month, we all expect profits to be strong. Why should our production volume affect our profits? We've got plenty of inventory and you accountants keep telling us that sales and profits are earned when we ship the product, not when we manufacture it. When the reported operating profit differs so much from our intuitive feel for profits, I'm afraid we all lose some confidence in your accounting reports!"

The controller was quick to defend his work. "Standard accounting conventions require that we use full absorption cost accounting," he pointed out. "Conservative accounting practice suggests that we charge any overabsorbed or underabsorbed overhead to this month's profit-and-loss statement. Moreover, it seems perfectly reasonable to me that the expenses associated with those idle production lines last month would hurt last month's profit."

"But," said the president, "the cost of our manufacturing facilities are there whether we produce anything or not. We laid off that part of our labor force that was affectd by the material shortages during those weeks; maybe your operating statement for the month doesn't reflect those savings."

"No, I double-checked that," responded the controller. "The reduced profit for the month has nothing to do with our direct costs of production—that is, direct labor and direct material—but only with our overhead. Because we didn't have enough production during the month to absorb all of our overhead, we simply ended up with a large volume variance for the month."

"Volume variances have always been difficult for me to understand, and I'm sure they are for the rest of our management team, as well." The president was obviously disturbed, and after studying the April statement for several more minutes, he turned to the con-

---

[1] Unabsorbed overhead = IPC volume variance.

troller and said, "Manny, I think you'd better try to figure out some method of reporting results to our managers that is easier to understand and better corresponds with our intuitive feeling for profit."

While the controller was somewhat surprised by the president's criticism, he realized that the opportunity now presented itself to recommend a major change in the cost accounting system at Killian, a change that he had been studying for several months. The controller was confident that if Killian had been using a variable costing system[2] the April operating results would have looked considerably different, and might in fact have resulted in profits above target, just as the president had anticipated.

The controller decided to rework the April figures. The operating statement that had been shown to the president (see Exhibit 1 below) was based upon the company's current full absorption, standard, job order cost accounting system. Exhibit 2 contains the controller's reworked statement, based upon a variable, standard, job order cost accounting system.

A comparison of these two exhibits indicates that the controller was correct in his expectations: the revised income statement showed a substantially improved operating profit, both by compari-

---

[2] Also referred to as a direct costing system.

Exhibit 1
THE KILLIAN COMPANY
Income Statement
April 19X7

Sales		$574,800
Cost of goods sold[1]		360,500
		$214,300
Less: Manufacturing variances		
Labor	($ 4,600)	
Material	5,100	
Indirect production costs		
Spending	($ 1,300)	
Volume	(36,300)	(37,100)
Gross profit:		$177,200
Operating expenses		
Selling	$79,600	
Administrative	38,100	
Engineering	29,600	147,300
Operating profit		$ 29,900

[1] At standard, full absorption cost.

Exhibit 2
THE KILLIAN COMPANY
Revised Income Statement
(Based on Variable Costing)
April 19X7

Sales		$574,800
Cost of goods sold[1]		266,200
Margin over variable costs		$308,600
Additional manufacturing expenses		
Fixed manufacturing overhead	$88,900	
Manufacturing variances:		
Labor	(4,600)	
Material	5,100	
Indirect production, spending	(1,300)	89,700
Gross profit		$218,900
Operating expenses		
Selling	$79,600	
Administrative	38,100	
Engineering	29,600	147,300
Operating profit		$ 71,600

[1] At standard, variable cost.

son with Exhibit 1 and by comparison with the targeted profit for the month.

When the controller showed the president the revised statement, the president first registered strong approval, and then said, "Maybe we'd better not make a radical change in cost accounting procedure based upon one month's results. Why don't you make a presentation to our management meeting next week, and let's get suggestions from the other managers as well."

As the controller prepared for the upcoming management meeting, he detailed what he thought were the primary advantages of the proposed variable costing system. The primary advantage, from his standpoint, was that the cost accounting procedures would be simpler: no longer would his staff have to develop a fixed overhead rate and apply it to the various production jobs. He also thought that the proposed system would cause the manufacturing managers to pay more attention to those costs which they could control in the short term: the variable costs of manufacturing. The fixed factory costs, composed largely of the costs of owning and operating the plant and equipment and of the salaries of the senior manufacturing management staff, were largely uncontrollable by middle management, as they arose from major decisions made by the president and the Board of Directors.

The controller also felt that the relative profitability of product lines was better measured by the margin over variable cost than by the margin over full absorption cost.

During the subsequent management meeting, this last advantage—assessing the relative profitability of product lines—was strongly supported by the sales manager. She believed these data would be much more useful for pricing than the full absorption cost data that the company had been using. Moreover, she was eager to have these variable cost data for use in pricing special large-volume orders that the company received from time to time; she felt that at times the company should take large orders at prices below full absorption cost, so long as the orders yielded a good margin over variable cost.

The company's treasurer jumped into the discussion at this point. "It is exactly this kind of dangerous thinking that is fostered by a variable costing scheme." He reminded the management group, in no uncertain terms, that "the fixed costs of Killian's operations have to be covered, just as much as the variable costs." He was strongly opposed to accepting orders priced below full absorption cost. He was concerned that the use of a variable cost accounting system would, over time, result in the company's lowering its prices, as the company had had a history of pricing so as to achieve a 45% margin over full factory cost.

The controller responded that, of course, the company's pricing rules would have to be changed to reflect the different basis of costing. The treasurer expressed skepticism that the sales department would in fact implement such an increase in markup. "Sales people always want to cut prices! Just remember," he said, "the fixed costs have to be covered. If you leave them out of our standard product costs, they are likely to be ignored as we make decisions on pricing and cost control."

The manufacturing manager then spoke up. "If we are really trying to reflect *full* cost in our standards, why don't we include selling, administrative, and research costs as well as manufacturing costs?"

The treasurer responded that while the manufacturing manager's idea was a good one for pricing purposes, accounting conventions required the clear separation of product and period costs.

Under further questioning from the treasurer, the controller admitted that variable costing was not a generally accepted accounting method and therefore inventory and cost-of-goods-sold data based upon variable costing would not be acceptable in the company's annual report. Further, the Internal Revenue Service would not permit the use of variable costing in determining the company's annual in-

come tax expense. The controller expressed his opinion that the
lack of acceptability of the variable costing method for external audiences—shareholders and taxing authorities—should not dissuade
the company from using the proposed cost accounting method for internal, month-to-month reports. He indicated that the adjustment
from variable to full absorption costing could be easily made at year-
end, for the purposes of reporting to its shareholders and filing its income tax return. He noted that the company's operating statements
already differed in a number of respects from the income tax statements: for example, accelerated depreciation was used for tax accounting purposes and straight-line depreciation was used for financial accounting purposes, and warranty reserves and expenditures
were accounted for differently in the two statements.

After an hour's discussion at the management meeting, the president suggested the controller undertake some additional study of
the matter. Specifically, he was curious to know how the operating
statement would appear for a month in which production exceeded
both expected levels and the rate of sales. He was worried that, if a
switch to variable costing improved profits when sales exceeded the
production rate, the same switch might decrease profits when the
production rate exceeded the sales rate.

He also wanted to explore further a possible change in the company's pricing policy. If the company made the cost-accounting
change recommended by the controller, the company would need to
price so as to achieve a margin of 50 to 55% over variable cost, rather
than a margin of 35 to 45% over full absorption cost. He was worried
that this pricing change might cause some significant pricing problems in the market. He decided to focus this part of his study on
products D, N, and S, the three primary products in Killian's broad
product line; these three products accounted for 62% of Killian's
sales. Product D involved relatively little processing by Killian; the
material was purchased in a semifinished state and Killian simply
performed a converting step. Product N involved somewhat more
processing, while product S was a proprietary product at Killian involving many processing steps and a good deal of specialized equipment. The standard costs per pound of each of these products were:

| | Products | | |
	D	N	S
Direct material	$2.30	$1.15	$0.73
Direct labor	0.70	1.00	1.41
Indirect production costs	1.05	1.50	2.12
	$4.05	$3.65	$4.26

The IPC rate at Killian was 150% of direct labor; IPC was estimated to be one-third variable and two-thirds fixed. The sales manager provided the following average list prices to the controller for use in his study.

Product	Price per Pound
D	$6.40
N	$5.80
S	$6.75

The controller was under some time pressure to complete the study requested by the president in order to report back to the management group at its next meeting.

Problems

1 Exhibit 3 on page 412 shows the balance sheets for the company as of March 31, 19X7 and April 30, 19X7. What are the effects on the balance sheet of a change to variable costing?

2 Approximately how busy, in relation to normal activity levels, was Killian's manufacturing department in April? (*Hint:* Consider the debit and credit entries in the IPC volume variance account that led to the unfavorable variance shown in Exhibit 1.)

3 In May the company's sales totaled $540,000 and production problems were overcome. Total production, as measured by direct labor wages, was $98,000, or about 10% above normal volume. If in May the expense levels and variances other than the IPC volume variance remained at approximately April's level, what profit would you expect Killian to earn:

  a Assuming variable costing

  b Assuming full absorption costing

4 What is the relative profitability per pound of products D, N and S as measured on the basis of:

  a Gross margin percentage

  b Sales − variable product costs

  c (sales − variable product costs) ÷ sales

  d (sales − variable product costs) ÷ direct labor cost

What is the relevance of each of these measures, and which do you feel is the best measure of relative profitability?

5 If Killian decided to price the three products so as to achieve a 53% margin over variable cost (i.e., sales less variable cost = 53% of sales), what would be the resulting prices? Would you recommend these prices? What procedures would you recommend to Killian for establishing the list prices of these three products?

Exhibit 3
THE KILLIAN COMPANY
Balance Sheets
(Based on Full Absorption Costing)
($000)

		As of
ASSETS	**March 31, 19X7**	**April 30, 19X7**
Current assets		
Cash	$ 29	$ 38
Accounts receivable	1,283	1,380
Inventory[1]	774	655
Total current assets	2,086	2,073
Plant and equipment, net	1,862	1,846
Total assets	$3,948	$3,919
LIABILITIES AND NET WORTH		
Current liabilities	$ 536	$ 501
Mortgage payable	756	750
Total liabilities	1,292	1,251
Owners' equity		
Capital stock	1,350	1,350
Retained earnings	1,306	1,318
Total owners' equity	2,656	2,668
Total liabilities and owners' equity	$3,948	$3,919

[1] The standard costs (by cost element) of inventory at each month end were:

Direct material	$199	$183
Direct labor	232	190
Variable overhead	111	92
Fixed overhead	232	190
	$774	$655

6 Which of the two cost accounting structures would you recommend to the management at Killian?

G IBBONS SYNDICATED NEWSPAPERS

Gibbons Syndicated Newspapers (GSN) owned and operated a large urban daily newspaper and 10 smaller newspapers located in suburbs of major metropolitan areas. Publishing frequency of these smaller papers was from four to seven days per week, depending upon the nature of the towns served and competition from nearby urban newspapers. Gibbons had in recent years placed increasing emphasis on improving financial control of its various operations. Ms. Lynn Schwartz, the financial manager at one of the suburban newspapers, was anxious to respond to this pressure for greater operational control and was particularly concerned about gaining a better understanding of the cost of newsprint.

The cost of newsprint typically represented between 15 and 30% of the total costs—both editorial and production—of operating the paper; at Ms. Schwartz's paper the figure was 25%, and thus careful attention to the control of newsprint costs was well warranted.

PRICE OF NEWSPRINT

Newsprint rolls were purchased from various paper mills and delivered by truck to each of the GSN plants. Most newspapers contracted for newsprint from a variety of paper mills. The mix of mills on which a newspaper relied was selected to optimize among several conflicting objectives: (1) minimize freight costs, (2) avoid undue dependency on a single geographic region, since poor weather or unsettled labor conditions in a region could restrict shipments for weeks or months, and (3) purchase sufficient quantity from the mills of a single manufacturer to achieve advantageous pricing without becoming too dependent on that manufacturer.

The price specified in the contracts with the mills was typically "prevailing market price" or a small discount off that price. Market prices changed frequently, depending upon supply and demand imbalances and general conditions in the world paper market. There also existed a "spot market" for newsprint—a market to which newspapers could turn to buy additional rolls of paper if their contracted supply proved inadequate or for some reason became unavailable. In periods of short supply, spot market prices were very much higher than the prevailing market price and rarely did the spot price fall below market price. Accordingly, newspapers attempted to avoid having to turn to the spot market. At the same time, newspapers tried to avoid overstocking newsprint in order to minimize both the space and dollar investment in inventory. Typically, a newspaper would maintain on hand a 30- to 40-day supply of newsprint.

The particular newspaper where Ms. Schwartz worked consumed about 8,000 tons of newsprint per year. At the time Ms. Schwartz undertook her analysis, the market price for newsprint was

$375 per ton. At this price, the newspaper's total cost of newsprint was about $3 million per year.

USE OF NEWSPRINT

The use of newsprint at the paper was dependent upon a number of variables. Minimum usage was not the objective. If the circulation and advertising staffs at the newspaper were able to increase circulation or increase the number of advertising pages, the increased usage of newsprint occasioned by these events was favorable. On the other hand, consumption of newsprint was also affected by efficiency in the pressroom, and varied according to the number of spoiled copies produced before the press reached full speed at acceptable quality and the number of "web breaks" (breaks in the sheet which required that the press be stopped and the paper rethreaded). Also, more newsprint was consumed without offsetting increases in income if a late-breaking editorial story required the paper to add additional pages without a corresponding increase in advertising.

ACCOUNTING PERIOD

Most newspapers used accounting periods based upon weeks rather than calendar months or quarters. The size of the paper varied substantially from day to day. Papers were larger on Wednesdays and Thursdays because of heavy grocery advertising. Few advertisers used the Saturday papers and thus these papers were small. Large papers were printed on Sunday because of heavy space and classified advertising. In order to assure comparability between accounting periods, newspaper publishers typically selected 13 four-week periods for their accounting year, or an accounting quarter that consisted of two four-week periods and one five-week period. Gibbons used the latter, described as a 4-4-5 system.

DESIGN OF VARIANCES

Ms. Schwartz set about to design a variance analysis system to highlight newsprint cost and usage. She felt that day-by-day analysis would not be useful and therefore she confined her analysis to weekly averages.

Purchase price variance Shipments of newsprint typically were received several times each week, and Ms. Schwartz thought a purchase price variance would be useful to management. This purchase price variance would be calculated at the time newsprint was received; thus, newsprint inventory would be valued at its standard purchase price (currently $375 per ton).

Usage variances   A single usage variance would be of limited value, since usage was affected by four primary factors, each of which needed to be highlighted:

1   Circulation gains and losses
2   Advertising increases and decreases
3   Editorial decisions
4   Pressroom efficiency

To isolate these factors, standard costs and quantities had to be established.

A standard circulation (number of newspapers) was easily set. Circulation was predominantly via home delivery, with few papers sold at newsstands. As a result, circulation week to week was quite steady, although some greater variation was experienced day to day. Ms. Schwartz settled on a standard circulation of 64,000 papers per day.

A standard cost per page produced could also be set. Newsprint was consumed at the rate of one ton per 180,000 pages. At the current market price of $375 per ton, each page cost $0.002083. This standard could be used to measure pressroom efficiency, since a total standard production cost for any size paper and any circulation could be calculated using this cost per page.[1] Each 50-page paper (the nominal size at this operation) with a standard cost of $0.104, and a standard run of 64,000 papers, each of 50 pages, should consume about $6,670 of newsprint (almost 18 tons).

To measure the effect of advertising sales and editorial decisions on newsprint consumption required the establishment of a standard paper size (number of pages). A single figure, however, could not apply to all days. By policy, the size of the paper was altered in response to advertising and editorial conditions. After considerable study, Ms. Schwartz hit on the idea of deriving for each day an "adjusted standard pages."

Adjusted standard pages   The number of pages in an edition of the paper was largely a function of the amount of advertising to ap-

---

[1] Newsprint that was spoiled during start-up or web breaks was sold for recycling. The pressroom weighed the amount of spoilage each day and reported these figures to accounting. Since Ms. Schwartz had some concern that not all of the spoiled paper was reported, she decided to ignore these data for the purpose of her analysis.

Exhibit 1
GIBBONS SYNDICATED NEWSPAPERS
Data on Edition Size and Newsprint Usage
(10th Accounting Period)

Date	Day	Newsprint Delivery		Edition Size (Pages)			Adjusted Standard Pages[1]	Circulation (000)	Actual Usage (Tons)
		Tons	$	Adv	Edit	Total			
10/6	Mon			28.0	20.0	48	48.0	63.5	17.1
10/7	Tues	81.5	30,560	31.0	21.0	52	51.7	64.0	18.5
10/8	Wed			41.5	22.5	64	69.2	65.2	23.2
10/9	Thur			31.5	20.5	52	52.5	64.0	18.3
10/10	Fri	58.2	21,936	36.5	23.5	60	60.8	66.1	22.1
Subtotal		139.7	52,496	168.5	107.5	276	282.2	322.8	99.2
Average for week		N/A	N/A	33.7	21.5	55.2	56.44	64.56	19.84
10/13	Mon			20.5	23.5	44	40.5	62.8	15.9
10/14	Tues	68.1	25,508	25.5	18.5	44	45.5	63.0	17.9
10/15	Wed			38.0	26.0	64	63.3	64.0	23.2
10/16	Thur	71.1	26,829	34.0	22.0	56	58.7	62.8	20.9
10/17	Fri	50.5	18,956	37.5	26.5	64	62.5	65.5	24.4
Subtotal		189.7	71,293	155.5	116.5	272	270.5	318.1	102.3
Average for week		N/A	N/A	31.1	23.3	54.4	54.1	63.62	20.46

Date	Day								
10/20	Mon	58.8	22,046	26.5	21.5	48	46.5	63.5	16.9
10/21	Tues			27.0	21.0	48	47.0	65.0	17.4
10/22	Wed	30.5	12,010	42.5	25.5	68	70.8	68.2	25.1
10/23	Thur			38.0	26.0	64	63.3	68.0	23.6
10/24	Fri	32.2	12,014	34.0	26.0	60	56.7	66.1	22.5
Subtotal		121.5	46,070	168.0	120.0	288	284.3	330.8	105.5
Average for week		N/A	N/A	33.6	24.0	57.6	56.86	66.16	21.10
10/27	Mon	60.6	22,930	30.5	21.5	52	50.8	64.1	18.6
10/28	Tues	48.8	18,390	33.5	22.5	56	55.8	64.0	19.9
10/29	Wed			42.0	22.0	64	70.0	67.8	24.3
10/30	Thur	32.9	12,671	36.0	24.0	60	60.0	65.0	22.0
10/31	Fri			37.5	22.5	60	62.5	70.0	23.8
Subtotal		142.3	53,991	179.5	112.5	292	299.1	330.9	108.6
Average for week		N/A	N/A	35.9	22.5	58.4	59.82	66.18	21.72
Totals		593.2	223,850	671.5	456.5	1,128	1,136.1	1,302.6	415.6
Average for 4-week period		N/A	N/A	33.58	22.82	56.4	56.81	65.13	20.78

¹ Derived as follows: (a) 20 pages editorial + actual advertising pages; or, if advertising pages exceed 30, (b) 20 pages editorial + actual advertising pages + 2/3 (actual advertising pages − 30).

pear in the edition. Typically, advertising constituted 60% of the space in each edition of the newspaper, and the remaining 40% was devoted to editorial material. This 60/40 ratio changed from day to day during the week (e.g., the ratio of advertising was higher on days that grocery ads appeared) and from season to season during the year; however, Ms. Schwartz decided to base her analysis on this typical ratio.

The number of pages in each edition was subject to another constraint: in no case should the editorial "hole" (the number of pages devoted to editorial material) fall below 20 pages. This size implied 30 pages of advertising in order to maintain the 60/40 ratio. Even if advertising fell below 30 pages in a particular edition, the size of the edition would be 20 pages plus the available advertising. If advertising exceeded 30 pages, editorial content of the edition would be increased in an attempt to maintain the 60/40 ratio.

The adjusted standard pages concept was designed to reflect these two policies: minimum editorial hole and 60/40 ratio of advertising to editorial content. The adjusted standard pages was defined as follows:

1   If advertising pages are less than 30:
    a   Twenty editorial pages, plus
    b   Actual advertising pages

or

2   If advertising pages exceed 30:
    a   20 editorial pages, plus
    b   actual advertising pages, plus
    c   Two-thirds (actual advertising pages − 30)

OPERATING DATA

Ms. Schwartz pulled together the various data relating to newsprint consumption over the most recent four weeks. These data are shown in Exhibit 1. The variance reporting form she designed is shown in Exhibit 2. Exhibit 3 contains her observations on the significance that each variance would have to management and what action might be prompted by each variance.

Exhibit 2
GIBBONS SYNDICATED NEWSPAPERS
Variance Report—Newsprint
Week Ending: _____

I. Purchase Price Variance
   A.   Quantity delivered (tons): _____ tons
   B.   Standard price per ton: $_____/ton
   C.   Total standard invoice (A × B): $_____
   D.   Actual invoice total: $_____
   E.   Variance: (D − C): $_____

II. Usage Variances
      (1) Efficiency Variance
   F.   Actual circulation: _____ papers
   G.   Actual pages: _____ pages
   H.   Standard cost per page: $_____/page
   I.   Standard material cost (F × G × H): $_____
   J.   Actual tons: _____ tons
   (B.) Standard price per ton: $_____/ton
   K.   Actual tons at standard price (J × B): $_____
   L.   Variance (I–K): $_____

      (2) Circulation Variance
   M.   Standard circulation: _____ papers
   (F.) Actual circulation: _____ papers
   N.   Difference (in papers): _____ papers
   (G.) Actual pages: _____ pages
   (H.) Standard cost per page: $_____/page
   O.   Variance (N × G × H): $_____

      (3) Editorial Usage Variance
   P.   Adjusted standard pages: _____ pages
   (G.) Actual pages: _____ pages
   Q.   Difference (in pages) (P − G): _____ pages
   (M.) Standard circulation: _____ pages
   (H.) Standard cost per page: $_____/page
   R.   Standard cost/Edition page (M × H): $_____/Edition page
   S.   Variance (Q × R): $_____

      (4) Advertising Volume Variance
   T.   Nominal pages: 50 pages
   (P.) Adjusted standard pages: _____ pages
   U.   Difference (in pages) (T − P): _____ pages
   (R.) Standard cost/Edition page: $_____/Edition page
   V.   Variance (U × R): $_____

Exhibit 3

GIBBONS SYNDICATED NEWSPAPERS

Explanation of Variances

Usage Variances

Purchase Price Variance[1]	Efficiency Variance[2]	Circulation Variance[3]	Editorial Overage Variance[4]	Advertising Volume Variance[5]
Actual invoice amounts	Actual tons × std price per ton	Actual pages × std cost per page × actual circulation	Actual pages × std cost per page × std circulation	Adjusted std pages × std cost per page × std circulation
Actual tons delivered × std price per ton	Actual pages × std cost per page × actual circulation	Actual pages × std cost per page × std circulation	Adjusted std pages × std cost per page × std circulation	Nominal pages × std cost per page × std circulation

[1] Debit balance indicates price in excess of list (currently $375/ton), typically as a result of having to purchase newsprint in the spot market. This action, in turn, may be caused by (1) circulation or advertising volume exceeding expectations—favorable events; or (2) inadequate inventory planning, efficiency problems, or interruptions in deliveries from the mills—unfavorable events.

[2] This variance is a traditional efficiency variance. A debit balance implies higher than standard wastage. This wastage may arise from problems with newsprint quality and several other sources.

[3] An actual printing run in excess of standard may be a favorable event (although resulting in a debit balance) if the papers are in fact sold and not wasted. This variance must be interpreted in light of the corresponding revenue variances (not available here).

[4] If actual pages exceed adjusted standard pages, an editorial decision caused this growth in paper size. A resulting debit balance, while unfavorable to short-term profitability, may have favorable long-term effects on circulation.

[5] The nominal size of the paper is that implied by the minimum editorial hole and the target advertising/editorial ratio. With a hole of 20 pages and a 60/40 ratio, the nominal size is 50 pages. The adjusted standard pages is the size of the paper implied by advertising exceeding 30 pages. A debit balance would generally be considered a favorable event. A credit balance suggests that editorial volume was not keeping pace with increased advertising, a condition that might improve short-term profitability at the expense of longer-term subscriber satisfaction.

Problems

1   What conclusions can you draw from an analysis of the variances for the full period (that is, using totals and averages for the four weeks)?

2   Do you think that the newspaper has had to turn to the spot market for newsprint purchases during this period?

3   Information more useful to operating management is derived from the weekly data, since conditions changed quite markedly from week to week.

   a   How would you rate the efficiency of the operation in the second week?

   b   How significant was the circulation variance in the third week?   What might have been the cause of this variance?

   c   During which week was the advertising variance most pronounced? What were possible causes?   What action, if any, might you propose on the basis of this variance?

4   To whom in the newspaper's organization is each of the variances most relevant?   Among the key managers at the newspaper are: the publisher (generally equivalent to the general manager), the editor, the financial manager, the circulation manager, the production manager, and the purchasing manager.

5   This case considers only variances associated with newsprint.   In what other areas of the newspaper's business might variance analysis be useful?

13

Budgeting and Analysis of Performance

All of us operate according to a plan, even if only an implicit plan in our minds. Well-managed enterprises operate to an explicit financial plan that is formally documented: a **budget.** The better-managed operations—businesses, schools, governmental units, and charitable and social organizations—also develop detailed reports to compare their actual financial performance to their budgets. This chapter focuses on the budgeting process and on the use of budgets in analyzing operating performance.

Chapters 11 and 12 included discussion of the design of standard cost accounting systems, and the use of standard cost data to analyze the efficiency of a manufacturing operation. We emphasized the desirability of management's focusing its attention on those segments of the operation that seem to be performing at variance with plan. Recall that the analysis of variances—the differences between standard and actual costs—facilitates *management by exception*.

As suggested in Chapter 12, if we set standards for all costs and expenses—not just product costs incurred in manufacturing, but the myriad expenses incurred in selling, marketing, administration, development, and so forth—we will have a basis or yardstick against which actual expenditures can be compared. The process of setting these standards is referred to as *budgeting*. The comparison of actual financial results with budgeted (or standard) results permits the analysis of performance of an organization or operating unit.

Managerial Accounting

The use of accounting data to assist management in making operating decisions is commonly referred to as **managerial accounting.** This chapter and the next (Cost Analysis for Operating Decisions) comprise the managerial accounting portion of this book. This chapter focuses on the establishment of operating plans, or budgets, and the use of budgets in determining if an organization is performing in accordance with plan or if corrective actions need to be taken. Chapter 14 looks specifically at ways in which accounting data can be selected, compiled, and analyzed to assist management in making some key operating decisions, such as the pricing of products or services, investing in new productive assets, and determining whether to add, delete, or redesign products.

Chapter 12 emphasized variance analysis and the types of management decisions to which these analyses may lead. For example, an unfavorable purchase price variance indicates that the company is spending more for the purchase of materials than planned. This unfavorable variance suggests careful review of the company's purchasing function to determine if alternative sources of supply can be located, if contracts with vendors can be renegotiated, or if substitute lower-cost materials can be used. Possibly the negative variance is caused by price inflation, over which the company's management has no direct control; if so, and if these price increases are being experienced by all competitors in the industry, the company may need to consider increasing selling prices. If no action is taken by management and these unfavorable purchase price variances persist, the company's realized profit will fall short of planned profit, unless offsetting favorable variances can be generated in other areas.

Thus, standard product costs provide management with a "road map" of what it should cost to manufacture the company's products or provide the company's services. Similarly, a budget provides management with a road map of what the company should be spending on period costs associated with marketing the company's output, administering its operations, and developing new products. When the company's operations deviate from these road maps, or plans, management is alerted to investigate that segment of the operation which is apparently off-plan and to take corrective action to steer the operation back on course. Deviations may suggest that plans be revised to capitalize on an emerging opportunity or to offset a recently encountered problem. In any case, carefully drawn budgets and subsequent comparison of actual results to these budgets facilitate the process of management by exception.

Guidelines for Budgeting

It is tempting to dive right into the details of budgets and budgeting. Many decisions need to be made: how much should be spent on salaries in certain departments, how should salary levels be set, how much should be spent on advertising and promotion, and how should that amount relate to the present size or future growth of the company. But the critical first step in budgeting is the same as the first step in most complex tasks: establishing the objectives. If you don't know where you're trying to go, you can't plan how to get there!

SETTING OBJECTIVES

In a profit-seeking enterprise, management will probably have in mind some profit objective, as well as certain other financial objectives. The profit objective may be measured in terms of return on equity or return on assets. Alternatively, it may be measured in relationship to profit earned in previous years—for example, a 10% increase from last year, a return to the record profitability level of three years ago, or a profit decline of only 15% in the face of an economic recession.

Profit may not be the overriding financial objective. Instead, the company may currently be geared more to growth in revenue or share of the market than to earning strong profits in the near term. For a fledgling company, the objective may be simply to break even this year, earning neither a profit nor a loss. Or, financial objectives may be measured in terms of the commitments that the company has to its creditors and shareholders for the repayment of loans and the payment of dividends.

In a nonprofit organization, the objective to which the financial budget is pointed may be simply a condition of balance between cash inflow and cash expenditures, or it may be to generate a certain level of surplus of inflow over outflow, or to increase sources of revenue by 10% in order to permit an expansion of services, or to reduce expenditures by 7% in light of declining membership. The budgeting objective for certain national governments in recent years, including that of the United States, has been to limit the amount of the government's operating deficit, the prospect of a balanced budget or surplus being so remote as to provide no realistic target for budgeting.

In any case, management needs to have in mind at the outset of the budgeting process a set of target financial objectives that represents a distillation in financial terms of the myriad qualitative and quantitive objectives to which the organization is committed.

BUDGETING: ONE ELEMENT OF PLANNING

Chapter 1 emphasized that financial statements cannot provide a full and complete history of a company or other organization. Much goes on in any operation that cannot be immediately reduced to monetary terms: personnel are hired or leave, stubborn technical problems are encountered or solved, and the firm's reputation within the marketplace is enhanced or eroded.

Financial statements are to history what budgets are to the future. An operating budget is simply an explicit estimate of what management believes future income statements will be. Thus, just as financial statements are not complete records of history, neither are budgets a complete set of plans regarding the future. Budgeting is just one element of the company's overall planning process. The budget describes the monetary consequences of the plans of the organization.

Budgeting cannot precede detailed operational planning, nor can it follow the conclusion of such planning. Financial budgets should not dictate plans, although operating plans often have to be tempered by financial realities as revealed by budgets. Nor should plans be finalized without a careful review of their budgetary implications. Budgeting must be integrated into the planning process. Thus, planning is typically an iterative process: some planning must be done as the basis for financial budgeting, but some replanning is typically required to adjust plans to budget restrictions. Sometimes several rounds of replanning and rebudgeting are necessary before management is satisfied that both operating plans and financial budgets are compatible with the organization's overall purposes, objectives, and available resources.

"BOTTOM UP" VERSUS "TOP DOWN"

Who sets the budget for the organization? How is an acceptable operating budget finally assembled? Just as one person cannot do all of the planning for any but the smallest of organizations, neither can one person establish budgets. All persons responsible for developing and refining operating plans must also be involved in developing and refining budgets.

Some top-level managers are inclined to impose on their subordinates detailed budgets and budgetary constraints. Once established they expect their subordinates to live within these budgets. At the same time, these top-level managers expect their subordinates to take responsibility for their individual segments of the operation, to make and revise plans, to be decisive, and to implement actions as required. These two views are incompatible. It is unreasonable to expect members of management to take responsibility for living within budgets that they had no hand in setting.

One cannot expect managers to take operating but not financial responsibility for their business segments. Therefore, an important budgeting guideline is that each manager should play a strong role in setting the budget for his or her segment of the operation and the budget of the entire operation should be built up from segment budgets. The total budget for the organization should not be established and then divided up among the operating segments.   The best and most useful budgets, then, are developed from the bottom up rather than from the top down.

To illustrate the importance of this guideline, consider the process of developing an annual selling expense budget for the Reynolds Company, a manufacturer of specialty chemicals.   The national sales manager, with offices at the Chicago headquarters, may be tempted to dictate to the regional sales managers a budget for both sales (or incoming orders) and for selling expenses for the coming year.   Consider the regional sales manager in Dallas, Texas, Mary Gonzalez.   Gonzalez is presumably more knowledgeable than the national sales manager about the Texas market; the position of the company and its competitors in that market; the need for additional training for the Texas sales force; the amount of travel, entertainment, and telephone expenses that will be incurred by the Dallas office during the coming year; and similar local matters.   Moreover, the national sales manager will undoubtedly want to hold the Dallas regional manager responsible for both sales and expense levels during the coming year.   If so, Gonzalez will want to have a say in establishing targets for sales and expenses for her region.

The nationwide budgets for sales and expenses, which are the responsibility of the Chicago-based national sales manager, will be both more realistic and more useful if they are built up from the budgets established in and by each of the regions.   Of course, Gonzalez in Dallas will need to work with the national sales manager and others throughout the organization in developing and refining her budget; while she may be particularly knowledgeable about conditions in the Texas market and the Dallas office, she will need to look to others for information on new product plans, national promotional plans for the coming year, expected actions by competitors, and, most importantly, the objectives and financial constraints of the overall company.   The process, then, of establishing the Dallas regional budget is a joint process, involving the Dallas regional sales manager and the national sales manager, and perhaps others at the Reynolds Company as well.

Most large organizations have a budget department or group within the financial function; this department may be headed by a person carrying a title such as Manager of Budgeting.   An observer might mistakenly conclude that this group is responsible for setting budgets for the organization; unfortunately, too many managers of budgeting see their role as imposing budgets on their organizations.   The budgeting department should see its role as that of facilitator and consolidator: articulating budgeting guidelines that are consistent with the organization's goals, assisting individual managers at all levels to develop realistic and workable budgets that are consistent with those guidelines, and building up the total budget for the organization from the segment budgets.

THE CORNERSTONE: THE SALES FORECAST

The cornerstone on which the remainder of the budget is built is the forecast or budget of revenue for the coming period. In a profit-seeking company, the forecast of sales typically becomes the critical first step in the budgeting process. A nonprofit organization must estimate revenue from dues, gifts, services, and all other sources.

Most operations must incur expenses to generate revenue, and the revenue provides the wherewithal to pay the expenses. Thus, neither the sales budget (or forecast) nor the expense budget can be set independently of the other. This situation has a tendency to cause chicken-first or egg-first arguments. Gonzalez, the Dallas regional sales manager, may be reluctant to estimate incoming orders or sales for the coming year without knowing for certain the level of expenses, and therefore the amount of sales effort, that will be budgeted for the coming year. At the same time, the national sales manager will be reluctant to define with Gonzalez permissable expense levels for the year without a reliable estimate of the sales to be generated by the region.

But revenue or sales is the place to start. The tentative sales forecast will provide the basis for establishing some guidelines for expense levels. Necessarily, the first sales forecast must be tentative. Once the entire budget is compiled, management may discover that resources will be available in the coming year to invest, for example, in opening several new sales offices or in launching a long-delayed new product; these investments may cause sales to be higher than the tentative forecast. Or management may discover that promotional expenses must be reduced in order to spend more on research and development, and that this reduction will make the tentative sales forecast difficult to achieve. In either case the tentative sales forecast will need to be modified, and in turn this revision may necessitate still another revision in the expense budgets. To repeat, budgeting is an iterative process.

Many companies develop both a sales target and a sales budget. The target, somewhat above the budget, represents a goal toward which the sales organization will be striving, but one to which the company's management might assign only a 50% or lower probability of achieving. Management will be unwilling to commit itself to expense levels based upon such a low-probability sales estimate. The sales budget—the sales forecast upon which the expense budget is based—will be lower than the target, a level that management is perhaps 80% confident will be met or exceeded. Such multilevel forecasting can be a useful tool for management.

HISTORY AS PROLOGUE

The budgeting process typically relies heavily on historical financial data. Since an operating budget is simply an estimate of the operating or income statement for a future period, past operating statements provide useful guides for budgeting. Frequently, budget levels for the coming year are established simply by incrementing last year's actual expenditures up or down. Every manager will want to have a detailed understanding of current expenditure levels as he or she considers appropriate budget levels for a future period. If Gonzalez knows that the Dallas office has been incurring about $700 per month of telephone expenses in the final months of 19X4, she will consider factors that may affect this expense item in 19X5: for example, telephone rates are expected to increase by 5%, one more salesperson will join the office early in the new year, the sales personnel are encountering fewer reasons to call the Chicago headquarters office. All factors considered, Gonzalez may decide that an appropriate budget level for 19X5 is about 7% more than current expense levels, or about $750 per month.

The technique of simply incrementing historical expenses to arrive at budgeted expenses has the unfortunate tendency to confirm present expenditure levels as appropriate and necessary. For example, Gonzalez may not question whether the office really needs to spend $700 per month on telephone expense. Perhaps the sales force would be just as efficient with less use of the telephone or, conceivably, the sales force should be encouraged to make greater use of the telephone in order to increase sales or decrease travel expenses. The national sales manager may encourage Gonzalez to think about such questions, but the inevitable tendency is to place primary reliance on present expense levels as the best indicator of what will be, or must be, spent in the future period.

A budgeting technique referred to as **zero-base budgeting** seeks to deemphasize the use of historical data as the basis for budgeting. The technique, originally introduced in certain agencies of the U.S. federal government but now gaining popularity in the private sector as well, requires that each manager justify each budget request by indicating why every dollar needs to be spent. Rather than simply referring to the amounts that have been spent in previous periods, the manager must justify from a zero base the need for each person who reports to the manager and for each expenditure to be made for supplies, telephones, travel, maintenance, computer time, and so forth. Under zero-base budgeting, Gonzalez would need to build up the telephone expense budget for the coming year by justifying the number of telephone lines coming into the office, the number of telephone sets in the office, the number and duration of long-distance telephone calls, and so forth. The advantage of such a procedure is that Gonzalez may thereby determine that, for example, a special line should be leased to connect the Dallas and Chicago offices in order to reduce long-distance telephone charges; or, that the office could get along with fewer telephone sets since the salespersons spend most of their time traveling away from the office. Zero-base budgeting is time-consuming and potentially frustrating to managers, but often the benefits in terms of more efficient use of resources—reducing expenditures in some areas and spending with good effect additional resources in other areas—far outweigh the costs.

COMMITMENT

The effectiveness of budgets and the budgeting process varies significantly from organization to organization. In some, budgeting is a meaningful part of the planning process and budgets become working documents that are both useful and used. In others, budgeting is simply a required but perfunctory exercise which is accorded little time and less thought on the part of management; the resulting budgets are filed away and seldom, if ever, referred to again. The difference in effectiveness is typically a function of the commitment that management makes to the budgeting process, commitment not just by the manager of budgeting but by all levels of management and particularly top management.

If the head of the organization—president, chairman of the trustees, mayor, principal, or whomever—is serious about budgeting, the balance of the management group will also take the process seriously. If the chief executive takes time to articulate meaningful objectives and guidelines for budgeting, to review and analyze budget requests, to require rebudgeting until an acceptable overall budget is compiled, and to monitor actual operating results in relationship to the budget, then lower levels of management will also devote the time required to develop and redevelop meaningful budgets and will use the budgets in operating their departments. On the other hand, if the top management sees budgeting as a necessary evil—a simple translation of already agreed-upon plans into monetary terms, an activity to be relegated to the clerical staff working for the manager of budgeting—then lower levels of management will find little time for budgeting and will pay little attention to budgets as they operate their departments.

Bottom-up budgeting requires the deep involvement of all levels of management. Each manager must understand that organization-wide financial results depend upon each segment of the organization performing—in terms of both revenue generation and expense control—in accordance with that segment's budget. Each department manager negotiates with his or her supervisor—the next manager up the management hierarchy—regarding the final budget for the department. Once agreed to, the budget becomes a kind of contract between the two individuals. The department manager gives the supervisor a commitment to operate the department in conformance with the budget, thereby helping to assure on-budget results for the total company; in turn, the supervisor commits that the department manager may spend the organization's resources in accordance with the budget. Where budgeting is effective, these commitments are taken seriously.

BUDGETING NONFINANCIAL PARAMETERS

It is worth repeating that, while budgeting is an integral part of the planning process, it is only a part. Plans contain much that cannot be reduced to financial terms. Just as management relies on reports other than strict financial reports in monitoring the operations of a company, so also management will need, as part of the budgeting process, to develop detailed estimates of certain nonfinancial parameters.

For example, a detailed labor forecast or budget, expressed in number of people (perhaps by job classification) rather than in dollars of wages and salaries, is a useful adjunct to financial budgeting. Detailed estimates may need to be made of percentage of late deliveries, number of new customers, square feet of warehouse required, process yield, average price discounts allowed, average markup, number of sales calls per day per salesperson, employee turnover rate, and rate of absenteeism. Indeed, to do a competent and realistic job of financial budgeting will require that these and many other parameters of the operation be budgeted.

FREQUENCY OF REVISION

Our discussion thus far has implied annual revisions to operating budgets. Most organizations do indeed undertake a major budgeting exercise just prior to the beginning of each fiscal year; however, many operations require interim rebudgeting as well, perhaps semiannually or even quarterly. The more volatile and unpredictable the operation, the more frequent and extensive must be the budget revisions. Revisions should not be undertaken so frequently—for example, monthly—that the budget is constantly in a state of flux and management is devoting unwarranted amounts of time to budgeting; nor should rebudgeting be so infrequent that the operating budget becomes unrelated to the changing set of operating conditions facing the company.

Responsibility Accounting

Bottom-up budgeting and commitment by intermediate levels of management require that the operation be defined for the purposes of both budgeting and financial reporting in terms of **responsibility centers;** that is, the total operation must be subdivided into departments, segments, or units for which a single responsible manager can be identified. Most businesses are operated in a manner quite consistent with responsibility centers: managers are assigned responsibility for a segment of the business and then are delegated the authority to carry out that responsibility. The first-line supervisor may be responsible for a relatively small segment of the business—perhaps only several employees and a few expenses. Managers farther up the management chain have responsibility for broader segments of the business, which are in turn composed of a number of small segments. Finally, the chief executive of the organization has ultimate responsibility for all operations.

Gonzalez, a middle-level manager of the Dallas office of the Reynolds Company, heads a responsibility center that includes all of the company's activities in Texas. Reporting to her are several managers, each in turn heading a responsibility center—for example, the service manager responsible for the service force, their travel, and associated expenses; the office supervisor responsible for the secretarial and clerical staff and the costs of supplies and janitorial services; and two area sales managers, each of whom is responsible for the activities and expenses of several salespersons. Gonzalez reports to the national sales manager, who has responsibility for overseeing all regional offices throughout the country.

As managers move up the management hierarchy, they typically become responsible for broader segments of the total enterprise and can, by their decisions, have greater impact on the overall financial health and success of the enterprise. The first-level supervisor in manufacturing has responsibility for only a modest set of resources and has relatively little direct impact on the revenues of the company or on its assets and liabilities. At the other extreme, the decisions of the chief executive, who commands all of the resources of the enterprise, can affect the revenues, expenses, assets, liabilities, and all other matters within the organization. Responsibility centers can be categorized on the basis of the extent of control exercised by the responsible manager. A segment of the business where the manager has responsibility only for expenses is referred to as a **cost center.** If the manager has responsibility for both expenses and revenue, but not for the investment of long-term resources, the center is referred to as a **profit center.** Finally, if the manager is responsible for the amount of the company's investment in the particular center, as well as for near-term revenues and expenses, the center is referred to as an **investment center.** The measure of performance of the manager will be different for each of the cost, profit, and investment centers.

COST CENTER

At a minimum, a manager is responsible only for expenses. One measure of a manager's effectiveness is the ability to operate the department in accordance with the budget of expenses. Good performance requires that the manager develop and obtain approval for a realistic budget, and then control expenditures according to that budget. In the example of the Dallas regional office, the office supervisor responsible for the secretarial and clerical staff is in charge of a cost center. The supervisor is not directly accountable for revenue and does not have authority to commit the office to additional assets (such as office machines).

PROFIT CENTER

A manager who is accountable for both revenue generation and expense control is responsible for a profit center. The manager is expected to make operating decisions with a view to the profit budget for the business segment and not solely with a view to either revenues or expenses. The Dallas regional office may be considered a profit center; Gonzalez is responsible both for the sales volume generated and the selling expenses incurred within the region. Her performance can be judged in terms of the profitability of the Dallas region. If the region is very successful in generating sales but at the sacrifice of very high selling expenses, profit from the region will be below budget and the manager's performance must be judged accordingly. If the region is frugal and incurs expenses 10% below budgeted level, the manager's performance cannot be applauded if this frugality leads to sales falling substantially below budgeted levels.

INVESTMENT CENTER

A manager who has authority for committing the investment resources of the enteprise along with responsibility for both revenues generated and expenses incurred is said to manage an investment center. Autonomous divisions of large companies are primary examples of investment centers; the division manager is held accountable for both the assets at his or her command and the profits generated by those assets. Gonzalez is not operating an investment center, nor presumably is her superior, the national sales manager; the division manager to whom the national sales manager reports, however, is in charge of an investment center. The financial performance of that division can be evaluated in terms of return on assets, or a similar measure of the effectiveness with which the division's assets are being utilized. It is not enough that the division manager control expenditures to budget or even that the profit target for the division be realized; it is also important that the profit be realized with a reasonable investment of resources. The successful division manager will focus both on the efficient management of assets and on profits.

Human Behavior Considerations

The budgeting process is ripe with human behavior complexities. Human motivations surround both the setting of budgets and the subsequent "living with" budgets. In our discussion of budgeting to this point, we have used many words that may elicit visceral reactions: commitment, responsibility, control, negotiate, performance evaluation. These are strong words, and they suggest personal interaction and possible confrontation. We are tempted to speak of an organization in impersonal terms: we speak of setting standards, exercising control, and altering direction. In fact, of course, an organization is not a machine that can be controlled or changed as one might a television set; it is neither more nor less than a collection of individuals, some of whom are designated as managers. Control is exercised by managers with respect to other employees, and if the organization is to change direction or correct problems, then individuals have to take action.

A popular tenet among students of human behavior is that people take action, in their professional lives as in their personal lives, only because they are motivated to do so. That motivation is derived from a desire to satisfy a need of some type, and each of us has a set of needs that we strive to satisfy. Budgets and budgeting create very personal needs. Some of the actions to which individuals are motivated in order to satisfy their needs may be beneficial to the organization, and others may be detrimental. Human behaviorists suggest that, whatever needs are created for the managers, the managers will inevitably take action that they believe will help fulfill those needs.

If the needs of an individual manager are closely aligned with the needs of the organization as a whole, then that manager's actions will be beneficial to the organization's goals. Conversely, if the needs of the individual deviate from those of the organization, the actions towards which the manager is motivated will not be in the best interests of the organization. When the manager's and the organization's needs are well aligned, the manager's goals are said to be congruent with those of the organization. Obviously **goal congruency** is a desirable condition, although absolute and complete goal congruency is an ideal that can seldom be achieved.

What types of actions will the manager be motivated to take because of the existence of budgets? The manager is expected to participate in the setting of the budgets, yet the manager's subsequent performance will be judged in part by reference to the budgets. The manager of the cost center will be evaluated in terms of his or her control of expenses, the manager of the profit center in terms of profits earned, and the manager of the investment center in terms of return on investment. Motivations will depend very much on the way in which top management views both budgets and performance analysis.

Suppose that top management decides to use budgets in a threatening manner, indicating implicitly or explicitly that if managers fail to meet budget (expense, profit, or return on investment), they will be disciplined and perhaps lose their jobs. Note that this attitude on the part of top management implies a quite pessimistic view of middle management. In essence, top management is saying, "Since middle managers are not really interested in doing a good job and are both somewhat incompetent and lazy, they can't be trusted to make decisions in the best interests of the company; therefore, we will impose tight budgets and coerce the managers into meeting budgets." Middle-level managers in such an environment will be motivated to take those actions necessary to avoid discipline and retain their jobs.

As budgets are established, the middle-level manager will be motivated to "sandbag" higher levels of management—to attempt to negotiate a budget that will be easily met. The manager of a profit center who thinks that a profit of $1,500,000 can be realized in the coming year will be motivated to negotiate for a budgeted profit of perhaps $1,300,000 or $1,400,000. In turn, the manager's superior will suspect sandbagging and will react by pressing for a profit budget of greater than $1,500,000. While some negotiation between two levels of management regarding budgets is both inevitable and healthy, carried to an extreme it can lead to much loss of time, poor communication, mutual suspicion, and a budget that may not be realistic.

Assuming that top management continues to view budgets as a tool to threaten or coerce management, what motivations will the middle-level manager have while attempting to live with the budget? Financial reports, particularly those that compare actual results with the budget, will be viewed as tools for top management, not as aids to help middle managers do a better job of managing. The accounting department may be viewed as a spying operation for top management, reporting financial figures that permit top management to coerce, dominate, and discipline. Middle-level managers will seek to take actions that will cause their operations to appear to fit the budget, in order to show minimum variance between budget and actual results. These actions may or may not be in the best interests of the operation and the company as a whole. The middle manager may be tempted to charge certain expenses to the wrong account, to defer certain discretionary expenses such as maintenance or training, to shift expenses to another profit center, or to speed up the recognition of income. All these actions will improve the *appearance* of the profit center's financial results without changing at all the fundamental economic position of the company. These actions represent a degree of dishonesty and moreover are simply wasted motion—the company as a whole and over the long run is not better off for them. If threatened sufficiently, however, most people will go to great lengths to "doctor up" financial results.

Alternatively, suppose that top management views budgets and internal financial reports primarily as tools to aid managers at all levels in doing a better job of managing their particular operations. Under this view, top management must believe that all levels of management are motivated to do a good job and will respond positively when presented with information that suggests corrective action. They must believe that managers are both competent and willing to work hard. This set of assumptions and view of the needs and motivations of middle-level management is a good deal more optimistic than the earlier set. Top management now does not believe that coercion must be used to cause managers to take actions that are in the best interests of the company. Rather, the assumption is made that the goals of the organization and the goals of the individual are sufficiently congruent that middle-level managers will, by seeking to satisfy their personal needs, take actions that will also satisfy the organization's needs.

Middle-level managers in this more optimistic and supportive environment will be more willing to communicate thoroughly and openly the problems and opportunities facing the operation, as budget levels are negotiated for the coming year; they will be confident that realistic budgets are sought by top management. With the threat of discipline greatly lessened, managers will be willing to take actions that are in the long-run best interests of the company, even if these actions will tend to impair the immediate financial results of their operations. They will welcome accurate financial reports from the accounting department, particularly those that compare budget and actual, because such reports help the managers to make better decisions. They will be confident that higher levels of management are willing to hear reasons why variances occurred and will be supportive of actions that may reflect negatively on the profit center's financial results but positively on the future of the overall company. The possibility that budget levels were inappropriate or that accounting data may be inaccurate is acknowledged. All of this communication takes place in an atmosphere free of threats or suspicion; the assumption is made that middle-level managers want to do a good job, are trying to do a good job, and will be assisted in these efforts by senior management.

In summary, then, budgets can be used by top management as a "blunt club" to force middle managers to take action, the motivation being the avoidance of discipline. On the other hand, budgets can be viewed as tools to assist managers in communicating with each other and in better running their operations, the motivation of the manager simply being the desire to do a good job.[1] Most middle-level managers prefer to operate in the second environment. There is good evidence that the budgeting pro-

---

[1] Students of human (or organizational) behavior will recognize that the first approach is consistent with the so-called theory X management style and the second with theory Y management style.

cess is much more efficient and useful when the management environment is supportive.

Recap: Reasons to Budget

Before we discuss the use of budgets in analyzing performance, it is useful to recap the primary benefits to be derived from a well-managed budgeting process, well-managed in terms both of setting budgets and of utilizing those budgets as working documents.

The single most important benefit of the budgeting process is to cause explicit planning. Operating plans have a tendency to be vague and somewhat indefinite until the financial implications of those plans are reduced to budgets. The Dallas regional manager may be inclined to talk about increasing the company's market share in Texas or utilizing more efficiently the sales force's travel time or making initial contact with 200 new customers. However, when Gonzalez turns to setting next year's budget for incoming orders and for selling expenses, she must become very explicit in planning: how many salespersons will be employed, how long will they be trained, who will make the contacts with new customers, how many cars will be leased and how many airplane trips will be taken, how much will telephone expense increase if the amount of travel is to be reduced, and so forth. This detailed and explicit planning has benefits far beyond simply setting budgets; Gonzalez needs to do this planning in order to make sensible staffing and other operating decisions.

This explicit planning is neither easy nor necessarily comfortable. Most of us do not enjoy budgeting because we do not enjoy detailed planning and the myriad small decisions that it requires. Moreover, once we commit plans to writing and numbers, we are less free to change our plans and we are increasingly accountable for the plans that we have made. Commitment and accountability are important parts of the budgeting process.

A second important benefit of budgeting is communication. Once plans are translated, to the extent possible, into monetary terms, these plans are more easily communicated. The Dallas regional manager communicates in part by budget, as well as orally and in writing, with the national sales manager. She also communicates with those persons working in the Dallas office; they understand the commitment that their supervisor has made to headquarters in terms of orders to be generated during the coming year and expense levels to be met. The Dallas regional budget also communicates to other groups within the company—the training department learns how much training support Dallas will need, the local advertising plans for the Texas market are communicated to the advertising department, and so forth.   Similarly, Gonzalez learns about plans in other departments of the company by referring to the budgets prepared by those departments.

Finally, budgets serve as a basis of comparison for actual results, permitting variance analysis and management by exception.   It is this third benefit of budgets that is most widely recognized and discussed, and the one to which we now turn.

Analyzing Performance: Budget versus Actual

Exhibit 13-1 shows an operating report that the manager of the Dallas regional office received early in August 19X4.   This report was prepared by

Exhibit 13-1
Operating Report: Actual versus Budget
Dallas Region
July 19X4
($000)

	July			Seven Months Year-to-Date		
	Budget	**Actual**	**Variance**	**Budget**	**Actual**	**Variance**
Sales	$1,250	$1,370	$120	$8,600	$8,450	($150)
Regional expenses						
Salaries	40.0	41.1	(1.1)	280.0	282.5	(2.5)
Sales commissions	25.0	27.4	(2.4)	172.0	169.0	3.0
Discounts and freight allowed[1]	5.0	5.4	(0.4)	34.4	33.5	0.9
Travel and entertainment	16.0	19.0	(3.0)	112.0	110.5	1.5
Telephone	4.0	3.8	0.2	28.0	29.0	(1.0)
Advertising	8.5	8.0	0.5	59.5	57.0	2.5
Rent and other occupancy	3.5	4.6	(1.1)	24.5	24.3	0.2
Sub-total	$102.0	$109.3	($7.3)	$710.4	$705.8	$4.6
Allocated Expenses						
Headquarters sales expense	20.0	20.5	(0.5)	140.0	142.5	(2.5)
National advertising	17.5	16.5	1.0	105.0	101.0	4.0
Trade shows	11.0	9.0	2.0	35.0	34.0	1.0
Sub-total	$48.5	$46.0	$2.5	$280.0	$277.5	$2.5

[1] Price allowances and allowances for freight expenses normally paid by customer

the home-office accounting staff and forwarded to the manager and to others in the organization, including the national sales manager. This report shows actual financial results for the month of July, as well as for the first seven months of the company's fiscal year, and compares those results to the budget for the corresponding periods.

The revenue section of this report indicates that the Dallas region was over-budget in shipments—a favorable condition—for the month, but continued to be under-budget for the year to date. Since the region was $120,000 over-budget for the month and $150,000 under-budget for the seven-month period, the region must have been $270,000 under-budget at the beginning of this month. July was a good month for sales.

In expenses, the region was over-budget for the month—an unfavorable condition—but under-budget for the seven-month period. The possibility that the over-budget condition in expenses was caused by the strong sales results for the month will be investigated shortly.

Note that the report contains two categories of expenses: regional expenses and allocated expenses. Gonzalez, the regional manager, is in charge of a responsibility center and is accountable for those expenses over which she has control. It is unreasonable to hold her accountable or responsible for expenses over which she exercises no control. Presumably she does control salaries, travel, telephone, and the other expenses within her particular region. On the other hand, she does not control the allocated expenses; she is not making the decisions with regard to the staffing at headquarters, the national advertising campaigns, or the trade-show schedule, and therefore she cannot be held responsible for any portion of these expenses, including the portion allocated to her region. It is the national sales manager or someone else in the organization, not the Dallas regional manager, who is responsible for these expenses. Thus, in judging the performance of the region in terms of expense control, attention should be focused on the regional expenses alone.

A number of expense categories have unfavorable variances for the month and favorable variances for the seven-month period. The reverse is true for telephone expenses. Both the monthly and year-to-date data are useful, since some variations in expenditure from month to month are inevitable. The under-budget condition for telephone expense in July might be explained by a number of salespersons being on vacation or it might be the result of improved management of telephone expenses. Similarly, rent and other occupancy expenses are very high for the month—almost 30% over budget. This condition may be explained by some major maintenance or repair expense that was incurred during the month. If the reason for the over-budget condition in July can be isolated, the Dallas regional manager can take comfort in the fact that the region is about on-budget for the seven-month period in occupancy expenses. The year-to-date data are very helpful in judging whether an over- or under-budget condition is persisting and whether a variance in a particular month is simply a random event.

Chapter 12 urged caution in the use of the terms *favorable* and *unfavorable* when referring to variances which increase and decrease profit. Note, for example, that the Dallas region was under-budget in advertising expense for July and for the seven-month period as well. Is this a favorable variance? It is favorable in the sense that the expense incurred was less than planned, but it may not be a favorable situation that the region is doing less advertising than originally planned. Could the reduced advertising level be contributing to the lower-than-anticipated sales volume for the year to date? Advertising is a discretionary expenditure, requiring management judgment. The precisely correct amount of advertising for the Texas market is difficult to ascertain. The Dallas regional manager can be commended if the planned advertising campaigns are being carried out at reduced cost; however, if the under-budget condition is achieved by reducing total advertising exposure, this may or may not be a favorable situation. Indeed, most selling expenses are discretionary in nature, and thus care must be exercised in interpreting these variances.

Consider Gonzalez's motivations. If she received great pressure (that is, if she is threatened or coerced) from the national sales manager to live within the expense budget each month, there is much that she could have done to avoid July's $7,300 over-budget situation. She might have reduced advertising, dismissed one salesperson, or foregone the repair of the facility. Each of these actions would have yielded short-term financial benefits —and reduced the threat of discipline—but they might not have been consistent with the long-term health of the company.

Parenthetically, note that the usefulness of the report shown in Exhibit 13-1 depends very much on the timeliness with which Gonzalez receives it. She is interested in seeing how her operation is performing relative to the plan to which she is committed; if the operation is off-plan she will be anxious to take corrective action. If she receives this report by, say, the tenth of August, she will still be able to recall the events of July that are reflected in monetary terms on the report. For example, she may recall why building maintenance and repairs were unusually large in July; when she receives the operating report for July, she is not surprised to see the rent and other occupancy variance, and decides that no corrective action is necessary. By contrast, she may be startled to see that travel expenses were well over-budget; not recalling any unusual circumstances that would have occasioned extra travel in July, she may want to take immediate corrective action. The longer the delay in obtaining financial feedback, the longer an out-of-control condition may persist and the more difficulty a manager will have in correlating the events of the accounting period with the financial report for the period. For these reasons, accounting departments should attach high priority to the timely reporting of budget-versus-actual information to operating managers.

Flexible Budgeting: Dealing with Fixed and Variable Expenses

Recall our discussion in earlier chapters of the need to separate fixed and variable costs. We recognized that product costs are composed both of costs which are unaffected by modest changes in volume of production and of costs which can be expected to vary directly with volume of production. Certain period expenses are similarly affected. It is necessary to recognize this condition when analyzing cost and expense variances.

Thus far in our discussion of budgeting, we have focused on setting budgets in absolute dollars for a subsequent accounting period. Exhibit 13-1 shows that the Dallas regional office budgeted $112,000 for travel expenses for the first seven months of 19X4 and $25,000 for sales commissions for July 19X4. But certain expenses will vary with volume of sales. Sales commissions are apparently paid at the rate of 2% of sales. Sales commission expense will always appear below-budget if sales revenue is below-budget, and over-budget, or unfavorable, if sales are above-budget.

It is tempting to argue that all expenses are variable with volume—salaries, travel expenses, and so forth. In reality, however, these expenses vary with some measure of sales *effort* but not directly with sales revenue realized. Salaries, travel expenses, and telephone expenses will vary as the Dallas region increases or decreases the amount of sales power in the region; this change in sales power may ultimately result in changes in sales revenue, but at best there will be a time lag between sales effort expended and sales realized and at worst there may be no relationship at all. Thus, these expenses vary with some discretionary decision made by management—for example, the number of salespersons in the field—but not with volume of sales. In the example illustrated in Exhibit 13-1 the only expense category besides sales commissions that varies with volume is discounts and freight allowed.

Exhibit 13-2 recasts the July operating budget of expenses for the Dallas region in order to separate variable and fixed expense elements. The exhibit also shows the percentage that each expense element is of budgeted sales volume for the month. For the purposes of budgeting, the key data for the variable expenses are the percentage figures; if sales for the month turn out to be different from $1,250,000, then sales commissions will be different from $25,000 but they should still be 2.0% of whatever sales turn out to be. On the other hand, the advertising budget of $8,500 for the month is independent of the volume of sales realized for the month; there is no rea-

Exhibit 13-2
Recast Expense Budget
Dallas Region
July 19X4

	July Budget	
	$000	%
Sales	$1,250	100%
Regional expenses		
Variable		
Sales commissions	$ 25.0	2.0%
Discounts and freight allowed	5.0	0.4%
	30.0	2.4%
Fixed		
Salaries	$ 40.0	3.2%
Travel and entertainment	16.0	1.3
Telephone	4.0	0.3
Advertising	8.5	0.7
Rent and other occupancy	3.5	0.3
	$ 72.0	5.8%
Total	$102.0	8.2%

son that advertising expenditures should be different from plan as a result of sales revenue being different from plan. Thus, the percentage figures in Exhibit 13-2 relating the fixed expenses to budgeted sales may be interesting, but they are not really germane to the budgeting process. The budget for fixed expenses should be stated in absolute dollar amounts.

The monthly budget, comprising both variable and fixed expenses, is best stated as a **flexible budget**—variable expenses in terms of percentages and fixed expenses in absolute dollar amounts.[2] The flexible budget for the Dallas region, according to Exhibit 13-2, is:

Budget = 2.4% of sales + $72,000

Volume-Adjusted Budgets

This flexible budget allows us to construct for the Dallas region what we shall call a **volume-adjusted budget,** giving effect to the impact that changes in sales volume have on budgeted expenses. The comparison of

[2] Note the similarity between flexible budgets of operating expenses and the IPC budget equation discussed in Appendix B of Chapter 12.

actual results for July (and the year to date) to the volume-adjusted budget will give us the most useful information for analyzing performance of the Dallas region. This same procedure was used to construct Exhibit 12-4 in the previous chapter.

Exhibit 13-3 is a reconstruction of Exhibit 13-1, comparing actual results to volume-adjusted budgets. A comparison of Exhibits 13-1 and 13-3 reveals that:

1 For the month, sales commissions are just equal to the volume-adjusted budget, although Exhibit 13-1 indicated they were $2,400 over budget. The over-budget condition in Exhibit 13-1 was fully explainable by the fact that actual sales exceeded budgeted sales.

2 Discounts and freight allowed were closer to plan for both the month and year to date than revealed in Exhibit 13-1. Exhibit 13-1 indicated a $400 unfavorable variance for July, but on a volume-adjusted basis this variance changes to $100 favorable.

Exhibit 13-3
Operating Report: Actual versus Volume-Adjusted Budget
Dallas Region, July 19X4
($000)

	July			Seven Months Year-to-Date		
	Volume-Adjusted Budget	Actual	Variance	Volume-Adjusted Budget	Actual	Variance
Sales	$1,370	$1,370	—	$8,450	$8,450	—
Regional expenses						
Variable						
Sales commissions (2.0%)	$ 27.4	$ 27.4	—	$169.0	$169.0	—
Discounts and freight allowed (0.4%)	5.5	5.4	0.1	33.8	33.5	0.3
	$ 32.9	$ 32.8	$0.1	$202.8	$202.5	$0.3
Fixed						
Salaries	$ 40.0	$ 41.1	($1.1)	$280.0	$282.5	($2.5)
Travel and entertainment	16.0	19.0	(3.0)	112.0	110.5	1.5
Telephone	4.0	3.8	0.2	28.0	29.0	(1.0)
Advertising	8.5	8.0	0.5	59.5	57.0	2.5
Rent and other occupancy	3.5	4.6	(1.1)	24.5	24.3	0.2
	$ 72.0	$ 76.5	($4.5)	$504.0	$503.3	$0.7
Total	$104.9	$109.3	($4.4)	$706.8	$705.8	$1.0

3 Overall for the month, regional expenses were $4,400 over the volume-adjusted budget—much closer to plan than indicated by the $7,300 unfavorable variance shown in Exhibit 13-1.
4 On the other hand, the $4,600 under-budget condition in total expenses year to date as shown in Exhibit 13-1 was misleading. The bulk of this under-budget condition was the result of lower than expected sales volumes. As compared to the volume-adjusted budget for the year to date, actual expenses have only been $1,000 under-budget.

A strong argument is made throughout this book for clearly identifying and separating variable and fixed costs. Such a separation is paramount to an accurate assessment of performance for virtually any enterprise, profit-seeking or nonprofit. The procedure for developing and utilizing a volume-adjusted budget is further emphasized by the following example.

Example: A Social or Residence Club

Suppose you are the president of a social or residence club on a university campus—for example, a sorority or a fraternity. The club employs a finance manager, but you are ultimately responsible for controlling the operations of the club and overseeing its financial well-being. You receive monthly financial statements from the finance manager. Moreover, since you are a competent and progressive manager, you have worked out, in cooperation with the finance manager, the social chairperson, the manager of the dining room, and others, a detailed month-by-month budget for your club. The finance manager prepares statements comparing each month's financial results with the corresponding monthly budget. Statements for two months are shown in Exhibit 13-4.

Exhibit 13-4 seems to be giving you, as president, conflicting messages. In October the club developed a $220 surplus, when break-even operations were budgeted, but control of expenses appeared to be poor, as the expense budget was overspent by $400. You can see that revenue was well ahead of budget, but of key concern to you is whether the management of the club is doing a good job of controlling costs—is the club operating in accordance with the plan that you worked out with your management team?

The November report in Exhibit 13-4 seems to be offering more conflicting evidence: the club incurred a deficit, but expenses were held to a level $200 below budget. Again, are expenses being well controlled in November?

The key is that in October, revenue—presumably a function of membership—was well above budget, while in November it was below budget. If each member is charged $150 per month, the club must have included 44

Exhibit 13-4
CAMPUS RESIDENCE CLUB
Operating Report: Actual versus Budget
October and November, 19X9

| | October | | | November | | |
	Budget	Actual	Variance	Budget	Actual	Variance
Revenue						
Revenue from members	$6,000	$6,600	$600	$6,000	$5,700	($300)
Other revenue	400	420	20	400	420	20
Total	$6,400	$7,020	$620	$6,400	$6,120	($280)
Expenses						
Food	$3,000	$3,200	($200)	$3,000	$2,800	$200
Wages and salaries	1,100	1,150	(50)	1,100	1,100	0
Supplies	600	650	(50)	600	650	(50)
Utilities	500	500	0	500	500	0
Occupancy	1,200	1,300	(100)	1,200	1,150	50
Total	6,400	$6,800	($400)	$6,400	$6,200	$200
Surplus (Deficit)	0	$ 220	$220	0	($80)	($80)

members in October (44 times $150 equals the $6,600 revenue from members) in contrast to the 40 planned (40 times $150 equals the budgeted $6,000 revenue) and only 38 members in November (38 times $150 equals $5,700). It is obvious that certain of the expenses will vary directly with number of members (and therefore with revenue from members). But these data still do not answer your (the president's) key question: Is the management of this club doing a good job of controlling expenses? A clear separation of variable and fixed expenses—those expenses that vary with number of members separated from those expenses that are independent of the number of members in the club—is needed to develop a more useful management control report.

Assume that food is a fully variable expense—the more members the club has, the more it must spend for food. On the other hand, assume that the number of persons employed is constant, as are the club's obligations to pay rent; utilities probably vary slightly with the number of members who are living in the house, taking showers and turning on lights, but the major portion of the utility expense is associated with operating the kitchen and heating the space. Thus, assume that wages and salaries, utilities, and occupancy are fixed. Supplies are probably semivariable; certain supplies, such as those used in the kitchen, are independent of the number of members, while other supplies, such as linen, soap, and toilet paper, vary directly with membership. The supplies expense might be divided into fixed and variable components—say, $200 per month fixed plus $10 per member per month. Because the budget shown in Exhibit 13-4 was predicated on membership of 40, supplies expense was budgeted at $600 per month: $200 fixed plus $400 variable (40 times $10). These assumptions

Exhibit 13-5

CAMPUS RESIDENCE CLUB

Operating Report: Actual versus Volume-Adjusted Budget
October and November 19X9

	Data for Volume-Adjusted Budget	October			November		
		Volume-Adjusted Budget[1]	Actual	Variance	Volume-Adjusted Budget[2]	Actual	Variance
Revenue							
Revenue from members	$ 150/member/mo.	$6,600	$6,600	0	$5,700	$5,700	0
Other revenue	$ 400/mo.	400	420	$ 20	400	420	$ 20
		$7,000	$7,020	$ 20	$6,100	$6,120	$ 20
Expenses							
Food	$ 75/member/mo.	$3,300	$3,200	$100	$2,850	$2,800	$ 50
Supplies	$ 10/member/mo. plus $200/mo.	640	650	(10)	580	650	(70)
Wages and salaries	$1,100/mo.	1,100	1,150	(50)	1,100	1,100	0
Utilities	$ 500/mo.	500	500	0	500	500	0
Occupancy	$1,200/mo.	1,200	1,300	(100)	1,200	1,150	50
		$6,740	$6,800	($60)	$6,230	$6,200	$ 30
Surplus (Deficit)		$ 260	$ 220	($40)	($130)	($80)	$ 50

[1] 44 members
[2] 38 members

and data are sufficient to develop a volume-adjusted budget for each of October and November.

In Exhibit 13-5 actual financial results for October and November are compared to budgets which have been adjusted to reflect the actual number of members in the club. Operations were in fact close to volume-adjusted budgets for both months. Given the composition of fixed and variable costs and the fact that membership exceeded expectations in October, the club should have generated a $260 surplus for the month; this figure appears at the bottom of the volume-adjusted budget column for October. In fact, the surplus was only $220, because the $60 unfavorable expense variance was only partly compensated by the favorable variance in other revenue. Similarly, given the expense structure of the club and the fact that membership in November fell below expectations, the club should have generated a $130 deficit that month; because of good expense control ($30 favorable variance) and a favorable variance in other revenue, the realized deficit was only $80.

You, as president of the club, might reasonably conclude that expenses are under quite good control. The club's problem appears to be much more one of variation in membership than control of expenses. Looking at the individual expense categories, you might conclude that the food operation is under particularly good control—actual expenditures were below the volume-adjusted budget level for both months. However, you also need to consider the degree of member satisfaction with the quality, quantity, and variety of the food served. Supplies, on the other hand, may deserve some additional attention, as the club has been over-budget both months. The other expense categories appear to be in good control; the variation, for example, in the Occupancy account from month to month is not unusual and you may want to ask the financial manager for year-to-date data to ascertain whether this expense category is under control.

Note that the flexible budgeting procedure can also help the club in establishing its membership fees or dues. If the club can anticipate total membership in excess of 40, it should be able to reduce its fees from the present $150-per-month level, assuming that the financial objective of the club is to generate neither a surplus nor a deficit. On the other hand, if membership will persist at the November level of 38, the club will have to increase membership dues as the total fixed expenses of the club will have to be spread over fewer members.

Other Types of Budgets

We have focused on operating budgets as established for individual months and for the accounting year. Operating budgets are analogous to income statements, the budget being prospective and the financial statement being historical. Just as other financial reports besides the income statement were discussed in the financial accounting section of this book, several other types of budgets should be mentioned briefly here.

LONG-TERM BUDGETS

While our discussion has centered on budgets for one year and portions of a year, most companies also devote much attention to longer-term operating budgets. As part of the annual budgeting procedure, managements often develop budgets for each of the next three or five years, although typically in less detail than the budget for the next year. Budgeting for only one year, without considering the longer-term financial consequences of the operating decisions to be made during the year, can be a dangerous proposition. A five-year budget can guard against this danger by causing management to think explicitly about the longer term. This exercise may reveal the need for additional facilities that have a long construction lead time, or for additional equity or debt capital that may or may not be obtainable, or for a substantial increase in the sales force, or for the introduction of new products to replace those nearing the end of their life cycles.

Of course, a budget established now for a period beginning four years hence will be tentative at best. The budget will be revised four more times, however, as the company proceeds through the intervening four annual budgeting processes.

PRO FORMA BALANCE SHEETS

An operating budget is a **pro forma** (estimated in advance) **financial statement.** Pro forma, or estimated, balance sheets can also be vital to the financial management of the company. Most companies will develop pro forma balance sheet statements as of various dates in the future, particularly at the end of the year and perhaps at critical dates during the coming year. These pro forma balance sheets will permit management to consider the need for increases or decreases in inventory, accounts receivable, accounts payable, and other working capital items; to judge whether the liquidity of the company will be adequate at these future dates; and to decide if the company will have to undertake additional short-term borrowing or can perhaps repay existing loans. The ability of the company to finance its projected operations will be revealed by pro forma balance sheets.

CASH BUDGETS

Operating budgets, being analogous to income statements, are prepared on an accrual basis. Yet every operation needs to keep a careful watch on the inflows and outflows of cash to (1) protect, on the one hand, against cash insolvency and (2) anticipate, on the other hand, cash surpluses that might be profitably invested. A cash budget is primarily a translation of the operating budget from an accrual basis to a cash basis of accounting (see Chapter 3 for a discussion of cash-basis accounting.) A seasonal business —for example, a toy manufacturer—must pay particular attention to the cash budget, as the inflows and outflows of cash throughout the year are very irregular, with most of the cash outflow occurring before and during the busy season and most of the inflows occurring at the end of or following the season. Remember that an operation can appear to be very profitable but still fail because it ran out of cash.

CAPITAL BUDGETS

The capital budget focuses on the longer-term need for and generation of investment capital. Typically, capital budgets need to be developed for several years, probably five and in some cases ten, in order to provide plenty of advance warning to management of capital shortages or excesses. Both the raising of additional capital and the judicious deployment of extra resources require considerable time and planning, and once commitments are made they cannot easily be changed. The capital budget will take into account not only the forecasted operating results for the company but also the many other decisions that do not immediately have impact on profit and loss: for example, the investment in or disposition of plant and equipment, the build-up or reduction in working capital as the volume of activity of the operation grows or shrinks, the payment of dividends and the scheduled repayment of borrowings, and anticipated changes in the capital structure of the operation.

Summary

Budgets are an integral part of the planning process, providing a road map in financial terms. They facilitate the process of managing by exception.

Key guidelines for the process of establishing and using budgets are:

1 The setting of objectives, generally both quantitative and qualitative, must precede the establishment of budgets.
2 Budgeting is only one element of planning. Much important planning cannot be translated into monetary terms. Planning, including budgeting, is typically an iterative process; successive revisions are undertaken until the plans and budgets are mutually consistent and are compatible with both the objectives and resources of the organization.

3 Budgets for an operation should be built from the bottom up—that is, from segment budgets—and not imposed from the top down.
4 While the setting of revenue and expense budgets must go hand-in-hand, typically the cornerstone of the process is the sales or revenue forecast.
5 Historical accounting data provide a basis for budgets. Nevertheless, managers should question the appropriateness of past expenditure levels, rather than simply setting budgets by incrementing past actual expenses.
6 The budgeting process involves negotiation between levels of management. The important end results of this negotiation should be commitment on the part of both managers.

The budgeting process is organized by responsibility center. Typically, as a manager ascends the management hierarchy, he or she takes on broader responsibility centers—from cost centers to profit centers and finally, at the division manager level, to investment centers.

The establishment and use of budgets is replete with human behavior considerations. Enlightened and supportive managements will view budgets, and subsequent reporting of operating performance, as tools to permit managers at all levels to do a better job of managing, rather than as devices to permit top management to coerce, control, and discipline lower-level managers.

The three primary reasons to budget are (1) to cause explicit planning, (2) to communicate plans, and (3) to provide a basis for comparing actual and planned results.

As managers compare "budget versus actual," they need to be aware that certain expenses vary with volume and others are fixed. Flexible budgeting provides for variable costs to be budgeted as percentages of revenue and fixed costs to be budgeted at absolute levels. Actual results are then appropriately compared to volume-adjusted budget data.

In addition to near-term operating budgets, several other types of budgets are useful planning documents for management: (1) operating budgets covering longer periods, say three to five years, (2) pro forma (or estimated in the future) balance sheets, (3) cash budgets that focus on the flow of cash rather than the flow of profit, and (4) capital budgets.

New Terms

Budget A description in monetary terms of the plans of an organization.
Cost center A responsibility center whose manager is accountable solely for the control of expenses and not for revenues or investments.

Flexible budget   A form of budget wherein variable expenses are stated in terms of their variation with volume (e.g., as percentages of revenue) and fixed expenses are stated in absolute dollar terms.

Goal congruency   The alignment of the goals (objectives) of the individual manager with those of the overall organization.

Investment center   A responsibility center whose manager is accountable for investment in assets as well as for profit (revenues and expenses).

Managerial accounting   The use of accounting data to assist management in making operating decisions.

Pro forma financial statements   Financial statements that are projected, or estimated in advance.   An operating budget is a pro forma income statement.

Profit center   A responsibility center whose manager is accountable for both revenues and expenses, and therefore profit, but not for investments.

Responsibility center   A segment of a business or other organization for which a single manager can be held accountable.

Volume-adjusted budget   A budget that has been revised to reflect actual volume of activity during the accounting period.   Volume-adjusted budgets are particularly useful when both fixed and variable cost elements are present.

Zero-base budgeting   A budgeting technique that requires justification for each dollar spent, rather than simply justification for increases or decreases of expenditures from the previous period.

Problems

1   Why is budgeting generally an iterative process, requiring several rounds of rebudgeting?

2   Explain the meaning of top-down budgeting.   Under what conditions might bottom-up forecasting be impractical or inappropriate?

3   Explain zero-base budgeting.

4   If you were designing the budgeting and financial reporting system for a university, determine which of the following segments or units you would classify as investment, profit, and cost centers:
  a   The math department
  b   The building maintenance group
  c   The student union
  d   The student-assistance department within the student union
  e   The university-owned bookstore
  f   The campus security force (police)
  g   The student-run organization that presents classic films at reduced fees
  h   The ticket office, selling tickets to both on-campus and off-campus cultural and theatrical events.

5   If you were designing the budgeting and financial reporting system for a large chain of hotels, determine which of the following segments or units you would classify as investment, profit and cost centers:
  a   The Pacific Coast operations, consisting of six hotels managed by a vice president

   b The hotel located in North Hempstead, California

   c The marketing department, headed by a marketing manager reporting to the Pacific Coast operations vice president

   d The centralized purchasing department, headed by a manager reporting to the Pacific Coast operations vice president

   e The Olde English Tavern (restaurant and lounge) at the North Hempstead hotel

   f The sports facilities department that oversees the swimming pool and tennis courts at the North Hempstead hotel

   g The gift shop in the North Hempstead hotel

   h The maid and janitorial department at the North Hempstead hotel.

6 Explain the meaning of the term *goal congruence* as it relates to budgeting.

7 What are the three primary reasons for budgeting?

8 Discuss situations in which each of the following managers might respond to budgetary pressures in a dysfunctional manner (i.e., a manner that is inconsistent with the broad financial and other goals of the organization):

   a The manager in charge of the vehicle pool (cars and trucks) at an electric power utility

   b The engineering department manager whose engineering staff is working concurrently on several important projects, each of which has been carefully budgeted

   c The manager of the state unemployment office in a particular town

   d The manager of the kitchen in a community hospital

   e The manager of the Des Moines branch sales office of a manufacturer of office machines.

9 A certain retail store typically earns a 34% gross margin on the merchandise it sells. The store's rental agreement provides for the store to pay as rent 3% of revenue, but not less than $1,500 per month. The store pays each retail sales clerk a base salary plus a commission of 1% of the clerk's sales. The budget for the store for a normal month is sales of $50,000 and operating profit (after all expenses except income taxes) of $3,000.

   a During the busy season, what operating profit should the store anticipate during a month when sales are $65,000?

   b During the slow season, to what level could sales fall before the store began to incur an operating loss?

   c In the month of October, when sales were $55,000, the gross margin of the store was $17,800 and operating profit was $4,100. What comments would you make to the store's manager about operations and cost control?

10 The O'Keefe Company utilizes flexible budgeting for its manufacturing operation. The budget for the production control department is described by:

> Monthly Budget $= 35,000 + (DL_1 - DL_n) \, 0.130$
> where: DL_1 is actual direct labor cost for the month and
> DL_n is normal direct labor cost for the month

   a What is the departmental budget during a normal month?

   b Assuming normal monthly direct labor cost is $157,000, reconstruct this flexible budget in the more traditional format: Budget = FC + vX, where X is actual direct labor cost for the month.

c By what percentage will the production control department manager be expected to reduce expenditures in a slow month when direct labor costs are reduced by 10% from the normal level?

d By subcontracting certain data processing services, the production control department manager would substitute a variable cost for the $4,400 per month fixed data processing costs at present. This change would not affect the total department budget for a normal month and normal monthly direct labor cost is $157,000. How would it affect the flexible budget formula? Under what conditions might it be wise to subcontract these data processing services?

11 Given the following operating data for six months for a fast-foods restaurant, develop a flexible budget for the restaurant. The restaurant employs a manager and several permanent staff whose monthly salary and wages total about $10,500; it also employs a large part-time staff, whose hours of work are increased and reduced as business fluctuates seasonally. (Dollar amounts in thousands.)

	March	**April**	**May**	**June**	**July**	**August**
Sales	$65.0	$67.3	$71.6	$74.3	$69.9	$68.0
Expenses						
Food	28.3	29.3	31.0	32.4	30.4	29.6
Labor	23.5	24.0	24.8	25.4	24.5	24.1
Occupancy	6.7	6.7	6.7	6.7	6.7	6.7
Supplies	7.2	7.4	7.6	7.7	7.5	7.4
Total expenses	65.7	67.4	70.1	72.2	69.1	67.8
Operating profit (loss)	($0.7)	($0.1)	$1.5	$2.1	$0.8	$ 0.2

12 Refer to problem 11. As schools reconvene in September, the restaurant manager anticipates a substantial increase in business and is hopeful of generating enough volume to earn a $3,000 operating profit for the month. What level of sales would the restaurant have to achieve in order to earn the manager's targeted profit?

13 The reported selling expense variance for June 19X1 at the Hazeltine Company was $4,200 credit, measured against the fixed dollar budget (that is, the budget *un*adjusted for volume). When selling expenses were measured against the flexible budget, adjusted for volume, the variance was $1,200 debit.

a Was activity at Hazeltine in June above or below expected levels?

b If the flexible budget for selling expense for a month was:

Expenses = $48,000 + (.06) Sales

What was the difference between actual sales and expected sales in June?

c How would you evaluate the performance of the selling department at Hazeltine during June?

14 The Sunridge Shopping Center leases space to numerous small retailers under rental contracts providing for a fixed monthly rental plus a percentage of the retailers' total receipts (sales) for the month. The general manager of the center indicates that the costs of operating the center (maintenance, utilities, promotion, depreciation, property taxes, and so forth) are independent of the volume of trade and are budgeted at $123,000 per month. During November 19X3 operating profits were $2,000 above the fixed dollar budgeted profit (that is, profit unadjusted for volume fluctuations) and $3,000 below the profit projected by the flexible budget.

   a Explain what happened to the level of activity at the shopping center in November.

   b If the rental contracts provided for 2% of receipts as the variable portion of rent, what was the difference between actual and expected receipts for all the retailers in the center in November?

   c Were operating expenses for the Center over- or under-budget for the month, and by what percentage?

15 The Mattson Maintenance Company, a contract janitorial service, reported actual and variance results for July 19X2 as follows:

	July 19X2 Actual	Variance from Fixed Dollar Budget[1]
Revenue	$53,000	$2,000
Expenses		
Wages	$31,000	(1,100)
Salaries	6,200	100
Supplies	5,100	(300)
Transport	1,800	(100)
Depreciation	3,000	0
Miscellaneous	1,400	100
Total expenses	48,500	(1,300)
Operating profit	$ 4,500	$ 700

[1] Debit, or unfavorable, variances shown in parentheses.

Wages were expected to vary directly with revenue. Management salaries were generally fixed, except that included in salaries was a bonus for the general manager equal to 1% of revenue. The general manager believed that janitorial supplies should be budgeted at 7% of revenue while the balance of supplies expense was fixed. The amount of transport expense depended, in part, upon the location of the particular jobs. Depreciation and miscellaneous expenses were fixed.

   a Construct a volume-adjusted budget for July 19X2.

   b How would you evaluate the general manager's operating performance in July?

16 The Franklin Corporation produces a standard line of large electrical equipment for power utility substations. The corporation's operating statement for 19X6 is:

	Year Ended September 30 19X6 ($000)
Sales	$45,630
Cost of goods sold	24,640
Gross margin	20,990
Operating expenses	
Selling	6,840
Development	2,970
Administrative	3,870
	13,680
Operating profit	7,310
Other income	110
Interest expense	1,150
Other nonoperating expenses	490
Profit before tax	5,780
Taxes on income	2,910
Net income	$ 2,870

Assume that Franklin's budget (in abbreviated form) for 19X6 (as developed in August 19X5) was:

	($000)	%
Sales	$43,500	100
Cost of goods sold		
Variable	17,400	40
Fixed	6,525	15
	23,925	55
Gross margin	19,575	45
Operating expenses		
Variable	2,175	5
Fixed	10,875	25
	13,050	30
Operating profit	$ 6,525	15

How well did the company control its expenses in 19X6? Explain.

17 Assume that you are the lending officer at a small bank. The controller of the Sanders Company, one of your customers, has just sent you the company's income statement for the year 19X5. You find in your files the company's budgeted (i.e., estimated) income statement for 19X5, which the controller sent to you about a year ago. Obviously, profits for Sanders turned out to be substantially below the estimate; however, 19X5 was a recession year, the company's sales were below the estimate, and therefore it is not surprising that profits are below the original estimate. You are concerned whether the profit decrease was caused by the sales decrease, or whether perhaps management has not done a satisfactory job of controlling costs.

	Estimate for 19X5	Actual for 19X5
Sales	$100,000	$85,500
Cost of goods sold	60,000	56,000
Gross margin	40,000	29,500
Selling expenses	15,000	14,000
General and administrative expenses	5,000	4,800
Income before taxes	$ 20,000	$10,700

In a telephone conversation with the controller of Sanders Company you gather the following additional information:

The company uses a full-absorption, actual cost accounting system.

The company sells all of its products through independent sales agents to whom it pays 10% commission on sales.

Because of poor economic conditions in 19X5, the company reduced prices by 5% on January 1, 19X5 and held these lower prices for the full year.

Inventories were approximately the same at the beginning and at the end of the year.

a Determine the effect on profit of:
  1 The price decrease
  2 Selling expenses
b Determine what portion of budgeted manufacturing and general and administrative expenses must be fixed if, in fact, the difference between the estimate and the actual expenditures for these cost elements is attributable solely to changes in physical volume.

18 A percentage analysis of the budget (operating plan) for the current year for Blodzett Corp. is:

Sales		100%
Costs of goods sold		
Variable costs	40%	
Fixed manufacturing overhead	15%	55%
Gross margin		45%
Selling expenses		
Variable	10%	
Fixed	10%	20%
General and administrative (all fixed)		15%
Operating profit		10%

At the beginning of the year, the company expected sales of 1 million units, total sales revenue of $3 million and, therefore, operating profit of $300,000. No variation in operations from season to season was anticipated.

At midyear, management of the company was pleasantly surprised to find actual operating results (below) at a rate substantially better than the budget:

Sales (580,000 units)	$1,700,000
Cost of goods sold	900,000
Gross margin	800,000
Selling expenses	350,000
General and administrative	275,000
Operating profit	$ 175,000

a Present a complete but *concise* analysis of the actual results to date and indicate the magnitude and nature of the variation from plan as well as possible reasons why profit is so much better than originally anticipated.

b Assume this is a period of very rapid inflation. What additional information regarding the accounting policies of the company would be helpful to you in your analysis? Be specific as to how this additional information would help you.

14

Cost Analysis for Operating Decisions

We conclude this book with a chapter on management's use of financial data in making certain operating decisions. This is not a new subject; we have been talking about managerial decisions throughout the book!

Chapter 9 discussed the many decisions that are influenced by analysis of the two primary products of the accounting system: the balance sheet and the income statement. Management's analysis of liquidity may lead to borrowing more money or repaying a portion of present indebtedness. A review of working capital may reveal that inventory is too high or too low, that customers should be pressed for speedier payments, or that more or less trade credit should be used. Capital-structure analysis indicates when more permanent capital should be raised, whether the company is making appropriate use of borrowed funds, and what the dividend policy of the company should be. And finally a review of profitability—expense categories in relation to sales, and profit in relation to investment—can lead to a whole host of operating decisions.

The chapters on cost accounting stressed management's use of cost reports to evaluate the efficiency of operations and to decide when and where corrective action should be taken. Information on the absolute and relative profitability of individual products and services provides a useful basis, although by no means the complete basis, for decisions regarding pricing, promotional emphasis, and product-line changes.

In addition to these important decisions, some of which have long-range implications for the company, management—and particularly middle management—is faced with a whole string of operating decisions, some of them day-to-day kinds of decisions, that collectively have much to do with the success and financial health of the operation. Accounting systems can be designed to yield data to assist operating managers in these day-to-day decisions. Parenthetically, note that not only must the data exist in the accounting system but they must also be disseminated in useful format to decision makers, who in turn must understand the relevance (and shortcomings) of the data.

Examples of Operating Decisions

The following are examples of prevalent operating decisions that will serve as the basis of our discussion in this chapter.

1 The production engineer is considering whether a particular part or subassembly should be fabricated by the company or subcontracted to a vendor—the classic make-or-buy decision. Important considerations are whether the company has the internal capability and capacity, or could acquire it, but the primary decision criterion is typically cost. The engineer can determine from the cost accounting department the standard cost factors for internal manufacture and can obtain price quotations from vendors, but is this the appropriate comparison?

2 The sales manager is considering whether to recommend acceptance of a particular large order from a nonregular customer. The price will be low, but at what price does the order become attractive business? Is there any argument for taking an order at a price that is below cost?

3 The financial analyst in the treasurer's department is analyzing the return on an investment proposal that calls for automating a production step. What are the true costs of the new and old methods?

4 The design engineer and the material manager are trying to determine when and if the redesign of a particular product should be introduced to the market. The decision is complicated by the existence of a good deal of raw and semifinished inventory that would be rendered obsolete by the new design.

5 The product-line manager in marketing is trying to evaluate the effect on sales and profit of varying the marketing inputs—price, promotional effort, product repackaging, change in incentive to the sales force, and so forth.

Many other types of operating decisions exist in contexts other than manufacturing. Service firms encounter pricing and product-line decisions, as well as make-or-buy decisions, and so do many nonprofit operations. Decisions regarding capital expenditures are prevalent throughout virtually all organizations. Interrelationships of volumes, prices, and costs permeate public activities and private, highly competitive companies and regulated ones, and service and manufacturing firms, both large and small.

Importance of Framing Alternatives

All of these operating decisions involve choices among alternatives: make-or-buy, accept or decline the special order, introduce the product or don't, accept or reject the capital equipment investment proposal, select among a spectrum of possible prices and promotional plans. Sometimes the decision is of the go–no go type, deciding either to take an action or not, and sometimes the decision is among a broad set of alternatives, one of which may be to do nothing.

The optimum decision can be reached only if the relevant alternatives are evaluated. If only suboptimal courses of action are considered, the decision will necessarily be suboptimal. One can hardly overemphasize the importance of properly framing the alternatives, taking particular care to include all relevant alternatives in the analysis. A common failing among decision makers is to consider only the obvious courses of action, without giving explicit consideration to other less-obvious but more beneficial options. Once a problem becomes framed as a choice between two mutually exclusive action alternatives, the tendency is to focus solely on that choice without considering the possibility of reframing the problem. Once the problem is reframed—generally in a broader context—other options may become apparent.

This admonition to consider all relevant alternatives before making a decision may seem so simple and obvious as to insult your intelligence. Poor problem definition is so prevalent, however, that a couple of examples, related to the operating decisions outlined above, may be useful to demonstrate the point.

1 The make-or-buy decision is typically viewed in its narrowest context: given the design of the part, in-house capabilities, and vendor quotations regarding price and specifications, should the work be subcontracted? Another alternative might be to improve, expand, or upgrade the in-house capabilities of the company, particularly if similar parts are used in other products, or if the redesign of other parts might use the new in-house capability. Still another alternative might be to redesign

the part to take particular advantage of a known vendor capability. Or perhaps the part could be combined with one or more other parts and subcontracted as a unit; or perhaps the search for vendors has been too restricted geographically, since the part's light weight makes air freight feasible.

2 The evaluation of automatic equipment may quickly narrow to a choice between the present method, at zero incremental investment, or the proposed method with high initial investment. Perhaps this decision should first be framed as a make-or-buy decision; that is, perhaps among the acceptable alternatives is subcontracting the operation so that no in-house method is used, present or proposed. Or perhaps a larger capital investment, involving equipment with broader capabilities, more versatility, or higher operating speeds, is an alternative worthy of complete evaluation.

3 The marketing manager, when considering the relative effect of price, promotion, and sales-force incentive, might consider entirely different methods of marketing: independent agents instead of a company sales force; direct-mail promotion instead of magazine-space advertising; "cents-off" coupons instead of price discounts to wholesalers.

Differential Cash Flows

Once all relevant alternatives have been framed, the decision maker must then focus on the differences in financial consequences among the alternatives. It is only the *differences* between alternatives that are relevant to the decision. Those conditions and financial flows that are unaffected by the particular decision may be ignored. All of the economic consequences of each possible course of action need not be defined, but only that subset that is affected by the choice.

For example, if the selling price and the volume of units sold is unaffected by the make-or-buy decision or the decision to redesign, total revenues, costs, and profits to be realized from the product need not be projected; only those cost elements that are affected by the decisions need to be considered.

If the present method of manufacture and the proposed automated method (necessitating a capital expenditure) both utilize the same amount of factory floor space and supervisory attention, these costs can be ignored. Attention should be concentrated on defining the differences in economic consequences that arise because the two methods utilize different amounts of power, direct labor, supplies, and so forth.

Moreover, those differences among the alternatives that have an impact on the *cash flow* of the operation are particularly relevant. Cash flow is the ultimate financial objective of the operation: it is cash flow that is used to repay borrowings, to pay dividends to shareholders, to support community and societal programs, and to pay salaries, wages, and bonuses to the staff.

Finally, the *timing* as well as the amount of those cash flows is critical; the inflow of a sum of cash today is preferred over the same inflow a year from now, since the cash can be used during the intervening year to make profitable investments, to repay borrowing, or to pay wages to owners and employees for them to spend or save. Money always has a time value to individuals, to profit-seeking companies, to nonprofit organizations, and to government units.

Important among the cash flows of a profit-making company are income taxes. To the extent that an operating decision affects taxable profits of the company, the cash flow is also affected. Thus, the decision to invest in new capital equipment will affect future depreciation expense for the company; depreciation expense itself is not a cash flow,[1] and thus need not be included in the analysis of alternatives, but the reduction in income taxes resulting from increased depreciation expense must be included. Scrapping (throwing away) inventory does not involve a cash flow, but because the book value of that scrapped inventory may be deducted from taxable income, the resulting cash savings in income taxes must be included in the analysis. Tax increases may also result; if a fixed asset is sold for an amount in excess of its book value, the difference will be taxable and the cash associated with this added tax must be considered in the decision. To repeat, it is the differences between alternatives in the timing and amount of cash flows that are the keys to operating decisions.[2]

Problems in Determining Differential Cash Flows

Accounting systems often do not report costs and expenses in a way that facilitates determining differential cash consequences of decisions. The problems arise for one or more of the following reasons:

---

[1] See discussion of tax shields in Chapter 7.

[2] This statement is probably a bit too global. Unusual situations may provide incentive for management to concentrate attention on parameters other than cash flow. For example, some management bonus plans are tied to current reported earnings (accrual, not cash-basis). The price paid by an acquiring company for the shares of an acquired company may be a multiple of current period profits. Other companies that operate in a regulated environment (e.g., utilities and certain government defense contractors) will respond to regulatory constraints or pressures, rather than to the immediate effects of their decisions on the timing and amount of cash flow; even here the long-term cash flow results are key, but these may be very difficult to evaluate.

1   Accounting systems are based upon the accrual concept of accounting, and yet many operating decisions would be better served by a cash-basis system. This statement is not meant to argue for abandoning accrual accounting; accrual-basis reports are more valuable for many purposes and particularly for those audiences external to the company. The statement does argue for maintaining records and issuing reports in ways that will facilitate the separation of cash and noncash expenses and revenues.

2   Some expenses—both product and period—vary with volume of activity, while others are fixed. If the operating decision being analyzed affects volume to a modest extent, variable costs will be affected and fixed costs will not.

3   Many expenses are allocated among products or segments of the business. For example, the IPC rate is used to prorate or allocate costs among products, and the operating reports for the Dallas region of the Reynolds Company discussed in Chapter 13 included allocations of corporate marketing expenses. These arbitrary allocations can lead to some faulty financial analyses.

Thus, frequently the decision maker cannot simply accept data from existing accounting reports and plug these data into the analysis. The five examples outlined at the beginning of the chapter will be used to illustrate the need to adjust accounting data in order to focus on differential cash flows.

THE MAKE-OR-BUY DECISION

The Arata Corporation is considering whether to produce part no. 4783 in its own shop or to subcontract the fabrication to Schreiber and Associates. Assume that other alternatives have been considered and eliminated and that quality, delivery, and other nonprice considerations are equivalent between the two alternatives. Schreiber has quoted $473 per hundred and the Arata analyst determines from cost accounting records that the standard full-absorption cost of in-house manufacture is $557 per hundred. The decision may seem obvious: subcontract.

Recall, however, that full-absorption costs include certain allocated indirect production costs (IPC). Will these costs be avoided if the part is subcontracted? Most will not be. If the decision is made to subcontract, part no. 4783 will no longer carry these allocations, but the costs will not evaporate. A reallocation of IPC will occur or negative IPC variances will result. What the analyst needs to know is the amount by which total IPC for the company will increase or decrease as a result of this decision.

Assume the detailed standard product costs for this part are:

Direct labor	$120 per hundred
Direct material	173 per hundred
Variable IPC	120 per hundred (100% of direct labor)
Fixed IPC	144 per hundred (120% of direct labor)
Total	$557 per hundred

The IPC vehicle here is obviously direct labor, and the total IPC rate is 220% of direct labor. What cash flows will be saved if Arata subcontracts? Assuming Schreiber supplies material as well as labor, these two product cost elements will be eliminated.[3]

The analysis of IPC savings is more difficult. Variable IPC includes those elements of overhead which vary with volume of production. If direct labor is eliminated by the decision to subcontract, it may be reasonable to assume that the associated variable IPC will also be saved. However, note that variablility is defined with respect to changes in total level of activity, not to changes in the mix of that activity. A decision to subcontract may increase the work of the purchasing and inventory control departments, but decrease the work of the factory supervisors and production control. Thus, even variable IPC costs may not be entirely differential with respect to this make-or-buy decision.

The analysis of the fixed IPC product costs is even more complex. Prominent among the fixed IPC cost elements are rent on the manufacturing space and depreciation of production equipment. If the factory and the equipment within it will remain unaffected by this decision—a reasonable assumption—then the portion of these costs that is allocated to part no. 4783 is irrelevant to the decision. It does not follow, however, that all fixed IPC costs are necessarily irrelevant. For example, if the shipping and receiving function is considered to be a part of fixed IPC, the decision to subcontract will increase fixed costs to the extent that the shipping and receiving function takes on added tasks. Any such difference in fixed costs should be considered.

Make-or-buy decisions are aided by a variable-cost system (or a full-absorption system that clearly separates fixed and variable IPC). The assumption that variable costs of manufacturing are differential to the make-or-buy decision, while fixed manufacturing costs are not, is typically a useful approximation, though not completely accurate. This approximation will almost surely be preferable either to ignoring all overhead in the analysis or to assuming that all IPC costs are differential. Applying the approximation to this example, the "make" alternative at $413 (total standard cost of $557 less the fixed IPC of $144) compares favorably with the "buy" alternative at $473. Part no. 4783 should be made in-house.

---

[3] Note that this statement assumes that Arata will shift the displaced direct-labor employees to other productive activities or will dismiss them; this assumption is typically valid, but labor contracts or government restrictions may sometimes eliminate even direct labor as a differential cash flow.

ACCEPT A LOW-PRICED ORDER?

The sales manager at Sedwick Company must decide whether to accept a particular order from a distant, foreign customer. The order is large, but the price is low. The customer is offering only $71,000 for merchandise that has a normal list price of $97,000. The sales manager learns from Sedwick's cost accounting group that the estimated standard manufacturing cost for this merchandise totals $75,000.

The marketing ramifications of this decision are numerous. Will Sedwick have trouble serving this foreign customer? If the order were not taken at this low price, might the customer return later and offer a higher price? Would Sedwick be setting a dangerous precedent for its other customers by accepting this low-priced business? In addition to all these important but noncash considerations (or, at least, nonimmediate-cash), the sales manager needs to know the present cash consequences before making a decision.

The decision seems to be framed simply: accept the order or decline it. This statement, however, is not a complete description of the possible alternatives. How busy is the company? If by accepting this order Sedwick commits its factory so that higher-priced orders from other customers would have to be declined, the consequences to the company are different than if, by accepting this order, Sedwick merely puts to use capacity which would otherwise remain idle. Of key importance to decisions of this type is the impact on the company's ability to serve other customers. Again, framing the alternatives is the important first step.[4]

Assume the following facts with respect to prices and costs:

Normal price	$97,000
Price offered	71,000
Standard manufacturing cost	
Direct labor	20,000
Direct material	25,000
Variable IPC	15,000
Fixed IPC	15,000
Total	$75,000

If Sedwick is operating below capacity and has no reasonable expectations of "selling" this added capacity, then the relevant alternatives are to take the order or do nothing. Under which alternative is the company better off? It is probable that direct labor, direct material, and variable IPC are incremental or differential to this decision. Since the sum of these three cost elements is $60,000 and the customer is offering to pay $71,000,

---

[4] In this case, the alternatives might be framed in terms of probability distributions, with probabilities assigned to the likelihood of utilizing the capacity in more profitable ways.

Sedwick is better off taking this order than not—better off by $11,000. If the labor force to be devoted to this job would, in the absence of the job, be standing idle, then even direct labor is not differential and a very compelling argument can be made for the acceptance of the order.

Assume on the other hand that, if this order is declined, Sedwick has a high probability of selling the merchandise at normal prices. Now the decision can be framed as the choice between two order opportunities. The decision is simple: decline the order since the normal-price order will cause Sedwick to be $37,000 better off ($97,000 price less $60,000 variable cost), while the foreign order will improve Sedwick's condition by only $11,000.

Note that the data on full-absorption product cost were not used. Would these data be relevant to the decision of whether to expand the capacity of the factory so that, for example, both the normal-price business and the foreign order could be accepted? No, the full-absorption costs are not differential to that decision either, because (1) they contain noncash expenses (primarily depreciation), (2) they involve arbitrary allocations, and (3) they do not allow for the immediate cash outflows to acquire the expanded facilities. For almost no operating decisions are full-absorption product costs differential.

A term that will be used throughout the balance of this chapter should be introduced at this point: **contribution.** The acceptance of this foreign, low-priced order *contributes* to Sedwick $11,000, the difference between the cash inflows and cash outflows brought about by the decision. The term *contribution* implies *contribution to fixed overhead and profit*. That is, the acceptance of this order will contribute to Sedwick $11,000 of cash that it otherwise would not have had.[5]

This type of contribution analysis is very useful in establishing bid prices during periods of slack activity. Under such conditions, accepting business at less than full cost may be essential to the survival of the operation. Exhibit 14-1 illustrates the dilemma created by blindly bidding as a mark-up of full costs. When times are lean and the company's business is slow, this bidding rule causes Skilling Construction to increase prices in a vain attempt to cover overhead, thus driving away more business. When the company is very busy and fixed overhead is spread over a larger volume of activity, total costs of construction are lower; the company then reduces its prices and more bids are won at exactly the time when the company will have difficulty handling the work. In fact, Skilling probably should be pricing just opposite to this decision rule: price lower when business is slack and raise prices when the company's capacity is being strained.

---

[5] The order will not provide $11,000 of reported profit to the company; in fact, the order itself will incur an accounting loss of $4,000 ($71,000 price less $75,000 standard manufacturing cost). The added activity (and absorption of overhead) will lead to a favorable IPC variance, but the cost accounting of the order itself will reveal a $4,000 loss.

Exhibit 14-1
"Bidding" by Marking-Up Full Costs
SKILLING CONSTRUCTION CO.

Basic Assumptions

Total estimated overhead for a period (assumed to be 100% fixed)	$180,000
Overhead applied as percentage of labor	
Bid Price = 120% of estimated total cost	
Job M: Estimated materials cost	$ 14,000
Estimated labor and direct supervision cost	$ 7,000

A.   Bid Price for Job M in Slow Period

Estimated total labor (all jobs) for period	$ 60,000
Overhead rate = ($180,000 ÷ 60,000)	$3 per direct labor $
Total cost of Job M:	
Material	14,000
Labor	7,000
Overhead ($3 × 7,000)	21,000
Total	$ 42,000
Bid Price of Job M = (120% or $42,000)	$ 50,400

B.   Bid Price for Job M in Busy Period

Estimated total labor (all jobs) for period	$ 90,000
Overhead rate = ($180,000 ÷ 90,000)	$2 per direct labor $
Total cost of Job M:	
Material	14,000
Labor	7,000
Overhead ($2 × 7,000)	14,000
Total	$ 35,000
Bid Price of Job M = (120% of $35,000)	$ 42,000

CAPITAL-INVESTMENT DECISIONS

Capital-investment decisions are prevalent throughout both the private and public sectors of the economy. Elegant procedures have been devised for evaluating such decisions; these are generally referred to as capital budgeting or engineering-economy techniques.[6] All of these procedures require that the analyst develop a complete outline of the cash inflows and outflows that will be occasioned by each investment alternative under study. Again, the emphasis is on the timing of and differences between cash flows.

Exhibit 14-2 presents the accounting data developed by the financial

---

[6] See for example: Grant, Ireson, and Leavenworth, *Engineering Economy,* 6th ed., Ronald Press Co., New York, 1976.

Exhibit 14-2
LIPINSKY MANUFACTURING CORP.
Proposal to Automate Operation R

Present cost of completing Operation R
Material	$ 2.00 per part
Labor	3.40
IPC (200% of labor)[1]	6.80
	$12.20 per part

Estimated cost of completing Operation R (after automation)
Material	$ 2.00 per part
Labor	1.40
IPC (200% of labor)[1]	2.80
	$ 6.20 per part

Investment to automate:
Equipment and installation	$600,000
Estimated life	6 years
Annual maintenance expense	$ 10,000
Estimated salvage value	0

Estimated annual volume	40,000 parts per year

[1] Assume one-half of total IPC is variable.

analyst at Lipinsky Manufacturing Corporation relating to a proposal to automate one step in the manufacturing process. Once again, these data require some reconstruction to isolate cash flow consequences, since they were developed on the accrual basis and include both noncash and allocated expenses. Note that the full cost of manufacture is $12.20 per part under the present method and $6.20 under the proposed method; the apparent savings is $6.00 per part. The investment required to automate is $600,000 for equipment with an estimated life of six years and estimated additional maintenance charges of $10,000 per year.

Exhibit 14-3, part A illustrates the type of analysis that might result from the uncritical use of the accounting data. This analysis assumes that IPC will be saved at a rate of 200% of direct-labor savings. It is probable that some of the variable IPC will indeed be saved, if much of the variable IPC is labor-related, including fringe benefits. It is equally probable that much of the fixed IPC that has been allocated to this operation R will continue to be incurred by Lipinsky even if the labor time required for Operation R is reduced; examples include rent, building maintenance, heat, and manufacturing management. Only savings that can truly be identified with this automation investment should be included in the cash flow.

The operating savings of $240,000 shown in the misleading analysis on Exhibit 14-3 have been overstated. Deducting depreciation on the new

Exhibit 14-3
LIPINSKY MANUFACTURING CORP.
Analysis of Proposal to Automate Operation R

A. *Analysis of Accounting Return*—Misleading

Operating Costs
Present (40,000 parts × $12.20) = $488,000
Proposed (40,000 parts × $6.20) = 248,000
Operating Savings $240,000
Less: Depreciation   (100,000)
       Maintenance   (10,000)
                                  $130,000

$$\text{Savings} \div \text{initial investment} = \frac{130{,}000}{600{,}000} = 21.7\%$$

$$\text{Savings} \div \text{average book value of investment} = \frac{130{,}000}{300{,}000} = 43.3\%$$

B. *Analysis of Cash Flows*—Required for Return on Investment Calculation

Annual Cash Flow	Present	Proposed	Difference
Material	$ 80,000	$ 80,000	0
Labor	136,000	56,000	80,000
Variable IPC	136,000	56,000	80,000
Annual maintenance	0	10,000	(10,000)
Net annual cash flow			$150,000
Initial (time-zero) cash flow		($600,000)	
Return on investment[1]		13.0%	

[1] Discounted cash flow or internal rate of return method.

equipment—$100,000 per year, assuming straight-line depreciation and zero salvage value—is also incorrect, since depreciation is a part of IPC; there is some double-counting here.

The misleading analysis indicates a ratio of annual savings to initial investment of 21.7%—a quite handsome accounting return. Indeed, the investment is still more attractive (43.3%) if the estimated annual savings is compared to the average book value of the investment—that is, the book value of the equipment at the end of three years when it is one-half depreciated.

The shortcomings of this analysis are several: (1) the operating savings associated with fixed IPC are illusory, since the decision to invest will not materially alter the company's fixed IPC expenditures; (2) the savings are reduced by the amount of depreciation expense, although the depreciation does not represent a cash outflow to Lipinsky; and (3) no recognition is given to the timing of the cash flows, the fact that the investment occurs at time zero while the returns are spread out over six years.

The second analysis in Exhibit 14-3 overcomes these deficiencies. Depreciation is ignored. The discounted cash flow or internal-rate-of-return technique[7] takes explicit account of the timing of the cash flows. The assumption is made that variable IPC will be saved in proportion to labor savings. (By no means is this assumption valid for all capital investments— each element of the IPC should be analyzed separately.) Apparent savings in allocated costs (fixed IPC) are omitted. The resulting return on investment is a much less attractive 13.0%.

Both of these analyses have still another shortcoming: the impact of income taxes has been ignored. Income taxes are very real cash costs and are affected both by the operating savings and by the depreciation expense which is deductible for tax purposes. Exhibit 14-4 extends the analysis of Exhibit 14-3 to derive an after-tax return on investment. Note that this exhibit assumes sum-of-the-years'-digits depreciation so as to accelerate the tax savings derived from depreciation.

The first part of Exhibit 14-4 is devoted simply to calculating the difference in income tax. The operating savings will add to taxable income, but

[7] A full description of these techniques is beyond the scope of this book. For an explanation of these techniques, see, for example, Chapter 8 of Grant, Ireson, and Leavenworth, op. cit.

Exhibit 14-4
LIPINSKY MANUFACTURING CORP.
Proposal to Automate Operation R: After-Tax Analysis

Calculation of Difference in Income Tax	Year						
	0	1	2	3	4	5	6
Operating savings (see Exh. 14-3, Part B)	—	150	150	150	150	150	150
Depreciation (SOYD)	—	171	143	114	86	57	29
Increase/(decrease) in taxable income	—	(21)	7	36	64	93	121
Increase/(decrease) in taxes (50% rate)		(10.5)	3.5	18	32	46.5	60.5
After-Tax Cash Flow							
Investment	(600)	—	—	—	—	—	—
Operating savings	—	150	150	150	150	150	150
Income taxes	—	10.5	(3.5)	(18)	(32)	(46.5)	(60.5)
Total cash flow	(600)	160.5	146.5	132.0	118.0	103.5	89.5

After-tax return on investment[1] = 7.5%

[1] Discounted cash flow or internal-rate-of-return method.

the depreciation will represent a shield against taxes; the difference between them will represent the net increase or decrease in taxable income. In the first year the depreciation is greater than the savings and thus Lipinsky receives both the benefit of the operating savings and a small income-tax benefit. In subsequent years the depreciation shield reduces. The second part of Exhibit 14-4 details year-by-year the amount and timing of the after-tax cash flows. These flows equate to an after-tax return on investment of 7.5%, a rate that would not be attractive to most companies. Thus, an investment proposal which at first seemed quite attractive becomes at best a marginal investment opportunity when a careful study is made of the net cash flows.

WHEN TO INTRODUCE A PRODUCT REDESIGN

The design engineer and material manager at Lipinsky Manufacturing are considering when they should introduce a product redesign. The marketing manager is pressuring for early introduction, but the production manager and controller are anxious to avoid having to scrap raw and semifinished goods inventory. Some facts relevant to this decision are outlined in Exhibit 14-5. The new model, designated Mark II, will be less expensive to manufacture but should enjoy the same reception and command the same price in the market as Mark I. Note that Exhibit 14-5 compares only the variable product costs, not the full-absorption costs.

Because of the design of Mark II, any raw or in-process material for Mark I that remains in inventory at the time of introduction will have to be scrapped. All of Lipinsky's management agrees that the new design should be introduced not later than six months from now, when all existing Mark I inventory has been exhausted, but the marketing manager is arguing for immediate introduction. The controller is asked to study the economic consequences of the decision.

The economic comparison shown in Exhibit 14-5 is inappropriate for making the decision, even though it correctly identifies the consequences to the company's income statements of the two alternatives. If introduction is delayed six months, all inventory will be used up, and therefore no inventory write-off will occur, but cost of goods sold will reflect the higher unit cost of Mark I. On the other hand, if introduction is immediate, the lower unit cost of Mark II will be reflected in the cost of goods sold for the full six months, but the inventory of Mark I materials, now carried on the balance sheet at a total of $140,000, will have to be written off.

The key consideration here is that inventory is carried at historical costs that cannot be affected by the decision to use or scrap the material. These are, in economists' terms, **sunk costs.** The inventory now on hand can be turned into finished units of Mark I for something less than total variable cost, as the inventory is a sunk cost. Therefore, the write-off does not

Exhibit 14-5
LIPINSKY MANUFACTURING CORP.
Introduction of Model Mark II

Facts	Mark I	Mark II
Variable cost of manufacture		
Direct material	$ 1.00	$ 1.40
Direct labor	2.00	1.30
Variable IPC	2.00	1.30
Total variable cost	$ 5.00	$ 4.00
Expected sales per month (units)	10,000	10,000
Inventory		
Raw (dollars)	$ 20,000	—
(units)	20,000	—
In-process (dollars)	$120,000	—
(units)	40,000	—

	Costs Throughout Next Six Months	
Erroneous Economic Comparison	**Introduction in 6 months**	**Immediate introduction**
Cost of goods sold: Mark I	$300,000	—
Mark II	—	$240,000
Write-off inventory: Raw	—	20,000
In-process	—	120,000
Total expenses	$300,000	$380,000

represent a cash flow, although it will affect the company's profit-and-loss statement.[8]

A more careful analysis of this decision recognizes that a third alternative may be attractive: introduce in four months, using up the in-process inventory and scrapping the raw material; it may be economic to convert the in-process material into finished Mark I units but uneconomic to convert the raw material into finished goods. Accepting the problem as first stated —introduce now or six months from now—without questioning whether other alternatives are viable may obscure the optimum decision.

A correct economic comparison requires more data than are available in Exhibit 14-5. What is needed is an analysis of the cash costs to the company of each of the three alternatives. Once again, variable product costs are more appropriate to the analysis than full-absorption costs. The cost to complete the in-process inventory will be less than the cost to complete the raw material inventory and both costs will be less than the $5.00 total variable cost of a Mark I unit.

[8] These sunk costs will be deductible for income taxes if the inventory is scrapped, resulting in a positive cash impact through a reduction in taxes.

Cash inflows can be ignored, as they are the same under all three alternatives. The analysis can be further limited to just those out-of-pocket (that is, future) cash costs for Lipinsky over the next six months; the comparison of costs beyond that period is unnecessary, as it is obvious that the lower-cost Mark II unit should by then be in production.

VARYING "MARKETING INPUTS"

The fifth example cited at the outset of this chapter involves the product-line manager's analysis of the effect that price, promotional effort, product redesign, and so forth may have on the sales volume and profit of the company. The product manager needs a clear understanding of the interrelationships of volume, price, costs, and profits. This understanding is fundamental to so many operating decisions that we shall devote the next section of the chapter to it. Operating managers can well use a simple model describing these relationships to assist them in analyzing a broad range of "what if" type of questions.

Interrelationship of Volume, Price, Cost, and Profit

Business is a complex financial system. Management decisions interact and opportunities for trade-offs exist. Changes in prices affect volume of sales and profits; changes in volume alone affect costs and profit; changes in cost may necessitate changes in price, which in turn will affect volume and profit; changes in cost (for example, increased marketing effort) may lead to increased volume along with or instead of higher prices. These interrelationships and trade-offs are constantly being explored by managers as they ask the "what-if" questions that are the appropriate prelude to so many operating decisions.

1 What if prices are increased by 5%, causing a 3% decline in volume; is the company better off?
2 What if commission rates paid to agents are increased by 2% (increased selling costs) and the agents' increased efforts result in a 5% increase in sales; will the company's profits be enhanced?
3 What if higher-cost materials are used in order to produce a higher-quality product that can command a higher market price; will profits be improved?
4 What if marketing expenses are increased 7% in order to increase sales volume by 4%; if resulting economies of scale cause a 5% reduction in variable production costs, will profits improve?

5   What if a portion of the facility is automated, thus adding $40,000 to annual fixed expenses and reducing variable manufacturing costs by 5%; will profits suffer if volume drops 3%?   If volume increases 3%?

6   What if the rental agreement on retail facilities provided for a lower monthly fixed rent in exchange for a percentage of sales; under what conditions would this be better for a retailer than continuing to rent space under the current fixed-rental plan?

There are endless questions of this type that might be asked.

The interrelationship of volume, price, cost, and profit for a sporting goods retailer, Sports World in Freeport, is pictured in Figure 14-1.   This graph of operating results displays physical volume along the x-axis and dollars (both revenue and cost) along the y-axis.   Revenue is represented by a straight line beginning at the origin; the slope of this line represents price.   Costs are layered: first the fixed costs of selling and administration, represented by horizontal lines, and then the variable costs represented by upwardly sloping lines.   The difference between the revenue line and the total expense line represents operating profit; at the left of the graph, the negative difference between revenue and total expense represents operating loss.   This graph is highly simplified and is useful primarily in thinking in a conceptual way about the interrelationships of volumes, prices, costs, and profits.   Costs do not in fact follow straight lines; fixed costs tend to be step functions and the slope of the variable cost lines will be different at different volume levels.   Nevertheless, a manager's primary concern is with

Figure 14-1   Sports World (Freeport)

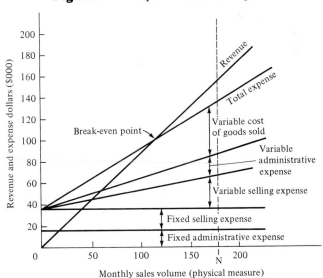

Monthly sales volume (physical measure)

Exhibit 14-6
SPORTS WORLD (FREEPORT)
Monthly Contribution Statement—Normal Operations

	$000		% of Sales
Revenue		$170	100.0%
Variable expenses			
Cost of goods sold	80		47.1
Selling expenses	7		4.1
Administrative expenses	15		8.8
Subtotal		102	60.0
Contribution		68	40.0%
Fixed expenses			
Selling expenses	18		
Administrative expenses	18		
Subtotal		36	
Operating profit		$ 32	

relatively small changes in costs, prices, and volumes around the company's present, or normal, operating point (represented by N on the graph). While fixed costs will not remain absolutely fixed as volume goes from zero to 120% of capacity, it is reasonable to assume that these costs are fixed for swings of, say, 10% around normal volume. Similar assumptions apply to variable costs and revenue.

This graph illustrates that there are really only four fundamental ways in which a company's profits can be changed: (1) increase or decrease prices, thus tilting up or down the revenue line; (2) increase or decrease volume, thus moving the operation to the right or left on the x-axis; (3) reduce or increase variable costs, thus tilting down or up the total cost curve (although the origin of the line will remain at the same point on the y-axis); and (4) reduce or increase fixed costs, thus shifting down or up on the y-axis the origin of the total cost curve. Simple enough. However, each of these actions will, as pointed out above, have second-order effects.

Exhibit 14-6 presents a contribution statement that displays the financial data for Sports World at normal volume; the cost-volume-profit relationships are those shown graphically in Figure 14-1. Note that *gross margin* is not shown in Exhibit 14-6, but *contribution*—revenue minus variable costs —is shown. The contribution at normal sales volume ($170,000 per month) is $68,000, and more importantly the **contribution margin** is 40% of revenue. This statement quickly indicates that a $10,000 increase in monthly sales should lead to a $4,000 (40% of $10,000) increase in contribution, and, if fixed costs truly remain fixed with this volume increase, operating profit should also increase by $4,000.

Algebraically, these relationships can be stated as:

Operating profit = CM × revenue − FC

where:

CM = contribution margin
FC = fixed cost in dollars

At normal volume, N, as shown in Figure 14-1 and Exhibit 14-6:

Operating profit = 0.4 (170) − 36 = 32

Now with these data consider some "what if" scenarios for Sports World. These are detailed in Exhibit 14-7.

A   Suppose management believes that it could substitute an increase of 1% in salespersons' commission (from 3.5% to 4.5% of sales) for $2,000 of advertising without affecting total sales volume. Contribution margin would be reduced to 39%, but fixed expenses would also be reduced.

Operating profit = (.39 × 170) − 34 = $32.3

The result would be a modest increase in operating profit from $32,000 to $32,300.

B   Because additional marketing effort seems appropriate, suppose the salespersons' commissions are increased still more—now by 1.5%—and advertising is not cut. Management feels that sales will then increase by 5%. The contribution margin is decreased, but sales volume is increased.

Operating profit = (.385 × 170 × 1.05) − 36 = $32.7

The result: a modest increase in operating profit. Note that if a lesser increase in volume (say 3.5%) is stimulated by increased commissions, the action would be unwise.

Operating profit = (.385 × 170 × 1.035) − 36 = $31.7

C   Suppose prices are changed, resulting inevitably in volume changes. Management believes that a 5% price increase will bring about only a 7% decrease in unit volume. Now the former contribution margin cannot be applied to the new sales volume figured at new prices; the pricing assumption upon which the contribution margin was originally calculated has been changed. The physical volume is expected to decrease by 7%, or to sales of $158,100, stated in terms of the former prices;

Exhibit 14-7
SPORTS WORLD (FREEPORT)
"What-If. . ." Scenarios

A. Increase salespersons' commission from 3.5% to 4.5%; decrease advertising (fixed selling expense) by $2,000.

Sales =	$170
Contribution margin (40% − 1%) =	39%
Contribution $(.39 × 170) =	66.3
Fixed expenses (36 − 2) =	34.0
Operating profit =	$ 32.3

B. Increase salespersons' commission from 3.5% to 5%; no change in advertising; increase sales by 5%.

New sales volume ($170 × 1.05) =	$178.5
Contribution margin (40 − 1.5) =	38.5%
Contribution $(.385 × 178.5) =	$ 68.7
Fixed expenses (unchanged) =	36.0
Operating profit =	$ 32.7

C. Increase prices 5%; decrease unit volume 7%.

New volume at old price (.93 × 170) =	$158.1
New volume at higher prices (158.1 × 1.05) =	166.0
Variable expenses (.6 × new volume at old price) =	94.9
Fixed expenses (unchanged) =	36.0
Operating profit =	$ 35.1

D. Decrease price 3%; increase unit volume 5%.

New volume at old price (1.05 × 170) =	$178.5
New volume at lower prices (178.5 × .97) =	173.2
Variable expenses (.6 × new volume at old price) =	107.1
Fixed expenses (unchanged) =	36.0
Operating profit =	$ 30.1

E. Renegotiate lease on retail space
from: $5,000 and 5% of sales
to: $12,000 and 0% of sales

Sales =	$170
Contribution margin (40% + 5%) =	45%
Contribution $(.45 × 170) =	76.5
Fixed expenses (36 + 7) =	43.0
Operating profit =	$ 33.5

F. Increase advertising (fixed selling expense) by $5,000 per month and sales commissions from 3.5% to 5.0%; lease adjacent space that will increase rent by $4,000 per month; increase volume by 20%; negotiate improved prices with vendors so that cost of sales reduces by 1.1 percentage points.

New sales (170 × 1.2) =	$204.0
Contribution margin (40 + 1.1 − 1.5) =	39.6%
Contribution $(.396 × 204) =	$ 80.8
Fixed expenses (36 + 5 + 4) =	45.0
Operating profit =	$ 35.8

the old variable cost percentage, 60%, can be applied to this figure to determine the total variable cost. The new contribution margin is substantially higher than before (42.9%) because prices have been increased without any increase in the cost of merchandise. This price increase appears attractive: operating profit increases from $32,000 to $35,100.

D   A price decrease of 3% to stimulate sales might also be contemplated. If this decrease will lead to only a 5% increase in unit volume, the operating profit at Sports World will suffer, as indicated in Exhibit 14-7. Again, the former contribution margin cannot be used directly.

E   Many retail leases, particularly in shopping centers and malls, provide for a fixed monthly rental plus an "override," or percentage of sales. For Sports World the lease arrangement is $5,000 per month plus 5% of sales. Suppose that Sports World renegotiates this lease to a fixed rate of $12,000 per month with no override. (Sports World would thereby be turning a variable expense into a fixed expense; the implications of this conversion are discussed later in this chapter.) Sports World's contribution margin will increase to 45%, more than enough to compensate for the increase in fixed expenses, and therefore the company's operating profit is improved by $1.5 thousand per month.

$$\text{Operating profit} = [(.40 + .05)170] - (36 + 7) = \$33.5$$

F   The last "what-if" scenario contemplates more far ranging and ambitious changes. Suppose that Sports World feels that increasing volume is the key to improved profits; to get the volume, management considers increasing sales commissions to 5% and also increasing advertising expenditures by $5,000 per month. To accommodate the added volume, additional space will have to be rented at an incremental fixed-rental cost of $4,000. Management believes these changes can lead to a 20% increase in unit volume, with no changes in price, and the higher volume in turn can permit Sports World to negotiate more favorable purchase terms with suppliers, reducing variable cost of goods sold from 47.1% of sales to 46.0%. The result: an erosion in contribution margin and somewhat higher fixed expenses are more than compensated by the increased volume.

$$\text{Operating Profit} = (.400 + .011 - .015) (170 \times 1.2)$$
$$- (36 + 5 + 4) = \$35.8$$

Operating profit as a percentage of sales is reduced from 18.8% to 17.5% by this series of changes, a rather substantial reduction. Remember too that Sports World may well have to invest somewhat more in inventory and perhaps accounts receivable (that is, invest more in working capital) in order to finance this expansion. Management needs to look at return on assets under this final scenario.

Similar "what-if" questions could be asked with respect to adding sales personnel, changing the mix of merchandise offered, extending more liberal credit terms to customers, and so forth.

"MODELING" AN OPERATION

The graph of operating results shown in Figure 14-1 represents a simple model of a company. It assumes a single product, sold at a single price, complete linearity in all costs and expenses, and a direct relationship between variable expenses and dollars of sales. In fact, of course, most businesses and other institutions are much more complex. Fortunately, it is increasingly possible to model these complexities, but the resulting model cannot be displayed on a two-dimensional graph! The business computer provides the means of developing, storing, and using a sophisticated model of an operation, including multiple products at multiple prices, step functions in expenses, and variability of expenses in terms of parameters other than sales volume. The result can be a highly useful tool for management in considering "what-if" scenarios. Increasingly, managements are able to sit at computer terminals and, using the financial model of the operation, test the financial consequences of alternative courses of action.

A USEFUL ANALYTICAL TECHNIQUE: BACKING INTO THE ANSWER

Arriving at some of the specific estimates regarding changes in sales or changes in margin that were used in the analyses above can be very difficult. The interrelationship among volume, price, cost, and profit is indisputable, but determining the degree of linkage and exact dollar effect is quite another matter. One way to avoid single-point or discrete estimates is to estimate and analyze in terms of probability distributions; a discussion of this approach is beyond the scope of this book.[9]

Another possibility is to rephrase the questions in terms of an indifference point. To illustrate, consider scenario B above. The original question was phrased as follows: Should management increase salespersons' commissions by 1.5% if such an increase will lead to 5% more sales? The difficult effect to measure is the amount of the sales increase. The question might be restated: By how much would sales have to be stimulated by a 1.5% commission increase in order for the change in commission rate to be

---

[9] See, for example, Bierman, Bonini, and Hausman, *Quantitative Analysis for Business Decisions,* 15th ed., Richard D. Irwin, Inc., Homewood, Ill., 1977, Chap. 2.

warranted? The contribution dollars must be sufficient to cover fixed expenses and present profits.

$$\text{Revenue} = \frac{\text{FC + present profit}}{\text{CM}}$$

$$\text{Revenue} = \frac{36 + 32}{(.40 - .015)} = \$176.6$$

Thus, sales must increase from the normal rate of $170,000 by $6,600, or 3.9%. From a profit standpoint, Sports World is indifferent as to whether it continues the present commission rate and $170,000 per month of sales, or increases the commission rate by 1.5% and achieves sales of $176,600. Now management can focus its attention on whether sales are likely to be stimulated beyond this indifference point. Management won't require 100% assurance before raising rates, but will certainly want a better-than-even chance that sales will exceed this indifference volume. Students of probability will see that the expected value of the distribution of possible sales levels should exceed this indifference point.

Any of the other scenarios discussed above could have been rephrased in terms of an indifference point. Decision makers often find it easier to make a go–no go judgment with respect to the single indifference point than to make single-point estimates regarding sales, prices, margins, volumes, competitor reactions, and so forth. Scenario D might have been rephrased to ask: By how much will sales have to increase in order to offset the margin erosion from a 3% price decrease? Or, alternatively: How much of a price decrease could Sports World withstand (i.e., operating profit to remain at present level) in return for a 5% volume increase?

Break-Even Point

In Figure 14-1 the intersection of the total revenue line and the total expense line is labeled the **break-even** point. At that break-even point, Sports World's sales revenue is just sufficient to cover all expenses with no profit or loss. Or, rephrased, at break-even sales volume the contribution earned by Sports World is just sufficient to cover the fixed expenses of the operation with no contribution to profit. The company's contribution margin is 40%, as shown in Exhibit 14-6. Therefore, the break-even point is:

$$\text{Revenue} = \frac{\text{Fixed costs}}{\text{Contribution margin}} = \frac{\text{FC}}{\text{CM}} = \frac{36}{.40} = \$90,000$$

If during a particular month the company's sales volume drops below this point, the company will incur a loss. For example, at a sales volume of $80,000:

Sales	$80,000
Variable expenses	48,000 (60% of sales)
Contribution	32,000
Fixed expenses	36,000
Operating profit (loss)	$ (4,000)

or

$$\text{Operating profit} = (\text{CM} \times \text{Revenue}) - \text{FC}$$
$$= (.40 \times 80) - 36 = \$4{,}000 \text{ loss}$$

Stated another way, the loss is equal to the contribution margin times the amount by which sales fell below the break-even volume:

$$(90{,}000 - 80{,}000) \times .40 = \$4{,}000 \text{ loss}$$

New companies and companies that are inadequately financed need particularly to focus on this break-even volume. If a company consistently operates below break-even, it will ultimately run out of financial resources and fail; the company will be marching a steady path to bankruptcy.

Two refinements of this break-even analysis are useful in many cases. First, note that this break-even point is stated in terms of reported profits, measured on the accrual basis. Of even more critical importance to a company is reaching *cash* break-even. If a company's noncash expenses (primarily depreciation) are large, it is possible for the company to operate for a long time below profit break-even so long as it is operating above cash break-even. If included among Sports World's $36,000 of fixed expenses are $10,000 of depreciation and amortization, the company's cash break-even is:

Cash fixed expenses = $26,000
Contribution margin = 40%
Required sales to break even = $26,000 ÷ .40 = $65,000

A second refinement involves considering points other than the zero-profit point. A company may have obligations beyond just meeting its expenses. For example, suppose Sports World's five-year term loan agreement requires monthly principal payments of $10,000. Sports World needs to earn sufficient after-tax income to fund these payments; if the company's income tax rate is 50%, it will need $20,000 per month in pretax profit to realize $10,000 per month in net income. The company's break-even with respect to this profit requirement is:

$$\text{Contribution required} = \text{fixed cost plus required profit}$$
$$= \$36,000 + 20,000 = \$56,000$$
$$\text{Contribution margin} = 40\%$$
$$\text{Required sales to service debt obligations} = \frac{56,000}{0.40} = \$140,000$$

Other companies may feel strongly about maintaining a certain dividend policy or funding a certain employee bonus plan or providing the resources for a capital investment program; a break-even-type of analysis can be useful in assessing the companies' risks in achieving these goals.

Operating Leverage

It should be clear from our discussion of break-even considerations that the higher a company's break-even point the greater the risk that the company will operate at a loss. That is, a high break-even point implies a high level of fixed costs, costs that will not be reduced if the expected volume of sales fails to materialize.

On the other hand, a high contribution margin coupled with a relatively high level of fixed expenses provides an opportunity to generate handsome profits if actual sales exceed the expected volume. That is, if most expenses are fixed, total expenses will not increase much as sales increase, and most of the increased sales volume will be reflected in higher profits.

The mix of fixed and variable expenses determines a company's **operating leverage.** If the company has high fixed costs—with attendant high risk of loss and opportunity for profit—the company has high operating leverage. To the extent that most of the company's expenses are variable, the company has relatively low risk of loss (expenses will decline as sales decline) and relatively low opportunity for extraordinary profits (expenses will increase as sales increase); such a company has low operating leverage. The conditions of high and low operating leverage are shown in Figure 14-2. The effects on profit and loss are demonstrated by the examples shown in Exhibit 14-8.

Recall our discussion of debt leverage in Chapter 9. A company has high debt leverage if a large proportion of its total capital is obtained from borrowings on which it is obligated to pay interest. A company has low debt leverage when most of its capital is obtained from shareholders; companies are not obligated to pay dividends unless the fortunes of the company permit their payment. While debt leverage and operating leverage

Company A (High operating leverage)   Company B (Low operating leverage)

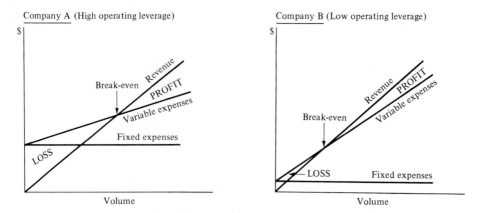

Figure 14-2   Illustration of Operating Leverage

are different phenomena, their effects are parallel.   Both high debt leverage and high operating leverage expose an operation to high risk, but both
create greater opportunity for profit.

Companies with high operating leverage tend to be those that are quite
capital-(as opposed to labor-) intensive, since expenses associated with capital equipment tend to be fixed.   As companies become more automated,
and increase their investment in plant, they also become more highly leveraged.   Electric and telephone utilities have high operating leverage,
since most of their expenses derive from fixed plant—generating and distribution facilities in the case of electric utilities and telephone lines, switching
facilities, and central offices in the case of telephone utilities.   The incremental expenses incurred by the utility—that is, variable costs—associated
with a customer making another long-distance telephone call or leaving the
porch light on overnight are very small.

Operations that are labor-(as opposed to capital-) intensive have low
operating leverage.   Personal-service firms, such as janitorial services or
secretarial services, are examples.   These companies require very little
capital equipment; most of their expenses are people-related.   If business
picks up, more janitors or secretaries are hired, and they are removed from
the payroll again when business slackens.   The wages and salaries paid to
employees of these operations represent the bulk of the expenses and they
are variable.

A company may seek to increase or decrease its operating leverage, depending on how management feels about the trade-off between accepting
higher risk of loss and seeking greater opportunity for profit.   In the Sports
World example, renegotiating the lease to a higher fixed monthly rent (from
a lower fixed rate plus a percentage of sales) will increase Sports World's
operating leverage.   Many new and smaller firms with limited financial resources are well advised to maintain variability in as many expenses as pos-

Exhibit 14-8
Effect of Operating Leverage

	Company A (High Operating Leverage)	Company B (Low Operating Leverage)
Normal Operations		
Sales	$1,000,000	$1,000,000
Expenses		
Variable	250,000 (25%)	600,000 (60%)
Fixed	600,000	250,000
	$ 850,000	$ 850,000
Operating profit	$ 150,000	$ 150,000
Break-even sales volume	$ 800,000	$ 625,000
Recession Conditions		
Sales	$ 750,000	$ 750,000
Expenses		
Variable	181,000 (25%)	450,000 (60%)
Fixed	600,000	250,000
	$ 781,000	$ 700,000
Operating profit (loss)	($ 31,000)	$ 50,000
Strong Economy Conditions		
Sales	$1,200,000	$1,200,000
Expenses		
Variable	300,000 (25%)	720,000 (60%)
Fixed	600,000	250,000
	$ 900,000	$ 970,000
Operating profit	$ 300,000	$ 230,000

sible, in order to reduce risk. On the other hand, a stable and secure larger company may choose to invest in ways that increase operating leverage and provide opportunities for increased profits, since they are able to accept the attendant higher risk. A company with high operating leverage may seek to offset this risk by arranging to finance with little debt leverage—that is, by reducing the financing risk. Another company with low operating leverage is in a good position to assume the risks associated with high debt leverage. Only companies with very stable and predictable revenue streams— such as public utilities—are able to tolerate both high operating leverage and high debt leverage.

Summary

The primary users of accounting data, operating managers, have been our focus throughout this book and particularly in this chapter. In addition to the traditional accounting statements—operating statement, balance sheet, and cost-accounting reports—detailed financial data should be available to permit managers to analyze economic consequences of operating decisions.

The key to such operating decisions is the difference in cash flows (both amounts and timing) between the relevant alternatives. The first challenge to management is to properly frame the alternatives, searching for less obvious options that may prove optimal. Deriving the differential cash flows from traditional accounting data is complicated by the following conditions: (1) accounting records are maintained on an accrual, not a cash basis, (2) variable and fixed expenses are likely to be affected quite differently by the decisions, and (3) many accounting reports, particularly cost-accounting reports, involve the allocation of expenses in an arbitrary way that can confuse the decision maker.

A clear understanding of the interrelationship of volume of sales or revenue, selling price, operating costs, and profits will be of particular help to the operating manager considering the many day-to-day operating decisions. Simple or sophisticated models that describe these interrelationships are now widely used by management to test alternative action plans before final decision—that is, to analyze "what-if" questions. Such models can also help management focus on the important issues of operating leverage and break-even points.

New Terms

Break-even Condition of zero profit or loss. Break-even occurs when total contribution equals total fixed costs.

Contribution The difference between total revenue (sales) and total variable costs.

Contribution margin Contribution as a percentage of total revenue (sales).

Operating leverage The extent to which a company's total costs and expenses are fixed. A company with high fixed costs but low variable costs is said to have high operating leverage. A company with high operating leverage has high risk of incurring operating losses but also high opportunities for profit.

Sunk costs Cash-flow expenditures incurred in the past that cannot be altered or affected by decisions now or in the future.

Problems

1 A production manager reporting to you (you are the manufacturing vice president) has recommended the investment of $10,000 in a new numerically controlled machine tool for her department. Her analysis compares production

costs on the proposed tool and on the tools currently owned by the company. What other alternatives might you suggest she explore?

2 Define and differentiate between:
   a Allocated costs and nonallocated costs
   b Period and product costs
   c Fixed and variable costs
   d Cash flow and profit (earnings)

3 The general manager of a small division of a large company is evaluating the introduction of a new product that is quite different from the other products the division produces. As he collects data to perform his financial analysis, he is struck with the variety of alternatives open to him; he must decide on final design, fabrication technique, and a host of marketing considerations. Discuss the nature of the alternatives that should be considered if the new product is:
   a A wheeled toy for small children
   b A small electrical appliance for the home
   c A medical electronics instrument to be used by clinics and hospitals
   d An innovative new accessory for automobiles
   e An electronics component for use in a broad range of electronics instruments and systems
   f A computer peripheral memory device
   g A line of safety shoes for the construction industry

4 A hospital administrator is evaluating bids from two contract building-maintenance firms for complete janitorial and external maintenance of the hospital for the next year. What other alternatives might the administrator consider besides selecting between the two bidders?

5 The Weinstein Company manufactures and markets standard wooden kitchen cabinets. The standard cost of the most popular of these units is:

Direct material	$17.50
Direct labor	10.30
IPC	8.75
Full-absorption cost	$36.55

The cost accountant at Weinstein estimates that the variable cost of the unit is $33.05. The IPC vehicle at Weinstein is direct-material dollars.
   a What is the ratio between variable and fixed IPC at Weinstein?
   b A large residential building contractor approached Weinstein during the early spring, Weinstein's slow season, and offered to buy 500 units at $35.00 per unit. What factors would you consider in deciding whether or not to accept this order?
   c During Weinstein's busy season, the company is considering whether, in order to meet demand, it should work overtime or subcontract the manufacturing of some units. The subcontractor has bid $39.70 per unit for 1,000 units; if these units were built in-house on overtime, labor costs would be about 150% of the standard shown above. Weinstein expects to be able to sell these units at $48.00 each. What would you do, and why?
   d A design engineer has proposed substituting less expensive material that would require the expenditure of some more labor. The effect of such a

substitution would be to reduce direct-material cost by $1.00 and increase direct labor by $1.10. What would be the new standard cost of the unit? What factors would you consider in making the final decision? Would your answer be different if the IPC vehicle were direct-labor dollars?

6 A convalescent hospital has 80 beds, and each patient is charged $78.00 per day for full care, including food and nursing. The cost of food is about $12.00 per day per patient. The number of hours nurses work varies with the patient load and they are paid by the hour. When the hospital is full, 240 nurse-hours are required per day at an average wage rate of $7.50 per hour. In April 19X4, the hospital averaged 63 patients and lost, $3,725. Assuming 30 days in an average month:

a What is the hospital's break-even patient load per day?

b If the nurses' wages are increased to $8.00 per hour, what is the new break-even patient load?

c If the nurses' wages are increased to $8.00 per hour and the hospital wishes to be able to break even at 60 patients per day, by how much will its daily patient charges have to be increased?

d Suppose the hospital subcontracts the feeding operation, thereby eliminating $27,000 per month in fixed costs, and the direct cost to the hospital of food. The subcontractor would charge $24.75 per patient per day. (Assume that nurses' wages remain at $7.50 per hour.)

  1 What would be the new break-even patient load per day?

  2 How much more or less profitable would the hospital be at full capacity if it enters into this subcontracting arrangement?

  3 Does the hospital have more or less operating leverage if it subcontracts the feeding operation?

e Suppose the hospital manager feels that providing increased services that would add $3,000 per month to fixed costs and $2.00 per patient per day to variable costs would allow it to compete effectively with hospitals charging higher fees. (Now assume that nurses' wages are increased to $8.00 per hour.)

  1 What will be the break-even patient load per day, if patient charges are increased to $80? $85? $90?

  2 If the manager feels that an average load of 60 patients (i.e., 75% occupancy) should be assumed, what is the break-even daily patient charge?

7 During the year just completed, the Grimes Company achieved sales of $4 million and total contribution to fixed costs and profit of $2 million. The company earned $500,000 before taxes. The company is now considering replacing its network of independent sales agents (who are paid commissions at the rate of 5% of sales) with a sales force to be employed by Grimes; the cost will be $170,000 plus a commission to the sales force of 1% of sales. At what sales volume will the company's before-tax return on sales be identical under both alternatives: selling through agents or employing its own sales force? (*Hint:* The new profit level will not be $500,000.)

8 A certain English company has capacity to produce 900,000 measures of paint per year. Last year the company produced 871,000 measures but produced a profit of only 4,197£ sterling (unit of money in England). Last year's income statement follows:

Sales (871,000 measures)	174,670	100%
Cost of goods sold		
Variable	97,906	56
Fixed	12,800	7
	110,706	63
Gross profit	63,964	37
Selling, general, and administrative expense		
Variable	12,100	7
Fixed	47,667	27
	59,767	34
Profit before tax	4,197	3%

a What is the company's break-even volume?

b The company is dissatisfied with its profitability. It wishes to earn 16,000 £ profit before tax when operating at full capacity. To achieve this level of profitability, by what percentage will the price of the product have to be increased, if operations of the company otherwise remain unchanged?

c If the company's volume next year is reduced by 10% from last year's level but fixed costs can only be reduced by 5%, what will be the company's profits assuming the price continues at last year's level?

9 The Kalison Kamper Company produces a single model travel trailer and has developed the following budget for 19X7:

Sales (50 units)	$100,000
Cost of goods sold	60,000
Gross margin	40,000
Selling expenses	10,000
General expenses	25,000
Profit before tax	$ 5,000

Mr. Kalison feels that his budgeted profit is inadequate. His accountant tells him that while the margin on full absorption costs is 40% (see above), the margin on variable production costs is 50%. He believes that with a 3% price increase and an increase in agents' commissions from 6% (assumed in the original budget) to 7½%, the same physical volume of sales can be achieved in 19X7. He feels that the other selling expenses and general expenses will remain constant with modest changes in volume.

a What is the break-even volume, based upon the budget shown above?

b What would be the budgeted pretax profit for 19X7 (expressed in percent), if the price and commission increases were instituted?

c What would be the budgeted contribution margin for 19X7, if the price and commission increases were instituted?

d Do you think the break-even volume for the company would change if a salaried sales force was used instead of commissioned agents? Explain.

10 Refer to problem 16 at the end of Chapter 13.

a According to the 19X6 budget, what is the Franklin Corporation's break-even volume, expressed in dollars of sales?

b Suppose that Franklin management wanted to increase its operating leverage. What actions might the management take and what would be the effect of these actions on the budget statement?

11 The Spacetravel Recreation Park derives revenue both from entrance fees and from a fixed percentage of the revenue earned by the concessions in the park. The concessionaires operate various rides, demonstrations, and food services. The park's fixed expenses for the season are:

Wages of ticket sellers and attendants	$300,000
Management salaries	60,000
Maintenance and janitorial services	60,000
Utilities	20,000
Advertising and promotion	200,000
	$640,000

The park's sources of revenue are:

Fixed rent from concessions	$100,000
Variable rent from concessions	7% of revenue
Admissions charge	$1.00 per person

a Assuming that each person who comes to the park spends $10.00 (in addition to the entrance fee) at the various concessions:

1 How many persons have to be admitted for the park to break even for the season?

2 If the desired profit before tax for the year is $170,000, how many persons have to be admitted?

3 If the desired profit before tax is 10% of revenue, how many persons have to be admitted?

b Assuming the park wishes to earn $170,000 in annual profit before tax and a reduction in the entrance fee to 50 cents would increase attendance, how many more persons would have to be attracted to the park for the management to be indifferent between an entrance fee of $1.00 and one of 50 cents? (Assume $10.00 is spent by each person at the concessions.)

c Again assuming the park wishes to earn $170,000 in annual profit before tax and can increase attendance by increased advertising, what is the maximum amount that the park could spend to increase annual attendance by 20,000? (Admissions charge remains at $1.00, and each person spends $10.00.)

d Would the operating leverage of the park be increased or decreased if the fixed rent from concessions were eliminated and the variable rent were increased to 9%? Draw graphs similar to Figure 14-2 to illustrate the two operating leverage situations. What would be the new break-even admittances for a year? (Admission fee remains $1.00 and each person spends $10.00.)

e The operators of the concessions have suggested that a reduction in the admissions fee to 50 cents would improve their business so much that they might be willing to increase their total fixed rent to the park by $200,000. Would such a move increase or decrease the park's operating leverage?

What would be the new break-even admittances for a year? (Each person spends $10.00.)

f Park management suggests to the operators of the concessions that they lower prices to induce persons to spend more than $10.00, and offers to undertake additional promotion of the park in return. If the park spends $50,000 more on promotion, how much more will each person have to spend in order for the park's profit before tax to remain at $170,000? (Assume attendance as calculated in a2 above and fixed rent from concessions remains at $100,000; admission fee remains $1.00.)

12 The News-To-You Company operates a chain of newsstands at regional airports, selling primarily newspapers and magazines. The space (including fixtures) is rented from the airport. The following expense and revenue relationships pertain to a contemplated expansion to Portville:

Fixed monthly expenses:

Space rental	$ 855
Wages to sales clerks	1,275
Payroll fringe costs: 10%	128
Other fixed costs	230
Total monthly fixed costs	$2,488

The gross margin on newspapers and magazines averages 40%. Consider each question independently.

a What is the monthly break-even point in dollar sales? If the average sale is 75 cents, what is the break-even point in number of sales transactions? If the stand operates 14 hours per day, what is the number of transactions per hour at break-even?

b If 10,000 transactions were completed in a particular month, what would be the company's income?

c If the space rental were doubled, what would be the monthly break-even point in dollar sales? In number of transactions?

d If, in addition to the fixed rent, News-To-You is required to pay to the airport 5% of its sales, what is the monthly break-even point in dollar sales? In number of transactions? (Refer to the original data.)

13 The Shanks Company, a television manufacturer, has always sold its products through distributors. In 19X1 its sales were $80 million and its net income was 10% of sales. Fixed expenses were $16 million, and the company's income tax rate was 50%. Because television sets are increasingly being sold through discount houses and other huge outlets, Shanks is considering the elimination of its distributors and selling directly to retailers. A financial analyst at the company estimates that this change would cause a 20% drop in number of units sold, but that the price realized per unit would increase by 10%. Fixed expenses would increase to $18 million because of the additional warehouses, distribution facilities, and sales force required.

a What was the break-even point (in dollars) under the situation prevailing in 19X1?

b What would the company's net income be under the proposed marketing plan?

c   What would be the break-even point (in dollars of sales) under the proposed situation?

d   What dollar sales volume must be obtained under the proposed plan to make as much net income as last year?

14   The Confections Company is a small specialty candy manufacturer. Sales are made principally to distributors throughout the country. The company's income statement for the past year is being analyzed by top management.

INCOME STATEMENT

For the year 19X1

Sales (1,500,000 pounds)		$900,000
Cost of goods sold		
Direct material	$450,000	
Direct labor	90,000	
Factory overhead		
Variable	18,000	
Fixed	50,000	608,000
Gross margin		$292,000
Selling expenses		
Variable		
Sales commissions (based on		
dollar sales)	$ 45,000	
Shipping and other	90,000	
Fixed		
Salaries, advertising, etc.	110,000	
Administrative expenses		
Variable	12,000	
Fixed	40,000	297,000
Operating income (loss)		($5,000)

Consider each of the following independently.

a   The president has just returned from a management conference at a local university, where he heard an accounting professor criticize conventional income statements. The professor had asserted that knowledge of cost behavior patterns was of key importance in determining managerial strategies. The president now feels that the income statement should be recast to harmonize with cost-volume-profit analysis. That is, the statement should have three major sections: sales, variable costs, and fixed costs. Using the 19X1 data, prepare such a statement, showing the contribution margin (i.e., sales less variable costs) as well as operating income.

b   The president is not pleased with 19X1 results. He says, "We need to take a fresh look in order to begin moving toward profitable operations. Let's concentrate on 19X1 results, and prepare 19X2 budgets under each of the following sets of assumptions:

1   A 5% average price cut will increase unit sales by 20%

2   A 5% average price increase will decrease unit sales by 10%

3   A sales commission rate of 10% and a $3\frac{1}{3}$% price increase will boost unit sales by 10%."

Prepare the budgets for 19X2, using a contribution-margin format. Assume that there are no changes in fixed costs.

c The advertising manager maintains that the advertising budget should be increased by $100,000 and that prices should be increased by 10%. Resulting unit sales will soar by 25%. What would be the expected operating income under such circumstances?

d A nearby large retail chain has offered to buy 300,000 pounds in 19X2, if the unit price is low enough. The Confections Company would not have to incur sales commissions or shipping costs on this special order. Confections' regular business would be undisturbed. Assuming that 19X2's regular operations will be exactly like 19X1's, what unit price should be quoted in order for the company to earn operating income of $5,000 in 19X2?

e The company chemist wants to add a special ingredient, an exotic flavoring that will add $.02 per pound to the candy costs. He also wants to replace the ordinary chocolate now used, which costs $.03 per pound of candy, with a more exquisite type costing $.04 per pound. Assuming no other changes in cost behavior, how many units must be sold to earn operating income of $5,000 in 19X2?

15 You are a financial analyst for Arundel Corporation. Arundel manufactures and markets a broad range of pressure gauges for industrial applications. The year 19X2 is typical of the company's recent history: strong growth in sales (a considerable portion of which is accounted for by inflationary price increases) and good profitability. All sales are made through independent agents who are paid an 8% commission on sales; these commissions are included in selling expenses.

INCOME STATEMENT ($000)	19X2
Sales	$12,100
Cost of goods sold	6,040
Gross margin	6,060
Operating expenses	
Selling expenses	1,950
Other operating expenses	2,550
Total operating expenses	4,500
Operating profit	1,560
Interest expense	100
Profit before taxes	1,460
Income taxes	730
Net income	$ 730

a Assume that in 19X2, cost of goods sold was composed of $3,300,000 variable costs and $2,740,000 fixed costs and that all operating expenses other than commissions to sales agents are fixed. What was Arundel's breakeven volume (in dollars of sales) in 19X2?

b You have been asked by the president of Arundel to assist in estimating (budgeting) the financial statements for 19X3, utilizing the historical figures from 19X2 and the following data:

1 Sales are expected to increase by 10% in physical volume. In addition, the company expects to institute a 5% price increase that will be applicable to all 19X3 sales.

2 Variable costs per physical unit sold should remain the same as in 19X2 (see *a*).

3 In 19X3 fixed costs in total dollars will increase 5% from their 19X2 level (see *a*).

16 A small community hospital has been operating at a deficit for several months and the hospital's administrator and Board of Trustees are concerned about the situation. The hospital controller projects the following operating results for the next three-month period:

	September	October	November
Percent occupancy	83%	85%	78%
Revenue	$24,900	$25,500	$23,400
Expenses			
Variable	6,225	6,375	5,850
Fixed	19,100	19,100	19,100
	25,325	25,475	24,950
Operating surplus (deficit)	($425)	$25	($1,550)

If the hospital authorities wanted to adjust operations in order to break even (just cover expenses with revenues) at 80% occupancy:

a By what percent would they have to reduce fixed expenses, assuming no change in fees or rate of variable expenses?

b What would the rate of variable expenses have to be, assuming no change in fees or fixed expenses?

c By what percent would they have to increase fees (prices), assuming no change in fixed expenses or rate of variable expenses?

What action would you recommend?

17 Shown below are the operating statement and volume-adjusted budget variances for Freeport Manufacturing Ltd. for May 19X8. The top managers at Freeport are dissatisfied with both actual and budgeted operating results and wish now to consider alternative operating strategies that might lead to improved results.

a What would Freeport's return on sales have been in May 19X8, had expenses been exactly in line with the company's flexible budget?

b Develop the volume-adjusted budget for May in contribution-statement format.

c What is the monthly break-even volume at Freeport, according to the flexible budget?

d If Freeport could raise prices by 2% without any loss in volume, what would be the company's new break-even volume, and what would the company's return on sales have been in May? Assume that variable selling expenses vary with total revenue, not with physical volume, but that general and administrative expenses vary with physical volume.

e Assuming prices remain unchanged, what would monthly sales volume have to be in order to:

	May 19X8 Actual ($000)	Volume-Adjusted Budget Variance
Sales	$470.0	—
Cost of goods sold		
Variable costs (at standard)	220.9	—
Fixed IPC	61.5	$1.1
Variances	3.0	(3.0)
Total cost of sales	285.4	(1.9)
Gross margin	$184.6	(1.9)
Operating expenses		
Selling		
Variable	33.4	(0.5)
Fixed	93.7	(1.6)
Total	127.1	(2.1)
General administrative		
Variable	9.2	0.2
Fixed	41.7	0.5
Total	50.9	0.7
Total operating expenses	178.0	(1.4)
Operating profit	$ 6.6	($3.3)

1 Earn an operating profit of $25,000?

2 Earn a return on sales (operating profit divided by sales) of 6%?

f If fixed costs could be reduced by 3% from their budgeted level, what would the company's new break-even volume be, assuming no changes in price or the rate of variable costs?

g Freeport has an opportunity to automate an operation in its plant. The result of this action would be to increase fixed IPC by $3,000 per month and decrease variable expenses by $\frac{1}{2}$ of 1%. What would be the effect of this change on the company's break-even volume? On May's profits? Would you recommend this action? Under what circumstances?

18 The Lange Corporation anticipated a contribution margin of 38% and fixed costs, including $25,000 of noncash expenses (principally depreciation), of $335,000. What volume of sales would be required to yield an after-tax cash flow (assume a 50% tax rate) equal to the company's obligation to repay $50,000 of borrowing?

T|RIPOLI TOY COMPANY

Ann Watcek was just completing her second month as a financial analyst for the Tripoli Toy Company. Ann was a recent graduate of the industrial administration program at a well-known university and was challenged by her position at Tripoli, a position that required her to formulate and defend recommended action regarding a broad range of operating problems and opportunities. During the course of her analyses, she was called upon not only to develop the relevant financial data but to consider the many subjective factors that surround most operating decisions. As a result, during her two months at Tripoli she had become very familiar with the accounting records and systems of the company and was gaining understanding of the marketing and production policies that guided the company.

Tripoli was a medium-sized toy manufacturing company. The United States toy industry was populated with a very great number of companies, most of which employed fewer than 20 people. Tripoli, with employment numbering about 75, was considered medium-sized, even though, of course, it was very much smaller than the several giants of the industry. Tripoli's products were concentrated in electrical games for children in the age range of about 8 to 14. These games were sold through the typical toy distribution channels (including direct sales to the major retail chains) and carried retail prices of about $20 to $70. Tripoli's manufacturing operations comprised a broad range of capabilities; however, the company found it necessary to rely on subcontractors for certain specialized operations and in instances where the subcontractor's equipment provided a significant efficiency advantage.

Ann reported to the controller but found that she spent a great deal of time working with people outside the financial function in order to get a better understanding of the considerations that affected their decisions, as well as to develop specific information regarding the analyses that had been assigned to her. When she first joined the company, Ann was told by the controller that she should bear in mind the need to "sell" her recommendations, as well as to make them analytically sound. He reminded Ann that the company was owned primarily by the three founders who continued to be the top executives of the company.

Tripoli had grown steadily, though not explosively. The company avoided "fad" toys, concentrating instead on toys and games that would typically have a five-to-eight-year life. The company had been consistently profitable and conservatively financed. Ann was told that the company had a very traditional set of financial objectives: grow in volume steadily, but moderately; emphasize cash flow, rather than reported earnings; invest in projects that promise attractive returns; and minimize income taxes.

The manufacturing facility comprised about 20,000 square feet and contained primarily sheet-metal fabrication, painting, silk-screening, and assembly operations. Electrical components, machined parts, and miscellaneous parts were all purchased from outside vendors. None of the operations was particularly complex or sophisticated and each member of the factory work force was competent to perform a number of different operations. Tripoli used a full-absorption, standard-cost-accounting system based upon job orders. The company used a plantwide standard direct-labor wage rate and overhead (or indirect production cost) rate. Ann had been given a copy of the 19X9 manufacturing department budget (shown in Exhibit 1), which she found helpful as she undertook her various studies.

Ann was now faced with three study assignments. The first required that she make a recommendation as to the appropriate time to switch from a sheet-metal to a molded-plastic frame for one of the company's most successful games. The sales manager was anxious to make the change as soon as possible (in order to save weight and improve appearances), while the manufacturing manager was anxious to utilize all of the existing raw and in-process material before switching to the new design. The second study involved a relatively straightforward make-or-buy decision. The purchasing department was anxious to use a new silk-screen vendor that had large and automated facilities. The manufacturing group felt that for reasons of quality, delivery, and flexibility, the silk-screening of all panels should

Exhibit 1
TRIPOLI TOY COMPANY
19X9 Budget
Manufacturing Department

Estimated direct labor hours:	46,000 hours
Average direct labor rate:	$6.25 per hour
Indirect production costs	
Variable	
Labor fringe benefits	$ 49,100
Power	13,600
Supplies	27,200
Indirect labor, shipping, and receiving	36,800
	$126,700
Fixed:	
Occupancy costs	$ 61,500
Supervision	78,300
Depreciation, equipment	47,700
Maintenance and repairs	43,700
Manufacturing engineering	52,500
	$283,700
Total:	$410,400

$$\text{IPC rate} = \frac{\$410,400}{46,000 \text{ hours}} = \$8.92 \text{ per direct labor hour}$$

be maintained at Tripoli. The third study again involved a difference of opinion between the sales and manufacturing departments. A large breakfast cereal company had offered to buy up to 10,000 units of a particular game, but at a price which was below the game's cost. The sales department was concerned about the impact on the company's other sales, while the manufacturing department was eager to have this order to carry some overhead during a period of the year that was typically slow.

PRODUCT REDESIGN

Tripoli's engineering department had been seeking opportunities for product cost reduction through redesign (i.e., value engineering). One of the more attractive opportunities was to substitute a molded-plastic chassis (or base frame) for the present fabricated sheet-metal chassis.

The engineering department had proven the technical and economic feasibility of the substitution. The tooling required for the molded-plastic chassis, purchased for $10,000, had already been used to manufacture prototype quantities.

The comparative manufacturing (full-absorption) cost data on a per-unit basis, as developed by Ann, were:

	Plastic	**Metal**
Material	$ .88	$ .41
Labor	.13 (0.02 hours)	.75 (0.12 hours)
IPC[1]	.18	1.07
	$1.19	$2.23
Tooling	$10,000	fully depreciated

Estimated annual usage was 12,500 units. The plastic unit would be molded by a subcontractor and only minor additional processing would be required at Tripoli. The raw material for the metal frame was sheared to size by a metal distributing company; it was then punched, formed, and finished at Tripoli. The 41 cents material cost was the amount charged by the metal distributor. The 0.12 hours of processing were represented by:

	.06 hours for punching
	.04 hours for forming
	.02 hours for finishing
Total	.12 hours

[1] See Exhibit 1 for IPC rate.

All managers agreed that the substitution should be made, but disagreement arose as to timing. The sales manager argued for immediate implementation to gain the slight sales-appeal and weight-reduction advantages, but primarily to realize the $1.04 per-unit cost advantage. The sales manager reminded the others of Tripoli's management-incentive compensation plan that provided for a bonus pool equal to 20% of year-to-year profit improvement, to be distributed among the key managers.

Ann's boss, the controller, argued that the substitution should be delayed until all existing inventory—both raw material and work in process—relating to this part had been used up. The controller was quick to rebut the sales manager's point by reminding him that any write-off of inventory would hurt profits and therefore the management bonus pool. At the controller's instructions, Ann developed the following information regarding present inventory positions.

	No. of Units	Inventory Value
Raw material	3,000	$1,230
Work in process[2]	4,200	5,544
		$6,774

Ann knew that the metals distributor would not take back the raw material (as it had already been sheared to size) and that the scrap value of the metal (even if it had been sheared and punched) was about $0.05 per unit.

Ann was faced not only with the need to make a recommendation as to timing but also to convince both the controller and the sales manager of the reasons.

MAKE-OR-BUY

Early in 19X9 Tripoli's designers had completed a game that required a silk-screened panel larger than any previously produced by the company. The manufacturing department indicated that they could perform the necessary silk screening but at some sacrifice in time, as the company's silk-screening equipment was particularly suited to smaller panels. The purchasing group had located an outside vendor who submitted what seemed to be quite an attractive price bid. Ann developed the following data for her analysis:

[2] Ann learned that these units, representing about a four-month's supply, had only been punched, but not formed or finished.

Estimated annual usage:
   Expected 3,000
   Minimum 1,000
   Maximum 12,000
Price bid from Art Ability, Inc.

Quantity	Price per Unit
100–499	$3.10
500–999	2.05
1,000–4,999	1.65
5,000–9,999	1.55
10,000 or more	1.45

Delivery: 45 days after receipt of order
Manufacturing time and cost estimate (Tripoli):

Material	$0.30 per unit
Labor	0.10 hours per unit
Tooling ("screen")	$300

The manufacturing manager was anxious to avoid subcontracting, feeling that control of quality and delivery was improved by in-house manufacture. He also pointed out that the quantities were difficult to estimate on new games and that outside vendors were less able or willing to respond to demand shifts than was Tripoli's own shop. Finally, he pointed out to Ann that just last year Tripoli had invested about $25,000 in the silk-screening department to increase capacity and upgrade quality. The equipment in the department was not being fully utilized and, if expected sales of 3,000 per year were realized, this panel for the new game would improve equipment utilization from about 50% of capacity to 60% of capacity, thus helping to carry the department's overhead.

CEREAL COMPANY OFFER

Breakfast Bounty, Inc. (BBI) had approached Tripoli with an offer to purchase up to 10,000 units of a small game that had been introduced by Tripoli in 19X7. Units sold to BBI would be modified slightly from Tripoli's standard design and would carry the BBI label, rather than the Tripoli label. BBI would offer these to its customers through a coupon or premium on or in cereal boxes at what would appear to customers as a bargain price.

The primary terms of the offer were:

Quantity:	Minimum 5,000 units
	Maximum 10,000 units
Price:	$5.35 per unit

Delivery:	During the months of April, May, and June; not less than 1,500 nor more than 3,500 in any single month; BBI would give 30-days' notice of the exact quantity required
Terms:	Net 30 days

Ann determined that the standard cost of Tripoli's comparable standard game was:

Direct material	$1.27
Direct labor (0.35 hours)	2.19
IPC	3.12
	$6.58

The design engineers told Ann that the savings to be achieved in the packaging for BBI (compared to standard packaging) would be about offset by the cost of having to make and apply special BBI labels.

Sales of the comparable standard game were 5,000 units in 19X7 (the year of introduction) and 12,000 units in 19X8. The sales manager anticipated sales of about 15,000 units for each of 19X9 and 19Y0, after which volume would be expected to fall off. The list price to the consumer was $28.50; Tripoli charged its distributors $11.00 and retailers paid $14.25 per unit to the distributors.[3] The sales manager was anxious that the company not jeopardize the near-term profit potential from this game by diverting either Tripoli's own production capabilities or retail customer demand to BBI. He knew that he would have some explaining to do to his distributors if the distributors discovered the bargain-price offer in BBI's cereal.

The manufacturing manager, on the other hand, was attracted by the timing of the deliveries requested by BBI: right in the heart of the slow season, after the Christmas and Easter toy and game seasons. He reminded Ann that much of Tripoli's indirect production costs were fixed and that this order would help carry that overhead, thereby reducing the overhead charged to other products. For example, if all 10,000 games were taken by BBI, Tripoli's total direct hours would be increased by 3,500, or about 7.6%; presumably, therefore, the fixed IPC portion of the overhead rate could be reduced by that percentage, not only for this order but for all of Tripoli's production during 19X9. He admitted that some problems might be encountered if BBI's demand peaked in June (or if BBI pressured Tripoli for additional units later in the summer), because by early or mid-June Tripoli was beginning to operate at or near capacity in anticipation of Christmas demand.

---

[3] Typically, games were sold as follows: from Tripoli to wholesaler to retailer to consumer. In the case of very large retail chains, the wholesaler step might be omitted, with Tripoli selling direct to the retail chain.

D ENNISON'S ICE CREAM PARLOR

As of early 19X2, Richard Allen was pleased with the success of his ice cream parlor venture, but anxious to learn more about how he could control his expenses and perhaps increase profits.   Allen had saved enough money by 19X0 to purchase a Dennison's Ice Cream Parlor franchise.   Dennison's was a relatively new chain of ice cream parlors similar to Baskin-Robbins and other franchise chains that had grown rapidly in the United States in the previous decade.   The company responsible for the development and franchising of the Dennison's chain was Cara Corporation.

Allen opened his parlor in late 19X0 and quickly learned how to run his store with the help of friends and some courses at the local community college.   In exchange for yearly franchise fees paid to Cara of $5,000 and 5% of gross sales, Allen received the benefit of the Dennison's national advertising, the right to use the Dennison name, extensive training before the store was opened, and continuing management assistance from Cara's regional manager.

Cara placed a number of restrictions on each Dennison franchise —e.g., a single-dip cone had to contain exactly $3\frac{1}{2}$ oz., and be priced at 40 cents.   While some of the restrictions were annoying to him, Allen enjoyed the opportunity of owning his own business and being responsible for its success.

Exhibit 1
DENNISON'S ICE CREAM PARLOR
Year Ending December 31, 19X1

Sales		$77,760
Cost of goods sold[1]		32,076
Gross margin		45,684
Labor, hourly	16,896	
Salary, manager	12,000	
Rent	3,540	
Utilities, including telephone	1,340	
Laundry	260	
Repairs	190	
Insurance	450	
License	100	34,776
Operating profit		10,908
Franchise fees	8,888	
Profit before taxes		$ 2,020

[1] Includes ice cream, toppings, cones, and supplies, but excludes labor and overhead.

Allen, like all other franchise owners, purchased from Cara the 37 Dennison ice cream flavors as well as cones, cups, toppings, and other supplies required in the store. Cara recommended appropriate order quantities for both ice cream and supplies and Allen had found these recommendations to be sound. Cara was able to determine with surprising accuracy the relative customer demand for various flavors and products. Although all Dennison outlets sold sundaes, milk shakes, and hand-packed pints and quarts of ice cream, the majority of sales was in single-scoop cones. Allen employed primarily high-school teenagers who were paid by the hour at or slightly above the minimum wage. Allen varied the number of employees and the hours worked in response to expected changes in sales volume.

The year 19X1 was Allen's first full year of operation, and Allen was pleased with both sales and earnings for the year. The 19X1 income statement is shown in Exhibit 1.

PROBLEMS

1   Which of Allen's expenses are variable, fixed, semivariable?
2   What were his total fixed expenses for 19X1?
3   Recast the 19X1 income statement in Exhibit 1 to a contribution statement.
4   What is the daily break-even volume in dollar sales (assuming 360 working days per year)? In gallons of ice cream sold (assuming single-scoop cones are the only product sold, and that a gallon is equivalent to 70 oz.)?
5   What would be the daily break-even volume is Allen were required to pay franchise fees of $2,000 per year and 8% of gross sales?
6   If the minimum wage is increased by 10%, and therefore Allen increases hourly wages by 10%, what would be the company's daily break-even volume? (Assume the 19X1 franchise fee arrangement prevails.)
7   What would Allen's profit have been had he averaged 34 gallons sold per day? (Make the assumptions as in question 4 above, but ignore the changes in franchise fees and labor costs discussed in questions 5 and 6.)
8   Several of the franchises have petitioned Cara for permission to increase cone prices to 45 cents. Allen feels that such a price increase would reduce his parlor's volume by 20%. If he is permitted to do so, should Allen increase his price? (Make your analysis on the basis of 19X1 actual results, assuming single-scoop cones are the only product sold.) How much loss in volume could Allen tolerate at the higher price and still earn as much profit as in 19X1?

Allen's courses had taught him how important budgeting can be in controlling costs. Based on 19X1 financial data and his own "feel" for the business gained over his months of experience, Allen drew up a budget for 19X2 as shown in Exhibit 2. He anticipated that with

Exhibit 2

DENNISON'S ICE CREAM PARLOR

Budget by Quarter

YEAR ENDING DECEMBER 31, 19X2

	First Quarter (Jan.–Mar.)	Second Quarter (Apr.–June)	Third Quarter (July–Sept.)	Fourth Quarter (Oct.–Dec.)	Total Year
Sales	$19,580	$22,720	$25,100	$21,400	$88,800
Cost of goods sold	8,077	9,372	10,354	8,827	36,630
Gross margin	11,503	13,348	14,746	12,573	52,170
Labor, hourly	4,250	5,000	5,400	4,650	19,300
Salary, manager	3,000	3,000	3,000	3,000	12,000
Rent	900	900	900	900	3,600
Utilities, including telephone	300	300	300	300	1,200
Laundry	50	50	50	50	200
Repairs	70	70	70	70	280
Insurance	120	120	120	120	480
License	30	30	30	30	120
Total	8,720	9,470	9,870	9,120	37,180
Operating profit	2,783	3,878	4,876	3,453	14,990
less: franchise fee	2,229	2,386	2,505	2,320	9,440
Profit before taxes	$ 554	$ 1,492	$ 2,371	$ 1,133	$ 5,550

Exhibit 3
Income Statement
DENNISON'S ICE CREAM PARLOR
January 1–March 31, 19X2

Sales		$18,810
Cost of goods sold		8,168
Gross margin		10,642
Labor, hourly	4,180	
Salary, manager	3,000	
Rent	900	
Utilities, including telephone	330	
Laundry	66	
Repairs	65	
Insurance	120	
License	27	
		8,688
Operating profit		1,954
Franchise fee	2,191	
Profit (loss) before tax		($237)

increased recognition in the community he could expect sales to increase approximately 15% over 19X1 figures. He also anticipated that fixed expenses would be held at about their 19X1 level in spite of inflation.

Allen was concerned when he discovered that his parlor had incurred an operating loss during the first quarter of 19X2, as shown in Exhibit 3. He was determined to learn the reasons for the loss and to consider what corrective action should be taken.

PROBLEMS

9 What are the primary factors that caused operating results during the first quarter to be well below budget? What operating problems or conditions might have caused the variances?

10 What was the first quarter's break-even sales volume implicit in the budget figures shown in Exhibit 2? Did the parlor operate above or below this break-even volume?

11 What profit should the parlor have earned on $18,810 of sales, if expenses had been well-controlled?

12 Allen consulted an advertising agency in the area. The agency projected that third-quarter sales (the peak season) could be increased by 10% from the budgeted amount with an advertising expenditure during that quarter of $900. Should the advertising program be undertaken, assuming the third-quarter contribution margin is as budgeted?

13 Allen's landlord has offered to renegotiate the parlor's lease to provide
for rent of $150 per month plus 2% of sales volume, instead of $300 per
month. What effect would the revised terms have on (a) first quarter's
actual profits, (b) third quarter's budgeted profits, (c) the parlor's quarterly break-even volume of sales? What are the advantages and disadvantages of accepting this offer? If you were Allen, what would you do?

Comprehensive Accounting Exercise

N EW CORP—FINANCIAL ACCOUNTING

You have just been appointed the accountant for New Corp for the month of March 19X7. You will find on the following pages:

a The company's financial statements (balance sheet and income statement) for the years 19X5 and 19X6

b A trial balance of the company's general ledger at February 28, 19X7

c The company's chart of accounts (by comparing the chart of accounts and the February 28 trial balance, you will find that not all of the accounts on the company's chart of accounts are currently being used)

d A list of entries describing all events and recognitions for the month of March (this list is, in effect, the set of source documents for your accounting system for March)

e Certain forms used in the company's accounting system, including journals (general, cash disbursements, and sales) and a subsidiary ledger for commissions payable

ASSIGNMENT

Using the trial balance at February 28, 19X7, you should begin by constructing a balance sheet as of that date and an income statement for the first two months of the company's year.

Your objective is then to develop a balance sheet at March 31, 19X7 and an income statement for the month of March. You can determine the income statement for March by deduction: develop the statement for the three-month period (January through March) and subtract the statement covering the first two months.

You are given the source documents but are to complete all of the other documents for your accounting system, including journals, ledgers, and subsidiary ledger. The company uses specialized journals to record sales and cash disbursements, but records all other transactions and recognitions (adjustments) in a general journal. You are *not* required to maintain a subsidiary accounts receivable ledger (the company maintains a file of copies of unpaid invoices to serve as an informal accounts receivable subsidiary ledger). You are required to maintain a subsidiary sales commissions payable ledger.

Background

Virgil Armstrong founded New Corp on January 1, 19X5, to manufacture and sell safety helmets used by the construction industry. Throughout 19X4, Mr. Armstrong spent a great deal of time during weekends and evenings perfecting a unique design for a safety helmet shell. Armstrong felt that his design would permit an unusual configuration of tooling for the injection molding presses and would result in a helmet that would be substantially more comfortable to wear. Rather than try to sell or license his helmet design to a company already in the market, Armstrong decided to use the design as the basis for a new business venture.

New Corp's original product line, introduced in the spring of 19X5, consisted of helmets for field-construction personnel. The federal law, as well as good construction practices, required all personnel on construction sites, including supervisory personnel and visitors, to wear safety helmets—typically referred to as "hard hats." Helmets were manufactured in a single size but incorporated a headband that was adjustable to fit the wearer's head.

This original helmet model, designated as product A in New's accounting records, sold well. Late in 19X6, the second year of the company's life, New introduced a line of safety helmets for industry. These helmets, also often referred to as hard hats and designated as product B at New, were used in heavy manufacturing companies, particularly where overhead cranes were used to move material. New's industrial safety helmets were lighter weight than construction hard hats and also were outfitted with more padding material to improve comfort. As a result, industrial safety helmets commanded a higher price than construction helmets.

Occasionally, a large contractor would approach New with a special order for helmets. Such special orders occurred when the contractor wished some specific configuration of strapping (perhaps to assure that the helmet would stay in place under unusual circumstances) together with special colors and the application of company identification logos.

The market for all safety equipment, including safety helmets, grew rapidly during the decade of the 19X0's, stimulated by increased governmental regulation and pressure from insurance companies for improved safety procedures.

The construction and industrial helmets were sold in somewhat different ways. Construction helmets were sold directly by New to the larger jobbers (distributors) of construction supplies. These jobbers bought for their own accounts, maintained inventory, and resold at a markup to the construction companies. In contrast, industrial safety helmets were sold by independent commissioned agents to industrial supply distributors; the sale transaction was actually between New and the distributor, and the agent (or "rep") was paid a commission by New. The industrial supply distributor bought the helmets for its own account, maintained an inventory, and resold to a wide variety of industrial customers. Occasionally, New would receive an order for product B directly from a large industrial company, rather than through an agent; on some of these orders New did not pay a sales commissions.

Initial capital for the company was provided by Mr. Armstrong ($20,000) and his brother-in-law ($20,000), with 60% of the original share issuance going to Armstrong. Soon after formation, an additional 10 shares (valued at $500 per share) were issued to A. T. Taster in partial payment of the initial tooling and related patent.

As the company grew during its first two years, New found it necessary to rely to an increasing extent on bank borrowing.

SUGGESTIONS FROM THE FORMER ACCOUNTANT TO THE NEWLY APPOINTED ACCOUNTANT

1 Post balances from the February 28 trial balance as opening balances in a set of general ledger accounts. Record all transactions and recognitions in journals before making any entries in the general ledger. Maintain the subsidiary commissions payable ledger as you record in the journals. When the journals are complete, add the columns, and check to be sure that within each journal the sum of the debit totals equals the sum of the credit totals.

2 Where possible, transfer the summary columnar totals (*not the detailed entries*) from the specialized journals (sales and cash disbursements) to the appropriate accounts in the general ledger. Transfer the detailed entries from the general journal and from the "Other" debit column in the cash disbursements journal to the general ledger. Check to determine that the subsidiary sales commissions payable ledger reconciles with the Sales Commissions Payable account in the general ledger.

3 Cost of goods sold is calculated by the end-of-period adjustment method. Transfer Purchases, Purchase Returns, Direct Labor Expended, and Indirect Production Costs Expended into Cost of Goods Sold (all of these accounts should have zero balances at the beginning of April). Then adjust inventories to correspond with ending physical inventory valuations by making appropriate adjustments in both the Inventory and Cost of Goods Sold accounts. All of these transfers and adjustments should be re-

corded in the general journal. Note that this adjusting entry cannot be made until the transfers (outlined in #2 above) from the journals to the general ledger have been completed, since you must know the month-end balances in each of the accounts affecting Cost of Goods Sold.

4 Draw up a trial balance at March 31, 19X7. Prepare a March 31, 19X7, balance sheet in appropriate format and a March and first-quarter (January–March) income statement in appropriate format.

Note: You are very persuasive! You have cajoled the former accountant into recording in the journals the transactions for the first 10 days of March. These entries should assist you in determining appropriate formats.

NEW CORP
Balance Sheet

	December 31	
ASSETS	19X6	19X5
Current Assets		
Cash	$ 8,300	$ 5,100
Accounts Receivable (net)	46,700	24,200
Inventory		
Raw and In-process	52,700	31,300
Finished Goods	20,100	9,900
Prepaid Expenses	10,600	7,200
Other	1,600	800
Total Current Assets	140,000	78,500
Fixed Assets		
Gross Plant and Equipment	68,100	36,800
less: Accumulated Depreciation	(10,300)	(2,100)
Net Fixed Assets	57,800	34,700
Intangibles	5,000	5,600
Other Assets	4,100	2,200
Total Assets	$206,900	$121,000

LIABILITIES AND OWNERS' EQUITY

Current Liabilities		
Accounts Payable	$ 47,900	$ 20,400
Short-Term Bank Loan	58,400	26,500
Current Portion of Long-Term Debt	6,800	4,100
Other	18,000	12,600
Total Current Liabilities	131,100	63,600
Long-Term Debt[1] (less current portion)	37,200	16,700
Owners' Equity		
Capital Stock (110 shares)	45,000	45,000
Retained Earnings (Deficit)	(6,400)	(4,300)
Total Owners' Equity	38,600	40,700
Total Liabilities and Owners' Equity	$206,900	$121,000

[1] Installment Contracts Payable

NEW CORP
Income Statement
($000)

	Fiscal Years Ended December 31	
	19X6	19X5
Sales		
Product A	$211.6	$127.4
Product B	43.1	0
Other	25.5	10.4
	$280.2	$137.8
Cost of Goods Sold	158.1	90.9
Gross Margin	122.1	46.9
Operating Expenses		
Selling Expenses		
Commissions	2.0	—
Fixed Expenses	85.4	37.2
G&A Expenses	37.8	14.8
	125.2	52.0
Operating Profit (Loss)	(3.1)	(5.1)
Other Income	1.0	2.4
Other Expense	—	1.6
Income (Loss) before Taxes	$ (2.1)	$ (4.3)
Income Taxes	—	—
Net Income (Loss)	$ (2.1)	$ (4.3)

NEW CORP
Trial Balance—February 28, 19X7
(After Adjusting Entries)

Account No.		Dr.	Cr.
101	Petty Cash	200	
105	Cash—First Bank	7,300	
111	Accounts Receivable—Trade	49,100	
112	Allowance for Doubtful Accounts		1,700
113	Accounts Receivable—Other	1,100	
115	Notes Receivable—Trade	2,500	
118	Travel Advances—Employees	800	
121	Inventory—Raw Material	42,200	
125	Inventory—In-process	11,100	
131	Inventory—Finished Goods	18,600	
141	Prepaid Expenses	10,100	
145	Other Current Assets	1,100	
147	Freight Clearing		300
151	Production Equipment	47,000	
153	Leasehold Improvements	15,000	
155	Motor Vehicles	8,000	
157	Office Furniture and Equipment	4,500	
161	Accum. Depreciation—Production Equipment		4,300
163	Accum. Depreciation—Leasehold Improvements		4,100
165	Accum. Depreciation—Motor Vehicles		2,000
167	Accum. Depreciation—Office Furniture		1,300
171	Intangible Assets	6,200	
181	Accum. Amortization—Intangible Assets		1,300
191	Other Noncurrent Assets	4,100	
201	Accounts Payable—Trade		49,900
211	Short-term Bank Borrowing		63,100
221	Accrued Wages and Salaries Payable		9,400
225	Sales Commissions Payable		800
227	Accrued Interest Payable		700
229	Accrued Rent Payable		1,600
231	Accrued Group Insurance Payable		0
233	Accrued Professional Fees Payable		3,600
235	Customer Down Payments		1,000
251	Installment Contracts Payable		45,000
261	Capital Stock		45,000
271	Retained Earnings (at prior year-end)	6,400	
301	Sales—Product A		38,300
305	Sales—Product B		16,100
321	Sales—Special Contracts		6,300
345	Sales Returns and Allowances	1,200	
351	Cost of Goods Sold	33,400	

371	Material Purchases—Current Month	0	
373	Purchase Returns—Current Month		0
375	Direct Labor Expended—Current Month	0	
379	Indirect Production Costs Expended	0	
401	Sales Commission Expense	800	
411	Sales Salaries	7,100	
413	Fringe Benefit Expenses—Sales	900	
415	Travel and Entertainment Expense	1,100	
421	Advertising (Space) Expense	2,800	
423	Promotional Literature Expense	600	
425	Miscellaneous Supplies	1,000	
429	Miscellaneous Outside Services	200	
431	Telephone and Telegraph Expense	1,100	
433	Occupancy Expense	800	
435	Depreciation Expense	400	
511	Research and Development (R&D) Salaries	800	
513	Fringe Benefit Expenses—R&D	100	
521	Development Materials	200	
611	General and Administrative (G&A) Salaries	2,900	
613	Fringe Benefit Expenses—G&A	400	
615	Travel and Entertainment Expense	500	
621	Accounting Supplies	300	
625	Miscellaneous Supplies	100	
629	Outside Services	1,200	
631	Telephone and Telegraph Expense	300	
633	Occupancy Expense	300	
635	Depreciation Expense	300	
701	Cash Discounts Earned		100
711	Interest Income		100
715	Gain (Loss) on Sale of Fixed Assets	0	
721	Interest Expense	1,500	
723	Bad Debt Expense	200	
731	Amortization of Intangible Assets	200	
		296,000	296,000

NEW CORP
Chart of Accounts

100-149 CURRENT ASSETS

101 Petty Cash
105 Cash (Checking)—First Bank
107 Cash (Savings)—Provident Savings and Loan
111 Accounts Receivable—Trade

112   Allowance for Doubtful Accounts—Trade
113   Accounts Receivable—Other
115   Notes Receivable—Trade
117   Notes Receivable—Other
118   Travel Advances—Employees
121   Inventory—Raw Material
125   Inventory—In-process
131   Inventory—Finished Goods
141   Prepaid Expenses
145   Other Current Assets
147   Freight Clearing

150–199   NONCURRENT ASSETS

151   Production Equipment—At Cost
153   Leasehold Improvements—At Cost
155   Motor Vehicles—At Cost
157   Office Furniture and Equipment—At Cost
161   Accumulated Depreciation—Production Equipment
163   Accumulated Depreciation—Leasehold Improvements
165   Accumulated Depreciation—Motor Vehicles
167   Accumulated Depreciation—Office Furniture and Equipment
171   Intangible Assets—Patents and Trademarks
173   Intangible Assets—Other
181   Accumulated Amortization—Patents and Trademarks
183   Accumulated Amortization—Other
191   Other Noncurrent Assets

200–249   CURRENT LIABILITIES

201   Accounts Payable—Trade
205   Accounts Payable—Other
211   Short-term Bank Borrowing
221   Accrued Wages and Salaries Payable
223   Accrued Payroll Taxes Payable
225   Sales Commissions Payable
227   Accrued Interest Payable
229   Accrued Rent Payable
231   Accrued Group Insurance Payable
233   Accrued Professional Fees Payable
235   Customer Down Payments
239   Other Accruals
241   Income Taxes Payable

250–259   LONG-TERM LIABILITIES

251   Installment Contracts Payable
253   Long-term Bank Loans
259   Notes Due Shareholders

261–299 OWNERS' EQUITY

261 Capital Stock
271 Retained Earnings

300–349 REVENUE (SALES)

301 Sales—Product A
305 Sales—Product B
321 Sales—Special Contracts
329 Other Sales
345 Sales Returns and Allowances
347 Sales Price Discounts

350–399 COST OF GOODS SOLD

351 Cost of Goods Sold—All Products
371 Material Purchases
373 Material Purchase Returns
375 Direct Labor Expended
379 Indirect Production Costs Expended

400–699 OPERATING EXPENSES
(400–499 Selling Expenses)

401 Sales Commission Expense
411 Sales Salaries
413 Fringe Benefit Expenses—Sales
415 Travel and Entertainment Expense
421 Advertising (Space) Expense
423 Promotional Literature Expense
425 Miscellaneous Supplies and Other Expense
429 Miscellaneous Outside Services
431 Telephone and Telegraph Expense
433 Occupancy Expense
435 Depreciation Expense

(500–599 Research and Development Expense)

511 R&D Salaries
513 Fringe Benefit Expenses—R&D
515 Travel and Entertainment Expense
521 Development Materials Expense
525 Miscellaneous Supplies and Other Expense
529 Miscellaneous Outside Services
531 Telephone and Telegraph Expense
533 Occupancy Expense
535 Depreciation Expense

(600–699 General and Administrative Expenses)

611 G&A Salaries
613 Fringe Benefit Expenses—G&A
615 Travel and Entertainment Expense
621 Accounting Supplies
623 Other Office Supplies

625   Miscellaneous Supplies and Other Expense
629   Outside Services—Legal and Accounting
631   Telephone and Telegraph Expense
633   Occupancy Expense
635   Depreciation Expense

700–799 OTHER INCOME AND EXPENSE

701   Cash Discounts Earned
705   Rental Income
711   Interest Income
715   Gain (Loss) on Sale of Fixed Assets
719   Miscellaneous Other Income
721   Interest Expense
723   Bad Debt Expense
729   Miscellaneous Other Expense
731   Amortization of Intangible Assets
761   Income Tax Expense

MARCH 1

Shipped 800 units of product A to Cox Supply Co. and issued an invoice for $4,000 plus $50 for freight.   Total: $4,050 (In this case New pays for the freight, when billed, but charges the customer.   The $50 credit should be to account no. 147, Freight Clearing.)

MARCH 1

Received from DuPont Corp. plastic raw material valued at $3,700. Total invoice of $3,900, including $200 freight charge.   (New includes freight in its Purchases account.)   New's terms of purchase with DuPont are net 60 days.

MARCH 2

Shipped 400 units of product B to General Mammoth Corporation (a large industrial concern that bought direct from New rather than through a distributor).   Total invoice: $3,200.   Commission of $150 is due to Finley Associates in connection with this sale.

MARCH 2

The company made the March payment on its installment contract payable to First Bank, as follows:

Principal repayment $600
Interest payment[1]   350
                          $950

Total payment = $950.00, check no. 257.

MARCH 3

A check for $100 was received from Mr. T. Hunt, the company's sales manager, to repay a travel advance that the company made to him in early February.

MARCH 4

Shipped 500 units of product A (sales value: $2,480) and 100 units of product B (sales value: $650). No commission is due on the sale of product B. The customer, Mansfield Distributors, is also billed $30 for freight. Total invoice: $3,160.

MARCH 4

New returned to its strapping supplier certain defective materials for which it has not yet paid. The supplier's invoice, previously recorded as an account payable, indicates that the purchase value of the returned materials is $400.

MARCH 7

The company issued a check (no. 258) to Sally Simond, the office manager, for $150 to reimburse the petty cash fund. Sally cashed the check and placed the $150 in the petty cash box to return the fund to a $200 balance. Receipts in the petty cash box indicate that $100 was spent on miscellaneous sales supplies and $50 on miscellaneous G&A supplies.

     Note: Petty Cash is referred to as an *imprest account:* the account, Petty Cash, is not affected by this transaction.

MARCH 8

Received from Consolidated Container packing materials (classified by New as raw material) valued at $300 plus freight charge of $50. Total invoice: $350. Terms of purchase: net, 30 days

---

[1] None of this interest has been accrued.

MARCH 8

Shipped to Foster Bros. Wholesalers 500 units of product A (sales value: $2,500) and 200 units of product B (sales value: $1,400). Total invoice: $3,900. Commission of $100 is due to Bace and Fruehauf on this sale.

MARCH 8

Shipped 500 units of product A to Willamette Supply Co., a newly appointed distributor. Total invoice: $2,600. Willamette agreed to pay $1,000 within 45 days and to pay the balance by executing a 12-month installment note (interest at 8%). A note form was sent to Willamette with the invoice.

MARCH 9

Received three checks from customers:

Cox Supply	$3,000
Greiner Brothers	3,500
Jackson and Co.	4,300
Total deposit	$10,800

MARCH 10

Paid freight bills arising from shipments to customers in February, as follows:

Check No.	Payee	Amount
259	Overland Freight	$100
260	NGT Lines	150
261	Kennedy Trucking	50
		$300

(When these charges were billed to customers, the credit entry was to Acct. no. 147, Freight Clearing.)

MARCH 10

The company's lawyers and accountants send bills to New on an irregular schedule. In order to avoid distorting monthly profit when one of these bills is received, the company accrues a certain amount for these professional services each month. Then, when a billing is received and paid, the accrued amount is reduced. Today New issued a check for $1,000 to Dean and Bulheley (lawyers). Total payment: $1,000. Check no. 262

MARCH 10

Paid two suppliers' invoices in order to earn cash discounts:

Check no.	Supplier	Gross	Discount	Net
263	Creative Publications	$2,000	$ 50	$1,950
264	Ajax Webbing	2,500	50	2,450
		$4,500	$100	$4,400

MARCH 10

Moore Supply returned 100 units of product A, which had originally been billed to them in February at $500. As Moore has already paid for this shipment, they requested a cash refund. Check was issued. Total payment: $500. Check no. 265.

Note: *Entries have already been made in the appropriate journals for all transactions up to this point.*

MARCH 14

Shipped to Interstate Pipeline Co. specially constructed helmets that the company had ordered on special contract. Total value of the contract is $3,500. Interstate Pipeline in January made a $500 down payment on this order. Order was sent "freight collect"; that is, the customer pays for the freight.

MARCH 14

Received invoice from Creative Publications for product advertising appearing in March. Total invoice: $1,300. Terms: 2% cash discount if paid by 10th of following month; net, 30 days.

MARCH 15

New Corp sold 20 shares of common stock at a price of $1,000 per share to the following individuals:

Production Manager	5 shares
Sales Manager	5 shares
Friend of Armstrong	10 shares

The proceeds of $20,000 were deposited in First Bank.

MARCH 15

Commission payments were made to the company's independent sales agents as follows:

Amount	Payee	Check No.
$200	Safety Suppliers	266
300	Finley Associates	267
100	Bace and Fruehauf	268
$600	Total	

MARCH 15

New shipped 300 units of product B (sales value $2,100) to Tormey Industrial. Shipment was made "freight collect." A commission of $100 is due to Finley Associates on this order. Total invoice: $2,100.

MARCH 15

New Corp contracts with First Bank to process the company's payroll, including the preparation of paychecks and required payroll tax forms. The Bank deducts from New's account the net amount paid to employees plus income taxes withheld and payroll taxes. Paydays occur on the 15th and last day of each month. The Bank sends a report to New for each pay period. The report for the period from March 1–March 15 follows:

Dept.	Wages/Salaries	Payroll Taxes[4]
Direct labor[2]	$3,000	$250
Indirect production[3]	1,500	150
Sales	1,800	200
R&D	200	0
G&A	750	100
	$7,250	$700

[2] Charge both wages and payroll taxes to Acct. no. 375
[3] Charge both wages and payroll taxes to Acct. no. 379
[4] An expense of New Corp, considered a fringe benefit expense

Gross Payroll	$7,250
less Income Tax Withheld	1,000
less Group Insurance Withheld	150
Net Payroll	$6,100

Amount deducted from New's account:

Net Payroll	$6,100
Income Tax Withheld	1,000
Payroll Taxes	700
	$7,800

MARCH 16

Received three checks from customers:

Gardiner Bros.	$2,000
Hess and Hess	1,200
Anderson and Co.	1,600

Total Deposit: $4,800

MARCH 16

New Corp repaid $20,000 (proceeds from the sale of common stock) of the company's short-term borrowing from First Bank. To effect this repayment, Armstrong delivered a letter to the bank instructing the bank to deduct the $20,000 from the company's checking account.

MARCH 16

Received from Ajax Webbing strapping material valued at $1,900. Freight was paid by Ajax. Terms of purchase are 2% if paid within 10 days, net 30 days.

MARCH 17

New made a no-charge shipment of 5 units of product A and 5 units of product B to Cody Supply. Cody is a prospective new distributor for New, and this shipment is made to provide Cody with inspection samples (it is not anticipated that Cody will return the helmets).

MARCH 17

Purchased miscellaneous supplies for the sales and G&A departments from Silva Supplies. Total invoice $1,000. Terms: net 30 days. Accountant determines that 60% of the invoice should be charged to sales and the balance to G&A.

MARCH 17

Rush Industrial Supply returned 40 units of product B requesting a $300 credit (the full amount of the invoice). As Rush is a steady customer, it did not request a cash refund, even though it had already paid this invoice. Commissions of $10 were paid to Safety Suppliers in connection with the original sale; in accordance with New's agreement with its independent sales agents, commissions earned by the agents on new shipments are offset by commissions on any returned merchandise.

MARCH 18

Sold to Erskine Corp. for $1,000 cash a hoist that New is no longer using. The hoist was purchased in 19X5 for $2,500 and accumulated depreciation to date is $1,150. Check deposited today.

MARCH 18

New discovered that certain office supplies purchased in January and paid for in February were defective. They were returned for credit to Miller Business Forms Corp. The supplies had been billed to New for $200 and New deducted $10 for prompt payment when paying the bill in February. These supplies were charged to Account no. 621 when purchased. New expects to use up the $190 credit at Miller within the next two months and therefore has not requested a cash refund.

MARCH 18

A check for $200 was received from Industrial Sentry, the company's insurance company, as payment on a claim resulting from an accident with one of the company's cars. The cost of repairing the car was paid in January, and at that time was charged to G&A Travel and Entertainment Expense (Account no. 615).

MARCH 21

The company took delivery of a new injection molding machine. The company had previously made a $2,000 down payment on this machine, and this amount is included in prepaid expenses at February 28, 19X7. The total cost of the machine is $10,000. The balance of $8,000 is financed through an installment contract at First Bank. The installment loan, signed by Armstrong today, provides for monthly payments of $168 for 60 months (effective interest rate of about 9.5%). The first payment is not due until next month.

Note: New Corp did *not* issue a check to the machinery supplier. The $8,000 was paid by First Bank as soon as Armstrong signed the installment note.

MARCH 21

Paid the following suppliers' invoices—no discounts earned:

Check no.	Supplier	Amount
269	Dupont	$5,000
270	Silva Supplies	1,500
271	Centerville Garage	400
272	Consolidated Container	2,300
		$9,200

MARCH 23

Shipped 300 units of product B to Rush Industrial Supply and issued an invoice for $2,100. (Rush now has a credit balance with the company—see entry at March 17). No commission is due on this sale.

MARCH 23

Shipped 2,000 units of product A to Cox Supply Co. and issued an invoice for $10,000 plus $100 for freight. Total invoice: $10,100

MARCH 24

Received checks from customers:

Phelps and Co.	$2,500
Saf-T-Co.	1,500
Milwaukee Mill Supply	2,800
Mansfield Distributors	8,300
Total Deposit	$15,100

MARCH 25

A check for $500 was received from Ace Distributors in Omaha, Nebraska. Ace owes New Corp a total of $1,500 arising from sales made in 19X5. Because New had been unable to obtain payment of this amount in 19X6, the company's accountant wrote off the $1,500 balance at year-end (against the Allowance for Doubtful Accounts). Mr. Armstrong continues to be doubtful that additional payments can be secured from Ace Distributors.

MARCH 29

The company received a check for $3,500 from Phelps Construction Supply Co. in full settlement of an invoice for $3,700 sent to Phelps in January. Phelps deducted $200 from the invoiced amount, explaining that certain of the helmets received were defective. Armstrong decided not to contest this allegation nor to request return of the defective merchandise, as Phelps is one of New Corp's best customers.

MARCH 30

New accumulates certain bills through the month and pays them all at month-end. These bills occur monthly, and New's accountant wants to make certain that one of each type of bill is included in each month. Furthermore, these bills require allocation of expenses among several departments, including production, sales, R&D, and G&A. Payments made were:

Check No.	Amount	Payee	Expense Category	Production	Sales	R&D	G&A
273	$ 900	Pacific Telephone	Telephone and Telegraph	100	600	—	200
274	500	Standard Oil	Travel and Entertainment	200	200	—	100
275	800	Ajax Janitorial	Occupancy	600	100	—	100
276	950	Pacific Gas and Electric	Occupancy	800	100	—	50
277	500	Auto Lease Co.	Travel and Entertainment	200	200	—	100
278	200	Air Travel Card	Travel and Entertainment	—	100	—	100
	$3,850			$1,900	$1,300	—	$650

MARCH 31

Interest was paid to First Bank for the months of January through March. Interest expense of $350 per month was previously accrued for January and February. Check no. 279: $1,050

MARCH 31

The report from First Bank for the pay period from March 16 to March 31 follows:

Dept.	Wages and Salaries	Payroll Taxes
Direct labor	$3,000	$250
Indirect production	1,500	150
Sales	1,800	200
R&D	200	50
G&A	750	50
	$7,250	$700

Gross Payroll	$7,250
less Income Tax Withheld	1,000
less Group Insurance Withheld	0
	$6,250

Amount deducted from New's account:

Net Payroll	$6,250
Income Tax Withheld	1,000
Payroll Taxes	700
	$7,950

MARCH 31

The quarterly rent for the company's facilities was paid to Sunshine Properties. Monthly rent is $800. Rent for January and February was accrued during each of those months. Fifty percent of rent expense is allocated to production (account no. 379) and 25% each to the sales and G&A departments. Total payment: $2,400. Check no. 280

AT MONTH END

The accountant for New collected the following information to be used in making month-end adjusting entries:

a Total depreciation expense for the month was $700 and comprised the following:

Depreciation on production equipment	$300
Depreciation on leasehold improvements	200
Depreciation on motor vehicles	100
Depreciation on office furniture	100

This depreciation was allocated to departments as follows:

Account no. 379	$400
Account no. 435	200
Account no. 635	100

b Amortization for the month of March on the company's intangible assets was $100.

c The accountant decided to add another $100 to the company's allowance for doubtful accounts.

d Following a careful review of the informal accounts receivable subsidiary ledger (files of unpaid invoices), the accountant decided that a $200 balance due from ABC Supply should be written off as uncollectible.

e The company's insurance policies had been prepaid in January for the full year. This prepaid account was to be reduced by $400 for March and charged to the following accounts:

Account no. 379	Indirect Production Costs	$200
Account no. 433	Occupancy—Sales	100
Account no. 633	Occupancy—G&A	100

f The accountant continued the practice of accruing for professional fees during each month. The accrual of $600 for March was charged to account no. 629.

g The accountant wanted to accrue for future vacation and holiday wages for New's employees. The appropriate addition to the Accrued Wages and Salaries account is:

Acct No.	Department	Amount
375	Direct Labor	$200
379	Indirect labor	100
411	Sales	200
511	R&D	100
611	G&A	100
		$700

h Inventories at month-end were physically counted and valued as follows:

Raw material	$40,500
In-process	11,000
Finished goods	19,300

See "suggestions from former accountant" for method of determining cost of goods sold.

NEW CORP
Cash Disbursements Journal
(Check Register)

Date	Payee	Check No.	Accounts Payable Amount	Other Acct.	Other Amount	Cash	Cash Discount Earned
			DEBIT			**CREDIT**	
Mar. 2	First Bank	257		251	600	950	
				721	350		
Mar. 7	Sally Simond	258		425	100	150	
				625	50		
Mar. 10	Overland Freight	259		147	100	100	
Mar. 10	NGT Lines	260		147	150	150	
Mar. 10	Kennedy Trucking	261		147	50	50	
Mar. 10	Dean and Bulheley	262		233	1,000	1,000	
Mar. 10	Creative Publications	263	2000			1,950	50
Mar. 10	Ajax Webbing	264	2500			2,450	50
Mar. 10	Moore Supply	265		111	500	500	

NEW CORP
Sales Journal

| DEBIT | | Date | Customer Name | CREDIT | | | | |
| 401 Commission Expense | 111 Acct. Rec'ble. | | | SALES | | 321 Special Contracts | OTHER | |
				301 Product A	305 Product B		147 Freight Clearing	225 Commissions Payable
	4,050	Mar. 1	Cox Supply Co.	4,000			50	
150	3,200	Mar. 2	General Mammoth Corp.		3,200			150
	3,160	Mar. 4	Mansfield Distributors	2,480	650		30	
100	3,900	Mar. 8	Foster Bros. Wholesalers	2,500	1,400			100
	2,600	Mar. 8	Willamette Supply Co.	2,600				

NEW CORP
General Journal
Month of March 19X7

Date		Description	Acct. No.	Debit	Credit
Mar.	1	Material Purchases	371	3,900	
		Accounts Payable—Trade	201		3,900
	3	Cash	105	100	
		Travel Advances—Employees	118		100
	4	Accounts Payable—Trade	201	400	
		Material Purchase Returns	373		400
	8	Material Purchases	371	350	
		Accounts Payable—Trade	201		350
	8	Notes Receivable (Willamette Supply)	115	1,600	
		Accounts Receivable—Trade	111		1,600
	9	Cash	105	10,800	
		Accounts Receivable—Trade	111		10,800
	10	Sales Returns and Allowances	345	500	
		Accounts Receivable—Trade	111		500

NEW CORP
Subsidiary Ledger—Sales Commissions Payable
Agnew & Associates

Date	Explanation	Debit	Date	Explanation	Credit
			Feb. 28	Balance	50

Bace and Fruehauf

Date	Explanation	Debit	Date	Explanation	Credit
			Feb. 28	Balance	100
			Mar. 8	Foster Bros.	100

Finley Associates

Date	Explanation	Debit	Date	Explanation	Credit
			Feb. 28	Balance	300
			Mar. 2	Gen'l Mammoth	150

Leigh Brothers

Date	Explanation	Debit	Date	Explanation	Credit
			Feb. 28	Balance	150

Safety Suppliers

Date	Explanation	Debit	Date	Explanation	Credit
			Feb. 28	Balance	200

Comprehensive Accounting Exercise

N EW CORP—COST ACCOUNTING

Mr. Armstrong has accepted your suggestions and is attempting to determine cost for helmets utilizing an actual, job order, full-absorption costing system. (See other New Corp cases for background on the company and its products.)

It is now early February 19X6 and you are the cost accountant for New Corp for this month.

You ask Mr. Armstrong what indirect production costs (IPC) vehicle he uses, and what the current IPC rate is. He replies as follows:

"Late in 19X5 we took a look at our production plans for 19X6. At the same time, of course, we were also doing our budgeting for 19X6. We expect to experience some fluctuation in production from month to month as we respond to seasonal fluctuations in orders. Because cash is tight around here we don't want to carry too much finished goods inventory.

"I believe that the most appropriate IPC vehicle for us is direct-labor hours and that is what we are using. We were tempted to use separate IPC rates for the injection molding department and for the assembly department, but finally, for the sake of simplicity, we decided to use a single factorywide rate. Also, we decided to maintain the same IPC rate throughout the year, in spite of seasonal fluctuations. We know that in the slower months, such as February, we will underabsorb our IPC, but we should correspondingly overabsorb during our busy months.

"Our planning for 19X6 indicated that we would produce about 45,000 units of our construction helmet and about 8,000 units of a new helmet that we are just now introducing to the industrial market. We call our construction helmet product A and our industrial helmet product B. We don't expect to sell quite as many helmets as we produce, so we will be increasing finished goods inventory through the year.

"Product A requires about 0.145 direct-labor hours (total for both molding and assembly), but product B requires about 0.260 direct-labor hours because the plastic resin we use takes slightly longer to mold and because the assembly process is somewhat more complicated. I also estimate that we will spend about 1,000 direct-labor hours on custom molding for the Edwards Company.

"Our budget for the production departments for 19X6 is:

Indirect labor salaries and wages	$29,600
Supplies	16,800
Power	4,100
Outside services	1,800
Rent	6,000
Depreciation	4,900
	$63,200

The 'rent' shown on production's budget is a pro-ration of total rent for that portion of the building occupied by the production depart- ments. Similarly, the other items such as power and depreciation have been pro-rated. Therefore, we came up with an IPC rate for 19X6 of $6.58 per direct labor hour. This rate seems high — it's more than 100% of direct-labor cost, since our average pay in injection molding is less than $6.00 per hour and our assemblers earn less than that — but my friends tell me that many companies have IPC (or over- head) rates of 200% or more of direct labor."

You tell Mr. Armstrong that you will double-check the IPC rate and familiarize yourself with the operation. You will also instruct a clerk in the accounting department regarding the maintenance of job cards on each job. The two of you agree that Mr. Armstrong or the chief accountant will call you when they need help.

On February 12, Armstrong calls to say that he must send out an invoice to Edwards Company for some custom molding that has just been completed. Armstrong is anxious to bill Edwards right away in order to shorten the time until payment is received from Edwards. Armstrong explains that the contract with Edwards calls for a price on all custom work equal to cost plus 25%; cost plus 25% means 125% of the sum of direct labor, direct material, and IPC.

Upon arriving at New Corp you ask for the job cost card on this custom molding. The job cost card is shown at the end of the case (see job no. 0635) and the sources of the data contained on the card are discussed in Appendix A.

The chief accountant at New Corp calls you several times during the month to ask some specific procedural questions. You respond over the telephone to the following questions, reminding the chief ac- countant that consistency from accounting period to accounting pe- riod should be stressed:

a For another custom-molding job for Edwards Company to be started in March, New Corp has placed an order for $2,000 of spe- cialized tooling. Should this expenditure be treated as (1) a direct material cost of the job, (2) an IPC expense (perhaps "supplies" or "outside services"), or (3) a capital expenditure to be depreciated over three or four years?

b Two bags of plastic resin, carried in beginning raw-material inventory at February 1, 19X6 at a value of $100 have become defective because they were stored incorrectly. How should this $100 expense be treated? The credit must be to Raw Material Inventory, but where should the debit go?

c At the end of the month 200 units of product A in inventory were found to be defective. A job has been opened for rework of these units in March. Should the costs to be accumulated on this job be shown as additional costs to produce these units when the units are returned to inventory? If so, the valuation of these units in inventory will be much higher than the valuation of identical units of product A that did not have to be reworked. Or should the rework cost be included in IPC or in administrative expenses?

d The designer in engineering has spent a great deal of time troubleshooting the production process on product B, the new helmet for the industrial market. He kept track of the amount of time that he spent on job no. 0636 during February and it amounted to over 40 hours. Should a portion of his salary be included as direct labor on job no. 0636? Should it be charged to Indirect Labor Salaries and Wages within IPC? At the moment these costs are just lumped in with other engineering salaries.

(Note: You should make no entries in the general ledger with respect to these four situations; these issues are raised for discussion only.)

At the end of the month Mr. Armstrong asks you to devote the time necessary to assist the chief accountant in completing the cost accounting for the month, valuing inventories and cost of goods sold and developing the income and balance sheet statements for February.

When you arrive at the office, the chief accountant presents you with the job cost cards for the month (jobs no. 0634 through 0638) and the (very) preliminary trial balance at February 28, 19X6. The accountant also tells you the following:

a All profit-and-loss accounts are closed monthly; therefore, the balances shown in these accounts are for February only.

b Direct material has been transferred to the jobs, but direct labor has not yet been transferred. Therefore, the balances shown in Job Cost accounts 0634–0638 on the trial balance (2/28/X6) are for direct material only. The balance shown in the Direct Labor account on the trial balance represents all direct labor for the month and it now needs to be transferred to the individual jobs.

c IPC has not yet been allocated to jobs for the month.

d Cost of goods sold has not yet been determined for the month. (Selling, general, and administrative expenses for the month have already been recorded.) Inventories are maintained on a FIFO basis. Finished goods inventory at February 1, 19X6 consisted of:

Product	Quantity	Cost/Unit	Extended Value
A	900	$2.524	$2,271.60
B	200	4.215	843.00
			$3,114.60

Shipments for the month were:

Product	Quantity
A	1,800
B	300

ASSIGNMENT

1 Do you agree with Armstrong's IPC rate and the way he derived it? If you would use a different rate, describe why and show the calculations that lead to your rate. (For the balance of this problem, however, use Mr. Armstrong's IPC rate.)

2 Calculate (as of February 12) the amount that Armstrong should bill Edwards for the custom-molding work. Show your calculations.

3 Answer the questions that the chief accountant posed to you (see pages 530–531). Do *not* make any entries in the general ledger regarding these questions.

4 Assist the chief accountant in the end-of-period closing and in constructing the financial statements for February 19X6. Suggested sequence of activities:

a Complete the job cost cards.

b Close Direct Labor and IPC accounts. Don't forget the IPC Variance account.

c Close Job Cost accounts, as appropriate, and record Cost of Goods Sold, thereby adjusting Finished Goods Inventory.

d Record in the T accounts your answer to question 2. (Note that all other sales have already been recorded.)

e Develop a new trial balance and construct financial statements. Ignore income taxes.

Appendix
Explanation of Job Cost Card

Job cost cards are used by New Corp to accumulate costs on individual jobs and to calculate unit costs when jobs are completed.

When the production control clerk initiates a job, he assigns a number (in sequence) to the job and sends an order to the production superintendent. A copy of this order goes to accounting and serves as a signal to initiate a job cost card. At this time the information at the top of the card is completed ("Product," "Quantity Ordered," "Job No.," and "Date Opened").

Machine operators and assemblers obtain material from the stockroom, as required. When material is removed from the stockroom, a material-requisition ticket is completed, and copies are sent to both the inventory control clerk (for maintenance of inventory records) and to accounting. Accounting transfers information from this ticket to the appropriate job cost card. The prenumbered ticket contains information on:

The date of the withdrawal

The job number to be charged

The part number (New Corp assigns its own part numbers to all materials purchased)

The unit of measure (pounds, feet or each, depending upon the particular material)

The cost per unit of measure (this cost fluctuates on any given part number as New Corp purchases from different vendors or vendors change their prices)

The quantity requisitioned

All production personnel are required to submit time cards each week. After review by the superintendent, these are sent to accounting where they are used (a) to compute wages and salaries for each employee and (b) as the source document for the direct-labor portion of the job cost card. Each time card shows the individual's name, employee number (assigned by New Corp when the employee joins the company), the date, the current wage rate per hour for the employee, and the number of hours spent by job.

When the job is completed, it is delivered to either the shipping department or the stockroom. The actual quantity produced is determined by the receiving clerk and noted on the original order form.

This order form is then routed to material control (for maintenance of inventory records) and to accounting, where it provides the final pieces of information required for the job cost card: "date closed" and "actual quantity realized."

A clerk in the accounting department can now do the necessary extensions, calculate the IPC absorbed by this job, and determine the cost per unit.

NEW CORP—COST ACCOUNTING
General Ledger
(at February 28, 19X6)

Raw Material Inventory	4,287.30
Finished Goods Inventory—A	2,271.60
Finished Goods Inventory—B	843.00
Other Current Assets	24,150.00
Plant and Equipment, Net	28,502.17
Other Assets	1,980.00
Current Liabilities	12,985.00
Other Liabilities	7,950.00
Invested Capital	45,000.00
Retained Earnings Prior Years	2,840.00
Retained Earnings —Year-to-Date	810.00
Sales—Product A	9,306.00
Sales—Product B	2,223.00
Sales—Custom	
COGS—A	
COGS—B	
COGS—Custom	
IPC Variance	
Direct Labor Exp.	2,774.80
Job 0634	591.40
Job 0635	262.70
Job 0636	486.18
Job 0637	593.35
Job 0638	402.50
IPC—Indirect Labor	1,543.00
IPC—Supplies	908.00
IPC—Power	335.00
IPC—Outside Services	240.00
IPC—Rent	500.00
IPC—Depreciation	388.00
Selling, General & Admin. Expenses	4,375.00

Job Cost Card

Product ____A____   Job no. ____0634____
Quantity ordered ____800____   Date opened <u>Feb. 2, 19X6</u>
          Date closed <u>Feb. 9, 19X6</u>

A.   Material

Date	Material Requisition No.	Part Number	Unit of Measure	Cost/Unit	Qty.	Extended Cost
2/2	1136	108-1	#	.570	560	319.20
2/5	1139	108-1	#	.570	20	11.40
2/6	1140	413-0	ft.	.175	1120	196.00
2/9	1144	423-1	ea.	.080	810	64.80
					Total	$

B.   Direct Labor

Week of	Employee No.	No. of Hours	Rate/Hour	Extended Cost
2/2	21	3.2	6.75	
2/2	26	39.0	6.80	
2/2	30	39.0	4.45	
2/2	31	16.5	6.75	
2/2	46	10.5	4.52	
2/2	49	2.9	4.50	
2/9	46	4.1	4.52	
2/9	49	8.0	4.50	
	Total	123.2	Total	$

C.   Indirect Production Costs

Direct-labor hours: _____
IPC rate   _____   _____
          Total IPC absorbed $ _____

          Total job cost $ _____
Actual quantity realized   ____820____
          Cost per unit   _____

Job Cost Card

Product <u>Custom (Edwards)</u>   Job no. ___0635___
Quantity ordered _____N/A_____   Date opened <u>Feb. 2, 19X6</u>
                                        Date closed <u>Feb. 12, 19X6</u>

A. Material

Date	Material Requisition No.	Part Number	Unit of Measure	Cost/Unit	Qty.	Extended Cost
2/2	1137	329-1	#	1.03	230	236.90
2/6	1141	640-0	ft.	.43	60	25.80
					Total	$

B. Direct Labor

Week of	Employee No.	No. of Hours	Rate/Hour	Extended Cost
2/2	45	12.5	5.95	
2/9	45	7.0	5.95	
2/9	49	22.7	4.50	
	Total	42.2	Total	$

C. Indirect Production Costs

        Direct-labor hours: _____
        IPC rate   _____   _____
            Total IPC absorbed $

                Total job cost $_____
        Actual quantity realized   ___N/A___
                Cost per unit   _____

Job Cost Card

Product _____B_____

Quantity ordered _____500_____

Job no. _____0636_____

Date opened __Feb. 3, 19X6__

Date closed __Feb. 25, 19X6__

A.   Material

Date	Material Requisition No.	Part Number	Unit of Measure	Cost/Unit	Qty.	Extended Cost
2/4	1138	193-0	#	.655	375	245.63
2/9	1142	193-0	#	.655	50	32.75
2/12	1145	415-0	ft.	.185	800	148.00
2/18	1147	415-0	ft.	.185	20	3.70
2/24	1151	428-0	ea.	.110	510	56.10
					Total	$

B.   Direct Labor

Week of	Employee No.	No. of Hours	Rate/Hour	Extended Cost
2/2	21	12.0	6.75	
2/2	45	20.0	5.95	
2/9	21	6.0	6.75	
2/9	45	30.0	5.95	
2/16	45	10.0	5.95	
2/16	49	38.2	4.50	
2/23	49	20.6	4.50	
	Total	136.8	Total	$

C.   Indirect Production Costs

Direct-labor hours: _____

IPC rate   _____

Total IPC absorbed $

Total job cost $_____

Actual quantity realized   _____510_____

Cost per unit   _____

Job Cost Card

Product _____A_____   Job no. ____0637____
Quantity ordered ____800____   Date opened Feb. 6, 19X6
                               Date closed Feb. 27, 19X6

A. Material

Date	Material Requisition No.	Part Number	Unit of Measure	Cost/Unit	Qty.	Extended Cost
2/9	1143	108-1	#	.570	560	319.20
2/17	1146	108-1	#	.575	30	17.25
2/18	1148	413-0	ft.	.175	1100	192.50
2/24	1150	423-1	ea.	.080	805	64.40
					Total	$

B. Direct Labor

Week of	Employee No.	No. of Hours	Rate/Hour	Extended Cost
2/9	21	3.0	6.75	
2/9	26	30.0	6.80	
2/9	30	30.0	4.45	
2/16	26	9.3	6.80	
2/16	30	9.3	4.45	
2/23	30	8.5	4.45	
2/23	46	12.8	4.52	
2/23	49	14.6	4.50	
	Total	117.5	Total	$

C. Indirect Production Costs

Direct-labor hours: _____
IPC rate _____   _____
   Total IPC absorbed $

      Total job cost $_____
   Actual quantity realized   ____800____
       Cost per unit   _____

Job Cost Card

Product _____A_____   Job no. _____0638_____
Quantity ordered ___1,000___   Date opened Feb. 20, 19X6
                                    Date closed _____

A.   Material

Date	Material Requisition No.	Part Number	Unit of Measure	Cost/Unit	Qty.	Extended Cost
2/23	1149	108-1	#	.575	700	402.50

Total $ _____

B.   Direct Labor

Week of	Employee No.	No. of Hours	Rate/Hour	Extended Cost
2/23	21	3.1	6.75	
2/23	26	22.4	6.80	
2/23	30	22.4	4.45	
2/23	53	21.5	6.30	
2/23	54	21.5	4.40	
	Total		Total	$

C.   Indirect Production Costs

Direct-labor hours: _____
IPC rate   _____   _____
   Total IPC absorbed $

         Total job cost $_____
   Actual quantity realized   _____
         Cost per unit   _____

NEW CORP—COST ACCOUNTING
Trial Balance
February 28, 19X6

	PRELIMINARY		ADJUSTED	
	Dr	Cr	Dr	Cr
Raw material inventory	4,287.30			
Finished-goods inventory—A	2,271.60			
Finished-goods inventory—B	843.00			
Other current assets[1]	24,150.00			
Plant and equipment, net	28,502.17			
Other assets	1,980.00			
Current liabilities		12,985.00		
Other liabilities		7,950.00		
Invested capital		45,000.00		
Retained earnings—prior years	2,840.00			
Retained earnings—year-to-date		810.00		
Sales—product A		9,306.00		
Sales—product B		2,223.00		
Sales—custom jobs		[2]		
Cost of goods sold—A	—			
Cost of goods sold—B	—			
Cost of goods sold—custom	—			
IPC variance	—			
Job 0634	591.40			
Job 0635	262.70			
Job 0636	486.18			
Job 0637	593.35			
Job 0638	402.50			
Direct-labor expense	2,774.80			
IPC—indirect labor	1,543.00			
IPC—supplies	908.00			
IPC—power	335.00			
IPC—outside services	240.00			
IPC—rent	500.00			
IPC—depreciation	388.00			
Selling, general, and administrative expenses	4,375.00			
	$78,274.00	$78,274.00		

[1] Includes cash, accounts receivable, and prepaids.
[2] Not yet recorded. Credit Sales and debit Other Current Assets with your answer to question 2.

Index

Index